GROLIER

ENCYCLOPEDIA
OF KNOWLEDGE

Grolier Incorporated
Danbury, Connecticut

ISBN 0-7172-5300-7 (complete set)
ISBN 0-7172-5305-8 (volume 5)

Printed and manufactured in the United States of America.

This publication is an abridged version of the *Academic American Encyclopedia*.

10 9 8 7 6 5 4 3

Ciudad Bolívar [see-oo-dahd' boh-lee'-var] The capital of the Venezuelan state of Bolívar, the city of Ciudad Bolívar (1981 pop., 181,864) is on the south bank of the Orinoco River at the narrows (*angostura*), which are spanned by the 712-m (2,336-ft) Angostura Bridge. The city is an administrative and cultural center, and attractions include the San Isidrio House, the Fortress of the Vulture, and the Talavera Museum. Exports include gold, diamonds, cattle, horses, and timber. Founded in 1764, and originally named Angostura, Ciudad Bolívar was in 1819 the site of Simón Bolívar's proclamation of the republic of Gran Colombia.

Ciudad Juárez [hwar'-ays] Ciudad Juárez is a city in Chihuahua state, northern Mexico. It is situated across the Rio Grande from El Paso, Tex., at an elevation of 950 m (3,117 ft), and has a population of 567,365 (1980). The city is linked to El Paso by bridge and railroad.

The Inter-American Highway begins in Ciudad Juárez, making it a major point of entry into Mexico and contributing to its popularity as a tourist center. Tourist attractions include a race course, markets, two bullrings, and the Mission of Our Lady of Guadalupe, founded in 1659. The city also has a museum of art and history and the Universidad Autónoma de Ciudad Juárez. Tourism is the major industry, but cotton is also grown in the area and processed here. The city was originally named El Paso del Norte. In 1888 it was renamed for Benito Juárez, who had his headquarters there during his exile in 1865.

Ciudad Victoria [vik-tor'-ee-ah] Ciudad Victoria (1980 pop., 153,206), capital of Tamaulipas state, northeastern Mexico, is in the Sierra Madre at an elevation of about 320 m (1,050 ft), 460 km (290 mi) north of Mexico City. The city is an important processing and commercial center for the surrounding mining and agricultural region where livestock is a principal product. Ciudad Victoria was settled in 1750.

civet [siv'-et] Civet is the common name for 16 genera of carnivores in the family Viverridae, a family that also includes the MONGOOSE. Civets are from 41 to 81 cm (16 to 32 in) long; the bushy tail often adds up to 76 cm (30 in) more. They have a catlike face.

The civet marks its territory with its musk. Civets may also ward off attackers with their powerful scent.

Anal scent glands open into a large pouch where musk accumulates. The animal uses MUSK to mark territory, and it may be a sexual attractant. The color of its coat varies but is usually grayish brown with dark stripes or spots.

Civets live in the forests and brush of Asia, Africa, and southern Europe. Palm civets climb trees, but others hunt on the ground. Civets feed on small animals and occasionally bulbs, corms, nuts, and fruits; some eat carrion. From one to six young are born in a litter. The life span is five or more years.

Civil Aeronautics Board The Civil Aeronautics Board (CAB), an independent U.S. government agency established under the Civil Aeronautics Act of 1938, regulated the fares and routes of commercial airlines for 46 years. The Air Transportation Deregulation Act of 1978 eliminated CAB authority over domestic routes by the end of 1981 and ended CAB regulation of domestic fares, mergers, and acquisitions by 1983. On Dec. 31, 1984, the CAB went out of existence.

civil defense Civil defense encompasses all measures taken by a government to protect its civilian population and its property against the destructive effects of enemy attack. (Recently the term has broadened in meaning to include rescue systems to counter the effects of natural disasters.)

Civil Defense in World War II. Little consistent attention was paid to the notion of civil defense until World War II, when bombing cities became a major factor in warfare. Citizens in many of the combatant countries were trained in civil defense techniques: fire fighting, first aid, and the rescue of bombing victims from ruined buildings. When air-raid sirens sounded the warning, the inhabitants of European cities learned to take shelter in designated protected areas, primarily subways and basements. The German bombings of London aroused fear that U.S. cities could also become targets of long-range attacks, and the U.S. Office of Civil Defense was established in 1941. Its program, which enlisted thousands of volunteers, was limited in effect, to the enforcement of blackout regulations in coastal cities.

Protection against Nuclear Attack. The atomic bombings of Hiroshima and Nagasaki forced the realization that civilian populations now suffered risks equal to those of military forces. The responsibility for creating and maintaining U.S. civil defense programs was given first to the U.S. Army (1946–48), then to a series of agencies, to the Department of Defense, and finally (1979) to the Federal Emergency Management Agency (FEMA). Interest in civil defense has been sporadic, and strategies have shifted from programs of private FALLOUT SHELTER building, to plans for massive evacuations of cities, to the establishment and provisioning of shelters in public buildings. In 1986, FEMA reported to Congress that U.S. civil defense capabilities were "low and declining."

Civil Defense in the USSR. Soviet efforts are believed to include drills for large parts of the population; training in bomb disposal; plans for evacuating cities and dispersing industries; and fallout shelters stocked with gas masks and other defense equipment. Information available to American experts, however, indicates that only a small proportion of the Soviet population would be effectively protected in case of nuclear attack.

Civil Defense Controversy. Some experts believe that the only rational measure in the event of nuclear attack would be the mass evacuation of cities. Others are convinced that a fully integrated civil defense effort, involving civilian training, adequate warning systems, and a large-scale shelter program, would substantially reduce losses. Opponents feel that such a program would be an indication that the United States accepts the inevitability of a nuclear war, thereby increasing the likelihood that war will occur. In addition, it is generally agreed that no civil defense program, however extensive, could be successful without adequate warning time for populations to take to shelters or be evacuated; warning time, in a surprise attack, might be only a matter of minutes. Therefore, the establishment of a civil defense system might imply to opposing governments that the United States is prepared to undertake a surprise attack, a "first strike."

Civil Defense in Other Countries. Other major countries maintain civil defense programs. Notably, only Switzerland—traditionally neutral—has a policy of protecting all citizens against nuclear blasts.

See also: NUCLEAR STRATEGY.

civil disobedience Civil disobedience is the act of disobeying a law on grounds of moral or political principle. It is an attempt to force society to accept a dissenting point of view. Although it adopts tactics of nonviolence, it is more than mere passive resistance since it often takes active forms such as illegal street demonstrations or peaceful occupation of premises. It is distinguished from other forms of rebellion because the civil disobeyer invites arrest and accepts punishment.

Civil disobedience is nearest to passive resistance when members of religious groups refuse to carry out legal obligations contrary to their beliefs, as when the DOUKHOBORS in Canada refused to send their children to state-operated schools. It can also take active forms: the same Doukhobors paraded nude in public to protest their prosecution for passive resistance to the school laws. The classic exposition of civil disobedience is Henry David THOREAU's *Resistance to Civil Government* (1849), later retitled *On the Duty of Civil Disobedience*. Thoreau said that when a person's conscience and the laws clash, that person must follow his or her conscience.

Resistance to war and military preparations is a frequent reason for civil disobedience; as such it can take the form of one's refusal to serve in the armed forces, generally known as conscientious objection, or unlawful demonstrations such as some of those against nuclear armament and the Vietnam War, in the 1960s and 1970s. (See CONSCIENTIOUS OBJECTOR.)

Civil disobedience has been a political force when people have sought to liberate themselves from foreign domination or from discrimination within their own countries. In such cases, civil disobedience has involved a mass withdrawal of cooperation, in forms such as strikes, boycotts, nonpayment of taxes, or mass resignation of public servants.

The most ambitious and perhaps most successful examples of mass civil disobedience were those of Mahatma GANDHI and Martin Luther KING, Jr. Gandhi called civil disobedience *satyagraha*, a term meaning "truth-force," and taught it as an austere practice requiring great self-discipline and moral purity. With a versatile use of disobedience, Gandhi led the campaign for Indian independence. In the 1940s American blacks and their white sympathizers began to use forms of civil disobedience to challenge discrimination in public transportation and restaurants, but the major movement began in 1955 with illegal sit-ins in support of boycotts of segregated establishments. King was the chief advocate of nonviolent civil disobedience in the CIVIL RIGHTS movement of the 1960s.

Civil disobedience is often an effective means of changing laws and protecting liberties. It also embodies an important moral concept—that there are times when law and justice do not coincide, and that to obey the law at such times can be an abdication of ethical responsibility.

See also: PACIFISM AND NONVIOLENT MOVEMENTS.

civil engineering Civil engineers design and construct major structures and facilities—bridges, dams, tunnels, tall buildings, factories, highways, airports, railroads, and so on. Over the course of history they have made a particularly significant contribution by creating sanitary systems to reduce disease and improve the environment. The profession has been known as *civil* engineering since the mid-18th century, when that designation was adopted to distinguish it from *military* engineering, which was then particularly active in building fortifications in Europe. The profession goes back to ancient times, however.

Specialties

The extent of knowledge required to solve various types of civil engineering problems makes subspecialties inevitable. TRANSPORTATION is one such branch, and it has divisions such as highway, bridge, and traffic engineering. A second major subspecialty is structural engineering, which concentrates on the design of bridges and large buildings. The structural engineer may cooperate with an architect, who concentrates on the aesthetic and functional aspects of design, whereas the engineer is concerned with materials, methods of construction, and other technical requirements. A third subspecialty is sanitary engineering, concerned with WATER SUPPLIES and SEWERAGE systems for collecting and processing human wastes. A fourth is construction. Other subspecialties include flood control, foundation, harbor, and pipeline engineering.

Education and Licensing

To become a civil engineer in the United States, a candidate must have four years of college leading to the bachelor of science degree in civil engineering. After four years' experience beyond a college education, a civil engineer may be licensed by a state board of registration for professional engineers. To assure uniformity, these state agencies are members of the National Council of Engineering Examiners. The American Society of Civil Engineers promotes the interests of the profession on a national level.

civil law Civil law, or code law, is the system of rules, courts, and procedures used in the legal systems of certain Western European countries and their offshoots in Latin America, Asia, and Africa. These systems are distinct from the COMMON LAW systems of English-speaking countries, but it is not easy to characterize the difference briefly. Civil law is customarily said to be based on ROMAN LAW. The difference between civil-law and common-law systems, however, is not simply the result of Roman influence. Civil-law systems also show varying degrees of influence from GERMANIC LAW and ecclesiastical, feudal, commercial, and customary law. Moreover, noncivil-law systems, such as the English legal system, were also heavily influenced by Roman law in the systematization of the law of CONTRACT. It is specifically the authority given to the *Corpus Juris Civilis* of the 6th-century Byzantine (East Roman) emperor JUSTINIAN, and not merely Roman influence, that distinguishes civil-law systems. (The term *civil law* is also used to mean private law, for example BUSINESS LAW, as opposed to public, or criminal law.)

The Influence of Justinian Law

The *Corpus Juris Civilis* was promulgated in 533–34. A codification of 1,000 years of Roman law, it consisted of three main parts: the *Institutes*, an introductory textbook; the *Digest*, a compilation of extracts from classical jurists; and the *Code* (see JUSTINIAN CODE), a collection of later imperial legislation. The *Institutes* has been particularly influential. From the 16th century onward it was revived as the main introduction to law for European students, and it influenced the development of modern law codes. Codification is now a typical feature of a civil-law system. (Some scholars even take it to be the distinguishing feature, but there is a codified common law in California, and the civil-law system of South Africa is not codified.) Modern codes tend to have a structure similar to that of the *Institutes*. They generally exclude the topics not dealt with in the *Institutes*, such as evidence, procedure, mercantile law, and public law. They tend to be similar to the *Institutes* in length and in amount of detail.

Academic explication of the law—the focus of the *Institutes*—stresses rules and principles; thus in modern civil-law cases the decision must be based clearly on rules and principles embodied in a code or statute. This makes civil law more accessible to the layperson than common law. Systematic academic treatises or monographs are also valued more highly than they are in common law.

The academic study of Roman law that began in Bologna in the 11th century has been the core of civil-law systems. The influence of Roman law on modern civil law is most apparent in the structure and divisions of the law: the sharp distinction between public and private law found in Roman law exists today in civil-law countries. Basic concepts such as contract, delict, possession, and ownership, and the substance of the law of contract and of individual contracts all show Roman influence. On the other hand, some parts of modern substantive civil law are largely free from such influence; these include law related to matrimonial property and acquisition of land ownership, mercantile law, and labor law.

Other Civil Law Codes

Codification is an event of the greatest significance in the life of a civil-law system, but part of its significance is that codes in the modern sense emerge at a late stage of civil-law development and that they necessarily involve a step toward a breakup of the international concept of civil-law systems. Even so, civil-law systems are markedly more international in character than are common-law systems; for example, books on the French civil code have frequently been translated for practical use in other countries, and the movement in this century for harmonization of law is stronger among civil lawyers. Moreover, civil codes have proved to be easy to borrow, and now most civil-law countries have codes that to a marked degree derive from others, particularly from those of France, Germany, Switzerland, and Chile.

French-Inspired Codes. In 1804, Napoleon I promulgated the French *Code Civil*, also known as the NAPOLEONIC CODE. It was to have an enormous influence for many reasons: Napoleon's charisma; French conquest; the ease with which law, especially in the form of a code, can be transmitted (and the absence for many years of a plausible rival code); and its high quality.

The Dutch issued their own Civil Code in 1838, but most of it is derived from the *Code Civil*; indeed, a majority of the provisions are literal translations. The structure of the *Code Civil* was improved in a way that brings the Dutch version closer to Justinian's *Institutes*. In parts of Germany and Switzerland the *Code Civil* also remained in force after the fall of Napoleon.

Despite the repeal in 1814 of the *Code Civil* in virtually all of French-occupied Italy, most Italian states issued codes based on it. The Civil Code (1865) of unified Italy was also substantially based on that of France. The new Italian Code of 1942 includes labor law and commercial law, but otherwise no real break with French tradition took place.

Spain and Romania, two nations outside of Napoleon's conquests, were also influenced by the *Code Civil*; Romania's civil law is simply a translation of the French. France also had a great colonial empire, and the possessions were given French law. Despite independence, these territories are still, in varying degrees, within the French legal tradition.

The South American countries that gained their independence from Spain in the 19th century also turned to French law. For political reasons Spanish law could not be the direct model, nor was Spanish law codified.

French law possessed the only satisfactory codification and was, moreover, very much like Spanish law. Thus the Code of Bolivia (1831) is virtually a translation. The Dominican Republic adopted the *Code Civil* in French in 1845 and had it translated into Spanish only in 1884. The Chilean Civil Code (1855) was much more original but still relied on French law; it served as a model for other South American codifications.

In North America, too, French law was influential. In Louisiana the Civil Code (1808) was modeled on either the *Code Civil* or an earlier draft. In Quebec the Civil Code (1884), which includes commercial law, owes much to the French *Code Civil*, but it is also indebted to the common law.

German-Inspired Codes. Modern civil law is sometimes divided into two families. French law and the systems allied to it form the Romanistic legal family; the Germanic legal family is the other division.

The oldest of the modern Germanic codes is the Austrian General Civil Code issued in 1811. The great code of this group, however, is the German Civil Code (*Bürgerliches Gesetzbuch,* or BGB), which became law in 1900. It has five sections: a general part, obligations (book 2), property (book 3), family law (book 4), and succession (book 5). The BGB is much closer to Roman law than is the French *Code Civil*, largely because Roman law had been received in the medieval period as the law of the Holy Roman Empire, which included most of Germany.

At first sight the general part of the BGB seems out of place in a system derived from Roman law, since nothing in Roman law corresponds to it. This part does not set out general rules or basic principles, but contains provisions on institutions that are common to much of private law—capacity, juristic persons, persons of limited capacity, things, and periods of time. The concept of the general part has been much criticized, and probably it is largely the arrangement that results from this feature that makes the BGB less accessible to the layperson than is the *Code Civil*.

Despite the admiration voiced (even in England) for the BGB, its influence abroad has been limited. It was most important in the Far East, where Siam (Thailand), China, and Japan all issued codes that, apart principally from family law, were derived from it; in Eastern Europe, in the various republics of the Soviet Union, and in Hungary; and, perhaps above all, in Greece, where the Civil Code of 1946 is closely based on it.

The Swiss Code. In the 19th century the various Swiss cantons had individual codes based on the Austrian and French models. The need for unification of law, however, was increasingly felt because of disputes involving the law of more than one canton, and a unified law of obligations took effect in 1811. In 1884 Eugen Huber was charged with the task of setting out the law of all the cantons as a preliminary step to a civil code. Even before Huber's last volume appeared he was given the task of preparing a draft code, which was ready by 1898, and the Swiss Civil Code (ZGB) was adopted in 1907. Before it came into force in 1912 the law of obligations was revised, amplified, and promulgated as a separate statute, but for all practical purposes, this law can be regarded as

part of the ZGB. In style and structure the ZGB usually has been regarded as superior to the BGB. The Turkish Civil Code (1926) is almost identical to the ZGB.

See also: LAW; LAW, HISTORY OF.

---

civil rights　Civil rights are those personal and property rights recognized by governments and guaranteed by constitutions and laws. Although these rights were once conceived of as civil liberties, as limits placed on the government on behalf of individual liberty, government is no longer the sole concern of civil rights policy. Recent legislation and court decisions have extended the zone of civil rights to include protection from arbitrary or discriminatory treatment by groups or individuals. Thus, in the broad sense, civil rights includes both rights against government and rights against individuals and groups.

The meaning of civil rights has changed greatly over the years. The original concept was rooted in 18th-century politics and philosophy. The decay of absolute monarchy led to efforts to check and limit royal power. In England the political philosopher John LOCKE gave shape to the new concept of individual natural rights against the state. Locke also believed that natural rights should be guaranteed against incursions by other persons as well as by the state.

In France, at the beginning of the revolution of 1789, the new Constituent Assembly issued its Declaration of the Rights of Man and of the Citizen. It stated that "men are born and remain free and equal in rights" and that the "aim of all political association is the conservation of the natural and imperscriptable rights of man," including "liberty, property, security, and resistance to oppression." Much of the Declaration was derived from the writings of DIDEROT, LAFAYETTE, MIRABEAU, Jean Jacques ROUSSEAU, and VOLTAIRE.

In America, Thomas JEFFERSON expanded the English and American views of civil rights. He emphasized the primacy of human happiness, by which he meant the opportunity of autonomous individuals to develop themselves to the fullest. He also advanced the concept of religious freedom and church-state separation as a key element of civil rights. Jefferson's thinking was embodied in the DECLARATION OF INDEPENDENCE (1776) and the Statute of Religious Liberty (1785) of the state of Virginia.

U.S. Constitutional Amendments. The BILL OF RIGHTS, as the first ten amendments to the Constitution of the United States are called, was largely the brainchild of James MADISON. The amendments restricted the power of the new national government (but not of the states) in the name of freedom of religion, speech, the press, assembly, and petition. In addition, citizens were assured against unreasonable or unwarranted intrusions by government officials into their homes or personal papers. Certain protections in criminal procedure were established, including the rights to a speedy trial, to a federal grand jury, to reasonable bail, and to confront one's accusers, as well as the right not to be placed twice in jeopardy of life or limb. None of these rights was absolute. Indeed, government restraints on the press and on speech were already well established.

The end of slavery marked a new chapter in the development of civil rights in the United States. After the Civil War a number of constitutional amendments were proposed. Eventually, three were ratified by the states; these were designed primarily to protect the newly freed African Americans. The 13th Amendment abolished slavery and involuntary servitude (including peonage). The 14th Amendment extended American citizenship to all those persons born or naturalized in the United States. It contained far-reaching provisions forbidding any state to "deprive any person of life, liberty, or property, without due process of law" or to deny any person "equal protection of the laws." The 15th Amendment extended the right of suffrage to blacks. The phrase "equal protection of the laws" became crucial in the 20th-century struggle against discrimination. Although the Supreme Court was slow to address the concept, it stands today as the major constitutional means for combating sex and race discrimination in America. In its decision in BROWN V. BOARD OF EDUCATION OF TOPEKA, KANSAS (1954), the Court declared that segregation in public schools was unconstitutional because separate facilities were inherently unequal.

Recent U.S. Civil Rights Laws. Rights have also been expanded through legislation. Since 1957, federal CIVIL RIGHTS ACTS and a VOTING RIGHTS ACT have been passed in an effort to guarantee voting rights, access to housing, and equal opportunity in employment. These have been accompanied by much state and local civil rights legislation.

Civil Rights Movements. Throughout recent history people have organized to struggle for rights to which they felt entitled. In the United States, black militancy spread in the 1950s and '60s through the activities of the CONGRESS OF RACIAL EQUALITY, the SOUTHERN CHRISTIAN LEADERSHIP CONFERENCE headed by Martin Luther King, Jr., and the Student Nonviolent Coordinating Committee (see SNCC). These groups achieved major successes in arousing national opinion against segregation and in stimulating the civil rights legislation of the 1960s.

The successes of black militants encouraged women activists. While the struggle for suffrage had achieved voting rights for U.S. women under the 19th amendment in 1920 (see SUFFRAGE, WOMEN'S), women now sought equal treatment in other social relationships such as employment and property rights (see WOMEN IN SOCIETY; EQUAL RIGHTS AMENDMENT).

A similar movement gained momentum among U.S. homosexuals that aimed at winning legal safeguards against discrimination in employment, housing, and public accommodations (see GAY ACTIVISM).

Civil Rights Outside the United States. Civil rights have been given broad recognition in many countries, particularly in Great Britain, Western Europe, Scandinavia, Australia, New Zealand, and Japan. In many other countries, however, civil rights are empty phrases in constitutions and other documents, and they are not recognized in practice. Nevertheless, even such lip service is a testimony to the growing consciousness of rights everywhere. The United Nations General Assembly gave expression to this consciousness in its Universal Declaration of Human Rights in 1948, and in subsequent convenants on civil and political rights and on economic, social, and cultural rights (see HUMAN RIGHTS).

See also: FREEDOM OF THE PRESS; FREEDOM OF RELIGION; FREEDOM OF SPEECH; INTEGRATION, RACIAL; PACIFISM AND NONVIOLENT MOVEMENTS.

Civil Rights Acts The Civil Rights Acts passed by the U.S. Congress include those of 1866, 1870, 1871, 1875, 1964, and 1968. The first two acts gave African Americans the rights to be treated as citizens in legal actions, particularly to sue and be sued and to own property. These rights were also guaranteed by the 14TH AMENDMENT (1868) to the Constitution, which conferred citizenship on the former slaves; and the 15th Amendment (1870), which declared it illegal to deprive any citizen of the franchise because of race. The Civil Rights Act of 1871 made it a crime to deny any citizen equal protection under the law by means of "force, intimidation, or threat." The act of 1875 further guaranteed African Americans the right to use public accommodations, but this legislation was declared unconstitutional by the Supreme Court in 1883.

By the mid-1880s, the political climate was such that the U.S. public had become indifferent to issues of social justice. This shift in attitude was exemplified by the Supreme Court decision in PLESSY V. FERGUSON (1896), which upheld the principle of "separate but equal" facilities for African Americans and whites and legally instituted the system of segregation. The system endured until it was overturned by BROWN V. BOARD OF EDUCATION OF TOPEKA, KANSAS (1954), in which the Supreme Court declared that separate educational facilities were "inherently unequal."

The 1965 civil rights march from Selma to Montgomery, Ala., was led by Martin Luther King, Jr. (waving at right, center). *One result of this march, which drew 25,000 demonstrators, was passage of the Voting Rights Act by Congress that August.*

Under intense public pressure brought about by massive demonstrations during the CIVIL RIGHTS movement of 1957 to 1965, Congress enacted new legislation in an attempt to overcome local and state obstruction to the exercise of citizenship rights by African Americans. These efforts culminated in the Civil Rights Act of 1964, which prohibited discrimination in employment and established the Equal Employment Opportunity Commission. This major piece of legislation also banned discrimination in public accommodations connected with interstate commerce, including restaurants, hotels, and theaters. The Civil Rights Act of 1968 extended these guarantees to housing and real estate.

See also: EQUAL OPPORTUNITY; RECONSTRUCTION; VOTING RIGHTS ACT.

---

civil service   The term *civil service* refers to nonelected civilian employees of federal, state, and local governments. Usually they qualify for positions by passing a written, oral, or performance test.

Early Origins. Civil service as a world institution dates from ancient times. In the greater river civilizations of Asia and the Near East, the operation of irrigation networks required bureaucracies composed of clerks, secretaries, and royal advisors. The ancient Egyptians assigned civil functions to principal officers under the monarch, and in China a centralized, pyramidal civil service with competitive examinations was introduced in the early centuries AD and lasted until 1912. The bureaucracy of the Roman Empire recognized five administrative categories: justice, military affairs, finance, foreign affairs, and internal affairs. Trainees for the bureaucracy of Holy Roman Emperor Frederick II came from the first European state university, which he founded at Naples in 1224. Peter the Great issued regulations for the Russian civil service in 1720. France developed national professional schools to supply qualified technicians. After the French Revolution of 1789, a body of administrative law developed that prescribed the organization, duties, and rights of civil servants.

The British System. Great Britain traditionally drew upon the aristocracy for its top-level civil servants (corresponding roughly to today's U.S. presidential appointees, who are exempt from examinations but subject to Senate confirmation). The Trevelyan-Northcote report (1854) led to the creation of the Civil Service Commission, which introduced difficult examinations based on the classics and humanities. This attracted university graduates who were trained, by daily confronting the administrative problems of empire, to become chiefs of ministries and advisors to cabinet members. Since 1968, however, British examinations have called for a more specialized background, particularly in management.

Overcoming the Spoils System. Both the United States and Canada long contended with a spoils system that began soon after 1800 (see PATRONAGE). In some state and provincial governments, successful office seekers gave jobs to supporters and eliminated officeholders of the defeated party, and the pattern spread to the federal level. The growing financial support of parties by business corporations, however, alleviated the need to sell offices as a means of filling a party's coffers. After a disappointed office seeker assassinated President James A. Garfield in 1881, Congress passed the Pendleton Act of Jan. 16, 1883. The act established the Civil Service Commission to conduct examinations and ruled out political interference in civil service appointments and removals. Political activities of federal employees were limited by the HATCH ACT (1939, amended 1940), intended to prevent them from using their power in order to bribe or intimidate voters.

The reform movement spread to Canada, where in 1908 Parliament instituted a Canadian Civil Service Commission. The early preoccupation with "fighting the spoilsmen" was replaced with a positive interest in personnel management. In the United States, by the end of the 1970s, most states had comprehensive merit systems, and all had adopted merit principles in departments receiving federal funds.

Recent Reform Efforts. Successive U.S. presidents have complained that the bureaucracy did not respond adequately to their policy initiatives. In President Truman's words, issuing a directive was sometimes "like pushing on a string." President Carter sought to develop a more efficient and responsive civil service. By the Civil Service Reform Act of 1978, Congress also regularized labor-management relations, increased transfer opportunities for senior officers, and abolished the Civil Service Commission, replacing it with the Office of Personnel Management and the Merit Systems Protection Board.

An important trend in both the state and the federal civil service was the hiring of more women and members of minority groups. In Canada the government was pressed to distribute appointments more equitably between the English- and French-speaking populations. Organized civil servants in the United States pushed toward collective bargaining. Several states granted employees—except those guarding the public safety—the right to strike if specified mediation and conciliation measures failed. In Canada, Parliament passed a similar law in 1967. In Britain, the Whitley Councils have played a prominent labor-management negotiating role since 1919. In these councils, middle- and lower-level employees have an equal voice with directing and supervising officers.

In Australia, before Federation (1901), Victoria was the first state to institute civil service examinations. When in 1901 the Australian Commonwealth assumed responsibility for foreign affairs, customs, and other functions that had previously been administered by the states, it absorbed the personnel of the corresponding state departments and also continued the state practice of requiring competitive examinations.

Civil War, English   see ENGLISH CIVIL WAR

Civil War, Spanish   see SPANISH CIVIL WAR

Civil War, U.S.

Civil War, U.S. The Civil War, in U.S. history, was a conflict that pitted the Northern states of the American Union against the Southern states. The war raged for 4 years (1861–65) and was marked by some of the fiercest military campaigns of modern history. Large armies were involved in large movements, and entire populations were engaged in supporting the war efforts of both sides. The war had international impact, not only because of the growing international stature of the United States, but also because war threatened world access to the South's cotton. Britain and France had particular interest in the war's outcome, but other nations were also affected by it.

Historians still argue over causes and effects of the war. A few have looked at the Civil War in a hemispheric and even world context. This perspective is enlightening, for the American Civil War fits into a general pattern of Western Hemispheric conflict in the 19th century that brought new political alignments to South America and new unity to Canada. The war's main effects, however, were felt in the United States, which entered the war as a nation on the threshold of industrial revolution and finished it as a world power. The South entered as a loose collection of agrarian states devoted to almost feudal protocols and lost everything. It is possible to view the Civil War as the war of American unification, because it forged a modern nation and wrought vast social and economic change.

Origins

Although historians commonly trace the coming of the Civil War through the 1850s, some roots of separation were present as early as the colonial period. Troubles between Tidewater (coastal region) and Piedmont (the interior) settlers often reflected differences in philosophies of

Henry Clay, a congressional leader from Kentucky, addresses the U.S. Senate during its debates over the Compromise of 1850. Devised by Clay, the legislation was intended to settle the controversy over the extension of slavery into new territories. The compromise, however, failed to alleviate tension between North and South.

John C. Calhoun, vice-president of the United States from 1825 to 1832, formulated South Carolina's opposition to the tariff acts of 1828 and 1832, claiming that states have the right to nullify federal legislation. Calhoun later argued that states also have the right to secede from the Union.

government: the Tidewater was an older, more settled region, and its citizens wanted little government interference; Piedmont people, on the other hand, looked to government for protection along the frontier, for ready money and light taxation. Those differences shifted with time. Under the ARTICLES OF CONFEDERATION, adopted while the American Revolution was still being fought, the "pluribus" theory of government prevailed. Sovereignty rested with the states, and they gave limited powers to a weak central administration. With the adoption (1787) and ratification of the federal Constitution, however, the "unum" theory came to the fore, and strong national government began in America.

State Rights. Old affections for loose administration and small government died hard. At the end of the 18th century, STATE RIGHTS ideas were supported in the KENTUCKY AND VIRGINIA RESOLUTIONS. Thomas JEFFERSON, who secretly wrote Kentucky's protest against aggressive federalism, suggested that the states ought to have a veto over offensive legislation. James MADISON, in Virginia's protest, shared the state supremacy idea. Not all the states agreed, and a national debate emerged with a decision only partially achieved by Jefferson's election to the presidency in 1800.

Jefferson was expected to restrain the federal government's interference in state and local matters. Responsibility changed some of his views, and he became a strong executive, as shown by the Louisiana Purchase (1803) and the Embargo Act (1807). Generally, however, he continued to feel "that government is best which governs least."

Economic Issues. Constitutional arguments centered on the uses of power, especially in economic matters. Troubles between the older and younger parts of emerging states usually had an economic origin; these troubles could be settled only by government intervention. Perhaps the best example is the WHISKEY REBELLION of 1794. In a test of federal authority over individuals, President George Washington called out troops to collect whiskey taxes in western Pennsylvania. Federal authority prevailed.

Taxes plagued federal-state-citizen relationships throughout the first half of the 19th century. The first

(Above left) *Fighting breaks out between "free soil" and pro-slavery factions in Fort Scott, Kans. The Kansas-Nebraska Act of 1854 aroused bitter sectional antagonisms by leaving to settlers the decision of whether to extend slavery into Kansas.* (Above right) *A fugitive slave arrives at a "safe house" in Indiana by means of the Underground Railroad, a clandestine system for aiding escaped slaves.*

protective tariff in 1789 brought the earliest of many clashes between Northern and Southern economic views. Southern producers wanted a tariff on hemp; Northern users wanted none. Gradually, tariff arguments pitted Northern manufacturing interests and small farmers against Southern planters and slaveholders. Friction increased with each new tariff bill until, finally, the so-called Tariff of Abominations of 1828 caused a confrontation between federal and state authority (see TARIFF ACTS). This bill forced Vice-President John C. CALHOUN to change his personal and political views. Earlier a strong nationalist, he now shifted to sectionalism and so broke with Andrew JACKSON, who had selected Calhoun to run again for the vice-presidency in the 1828 election.

Nullification Controversy. Despite his position in the federal government, Calhoun wrote the "South Carolina Exposition and Protest," which the South Carolina legislature adopted (1828) as its manifesto against bad federal laws. In it Calhoun ingeniously claimed the right of

John Brown, an extremist abolitionist, became a martyr to the cause of black freedom when he was hanged for treason after his seizure of the federal arsenal at Harpers Ferry, Va. (now W. Va.), in 1859.

states to nullify federal laws that they deemed unconstitutional. The NULLIFICATION controversy came to a head in 1832 when South Carolina declared the tariff laws null and void and President Jackson responded with the threat of force. By this time Calhoun had resigned the vice-presidency and become a South Carolina senator. His theories of government shaped South Carolina's views, and at length he devised a theory of secession that prescribed the steps for leaving the Union. Although a compromise solution to this particular crisis was found, Calhoun's ideas were to be invoked again in 1861.

Slavery and Territorial Expansion. Politics and economics conspired against the Union in the next 30 years. Politics became inextricably mixed with the SLAVERY issue in the years after the MISSOURI COMPROMISE (1820–21), by which Maine entered the Union as a free state and Missouri as a slave state, but slavery was forbidden in the rest of the Louisiana Purchase territory north of 36°30' north latitude. Southern leaders feared their power in the House of Representatives would dwindle as new free states were created. They resisted in the Senate by calling for a Southern slave state to balance every Northern free one and by upholding the ideas of state sovereignty and the sanctity of private property—even slaves.

These issues were involved in the debates over annexation (1845) of TEXAS and the MEXICAN WAR, by which the United States acquired a large block of territory not affected by the Missouri Compromise. Having unsuccessfully opposed both the annexation and the war, antislavery forces sought by the WILMOT PROVISO (1846) to bar slavery in the new territories. When this failed, the COMPROMISE OF 1850 was worked out, whereby California entered the Union as a free state, the question of slavery in New Mexico and Utah was left open, and a new FUGITIVE SLAVE LAW was passed to appease Southern interests.

The adjustment of the border with Mexico by the GADSDEN PURCHASE (1853) introduced another element into the sectional dispute, because it made possible a

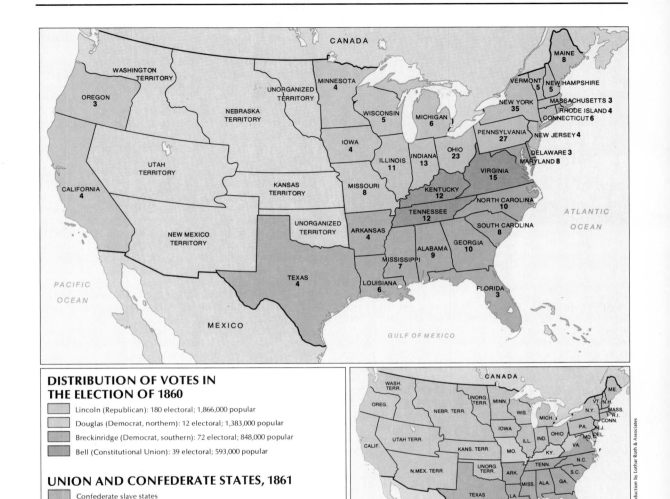

DISTRIBUTION OF VOTES IN THE ELECTION OF 1860

Lincoln (Republican): 180 electoral; 1,866,000 popular

Douglas (Democrat, northern): 12 electoral; 1,383,000 popular

Breckinridge (Democrat, southern): 72 electoral; 848,000 popular

Bell (Constitutional Union): 39 electoral; 593,000 popular

UNION AND CONFEDERATE STATES, 1861

Confederate slave states

Union slave states

Union free states and territories

southern route for the proposed TRANSCONTINENTAL RAIL- ROAD. In addition to its economic value to the South, this route would have carried Southern settlers to the West. The building of such a railroad was blocked until 1862. The slavery issue thus impinged on many developments of the era, although other major influences were also at work—for example, the westward movement (see FRON- TIER) and the burgeoning spirit of MANIFEST DESTINY.

Like the lingering legal case of DRED SCOTT V. SAND- FORD, the Union's troubles persisted. As slave Scott's pe- tition for freedom, made because of temporary residence in a free state, meandered toward the Supreme Court (where it was finally denied in 1857), the Compromise of 1850 began to crumble. The existence of personal liberty laws in many Northern states nullified the effect of the Fugitive Slave Act of 1850, the South's keystone of com-

promise. Moreover, new controversy arose over the status of Kansas and Nebraska, through which a powerful North- ern segment wished to run the transcontinental railroad. These territories were covered by the Missouri Compro- mise, but in order to win Southern support for the route, Sen. Stephen A. DOUGLAS of Illinois proposed that the principle of POPULAR SOVEREIGNTY be applied, allowing the settlers in each territory to decide for or against slavery. The resulting KANSAS-NEBRASKA ACT (1854), which in ef- fect repealed the Missouri Compromise, enraged the an- tislavery forces, who coalesced to form the new REPUBLI- CAN PARTY, and led to a rush of proslavery and antislavery settlers into Kansas. Armed conflict soon followed, turn- ing that territory into "Bleeding Kansas."

The Antislavery Movement and Southern Response. By the mid-1850s the spirit of accommodation had all but

Abraham Lincoln argued against the extension of slavery into new territories during debates with Stephen A. Douglas (seated left) *in the 1858 Illinois senatorial campaign. Although Douglas won the election, Lincoln gained national prominence.*

vanished. Northern interest in emancipation, pushed by ABOLITIONISTS, eroded relations between families north and south. William Lloyd GARRISON's *Liberator* was the extremist voice of abolitionism, calling for immediate emancipation of the slaves by extralegal means if necessary. Although not representative of majority abolitionist opinion, this voice roused the deep-seated fear of slave insurrection among Southerners, who pointed to the actions of Denmark VESEY, Nat TURNER, and finally John BROWN as examples of what could become a bloodbath.

As the Northern antislavery movement changed its tactics from direct political action—for example, attacks on slavery in the state legislatures—to general moral condemnation of all Southerners, Southern attitudes began to set. In the early 1830s the South had claimed the largest number of antislavery societies; by the mid-1850s all such societies were north of the Mason-Dixon line. From an uneasy mood over slavery, Southerners evolved a "positive good" philosophy and argued that slaveowners provided shelter, food, care, and regulation for a race unable to compete in the modern world without proper training. After Harriet Beecher STOWE's *Uncle Tom's Cabin* (1852) indicted all slaveowners to the world, most creative Southern minds turned toward the defense of slavery. Increasingly threatened by a wealthy and developing North, Southerners evolved almost a "garrison philosophy" as they clung to the past for protection.

There was much to cherish in the society of the Old South—an agrarian humanism, a leisurely pace of life for the privileged, gracious manners, and the stability that came from a sense of kin and place. Yet this fading Eden existed on the backs of the slaves who worked the cotton plantations. The South wore slavery as a badge of tradition that it stood ready to defend. In that frame of mind, it faced the election of 1860, an election made fateful by the emergence of the Republican party and its new standard-bearer, Abraham LINCOLN.

The 1860 Election. Lincoln, the Illinois small-town lawyer, had run a stiff but unsuccessful senatorial race against Stephen A. Douglas in 1858 and gained much renown in their publicized debates. He came to national candidacy apparently as a champion of freedom; his new party united the remnants of the old FREE-SOIL PARTY and LIBERTY PARTY.

Douglas wanted the Democratic nomination in 1860, but he had alienated much Southern opinion by his denunciation of Kansas's proslavery LECOMPTON CONSTITUTION. He finally gained the support of a fractured Democratic party. The Democratic national convention in Charleston, S.C., ruptured. A Southern Democratic party emerged with John C. BRECKINRIDGE as its presidential candidate, and another group, the CONSTITUTIONAL UNION PARTY, also contested the election. So splintered were the Democrats that Lincoln captured the election with 180 electoral votes against 123 for his combined opponents, although in popular vote he garnered only 1,866,452 against his major opponents' 2,815,617.

War Comes

News of the election returns spread rapidly. The loudest alarm rang in South Carolina, but secession fires were stoked across the South.

Secession. Calhoun's doctrine of a Union based on a compact between equals seemed logical to Southerners. Most believed that secession was legal—New Englanders were thought to have debated secession at the HARTFORD CONVENTION (1814–15)—but the timing had to be right. Some Southerners had talked of secession during the crisis of 1850, but sentiment had not yet congealed, nor

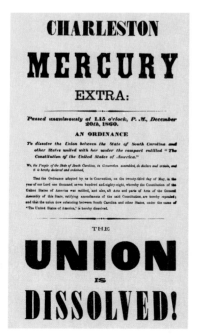

The Charleston Mercury *printed a special one-page edition on Dec. 20, 1860, to announce South Carolina's secession. On that day a special state convention had resolved that "the union now subsisting between South Carolina and other States under the name of the United States of America is hereby dissolved." (New York Public Library.)*

(Above) *Jefferson Davis* (left), *a former U.S. senator from Mississippi, was elected president of the Confederacy on Feb. 8, 1861.* (Right) *President Davis and Gen. Robert E. Lee appear in this lithograph with the original Confederate cabinet:* (left to right) *Stephen Mallory, secretary of the navy; Judah P. Benjamin, attorney general; Leroy P. Walker, secretary of war; Davis; Lee; John H. Reagan, postmaster general; Christopher Memminger, secretary of the treasury; Vice-President Alexander Stephens; and Robert Toombs, secretary of state.*

was the South in any sense prepared for independence. Moderates counseled caution; realists counseled discretion—there were not enough factories, shipyards, railroads, or guns in the South to wage war.

By 1860 many conditions were different. Political attitudes about slavery had now hardened, and the Southern economy seemed strong. The South's international importance as the leading supplier of cotton was also now clear. Moreover, a major financial panic in 1857 had disrupted the Northern economy but touched the South only lightly. If secession were necessary—and the election of Lincoln, a "black Republican" apparently made it so—late 1860 might be the best moment.

Secession brought anguish to many but exultation to the "fire-eaters" of the South. Many Southerners hoped that the threat of secession would force acceptance of Southern demands; others worked to assure cooperation among many Southern states before a single one committed itself—and perhaps suffered South Carolina's 1832 isolation. The South also had its Unionists, who worked to prevent disruption. Old-time Whigs were often Unionists, as were some individuals such as Sam HOUSTON of Texas. Excitement and fear finally overwhelmed the moderates and temporizers, however, and on Dec. 20, 1860, a South Carolina convention unanimously adopted an ordinance of secession. Mississippi seceded on Jan. 9, 1861, followed by Florida on January 10, Alabama on January 11, Georgia on January 19, Louisiana on January 26, and Texas on February 1. On Feb. 4, 1861, delegates from these states met in Montgomery, Ala., where they drafted a constitution for the CONFEDERATE STATES OF AMERICA.

Jefferson DAVIS of Mississippi was selected provisional president and inaugurated on February 18.

Confederate Leadership. President Jefferson Davis seemed to have all the necessary qualifications for success. A West Point graduate with a record of heroic service in the Mexican War, he had served long and ably in the U.S. Senate and as secretary of war in Franklin Pierce's cabinet. An admitted disciple of Calhoun, Davis had nimbly and eloquently defended the South's position in national debate and ranked among the most influential politicians of the country in 1861. Not an extremist on the slave issue, he was nonetheless a defender of the Southern "way of life," and his reputation lent stature to the new nation.

Davis formed his cabinet—generally able and industrious men—and sought peaceful relations with Lincoln's government, but he also prepared for war. Early military legislation created regular and "provisional" land and naval forces, assumed Confederate control of all military operations affecting the South, and set quotas for state militia contributions to a 100,000-man army. In the weeks after he took office, Davis focused increasingly on Confederate control of public property, especially military installations such as Fort Pickens, in Pensacola harbor, and FORT SUMTER, in Charleston harbor. The latter was especially important; without control of Charleston harbor, a key international port, the Confederacy could scarcely claim sovereignty. Sumter became the supreme symbol of independence.

Everything Davis did, however, had to be balanced against statistical realities. Seven Southern states (11

Abraham Lincoln became president on Mar. 4, 1861, by which time seven states had seceded. In his inaugural address Lincoln reminded the South that his oath of office bound him to "preserve, protect and defend" the Union.

Fort Sumter. After inauguration, Lincoln labored under the handicap of stronger subordinates. William H. SEWARD, as secretary of state, tried to run the government and involved himself in prolonged duplicity with Southern representatives over the Fort Sumter issue. Dangling possibilities of negotiation before Davis's emissaries, Seward virtually compromised the honor of the government. Lincoln stayed aloof, considered the Sumter question in proper political terms, and decided to push at that point. The Confederates, almost fooled, realized at last that a Federal expedition would come to the fort's aid and that forbearance by the South would appear to the world as weakness. On Apr. 12, 1861, Confederate cannons opened fire, and Fort Sumter became the first battle of the American Civil War. Historians still argue over whether Lincoln maneuvered the South into firing the first shot.

Lincoln called out 75,000 volunteers on April 15 to suppress "combinations too powerful to be suppressed by the ordinary course of judicial proceedings." By calling troops to put down insurrection, Lincoln set the nature of the war; he officially denied the existence of the Confederacy and conceded only that the South contained "combinations" in rebellion. No declaration of war was necessary.

Initial Strategy. Lincoln had an almost geopolitical grasp of the Union's dilemma in the summer of 1861. The loss of Virginia was a serious blow, but Lincoln felt that the border states, especially Kentucky, were the keys to success. Should Kentucky go, communication with the West would be impaired and Confederates would threaten the heart of the North. He played a careful game to save the border and at length retained both Kentucky and Missouri, although the latter became a theater of war. The

On Apr. 12, 1861, Confederate troops in Charleston fired on Fort Sumter. The bombardment marked the first military engagement of the Civil War.

when Virginia, North Carolina, Tennessee, and Arkansas seceded in the spring) would stand against 23 Northern states, would pit 9 million people—3 million of them slaves and hence not military assets—against 22 million. Industrial and manufacturing advantages were all with the North, along with twice as many miles of railroad and a better managed and equipped agriculture. The South boasted no more than $27 million in specie, mostly in New Orleans banks. The North had diplomatic relations with foreign powers and hence had unlimited credit. It was not clear where, if anywhere, a rebel group of cotton states could borrow money.

Lincoln's Position. Davis had no monopoly on problems. In the months following his election Lincoln juggled office seekers, party promises, and the doings of the lame-duck incumbent, James BUCHANAN. Sympathetic to Southern views, Buchanan suffered a paralyzing view of the Constitution and secession—he thought secession unconstitutional, but he believed that the constitution gave him no power to prevent it. By doing nothing, he permitted secession to run its course. He gave no help to the Peace Convention that assembled in Washington during February 1861 and no leadership to a Congress struggling with various compromises.

Lincoln also played a part in the failure of compromise. Trying to avoid committing himself to anything before gaining power, he nonetheless let others "attribute" ideas to him, including opposition to compromises that might result in extending slavery. Republican leaders in Congress adopted his apparent intransigence and steadily opposed compromise. In fact, Lincoln was willing to protect slavery where it existed, even by constitutional amendment, and thought the Fugitive Slave Act should be enforced. Neither he nor his spokesmen made his views clear, however, and the South came to see him as being against compromise of any kind.

(Left) *A colorful Zouave regiment leads a parade of Union troops through Washington, D.C., shortly before the First Battle of Bull Run. The Zouaves, whose uniforms were patterned after those worn by French soldiers of the era, were organized by Col. Elmer Ellsworth.* (Right) *Gen. Irvin McDowell was the first commander of the large Union army in Virginia. He was defeated by two smaller Confederate forces in the First Battle of Bull Run (July 21, 1861).*

slave states of Delaware and Maryland also remained in the Union, and the western section of Virginia seceded from that state and entered the Union as West Virginia in 1863.

Shortly after calling for volunteers, Lincoln proclaimed a blockade of Southern ports—the U.S. Navy boasted 42 commissioned ships in March—and pushed war taxes. Volunteers abounded, and a large army gathered near Washington.

Lincoln's military experience was limited, and he turned to career soldiers for advice on the next step. Venerable Winfield SCOTT, the ranking general in the U.S. Army, attempted to persuade Col. Robert E. LEE to assume command of federal forces, but Lee decided in favor of his native Virginia. Scott struggled to produce an overall strategy for the North, but then yielded to the "On to Richmond" outcry that summed up Northern sentiments. General Irvin McDOWELL took command of the main federal army and fitted it for a Virginia offensive.

Davis, on the other hand, pushed Confederate military preparations against some apathy. Although martial excitement spread across the South, few people thought of a serious war. Davis collected almost as many volunteers as did Lincoln and sent them to Virginia. He wanted to convince Virginians of the South's intent to defend the northern border of the Confederacy, and he also wanted to protect the Tredegar Iron Works and other munitions factories in Richmond—the nascent industrial heart of the South. Many officers resigned from the U.S. Army and joined the South; Davis looked to Gen. P. G. T. BEAUREGARD of Louisiana, who had commanded the action against Fort Sumter, to organize Confederate legions arriving near Richmond. Logistics and administration were as vexing to Southerners as to their enemies, and

effective ranks took shape slowly. Initial Southern strategy was simply to fend off the enemy, to win by not losing. Energetic offensives might have been the better course, but Davis's government wanted to show nonaggressive intent.

Military Operations

Historians have called the U.S. Civil War "the first modern war," with good reasons: railroads were first used in large-scale movement of troops and supplies; technological advances in ordnance and weaponry were marked; trench warfare was used; steam and ironclad warships

P. G. T. Beauregard was the Confederate commander in Charleston, S.C., who ordered the bombardment and capture of Fort Sumter. Beauregard's victories in Charleston and the First Bull Run made him a hero throughout the South.

General George B. McClellan succeeded McDowell as commander of the Union's Army of the Potomac in July 1861. Although McClellan organized the largest fighting force ever assembled in the Western Hemisphere, he deployed it with extreme caution. Removed from command in November 1862, McClellan ran for president against Lincoln in 1864.

became commonplace; whole populations were directly involved in supporting the war efforts of both sides; and new ways of raising, sustaining, and commanding massive armies were devised.

First Bull Run. On July 21, 1861, roughly equal forces met near Manassas, Va., in the first major land battle of the war. McDowell's army (soon to be known as the Army of the Potomac) attacked Beauregard's lines along Bull Run Creek. Successful early in the day, the Federals were at last held on the Confederate left by Gen. Thomas J. Jackson's brigade, rushed to the field by rail from the

Shenandoah Valley. Jackson's men held off repeated attacks, and as Gen. Barnard E. Bee (1824–61) of South Carolina sought to rally his own men, he cried: "There is Jackson standing like a stone wall. Let us determine to die here, and we will conquer." Stonewall JACKSON became an internationally known hero in the wake of that rebel victory, but it proved to be costly. Southerners became overconfident, and Northerners buckled down for a long, hard war. (See BULL RUN, BATTLES OF.)

Following Bull Run, or Manassas, as it was called in the South (Northerners named battles after nearby bodies of water, Southerners after nearby places), both sides reorganized. Lincoln called Gen. George B. MCCLELLAN, fresh from small successes in western Virginia, to command the main Union force. Davis combined Beauregard's force with Gen. Joseph E. JOHNSTON's troops, and Johnston took the senior command of the Confederate forces in Virginia.

Other Activity in 1861. Major military activity centered in Virginia throughout the rest of 1861. McClellan built an enormous army to hurl against Richmond. Davis, advised by Robert E. Lee of Virginia's army, concentrated increased forces to defend that city, which became the Confederacy's new capital in May 1861. The sheer mass of troops numbed commanders. So much was needed to support so many that traditional organization simply could not sustain demand. With no time for innovative theorizing, offices and officers proliferated on both sides.

Distances, too, unnerved old army hands. While the heaviest preparations for battle continued in Virginia, conflict flickered along the border. In Missouri, where the secessionists had taken up arms against the Unionist majority, the Confederate militia defeated the Unionists

(Left) *Thomas J. "Stonewall" Jackson won his nickname at First Bull Run. A brilliant tactician, he played a key role in the early Confederate victories in Virginia.* (Right) *Union troops fled during the first major engagement of the Civil War, the First Battle of Bull Run. This triumph for the combined confederate armies of P. G. T. Beauregard and Joseph E. Johnston confirmed suspicions of the Union army's lack of discipline and dashed Northern hopes for a swift victory. (Library of Congress.)*

at Wilson's Creek on Aug. 10, 1861. Union control of Missouri was not assured until Confederate forces were defeated at Pea Ridge, Ark., in March 1862.

Grant in the West, Spring 1862. The Union general Ulysses S. GRANT opened the 1862 campaign west of the Appalachian Mountains by capturing FORT HENRY AND FORT DONELSON on the Tennessee and Cumberland rivers in February. Grant then began to advance southward toward Corinth, Miss., while part of the Union army under John POPE undertook to expel the Confederates from the upper Mississippi. Supported by a naval flotilla under Andrew Hull FOOTE, Pope besieged and captured Island No. 10 in the Mississippi (March 16–April 7). In the meantime, however, the Confederate general Albert Sidney JOHNSTON concentrated his forces near Pittsburg Landing, Tenn., and on April 6 he launched a suprise attack against Grant's army at Shiloh Church (see SHILOH, BATTLE OF). One of the worst battles of any American war, Shiloh raged for two days.

Although the Confederates were initially successful, Johnston was mortally wounded on the first day, and command passed to Beauregard. Confusion and exhaustion sapped Confederate strength, and on April 7, Grant, reinforced by Gen. Don Carlos BUELL's army, counterattacked with great success. Beauregard withdrew, and the Union Army followed slowly, taking Corinth in May. The fall (April 26) of New Orleans to a U.S. fleet under David G. FARRAGUT was a third major blow to Confederates in the West. However, the war then stabilized in this theater.

Peninsular Campaign. In the east, McClellan had at last begun to move his vast army in March 1862. He planned a giant amphibious operation aimed at capturing Yorktown and moving on Richmond from the south. The water

Ulysses S. Grant gained the attention of Lincoln by his victories at Fort Henry and Fort Donelson (February 1862) and at Shiloh (April 1862).

route to Richmond up the James River was closed by the presence of the Confederate ironclad *Virginia* (formerly the U.S.S. *Merrimack*, which survived a 4-hour engagement with the U.S.S. *Monitor* on March 9; see MONITOR AND MERRIMACK). However, McClellan intended to advance up the peninsula between the York and James rivers. By early April his forces had been transported by sea to the end of the peninsula and were massed to take Yorktown.

For the Confederates, grand tactics demanded some kind of diversion to fend off the Yankees from Richmond. Lee, serving as military advisor to Davis, encouraged Stonewall Jackson to conduct such a campaign in the Shenandoah Valley, where his activities would threaten

Union troops stand firm against a Confederate assault during the Battle of Shiloh (April 6–7, 1862), one of the bloodiest battles in the Civil War. (Chicago Historical Society.)

Rear Adm. David Farragut (leaning from rigging) watches as the Confederate ironclad Tennessee passes by his flagship, the Hartford, during the battle for Mobile Bay (Aug. 5, 1864). Farragut's Union fleet forced the Tennessee to surrender and sealed off the port city of Mobile to Confederate shipping. (Wadsworth Atheneum, Hartford, Conn.)

Washington. In a brilliant series of actions from March to June 1862, Jackson, with never more than 16,000 men, confused and stalled about 50,000 Union troops in the valley. As a result, McClellan, who had hoped for aid from a force under McDowell at Fredericksburg, did not receive any reinforcements for his campaign.

Having occupied Yorktown on May 4, McClellan began his cautious advance up the peninsula with more than 100,000 men. After a rear-guard action at Williamsburg (May 5), the Confederates, under Joseph E. Johnston, withdrew slowly until McClellan reached Seven Pines, about 14 km (9 mi) from Richmond. There, on May 31–June 1, Johnston checked McClellan's advance in a pitched battle. Johnston, however, was severely wounded,

Robert E. Lee assumed command of the Confederate Army of Northern Virginia on June 1, 1862. Charged with the defense of Richmond, the Confederate capital, Lee defeated several numerically superior Union armies and even launched two invasions of federal territory.

and command of what would soon be known as the Army of Northern Virginia passed to Lee.

Applying Napoleonic tactics of flanking and fighting, Lee called Jackson to Richmond and planned a great wheeling turn of 95,000 men to flank McClellan's right and pin part of his army against the Chickahominy River. The plans were formulated on the basis of information from J. E. B. STUART, who had made a complete circuit of the Union positions. Inexperienced staff officers, unexpected delays, and stiff Union resistance prevented the total envelopment Lee had hoped for, but the Seven Days' Battles (June 26–July 1) forced McClellan to retreat from the peninsula, removing the threat against Richmond, and gave the Confederacy new hope. (See PENINSULAR CAMPAIGN.)

Second Bull Run. Almost in despair of finding a winning general or combination, Lincoln appointed Henry W. HALLECK commanding general on July 11. Halleck put another Union army into Virginia under John Pope. As Pope advanced from Washington, Lee detached Jackson with more than half the Army of Northern Virginia to meet him. At Cedar Mountain on August 9, Jackson drove Pope back toward Manassas Junction. Having moved up to join Jackson, Lee sent him ahead again to flank Pope and outmarch him to Manassas. There, Jackson destroyed the Union supply depot and took position near the old Bull Run battlefield. While Pope moved to attack Jackson on August 29, Lee sent forward James LONGSTREET's wing of the army, which hit Pope's left flank on August 30. Pope was smashed back across the Potomac. With McClellan's force already withdrawn from Virginia, that Confederate state was now virtually free from invaders. Davis and Lee pondered how to exploit success.

The South's Double Offensive of 1862. Lee was an apt student of Napoleonic teachings, including the French general's call for constant audacity in small powers fighting large ones. In September 1862 the Confederacy

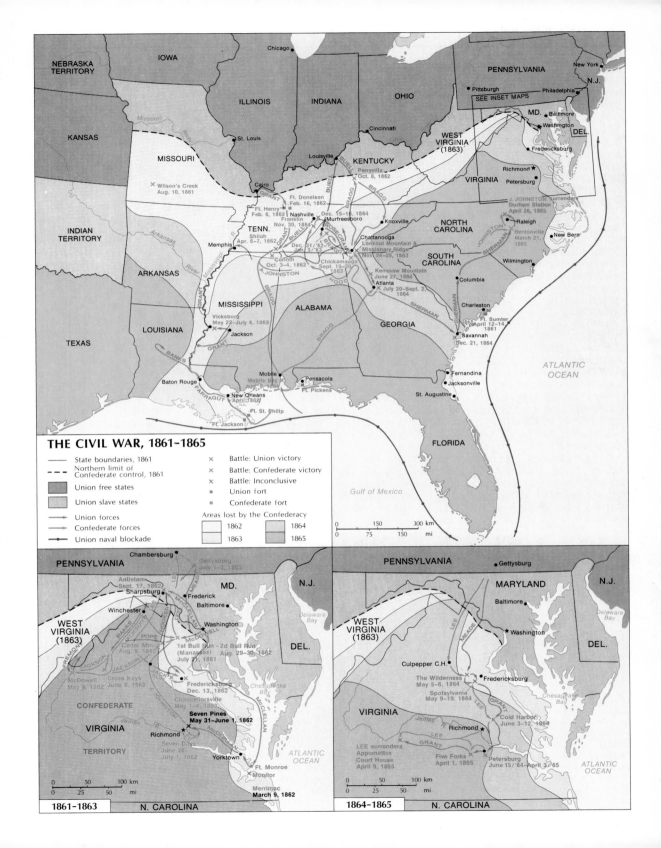

THE CIVIL WAR, 1861-1865

State boundaries, 1861
Northern limit of Confederate control, 1861

Union free states
Union slave states

Union forces
Confederate forces
Union naval blockade

× Battle: Union victory
× Battle: Confederate victory
× Battle: Inconclusive
■ Union fort
■ Confederate fort

Areas lost by the Confederacy
1862
1863
1864
1865

0 75 150 300 km
0   75   150 mi

NEBRASKA TERRITORY
IOWA
Chicago
ILLINOIS
INDIANA
OHIO
PENNSYLVANIA
New York
N.J.
KANSAS
Pittsburgh
Philadelphia
SEE INSET MAPS
MD. Baltimore
Washington
DEL.
St. Louis
Cincinnati
WEST VIRGINIA (1863)
MISSOURI
Louisville
KENTUCKY
Fredericksburg
Richmond
Petersburg
VIRGINIA
Wilson's Creek Aug. 10, 1861
Perryville Oct. 8, 1862
Cairo
Ft. Donelson Feb. 16, 1862
Ft. Henry Feb. 6, 1862
Nashville
Franklin Nov. 30, 1864
Dec. 15-16, 1864
Murfreesboro
Knoxville
J. JOHNSTON surrenders Durham Station April 26, 1865
Raleigh
NORTH CAROLINA
New Bern
TENN.
Shiloh Apr. 6-7, 1862
Memphis
Chattanooga
Lookout Mountain & Missionary Ridge Nov. 24-25, 1863
Bentonville March 21 1865
Corinth Oct. 3-4, 1862
A. JOHNSTON
Chickamauga Sept. 19-20, 1863
Dec. 21, '62- Jan. 3, '63
SOUTH CAROLINA
Wilmington
ARKANSAS
Kenesaw Mountain June 27, 1864
Columbia
MISSISSIPPI
ALABAMA
Atlanta July 20-Sept. 2, 1864
Charleston
Ft. Sumter April 12-14, 1861
Vicksburg May 22-July 4, 1863
GEORGIA
Savannah Dec. 21, 1864
Jackson
TEXAS
LOUISIANA
Mobile
Mobile Bay Aug. 5, 1864
Pensacola
Ft. Pickens
Fernandina
Jacksonville
St. Augustine
Baton Rouge
New Orleans April 1862
Ft. St. Philip
Ft. Jackson
ATLANTIC OCEAN
FLORIDA
Gulf of Mexico

1861-1863

PENNSYLVANIA
Chambersburg
Gettysburg July 1-3, 1863
Antietam Sept. 17, 1862
Sharpsburg
MD.
Frederick
Baltimore
N.J.
Winchester
Washington
Delaware Bay
DEL.
WEST VIRGINIA (1863)
McDowell
Cedar Mtn. Aug. 9, 1862
1st Bull Run - 2d Bull Run (Manassas) Aug. 29-30, 1862
July 21, 1861
McDowell May 8, 1862
Cross Keys June 8, 1862
Fredericksburg Dec. 13, 1862
Chancellorsville May 1-4, 1863
Chesapeake Bay
CONFEDERATE
VIRGINIA
Seven Pines May 31-June 1, 1862
TERRITORY
Richmond
Seven Days June 26-July 1, 1862
Yorktown
Ft. Monroe
Monitor
Merrimac
March 9, 1862
ATLANTIC OCEAN
0 50 100 km
0 25 50 mi

1864-1865

PENNSYLVANIA
Gettysburg
MARYLAND
Baltimore
N.J.
Washington
Delaware Bay
DEL.
WEST VIRGINIA (1863)
Culpepper C.H.
The Wilderness May 5-6, 1864
Fredericksburg
Spotsylvania May 9-19, 1864
Chesapeake Bay
VIRGINIA
Cold Harbor June 3-12, 1864
Richmond
LEE surrenders Appomattox Court House April 9, 1865
Five Forks April 1, 1865
Petersburg June 15/'64-April 3/'65
ATLANTIC OCEAN
0 50 100 km
0 25 50 mi

N. CAROLINA

seemed to have a unique chance for a double offensive. In the west Gen. Braxton BRAGG, with the army that Albert Sidney Johnston and Beauregard had commanded (now known as the Army of Tennessee), was about to move north from Chattanooga, Tenn., into Kentucky. If Lee and Bragg moved in concert, the South might exploit its inner lines and concentrate more troops at crucial points than the enemy. Invasions of Maryland and Kentucky could be defended to the outside world: both were considered Confederate states, and the South would simply be seeking natural boundaries.

Moreover, such a combined offensive conformed to Davis's evolving strategy of the "offensive-defensive," which would permit the South to hoard its thin resources on the defensive and use them for attacks when special opportunities offered. Bragg moved north in late August, and Lee crossed the Potomac in early September.

Everywhere Union forces were on the defensive. The Army of the Potomac, once more under McClellan, reorganized near Washington. Buell's army retreated in confusion ahead of Bragg and was soon in what appeared to be a losing race for Louisville, Ky. If Louisville fell, all of Indiana and Ohio would be open to rebels, the Baltimore and Ohio rail link would break, and the Confederate flag might wave over the Great Lakes. If McClellan failed to halt Lee, Washington might fall. McClellan and Buell could lose the war.

Perryville and Antietam. As it happened, the rebel gamble failed. Bragg maneuvered Buell deftly out of Tennessee, but he avoided battle until too late and was defeated at Perryville, Ky., on Oct. 8, 1862. He retired toward Chattanooga.

Lee's invasion of Maryland went well at first. At Frederick he divided his army of 55,000, sending Jackson to take Harpers Ferry and open up a possible line of retreat to the Shenandoah Valley. However, a copy of Lee's order detailing troop dispositions fell into McClellan's hands,

Confederate dead sprawl before a cannon near Dunker Church, the scene of early fighting in the Battle of Antietam (Sept. 17, 1862). This battle resulted in more casualties than any other one-day engagement of the Civil War.

giving the latter an unusual chance of success.

Concentrating about 70,000 troops quickly in front of Lee at Sharpsburg, Md., along Antietam Creek, McClellan almost wrecked Lee's army, which Jackson had rejoined on September 17. The last-minute arrival of an absent division under A. P. HILL saved Lee (see ANTIETAM, BATTLE OF), but he was forced to retreat across the Potomac into Virginia on September 18–19. Incompetence and bad luck had ruined Davis's plan, but he did not lose heart.

Command Dilemmas. Lincoln nearly lost patience through the fateful summer of 1862. His grasp of strategy, untutored but sound, allowed him to see the chance offered Buell and McClellan. When both failed to seize

During the Battle of Antietam, Confederate troops stalled Union attempts to force a crossing of Burnside Bridge long enough to allow Lee to reinforce his threatened positions.

(Left) *After McClellan's abortive Peninsular Campaign, Henry Halleck was appointed commander of the Union armies, and John Pope was given command of the Army of Virginia. Pope, advancing on Richmond, confronted a Confederate army entrenched near Bull Run. In the ensuing engagement* (right), *the Second Battle of Bull Run (Aug. 29–30, 1862), Pope was trapped between forces led by Stonewall Jackson and James Longstreet and suffered a humiliating defeat.*

that chance after victory, he replaced Buell with William S. ROSECRANS in late October, and put Ambrose E. BURNSIDE in McClellan's place in November. Rosecrans finally forced Bragg's withdrawal from central Tennessee with a costly victory at Stones River (Murfreesboro; December 31–January 3). Burnside, however, who attempted a new drive on Richmond, failed to cross the Rappahannock River with necessary speed at Fredericksburg and found Lee's army concentrated against him. Undaunted, Burnside launched a series of assaults against the entrenched Confederate lines on December 13. The Confederates held their position without difficulty, while Burnside sacrificed more than 12,000 men. A month later he was relieved of command. (See FREDERICKSBURG, BATTLE OF.)

Thus, Lincoln still looked for someone willing to take the initiative and use effectively the massive strengths of the North. Strategy dictated combined use of army and naval forces to keep the Confederate units constantly occupied, to crush the South in a closing vise. As long as the Union armies fought individually, Southern armies, moving on inner lines, could concentrate against them.

Davis perceived the same problem. He developed a novel command structure that was ahead of its time—the theater command. He had followed traditional usage early when he adopted geographical departments as the main command components of the armies. Historically, geographical commands permitted commanders and forces within certain geographical limits to make combined use of military, civil, financial, and other resources; the Civil War's size, however, outstripped this older no-

In this sketch by Henri Lovie, General William Rosecrans (third from left), commander of the Union's Army of the Cumberland, leads a charge during the Battle of Murfreesboro (Dec. 31, 1862–Jan. 3, 1863). (New York Public Library.)

tion. In a large-scale theater of operations, several armies, as well as all other resources of government, would be available to the overall commander. Wise leadership could negate weaknesses in communications and logistics. A special commander, a general of experience and renown, was needed to make the novel idea successful. In November 1862, Davis picked Joseph E. Johnston as commander of the Department of the West, stretching from the Gulf of Mexico as far north as possible and from the Chattahoochee River to the Mississippi.

Davis and Johnston irritated each other, but Johnston had the requisite qualities for the job. Had he risen to the occasion, he might have made the summer of 1863 decisive to Confederate success. Instead, misunderstanding the vast powers bestowed on him, he lapsed into the role of inspector of armies in his domain and did not adequately coordinate reaction to General Grant's brilliant Vicksburg campaign in May, June, and July 1863.

Vicksburg Campaign. After Shiloh, Grant had been relegated to a subordinate position under Henry Halleck. When Halleck went to Washington in July 1862, Grant assumed command of the Army of Tennessee. In October, while Rosecrans (before he succeeded Buell) held Corinth against Confederate assault, Grant began to plan a thrust toward the last fragment of the Mississippi River held by the Confederacy. Although the mouth of the river was now in Union hands, the rebels still held a sufficient stretch to allow communication with the far West. The key point on this stretch was Vicksburg, Miss.

Grant's first two attempts to take Vicksburg failed (December 1862, January–March 1863). In the summer of 1863, however, he determined to stick to his plan until he succeeded. Daring tactics and unusual logistics learned from Winfield Scott in the Mexican War enabled Grant to cross the river south of Vicksburg on April 30 and march swiftly northeast toward Jackson, Miss., thus cutting Gen. John C. Pemberton's Vicksburg army off from the interior. Turning west, he penned Pemberton into Vicksburg and initiated a siege of the city on May 22. Johnston reacted timidly, failing to move Confederate forces south to trap Grant against the river. Vicksburg fell

(Left) *Ambrose E. Burnside, best known for his distinctive whiskers, led the Union Army of the Potomac to defeat in the Battle of Fredericksburg (Dec. 13, 1862). (Below) At Fredericksburg, Burnside's forces suffered thousands of casualties in futile assaults against Confederate positions (Historical Society of Pennsylvania.)*

Stonewall Jackson was accidentally shot by his own troops while reconnoitering during the Battle of Chancellorsville (May 1–4, 1863). His death on May 10 cast a pall over the Confederate success in that battle. (Library of Congress.)

on July 4, 1863, and the Union captured 30,000 prisoners and much booty. (See VICKSBURG CAMPAIGN.)

Chancellorsville. Grant's operations had been loosely connected with the spring offensive of the Army of the Potomac. Gen. Joseph HOOKER, Burnside's successor, had planned to flank Lee, who was still entrenched near Fredericksburg, and get between him and Richmond. However, Lee came out to meet Hooker in Virginia's Wilderness,

detaching Jackson for a flanking attack. On May 1–4, Hooker was decisively beaten at Chancellorsville, but Jackson was mortally wounded, and gloom tinged the Southern success. (See CHANCELLORSVILLE, BATTLE OF.)

Gettysburg. On the heels of this victory, Lee seized the initiative by reorganizing his army and invading Pennsylvania. Pemberton needed a diversion to loosen the bonds at Vicksburg; Virginia was picked clean of food; and Lee thought he could reprovision his army as well as aid the West by moving north. He might have detached men to send west, but he persuaded Davis to try for a quicker decision.

At Gettysburg, Pa., on July 1, 1863, Lee's men met the Army of the Potomac, now commanded by George G. MEADE. Three days of fierce fighting resulted. On the first day the Confederates drove the Union forces back, until the latter reached a strong defensive position on Culp's Hill and Cemetery Hill. On the second day, Confederate attacks on the Union flanks failed to dislodge Meade. Finally, on July 3, Lee ordered Gen. George E. PICKETT to lead a charge against the Union center on Cemetery Ridge. About 15,000 dared the hill; approximately 6,000 were killed or wounded in the repulse. Lee lost a total of 28,000 in casualties, as well as many weapons. His train of wounded was miles long as his army retreated back to Virginia. (See GETTYSBURG, BATTLE OF.)

Chickamauga and Chattanooga. Vicksburg and Gettysburg were staggering blows to the Confederacy. The remainder of 1863 held little good news for the South, except for the flickering hope offered by a victory near Chattanooga in September.

General Grant (lower right) watches as Union troops lay siege to Vicksburg, the last major Confederate stronghold on the Mississippi River. The commander of Vicksburg's Confederate defenders, John C. Pemberton, surrendered the city on July 4, 1863. (Library of Congress.)

Gen. Meade was given command of the Army of the Potomac only three days before engaging Lee's Army of Northern Virginia in the Battle of Gettysburg (July 1–3, 1863).

William Tecumseh Sherman was given command of the Union armies in the West in March 1864. Sherman hastened the war's conclusion by invading Georgia, capturing Atlanta, and leading his army on the famous "March to the Sea," which devastated Georgia.

In early September, Rosecrans maneuvered Bragg out of Chattanooga and pursued him into northwestern Georgia. Bragg, however, was reinforced by Longstreet's corps from Lee. Catching Rosecrans in an exposed position along Chickamauga Creek on September 19–20, Bragg smashed the Union forces back into Chattanooga's defenses. Bragg lost the impetus of success, however. Clapping an incomplete siege around Chattanooga, he frittered away his men in peripheral ventures. Longstreet, for example, was sent to lay siege to Burnside at Knoxville.

In mid-October, Grant, newly appointed as commander of all the Union forces in the West, replaced Rosecrans with George H. THOMAS and sent a relief force into Chattanooga. A month later, reinforced Union troops dislodged Bragg's forces from Lookout Mountain and Missionary Ridge (November 24–25). Longstreet abandoned the siege of Knoxville in early December, and the Confederate Army of Tennessee took refuge for the winter near Dalton, Ga. (See CHATTANOOGA, BATTLES OF; CHICKAMAUGA, BATTLE OF.)

Grant Takes Command. Lincoln had noted that Meade failed to press victory after Gettysburg, while Grant at Vicksburg had stuck to his campaign until victorious. Grant seemed to be the commander that Lincoln was looking for, and in March 1864 he became general in chief of all the Union armies. His task was to concentrate the North's massive resources in men and material and keep throwing them at the enemy.

When he gave Grant supreme command of the North's armies, Lincoln made a quantum advance in democratic command. Keeping the constitutional responsibility himself, he turned active charge of operations over to a man he trusted. This scheme, combined with Davis's theater struc-

A. P. Hill's Confederate divisions charge the Union positions at Gettysburg. Union troops retreated to the surrounding hills and held off repeated assaults by Lee's forces. (West Point Museum Collection, U.S. Military Academy.)

Confederate soldiers captured during the Battle of Gettysburg were photographed before being assigned to a prison camp. (Library of Congress.)

ture, set the pattern for management of future U.S. wars.

Grant wasted no time. He placed the western armies under his old lieutenant, William Tecumseh SHERMAN, who had played a key role at both Vicksburg and Chattanooga. Meade was left in charge of the Army of the Potomac, but Grant established his own headquarters nearby. His plan was simple: keep pressure on the South's two major armies, prevent them from reinforcing each other, and fight throughout the summer. The offensive would start in May 1864.

Confederate Strategy, 1864. Reduced in strength and resources, Lee and Joseph Johnston, the latter again in command of the Army of Tennessee, hoped to beat Grant to the attack, but sufficient wagons and supplies were not available for an offensive. Late in 1863 Lee had a chance to trap Meade at Mine Run in the Virginia Wilderness, but he discovered that he lacked skilled commanders for the first time. Casualties had whittled away the experience in his top echelons; the younger men could only gain experience in the coming summer. Johnston was also unable to amass the men or transport to take the initiative that was so strongly urged by Davis.

In the campaigns that followed, both Confederate armies fended off the enemy bravely. Their chief hope was to run up the cost of Union success beyond Northern patience as the presidential election of 1864 approached. Lincoln was under attack from Radical Republicans, who thought he had temporized too long on the question of emancipation of the slaves and disliked his moderate plan for postwar RECONSTRUCTION. On the other extreme, he had offended conservatives by suspending habeas corpus and by introducing (1863) conscription and his EMANCIPATION PROCLAMATION. Antiwar feeling had been apparent in the DRAFT RIOTS of 1863, and even the northern victories of that year had not offset the high casualties. The South could at least hope that continuing high casualties would convince Northerners to elect George B. McClellan, who was the Northern Democrat's standard-bearer on a peace platform.

Virginia Campaigns of 1864–65. Casualties were running high. Launching a new drive on Richmond, Grant and Meade suffered heavy losses in the WILDERNESS CAMPAIGN of May–June 1864. At Cold Harbor on June 3, Grant made a mistake that cost the Union more than 6,000 killed and wounded in less than an hour. Instead

General Joseph Hooker (on white horse) directs artillery fire against the Confederate positions atop Chattanooga's Lookout Mountain (Nov. 24, 1863). (Office of Military History, Department of the Army.)

Abraham Lincoln reads a preliminary draft of his Emancipation Proclamation before cabinet members. The document, which went into effect on Jan. 1, 1863, provided for the abolition of slavery only in the Confederate States of America not under federal control.

of retiring to lick its wounds, however, the Army of the Potomac pushed on across the James River, intending to capture Petersburg, about 40 km (25 mi) south of Richmond. The Confederate capital's rail connection to the south ran through Petersburg. If direct approaches were impossible, Richmond might be toppled by sealing it off from outside help.

The initial assault on Petersburg was repelled (June 15) by a force of old men, boys, and casuals under Beauregard. They held on until Lee sent help and established fortified lines that stopped Grant's main attack on June 18. Grant then dug in for a siege. (See PETERSBURG CAMPAIGN.)

Lee knew that his only hope lay in restoring maneuverability to his army. He tried to divert some of Grant's strength by detaching Jubal EARLY, with Jackson's old corps, against Washington in mid-June. Early, who had some of Jackson's dash, stormed down the Shenandoah Valley and in July bombarded Washington's defenses—some of his sharpshooters even fired on Lincoln, who was watching from Fort Stevens's parapet. But the attack on Washington was no more than a raid. In August, Grant dispatched Philip SHERIDAN to the valley, where he conducted a campaign of systematic devastation. He finally defeated Early at Cedar Creek on October 19. Three weeks later the Northern presidential election took place, and Lincoln won comfortably.

On Feb. 3, 1865, a Southern delegation met Lincoln and Seward on a ship in Hampton Roads, but Davis's insistence on recognition of Southern independence prevented effective negotiations. The siege of Petersburg, however, was wearing Lee down. His lines finally broke at the end of March 1865; he evacuated Richmond on April 2 and retreated west, hoping to join Johnston's army somewhere in the Carolinas. A week's desperate quest for rations brought the Army of Northern Virginia to APPOMATTOX COURT HOUSE, where it was virtually surrounded. Only 9,000 of Lee's 20,000-odd troops carried muskets at the last roll call. On Apr. 9, 1865, Lee surrendered his army to Grant.

Georgia and Carolina Campaigns. Leaving Chattanooga in early May 1864, Sherman invaded Georgia with three armies totaling 100,000 men. With an army of only 60,000, Johnston fell back mile by mile, stalling Sherman repeatedly. At Kennesaw Mountain, on June 27, he fought a pitched battle that cost Sherman dearly. Finally, Johnston settled into Atlanta's defenses in early July. Davis, however, was furious at Johnston's unexplained re-

Confederates (top) under Gen. John B. Hood surge forward to check the advance of Union troops toward Atlanta. Despite a stubborn defense, on Sept. 2, 1864, the city fell to Sherman's Union armies, providing Abraham Lincoln with a much-needed victory to boost his campaign for reelection. (Detail from the Atlanta Cyclorama: City of Atlanta.)

Southern forces and members of the Confederate government flee across the James River as Richmond burns (Apr. 2, 1865). Richmond's factories, mills, and arsenals were set afire before the evacuation.

treat and made the error of replacing him with Gen. John B. HOOD on July 17. A gallant but reckless officer, Hood attacked furiously and lost. In early September he was forced to abandon Atlanta. Sherman's occupation of that key city buoyed Northern morale and contributed to Lincoln's success in the presidential election two months later. (See ATLANTA CAMPAIGN.)

Hood then tried a strategic diversion, in the best sense of the offensive-defensive: he invaded Tennessee, hoping to draw Sherman after him. Sherman, however, left George H. Thomas to deal with Hood, while he marched virtually unopposed to the sea. Laying waste as he went,

In this painting by the artist Louis Guillaume, Grant accepts Lee's surrender of the Army of Northern Virginia on Apr. 9, 1865. The dramatic encounter took place at Appomattox Court House, Va.

Sherman's intent was to make "Georgia howl." He reached Savannah and occupied it on December 21.

In Tennessee, Hood won a costly battle at Franklin on November 30, but at Nashville on Dec. 15–16, 1864, his army was wrecked, and its remnants streamed toward Georgia.

Restored to Johnston's charge, the tiny Army of Tennessee sought to delay Sherman's powerful columns as they coursed through the Carolinas in the spring of 1865. At Bentonville, N.C., on Mar. 19–21, 1865, Johnston won his last victory, but Sherman kept pushing forward. On April 13, the day before Lincoln's assassination in Washington, Sherman occupied Raleigh. At Durham Station, N.C., on Apr. 26, 1865, Johnston formally surrendered his army to Sherman. The main land campaign ended that day. Fighting west of the Mississippi continued to the end of May, but it was peripheral to the war's outcome.

Diplomacy and Naval Policy

Somehow the end seemed inevitable at Appomattox and at Durham Station, yet the issue had often hung in doubt. When Lincoln issued (Sept. 22, 1862) his Preliminary Emancipation Proclamation on the heels of dubious success at Antietam, he foiled the Confederacy's best chance for British recognition. The British cabinet, divided in sentiments toward the Civil War, was about to debate either outright recognition of the Southern government or an offer of mediation. Either would have vastly boosted Southern stock in the world.

Lincoln's proclamation did not actually free any slaves, since its provisions were confined to states not in Union control by January 1863, but the proclamation had dramatic domestic and foreign impact. When Lincoln followed it in January with a full document outlining emancipation as victory progressed, he changed the course of

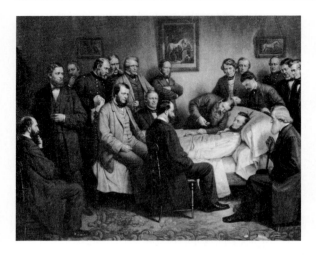

Medical specialists and distraught cabinet officers crowd around the deathbed of Abraham Lincoln. Lincoln was mortally wounded by John Wilkes Booth as he attended a play at Ford's Theater in Washington, D.C., Apr. 14, 1865.

the war. Up to that time not all Northerners knew what they were fighting for; now they were on the side of freedom. The South could not wholly slip the stigma of slave ownership.

The Confederacy's Foreign Supplies. Confederate diplomatic efforts were deft after an initial fumbling period. When Judah P. BENJAMIN became Confederate secretary of state in March 1862, he brought a canny realism to diplomacy. He realized that European recognition would depend on martial success; while he waited for that success, he turned to active secondary diplomacy. Commercial agents were sent abroad to increase the amounts of supplies purchased there.

From early in the war the Confederate Ordnance Department, under the brilliant leadership of Josiah Gorgas (1818–83), had sent small, fast ships (blockade runners) to Bermuda, the Bahamas, and Cuba. At those islands, the runners picked up cargoes of munitions and other stores brought from Europe in large freighters. Private contractors who ran the blockade with luxury items or staples made fantastic profits; the business gained a dubious glamour as the South's resources dwindled and everything became scarce.

Benjamin at last determined to systematize this haphazard traffic. He sent a special agent, Colin McRae (1812–77), to Europe to manage all monies raised abroad and expenditures and orders for supplies. This system, inaugurated in 1863, produced remarkable results. Between 1861 and 1865, 330,000 small arms were imported for the government and perhaps another 270,000 for states and private firms.

In early 1864 the normally laissez-faire Confederate Congress passed laws commandeering room on outgoing and incoming runners for government cargoes, but this important centralizing step came too late. Had such bold

steps, including the creation (March 1864) of a Bureau of Foreign Supplies been taken earlier, the system that provided much might have provided enough.

Confederate Cruisers. The United States wanted to stop the South from buying blockade runners and warships in Britain. U.S. agents operating along the Clydeside in Scotland fought clandestine skirmishes with Confederate naval agents. At first the British government refused to intervene in this situation, but in September 1863 it ordered that Confederate warships under construction in Britain be held in port.

Before this blow the South had put about 20 warships to sea, many of them built in Britain. The most famous of these Confederate cruisers was the *Alabama*, which slipped out of Liverpool in the summer of 1862. Commanded by Raphael SEMMES, it is a legend in sea warfare, capturing almost 70 U.S. merchant ships. So successful were the *Alabama* and other cruisers in raiding U.S. merchantmen that most of the latter "fled the flag" to other registries. If more cruisers had been built, they might have destroyed the U.S. merchant marine.

Naval Innovations. Commerce raiding was a novel weapon and a splendid example of the original sea warfare doctrine espoused by the Confederate navy secretary Stephen R. MALLORY. Mallory recognized that naval warfare was at a turning point. The day of the iron ships was coming, and Mallory backed his vision by converting the captured U.S.S. *Merrimack* into the ironclad C.S.S. *Virginia*. Although Mallory built other iron ships, he was hampered by the unreliable engines produced by Confederate shops, and metal was needed for cannon. Southern efforts to buy ironclads abroad were only partially successful. Nonetheless, Mallory and his officers deserve credit for spearheading the seapower of the future. Their innovations also included the torpedo boat; the water mine; and the first modern submarine, the *H. L. Hunley*, which sank a U.S. ship—and itself—in Charleston harbor in 1864.

In this Currier & Ives print, the U.S.S. Kearsarge (left) fires a broadside at the Alabama, a Confederate raider that had been preying on Union shipping. After an 80-minute battle on June 19, 1864, the Kearsarge sank the Alabama in the English Channel.

In the first engagement between ironclad warships, the U.S.S. Monitor (left) and the Merrimack *(refitted by the Confederates as the* Virginia*) fought (Mar. 9, 1862) to a draw off Hampton Roads, Va.*

The North responded with its own originality. The U.S.S. *Monitor* was quickly designed to do battle with the *Merrimack/Virginia* in the first clash of floating iron. In time, special river ironclads enabled the North to range Southern waterways almost at will. In time the Union navy became the best in the world. Its steadfast opponent, however, did not finally strike its colors until the *Shenandoah*, the last Confederate cruiser, lowered its flag in Liverpool on Nov. 6, 1865.

Former slaves were often unable to cope with their new status after the war. The Freedmen's Bureau was founded by the government in 1865 to ease the transition of Southern blacks from slavery to citizenship.

Economic Factors

With few industrial resources at the start, Southern officials made remarkable strides in creating a small industrialized nation. Logistics, however, finally defeated the Confederacy.

The Money Problem. Money was not always plentiful in the North. Paper money gradually intruded on specie, and large loans had to be floated to sustain the war effort, with financiers such as Jay COOKE serving as agents and making fortunes. However, money could be obtained in the North.

In the South money had to be printed. From a par level at the beginning, Confederate dollars constantly sagged as inflation paced defeat; by 1865, a Confederate dollar was worth about 1.5 cents in Union money.

Costs of the War

The statistics of death and destruction are grim, cold, and not necessarily accurate. By some counts more than 2.25 million white, black, and Indian men were in the Union armies and navy. Of these more than 650,000 died from all causes or were wounded. Confederate statistics are vague. The historian E. B. Long, a careful student of war strengths, suggests that "perhaps 750,000 individuals would be reasonably close" as an estimate of Southern enrollments in the armies and navy.

Civilian Conservation Corps The Civilian Conservation Corps (CCC) was established in 1933 as a NEW DEAL program to combat unemployment in the United States during the DEPRESSION OF THE 1930s. Unemployed, unmarried young men were enlisted to work on conservation and resource-development projects such as soil conservation and flood control. Enrollees were provided with food and lodging and were given a small salary. In 1935, 2,600 CCC camps had an enrollment of 500,000. The CCC was abolished in 1942.

---

civilization   The term *civilization* designates a condition of human society characterized by a high level of cultural and technological achievement and correspondingly complex social and political development.

Theories about Civilization. In the 1920s the British archaeologist V. Gordon CHILDE defined civilization in terms of the elements that he believed fundamental in transforming a CULTURE into a civilization. These traits include the invention of writing, metallurgy, standard units of weights and measures, mathematics, monumental architecture, long-distance trade, wheeled carts, specialized artisans, irrigation technology, surplus production, and the use of the plough.

Contemporary scholars cite the following set of interrelated social institutions as basic to the definition of a civilization: (1) class stratification, with each stratum differentiated by the degree of its ownership or control of the main productive resources; (2) political and religious hierarchies that complement each other in the administration of territorially organized states; (3) a complex division of labor, with full-time artisans, soldiers, and bureaucrats existing alongside the mass of primary peasant producers.

Civilizations of the Past. Anthropologists in the 19th century formulated a theory of cultural evolution in which they divided human development into three stages: savagery, barbarism, and civilization. The stage of civilization was at that time believed to be restricted to the Egyptian, Assyrian, Greek, and Roman peoples of antiquity.

Within the past 100 years archaeological research has more than doubled this list. The earliest civilization, that of the SUMERIANS in Mesopotamia (*c.*5000–4000 BC), was rediscovered in the early part of this century. The Minoan and Mycenaean civilizations that preceded classical Greece in the Aegean and date from *c.*3000 to *c.*1000 BC, also became known at about the same time (see AEGEAN CIVILIZATION). The SHANG civilization of the Huang He (Hwang Ho) valley in North China, which emerged in about 1600 BC, was discovered through archaeological excavations in the late 1920s. As recently as 1924 the British archaeologist John MARSHALL announced the discovery of the INDUS CIVILIZATION (at its peak from *c.*2300–1700 BC); it has the largest geographical distribution of all Old World civilizations. The ancient civilizations of the New World are those of MESOAMERICA and of the Andean region of South America (both *c.*1200 BC–Spanish conquest). Archaeologists have spent much effort excavating the remains of these civilizations and attempting to understand their nature and the processes that led to their formation and eventual decline.

Historians have differed greatly in enumerating past civilizations. In *The Decline of the West* (2 vols., 1918–22; Eng. trans., 1926–28), the German philosopher Oswald SPENGLER acknowledged only 8 civilizations in history. The English historian Arnold TOYNBEE, in his monu-

mental work *A Study of History* (12 vols., 1934–61), named 26. It is therefore clear that, depending on the criteria used, one can judiciously increase or decrease the number of past and present civilizations. Prevalent in the Victorian age was the view that the pinnacle of civilization was that of the Western world, rooted in ancient Greece and Rome. This ethnocentric view overlooked the civilizations of Islam, Byzantium, India, China, Japan, and the West African kingdoms.

Civilization and Its Discontents   In *Civilization and Its Discontents* (1930), Sigmund FREUD expounded the psychological theory that complex societies and their attendant cultures spring from the channeling of socially proscribed erotic and aggressive urges into constructive works. Because such sublimations are never entirely satisfactory substitutes for the desire, tension remains, sometimes released in antisocial or nonsocial behavior. Freud's psychological history contrasts with other theories of history, such as the economic determinism of Karl Marx.

Cixi, Dowager Empress of China   Commonly known among Western historians as "The Old Buddha," the Empress Dowager Cixi, b. Nov. 29, 1835, d. Nov. 15, 1908, used a series of "regencies" to rule de facto for the final five decades of the QING (Ch'ing) dynasty in China. As concubine to the Zianfeng (Hsien-feng) emperor, Cixi bore his only son. In 1861, when the 5-year-old boy became the Tongzhi (T'ung-chih) emperor, Cixi contrived to become coregent with the empress. When the emperor died in 1875, Cixi remained in power by manipulating the succession to put her infant nephew on the throne as the Guangxu (Kuang-hsü) emperor.

Her rule was autocratic, ruthless, and extravagant. In 1898, Cixi nullified the decrees issued by the Guangxu emperor in collaboration with KANG YOUWEI (Kang Yu-wei) to modernize China (since called the Hundred Days of Reform) by seizing the emperor in a coup d'état to begin her third regency. In 1900 she supported the antiforeign BOXER UPRISING because she believed that the foreign powers intended to demand her retirement. The day before her death Cixi appointed the 2-year-old Henry Buyi (Pu-yi) to succeed his uncle, the Guangxu emperor, who had suddenly and mysteriously died.

Clackmannan   [klak-man'-uhn]   Clackmannan (also called Clackmannanshire), the smallest county in Scotland until 1975, when it became part of the CENTRAL administrative region, was in the east central part of the country, at the head of the Firth of Forth. Alloa was the county town. The Ochil Hills (average elevation 600 m/ 2,000 ft) cover the northern portion of the area. Coal mining is the economic mainstay, although sheep raising, agriculture (on land reclaimed from the firth), and light manufacturing, particularly of woolen worsted and beer, are also important. The Picts, who inhabited the area by the 7th century, were defeated there in 843 by Kenneth MacAlpin, the Scottish king.

Clair, René   René Clair, b. Nov. 11, 1898, d. Mar. 15, 1981, originally named René Chomette, was a French filmmaker best known as a director and writer of ironic comedies. He directed his first film, *Entr'acte*, in 1923. His best-known silent film is *The Italian Straw Hat* (1927). Clair, with such comedies as *Sous les toits de Paris* (Under the Rooftops of Paris, 1930) and *Le Million* (1931), was among the first to make films with sound tracks. His satire on modern technology, *À nous la liberté* (Freedom Is Ours, 1931), is thought to have inspired Charlie Chaplin's *Modern Times* (1936). Clair's later comedies include *Le Silence est d'or* (Silence Is Golden, 1947) and *Les Grandes Manoeuvres* (Grand Maneuvers, 1955). In 1960 he became the first film director elected to the Académie Française.

clairvoyance   SEE PARAPSYCHOLOGY

clam   Clams comprise a large group of often edible, mostly marine MOLLUSKS in the class Bivalvia, or Pelecypoda (see BIVALVE). Different species are called geoducks, quahogs, hard-shell or soft-shell clams, littlenecks, cherrystones, and other names.

The clam body is enclosed by a mantle tissue and two

A clam is a shallow-water marine mollusk represented by more than 12,000 species, most of which are edible. A clam has two shells that open and close by muscle action; a muscular foot; and gills that filter oxygen and food from water.

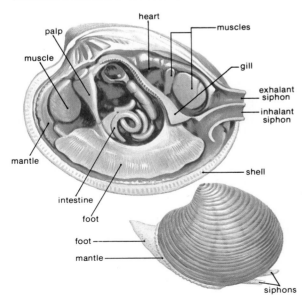

symmetrical shells (valves) held closed by two large muscles and joined by a dorsal hinge joint. The muscular foot is used to burrow in mud or sand. Buried clams extend siphons above the surface to maintain water currents needed for respiration and feeding. Most clams are only a few centimeters long, but the giant clam of the Indian and Pacific oceans may be nearly 130 cm (50 in) long and weigh 227 kg (500 lb).

As filter feeders, clams use their greatly enlarged gills as food collectors. Particulate matter, especially protozoans and organic wastes, clings to the gill filaments and eventually is engulfed in a mucous mass and passed to the mouth.

The clam has a three-chambered heart. Its nervous system consists of three pairs of ganglia with connectives (there is no defined head region); sense organs are concentrated in the mantle tissue. The animals are either male or female. During reproduction eggs and sperm are released into the ocean, where fertilization takes place.

clan   A clan is a kin group whose members claim common ancestry. An important unit of the SOCIAL STRUCTURE of societies throughout the world, a clan is generally composed of numerous LINEAGES of varying size. Most stress collective rights and obligations and provide members with mutual support during FEUDS or other conflicts. The term (from Gaelic *clann*, "offspring") originally referred to Irish and Scottish family groups, known from as early as AD 1000, with common names and ancestors. Scottish Highland clans early developed distinctive identifying TARTANS (plaid designs), for which they are famous.

Anthropologists define a clan as a social group whose members trace their descent unilineally, or exclusively through one line—through males (a patriclan) or through females (a matriclan)—back to a remote ancestor whose name has been forgotten, or to a supposed ancestor, or to a mythical figure or animal (see TOTEM).

Membership in a sib, as clans thus defined are also called, is based solely on descent. Clans are also sometimes defined as compromise kin groups in which membership is based on two principles, a rule of descent and a rule of residence.

Clapton, Eric   British guitarist, singer, and composer Eric Clapton, b. Eric Patrick Clapp on Mar. 30, 1945, is one of rock music's most accomplished guitarists. Basing his style in the folk-blues tradition of Muddy Waters, Clapton achieved cult status—"Clapton is God" was common graffiti—with several popular and influential bands: the Yardbirds (1963–65), John Mayall's Bluesbreakers (1965–66), Cream (1966–68; comprising Clapton, Jack Bruce, and Ginger Baker), Blind Faith (1969), and Derek and the Dominos (1970–71). Since 1974 he has performed solo. The songs "Sunshine of Your Love" (1967), "After Midnight" (1970), "Layla" (1970), "Lay Down Sally" (1977), and "Cocaine" (1977) are among his most famous.

Clare   Clare (Irish: Chláir) is a county in western Ireland, between the Atlantic coast and the River Shannon estuary, in Munster province. It covers 3,188 km^2 (1,231 mi^2), and the population is 91,343 (1986). Ennis is the county town.

The Burren, a flat limestone plateau with little vegetation, is in the north. Clare's hilly, lake-filled center gradually slopes down to fertile coastal plains, which are farmed. Coastal fishing is important, and lead, marble, and slate are mined.

Vikings invaded Clare late in the 8th century. From the 11th to 17th century, the O'Brian clan controlled the county.

Clare, John   John Clare, b. July 13, 1793, d. May 20, 1864, was an English romantic poet noted for his simple but expressive nature poems. A farm laborer with little education, he achieved fame as the so-called Northampton peasant poet with his first volume of verse, *Poems Descriptive of Rural Life and Scenery* (1820). Clare was confined to a mental asylum from 1838 until his death, but much of his later poetry has become known and appreciated in the 20th century.

Clare of Assisi, Saint   A follower of St. Francis of Assisi, Clare, b. 1194, d. Aug. 11, 1253, left her noble Italian family to found the women's religious order known as "Poor Clares." She led a life of austerity and prayer according to the Franciscan rule. Devoted to the Eucharist, Clare is often pictured with a monstrance, a eucharistic vessel. She was canonized in 1255. Feast day: Aug. 11.

Claremont Colleges   The Claremont Colleges are six associated colleges on contiguous campuses in Claremont, Calif. Each is an independent school with its own administration, faculties, and curricula, and each maintains a separate identity in character and in academic offerings. Four coeducational undergraduate colleges offer separate, distinct programs: **Pomona** (1887) has a liberal arts curriculum; **Claremont McKenna College** (1946), a men's college until 1976, has liberal arts studies with particular emphasis on political science and economics; **Harvey Mudd** (1955) concentrates on sciences, mathematics, and engineering; and **Pitzer** (1963) stresses social and behavioral sciences in its liberal arts program. **Scripps** (1926) is a liberal arts school for women. The **Claremont University Center** houses the **Claremont Graduate School** (1925), as well as the central library used by all the Claremont Colleges, some of which have their own libraries.

Clarendon, Edward Hyde, 1st Earl of   Lord Clarendon, b. Feb. 18, 1609, d. Dec. 9, 1674, was a leading English statesman of the Restoration period. He entered Parliament in 1640 and as chancellor of the exchequer (1643) worked unsuccessfully to reconcile King Charles I with Parliament during the English Civil War. He followed Prince Charles (later Charles II) into exile in 1646 and negotiated his restoration to the throne in 1660. Hyde, who was created earl of Clarendon in 1661, served as lord chancellor from 1660 to 1667; the Clarendon Code was named for him, although he actually disapproved of the laws, which penalized religious dissenters. Reverses in the Second Anglo-Dutch War led to his dismissal in 1667. He fled to France, where he completed his *History of the Rebellion* (1702–24), still a standard source on the English Civil War. Clarendon's daughter Anne was the first wife of the duke of York (later James II) and the mother of queens Mary II and Anne.

Clarendon Code   The Clarendon Code is the name given to four English statutes passed by Parliament after the Restoration of the monarchy in 1660 to reestablish the Anglican church (see England, Church of) and penalize the Puritans. The laws were named after Charles II's chief minister, the 1st earl of Clarendon.

The Corporation Act of 1661 required all holders of municipal office to take communion according to the rites of the Church of England and to abjure the Solemn League and Covenant of 1643, whose subscribers had sworn to promote Presbyterianism as the established church. The Act of Uniformity of 1662 provided for the ejection from their parishes of all clergymen who refused to subscribe to all tenets of the Book of Common Prayer. As a result, about 2,000 clergy left the church; these were the original Nonconformists. The Conventicle Act of 1664 set penalties for attending non-Anglican religious services. Finally, the Five Mile Act of 1665 prohibited clergymen who had not subscribed to the Act of Uniformity from residing within 8 km (5 mi) of the town, borough, or parish from which they had been ejected.

clarinet [klair-i-net']   The clarinet is a wind instrument consisting of a cylindrical wood (or occasionally metal) pipe with a bell-shaped opening at one end and a mouthpiece at the other end, to which a reed is attached. Generically, the clarinet is any member of the woodwind family, whose enclosed air column is activated by a single reed, as opposed to the double-reed instruments of the oboe family. It is a versatile member of the orchestra, the principal treble woodwind of the concert band and is used extensively in solo, chamber, and popular music. The clarinet is a transposing instrument—its part in the score is written at a pitch different from the one actually sounded.

The immediate ancestor of the clarinet was the chalumeau, a short, cylindrical pipe with seven finger holes and a reed cut in its upper side, but without a bell-shaped opening. The clarinet was invented when Johann C. Denner (1655-1707) doubled the length of the chalumeau and added two keys, making possible the clarino, the upper or trumpetlike, register.

Early clarinets were made in many more sizes than are

The clarinet is a versatile, single-reed wind instrument equally adaptable for use by orchestras, jazz ensembles, and dance bands. The B-flat clarinet (left) is the most common member of the family; less common is the alto clarinet (right).

George Rogers Clark, a general during the American Revolution, led several successful expeditions in the Illinois country of the Old Northwest. Fighting against the British and later against Indian tribes, Clark was instrumental in gaining the midwestern lands for the United States.

produced today. The number of different sizes needed was reduced in the early 19th century by adding more keys to the instrument. The B-flat clarinet is most common today; next is the clarinet in A. The B-flat clarinet is about 60 cm (23.6 in) long and has a range of more than three octaves. Since the end of the 19th century, a D clarinet and a bass clarinet in B-flat have been used in large orchestras. Concert bands commonly use a small E-flat clarinet, pitched a fourth above the B-flat clarinet; an alto clarinet in E-flat, pitched a fifth lower than the B-flat clarinet; and a bass clarinet, pitched an octave lower than the standard instrument; these constitute the "clarinet choir." A double-bass, or contrabass, clarinet is pitched two octaves lower than the standard B-flat clarinet.

Clark, Francis Edward   Francis Edward Clark, b. Aylmer, Quebec, Sept. 12, 1851, d. May 26, 1927, was the founder of the CHRISTIAN ENDEAVOR movement. As a clergyman he organized (1881) the young people of his Congregational church in Portland, Maine, into a society dedicated to practical religious activity. Clark eventually became president of the World's Christian Endeavor Union and editor of the *Christian Endeavor World*.

Clark, George Rogers   George Rogers Clark, b. near Charlottesville, Va., Nov. 19, 1752, d. Feb. 13, 1818, was a military leader on the American frontier, renowned for his dramatic expedition from Kentucky into the Illinois territory during the American Revolution. Clark moved to Kentucky in 1775. After organizing and leading Kentucky militiamen in the defense of their settlements,

he decided to carry the war to the British by attacking posts in Illinois. Leaving Louisville in June 1778 with fewer than 200 men, he took Kaskaskia without resistance in July. This success convinced the French inhabitants of Cahokia and Vincennes to transfer their allegiance to the Americans. Henry Hamilton, the British commander at Detroit, then led an expedition that captured Vincennes in December 1778. In February 1779, however, Clark led a small force across the harsh winter terrain, retook Vincennes, and captured Hamilton. After the war Clark returned to Louisville, where he lived until his death.

Clark, Jim   James Clark, b. Mar. 4, 1936, d. Apr. 7, 1968, was a Scotsman who was the foremost race-car driver of the 1960s. He is judged by many to have been the greatest driver of all time. At the age of 25 he won four 1962 Grand Prix races in Formula One cars. A year later he won seven Grand Prix events and the world title. In 1965 he became the first non-American since 1916 to win the Indianapolis 500, and once again he won the world driving championship for Grand Prix cars. In all, he set a record by winning 25 Grand Prix events before his death in a race in West Germany when he was only 32 years of age.

Clark, Joseph   Charles Joseph Clark, b. High River, Alberta, June 5, 1939, served as prime minister of Canada for 9 months in 1979–80.

In 1967, Clark became executive assistant to Robert Stanfield, leader of the Progressive Conservative Party (PCP). In 1972 he was elected to Canada's House of Commons, and in 1976, after Stanfield's resignation, he became leader of the PCP. In 1979 he led the PCP to a narrow victory over Pierre Elliot Trudeau and the Liberal party.

From the outset Clark's government was shaky because it did not have a majority in parliament and had to rely on the support of smaller parties. In elections held in

Leader of Canada's Progressive Conservative party from 1976 to 1983, Joe Clark was prime minister of Canada in 1979–80. He was the youngest man to hold that office in Canadian history.

February 1980 he was defeated by Trudeau because of strong oppostition to his proposed increase in the excise tax on gasoline. Clark resigned as party leader in February 1983. When Brian MULRONY, the new PCP leader, became prime minister in 1984, Clark was appointed external affairs minister. He continued in that post after the PCP's victory in 1988.

Clark, Kenneth B.   Kenneth Bancroft Clark, b. Panama Canal Zone, July 24, 1914, is an American psychologist who studies racial segregation. A participant from 1939 to 1941 in Gunnar MYRDAL's study of the race problem in the United States, in 1942, Clark started teaching at the College of the City of New York and was promoted to full professor in 1960. He became professor emeritus in 1975.

A report prepared by Clark, arguing that segregation impairs the development of both white and black students, figured prominently in the 1954 U.S. Supreme Court decision barring segregation. In 1954 he charged de facto segregation in New York City schools, an accusation that precipitated sweeping reforms in the system. Clark wrote *Dark Ghetto* (1965) and *King, Malcolm, Baldwin* (1984).

Clark, Kenneth M.   The British scholar Kenneth Mackenzie Clark, Baron Clark of Saltwood, b. July 13, 1903, d. May 21, 1983, was a leading art critic and art historian. Among his critical studies are *Leonardo da Vinci* (1939), *Landscape into Art* (1949), *Piero della Francesca* (1951), *The Nude* (1955), and *Rembrandt and the Italian Renaissance* (1966). Lord Clark served (1934–45) as director of London's National Gallery. He became famous as the writer and narrator of the television series "Civilisation" (1969) and "The Romantic Rebellion" (1973). In addition to his more than two dozen volumes on art history, his two autobiographical volumes, *Another Part of the Wood* (1974) and *The Other Half* (1977), are accounts of the 20th-century art world.

Clark, Mark W.   Mark Wayne Clark, b. Madison Barracks, N.Y., May 1, 1896, d. Apr. 17, 1984, graduated (1917) from West Point and served in both world wars. By 1942 he was chief of staff of the army ground forces. After commanding the U.S. Fifth Army in its successful North African and Italian campaigns, Clark became (1944) Allied commander in Italy. He was promoted to full general in 1945 and placed in command of the Allied occupation forces in Austria. In 1952–53 he was supreme commander of the United Nations forces in Korea and signed the armistice ending the Korean War. From 1954 to 1966, Clark was president of The Citadel, a military academy in Charleston, S.C. His memoirs are titled *Calculated Risk* (1950) and *From the Danube to the Yalu* (1954).

Clark, Tom Campbell   Tom Campbell Clark, b. Dallas, Tex., Sept. 23, 1899, d. June 13, 1977, was an associate justice of the U.S. Supreme Court from 1949 to 1967. Clark's son Ramsey served as U.S. attorney general from 1967 to 1969, a post the elder Clark had held from 1945 to 1949. Clark resigned from the Court to prevent any conflict of interest.

Clark, Walter van Tilburg   Walter van Tilburg Clark, b. East Orlando, Maine, Aug. 3, 1909, d. Nov. 10, 1971, was a writer of prose fiction and a professor of English. His novel *The Ox-Bow Incident* (1940; film, 1943) is a minor classic. Set in 1885 in Nevada cattle country, where Clark was raised, it is a perceptive analysis of mob violence that centers on the lynching of three innocent men accused of cattle rustling. Clark employs some conventions of the Western drama but uses psychological realism to strip the glamour from the stereotyped cowboy. Clark wrote two other novels, *The City of Tumbling Leaves* (1945) and *The Track of the Cat* (1949; film, 1954), and his short stories are collected in *The Watchful Gods* (1950).

Clark, William   William Clark, b. Caroline County, Va., Aug. 1, 1770, d. Sept. 1, 1838, was co-commander, with Meriwether LEWIS, of the first American expedition to explore the territories between the Mississippi River and the Pacific Ocean. He was the younger brother of George Rogers Clark. During the LEWIS AND CLARK EXPEDITION (1804–06), Clark assumed responsibility for mapping the terrain and for maintaining military discipline. Upon the expedition's return, and following Lewis's death, the task of arranging publication of the records of the journey also fell to Clark. Appointed superintendent of Indian affairs in 1807, Clark held the post for three decades and was instrumental in shaping the federal government's policy in the West. He was respected by the Indian tribes, among whom he was familiarly known as "red-haired chief." From 1813 to 1821 Clark served as governor of the Missouri Territory.

Clark, William Andrews William Andrews Clark, b. Fayette County, Pa., Jan. 8, 1839, d. Mar. 2, 1925, was a U.S. senator and financier who gained wealth and power through the development and control of copper mines in Montana. He vied with Marcus DALY, also a copper magnate and also a Democrat, for domination of Montana politics. Clark helped win statehood for Montana in 1889, but his opponents blocked his election as one of the state's first senators. He finally served in the U.S. Senate from 1901 to 1907. Clark's business interests in Montana extended beyond copper to include banks, timberlands, oil refineries, utilities, and newspapers. His major art collection eventually went to the Corcoran Gallery in Washington, D.C.

Clarke, Arthur C. Arthur Charles Clarke, b. Dec. 16, 1917, is an English writer of science fiction and of nonfiction devoted to scientific speculation. In a 1945 paper, he predicted the use of communications satellites. The conviction that humanity has been touched by a higher intelligence is evident in his early novel, *Childhood's End* (1953), as well as in *2001: A Space Odyssey* (screenplay and novel, 1968) and its sequels, *2010* (also a film, 1984) and *2063* (1988).

Clarke, Bobby A professional ice hockey player, Robert Earle Clarke, b. Flin Flon, Manitoba, Aug. 13, 1949, was one of the highest-scoring stars of the 1970s when he played center for the Philadelphia Flyers of the National Hockey League. In 1972, Clarke became the youngest team captain in NHL history. During his career (1970–84), all of it with the Flyers, he scored 1,210 points (358 goals, 852 assists) and was voted the league's Most Valuable Player 3 times (1973, 1975–76). With Clarke, the Flyers won 2 Stanley Cups (1974–75)—NHL titles— and Clarke himself was a 1st-team All-Star twice.

Clarke, James Freeman James Freeman Clarke, b. Hanover, N.H., Apr. 4, 1810, d. June 8, 1888, was an American Unitarian minister and author. After studying at Harvard he served the Unitarian church in Louisville, Ky., from 1833 to 1840 and the Church of the Disciples in Boston for most of the period from 1841 to 1888. Clarke was active in the transcendentalist movement. He published the works of several friends, including Ralph Waldo Emerson and Oliver Wendell Holmes, in the *Western Messenger*, a magazine that Clarke edited for 3 years. He was also active in the antislavery and other reform efforts. With his *Ten Great Religions* (2 vols., 1871–83), Clarke pioneered the study of non-Christian religions.

class, social A social class is a category of people similar in socioeconomic status when compared to other such categories in a stratified society. All societies larger than the tribal are characterized by an unequal distribu-

tion of material goods, prestige, and power over others. The formation of a hierarchy of groups differentiated by their possession of greater or lesser amounts of these advantages constitutes the class structure of a society. The most famous of class theorists, Karl MARX, understood class in this sense when he wrote in *The Communist Manifesto* "The history of all hitherto existing society is the history of class struggles," and then enumerated as examples "free man and slave, patrician and plebeian, lord and serf, guild master and journeyman." Marx's major contribution was to add the two specifically modern classes produced by industrial capitalism, the BOURGEOISIE and the PROLETARIAT (see MARXISM).

In a more restricted sense the term *social class* refers to the kinds of stratified groups peculiar to modern economically developed societies that have, since the French Revolution, abolished political and legal distinctions of rank and privilege. Classes in this usage are contrasted with the hereditary estates of premodern Europe, the CASTES of traditional Hindu India, and free and unfree groups in societies where slavery has existed. Social classes in the modern world coexist with equality before the law and the right of individuals to move from one class to another regardless of their parents' class.

Marx saw classes as products of a capitalist economy, but other theorists have stressed different origins. Max WEBER recognized what he called "status groups"— groups sharing a common style of life and collective identity—as being partially independent of their economic position. He regarded the European ARISTOCRACY, surviving as a social and political force after it had lost its legal and economic privileges, as one such status group. The term has also been applied to ethnic groups in societies where ethnicity is positively or negatively valued, and to groups sharing a common cultural outlook rooted in educational experience.

The combined status and income or occupational divisions in capitalist industrial societies are sufficiently alike to permit sociologists to identify four main classes: an upper class of owners, managers, and top public officials; a middle class of white-collar workers and owners of small businesses; a manual working class; and a lower class, or underclass, of the irregularly employed and the rural poor. In noncapitalist or state socialist societies, the upper class comprises the political elite and industrial managers; nonmanual workers form a middle class; manual workers are below them; and a large farm population is at the bottom.

class action A class action, in law, is a suit brought by one or more members of a group of people on behalf of all the members of the group, or "class." It has been used in recent years by lawyers litigating for consumers who claim that they have been cheated, for stockholders in corporations, for tenants in apartment houses, and for environmentalists protesting oil spills and other nuisances. The attraction of a class-action suit is that a lawyer can represent the combined claims of a large number of people whose individual claims might be too small to pay the costs of separate suits.

classical period in music   In common usage the term *classical music* denotes "art music," as opposed to popular or folk music. Music historians, however, use the term to mean a specific style and period in music history, roughly 1750 to 1825, that followed the baroque era and preceded the romantic. Its greatest masters were Christoph Willibald GLUCK, Franz Josef HAYDN, Wolfgang Amadeus MOZART, and Ludwig van BEETHOVEN. The latter three composers are often referred to as the "Viennese classical school."

An essential characteristic of classical music is a balance between the content of the music and the form in which it is expressed. The classical period saw the rapid flowering of the SONATA form and the first maturity of the SYMPHONY, the solo CONCERTO, the solo piano sonata, the STRING QUARTET, and other forms of CHAMBER MUSIC. During this time the ORCHESTRA was expanded, in both the number and the variety of instruments, and the PIANO supplanted the HARPSICHORD as the most popular solo keyboard instrument.

Rococo, an 18th-century style of building decoration characterized by elaborately sculptured and elegant detail, left its mark on music in the form of light and delicate textures, profusely ornamented melodies, and an elegant sentimentality; it is often referred to as the *style galant*. Another source of the classical style is the *empfindsamer Stil* ("sensitive" or "sentimental style") that appeared in Germany about 1740 and is exemplified in the keyboard works of Carl Philipp Emanuel BACH. This style was emotional, passionate, even boisterous.

Composers of the classical period developed a new way of composing with contrasting melodic fragments, or motives. These melodic fragments could be combined and manipulated in various ways, giving rise to the technique of development, a crucial element of the emerging classical style, and of the sonata form, the most important musical structure of the classical period. Used in symphonies, sonatas, concertos, and chamber works, sonata form appears almost invariably in the first movement, and sometimes in other movements.

The classical period in music coincided with two important developments—the emergence and spread of public concerts and the emancipation of musicians as artists. From Beethoven on, they appeared before the public as independent creators and performers, no longer dependent for recognition on the favor of rulers or officials.

During the classical period in music (c.1750–1825), composers strived for clarity and simplicity of expression and for stylistic refinement. Franz Josef Haydn (right) is considered a master of classical composition, particularly in his development of the sonata form.

classicism [klas'-i-sizm]   Classicism denotes the aesthetic ideals and styles of ancient Greece and Rome: simplicity, harmony, restraint, proportion, and reason. Other meanings of *classicism* (and of *classic* and *classical*) include the idea of the best. The Latin word *classicus* meant the highest rank of citizenry, and *classic* came to signify anything that was best. Thus, the period during which a society or an art reaches its peak is often called "classical," as in "classical Greece"—Greece of the 5th century BC, when its art and culture reached their high point.

As a recurring theme among the makers of art and literature, classicism has had a long history beginning with the Romans, who copied Greek styles of architecture and statuary. During the Renaissance, rediscovered ancient texts and sculptures inspired efforts to imitate the Greeks and Romans. ARISTOTLE's *Poetics* was widely read, as was HORACE's *Ars poetica*. Literature received a set of rules derived from these ancient writers by Nicolas BOILEAU-DESPREAUX in his *The Art of Poetry* (1674). Renaissance Italian painters and architects abandoned the starkness of the Gothic for the more humanistic styles they associated with the ancients. Sculptors created idealized figures in homage to the perfection they found in Greek figural works. RAPHAEL was considered the chief classicist of the Renaissance painters, and Nicolas POUSSIN of the baroque period that followed.

The 18th century saw a revival of classicism, spurred by the discoveries at Pompeii and Herculaneum and by the work of Johann WINCKELMANN, an art historian who, like Boileau, translated his perceptions of Greek art and literature into a program for artists and writers of his own time. The new classicism, or NEOCLASSICISM, took its inspiration as much from Renaissance classicism as from the genuine classic. Architects turned to the Italian Renaissance designer Andrea PALLADIO for their models; artists, to Raphael and Poussin.

The AUGUSTAN AGE in English literature was that period when poets and writers emulated Roman models, creating literature of great clarity and formal perfection. Gotthold LESSING, Johann von GOETHE, and Friedrich SCHILLER were notable German literary classicists. The ENLIGHTENMENT, with its belief in the power of reason and its search for rational principles in the pages of Plato, Aristotle, Cicero, and Lucretius, can be seen as a final flowering of classicism. ROMANTICISM followed in the early 19th century.

—

classification, biological Biological classification is the arrangement of living organisms into categories based on natural similarities, such as structure, development, biochemical or physiological functions, and evolutionary history. The branch of biology dealing with classification is called taxonomy or systematics. Biologists classify living things to show relationships between different ancient and modern groups; to indicate the evolutionary pathways along which present-day organisms may have developed; and to provide a basis for comparing experimental data about different plant and animal groups.

The first scheme for classifying animals into logical groupings may have been proposed by Aristotle more than 2,000 years ago. Since his time, many new classification systems have been proposed; none, however, has succeeded in fitting all plants, animals, and microorganisms into a single, completely satisfactory scheme. For example, many organisms can be conveniently classified as either animals or plants, depending primarily on the presence or absence of a cell wall, and the relationships of several groups of microorganisms are not at all clear and are therefore open to conflicting interpretations. Some taxonomists, for example, prefer to classify fungi in a separate group, whereas others file them with plants.

In practice, taxonomists use as many separate characteristics as possible to classify organisms. The types of information commonly used are the organism's anatomy, biochemistry, embryology, molecular biology, behavior, and distribution.

The present-day system of classification was introduced by Swedish biologist Carolus LINNAEUS in 1753. The basic unit in the classification of living forms is the species: a group of organisms both resembling each other more closely than the organisms of any other group and capable of mating with one another to produce fertile offspring. This capability is probably the most important single criterion for deciding that individuals belong to the same species, for it implies a close resemblance in genetic makeup and evolutionary history.

Binomial Nomenclature

According to internationally accepted rules, a species is identified by two technical Latin names, or a binomial. For example, the species of grass frogs is *Rana pipiens*; the species of humans is *Homo sapiens*. The first word identifies the genus, which is a group of species more closely related to one another than to any other group. The second word identifies a particular species within a genus. Thus, grass frogs belong to the genus *Rana*, and the human species to the genus *Homo*. *Rana* contains many other species besides *Rana pipiens*; *Homo sapiens* is the only living species within the genus *Homo*.

Species are arranged into higher groupings that are progressively more inclusive. Ideally, all the organisms grouped together should have common evolutionary origins.

Species that are closely related are grouped together into a genus (plural, genera). Genera with similar characteristics and origins are grouped into families. Families, in turn, are grouped into orders, orders into classes, and classes into phyla in animals and into divisions in plants. Finally, related phyla or divisions are placed together into kingdoms.

Sometimes it is desirable to make finer distinctions between two consecutive ranks. In that case an additional rank may be inserted between the original two, and the prefix sub- or super- is then added to one of the main ranks. Between an order and a family, for example, the order may contain several suborders, each suborder several superfamilies, and each superfamily several families.

Homology and Analogy

The members of a phylum or a division may live in radically different environments. Both humans and fish are chordates, for example. But all organisms within a phylum or a division use the same kinds of anatomical structures in adapting to their different environments. The fins of a fish and the arms of a human are basically similar structures that have evolved from a common, ancestral type of body appendage.

When given body parts of different organisms correspond to one another in terms of ancestry and basic development, they are termed homologous. Homology implies descent from the same ancestral line and thus serves as an important basis for classification. By contrast, structures of different organisms that possess a similar function but are basically different in origin and structure—bird wings and butterfly wings, for example—are called analogous.

Major Kingdoms

Several classification systems are now in use, but many biologists favor the five-kingdom system proposed by R. H. Whittaker in the 1950s. In this system, organisms are classified according to whether they are prokaryotic—meaning single-celled, such as bacteria, with neither internal membranes nor organelles—or eukaryotic, meaning composed of one or more cells containing membrane-bound nuclei and organelles; whether they are unicellular or multicellular; and whether they obtain food by photosynthesis, ingestion, or absorption of organic matter from their surroundings.

The five kingdoms established according to these properties are the MONERA, including bacteria and blue-green algae; the Protista, including protozoans and some single-celled algae; the Fungi; the Plantae (plants); and the Animalia (animals).

Monera are single-celled or colony-forming prokaryotes; if colonial, no specialization or division of labor occurs among the cells. Protista, and all other living things except Monera, are eukaryotes. Protista are divided into two major subgroups by mode of nutrition: algae carry out photosynthesis; protozoans are nonphotosynthetic and live by ingesting or absorbing organic matter from their surroundings.

The fungi are plantlike, many-celled organisms that live by absorbing nutrients from their surroundings. These organisms include yeast, slime mold, mold, and mushrooms.

The plants are many-celled organisms that live by photosynthesis. They fall into two major groups: the bryophytes (liverworts and mosses), which have no vascular tissues, or tissues for transporting water and minerals from roots; and the far more numerous and important tracheophytes, or vascular plants, which include FERNS and seed plants.

The animal kingdom comprises the following main groups: sponges; coelenterates, such as jellyfish; annelids, such as earthworms and leeches; mollusks, such as clams, snails, and squid; arthropods, such as insects, spiders, and lobsters; echinoderms, such as starfish and sea urchins; and vertebrates—the fish, amphibians, reptiles, birds, and mammals.

clathrate compounds [klath'-rayt] Clathrate compounds, or inclusion compounds, are formed by the combination of two or more component compounds without normal electron-sharing or electron-transfer chemical bonds. In most cases, one component forms a rigid framework with holes into which molecules or ions of the other component fit. Because of this unusual type of bonding, the name *clathrate* was proposed (from the Latin *clathratus*, meaning "enclosed or protected by the crossbars of a grating").

Claudel, Paul [kloh-del'] Paul Claudel, b. Aug. 6, 1868, d. Feb. 23, 1955, was a French Catholic dramatist, poet, essayist, and diplomat whose works express both religious and sensual fervor. He viewed the world as a vast poem in the process of creation and, through metaphors, attempted to establish mystical relationships between objects and humanity and between humanity and God.

Both *Tidings Brought to Mary* (1912; Eng. trans., 1916), a revision of *La Jeune fille Violaine* (Young Violaine, 1901), and the panoramic drama *The Satin Slipper* (1924; Eng. trans., 1931) reveal Claudel's theme of spiritual salvation through physical renunciation. He collaborated with Darius MILHAUD on the opera *Christopher Columbus* (1928) and with Arthur HONEGGER on the dramatic oratorio *Joan of Arc at the Stake* (1935). Claudel employed a verse form, *verset claudélien*, characterized by irregular rhyme and meter, powerful images, exotic landscapes, and musical overtones, as seen in *Cinq grandes odes* (Five Great Odes, 1910).

Claudius I, Roman Emperor Claudius, b. Aug. 1, 10 BC, d. Oct. 13, AD 54, was Roman emperor from AD 41 to 54. His full name was Tiberius Claudius Drusus Nero Germanicus. The younger son of Nero Claudius DRUSUS, and a great-nephew of AUGUSTUS, he suffered from a kind

of paralysis and was considered unfit for a public career. He survived the purges under his uncle, TIBERIUS, and his nephew CALIGULA. When Caligula was assassinated in AD 41, Claudius also expected to be murdered. Instead, the Praetorian guard proclaimed him emperor while the Senate was debating the possibility of restoring the republic.

Claudius was unpopular with the Senate not only because of the circumstances of his accession but also because of the political power of his wives and freedmen, to whom he entrusted positions as ministers of state. But Claudius was a shrewd administrator; he pursued the policies of extending Roman citizenship and of founding Roman cities in the provinces, which he rightly regarded as the keystone of Roman imperial power. He incorporated Britain, Mauretania, and Thrace into the Roman Empire.

In 48 his third wife, Messalina, was executed on the charge of conspiracy, and Claudius married his niece AGRIPPINA II. He adopted her son NERO, thus paving the way to the throne for him and excluding from succession his own son, Britannicus. It is believed that Claudius was poisoned by Agrippina.

Claudius was perhaps the most erudite of all Roman emperors. In his youth he met Livy and gained extensive knowledge of Roman antiquities; he also wrote on Etruscan and Carthaginian history. He is the subject of two novels by Robert Graves, *I, Claudius* and *Claudius the God* (both 1934).

Clausewitz, Carl Philipp Gottfried von [klow'-zeh-vits] Carl Philipp Gottfried von Clausewitz, b. June 1, 1780, d. Nov. 16, 1831, was a Prussian general and a writer on warfare. He joined the army at the age of 12, studied at the War College in Berlin, and took part in the Napoleonic Wars. He was in the service of the Russians from 1812 to 1814 but fought in the Prussian army at Waterloo (1815). From 1818 to 1830 he was director of the War College in Berlin.

In Clausewitz's classic study, *On War* (*Vom Kriege*, 1833; Eng. trans., 1976), he analyzed what determines success in war. Even though Clausewitz held that the best way to conduct a war is to apply maximum force to the destruction of the enemy, he also emphasized that war must be an instrument of policy. In the final section of *On War*, he wrote: "war is simply a continuation of political intercourse, with the addition of other means.... The main lines along which military events progress, and to which they are restricted, are political lines that continue through the war into the subsequent peace." He also distinguished between total war, in which the aim is the destruction of the enemy's forces, and more limited kinds of war, in which the purpose is to conquer territory or perhaps only to occupy it until some political end is achieved.

Clausius, Rudolf [klow'-zee-us] The German physicist Rudolf Julius Emmanuel Clausius, b. Jan. 2, 1822, d. Aug. 24, 1888, is credited with creating the science of THERMODYNAMICS. In 1850 he published a major paper rejecting the then widely accepted caloric theory of heat, which held that the total amount of heat in the universe always remains constant. Clausius accepted James JOULE's experiments, which showed that heat and work are interconvertible, so that when work is produced by heat, an amount of heat is consumed. This same paper also contained Clausius's principle that "heat cannot of itself pass from a colder to a hotter body," which became known as the second law of thermodynamics. In another paper (1854) he developed this notion into the concept later called ENTROPY. Clausius also incorporated Sadi Carnot's (see CARNOT family) work on ideal engines into his theory of heat.

claustrophobia   see PHOBIA

▬

Claver, Saint Peter [klah-vair']   Saint Peter Claver, b. 1581, d. Sept. 4, 1654, was a Spanish Jesuit missionary who became known as the "Apostle to the Negroes." In 1610 he went to Cartagena, in what is now Colombia, where he worked among the African slaves who had been brought there. Despite opposition from slaveowners, Claver cared for the slaves and was said to have instructed and baptized more than 300,000 of them. He was canonized in 1888 and declared the patron saint of all black missions in 1896. Feast day: Sept. 9.

▬

clavichord [klav'-i-kord]   The clavichord is the simplest of the keyed stringed instruments. Contained in a shallow, rectangular box, its strings are suspended over a

The clavichord, one of the oldest keyboard instruments, was popular from the 15th to the 18th century. Admirably suited for practice and instruction because of its sensitive touch and delicate tone, it was rarely used in concert ensembles except for vocal accompaniment. A string sounds when a key (A), pivoted at (C), is depressed. The tangent (B) strikes the string, which vibrates until the key is released.

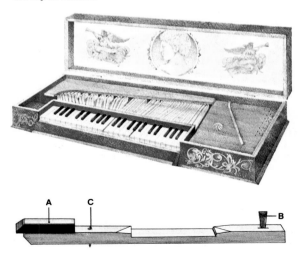

shallow bridge and extend past felt dampers. Pressing a key raises a thin brass tangent, or blade, that activates the string, dividing it into two sections; one is free to vibrate, and the other is damped. The pitch is determined by the length of the string from the end that is free to vibrate to the blade of the tangent. When the key is released, the string is stopped by the damper. Because of the short distance of the stroke, and the location of its point of contact, the tone is soft and lovely. The instrument is capable of some variation in dynamics (soft and loud) and of vibrato effects (rapid and minute fluctuation in pitch).

The clavichord was developed in the late 14th century by adding a key mechanism to the monochord, an instrument with one or more strings that produces different pitches by the use of a movable bridge.

Clay, Cassius   see ALI, MUHAMMAD

▬

Clay, Cassius Marcellus   Cassius Marcellus Clay, b. Madison County, Ky., Oct. 19, 1810, d. July 22, 1903, was an American politician, diplomat, and abolitionist. The son of a slaveholder and a lifelong resident of Kentucky, he entered the Kentucky legislature in 1835, but was defeated in 1841 because of his opposition to slavery. He continued his crusade against slavery in the *True American*, a newspaper he founded in 1845, later renamed the *Examiner*. Clay served with distinction in the Mexican War. After 1856 he joined the Republican party, and his friendship with Abraham Lincoln brought him the position of minister to Russia (1861–62, 1863–69). Shortly before his death, Clay was declared legally insane.

▬

Clay, Henry   Henry Clay, b. Hanover County, Va., Apr. 12, 1777, d. June 29, 1852, was a key figure in U.S. politics during the first half of the 19th century. A master of the art of political compromise, he studied law in Richmond and moved to the frontier state of Kentucky in 1797. Clay rose rapidly in Kentucky politics, becoming speaker of the state assembly in 1807, and winning election to the U.S. House of Representatives in 1811.

In the capital, Clay soon became the leading spokesman of the West. He was a leader of the "War Hawks" in Congress who pushed for war with Britain in 1812, hoping to conquer Canada. He supported the War of 1812 when it came, and served on the peace commission to Ghent that negotiated an end to the conflict in 1814. Clay returned to the House in 1815, where he sponsored a program for national economic development known as the American System. The program called for federally financed roads to link east and west, protection of American manufacturing through a high tariff, and a national bank. In 1820 Clay was instrumental in devising the MISSOURI COMPROMISE, which resolved a bitter sectional dispute over the extension of slavery into western territory.

Clay made his first try for the presidency in 1824. Four men ran, including Andrew JACKSON of Tennessee. When no candidate won a majority, Clay threw his support

Henry Clay, an American congressional leader, developed the compromises that helped ease the sectional rivalries plaguing the U.S. during the first half of the 19th century.

to John Quincy ADAMS. Adams won and promptly named Clay his secretary of state. At once, Jackson's followers cried "corrupt bargain," an accusation Clay never fully lived down. Both Adams and the Congress supported Clay's American System, but the program was not widely popular, and it thus contributed to Adams's defeat by Jackson in the presidential contest of 1828.

In 1831, Clay won election as senator from Kentucky and became leader of the opposition to Andrew Jackson. He ran against Jackson for the presidency in 1832, campaigning on behalf of the BANK OF THE UNITED STATES, which had been reconstituted in 1816 but which Jackson wanted to dissolve, and against the growth of presidential power. Clay lost. His skill at political compromise proved crucial in 1833, when South Carolina nullified the federal tariff law and Jackson threatened to send troops to suppress NULLIFICATION. Clay helped devise the lowered tariff that settled the dispute.

Frustration plagued Clay throughout the 1840s. Unable to work with President John TYLER, he had Tyler expelled from the WHIG PARTY, a party Clay had helped to found, and he himself resigned from the Senate in 1842. When Clay ran for the presidency in 1844, Tyler had his revenge. The deserted president forced into the campaign his proposal to annex the slaveholding Republic of Texas. Clay vacillated over the controversial issue and lost the election to James K. POLK.

Clay returned to the Senate in 1849 and for the last time played the role of great compromiser. Victory in the Mexican War had brought bitter division over whether slavery would be allowed in the conquered Southwest. Clay helped persuade the Congress to accept the COMPROMISE OF 1850, which preserved the Union for another decade.

Clay, Lucius D.   Lucius Dubignon Clay, b. Marietta, Ga., Apr. 23, 1897, d. Apr. 16, 1978, was the U.S. Army general who directed the Berlin Airlift in 1948–49. A graduate of West Point (1918), he rose in rank through the U.S. Corps of Engineers and served as U.S. director of materiel during World War II. In 1947 he was made mili-

tary governor of the U.S.-occupied zone of Germany and directed the massive airlift of food and supplies to West Berlin, a tactic ordered by President Truman in response to the Soviet blockade of the city. After retiring as a full general in 1949, he wrote *Decision in Germany* (1950).

clay minerals   Clay, a natural, earthy, fine-grained material consisting primarily of a particular group of crystalline minerals, is a major component of the sedimentary rock known as SHALE. The clay minerals are hydrous SILICATE MINERALS consisting mainly of silica, aluminum, and water, sometimes with amounts of iron and alkali and alkaline earth compounds as well. Clay minerals form naturally by the WEATHERING of rocks that contain FELDSPAR and MICA.

Clays rank among the leading industrial minerals, both in tonnages produced and in total value. A complex group, they consist of several mineral varieties, each having somewhat different mineralogy, geologic occurrence, technology, and uses. Their value, depending as it does on mineralogical and chemical composition, is adversely affected by the presence of minor amounts of mineral or soluble salt impurities.

The term *clay* also refers to the typical grain size of clay minerals, and in this sense may also refer to substances other than typical clay minerals. Clay grains are of microscopic size and smaller, generally less than 0.004 mm (0.00015 in) across, with most grains less than half this size.

Kaolin Clays. Several clays in commercial use consist largely of kaolinite, a hydrated aluminum silicate. Large deposits of this mineral occur in China; Czechoslovakia; Cornwall, England; and at several places in the United States. Various grades of kaolin clays may be distinguished. White kaolin clays are composed of microscopic particles that are soft, nonabrasive, and chemically inert over a wide pH range. Their largest consumer is the PAPER industry, which uses them as a coating to make paper smoother, whiter, and more printable. Ball clays have excellent plasticity and strength, and they fire to a light cream to white color. They are used extensively in CERAMICS in whitewares, sanitary ware, and wall tile. Fireclays are soft, plastic clays used primarily in making REFRACTORY MATERIALS.

Bentonites. Bentonite, an important industrial clay, is made up mainly of the mineral smectite (montmorillonite) and formed by the alteration of volcanic ash. One of its most important uses is as DRILLING mud in the petroleum industry. Bentonite is also used as a bonding agent in foundries and smelters, as an adsorbent, as a decolorizer for fats and oils, and as a liner for ditches and ponds to prevent water loss. In addition to fine particle size, bentonite has the unique capability of swelling when wet.

Other Varieties. Some clays, such as attapulgite and sepiolite, are hydrated magnesium aluminum silicates consisting of long, tubular particles. Mined in Florida, Georgia, and Nevada, they are used as drilling mud and as additives in adhesives, fertilizers, pharmaceuticals, and PAINT. Most other clays consist of mixtures of illite (a hydrated potassium–iron–aluminum silicate), CHLORITE, kaolinite, and smectite. By far the largest use for these miscellaneous clays is in the manufacture of structural clay products, such as brick and sewer pipe. The CEMENT AND CONCRETE industry also uses these and other clays, mostly as a source of aluminum and silica for the charge that is added to cement kilns.

Clearchus [klee-ahr'-kuhs]   Clearchus, d. 401 BC, was the Spartan general who led the Greek mercenary army called the Ten Thousand in support of CYRUS THE YOUNGER's claim to the Persian throne. Appointed (410) governor of Byzantium by the Spartans, he was so tyrannical that the people opened the city to the Athenian general ALCIBIADES in 408. At the conclusion of the PELOPONNESIAN WAR (404), Clearchus returned to Byzantium but was expelled by the Spartans for disobeying orders. He took refuge with Cyrus, for whom he recruited the Ten Thousand and fought at Cunaxa (401). Defeated there, he led the army in the famous retreat described by XENOPHON in the *Anabasis*. During truce negotiations with the satrap TISSAPHERNES, he was seized and turned over to the Persian king ARTAXERXES II, who executed him.

cleavage, mineral   see MINERAL

Cleaver, Eldridge   Leroy Eldridge Cleaver, b. near Little Rock, Ark., Aug. 31, 1935, is a writer and black activist who is best known for his book *Soul on Ice* (1968), written while he was an inmate at California's Folsom Prison. Sensitive to the symbols of American culture, Cleaver discusses subjects ranging from the Vietnam War to his motives for raping white women. Fleeing abroad when his parole was revoked in 1968, Cleaver returned in 1975 and turned to lecturing and writing on his conversion to Christianity. He published *Soul on Fire* in 1978.

Eldridge Cleaver, an American writer, presented a vivid exposition of black experience in a white society in Soul on Ice *(1968). He is shown here with a later work,* Soul on Fire *(1978), which describes his disillusionment with radical politics and his spiritual rebirth as a Christian.*

Photo Jill Krementz © 1974

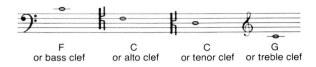

F or bass clef	C or alto clef	C or tenor clef	G or treble clef

clef   The clef is a musical symbol that identifies the position on the STAFF of a single pitch for which the clef is named. In early music, up to ten different positions were used in order to keep most of the notes on the staff. As the range of the parts increased, ledger lines above or below the staff were used to lessen the need for so many clefs. The F, C, and G clefs are now in common use, with the C clef used in two positions. The clefs are shown in their relation to middle C.

The BASS clef is used for the low range, the C clef for the middle range, and the G clef for the high range. With keyboard instruments, the F clef is used for the left hand, and the G clef for the right hand.

cleft lip and palate   Cleft lip, or harelip, is a BIRTH DEFECT in which the upper lip is split on one or both sides. It may occur with cleft palate, a partial to complete split of the roof of the mouth. Cleft lip occurs about once in every 1,000 births and is more common in males. Cleft palate, when observed alone, is more common in females and occurs about once in every 2,500 births. The defects result from incomplete fusion of tissue or bone, or both, during fetal development. Early surgery usually can repair the defects, but cleft palate in particular may also be linked with hearing, breathing, or tooth-placement problems. The defects are genetic in origin in some cases.

Cleisthenes [klys'-thuh-neez]   The Athenian statesman Cleisthenes, 570–508 BC, played a leading role in the founding of Athenian democracy. Head of the Alcmaeonidae, a prominent family, he assumed leadership after the Spartan king Cleomenes I overthrew (c.510 BC) the Athenian tyrant Hippias. He reorganized the Athenian tribes into *demes*—political divisions based on locality— and extended citizenship to nearly all resident aliens.

Cleland, John [klel'-uhnd]   English writer John Cleland, b. 1709, d. Jan. 23, 1789, is best known as the author of *Fanny Hill; or, Memoirs of a Woman of Pleasure* (1748–49), a classic of erotic literature. Frequently suppressed as pornographic, the novel was not cleared by the U.S. Supreme Court until 1966. Cleland's other works include historical plays and the novels *Memoirs of a Coxcomb* (1751) and *Surprises of Love* (1765).

clematis [klem'-uh-tuhs]   Clematis, genus *Clematis*, is any of several deciduous climbing or bush plants that belong to the buttercup family, Ranunculaceae. They are

Clematis is often planted to climb fences and trellises. Henryi (left) may have vines 6 m (20 ft) long. The vines of Beauty of Worcester (right) grow up to 2.5 m (8 ft) long.

widely distributed throughout temperate zones. Many species, varieties, and hybrids exist with varying habits and flowering forms. Climbing forms are well adapted to cover fences, arbors, or porches; bush types are used in flower borders. Although *Clematis* vines like sunlight, the roots must be cool. The peak flowering time is early summer.

Clemenceau, Georges [kle-mahn-soh'] The French statesman Georges Clemenceau, popularly known as "the Tiger," b. Sept. 28, 1841, d. Nov. 24, 1929, contributed to the Allied victory in World War I and helped formulate the Treaty of Versailles. Clemenceau received a medical education and spent several years in the United States. In 1870, after the overthrow of Napoleon during the Franco-Prussian War, he became mayor of Montmartre.

As a journalist and, from 1876, a Radical deputy, Clemenceau uncompromisingly opposed clericalism. In

Georges Clemenceau was premier of France from 1906 to 1909 and again from 1917 to 1920. Clemenceau was a vigorous leader who bolstered French morale during World War I and, as a framer of the Treaty of Versailles, advocated strong measures against Germany at the Paris peace negotiations.

1892 he was caught in a scandal involving bribes to the press and the deputies by the company constructing the Panama Canal. Clemenceau lost his seat in the chamber in 1893 but was returned to politics by the DREYFUS AFFAIR. In 1898 he published Émile ZOLA's open letter "J'accuse" in his newspaper *L'Aurore*. His support of Dreyfus not only helped clear the latter's name but restored his own reputation.

Elected to the Senate in 1902, Clemenceau served as premier from 1906 to 1909. He strengthened cooperation with Britain and approved the Anglo-Russian agreement of 1907 that created the TRIPLE ENTENTE of France, Russia, and Britain. Labor unrest during Clemenceau's term culminated in strikes in 1908–09. His use of troops to break one strike cost him the support of the Radicals, and he lost office.

In November 1917, President Raymond POINCARÉ again called Clemenceau to the premiership, knowing that only Clemenceau could maintain French national unity. In a short time the new premier raised national morale, sustaining it through the onslaught of a fresh German offensive of March 1918. The next month he unified the Allied command under Gen. Ferdinand FOCH.

Clemenceau led the French delegation at the PARIS PEACE CONFERENCE. There he advocated the establishment of French-occupied buffer states on the Rhine River and the creation of strong states on Germany's eastern border. He also demanded REPARATIONS from the Germans for French war damages. Although Clemenceau was much harsher toward the Germans than either President Woodrow WILSON or Prime Minister David LLOYD GEORGE, many in France criticized him as being too lenient. Old political grievances brought the Tiger down. Clemenceau had denounced some members of the Left as defeatists in 1917; in 1920 they defeated him in the presidential election, and he retired from politics.

Clemens, Samuel Langhorne   see TWAIN, MARK

Clement of Alexandria, Saint   Clement of Alexandria, c.150–c.215, was a Greek theologian who made an early attempt to synthesize Platonic philosophy and Christian thought. According to Pantaenus, religious knowledge, or *gnosis*, prepares for the stage of ecstasy in which perfect identity with God is achieved. He held that the only true *gnosis*, however, was to be found in the Christian faith (see GNOSTICISM). Clement succeeded Pantaenus as head of the school about 190. About 202, during the persecution of Roman emperor Septimius Severus, he was forced to flee to Cappadocia, where he died.

Clement was among the founders of the Alexandrine tradition in Christian theology. His best-known works are the *Protrepticus* (Exhortation to the Greeks), in which he attempted to convert worshipers of pagan gods; the *Paedagogus* (Tutor), an explanation of the world in terms of the LOGOS, or mind of God; and the *Stromata* (Miscellanies), in which he argued that philosophy was God's gift to the Greeks. Clement is considered one of the FATHERS OF THE CHURCH.

Clement I, Saint   Clement, d. AD 101, called Clement of Rome, was the bishop of Rome, or pope, from c.92 to 101. His *Epistle to the Corinthians* (c.96) is the earliest piece of Christian literature other than New Testament writings for which the name of the author is certain. He is one of the Apostolic Fathers of the church. The epistle was written because of internal discord and division in the Corinthian church. Clement intervened in the name of the church at Rome and appealed for restoration of peace, harmony, and order. The document, which demonstrates Clement's familiarity with Greek Stoic philosophy and mythology, gives a valuable picture of early church organization, belief, and practice. Feast day: Nov. 23 (Western); Nov. 24 or 25 (Eastern).

Clement V, Pope   Clement V, b. c.1260, d. Apr. 20, 1314, was pope from 1305 to 1314. He was a Frenchman named Bertrand de Got. When he moved his administration from Rome to Avignon in 1309, he initiated the controversial 70-year residency of the papacy in France. Although Clement served the interests of the French, he nevertheless supported (1312) the election of HENRY VII as Holy Roman emperor rather than Philip V of France. During his pontificate, the Knights TEMPLARS were suppressed (1311–12), at Philip's insistence. In making church appointments, Clement openly favored Frenchmen, as well as his relatives. He promulgated (1314) the *Clementinae*, a collection of decretals that were later incorporated in canon law.

Clement VII, Pope   Clement VII, b. May 26, 1478, d. Sept. 25, 1534, was pope from 1523 to 1534. Named Giulio, he was the illegitimate son of Giuliano de'Medici. After a successful career as manager of the affairs of the Medici family and as vice chancellor of the church, he was elected pope. Although Clement was devout and was judged extremely capable before his election, his pontificate was marked by indecision and miscalculation.

Clement tried to follow a middle road in the political struggles between FRANCIS I of France and Holy Roman Emperor CHARLES V, but his faulty diplomacy led to the sack of Rome in 1527 by imperial troops. He failed to take any vigorous measures to meet the demands of the Protestant Reformation. The same kind of indecision marked his relations with HENRY VIII of England over the annulment of Henry's marriage with CATHERINE OF ARAGON. Clement was a patron of artists, including Cellini, Raphael, and Michelangelo.

Clement VIII, Pope   Clement VIII, b. Feb. 24, 1536, d. Mar. 5, 1605, was pope from 1592 to 1605. His name was Ippolito Aldobrandini. As pope, he inherited the task of consolidating and implementing the reforms decreed by the Council of TRENT (1545–63) as part of the COUNTER-REFORMATION.

Clement's recognition (1595) of HENRY IV as the legitimate king of France was his most important diplomatic action. Since PHILIP II of Spain was one of the claimants to the French throne, Clement thus undercut the influence of Spain over the affairs of the papacy. Clement won respect because of his kindness and high moral character.

Clement XI, Pope   Clement XI, b. July 23, 1649, d. Mar. 19, 1721, was pope from 1700 to 1721. His name was Giovanni Francesco Albani. Clement is mainly known for two controversial actions. In 1704 he settled the long-standing Chinese Rites Controversy by forbidding Chinese Roman Catholics to participate in Confucian ceremonies, a ban that remained in effect until 1939. His bull *Unigenitus* (1713) condemning JANSENISM met with strong resistance in France and divided the French church for decades.

Clement XIV, Pope   Clement XIV, b. Oct. 31, 1705, d. Sept. 22, 1774, was pope from 1769 to 1774. His name was Giovanni Vincenzo Antonio Ganganelli. He is remembered chiefly for ordering the suppression of the JESUITS in 1773. A member of the Franciscan Order, he was prominent in papal affairs as a consultor for many years before being appointed a cardinal in 1759.

Clemente, Roberto   Roberto Walker Clemente, b. Carolina, Puerto Rico, Aug. 18, 1934, d. Dec. 31, 1972, became one of baseball's greatest right fielders during his 18-year career (1955–72) with the National League's Pittsburgh Pirates. Clemente won 4 NL batting titles (1961, 1964–65, 1967) while compiling a .317 lifetime batting average, precisely 3,000 hits, and 1,305 runs batted in. He was the league's Most Valuable Player in 1966 and was selected to the All-Star team 12 times. He also won 12 Gold Glove awards as the NL's premier right fielder, and he was frequently cited by experts as having the best outfielder's throwing arm they had ever seen. After his death in an airplane crash while aiding Nicaraguan earthquake survivors, Clemente was elected to the Hall of Fame in an unprecedented special vote.

Clementi, Muzio   The Italian composer and pianist Muzio Clementi, b. Jan. 23, 1752, d. Mar. 10, 1832, has been called "the father of the piano" because his brilliant keyboard performances and his compositions and teaching popularized the piano and established a body of techniques for this relatively new instrument. Clementi became renowned in England, where he lived from 1766. With John Longman, he founded (1798) a music publishing and piano manufacturing firm. His subsequent concert tours throughout Europe were undertaken in large part to introduce his audiences to the firm's instruments. His more than 100 sonatas and his collection of pedagogical études in *Gradus ad Parnassum* (1817–26) are his major works.

Cleomenes III, King of Sparta

Cleomenes III, King of Sparta [klee-ahm'-uh-neez] Cleomenes III, 260–219 BC, succeeded his father, Leonidas II, as king of Sparta (r. 235–222). He instituted social reforms and sought to increase Sparta's power. After defeating the armies of Achaea at Mt. Lycaeus and Ladoceia in 227, he made the kingship the supreme power in Sparta by eliminating the EPHORS. He extended citizenship, redistributed land, canceled debts, and restored Spartan prestige until Antigonus III of Macedonia intervened on behalf of the Achaean League. Cleomenes was defeated in 222 at Sellasia and fled to his patron, PTOLEMY III Euergetes, in Egypt. There Cleomenes was imprisoned by Euergetes' successor. He escaped and attempted unsuccessfully to muster a revolt, then committed suicide.

Cleon

Cleon Cleon, d. 422 BC, was an Athenian politician who opposed PERICLES and assumed leadership of the democracy after the latter's death in 429. The son of a tanner, he was the first member of the commercial class to attain such prominence. Cleon was brutal toward Athens's subject states: in 427, after a revolt of the city of Mytilene on Lesbos, he decreed that all the Mytilene men be killed and the women and children enslaved; although this decree was reversed, he later ordered (423) the same fate for the rebellious population of Scione. Continuing the PELOPONNESIAN WAR despite Spartan peace proposals, he personally commanded the Athenian forces in the victory at Sphacteria in 425. He was defeated, however, and killed at Amphipolis in 422. Thucydides and Aristophanes portrayed Cleon as a vulgar and dishonest demagogue, but their accounts are considered biased.

Cleopatra, Queen of Egypt

Cleopatra, Queen of Egypt Cleopatra was the name of the seven queens of ancient Egypt. By far the most famous was Cleopatra VII, b. 69 BC. Her extraordinary efforts to revive Ptolemaic power through her forceful personality and political skill, and the romantic liaisons with prominent Romans that this policy involved, have been the subject of such dramatic masterpieces as Shakespeare's *Antony and Cleopatra*, Dryden's *All for Love*, and George Bernard Shaw's *Caesar and Cleopatra*.

The daughter of PTOLEMY XII, Cleopatra became joint ruler with her younger brother PTOLEMY XIII in 51 BC. Three years later they fought each other in a civil war, during which the Roman general POMPEY THE GREAT came to Egypt and was assassinated by Ptolemy. Julius CAESAR then invaded Egypt and defeated Ptolemy, who drowned in the Nile. Cleopatra married another brother, Ptolemy XIV, but she also became Caesar's mistress and followed him to Rome, where she stayed until his assassination (44 BC).

Returning to Egypt, Cleopatra ruled with her son by Caesar, Ptolemy XV, called Caesarion, as joint king, Ptolemy XIV having been murdered on her orders. In 42 BC, when Mark ANTONY came to Egypt, she became his mistress. They planned to set up a vast kingdom to be inherited by her sons by Caesar and Antony. Octavian (later

Cleopatra VII, queen of ancient Egypt, appears as the goddess Isis in this Egyptian bas-relief. Although Cleopatra passionately strove to restore Egypt's power and to preserve its independence from Rome, she ultimately undermined her own efforts. The Ptolemaic dynasty was extinguished, and Egypt fell under Roman dominion.

AUGUSTUS), however, defeated Antony and Cleopatra in the Battle of Actium (31 BC) and pursued them to Egypt. Antony committed suicide. Cleopatra surrendered and sought to establish a relationship with Octavian. Failing, she killed herself in August of the year 30 BC, allowing herself to be bitten by an asp (cobra), the royal symbol of ancient Egypt. On the murder of her son Caesarion the Ptolemaic dynasty ended.

clepsydra

clepsydra [klep'-suh-druh] The clepsydra is a water clock (see CLOCKS AND WATCHES) that has been reliably dated to 1600 BC in Egypt. It functioned by water dripping through a hole in the base of a container, which lowered the water level past markings on the container sides. These markings were spaced to indicate fixed periods of time. Many variations were based on this design. Before the 3d century BC the clepsydra was used by the Greeks to indicate intervals of time, especially in law court; later it functioned as a clock. Clepsydras were later used in Rome, the Arab world, and China.

clerestory

clerestory [kleer'-stohr-ee] A clerestory is the uppermost portion of the nave walls of a church. Rising vertically above the roofs of the side aisles, the clerestory is penetrated by windows. In Romanesque churches the clerestory often contains a narrow passageway that is distinct from the arcaded wall passage immediately below and known as the triforium.

clergy

clergy see MINISTRY, CHRISTIAN

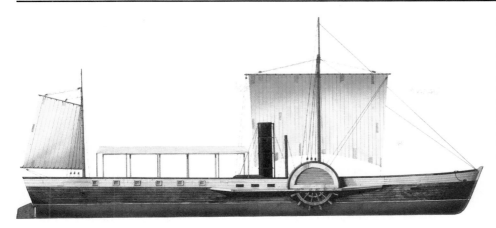

Steam navigation became economically feasible when Robert Fulton's steamship, Clermont, *made its maiden voyage in 1807. Powered by a British-built engine that generated 20 hp, the Clermont averaged nearly 8 km/h (5 mph) during its voyage up the Hudson River and back.*

Clermont   The *Clermont*, designed by Robert FULTON, was the first commercially successful STEAMBOAT. Originally named *Steamboat* and then *North River*, it made its maiden voyage up the Hudson River from New York City to Albany on Aug. 9, 1807, covering the 240 km (150 mi) at an average speed of 8 km/h (5 mph). The *Clermont* was equipped with a woodburning steam engine, purchased from Boulton & Watt in England, that drove two side paddle wheels. The vessel's only innovation was its hull design, which was the result of Fulton's studies of friction. The *Clermont* was 41 m (135 ft) long and 5 m (16 ft) wide. It was low, flat-bottomed, and wall-sided, with a draft of 2 m (7 ft).

Clermont-Ferrand [klair-mohn'-fe-rahn']   Clermont-Ferrand is a French industrial center and capital of Puy-de-Dome department, located about 320 km (200 mi) southeast of Paris. The population of the city proper is 151,092, and that of the metropolitan area is 256,189 (both 1982). The city's diverse industries produce chemicals, textiles, and metals, but rubber and tire manufacturing dominates Clermont-Ferrand, headquarters of the Michelin company. Many of the city's old buildings, including the Gothic cathedral, are constructed from a locally quarried dark lava rock. The university was established in 1810. Blaise Pascal (1623–62) is a native son.

Founded by the Romans, Clermont became, during the Middle Ages, the seat of a powerful bishopric and of the counts, later dukes, of Auvergne. Pope Urban II preached the First Crusade there in 1095. The present city dates from the merging (1731) of Clermont with neighboring Montferrand.

Cleveland (city)   Cleveland is a city in northeastern Ohio that is situated at the mouth of the Cuyahoga River on the south shore of Lake Erie. The seat of Cuyahoga County, it is the second-largest city in Ohio, with a population of 505,616 (1990). Cleveland's metropolitan area has a population of 2,759,823.

A major port on the St. Lawrence Seaway, Cleveland is an industrial center producing such manufactured goods as electrical machinery, primary and fabricated metals, transportation equipment, motor vehicles, aircraft, and electric motors.

The city is the home of several institutions of higher learning, including Case Western Reserve University (1826), Cleveland State University (1923), and John Carroll University (1886). Many of its cultural, educational, medical, and religious institutions are clustered in the University Circle area. Besides Case Western Reserve, these include the Cleveland Institute of Music, Severance Hall (home of the renowned Cleveland Orchestra), the Cleveland Museum of Art, the Shakespeare and Cultural Gardens, and the Cleveland Museum of Natural History. The city is home to three professional sports teams, the Cleveland Indians of baseball's American League, the Cleveland Browns of the National Football League, and the Cleveland Cavaliers of the National Basketball Association.

Cleveland, laid out in 1796 by Moses Cleaveland, grew rapidly as a production center for metals and as the most important shipping center in Ohio after the opening of the Erie Canal in 1825 and the building of a canal between Lake Erie and the Ohio River in 1830. The arrival (1840) of the railroad further spurred the city's growth. In 1870, John D. Rockefeller established the Standard Oil Company of Ohio in Cleveland.

By the middle of the 20th century, the suburbs were growing rapidly to accommodate the new businesses and the residents who were leaving the center city. Since the 1960s, urban-renewal programs have attempted to stop the flight and protect the city's eroding tax base. Following racial disorders in 1966, Carl B. Stokes became (1967) the first black mayor of a major U.S. city. Through the 1980s Cleveland's downtown area underwent renovation and experienced a construction spurt.

Cleveland (county)   Cleveland is a county situated in northeastern England along the North Sea coast. It has a population of 553,100 (1988 est.) and covers an area of 583 km^2 (225 mi^2). Cleveland is heavily industrialized,

GROVER CLEVELAND
22d and 24th President of the United States (1885–89, 1893–97)

Born: Mar. 18, 1837, Caldwell, N.J.

Profession: Lawyer

Religious Affiliation: Presbyterian

Marriage: June 2, 1886, to Frances Folsom (1864–1947)

Children: Ruth Cleveland (1891–1904); Esther Cleveland (1893–1980); Marion Cleveland (1895–1977); Richard Folsom Cleveland (1897–1974); Francis Grover Cleveland (1903–   )

Political Affiliation: Democratic

Writings: *Presidential Problems* (1904)

Died: June 24, 1908, Princeton, N.J.

Buried: Princeton, N.J.

Vice-Presidents: Thomas A. Hendricks (1885–89); Adlai E. Stevenson (1893–97)

with iron and steel produced at the port city of HARTLE-POOL and chemicals produced at Billingham, located on the River Tees. Cleveland was created in 1974 from the county boroughs of Hartlepool and Teesside and parts of County Durham and Yorkshire.

Cleveland, Grover   The 22d and 24th president of the United States, Grover Cleveland is the only American chief executive to have served nonconsecutive terms (1885–89 and 1893–97).

Early Life. Stephen Grover Cleveland was born on Mar. 18, 1837, in Caldwell, N.J. His father, a Presbyterian clergyman, took the family to New York State in 1841. On the father's death in 1853, the family was in difficult financial straits, and young Grover left home. He worked one year in New York City at the New York Institution for the Blind before moving to Buffalo in 1855 to live with a wealthy uncle. He studied law and was admitted to the bar in 1859.

Entering politics as a Democrat, Cleveland became assistant district attorney of Erie County in 1863. In the same year he was called for military service in the Civil War, but he paid to have a substitute go in his place so that he could support his mother and sisters.

Political Rise. Cleveland's meteoric rise to the presidency began in 1881 when he won election as a reform mayor of Buffalo. True to his campaign promises to deal firmly with corruption and to cut the city's budget, he be-

came known as the "veto mayor," refusing to approve several expensive measures passed by the city council. Although still little known outside Buffalo, he caught the eye of state Democratic leaders, who saw Cleveland as the perfect foil to the Republican gubernatorial candidate, a machine politician. In 1882, therefore, Cleveland received the Democratic nomination for governor and won.

Taking office in 1883, Cleveland angered some voters by vetoing a bill to reduce fares on New York City elevated railroads to 5 cents. Even this unpopular act, however, served to establish his reputation as an independent man of principle. He was persistently at odds with the leadership of New York City's Democratic machine (Tammany Hall) and thus antagonized a powerful faction in his party. He simultaneously strengthened his public image, however, as an opponent of the spoils system.

When the 1884 Republican presidential nomination went to James G. BLAINE, a senator accused of influence peddling, the Democrats sought to highlight the issue of public morality, and Cleveland was again their logical choice. The campaign that followed his nomination was marked by mudslinging, including the revelation that Cleveland had fathered an illegitimate child and further exposures of Blaine's shady bond deals as a congressman. In a close contest, Cleveland won by a plurality rather than a majority of the popular vote.

First Presidency. During his first term Cleveland was unable to preserve or expand his coalition of support. Elected under a reform banner, he was pressed by civil service reformers to distribute PATRONAGE on the basis of merit. On the other hand, most Democratic leaders, hungry for spoils after 24 years without a Democratic president, clamored for the removal of all Republican appointees from federal positions. Cleveland gradually gave in to his party's majority, dispensing most of the patronage to "deserving" Democrats.

He was more successful in dealing with Congress on the issue of executive prerogative, bringing about repeal of the TENURE OF OFFICE ACT. As a matter of principle he also resisted congressional efforts to distribute the federal treasury surplus by granting new veterans' pensions, thus antagonizing many potential recipients.

In December 1887, Cleveland sent Congress a message urging reduction of tariff levels. Since tariffs were then the chief source of federal revenue, he argued that the treasury's surplus would thus be reduced; at the same time lower tariffs would save consumers money and end special federal privileges for favored, or protected, industries. The message was a bold stroke, but Cleveland then turned the issue over to congressional leaders who were either unable or unwilling to produce a reform bill. Running for reelection in 1888, he further weakened his stand by allowing the prominent protectionists William H. Barnum and Calvin S. Brice to manage his national campaign. In the end the tariff issue probably did him more harm than good. Cleveland was defeated in the election, winning a plurality of the popular vote but losing in the electoral college to the Republican Benjamin HARRISON.

Between Terms. While Cleveland retired to private law practice in New York City, Harrison's administration produced several pieces of activist legislation, including the Sherman Silver Purchase Act, the McKinley Tariff (see TARIFF ACTS), and record high budgets. For voters who considered these acts excessive, Cleveland's low-tariff and hard-money views seemed very attractive by comparison. Cleveland easily won the Democratic nomination in 1892, and discontent within the Republican party enabled him to defeat Harrison.

Second Presidency. Upon taking office for the second time, Cleveland was faced with a national crisis. The treasury's gold reserves were rapidly dwindling, and a national depression was beginning. Cleveland responded by calling a special session of Congress in 1893 and pressed for repeal of the Sherman Silver Purchase Act. By exerting an unusual degree of presidential pressure, Cleveland accomplished his goal, but in bludgeoning Congress into accepting repeal he alienated the FREE SILVER wing of his party and expended most of his political capital. In seeking his second major legislative goal, tariff reform, Cleveland received little cooperation from Congress. A tariff bill, the Wilson-Gorman Tariff, passed Congress in 1894, but because it achieved few significant tariff revisions, it greatly disappointed Cleveland. He let it become law without his signature.

In foreign affairs Cleveland generally resisted the growing expansionism of the 1890s. His administration withdrew recognition of the revolutionaries who had overthrown the native Hawaiian monarchy in hope of forcing the United States to annex the islands. He also refused to intervene in Cuba in the struggle between the Cuban insurgents and the Spanish colonial government. Ironically, possibly the most popular act of Cleveland's second administration was a departure from this cautious foreign policy. Late in 1895 Cleveland issued a belligerent warning that the United States would not tolerate British intervention in the VENEZUELA BOUNDARY DISPUTE. The British, having little interest in challenging Cleveland's interpretation of the MONROE DOCTRINE, agreed to arbitrate the dispute.

Cleveland's handling of the nation's economic crisis sharpened the division between his administration and Democrats from the South and West. The president defended the gold standard by selling bonds through syndicates of New York bankers, including one led by J. P. Morgan (see MORGAN family). He endorsed the hostile treatment given COXEY'S ARMY of the unemployed when it reached Washington, D.C., in 1894. During the PULLMAN STRIKE of the same year, his administration used an injunction against the strikers and sent federal troops to Chicago over the protests of Gov. J. P. ALTGELD of Illinois. Disaffection with Cleveland increased until, in 1896, the Democrats nominated William Jennings BRYAN for president, thus repudiating Cleveland's leadership.

Later Years. After leaving the presidency, Cleveland moved to Princeton, N.J. He resumed his legal practice, became a member of Princeton University's board of trustees, and played the role of elder statesman through writings and speeches. He died in Princeton on June 24, 1908.

Cleveland Museum of Art

The Cleveland Museum of Art, a private institution opened to the public in 1916, is located in Wade Park in a neoclassical marble structure built by Hubbell and Benes, to which a new wing was added in 1958. One of the finest collections in the United States, the museum's holdings cover painting from the 15th to the 20th century; prints and drawings; decorative arts; Egyptian, Near Eastern, and classical art; Oriental art and textiles; Early Christian, Byzantine, Romanesque, and Gothic sculpture, ivories, and miniatures; modern sculpture; and pre-Columbian art. It is particularly rich in medieval works.

Cleveland Orchestra, The

The Cleveland Orchestra, founded in 1918, has played its regular season at Severance Hall since 1931. Nikolai Sokoloff, its first conductor, was succeeded in 1933 by Artur Rodzinski, whose 10-year tenure as conductor brought the orchestra national prominence. Erich LEINSDORF assumed the post in 1943 and remained until Georg SZELL was made musical director and conductor in 1946. Under Szell, whose reign lasted until his death in 1970, the orchestra achieved international celebrity from its world tours and many fine recordings. Following a season in which Pierre Boulez was principal guest conductor, Lorin Maazel served (1972–82) as musical director and conductor, expanding the orchestra's repertory and further enhancing its reputation. In 1982, Christoph von DOHNÁNYI was appointed Maazel's successor.

Cliburn, Van [kly'-burn]   The pianist Van Cliburn, originally named Harvey Lavan Cliburn, Jr., b. Shreveport, La., July 12, 1934, was the first American to win (1958) the International Tchaikovsky Prize. Cliburn studied piano with Rosina Lhévinne at Juilliard and graduated in 1954. He debuted with the Houston Symphony in 1947 and in Carnegie Hall the following year.

cliff dwellers   Cliff dwellers are people who make their homes in shallow natural caves in cliffs or under cliff overhangs. Although such dwellings have been found in many areas, including the well-known rock shelters of the Dordogne and central Pyrenees regions of southwestern France, the term *cliff dwellers* is usually associated with prehistoric inhabitants of cliffs in the American Southwest (see ANASAZI; PUEBLO Indians). The cliff dwellings are found from southern Colorado and Utah to northwestern New Mexico and northern Arizona. They are concentrated on the Colorado Plateau, where box canyons with vertical sides have been created by erosion.

These shallow caves in the recessed cliffs served as natural shelters from the wind and rain; in addition, caves facing east or south were warmed by the morning sun and cooled in the evening. Many were situated near a spring, above a river valley with arable land. Most were inaccessible from above and had to be entered either by removable ladders or by hand- and footholds cut into the cliff faces. As homesites, these cliff dwellings perched high on ledges of the canyons were virtually inaccessible to outsiders and were easily defensible against nomadic, predatory peoples.

The masonry houses of cliff dwellers are found in the Four Corners area of the southwestern United States. They were built into the sheer cliffs beneath overhanging rock as natural protection against invading peoples.

Clifford, Clark   Clark McAdams Clifford, b. Fort Scott, Kans., Dec. 25, 1906, is a lawyer who held numerous posts in the administrations of Presidents Franklin Roosevelt, Harry Truman, John Kennedy, and Lyndon Johnson. After serving in the U.S. Navy during World War II, he was named (1946) naval aide to President Truman, and in 1948 he became special counsel to the president and helped manage Truman's successful election campaign. He was also prominent in the 1960 presidential election campaign of John F. Kennedy. In 1963, Clifford

was appointed chairman of the Foreign Intelligence Advisory Board. President Johnson appointed him to succeed Robert S. McNamara as secretary of defense in 1968; in that post he was influential in changing the direction of U.S. policy in Vietnam.

climate   Climate is the general state of the ATMOSPHERE over a long period of time. Whereas weather is the expression of day-to-day conditions, climate is a composite of averages and extremes during a specified number of years. Like weather, climate results from energy and mass exchanges within the atmosphere and between the atmosphere and the Earth's surface.

As a factor in the natural environment, climate not only affects world patterns of vegetation, soils, and water resources, but also directly or indirectly influences every human endeavor. Climate determines an area's suitability for settlement and for agriculture, manufacturing, transportation, and other economic activities. Knowledge of past climatic fluctuations has helped to explain ice ages, changes in sea level, famines, and migrations. Increasing evidence indicates that human impact on the environment is causing local and perhaps worldwide changes in climate.

Climatology

No two places on Earth have the same climate. In order to communicate information about different climates, an organized system of generalizations—that is, a classification—must be used. The three main approaches to climatic classification are genetic, empiric, and applied. Genetic systems group climates according to their presumed causes—for example, tropical, highland, continental, and monsoonal. The ancient Greek division of the world into torrid, temperate, and frigid zones was an early attempt at genetic classification based on the effects of latitude on temperature.

Empiric classifications identify climates in terms of their observable characteristics, treated either singly or in combination. Empiric classifications commonly fix quantitative limits for descriptive categories with reference to temperature, precipitation, sunshine, wind, or other elements. Applied, or technical, classifications employ any criteria relevant to the effects of climate on other phenomena. Climates may thus be defined according to their influence on landforms, vegetation, agriculture, human comfort, energy consumption, air pollution, or urban environments.

Any climatic classification must provide for different scales of space and time. Broadly generalized regional climates encompassing large areas are macroclimates and may be subdivided into mesoclimates of intermediate scale. Microclimates are climates of small areas, often limited to shallow surface layers of the atmosphere for the purposes of applied studies. Paleoclimates, or prehistoric climates, are usually subdivided according to geologic or biologic time scales (see GEOLOGIC TIME; PALEOCLIMATOLOGY). Evidence from archaeology, recorded history, and statistical analyses of observational data have fixed the limits of climatic periods since humans first appeared.

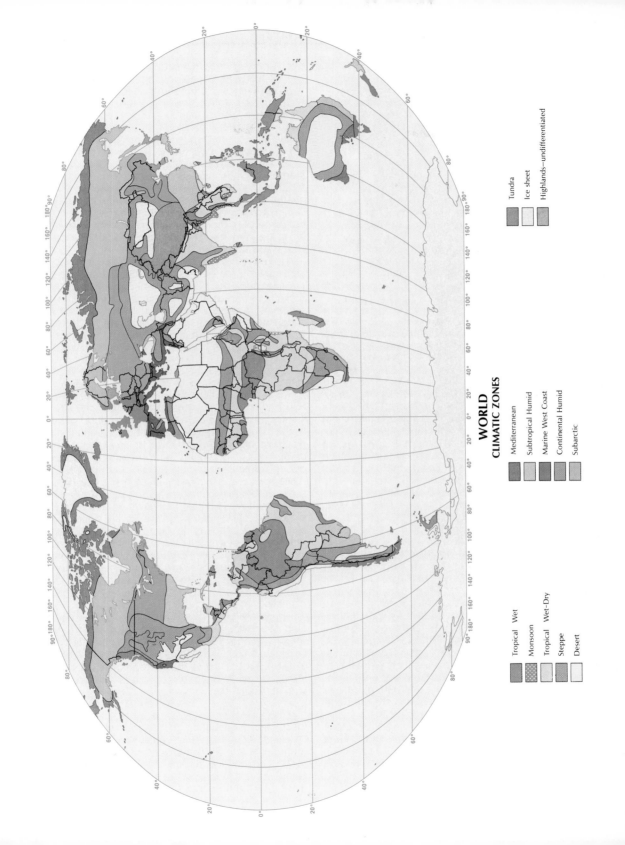

WORLD
CLIMATIC ZONES

Tropical Wet
Monsoon
Tropical Wet-Dry
Steppe
Desert

Mediterranean
Subtropical Humid
Marine West Coast
Continental Humid
Subarctic

Tundra
Ice sheet
Highlands—undifferentiated

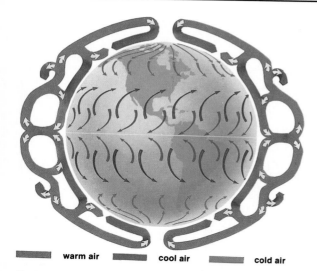

warm air   cool air   cold air

The Earth's atmospheric circulation depends primarily on a continuous exchange of hot equatorial air with cold polar air. The Earth's rotation affects wind direction, however, causing wind currents to be deflected to the right in the Northern Hemisphere and to the left in the Southern Hemisphere as a result of the Coriolis effect.

The best known and most widely used climatic classification is that developed by Wladimir KÖPPEN in the early 20th century. Köppen defined values of temperature and precipitation that set boundary conditions between major vegetation formations. The accompanying map shows the world distribution of 13 main classes of climate, based on a modification of Köppen's system by the American geographer Glenn T. Trewartha. These climatic types fall into 6 major categories that combine broadly similar characteristics of temperature or precipitation and the associated natural vegetation: humid subtropical, dry, humid mesothermal, humid microthermal, polar, and highland.

The humid tropics are constantly warm and receive large annual totals of rainfall. In the tropical-wet type, adequate moisture throughout the year supports dense tropical JUNGLES AND RAIN FORESTS such as those of the Amazon and Congo river basins. MONSOON climates prevail along certain tropical coasts where a strong onshore flow of moist air occurs during a distinctly wet summer season. Rainfall and soil-moisture storage generally are sufficient to maintain evergreen forests. Tropical wet-dry regions experience great contrasts in precipitation through the year. Summers are rainy, whereas winters are extremely dry. Tall grasses and scattered trees of the savanna vegetation are adapted to the alternating wet and dry periods. Representative savanna areas are the Campos of Brazil and the Sudan of northern Africa.

Dry climates extend from the tropics well into the middle latitudes and therefore vary widely in temperature characteristics. Steppe, or semiarid, climates occur along the slightly wetter margins of tropical deserts and in broad belts of western North America and Central Asia. Shrubs and short grasses are the principal native vegeta-

tion. Desert, or arid, climates include the hot deserts of the tropics and subtropics and cold-winter deserts of middle latitudes. Thorny shrubs and scattered grasses are typical desert plants.

Humid mesothermal climates are found in the middle latitudes, where winters are mild and short. Mediterranean climates are distinguished by rainy winters and hot, dry summers; another name for these regions of scrub forest along the west coasts of continents is "dry summer subtropics." On continental east coasts in comparable latitudes are the subtropical humid climates, which have adequate rainfall throughout the year for forests. The hot, wet summers are much like those of the humid tropics, but winters are cooler. Poleward of Mediterranean-climate areas are marine-west-coast areas of cool forest climates with wet winters.

Humid microthermal climates extend in broad bands across North America and Eurasia. Winter temperatures are low, and they decrease with both latitude and distance from oceans. Interior areas experience great annual temperature ranges. Continental humid climates may be subdivided into "long" and "short" types, reflecting latitudinal effects on the growing season. Tall grasses and mixed forests are the natural vegetation. Farther poleward, subarctic climates are associated with the boreal forest (taiga), consisting mainly of conifers. Winters are very cold; summers are short and cool.

Polar climates form belts surrounding the North and South poles. Winters are long and dark; the short, cool summers have long daylight periods. Grasses and lichens of the TUNDRA can grow on hummocky ground that overlies permanently frozen subsoil, or PERMAFROST. Ice sheets cover most of Greenland and Antarctica. Temperatures during the short summers are not high enough to melt these ice caps, which are maintained by relatively light snowfall that may come in any season.

Regions with highland climates are mosaics of many different local climates that vary with slope, exposure, and altitude in the world's MOUNTAIN ranges and PLATEAUS. Windward slopes usually are wetter than those on the lee sides. In general, temperatures decrease and precipitation increases with altitude, resulting in a vertical zonation of plant life. Seasonal distribution of temperature and precipitation approximates that of adjacent lowland climates.

Numerous other classifications have been devised for climate research and for applied studies of natural resources, economic activites, or environmental problems. No single system can suit all purposes; rather, the system of organization and selection of criteria depend on the intended use: explanation, description, or application of climatic knowledge.

Why Climates Differ

Incoming solar radiation, or insolation, is the basic source of energy for atmospheric processes. The Earth's orbital revolution around the Sun and its rotation on a tilting polar axis produce seasonal and daily changes in the amount of insolation. Gases, clouds, and suspended particles in the atmosphere scatter and reflect about 26 percent of insolation into space. The Earth's surface reflects another 4 percent, although the proportion varies with the angle of the Sun and the reflectivity of different materials. The atmosphere and the Earth's surface together absorb about 70 percent of insolation, which is converted to the heat and kinetic energy that create weather and climate. Absorption by the atmosphere of energy emitted from the Earth's surface delays the energy's return to space, creating a GREENHOUSE EFFECT. Eventually all absorbed solar energy returns to outer space as long-wave radiation, maintaining a long-term global energy balance and a nearly constant average global temperature.

The actual energy budget and resulting effects on climate at a given place depend on additional factors. Latitude determines the duration of daylight as well as the angle of the Sun's rays, which are more effective when the Sun is near the zenith. Altitude is also a factor in climate, because air temperature normally decreases with elevation at a rate of about 6 C degrees/1,000 m (3.3 F degrees/1,000 ft). General atmospheric and oceanic circulation systems redistribute heat and moisture, helping to prevent overheating in the tropics and intense cold near the poles. Prevailing winds, especially TRADE WINDS and WESTERLIES, transfer temperature and moisture properties between the continents and the oceans. Because water is slower to heat and cool than land and affords a ready supply of moisture, regions downwind from oceans usually have more moderate temperatures and more precipitation than do the interiors of the continents. This maritime influence is marked in middle latitudes. OCEAN CURRENTS and drifts further promote the transfer of heat.

Climate Change

The elements of climate change through time as well as from place to place. Indirect evidence of climatic trends in the distant past is revealed in fossils, lake and ocean beds, peat bogs, glacial deposits, and soils. Widths of annual growth rings in trees correlate with temperature and rainfall fluctuations, especially along the drier margins of forests, and fossil trees provide records of dramatic climatic events in the past. Archaeological remains and written history offer clues to climatic conditions during the human era, and modern instrument records now provide direct evidence of climatic change.

Different explanations have been offered for the changes that have been observed or inferred. The Milankovitch theory, for example, suggests that differences in the shape of the Earth's orbit, the tilt of the polar axis, and the time of year when the Earth is nearest the Sun effect changes in insolation that have brought on the ICE AGES.

Within the atmosphere, fluctuations in the amount and distribution of gases, clouds, and solid particles would be expected to alter the energy budget. Among the possible natural causes of such fluctuations are volcanic eruptions and meteor impacts. The Earth's surface exerts immense influence on the heat and moisture budgets. Geologic changes in the size, position, and elevation of the continents have been studied as causes of paleoclimatic change (see PLATE TECTONICS). Changes in reflectivity resulting from shifting patterns of plant cover, water, or

ice are other possible factors in climatic variability.

Human activity has the potential of affecting large-scale climate patterns through the introduction of materials into the atmosphere and the depletion of forest cover. Scientists now clearly recognize that the greenhouse effect, mentioned above, is being enhanced by human activities. The regional effects on climate of large urban centers have also been the subject of research for many years (see URBAN CLIMATE).

clinical psychology   see PSYCHOLOGY

Clinton (family)   The Clinton family dominated New York politics during the first half-century of its statehood. The founder of the family was **Charles Clinton**, b. 1690, d. Nov. 19, 1773, an Irish immigrant who in 1731 settled Little Britain in Ulster (now Orange) County. A judge, militia officer, surveyor, and land speculator, he had two famous sons, James and George.

James Clinton, b. Aug. 9, 1733, d. Dec. 22, 1812, earned distinction as an officer during the French and Indian War and the American Revolution. **George Clinton**, b. July 25, 1739, d. Apr. 20, 1812, was an undistinguished officer in the same wars but was a brilliant politician. After serving as assemblyman and member of the Provincial and Continental congresses, he was elected governor of New York seven times between 1777 and 1804. An ardent Anti-Federalist, he was the author of seven letters signed "Cato" in the *New York Journal* opposing ratification of the federal Constitution. He later served as vice-president (1805–12) under Thomas Jefferson and James Madison. George Clinton's achievements as revolutionary governor earned him the title "father of the state."

James's son, **DeWitt Clinton**, b. Mar. 2, 1769, d. Feb. 11, 1828, served as his uncle's private secretary from 1790 to 1795 and then embarked on a similar career. In addition to a brief term (1802) in the U.S. Senate, DeWitt held every major elective office in New York between 1797 and 1828—assemblyman, senator, mayor of New York City, lieutenant governor, and governor. He was a

DeWitt Clinton, who held almost every important public office in New York State, is remembered chiefly for his achievements as governor of New York, which include the institution of a public school system and the construction of the Erie Canal. (National Portrait Gallery, Washington, D.C.)

philanthropist and patron of the arts and science and, as canal commissioner, championed (1825) construction of the Erie and Champlain canals.

Clinton, Sir Henry

Sir Henry Clinton, b. *c*.1738, d. Dec. 23, 1795, was a British general in the American Revolution. He began his military service in the New York militia because his father was governor of that colony. He served in Germany during the Seven Years' War and rose to the rank of major general in 1772.

When the American Revolutionary War broke out, Clinton was sent to Boston and distinguished himself in the Battle of BUNKER HILL (1775). For his part in the Battle of Long Island (1776; see LONG ISLAND, BATTLE OF) he was made a lieutenant general and was knighted. When William HOWE resigned in 1778, Clinton succeeded him as commander in chief of the British forces in America.

Clinton shifted his theater of operations to the south, capturing Charleston in 1780. He quarreled constantly with Charles CORNWALLIS, which may have contributed to the latter's surrender at Yorktown. Clinton resigned in 1781 and returned to England.

clipper ship

The clipper ship was an exceptionally fast, graceful sailing SHIP. This type of vessel "moved at a good clip" and could "clip" time from long ocean voyages, hence its name. The first clippers were wooden schooners built in Virginia and Maryland and were known as Baltimore clippers. Having first gained fame as blockade runners and privateers during the War of 1812, these schooners later earned notoriety as West African slave ships. They were not, however, true clippers. The first true clipper was the *Rainbow*, built in New York in 1845. Typical clippers had a length of 64.6 m (212 ft) and a beam of 6.4 m (21 ft), giving them their characteristic long, narrow hulls and high sharp bows. With their three masts carrying full sail, they could outrun any other sailing vessel and were used at first for high-speed transportation to and from the gold fields of California (1848) and Australia (early 1850s). Best known were the *Flying Cloud* and the *Flying Fish*, built by Donald MCKAY of Boston, and the *Sovereign of the Seas*, which sailed across the Atlantic in under 14 days. The 1854 record set by the *Flying Cloud*—89 days from New York to California via Cape Horn—was broken only in 1989 by a modern yacht.

When British firms began ordering U.S. clipper ships for the China tea trade, Scotland's shipyards were spurred to design their own clippers. The high prices obtained in London for the first of each season's tea crop led to races from China to Great Britain. The most famous race took place between the *Thermopylae* and the *Cutty Sark* in 1868.

The U.S. Civil War (1861–65) had disastrous consequences for U.S. shipbuilders, who were no longer able to compete with British shipyards. Then, in 1869, the opening of the Suez Canal deprived British tea clippers of their handsome profits.

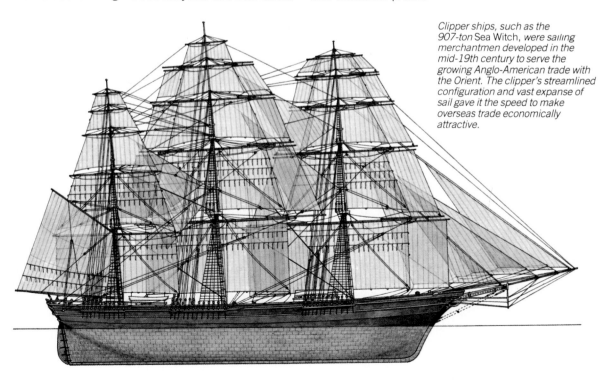

Clipper ships, such as the 907-ton Sea Witch, *were sailing merchantmen developed in the mid-19th century to serve the growing Anglo-American trade with the Orient. The clipper's streamlined configuration and vast expanse of sail gave it the speed to make overseas trade economically attractive.*

Clive, Robert Robert Clive, b. Sept. 29, 1725, d. Nov. 22, 1774, was an English soldier and administrator who established early British hegemony in India. He went to India as a clerk for the British East India Company in 1743. Commissioned in the company's army four years later, he fought (1751–52) with distinction against the French under Joseph François DUPLEIX. In 1755 he was appointed lieutenant governor of Fort St. David, near Madras. When the nawab of Bengal captured Calcutta in 1756, Clive was sent to retake the city, which he did in January 1757. His victory over the nawab at Plassey in June of that year brought Bengal effectively under British rule. Although a puppet nawab was installed, Clive became the British governor and during the next few years extracted a large fortune from the nawab. After defeating the Dutch near Chinsura in 1759, he returned (1760) to England where, in 1762, he was created Baron Clive of Plassey.

Reappointed governor of Bengal in 1765, Clive obtained for the East India Company the right to collect revenue in Bengal, Bihar, and Orissa. He also tried to curb the financial corruption from which he had benefited earlier. Upon his return to England in 1767, Clive himself was charged with corruption, but after an investigation by Parliament that lasted six years, he was acquitted. An opium addict, he committed suicide.

clocks and watches Clocks and watches are mechanical, electrical, or atomic devices that measure the passage of TIME. In the quest for more accurate ways to measure time, humans have progressed from watching the Sun, Moon, and stars move across the sky to con-

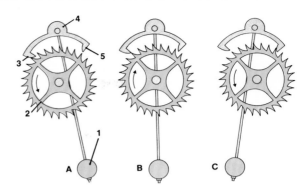

The anchor, or recoil, escapement (2 and 3 on the long-case clock mechanism) ensures uniform movement of the entire set of wheels and keeps the pendulum moving despite friction. As the pendulum (1) swings to the right (A), a tooth on the escapement wheel (2) is engaged by the left pallet (3) of the anchor (4) and is moved counterclockwise against the opposing force of a spring. The spring recoil action shortens the pendulum swing and moves it back to the left (B). The wheel is then freed from the left pallet and is moved clockwise by the spring. As the pendulum moves to the far left (C) the right pallet (5) locks the escape wheel, which reverses direction. The recoil swings the pendulum back to the right, and the cycle is repeated.

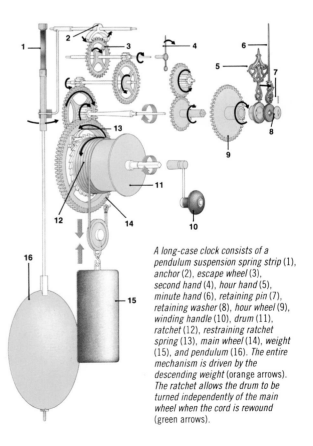

A long-case clock consists of a pendulum suspension spring strip (1), anchor (2), escape wheel (3), second hand (4), hour hand (5), minute hand (6), retaining pin (7), retaining washer (8), hour wheel (9), winding handle (10), drum (11), ratchet (12), restraining ratchet spring (13), main wheel (14), weight (15), and pendulum (16). The entire mechanism is driven by the descending weight (orange arrows). The ratchet allows the drum to be turned independently of the main wheel when the cord is rewound (green arrows).

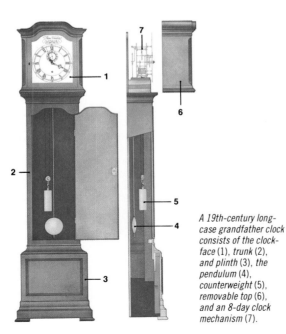

A 19th-century long-case grandfather clock consists of the clockface (1), trunk (2), and plinth (3), the pendulum (4), counterweight (5), removable top (6), and an 8-day clock mechanism (7).

structing ingenious mechanical devices and measuring small energy oscillations in atoms.

The Babylonians and Egyptians used SUNDIALS, or shadow clocks, to divide daylight into short, defined periods. The Egyptians used the water clock, or CLEPSYDRA, to measure time at night, and the Greeks designed fine ASTROLABES. Modern mechanical clocks date from the late Middle Ages. All such clocks must have a source of energy—a falling weight, a wound spring, or an alternating current—which must be carefully regulated in order for the clock to run accurately. The weight, spring, or current turns a wheel and a system of gears that move the hands of the clock and are controlled by an arresting mechanism called an escapement, which allows the teeth of one of the gears to "escape" one by one.

Weight-Driven Clocks. The first major advance in clock construction occurred in Europe in the 14th century. It was discovered that the speed of a falling weight could be controlled by using an oscillating horizontal bar (foliot) attached to a vertical spindle (verge) with two protrusions (pallets) as an escapement. When a pallet meshed with a tooth of the gear driven by the weight, it momentarily halted the revolving wheel and hence the weight. The oldest existing examples of this arrangement, which is known as the verge escapement mechanism, are found in ornate clocks at Rouen, in France (1379), and at Salisbury (1396) and Wells (1392), in England.

Accuracy was improved considerably when the Dutch scientist Christiaan HUYGENS introduced the PENDULUM into weight-driven clockmaking. About 1660 the Englishman Robert HOOKE invented the anchor, or recoil, escapement, which improved the functioning of the gear train. About 1715, George Graham introduced the Graham, or deadbeat, escapement, the purpose of which was to let the pendulum oscillate with as little interference as possible. It is still used in precision clocks.

Spring-Driven Clocks and Watches. By the end of the 15th century the spring had replaced the weight in some clocks, allowing them to be built small enough to be carried. Since the verge escapement mechanism can operate only with a constant force, it was necessary to compensate for the loss of power as the mainspring unwound. An extra spring (the stackfreed) and, later, a chain coiled around a drum (the fusee) were devices that balanced varying mainspring strength.

During the 16th and 17th centuries the demand for accurate timekeeping devices for NAVIGATION at sea stimulated the development of portable timepieces, which were first made about 1500. Only in the late 18th century did timepieces for navigation become practical. John Harrison's CHRONOMETER no. 4, with a balance spring made of a bimetallic strip to lessen temperature effects, was in error by only 54 seconds after a sea voyage of 156 days.

The balance wheel, hairspring, and mainspring, together with the anchor escapement, or improved escapements, constitute the essentials of the modern mechanical watch. Beginning in the 18th century the friction in the gears was reduced by using jewels as spindle bearings, a feature incorporated in all modern watches. The principle behind self-winding watches had been known

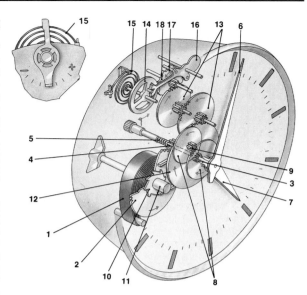

In a clock movement, the mainspring (1) drives a great wheel (2), which rotates a center spindle (3), gear (4), and friction spring (5), driving the minute hand (6). The hour hand (7) is driven by the second and third wheels (8) and a gear (9). A ratchet (10) on a spindle (11) prevents the mainspring from uncoiling too fast. Release of the mainspring's energy is controlled by an escapement, through a center wheel (12) and a double-geared set of wheels (13). Oscillation of the balance wheel (14), stabilized by a balance spring (15), causes a lever (16) to rock. Lever pallets (17) allow the escape wheel (18) to turn in fixed increments. A small lever on the balance spring (see detail) controls its tension and thus the movement speed.

for about two centuries, but it was not widely applied until the 1920s, when wristwatches became popular. Watches run by small batteries were introduced in the 1950s. The balance of such an electric watch is kept in motion electromagnetically by a coil that is energized by an electronic circuit. The modern electronic watch is driven by a quartz crystal, which is made to vibrate at its natural frequency, using the PIEZOELECTRIC effect. Digital quartz watches display time in numbers, using LEDs (light-emitting diodes) or an LCD (liquid-crystal display). All digital clocks use either these display methods or gears turning numbered sheets.

Electric Clocks. The domestic electric clock uses electric current as a power source instead of a weight or spring. In essence, the clock is an electric motor synchronized with the alternating current (AC) power line, the frequency of which in the United States is 60 hertz (cycles per second). The rotational speed of the motor is reduced by gears to the appropriate rotational speed of the hour, minute, and second hands. The accuracy of such clocks depends entirely on the stability of the AC frequency.

Atomic Clocks. The most accurate timepieces yet devised are ATOMIC CLOCKS, which measure time in terms of the oscillations of cesium, rubidium, hydrogen, or other elements. Such clocks may be accurate to within 1 second in many thousands or even millions of years.

Clodion [klawd-yohn'] The sculptures of Claude Michel, called Clodion, 1738-1814, were the counterpart to the ROCOCO paintings of Jean Honoré Fragonard. After studying with his uncle Lambert Sigisbert Adam in 1755 and Jean Baptiste Pigalle in 1759, he won the Grand Prix de Sculpture and lived (1762–71) in Rome. Clodion produced gaily colored terra-cotta statuettes of allegorical subjects often tinged with erotic overtones. As in *Satyr and Bacchante* (*c*.1775; Metropolitan Museum of Art, New York City), he emphasized light-hearted and witty interpretations of mythology suited to private rather than public commissions.

Clodius, Publius [klohd'-ee-uhs] Publius Clodius, called Clodius Pulcher, b. *c*.92 BC, sought power by unorthodox means during the late Roman republic. In 68 he instigated mutiny among the troops of Lucius Licinius LUCULLUS. Apparently having an affair with Julius CAESAR's wife Pompeia, in 62 Clodius entered Caesar's house disguised as a woman during a ceremony honoring the women's goddess, Bona Dea. Charged with sacrilege, he was acquitted by a jury probably bribed by Marcus Licinius CRASSUS but became a bitter enemy of CICERO, who had given evidence against him.

As tribune for 58 BC Clodius obtained passage of several popularly supported measures, including Cicero's exile. Although relatively powerless after 56, he was murdered on Jan. 18, 52 BC, by street fighters in the pay of POMPEY THE GREAT's friend Milo.

cloisonné see ENAMEL

cloister A cloister, from the Latin word *claustrum* ("hidden"), is a covered walkway along the walls of an interior courtyard. Prominent design elements in early monasteries, cathedrals, and churches, cloisters were built between the enclosed areas of a structure. Often arcaded or colonnaded, the cloister walkways surrounded an open-air courtyard.

cloning Cloning is the production of a group of genetically identical cells or organisms, all descended from a single individual. The members of a clone have precisely the same characteristics, except where mutation and environmentally caused developmental variation have occurred.

Examples from Nature

Primary Reproductive Mode. In species whose reproduction is strictly asexual, each population consists of one or more clones, depending on the number of ancestral individuals. Such species include all bacteria and blue-green algae, most protozoans and other algae, some yeasts, and even some higher plants and animals, such as dandelions and flatworms.

Supplementary Reproductive Mode. Some algae reproduce sexually and asexually. Those individuals formed by asexual reproduction constitute a clone. In the club mosses and some higher plants, a "runner," or stem, grows horizontally along the surface of the soil and at intervals produces roots and upright stalks. When the sections of stem between stalks disintegrate, the separated individuals constitute a clone.

Some animals have tremendous powers of REGENERATION. If the body of certain starfish is cut up into its five arms, each arm will regenerate a complete individual. Another type of asexual reproduction found in all animals, human beings included, is the formation of identical twins, triplets, and so on. Identical siblings constitute a clone. Some forms of PARTHENOGENESIS can also produce clones.

Tissue-level Reproductive Mode. The growth of a tumor is, in effect, the formation of a clone of malignant cells. Another clone is the proliferation of a single B lymphocyte (a cell type of the immune system), producing identical specific monoclonal ANTIBODIES, against a particular antigen.

Artificial Techniques

In one method of artificial cloning used in PLANT BREEDING, cells are cut from a plant and placed in a flask with nutrient medium. The cells grow and divide, forming embryonic tissues that are transferred to soil where they produce complete plants. GRAFTING is another method. Cuts are made in the stems of two plants, which are then fitted together so that their transport systems are in contact. The wounded area heals, and the two stems become a single physiological unit.

In the "nuclear transplantation procedure" used with animals, nuclei from cells of one individual are transferred to unfertilized eggs whose nuclei have been removed. All the transplanted nuclei are generally identical, and therefore the resultant individuals constitute clones. This procedure has been successfully carried out in frogs and mice.

In recombinant-DNA formation, genetic material from one organism is transferred to a host cell, which then divides many times, forming a clone, all of whose members contain the donor DNA and produce its encoded protein. Thus, human genes have been transferred to bacteria whose subsequently formed clones have produced such medically important substances as INSULIN, INTERFERON, and growth hormone. Genes have also been cloned from bacteria in preserved tissues of long-dead humans and extinct animals, yielding copies for comparisons with related organisms. Another procedure involves the somatic-cell fusion of a B lymphocyte with a cancer cell, forming a "hybridoma" whose descendant cells produce large amounts of monoclonal antibodies.

Great concern has been voiced over the potential for human cloning. The possibility that the technology required for human cloning will be perfected in the foreseeable future is remote, however.

Close, Chuck Chuck Close, b. Monroe, Wash., July 5, 1940, is a leading American photorealist painter.

Close enlarges color photographs, almost exlusively of faces, into enormous images of soft-focus flesh and pore-and-wrinkle detail, as in *Phil* (1969; Whitney Museum, New York City). After using other materials for some 20 years, Close returned to oil painting, creating the acclaimed portrait *Stanley* (1981; Solomon R. Guggenheim Museum, New York City).

closed shop In labor-management relations, a closed shop means that an employer must hire only workers who are members in good standing of a specific labor union. The closed shop is common in the United States among craft unions in the building trades and the arts. It also exists where employers hire from a union hall for short periods of time, as with construction workers and dockworkers. The Taft-Hartley Act of 1947 made the closed shop illegal in the production of goods that entered or affected interstate commerce, but it still exists in some industries on an informal basis. Elsewhere it has been replaced by the UNION SHOP.

clothing industry The contemporary system of industrialized clothing production did not exist before the mid-19th century. Although important advances in the mechanization of spinning and weaving had been taking place during the previous centuries, clothes making continued to be a hand skill. Except for the introduction of metal needles in the Middle Ages, no new technology had been successfully utilized until Isaac M. SINGER designed a treadle-powered sewing machine in 1851. At first his machines were used only for straight-seam stitching, but gradually other machines were introduced: a band knife that could cut several layers of cloth at one time; a machine to spread the fabric in layers on the cutting table; a machine for sewing buttonholes, and another for sewing on buttons; a pressing machine to replace the hand flat-iron. By the end of the 19th century, the basic conditions and technologies for the creation of a giant clothing industry were present.

Development of the American Clothing Industry

In the early 1800s, a small industry in Boston produced off-the-rack rainwear for sailors and whalers. The demand for secondhand clothing for working people had always exceeded the supply, and gradually, a market grew for cheap, new ready-to-wear work clothing. Soon men's tailors started to stock easy-to-fit items for their middle-class customers. Cutting was usually done in the shops; the sewing was jobbed out to women and journeymen tailors, who still did their work by hand.

The sewing machine that Singer introduced in the 1850s transformed the garment trade. Singer's machine, with its foot treadle, left both hands free to feed cloth into the machine. Gradually, tailoring and dressmaking shops were transformed into small factories as owners bought a few machines and trained operators to use them.

The American textile industry made a variety of inexpensive fabrics, and the Civil War created new impetus for the expansion of both the textile and clothing industries. Government contracts were awarded for the production of army uniforms, and manufacturers quickly discovered the advantages of assembly-line techniques that required little skill on the part of individual workers and increased their output.

Women's Clothing. The manufacture of women's and children's clothing developed more slowly. Cloaks had been produced in the 1840s, but until the turn of the century, seamstresses continued to sew for the women who could afford them, and fashionable women utilized the talents of the French-influenced couturiers who had shops in the large cities. Mass-produced underwear and silk kimonos were available, however, and the popularity of the Gibson girl of the 1890s persuaded a generation of women to wear shirtwaists. By the beginning of the 20th century, clothing factories existed in most cities, where large immigrant populations were available as cheap labor, and New York City became the center of the industry.

Growth of Garment Unions. In 1891 a merger of many small trade unions created the United Garment Workers of America, the first industry-wide garment labor union. The INTERNATIONAL LADIES' GARMENT WORKERS' UNION was organized in 1900, with a membership of 2,000. The tragic fire in the loft building that housed the Triangle Shirtwaist Co. (Mar. 25, 1911), which caused the deaths of 146 workers, drew public attention to conditions in the sweatshops; in reaction to the fire, large numbers of garment workers joined unions. In 1914 the Amalgamated Clothing Workers of America broke away from the more conservative United Garment Workers and became the most important union in the menswear industry.

Seventh Avenue. In the 1920s, a group of real-estate investors constructed a number of buildings on New York City's Seventh Avenue, designed specifically to house the workrooms and showrooms of apparel manufacturers. A 16-block area on the avenue and the streets around it became the center of the women's garment trade in the United States.

In the 1930s, the women's fashion industry began to free itself from France. Certain upper-level department stores began to promote American fashion designers by name. Today, although Paris is still a major style center, it no longer holds absolute sway over the way Americans dress.

The Production of a Line

A line is a group of garments created either by a single designer or by a manufacturing house. Lines are produced for the seasons—spring, summer, fall, and resort or holiday.

Inexpensive apparel begins with basic patterns, or slopers, modified to current taste or copied directly from a designer's best-seller. The designer's original sketch for a garment is translated into muslin, which is marked, cut, and sewn into a sample garment. The sample is fitted on a model, and if the design works, duplicate samples are created and then corrected to ensure that the pattern is true. The duplicate is then graded into a range of pattern sizes.

Decisions about all the sample garments in a line have to take several cost factors into account. Once a sample has been approved, the production process begins. Each pattern size is laid out in a way that will fit the most pattern pieces on the least amount of fabric. This layout, or marker, is used to guide the actual cutting.

The process of assembling a garment is also being rapidly automatized. Most clothing is still stitched together on sewing machines. The machines, however, have become increasingly sophisticated. Many can now be programmed to perform a sequence of steps automatically. Large manufacturers, especially those in the United States, are depending more and more on sophisticated machines that reduce the number of operators.

The U.S. Industry Today

Since about 1950, the U.S. industry has changed radically. Although New York City is still the focus for FASHION DESIGN, promotion, and merchandising, manufacturing has moved steadily away from the city and into the South and West. Overseas manufacturing has become the single most pressing problem for both U.S. apparel manufacturers and clothing workers. Estimates indicate that approximately one-third of all garments sold in the United States are made abroad.

The Industry in Europe

Germany produces almost one-quarter of the total clothing output in Western Europe. In France, the couturier houses continue to set trends, but most of the clothing sold is ready-to-wear. Italy still maintains large numbers of tailors and dressmakers, but its ready-to-wear industry is large, and much of its production is sold outside the country.

———

cloture [kloh'-chur]   Cloture, or closure, is a means to end debate in a deliberative assembly. It is invoked to prevent obstruction of legislation by a minority. One method, used since 1789 by the U.S. House of Representatives, is the parliamentary device of "moving the previous question" to end debate. The U.S. Senate employed the same device until 1806. Thereafter it had no cloture rule until 1917, when a rule was adopted by which speeches could be limited to one hour for each person, if a proposal to do so was supported by 16 senators and agreed to by two-thirds of those present. A new rule (1949) provided for cloture by a two-thirds vote; in 1975 the requirement was changed to three-fifths of the full Senate membership. However, efforts to end debate in the Senate have seldom been successful in the face of a FILIBUSTER. Legislative bodies in Canada, Great Britain, and France require only a majority vote to end debate.

———

cloud   A cloud is any concentration of gas, liquid droplets, or solid particles suspended as a distinct body in a gas or liquid. Generally, however, the term *cloud* is used to refer to the suspension of small ice or water particles in the ATMOSPHERE.

Cloud Formation. Clouds in the atmosphere form whenever the relative HUMIDITY of an AIR MASS, or parcel, reaches slightly more than 100 percent. This can occur for a number of reasons: the upward motion of air, which causes expansion and cooling; input of water from outside the parcel; or loss of heat by radiation. Among the major producers of the upward motion that results in clouds are the low-pressure systems (see LOW-PRESSURE REGION) with their cold, warm, and occluded FRONTS; tropical disturbances such as hurricanes (see HURRICANE AND TYPHOON); and the lifting of air as it flows over hilly and mountainous terrain.

The size of cloud droplets and ice crystals ranges from about 1 to 100 micrometers (4/100,000 to 4/1,000 in). Particles this small fall to the ground so slowly that they appear suspended in air, tending to move with the wind. The fall of larger water or ice particles, at much greater speeds, is called PRECIPITATION.

Cloud droplets and ice crystals first form on certain types of small particles of dust or other airborne materials. They are called condensation nuclei when water droplets are formed and ice nuclei when ice crystals result. The nuclei generally range in size from as small as 0.01 micrometer to about 1 micrometer (4/10,000,000 to 4/100,000 in). The number of nuclei varies widely, depending on the source of the air mass in which the particles are imbedded. The atmosphere over the ocean generally has the lowest number of nuclei, whereas polluted air has the highest.

The more nuclei, and therefore the more water droplets or ice crystals, the slower the process of formation of precipitation-sized particles, because the competition for the available water is greater. Thus, although RAIN often falls shortly after a cloud forms over the ocean, a much longer time is required for it to fall over continental areas.

Cloud Classification. Clouds, defined in terms of their gross physical characteristics, can be classified as stratiform or cumuliform. Stratiform, or layered, clouds form when the upward motion is relatively uniform over an area, and cumuliform, or cottony, billowing clouds develop when upward and downward air currents are relatively close together.

When clouds form at ground surface they are called FOG. Clouds that form in the middle TROPOSPHERE are called altostratus and altocumulus, and those in the upper troposphere are referred to as cirrocumulus, cirrostratus, or CIRRUS. For those with bases in the lower troposphere, the terms STRATUS and CUMULUS are used. When precipitation is falling from these clouds, they are referred to with such terms as nimbostratus or cumulonimbus. Nimbostratus are the gray, leaden-sky clouds often produced by large-scale winter CYCLONES in which precipitation is fairly steady and long lasting. Cumulonimbus clouds, on the other hand, are associated with typical summertime THUNDERSTORMS, in which rainfall is generally brief but heavy. (See art on page 58)

See also: METEOROLOGY; WEATHER FORECASTING.

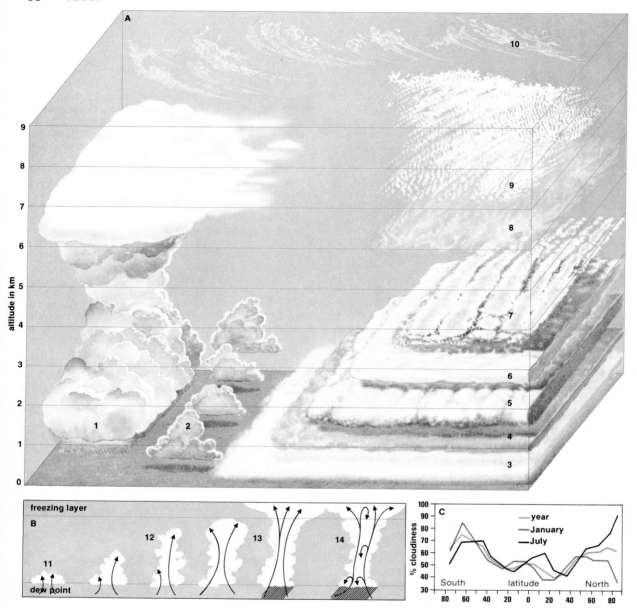

Clouds are formed as a result of the virtual suspension of large quantities of water droplets or ice crystals in the atmosphere. (A) Cloud forms vary from the towering cumulonimbus (1) to the smaller cumulus clouds (2). Other varieties found (in order of increasing altitude) are stratus (3); nimbostratus (4); stratocumulus (5); altostratus (6); altocumulus (7); cirrostratus (8); cirrocumulus (9); and cirrus (10). (B) Fair weather (11) is associated with clouds near the dew-point level (12). Clouds that form well above the dew point produce heavy rainfall. If moist air rises to the higher, freezing altitudes (13), cumulonimbus clouds may develop, resulting in thundershowers or hail (14). (C) The average annual and seasonal cloud-cover values for various latitudes indicate the presence of few clouds near the equator.

cloud chamber The cloud chamber is an instrument widely used in nuclear-physics research to observe the paths of fast-moving ionized, positively charged atomic and subatomic particles of matter that are charged in an ACCELERATOR. It is based on the principle that supersaturated vapor condenses readily on an electrically charged atom, molecule, or subatomic particle to produce droplets that can be photographed.

The cloud chamber was devised by the Scottish physicist C. T. R. WILSON in 1897, while he was conducting cosmic-ray research. It led in 1932 to the discovery of the positron, or positive electron, by Dr. Carl D. ANDERSON at California Institute of Technology. The Wilson chamber typically consists of a small cylinder with a glass window at the top and a retractable piston below. When the piston is suddenly withdrawn, the enclosed gas expands and cools, causing it to retain more vapor in a supersaturated state than it would normally hold at a lower temperature. If ionized particles are produced simultaneously, droplets will form on them and will persist long enough so that their paths can be recorded on a photographic plate.

Clouet (family) [kloo'-ay]   The Clouets were a family of portrait painters whose most distinguished members, Jean and his son François, were active at the court of Francis I of France.

Jean Clouet, c.1485–c.1540, is believed to have come from Brussels. He is recorded in the French royal accounts from 1516 to 1536 and by 1522 had been appointed chief court painter. He was apparently involved primarily in portrait commissions, and there survives a remarkable group of more than 500 red and black chalk portrait drawings, now housed in the Musée de Condé, Chantilly; at least 130 have been attributed directly to

The Portrait of Francis I (c.1525–30) is one of the few existing panel paintings that may be attributed to Jean Clouet. The painting reveals the dignity and sensitivity characteristic of Clouet's portraits of the Valois kings of France. (Louvre, Paris.)

Jean. His achievements in portrait drawing parallel those of his great German contemporary, Hans HOLBEIN the Younger. The portrait of *Guillaume Bude* (c.1536; Metropolitan Museum of Art, New York City) is Jean's only documented painting.

François Clouet, fl. 1536–72, served Francis I, Henry II, Francis II, and Charles IX. His paintings reflect a response to the Italianate MANNERISM of the school of Fontainebleau established by Francis I. Among François Clouet's best-known paintings are the signed portrait of the apothecary *Pierre Quthe* (1562; Louvre, Paris), the full-length portrait *Charles IX* (1570; Kunsthistorisches Museum, Vienna), and *Lady at Her Bath* (c.1570; National Gallery of Art, Washington, D.C.).

---

clove   Cloves are the dried buds of a tree, *Syzygium aromaticum*, of the myrtle family. Native to the Moluccas (the Spice Islands) in Indonesia, *S. aromaticum* is cultivated primarily in Zanzibar and Madagascar. The tree may reach a height of 12 m (39 ft). The clusters of small red flower buds are gathered before opening and dried to produce the dark brown, nail-shaped spice clove. Whole and ground cloves are used as food seasonings. Almost 20 percent of the clove's weight is ESSENTIAL OIL, used in perfumes, spice blends, medications, and candies and as a local anesthetic for toothache.

The clove tree, a small tropical evergreen, is the source of the spice clove. The flower buds (top right) are picked by hand and sun-dried into hard, dark-brown cloves (bottom right).

---

clover   Clover, genus *Trifolium*, belongs to the pea family, Leguminosae. (The term clover also is applied to other plants with three-lobed foliage.) There are approximately 300 species of *Trifolium*, which are widespread in temperate and subtropical regions. Some species are valuable forage and cover crops; others are grown in lawns as ornamentals. As a LEGUME, clover is useful for building up nitrogen in the soil.

White clover is a creeping perennial used in crop rotation to improve soil. Also used to feed livestock, white clover has a high protein content. During the great potato famine in Ireland, its seeds and white flowers were dried and made into bread.

Clovers are annual, biennial, or perennial herbs. Some are low growing and trailing; others may grow up to 1 m (3 ft) tall. Leaves normally have three parts. The small white, pink, red, or yellow flowers are borne in dense, soft, rounded, or elongated heads. The most important forage clovers are red clover (*T. pratense*), crimson clover (*T. incarnatum*), and alsike clover (*T. hybridum*). White clover (*T. repens*; the original Irish SHAMROCK) is included in some lawn-seed mixtures. Other plants called clover are the leguminous *Melilotus* (sweet clover) and *Lespedeae* (bush or Japanese clover) and the nonleguminous *Orthocarpus* (owls clover).

Alsike clover is an upright perennial that may grow to a height of 60 cm (2 ft). Also called Swedish clover, it thrives in cool climates and has pink globular flowers. Alsike clover is an important hay and forage crop and is also used for soil improvement.

Clovis [kloh'-vis]   Clovis, *c.*466-511, of the MEROVINGIAN dynasty, was the first generally recognized king of the FRANKS. He united most of present-day France under his rule. Clovis succeeded his father, Childeric (d. 481), a Salian Frankish chief, as ruler of Tournai. During the next three decades he destroyed (486) the Roman kingdom of Soissons and defeated the Alamanni at the Battle of Tolbiac (496?) and possibly again in 506. Soon after Tolbiac, Clovis converted to Christianity, having married Clotilda, a Christian Burgundian princess. He later turned against the Visigoths (see GOTHS) in southern France. After defeating (507) them at Vouillé, he controlled all of France except Burgundy, Provence, and Septimania. During the remainder of his reign, Clovis eliminated the Frankish chiefs who might contest his position. He regularized the relations of his kingdom with the episcopate in Gaul and had the Salian law (see GERMANIC LAW) written down. Upon his death, Clovis's kingdom was divided among his four surviving sons.

Clovis culture   Clovis culture—named for a site in Clovis, N.Mex., where Clovis artifacts were first uncovered—refers to a stone tool complex associated with Paleo-Indians who settled in North America about 11,500 years ago (see NORTH AMERICAN ARCHAEOLOGY). Big-game hunters, the Clovis people produced distinctive spear points—thin and tapered, flaked on both sides, and fluted at the base to facilitate attachment to a shaft—that typify Clovis sites and are often associated with the killing of mammoths. The Clovis people apparently came to North America over the BERING LAND BRIDGE. Within 1,000 years the Clovis people had spread as far south as central Mexico. Clovis artifacts have been unearthed in all 48 contiguous U.S. states.

clown   The clown, a CIRCUS entertainer whose function is to evoke laughter, is older than the circus itself, but the origins of this role are obscure. Attempts have been made to link the clown to the COMMEDIA DELL'ARTE, to the HARLEQUIN actor Joseph GRIMALDI, and even to the FOOLS and jesters of the Middle Ages and the Renaissance. The clown was an indispensable part of the burlesque equestrian interludes that entertained audiences in 18th-century London and Paris.

The many kinds of circus clowns are all descended from two basic types. The earlier, white-faced clown, in an elegant and bizarre costume, was the dominant type during the first half of the 19th century. Assisting in a comically perverse manner during the equestrian acts, this clown excelled at energetic displays of tumbling and leaping and was a foil to the more conservative ringmaster. About 1865 the second type of clown came into being as "Auguste," whose bulbous nose, oversized shoes,

Oleg Popov, one of the most popular clowns in the USSR, has relinquished the traditional slapstick and outlandish costume of the Auguste clown, relying on subtlety and sharp satire to evoke laughter.

ill-fitting clothes, and clumsy attempts to be of use in the ring are familiar to circus goers today. The sadfaced tramp portrayed by Emmett KELLY, sometimes called "the clown's clown," is a variation of this type.

The interplay between the white-faced clown and Auguste, the so-called straight man and his fool, has carried over into the music hall, drama, and film. In the modern circus of the USSR, a more natural clown has evolved; the grotesque costume and makeup have been discarded, and emphasis is more on satire and even lyricism than on slapstick and buffoonery.

club moss

Club mosses, genus *Lycopodium*, are evergreen, flowerless, seedless plants with simple scalelike leaves, belonging to the club moss family, Lycopodiaceae. Some species, particularly those resembling miniature trees, are also known as ground pines. Club mosses have a primitive, but definite, vessel system for the transport of water and nutrients. The plants are abundant on the coniferous forest floor of temperate regions. Some tropical species are epiphytic.

Club mosses are related to the ferns and propagate in a similar ALTERNATION OF GENERATIONS pattern, in which unlike generations follow each other repeatedly. Some common species of club moss are *L. clavatum*, which grows to 7.5 cm (3 in) tall but has a running ground stem nearly 3 m (9 ft) long; *L. complanatum*, with stalks divided into fanlike evergreen sprays; and *L. obscurum*, which forms underground creeping stems with some erect branches up to 25 cm (10 in) tall. Club mosses are often used in Christmas decorations.

The ground pine Lycopodium clavatum *is shown with roots, cones of sporophylls (spore-bearing leaves), and a leaf* (right, enlarged). *The stem of the fossil club moss* Lepidodendron (detail top left), *abundant during the Carboniferous Period, shows leaf scars.*

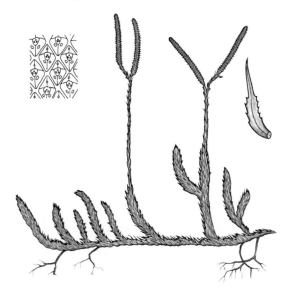

clubfoot

Clubfoot is a BIRTH DEFECT that occurs in approximately 1 in 1,500 children. It is more common in males. The term clubfoot, or *talipes*, includes several types of deformity of the foot and ankle (see FOOT DISORDERS).

In 95 percent of the cases, the defect is *talipes equinovarus*, in which the foot flexes inward and the toes turn down. Another is *talipes calcaneovalgus*, in which the foot is flexed outward and the toes turn up. There is a 2 to 8 percent chance of recurrence in a family with one affected child. Inherited factors and physical limitations during gestation play a role in development of clubfoot. Treatment ranges from casts to corrective surgery, depending on severity.

Cluj-Napoca

[kloozh]   Cluj-Napoca (1986 est. pop., 310,017) is a city in the Someşul Mic valley in the Transylvania region of northwestern Romania. Refrigeration equipment, leather goods, china, and cigarettes are produced. Cluj-Napoca is the site of numerous colleges and has many buildings of historic interest, such as the Gothic Church of St. Michael. The botanical gardens are Romania's most extensive.

Once the site of an ancient Dacian settlement, Cluj later came under Roman rule. German colonists settled on the site during the 12th century, and in 1405, Cluj became a free city. In the 16th century the autonomous principality of Transylvania was created, with Cluj as its capital. The city and region were unified with Austria-Hungary in 1867 and incorporated into Romania in 1920. Cluj was again held by Hungary from 1940 to 1945. The city of Cluj was combined with neighboring Napoca in the mid-1970s.

Clumber spaniel

The Clumber is one of the rarest and most massive spaniels, with males weighing up to 29.5 kg (65 lb). A long, low, heavy dog with a head not unlike a St. Bernard's in appearance, the Clumber is white with lemon or orange ticking. The coat is flat and silky, with feathering on the chest, legs, and tail.

The Clumber spaniel is a hunting breed developed during the 19th century and named for the Nottinghamshire estate—Clumber Park—of the dukes of Newcastle.

Slow in movement and dignified in action, the Clumber is a sedate breed. The massive Clumber may have been developed because a strong, solid worker was needed to hunt in dense undergrowth and bramble tangles.

Cluny   Cluny was an influential Christian monastery founded in 909 near Mâcon, France. The high standards of monastic observance adopted by its first abbot, Berno of Baume, became a model for a number of other monasteries throughout Europe and England. The monks and nuns under the jurisdiction of Cluny followed the BENEDICTINE rule and were known as the Order of Cluny. In the 11th and 12th centuries, they encouraged the reform of church abuses, especially simony and the lax observance of clerical celibacy. During the French Revolution the order was suppressed, and the abbey at Cluny, which had become known for the splendor and beauty of its liturgy, was destroyed. Parts of the abbey church (12th century), the largest church in Christendom until the 16th century, remain, as well as the abbey, which now houses a national trade school. The population of the present town of Cluny is 4,133 (1982).

Clurman, Harold   Harold Edgar Clurman, b. New York City, Sept. 18, 1901, d. Sept. 9, 1980, was one of the most prominent theater directors and critics in the United States. He joined with Lee Strasberg and Cheryl Crawford to found The GROUP THEATRE (1931–41). He made his directing debut (1935) with Clifford Odets's *Awake and Sing.* Thereafter he directed plays by Eugene O'Neill, Tennessee Williams, and Arthur Miller, among others. From 1953, Clurman was drama critic for *The Nation.*

cluster, star   Of the stars in the Milky Way GALAXY, about 1 in every 100,000 is in a dense grouping called a star cluster. For the most part, star clusters can be divided into two types, galactic and globular. The distinction is based primarily on the location of a cluster and its orbital motion in the Galaxy; galactic, or open, clusters are found in the relatively thin disk of the Milky Way orbiting about its center in nearly circular orbits, whereas globular clusters inhabit a spherical halo around the Galaxy and have highly elliptical orbits.

Globular Clusters. Globular clusters usually consist of several hundred thousand to more than a million stars and have a full, round appearance. The clusters are concentrated toward the center of the Galaxy but extend outward at least 50,000 light-years from the center. About 10 to 15 billion years old, they are among the oldest objects in the Galaxy. The brightest visible stars are the huge, evolving red giants, which have masses approximately 1.5 times that of the Sun. Globular clusters usually contain a few hundred red giants, but most of the stars are much fainter and of lower mass and are still in the long-lived state of equilibrium represented by the main sequence.

The M3 globular cluster in the constellation Canes Venatici, a dense group of approximately 100,000 stars, lies 35,000 light-years away from Earth and is faintly visible to the naked eye.

Galactic Clusters. Galactic clusters are younger (almost 10 billion years for the oldest, but most are much younger) than globular clusters. Thus, they are made up of stars built from material enriched in heavy elements by generations of stellar evolution; they contain up to 100 times the amount of heavy elements found in globular clusters. Galactic clusters are small, averaging only 15 light-years in radius, and most have between 100 and 1,000 stellar members.

Clwyd   [kloo'-id]   Clwyd is a county in northeastern Wales bounded by the Irish Sea on the north and England on the east. It covers 2,424 km^2 (936 mi^2), and the population is 407,000 (1988 est.). Mold is the county town. Drained by the River Clwyd, the county has a central plateau with fertile river valleys that gives way in the south to uplands that reach 827 m (2,713 ft) at Moel Sych. Coalfields are found in the eastern part of the county. Agriculture is carried on in the river valleys, where dairy cattle are raised and wheat and oats are grown. Sheep and beef cattle are raised in the uplands. Iron and steel are manufactured at Brymbo and Shotton, and Llangollen has a wool industry. Tourism is important because of resorts along Colwyn Bay and historic landmarks including OFFA'S DIKE, the remains of an Anglo-Saxon defense line.

The area was conquered by the English during the reign of King Edward I (1272–1307). The county of Clwyd was created in 1974 out of most of what was formerly FLINTSHIRE and Denbighshire.

Clyde, River   The 171-km-long (106-mi) River Clyde is Scotland's most important river. It rises in the moors of the southern uplands, flows generally northwestward, and in its middle course crosses the rich farming region of Clydesdale before reaching its estuary, the Firth of Clyde, an arm of the North Channel. The Falls of Clyde, which drop 76 m (250 ft) in 6 km (4 mi), supplied power for cotton mills in the 19th century; today the falls serve the same purpose for several hydroelectric plants. In the 18th century the river was dredged and made navigable for ocean vessels going to Glasgow. The river is still used to transport coal and other industrial goods.

Clydesdale   see HORSE

Clytemnestra [kly-tem-nes'-truh]   In Greek mythology, Clytemnestra, the sister of HELEN OF TROY and wife of AGAMEMNON, king of Mycenae, was one of the tragic women in the TROJAN WAR. While Agamemnon was away in the war, Clytemnestra took Aegisthus as her lover, and together they plotted to murder Agamemnon when he returned. Clytemnestra was motivated in part by the desire to avenge her husband's sacrifice of their daughter IPHIGENIA. When Agamemnon arrived with the captive Trojan princess CASSANDRA, Clytemnestra pretended to welcome them. Later, as Agamemnon bathed, Clytemnestra murdered him and then together with Aegisthus killed Cassandra. Clytemnestra's daughter ELECTRA persuaded her brother, ORESTES, to avenge their father's death by killing his mother and Aegisthus. The most famous depiction of Clytemnestra is in Aeschylus's ORESTEIA.

Cnidosporidi [ny-doh-spor-id'-ee-uh]   Cnidosporidians comprise about 1,100 known species of parasitic PROTOZOA in the subphylum Cnidospora and are divided into four subgroups: Heliocosporida, insect and mite parasites; Microsporida, arthropod and fish parasites; Myxosporida, mainly fish parasites; and Actinomyxida, worm parasites. They have walled spores, contain hollow filaments, and are believed to have arisen from somatic cells rather than germ cells. The filaments seem to serve as a passageway used by the sporoplasm (the infective stage) to travel from the cnidosporidian to the host's tissue cells. The sporoplasm develops into a plasmodium (a multinuclear cytoplasm). Cnidosporidian infections can occur in epidemic form among honeybees and commercial fish.

Cnidus [ny'-duhs]   Cnidus (Knidos) was an ancient Greek city located on the southern shore of the Gulf of Kos in the southwest corner of present-day Turkey. It was founded possibly as early as 900 BC and inhabited until the 7th century AD. A prosperous trading center, Cnidus was subject to Persia, then Athens, and later Rome. In 394 BC, Athens destroyed Sparta's sea power in a battle off Cnidus. Ruins at the site were first excavated by Charles T. Newton between AD 1857 and 1859. The layout of the city is easily visible, and many buildings are preserved. The famous statue of Aphrodite by PRAXITELES was discovered there.

Cnut   see CANUTE

coach and carriage   The term *carriage* generally refers to any wheeled vehicle, especially a horse-drawn one for transporting people. The term *coach* is slightly more specific: a coach is a large, usually closed, four-wheeled carriage having side doors, with the body suspended on springs for a smoother ride.

The carriage evolved from the early sledge, or SLED, as did the wagon, which is a similar, animal-drawn, wheeled vehicle. According to popular belief, coaches were first produced in the township of Kocs in Hungary in the 15th century. Developed from the chariot, the coach could carry up to eight persons. Regular stagecoach lines were gradually established to transport passengers and mail on a regular schedule.

Following is and alphabetical listing of some of the main types of coaches and carriages used during various periods, from ancient times to the present.

Berlin. Originating in Berlin in 1660, it was a light, fast, pair-horse, four-wheeled coach, with glass windows, that carried one or two people.

Brake. Commonly in use from about 1880 to the advent of the automobile, the brake was essentially a large version of the wagonette.

Britska. Introduced into Great Britain from Austria about 1818, the britska could carry four passengers.

Brougham (pronounced broo'-uhm). Named for Lord Brougham, one-time lord chancellor of England, the brougham was a closed, four-wheeled carriage light enough to be drawn by a single horse.

Buckboard. A light, four-wheeled carriage, the buckboard utilized a springy plank between two axles and had a single seat. It was used mainly in the United States between 1850 and 1900.

Cabriolet. A light, two-wheeled, pair-horse vehicle, the cabriolet had a shell-shaped body and could seat two people.

Cart. The general name for two-wheeled goods vehicles, the cart was used until the advent of the motorized tractor.

Chaise (full name *post chaise*). The chaise was a two-wheeled, two-horse, covered pleasure carriage for one or two people with the body slung on leather straps.

Dog cart. A high, one-horse, two-wheeled carriage having two seats, this cart had a space between the seats for carrying dogs.

Gig. This form of light, two-wheeled carriage was known in France as early as 1670. It became popular in England as a one-horse, open carriage. The buggy, shay, stanhope, tilbury, and trap were all slight variants of the basic gig.

Hackney carriage. This was a passenger vehicle for public hire. Coaches for hire first appeared in 1634 in London. Hackney carriages had a monopoly in London until 1823, when 12 cabriolets were licensed for hire. The carriages were eventually replaced by Hansom cabs.

Hansom cab. In 1834 an Englishman named Joseph Hansom designed a cab in which a covered body was slung between two large wheels, with the driver sitting on top. A modified version with smaller wheels and the driver placed behind the cab's body was the standard London cab for many years.

Landau. An elegant, pair-horse, four-wheeled carriage usually driven by a coachman in livery, the Landau seated four passengers, two facing forward and two backward. It takes its name from the Bavarian town where it originated

The English stagecoach (1), a variation on the heavier mail coach, was modified to accommodate passengers on top of the vehicle as well as within it. These coaches were brightly colored, and the names of the way stations were emblazoned on the sides. They became known as "stage" coaches because the long-distance journeys were divided into stages; at each stage the horses and drivers were changed.

The introduction of elliptical, or under, springs in 1804 enabled coaches and carriages to be lighter and more comfortable to their passengers. The surrey (2) and the buggy (3), both of light construction, were American adaptations of, respectively, the English phaeton and gig. The surrey was designed for family use and was often topped with a fringed roof; the buggy sometimes featured a folding hood and a rear seat for a groom. Each vehicle was drawn by a single horse, although the surrey could be modified to accommodate two horses.

The English phaeton, a light, four-wheeled carriage driven by the owner, became popular during the 19th century. Both the lady's, or park, phaeton (4) and the Stanhope phaeton (5) were elegant town carriages. The mail phaeton (6), the heaviest of the type, was drawn by two horses and more closely resembled a coach. A governess, or tub, cart (7) was designed for children; it was entered through a back door and lacked a front-facing driver's seat.

in 1757. Today the term indicates a similar type of automobile body.

Omnibus. See separate article BUS.

Phaeton. Introduced c.1757, the phaeton was an elegant, open, horse-drawn carriage with an extremely high seat.

Wagonette. The wagonette was a lighter version of the wagon.

In modern times, animal-drawn vehicles, such as carriages, coaches, and wagons, have largely been replaced by automobiles, trucks, buses, and tractors. See separate articles for these and other motorized vehicles.

See also: CHARIOT; STAGECOACH; WAGON.

Coahuila [koh-ah-wee'-lah]   Coahuila is a state in northern Mexico south of the U.S. border. It covers 149,982 km^2 (57,908 mi^2), and the population is 1,937,209 (1989 est.). SALTILLO is the capital city. Most of Coahuila is an arid plateau except in the east, where the Sierra Madre Oriental reaches 3,050 m (10,000 ft). Coahuila is traditionally a stock-raising area, but irrigation has now made agriculture possible, and beans, cotton, grains, grapes, and sugarcane are grown. Coahuila is Mexico's leading coal producer, and copper, iron, lead, and silver are also mined.

In 1575 the Spanish settled Saltillo, and from 1824 to 1836, Coahuila and Texas were united. Coahuila became a Mexican state in 1868.

coal and coal mining   Coal, one of humankind's primary ENERGY SOURCES, is a rock derived from vegetable matter through the process of metamorphism, which requires that heat and pressure act over long periods on this matter, altering both its chemical and physical characteristics. Because the final product may have a variety of chemical compositions and is not crystalline, coal is classified as a rock rather than as a mineral. Coal is further classified according to grade, or purity, defined as the percentage of carbon content; according to type, depending on variations in the original plant composition; and according to rank, depending on the degree of metamorphism. Of these three criteria, purity (grade) and degree of metamorphism (rank) are most important in practice.

Formation and Distribution

The initial stage of coal formation is PEAT, decomposed organic matter, itself not regarded as a variety of coal. All types of peat easily retain water, and in saturated natural deposits include more than 75 percent moisture. Coal forms by the dehydration and alteration of the plant parts that are initially conserved in peat deposits. These processes begin operating when a peat deposit has become buried beneath a thick, heavy cover of sedimentary materials.

Conditions that led to coal formation have existed from Devonian times, 390 million years ago, when the first peat deposits were formed from terrestrial vegetation (see GEOLOGIC TIME). Coal of Permian age (280 to 230 million

years ago) is found in Antarctica, Siberia, China, Australia, India, and South Africa. Tertiary-age coal (65 million to 2 million years old) is mined in Spitzbergen, and much of the low-sulfur coal now being exploited in the western United States is also from the older Tertiary Period. Much of the higher-rank coal of the western United States occurs in Cretaceous deposits, 140 million to 65 million years old.

The most extensive and most important deposits of coal, however, are in the Appalachian Trough and the interior basins of North America; in Nova Scotia; in Great Britain; in the Belgian, Dutch, and Ruhr deposits in Germany; in Silesia; and in the great Donetz field of southern Russia. All of these deposits were formed in the Carboniferous Period, 340 to 280 million years ago.

Coal is thus widely distributed and generally available in ample supply. The United States has approximately 31 percent of the known recoverable coal reserves of the world. The USSR produces more coal than the United States, however; it has 23 percent of the known recoverable coal reserves. Europe has 13 percent and China 22 percent. At an annual production rate of about 3.5 billion metric tons (3.8 billion U.S. tons) worldwide, serious depletion of resources will take several hundred years. However, coal resources are not inexhaustible; in many areas the best and most accessible coal has already been depleted.

Ranks and Characteristics

In order of increasing coalification—that is, of increasing geological compression and loss of volatile constituents—the three main ranks of coal are lignite, bituminous coal, and anthracite.

Lignite is closely related to peat but has a lower moisture content. Also called brown coal because of its dark-brownish color, it has a layered appearance in which fragments of the original plant remains may be observed. Lignite burns with a smoky flame and tends to crumble after long exposure to air. It has the lowest heating value of any of the ranks of coal, not exceeding about 4,600 calories per gram (cal/g), or about 8,300 British thermal units per pound (Btu/lb). In the United States, the largest deposits of lignite occur in Montana and the Dakotas, Arkansas, and Texas.

Bituminous coal is more dense than lignite and is black in color; in deposits it has a banded appearance. Many grades of bituminous coal are defined in various classification systems. The heating values of these different grades range from about 5,600 cal/g (about 10,000 Btu/lb) to more than 8,000 cal/g (about 15,000 Btu/lb). Bituminous coal is the most commonly used of the ranks of coal for industrial purposes, both for the generation of electrical power (unless prohibited because of sulfur or other impurities) and for the production of COAL TAR and COKE through destructive distillation. In the United States, bituminous coal is mined in the Appalachian region and in the basins of the continental interior.

Anthracite is the hardest of all the ranks of coal and typically has a lustrous-black appearance. Although the heating values of the highest grades of bituminous coal may exceed the heating value of anthracite, the latter has

The formation of coal begins as thick deposits of partly decomposed plant material, or peat (1), accumulate on swamp bottoms. Compression increases with depth, and the peat successively becomes lignite (2) at about 1,000 m (3,280 ft), bituminous coal (3) at about 3,000 m (10,000 ft), and anthracite (4) at about 6,000 m (20,000 ft).

the highest carbon content of any of the coals and burns with the cleanest flame. For this reason, anthracite has been the preferred coal for use as a domestic fuel, although the main reserves in the United States, which are in eastern Pennsylvania, have largely been depleted, limiting both the domestic and industrial use of anthracite.

Underground Mining

In modern mining, access to underground mines is gained by three primary methods. In the drift-mine method, the seam of coal is exposed to the surface on the side of a hill or mountain, and the mine opening is made directly into the coal seam. This is generally the easiest and least expensive way to open an underground coal mine. In the slope-mine method, an inclined opening through rock strata is used to gain access to the coal seam. If the coal seam itself is inclined, the slope may follow the seam. Slope-mine access is usually used where less overburden is present. In the mine-shaft method, the coal seam is reached by a vertical opening from the surface. Combinations of access methods may be used, depending on conditions of the coal seams.

Once access is gained to the coal bed, three primary mining systems are used in the United States. Classified according to the equipment used, they are the conventional, continuous, and longwall methods.

Conventional Mining. In conventional mining the coal is first cut with an undercutter, a large chain saw on wheels.

Holes are then drilled in the coal, using mobile or hand-held electric or hydraulic drills. The holes are loaded with explosives, and blasting or other breaking methods are used to dislodge the coal from the seam. A loading machine places the coal into a specially designed shuttle car, which transports it either to a conveyor belt or to mine cars for transportation to the surface.

Continuous Mining. The continuous-mining system uses a single machine, called a continuous miner, that replaces the undercutter, drill, explosives, and loading machine used in the conventional mining system. This machine breaks the coal and loads it into shuttle cars for transportation to either conveyor belts or mine cars.

The three types of continuous miners are the boring, ripper, and milling machines. The boring machine cuts or breaks the coal with arms that rotate flat against the coal face. This machine produces an arched opening in the working place and provides advantages in roof support, but the height and width of the opening created is restricted. The ripper miner cuts the coal with a series of chains operating vertically on the coal face. This machine, similar to an undercutter, can load the coal that it cuts or breaks. The ripper miner is more flexible in the height and width of the mine opening it can create. The milling or drum miner cuts the coal with tool bits mounted on heads or drums rotating vertically parallel to the coal face. It is widely used in the industry today.

Longwall Mining. In the longwall-mining system, large blocks of coal, 100 to 200 m (300 to 600 ft) in width, are extracted that had been exposed previously by other mining systems. These blocks are completely extracted by continuous operations, using self-advancing hydraulic jacks to provide roof support during the mining operations. These jacks (chocks) advance as the coal is mined, thus allowing the roof behind the jacks to collapse. Longwall-mining machines cut the coal parallel to the coal face. The broken coal falls into a chain conveyor that removes it to a conveyor belt.

The two general types of longwall-mining machines are plows (planers) and shearers. The plow is a blade arrangement pulled across the face by a heavy chain; it is similar to the plow used by farmers. This machine, which cuts to a depth of about 8 to 15 cm (3 to 6 in), also forces the broken coal into the chain conveyor. The shearer is a rotating drum with either a single or a double drum; it is similar to a drum miner. The shearer can cut to a depth of 69 cm (27 in).

Developing the Mine. Using the abovementioned techniques, mine development follows a "room and pillar" plan. Rooms are the openings from which coal is extracted, and pillars are the blocks of coal that are left for roof support. Sets of rooms are connected with cross cuts (openings driven at an angle to rooms); pillars are left between rooms and cross cuts.

To open a coal mine, development mining is done. When the mine has been developed, pillars that were left during the development may be mined. This is known as retreat (second) mining. Often two or more seams must be mined; if the upper seam is mined first, the lower seams will not be affected.

Surface Mining

Surface mining, commonly known as strip mining, is divided into three general classifications: area, contour, and open-pit mining. Area mining prevails in the West and Midwest, where the minable coal seams are relatively flat under either a level or gently rolling surface. The depth from the surface to the coal remains relatively constant. With these conditions, the property can be mined using either a dragline or a shovel to excavate the overburden in a series of parallel openings. The topsoil is removed first and stockpiled for later reclamation. The overburden from each opening is deposited into the previous opening after the coal has been extracted. Peaks created by this deposition must be leveled and covered with topsoil for reclamation.

Contour mining is used in hilly and mountainous terrain, as in the eastern United States, where coal outcrops on the side of a hill. The mining begins on the outcrop and follows it along its contour. The topsoil is first re-

moved and stockpiled for later reclamation; the overburden is then removed by shovel, dragline, scraper, trucks, front-end loaders, or bulldozers. This material is saved and eventually placed into another excavation. Succeeding excavation material is placed into the preceding excavation and leveled; topsoil is then distributed over the area.

Open-pit mining is similar to quarrying. In the western states, coal seams vary from 12 to 30 m (40 to 100 ft) in thickness, with thin overburden. Because the coal seam is so thick, it is impossible to completely backfill the mined-out area with overburden. The overburden may be transported directly to mined-out areas by scrapers or trucks.

Coal-Mining Safety

Underground coal mining is the most hazardous industrial occupation in the United States. The principal hazard is explosion, caused by the presence of coal dust and methane gas. The technology exists to prevent dangerous concentrations of both substances, but it is not always

Although coal is widely distributed throughout the world, 76 percent of the known, recoverable coal deposits are found in the United States, the USSR, and China, three nations that are not only the largest producers of coal but also the largest consumers.

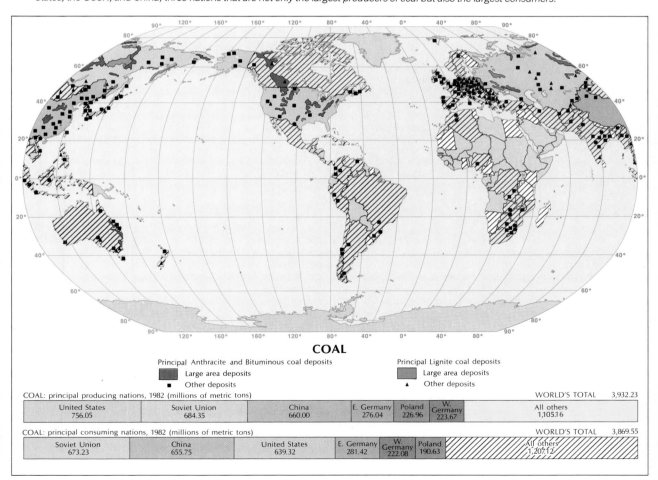

COAL

Principal Anthracite and Bituminous coal deposits
- ▨ Large area deposits
- ■ Other deposits

Principal Lignite coal deposits
- ▨ Large area deposits
- ▲ Other deposits

COAL: principal producing nations, 1982 (millions of metric tons)   WORLD'S TOTAL   3,932.23

United States 756.05	Soviet Union 684.35	China 660.00	E. Germany 276.04	Poland 226.96	W. Germany 223.67	All others 1,105.16

COAL: principal consuming nations, 1982 (millions of metric tons)   WORLD'S TOTAL   3,869.55

Soviet Union 673.23	China 655.75	United States 639.32	E. Germany 281.42	W. Germany 222.08	Poland 190.63	All others 1,207.12

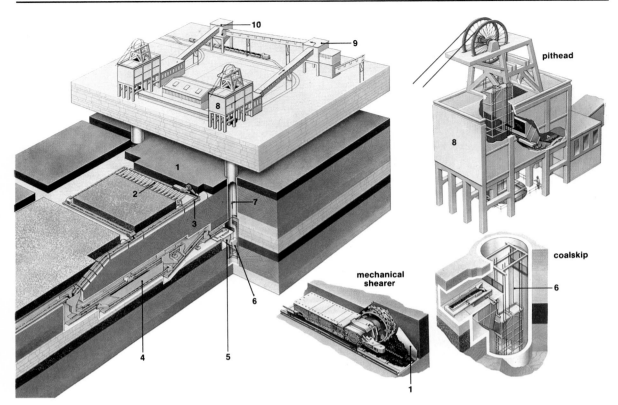

In longwall mining, where a large rock face has already been exposed, a mechanical shearer (1) is pulled along a guide chain as it strips off a layer of coal parallel to the coal face. As the shearer moves along the face, a line of hydraulic jacks supporting the roof (2) automatically keeps pace with it. The broken coal is guided by a scoop onto a conveyor belt (3), which moves it into a storage bunker (4). The bunker delivers a constant stream of coal to a measuring hopper (5), which feeds it into a coal skip (6). The skip is then lifted up a concrete shaft (7) to a pithead (8) on the surface. Here, the coal is dropped from the skip onto a conveyor and moved first to a washing and grading plant (9) and finally to the train-loading tower (10), a giant hopper that feeds coal into the gondolas of a waiting freight train.

used effectively. Coal dust is also the cause of the disease BLACK LUNG.

The passage of the Federal Mine Health and Safety Act (1969) established the Mine Safety and Health Administration (MSHA), which laid down minimum mine safety and health standards, mandated a schedule of frequent mine inspections, and set rigorous civil and criminal penalties for mine operators and miners who violated the standards. The act also provided compensation for miners suffering from black lung.

Environmental Considerations

Both the mining of coal and the use of coal for fuel are processes that have the potential for causing environmental damage. The problems associated with coal mining include the destruction of land when it is strip-mined and the various surface effects of underground mining: slag heaps, long-burning mine fires, and the occasional undermining and collapse of the surface into abandoned mines. The environmental effects of coal burning are less visible but perhaps more serious. They include the dis-

persal in the air of particulate matter from coal smoke, the venting of sulfur compounds into the atmosphere with the subsequent acidification of atmospheric moisture (see ACID RAIN), the pollution of water used in coal-fueling operations, and the pollution of land used to store coal residues, such as ash and the sludge from smokestacks. Smokestack scrubbers can remove particulates and sulfur and nitrogen compounds from flue gases (see SMOKE), but few coal-burning plants have installed them because of their high cost. New technologies are being developed, however, for burning coal without producing airborne pollution. Among the most promising is FLUIDIZED BED COMBUSTION, which burns coal and limestone on an incandescent bed of sand and air.

Coal Gasification

Coal gasification is a process for converting coal to combustible gases that can be used as SYNTHETIC FUELS or as raw materials for the manufacture of chemicals and fertilizers. (Coal liquefaction uses similar processes to produce liquid oil products as well as fuel gases.) Simple gasification processes have been in use since the early 19th century, and until the 1940s—when natural gas first became widely available—almost all European and U.S. fuel gas was produced from coal.

In order to convert coal into gas, the heavy coal hydrocarbon molecules must be "cracked," or converted into lighter molecules in high-temperature, high-pressure processes involving the reaction of coal with water and oxygen. Advanced gasification techniques for the large-scale production of fuel are still in the experimental stage, but they offer the potential for the pollution-free use of all grades of coal, including the high-sulfur grades that are now unsuitable for use because of the pollution they produce.

Coal Production

In the decade 1950–60 the use of oil for energy began to soar in the United States, and U.S. coal production fell from 508 to 394 million metric tons (560 to 434 million U.S. tons). Production crept up in the 1960s, with most of the additional coal being used to fuel steam-powered electric generating plants (see POWER, GENERATION AND TRANSMISSION OF). The 1973 Arab oil embargo and the subsequent steep increases in oil prices, however, made the cost of coal competitive with that of oil for the first time since World War II. The United States produced about 925 million metric tons (over 1 billion U.S. tons) of coal annually in the early 1990s. Eighty-five percent of this total production was used for electricity generation, and about 9 percent was exported.

———

coal tar   Coal tar is a viscous liquid mixture of hydrocarbon compounds, derived, along with COKE, from the destructive distillation of coal (see COAL AND COAL MINING). The distillation process, also known as carbonization, consists of heating coal in the absence of air to temperatures ranging from 900° to 1,200° C (1,650° to 2,200° F) and is carried out in coking ovens. The coal tar is cooled, collected, and then distilled to yield four fractions and a residue. The first fraction, containing benzene, toluene, xylene, and other substances, distills off at temperatures up to 200° C (390° F). The second fraction, obtained at 200° to 250° C (390° to 480° F), contains naphthalene and tar acids and bases. Temperatures from 250° to 300° C (480° to 570° F) yield the CREOSOTES and the methylnaphthalenes; in the 300° to 350° C (570° to 660° F) range, quinoline, anthracene, phenanthrene, and carbazole distill off. The residue after distillation is called coal-tar pitch, which becomes less viscous when heated. It does not absorb water or steam but can be modified by the addition of oils or solvents. Coal-tar pitch is used in the production of steel, coal, coke, carbon electrodes for batteries, roofing, and protective coatings.

———

coast   see BEACH AND COAST

———

Coast Guard, U.S.   The United States Coast Guard is the principal federal agency for national maritime transportation policy and for marine safety and maritime

The U.S. Coast Guard dispatched fire-fighting vessels and a rescue helicopter to assist the Fernview, a Norwegian freighter, after it collided with the American tanker Dynafuel in 1963 at the entrance to Buzzards Bay in Massachusetts.

law enforcement on the high seas and in all waters under the jurisdiction of the United States. In peacetime the Coast Guard is part of the Department of Transportation, but in time of war, or when the president so directs, it operates under the Department of the Navy. Founded on Aug. 4, 1790, by Alexander Hamilton as a fleet of cutters to prevent smuggling, it is the oldest continuous seagoing federal armed force.

The operations of today's Coast Guard include the following tasks: developing construction standards and operational rules for American deepwater ports; conducting the International Ice Patrol in the North Atlantic; cooperating with the Drug Enforcement Administration and the Customs Service to detect and intercept drug smugglers; providing patrol and law enforcement in the 200-mi Fishery Conservation Zone off the coasts of the United States; and performing icebreaking services for commercial and scientific ships in the Great Lakes, in the Gulf of Alaska, and in the Arctic and the Antarctic.

Preventing and controlling pollution of U.S. waters is a Coast Guard responsibility, as is installing and maintaining more than 46,000 aids to navigation—from LORAN stations to river channel markers. Merchant vessels built in the United States must obtain Coast Guard approval at various phases of construction. U.S. merchant ships are also periodically inspected for safety by the Coast Guard, and all U.S. licensed merchant marine personnel obtain their licenses by passing examinations conducted by the Coast Guard. Recreational boats are also subject to Coast Guard safety regulations.

The peacetime strength of the Coast Guard is about 38,000 military members and 6,000 civilians. The service operates ships, specialized vessels, rotary and fixed-wing aircraft, research and development facilities, and shore installations throughout the Atlantic and Pacific. The UNITED STATES COAST GUARD ACADEMY is located in New London, Conn.

Coast Ranges   The Coast Ranges are a belt of long, narrow mountain ranges that parallel the Pacific coast of North America from Alaska to Baja (Lower) California in Mexico, a distance of about 7,200 km (4,500 mi). The mountains are generally rounded in form and varied in height, and the average elevation is about 1,000 m (3,300 ft). In Canada some peaks rise much higher. Mount LOGAN in Yukon Territory is the second highest peak in North America (6,050 m/19,850 ft). On the coasts of southern Alaska and British Columbia the ranges consist of peaks of offshore islands. Throughout their length the ranges are subject to earthquakes. The CASCADE RANGE in the U.S. Northwest contains several active volcanoes.

coastal plain   Coastal plains are areas of low relief, bounded on one side by the sea and on the other by highlands. They are underlain by marine SEDIMENTS that dip gently seaward. Structurally, coastal plains are the dry-land extensions of the submerged CONTINENTAL SHELF.

coastal protection   Coastal erosion from natural causes, especially wave action, modifies the features and outlines of coasts, as do such human activities as offshore dredging, exploiting sand, gravel, or shingle from beaches, and constructing harbor works and housing. Furthermore, the spoliation of beaches and shores through OIL SPILLS has brought a new dimension to coastal protection.

The primary problems of beach and shore erosion are longshore drift and wave damage caused by storms. Longshore drift transports sand along the shore, denuding beaches in some areas and building them up in others. It can be combatted by replenishing the sand or building jetties, or groins. Such structures, although useful locally, tend to increase the erosion rate of beaches farther down the shore by cutting off their supply of sand. Wave damage is controlled by building breakwaters or seawalls. Breakwaters may be huge, elongated dikes built of rock rubble and soil. Seawalls are masonry structures that de-

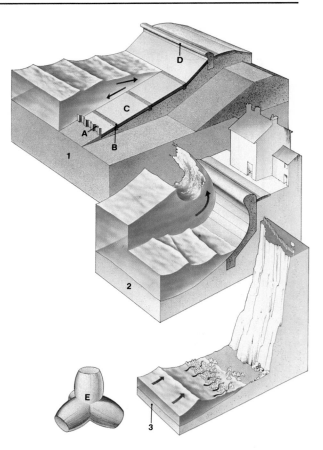

Three major techniques used in retarding coastal erosion are illustrated. The energy-absorbing wall (1) protects against wave damage by means of a series of defenses. As waves roll shoreward, a steel-sheet piling (A) absorbs and deflects some of the initial energy. A series of reinforced concrete strips (B) and concrete blocks set in asphalt (C) absorb additional wave energy while holding the coastline intact. As waves finally break, they are contained by a reinforced, concrete retaining wall (D). The reflector wall (2), designed for waves at high tide, deflects the energy of waves outward by means of its curved construction. A heavy, permeable apron (3) is used in areas where heavy construction is too expensive. Rows of massive, concrete tetrapods (E) are positioned along the shoreline so that they, rather than the beach, bear the brunt of the waves' destructive force.

Groins, such as the zig-zag groin (1) and the straight groin (2), are placed perpendicular to the shoreline to reduce erosion from waves or to trap sand and sediment in order to improve a beach.

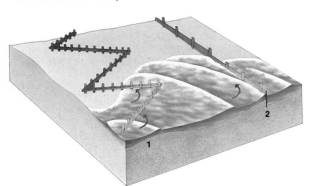

flect wave energy.

See also: BEACH AND COAST; EROSION AND SEDIMENTATION; POLLUTION, ENVIRONMENTAL; WATER WAVE.

coat of arms   see HERALDRY

coatimundi   [koh-ah'-tuh-mun'-dee]   The coatimundis, relatives of the raccoon, include three species in the genus *Nasua* of the family Procyonidae, order Carnivora. *N. nasua* inhabits most of South America, *N. narica* ranges from the southwestern United States to South

The white-nosed coatimundi is a raccoonlike mammal that ranges from the southwestern United States to Panama. The coatimundi has a flexible snout and walks with its tail held vertically.

America, and *N. nelsoni* lives on Cozumel Island off Yucatán. Coatimundis are 41 to 66 cm (16 to 26 in) long, with a tail 31 to 69 cm (12 to 27 in) long. They weigh about 11 kg (25 lb).

All species have reddish brown coats with white marks on the muzzle and chest and whitish rings on the tail. The snout is mobile, and the omnivorous coatimundi pokes it into crevices and tree hollows in search of food. The rare mountain coatimundi, *Nasuella olivacea*, of the Andes is closely related.

---

cobalt   The chemical element cobalt is a hard silver metal with a bluish sheen. Its chemical symbol is Co, its atomic number is 27, and its atomic weight is 58.9332. Cobalt is a TRANSITION ELEMENT, in Group VIII of the periodic table.

Occurrence. Cobalt is 0.001% to 0.002% of the Earth's crust. Never found in pure form, cobalt is usually bonded to arsenic and sulfur. Cobalt minerals include cobaltite (cobalt glance), $CoS_2 \cdot CoAs_2$; linnaeite (cobalt pyrite), Co_3S_4; smaltite, $CoAs_2$; and erythrite, $Co_3(AsO_4)_2 \cdot 8H_2O$ (see ORE DEPOSITS). Cobalt is also a constituent of many meteorites and is found in the Sun and the atmospheres of stars.

The name cobalt, derived from the German *kobold* (a malicious underground goblin or demon), originated in the 16th century, when arsenic-containing cobalt ores were dug up in silver mines of the Harz Mountains. Believing that the ores contained copper, miners heated them and were injured by the toxic arsenic trioxide vapors that were released.

Uses. Cobalt is a relatively expensive metal used in the manufacture of valuable alloys. Cobalt-iron alloys have special magnetic properties. Alloys of titanium, aluminum, cobalt, and nickel, such as alnico and ticonal, can be made permanently magnetic. Stellite, an alloy of cobalt, chromium, tungsten, and molybdenum, is very hard and retains its hardness even at high temperatures. It is used in cutting tools, combustion-engine valves, and parts for gas turbines.

Cobalt Isotopes. ^{59}Co is the only naturally occurring cobalt isotope. Other isotopes, all of them radioactive, have been artificially produced. Among these, ^{60}Co is especially important for its use in cancer research and as a source of X rays for RADIATION THERAPY.

Chemical Properties. Chemically, cobalt resembles iron and nickel. The most common valence of cobalt is +2; trivalent cobalt salts are usually strong oxidizing agents, and a valence of +4 occurs in rare instances.

Cobalt salts have a strong tendency to form COORDINATION COMPOUNDS. Many coordination compounds of cobalt are intensely colored; several of them are used as dyes, such as Thenard's blue, $CoO \cdot Al_2O_3$; Fischer's salt, or cobalt yellow, $K_3Co(NO_2)_6$; cobalt blue, $CoSnO_3$; and cobalt red, $Co_3(PO_4)_2$. The color of some cobalt salts depends on the number of molecules of water or crystallization present. Thus, cobalt(II) chloride varies from dark violet ($CoCl_2 \cdot H_2O$) to light red ($CoCl_2 \cdot 6H_2O$).

Cobalt is a common trace element in food and, as a component of vitamin B_{12}, or cyanocobalamin, is important to health, since lack of this vitamin can cause pernicious anemia. On the other hand, excessive amounts of cobalt or its compounds can cause nausea; damage to the heart, kidneys, and nerves; and even death.

Pure cobalt, a blue-tinged silvery metal, is normally found combined with other elements and must be extracted by a chemical process.

Cobb, Lee J.   Lee J. Cobb, b. Leo Jacoby in New York City, Dec. 9, 1911, d. Feb. 11, 1976, was an American actor who began his career on the stage but later moved to films. He became a familiar Hollywood character actor noted for his gruff characterizations. Cobb's most famous stage appearance was as Willy Loman in Arthur Miller's *Death of a Salesman* (1949). His noteworthy film roles were in *Golden Boy* (1939), *The Moon Is Down* (1943), *The Dark Past* (1948), *On the Waterfront* (1954), and *Twelve Angry Men* (1957).

Cobb, Ty   Tyrus Raymond Cobb, b. Narrows, Ga., Dec. 18, 1886, d. July 17, 1961, nicknamed the "Georgia Peach," is considered by many experts the greatest baseball player of all time. He was an outfielder for the Detroit

Ty Cobb, who played the outfield for the Detroit Tigers and the Philadelphia Athletics, excelled in almost every area of baseball. During his 24-year career in the major leagues, Cobb established records that still stand for lifetime batting average (.367), runs scored (2,245), and number of batting titles won (12).

Tigers from 1905 through 1926, then played with the Philadelphia Athletics until 1928. Cobb held numerous baseball records. Three times he batted over .400 and 23 times he hit over .300—feats no other player has accomplished. Cobb was an outstanding base stealer; his total of 892 was a major league record until it was broken by Lou Brock of St. Louis in 1977. In 1936, Cobb was chosen to be the first member of the Baseball Hall of Fame.

Cobbett, William   William Cobbett, b. Mar.9, 1763, d. June 18, 1835, was an English reformer and journalist noted for his evocative essays *Rural Rides* (1830), in which he mourned the changes in rural life that resulted from the INDUSTRIAL REVOLUTION.

The son of a farm laborer, he served (1784–91) in the army but resigned in order to expose corruption among the officers. He was forced to flee abroad, ultimately to the United States, where he defended the British monarchy in publications such as *Observations on Priestly's Emigration* (1794) and *Porcupine's Gazette* (1797–99). He returned (1800) to England after losing a libel suit to Dr. Benjamin RUSH.

In England the TORY patriot reverted to radicalism and became an embarrassment to the Tory governments. He spent the years 1810–12 in prison and 1817–19 in the United States because of his writings, especially the influential reform journal *Political Register*, which he published from 1802 until his death. He also began (1804) an unofficial record of the parliamentary debates, which later became the official record of Parliament.

Cobbett led the agitation for parliamentary reform and, after passage of the REFORM ACT of 1832, was elected to Parliament as a Radical. To the end, however, he regretted the passing of the beneficent elements in early 18th-century Toryism and detested the rising bourgeoisie.

cobble   In a general sense, cobbles are somewhat rounded rocks suitable for use as paving stones. The size of such rocks is not precisely defined. Geologists, however, grade SEDIMENTARY ROCKS according to the size of their constituent particles. They define cobbles as rock fragments from 64 to 265 mm (2.5 to 10 in) wide, smaller than boulders but larger than pebbles.

Cobden, Richard   [kahb'-den]   Richard Cobden, b. June 3, 1804, d. Apr. 2, 1865, was a British reformer who, as a leader of the so-called Manchester school of FREE TRADE and in association with John BRIGHT, secured the repeal (1846) of the protectionist CORN LAWS. Active in the Anti–Corn Law League from its foundation (1838), he entered Parliament in 1841. Cobden opposed the Crimean War, supported the North in the U.S. Civil War, and argued that Parliament should be radically reformed. Believing that free trade would promote international peace, he negotiated an important treaty (1860) with France that reduced tariffs.

Coblenz   see KOBLENZ

COBOL   see COMPUTER LANGUAGES

CoBrA   CoBrA was an international movement in the arts (1948–51), begun by a group of northern Europeans as a protest against the formalism and aesthetics of the Parisian painters who had dominated modern art since the early years of the 20th century. The movement also rejected the theories of the DE STIJL artists. CoBrA's members included the Danish painter Asger Jorn; the Dutch artists Karel APPEL, Constant (C. A. Nieuwenhus), and Corneille (C. Guillaume van Beverloo); the Belgian painter Pierre ALECHINSKY; and the Dutch poet-painter Lu-

William Cobbett, a British pamphleteer and journalist, founded (1802) Cobbett's Weekly Political Register, *in which he excoriated Britain's government for its disregard of the working classes and advocated parliamentary reform.*

cebert (L. J. Swaanswijk). The group derived its name from the first letters of members' native cities; *C*open-hagen, *B*russels, and *A*msterdam.

cobra Cobra is the name popularly applied to African and Asian snakes of the family Elapidae that are capable of spreading long ribs to flatten their necks into a hood when threatened. Included are six species of the genus *Naja*, as well as the South African ringhal (*Hemachatus*), king cobra (*Ophiophagus*), water cobra (*Boulengerina*), tree cobra (*Pseudohaje*), and shield-nose cobra (*Aspidelaps*).

Cobra bites are potentially dangerous to humans. A few species—the ringhal, black-necked cobra, and some species of Asian cobra—can spray venom from their fangs accurately to a distance of 2 m (6.6 ft). Venom coming in contact with human eyes causes immediate, severe irritation of the conjunctiva and cornea. If untreated, permanent blindness may result.

Cobras are large snakes, usually 1 m (3.3 ft) in length or longer. The king cobra, or hamadryad, holds the record length of 5.58 m (18.3 ft) for a venomous snake. Cobras are famous for their use by Oriental snake charmers. Like all snakes, they are deaf, but they respond to visual cues, have a rather slow strike, and are of spectacular appearance.

The Indian cobra is a favorite of snake charmers because daylight hampers its ability to make an accurate strike. At night, however, the venomous snake is extremely dangerous. Only 10% of cobra bites are fatal. Yet it is estimated that cobras kill 10,000 Indians each year.

coca Coca is the common name of a shrub, *Erythroxylon coca*, of the coca family, Erythroxylaceae. Coca is densely leaved and grows to heights of 2.5 m (8 ft). It is cultivated in its native South America and in Africa, Southeast Asia, and Australia for the narcotic alkaloids of its leaves, particularly cocaine. Whole or powdered dried leaves, usually mixed with lime, are chewed to dull the sense of hunger and to lessen fatigue. The coca shrub should not be confused with the cacao tree, the source of cocoa and chocolate.

cocaine Cocaine, an alkaloid drug found in the leaves of the coca plant, was first used medically in 1884 by

Carl Koller, an Austrian ophthalmologic surgeon. Historically, its chief medical use has been as a local anesthetic, especially for the nose, throat, and cornea, because it blocks nerve conduction. It has been largely replaced by less toxic, synthetic local anesthetics. Used systemically, cocaine stimulates the central nervous system, producing feelings of excitation, well-being, and enhanced physical strength and mental capacity and a lessened sense of fatigue. It also causes increased heart rate, blood pressure, and temperature; in large doses, it can cause death.

Those who abuse cocaine because of its stimulating effects frequently do so by sniffing its fine white powder, often called "snow." In the mid-1980s, however, the use of "crack," a new, relatively inexpensive form of cocaine, surged. Crack is highly concentrated, chemically reconstituted cocaine, in pebblelike shape, that users smoke. By 1990 the use of the highly addictive crack was widespread in the United States and had become a national issue. A principal cause of concern was the increase in the rates of violent crime in the deteriorated urban areas in which crack dealers were active. Crack also bore much responsibility for such social ills as addicted newborns and child abuse.

The chronic user of cocaine can develop a full toxic paranoid psychosis. Long-term use can also result in weight loss and deterioration of the nervous system. Cocaine is psychologically addictive. Abrupt cessation of use of the drug, or withdrawal, can be followed by depression.

See also: DRUG ABUSE.

coccidioidomycosis [kahk-sid'-ee-oy-doh-my-koh-sis] Coccidioidomycosis is an infection caused by inhaling the spores of the fungus *Coccidioides immitis*. Although prevalent in the San Joaquin Valley of California, and thus sometimes called valley fever, the disease also occurs in other southwestern states, in Mexico, and in Central and South America. Infected individuals develop fever, malaise, loss of appetite, chest pain, dry cough, headache, weight loss, and, occasionally, a rash on the palms, soles, and other areas. New medications have greatly reduced the high mortality rate.

coccyx see SKELETAL SYSTEM

Cochabamba [koh-chah-bahm'-bah] Cochabamba (1986 est. pop., 329,941) is Bolivia's third largest city and the capital of Cochabamba department. Noted for its pleasant climate, beautiful parks and plazas, and large Indian market, La Concha, Cochabamba is the region's commercial center and contains an oil refinery, textile mills, and a shoe factory. It was founded as Oropeza by the Spaniards in 1574 in a broad valley on the eastern slopes of the Andes at an altitude of 2,558 m (8,392 ft).

Cochin (city) [koh'-chin] Cochin (1981 pop., 513,081) is a port city in Kerala state, southern India, on the Malabar Coast of the Arabian Sea about 250 km (155 mi) from the southern tip of the Indian subcontinent. Cochin has one of India's safest and most prosperous ports, exporting coconut products, nuts, and tea. Industries include shipbuilding and chemical, paper, and tire manufacturing. Tourism is also important. An Indian naval base and the University of Cochin (1971) are there.

Cochin became the first European community in India when the Portuguese explorer Vasco da Gama established a trading station there in 1502. The city passed to the Dutch in 1663, who made it a prosperous port. It was held by the British from 1795 until Indian independence (1947).

Cochin China   see VIETNAM

Cochise [koh-chees']   Cochise, chief of the central Chiricahua in southeastern Arizona, was one of the most famous APACHE leaders to resist intrusions by whites into the southwestern United States during the 19th century. He kept peace with the Anglo-Americans until 1861. In that year, Cochise and several of his relatives had gone to an encampment of soldiers in order to deny the accusation that they had abducted a child from a ranch. The boy was later proved to have been kidnapped by another band of Apaches. During the parley Cochise and his fellows were ordered held as hostages by Lt. George Bascom, but Cochise managed to escape almost immediately by cutting a hole in a tent. Bascom later ordered the other Apache hostages hanged, and the embittered Cochise joined forces with MANGAS COLORADAS, the leader of another Chiricahua band. For ten years Cochise and his warriors harassed the whites by raiding lonely ranches and attacking stagecoaches and miners. They did not surrender to the troops until 1871. Cochise died on the new Chiricahua reservation in 1874.

Cochran, Jacqueline   Jacqueline Cochran, b. Pensacola, Fla., 1912, d. Aug. 9, 1980, was an American aviatrix who organized the Women's Airforce Service Pilots, WASP, during World War II. She was also the first woman to ferry a bomber to England. Reared in a foster home, Cochran left school after the third grade to work in a cotton mill. She acquired her pilot's license in 1932 after only three weeks of training. Two years later she entered the Bendix Transcontinental Air Race, and in 1938 she won that race. She held more speed, distance, and altitude records than any of her contemporaries and was voted the world's leading aviatrix in 1937, 1938, and 1939. Cochran was named (1971) to the Aviation Hall of Fame.

cockatoo   Cockatoos are tropical birds in the parrot family, Psittacidae. Native to an area extending from Malaysia and Australia to the Philippines, they have long been popular cage birds because of their ability to mimic human speech. Many common species belong to the genus *Cacatua*.

One of the largest cockatoos is the great black, or palm, cockatoo, *Probosciger aterrimus*, of Australia and

The sulfur-crested cockatoo, found in Australia, New Guinea, and New Britain, is a boisterous trickster familiar to many as a cage bird. It can even be taught to talk, although this is rare. When flying over the rain forest in search of food, it communicates with others of its species so as not to get lost.

New Guinea; it is about 63 cm (25 in) long and has black feathers with exposed patches of bright red skin on its cheeks. The smallest cockatoo is the cockatiel, *Nymphicus hollandicus*, of central Australia; gray with a yellow head, it is only about 30 cm (12 in) long. All cockatoos have feathered crests, which they can raise or flatten. They also have large, curved, sharply pointed bills that are used to crack nuts. Most cockatoos feed on fruits, vegetables, and roots. In some parts of the world they are considered agricultural pests.

Cockcroft, Sir John Douglas   John Douglas Cockcroft, b. May 27, 1897, d. Sept. 18, 1967, was an English physicist known for his early work with Ernest Walton on atomic particle ACCELERATORS, for which they received the 1951 Nobel Prize for physics. In 1932, Cockcroft and Walton achieved the first successful disintegration of atomic nuclei by artificial means. Using a voltage multiplier to generate 150,000 volts of electricity, they bombarded lithium atoms with accelerated protons to produce beryllium. The beryllium immediately split into two alpha particles, which were identified by bright scintillations on a zinc sulfide screen and by the density of their tracks.

cocker spaniel   The cocker spaniel is one of the smallest of the sporting dogs. Its name is derived from one of its early functions, hunting woodcock. Cocker spaniels are divided on the basis of color into three varieties: black, any solid color other than black, and parti-color.

Once indistinct from the larger ENGLISH COCKER SPANIEL, the American breed was developed into a specific type by U.S. fanciers. It has a rounded skull, hanging ears, a docked tail, and heavy feathering on the chest and

The cocker spaniel, named for its ability to hunt woodcock, is one of the smallest of the sporting dogs.

legs. Cocker spaniels are about 31 to 38 cm (14 to 15 in) high at the shoulders and typically weigh about 11 kg (25 lb).

cockfighting Cockfighting, a sport or pastime that pits gamecocks against each other, is popular in Asia and Latin America. Although in the United States it is illegal in all but three states, it is still practiced in some other areas. Fights are usually held in small, circular, earthen pits. Two cocks specially bred for fighting—and equipped with sharp metal spurs over their own natural spurs—are placed in a pit. Spectators around the pit wager on the outcome. Fights are usually over in a matter of minutes, the outcome decided when one fowl is killed, unable to fight anymore, or refuses to continue.

The sport probably originated in Asia more than 3,000 years ago and was popular in Persia, Rome, and parts of Greece. In 16th-century England cockfighting was a favorite pastime of members of the aristocracy. When colonists came to America in the 17th century they brought the sport with them. In 1836, Massachusetts barred cockfighting, and many other states followed. Similar legislation was passed in Great Britain in 1849.

cockle see MOLLUSK

cockney The term *cockney* refers to certain long-established London residents and to the dialect of English spoken by them since at least the 16th century. Distinctive pronunciations include long *i* for *a* (*nyme*), *ah* for *ou* (*abaht*), *f* or *v* for *th* (*mouf*), and short *i* for *e* (*cimetery*). Another characteristic is dropping or adding initial *h* (*'uman, hup*). Cockney is also characterized by rhyming slang (*artful dodger* for *lodger*) and has contributed many words to English and American slang, such as *crook* for *thief* and *kid* for *child*.

cockroach Cockroaches are long-legged, flattened insects of the family Blattidae, order Orthoptera, common in tropical climates but numerous indoors even in temperate and sub-Arctic zones. Fewer than 1 percent of

cockroach species are considered pests. Most cockroaches live outdoors, hiding under logs, stones, and bark, or in palm fronds and ant and termite nests.

The common cockroach pests are the American, Oriental, Australian, German, Asian, and brown-banded cockroaches. They have spread throughout most of the world as a by-product of commerce, being carried in ships, wagons, trucks, and airplanes. All the pest species are scavengers, feeding on garbage, dead insects, or human food, which they contaminate with their excrement.

Asian cockroaches, unlike other cockroaches, are attracted to artificial lights. Common in many parts of Asia, they invaded the United States and were first seen in central Florida in 1985. Within two years their range extended more than 800 km (500 mi), and they are expected eventually to spread as far north as Maryland.

Evidence linking cockroaches to the transmission of diseases is circumstantial, but because of the threat, much effort and expense are invested in the chemical control of cockroaches. Insecticides are usually effective, though in some places cockroaches have developed resistance to the most widely used poisons.

The Central American cockroach (A), *one of the larger roaches, measures 5 cm (2 in) in length, with a 7.5-cm (3-in) wingspan. It is among the majority of cockroaches not considered pests to humans. The Oriental cockroach* (B) *is a cosmopolitan pest that damages food, paper, and clothing and spreads infectious diseases. Fifteen to 40 cockroach eggs mature within a hard case, or ootheca* (C), *from which white nymphs emerge. Adults usually have squat, oval bodies; the tarsus of each leg* (D) *has five segments.*

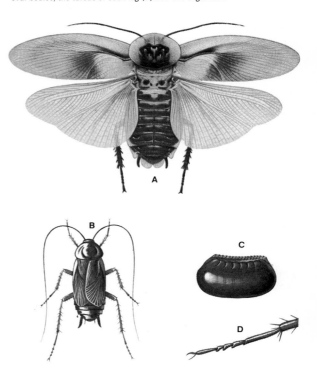

Cockroaches lay their eggs in an egg case, or ootheca. The eggs hatch into nymphs that look like miniature adults without wings. The nymphs grow through several molts, usually taking several months to reach adulthood. Some cockroaches are wingless as adults; others have well-developed wings. Cockroaches are among the oldest insect groups, having survived basically unchanged for 300 million years.

cocoa Cocoa is finely pulverized, defatted, roasted CACAO kernels, to which natural and artificial spices and flavors may be added. It is commercially manufactured by pumping hot CHOCOLATE liquor (semiliquid ground cacao kernels) into presses where, under extreme pressure, part of the fat, or cocoa butter, is removed. Cocoa may be Dutch-processed by mild alkali treatment to change and darken color and improve flavor. Cocoa is the flavoring ingredient in many confections, baked goods, ice creams, puddings, and beverages.

The coconut palm tree (1) produces large fruit (2) encased in a tough outer pod (3) and a fibrous inner shell (4). The fruit yields a refreshing liquid and a sweet flesh, which yields coconut oil and is eaten raw or dried.

The cacao tree is the source of chocolate and the chocolate product, cocoa. The woody fruit, which may grow to a length of 30 cm (1 ft), contains numerous small seeds that are fermented and roasted before being processed into chocolate liquor and cocoa.

growing point that produces huge pinnate leaves, or fronds, and yellow or white flowers that form the fruit bunch. The fruit is a large, single-seeded drupe with a hard stony "shell" and a fibrous husk. The abundant liquid inside the shell becomes solid and oily to form the coconut meat, which is subsequently dried to make commercial copra.

The coconut forms the very basis of life for many people, particularly in the Pacific area. Its liquid provides food and drink; the shell, domestic utensils and fiber; the leaves, thatch and plaiting. The wood is often the only available timber, and the sap bled from its bud produces a sweet drink, alcoholic beverages, and sugar syrup.

Because of its high content of saturated fatty acids and its good keeping quality, coconut oil is valued as a principal ingredient of margarine and cooking and salad oils, as well as in soap and shampoo manufacture.

coconut The coconut is the fruit of the most economically important member of the great PALM family, Palmae. The genus *Cocos* is Southeast Asian and contains only one species, *C. Nucifera*. Cultivated in tropical lowlands, almost always near the sea, the coconut has long been distributed throughout Southeast Asia and along the tropical African and American coasts. Much of its propagation has occurred through the distribution of its fruits—which can remain viable in seawater for several weeks—by ocean currents.

The coconut tree grows to 30 m (98 ft) in height and may live as long as 100 years. It has a single (terminal)

cocoon [kuh-koon'] A cocoon is a protective covering constructed by an insect larva prior to transformation from the larval to the pupal life stage (see PUPA). The cocoons may be woven entirely of silk produced by the larva, or may include mud, sand, bits of chewed wood, or other debris. Some cocoons consist of a rolled leaf held together by silk. Inside the protective cocoon, the larva molts and transforms into the pupal stage, then molts again, and emerges as an adult. Cocoons are also made by leeches and other ANNELID worms.

Jean Cocteau possessed one of the outstanding creative minds of the 20th century. The range of his genius is indicated by his highly regarded plays, poetry, essays, and criticism. In his later years the French virtuoso turned his creative energies toward filmmaking.

Cocteau, Jean [kawk-toh']   Jean Cocteau, the French litterateur and artist, b. July 5, 1889, d. Oct. 10, 1963, was an inventor and facilitator of art in many poetic forms: design, verse, prose, theater, dance, and cinema. His first volume of poetry was published in 1909, and his involvement as a librettist for the Ballets Russes and its impresario Serge Diaghilev began the same year. After serving as an ambulance driver on the Belgian front during World War I, Cocteau returned to Paris in 1917 produced his ballet *Parade*, with music by the modernist Erik Satie and scenery by Picasso. As a poet and novelist, he illustrated many of his books himself. In 1934 he produced what is considered his finest play, *The Infernal Machine* (Eng. trans., 1936), a unique rendition of the myth of Oedipus. In 1931 he wrote and produced his first film, *Blood of a Poet*, in which he asserts through a series of powerful surrealist images the themes that are repeated throughout his work and that are particularly visible in the films he was to make in the following decades: the poet as a special being who is in touch with supernatural forces, and the power of art to survive time and death. Later films include *Blood of a Poet; The Eternal Return* (1944), a sensual retelling of the Tristan legend; *Beauty and the Beast* (1946), a fairy tale recast as a surreal romance; *Orpheus* (1950); and *The Testament of Orpheus* (1960). In 1955 the French literary establishment—which had for many years considered Cocteau merely a literary *poseur*—finally recognized his importance by electing him to the French Academy.

cod   Cod is the common name for ten families of fishes in the order Gadiformes and five families in the suborder Gadoidei. The families comprise about 150 species, including some of the most heavily harvested fish the world over. The many families include the true cod, Gadidae; the deep-sea cod, Moridae; the Bregmacerotidae; and the HAKE. The true cod include the common cod (the most important of which are the Atlantic cod and the Pacific cod), HADDOCK, and pollack. Members of this family generally inhabit shelf regions off the coasts.

The haddock population in New England waters has declined drastically as a result of overfishing. From 1935 to 1960 the haddock population of Georges Banks (a fishing ground off the New England coast) averaged 140 million, and by 1987 it had declined to about 13 million. Deep-sea cod live primarily at depths of more than 500 m (1,640 ft), below the commercially fished zones. The Bregmacerotidae are found only in the tropical and subtropical regions of the Atlantic, Indian, and Pacific oceans. The hake, like the common cod, is commercially important. Hakes tend to live in deeper waters than do other cods.

Congregating in vast shoals, the Atlantic cod may reach lengths of 1.8 m (6 ft) and weights of more than 90 kg (198 lb) but averages from 1 to 11 kg (about 2 to 25 lb). Its round body is olive green to brown; the back and flank are spotted, and the belly is silvery. A single cod may lay up to 9 million eggs in a season. The eggs float freely in the sea, where they are fertilized by the male, and in many cases they are consumed by predators or else carried by currents away from the plankton on which the young fish feed. Fertilized eggs hatch in 10 to 20 days. Adult cod feed mainly on other fish, especially herring and mackerel, as well as on shellfish and worms.

The Atlantic cod (A) is widely distributed in the North Atlantic and is most abundant off the coasts of Iceland, Newfoundland, and Norway. World stocks of haddock (B) and European hake (C) have been greatly depleted in recent decades.

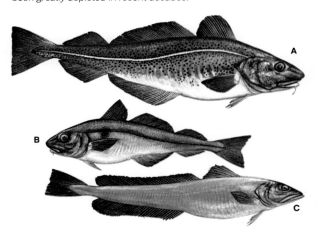

coda   see SONATA

Coddington, William   William Coddington, b.1601, d. Nov. 1, 1678, was the founder of Newport, R.I. Initially a resident of the Massachusetts Bay Colony, he supported Anne HUTCHINSON in the antinomian controversy and was part of the group that moved to the island of Aquidneck (Rhode Island) in 1638. The following year, he and some followers started a settlement at Newport. A longtime rival of Roger WILLIAMS, the leader of nearby Providence Plantations, Coddington was governor of Aquidneck Island (1640–44, 1651–52). He opposed the unification of Aquidneck and Providence Plantations but later served as governor of united Rhode Island (1674, 1675, 1678).

Code Napoleon   see NAPOLEONIC CODE

codeine [koh'-deen]   Codeine is a narcotic drug, one of two clinically useful phenanthrene alkaloids in OPIUM. (The other is morphine.) Discovered (1832) in opium by French chemist Pierre Jean Robiquet, codeine constitutes about 0.5 to 2.5 percent of this plant substance. The drug shares most of the pharmacologic characteristics of morphine but is only about one-tenth as potent on a weight-to-weight basis when given by injection; it loses one-third of its potency when taken orally.

Codeine is a frequently prescribed oral analgesic for treatment of mild to moderate pain and can be used alone or in combination with salicylates, such as aspirin. It is also an effective cough suppressant, at doses lower than those needed for treatment of pain, but it has been partly replaced by effective nonnarcotic, nonaddictive antitussives.

Codeine is addictive, capable of producing physical and psychological dependence and tolerance. Withdrawal symptoms are similar to, but milder than, those of morphine addiction.

codes and ciphers   see CRYPTOLOGY

Cody, William Frederick   see BUFFALO BILL

Coe, Sebastian   The British runner Sebastian Newbold Coe, b. Sept. 29, 1956, was one of the greatest and most versatile middle-distance runners in track history. Within 41 days in the summer of 1979, Coe set three world records: at 800 m, 1,500 m, and the mile. In July 1980 he set a fourth—at 1,000 m. At the 1980 Olympics he won gold (1,500 m) and silver (800 m) medals, and at the 1984 Games he became the first to repeat victory at 1,500 m. As of 1991, Coe still held world records at 800 m (1 min 41.73 sec) and 1,000 m (2:12.18).

coeducation   Coeducation is the education of males and females together at the same institution. This practice, at the college or secondary level, did not gain widespread acceptance in the United States until the late 19th century. Previously, the few women who attended college were likely to be enrolled in exclusively female institutions that sought to provide an education equal to that given men. Oberlin, in Oberlin, Ohio, the oldest coeducational college in the United States, admitted four women in 1837. By the turn of the century, women were accepted in larger numbers by such state universities as Iowa, Michigan, and Wisconsin, but the presence of "coeds" in college classes was still something of a novelty. Some universities in the East admitted women to their coordinate colleges, a compromise that permitted women to receive essentially the same education as men.

At the secondary level, college-preparatory grammar schools and vocationally oriented academies in the United States and their counterparts in other countries were ordinarily closed to girls. Not until the 18th century did girls begin to attend common schools in any great number, although they usually did so for only a few years. By the 19th century the principle of formal education for girls was generally accepted, but girls were often taught apart from boys. In the early 1800s several female academies were established, and some schools provided "female departments." Coeducational high schools developed during the 1840s, but for several decades the idea persisted that education beyond the elementary level was unnecessary for girls.

Although coeducation at all levels is now taken for granted throughout much of the world, males and females are still likely to be segregated, especially at the secondary level, in countries with predominantly Muslim or Roman Catholic populations. In the United States hundreds of private schools still admit only one sex, although since the 1950s many single-sex high schools and colleges have opened their doors to students of both sexes. The trend toward coeducation, accelerated by changing concepts of sex roles, concern for sexual equality, and evidence that the educational interests and abilities of men and women are about the same, resulted in a decline from 300 U.S. women's colleges in 1960 to about 100 by 1988.

coelacanth [se'-luh-kanth]   The coelacanth is a crossopterygian (lobe-finned) fish, *Latimeria chalumnae*, whose fossil record dates back more than 350 million years to the Devonian Period. Paleontologists once assumed that it had become extinct at the end of Cretaceous time (about 65 million years ago). Then, in 1938, a living coelacanth was netted off southeast Africa. The fish was about 1.5 m (5 ft) long, weighed 57 kg (126 lb), and was covered with deep-blue scales. Several others have since been caught in waters between Africa and Madagascar. Underwater pictures of the fish were taken in 1987.

Coelacanth is the only surviving species of a prehistoric group of fishes, the Crossopterygii, from which scientists conjecture the first land vertebrates evolved.

The coelacanth has a deep and stocky body, and its paired dorsal fins are rounded and lobelike as in fossilized members of the order Crossopterygii. The dorsal and anal fins are fan-shaped. The first spine of the dorsal fin is hollow. The skeletal structure of the pectoral and pelvic fins indicates a close evolutionary relationship between the coelacanth and four-limbed land vertebrates (see EVOLUTION). The underwater pictures show the fish moving like four-legged animals.

Coelacanths also have symmetrical three-lobed tails. The head is short and deep, and the skull bones are considerably reduced. The coelacanth is carnivorous.

coelenterate [suh-len'-tur-ayt]   Coelenterates are INVERTEBRATE animals comprising some 9,000 species in the phylum Coelenterata, a name derived from Greek words meaning "hollow gut." An alternate, more recent name for the phylum is Cnidaria, meaning "nettle." Both names refer to important attributes of the group: the possession of an internal gastrovascular cavity and the ability to sting prey or enemies. Most coelenterates, such as hydroids, SEA ANEMONES, and the various types of CORAL, are sedentary and marine. JELLYFISH, however, are modified for swimming. HYDRAS, although sedentary, inhabit fresh water.

Structures and Functions

The coelenterate's body wall is composed of two cell layers—an outer layer (ectoderm) and an inner layer (endoderm)—separated by a middle layer (mesoglea) of varying thickness. Various internal or external supporting skeletal structures are also common.

Two body forms are found among coelenterates: the polyp, and the medusa, or jellyfish. The polyp is a cylindrical, saclike structure adapted for a sedentary life. A mouth surrounded by tentacles leads into a central gastrovascular cavity in which food is digested and incorporated. The medusa is a sexually reproducing stage that occurs in the life cycle of many coelenterates. It is structurally similar to the polyp stage but is specialized for swimming and drifting in water. A typical medusa is shaped like an inverted bowl with a ring of tentacles around the outside and a mouth projecting downward in the center. Many medusae have an enlarged, gelatinous mesoglea, hence the name jellyfish.

Coelenterates are mainly carnivorous, collecting planktonic animals from the surrounding water. Feeding, as well as defense, relies largely on special cells, the cnidocytes. These are concentrated in the ectoderm of the tentacles and mouth region and contain a thin, coiled, inverted thread called a nematocyst. In response to touch or chemical stimulus, the nematocyst everts and extends out beyond the cell. One type of nematocyst is the hollow penetrant that injects poison into a prey organism, subduing it before ingestion. Other types contain adhesive substances or entangle prey.

Reproduction

Reproduction occurs both sexually and asexually. Asexual reproduction is by the process of budding, in which a new

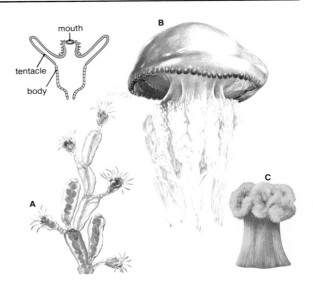

The phylum of coelenterates consists of invertebrate animals such as hydroid polyps (A), jellyfish (B), and sea anemone (C). Although they look very different, all coelenterates have a soft, hollow body and tentacles that contain stinging cells to paralyze prey (sketch at upper left).

polyp is formed from some part of an existing one. The newly formed polyp may break loose, producing an independent organism (for example, hydra), or remain attached, eventually producing a colony of several or even thousands of polyps, all derived initially from a single animal.

Sexual reproduction occurs in all coelenterates. In some species the polyp stage buds off medusae. After a period of growth and maturation the medusae produce eggs or sperm, which unite to form a small, ciliated larva, the planula, that eventually settles and develops into a sedentary polyp. In many species, however, there is no free-swimming medusa stage. Instead, male polyps release sperm that fertilize eggs retained by female animals or colonies. This results finally in a free-swimming planula, which leaves the female and, after a period of drifting in the plankton, attaches to the substrate and grows into a polyp.

Classification of Coelenterata

Class Hydrozoa. The most common Hydrozoa are the hydroids, bushy colonies of polyps commonly attached to rocks and pilings in shallow, salt water. Hydroid polyps are specialized for different functions, such as feeding, reproduction, and defense. In many species, the outer cell layer secretes a nonliving outer covering that strengthens and protects the colony. In some hydroids, small, free-living medusae are budded off and carry out sexual reproduction, but sometimes eggs and sperm are produced directly by certain kinds of polyps. Other interesting hydrozoans include the stinging coral, the PORTUGUESE MAN-OF-WAR (a floating colony of specialized polyps), and the hydra.

Class Scyphozoa. Scyphozoa include the large jellyfish. Here the medusa stage is dominant and the polyp stage inconspicuous or absent.

Class Anthozoa. Anthozoa include the sea anemones and most types of coral. These animals are solitary or colonial polyps. A medusa stage is not present, and eggs and sperm are produced directly by the polyps.

See also: CORAL REEF; FOSSIL RECORD.

coelom [see'-luhm]   The coelom, in zoology, is the body cavity that lies between the digestive tract and the outer body wall in all animals more advanced than flatworms on the evolutionary scale. The term comes from a Greek word meaning "cavity." The coelom's form and its mode of embryonic DEVELOPMENT are useful in indicating evolutionary relationships among ANIMAL phyla. In all higher animals the coelom is lined by the peritoneum, a membrane that develops from the mesoderm, a layer of tissue in the embryo. The peritoneum separates the coelom walls from all the body organs contained in the cavity. In adult animals the coelom may also be divided in distinct parts, such as the pericardial cavity around the heart in humans.

Some lower animals, such as roundworms, also have a coelomlike space in their body, but this space lacks a definite mesodermal lining and is not a true coelom. Very simple forms of life, such as jellyfish, have only a basic gastric cavity and completely lack any form of mesodermal tissue.

coenzyme   see ENZYME

Coercive Acts   see INTOLERABLE ACTS

coesite [koh'-e-syt]   Coesite is a rare, monoclinic variety of QUARTZ (SiO_2). With a specific gravity of 2.93, it is the densest known form of quartz except for stishovite. Like stishovite, it was first synthesized (1953) before being found (1961) in METEORITE CRATERS, where it had been formed by meteorite impact. The minerals, products of high temperature and pressure, suggest the different mineral forms to be found deep in the Earth's interior.

Coetzee, J. M.   Joseph Michael Coetzee, b. Feb. 9, 1940, is a South African writer whose novels have won wide international praise. *Waiting for the Barbarians* (1980) describes in Kafkaesque terms a society that justifies its brutality by raising the threat of nonexistent barbarians. *The Life and Times of Michael K* (1983) again refers to Kafka, through the name of its protagonist and the nature of his journey, an attempt to live a life not defined by those who have always dominated. *Foe* (1987) is a symbolic retelling of the Robinson Crusoe tale. Coetzee has also written a work of criticism, *White Writing* (1988), on literary culture in South Africa, and, with fellow novelist André Brink, has edited *A Land Apart: A South African Reader* (1987), an anthology of work by younger black and white writers.

coffee   The coffee bean is the world's most valuable agricultural commodity. In the late 1980s coffee imports into the United States alone cost more than $4 billion annually. Of the many varieties of the genus *Coffea* (family Rubiaceae) known to exist, only two species have significant commercial importance: *C. arabica* and *C. robusta*, which together constitute 99 percent of the total world output.

Coffee Cultivation. The coffee plant is an evergreen shrub or small tree, cultivated in hot, moist climates. The most flavorful beans are produced between 900 and 1,800 m (3,000 and 6,000 ft) above sea level, especially on volcanic soil.

A coffee tree, propagated from seed, bears its first fruit in 5 to 8 years and annually yields more than 2 kg (about 5 lb) of fruit—the red, seed-bearing coffee "cherries"—from which about 0.5 kg (1 lb) of green coffee seeds, or beans, is obtained. The cherries must be har-

The coffee tree is cultivated in tropical regions for its bean, a principal agricultural export of several countries. The shrub or small tree reaches a height of 4.5 m (15 ft) and has fragrant, white flowers that give way to pulpy "cherries" containing the bean. After the fruit is harvested and the pulp removed, the beans are dried and shipped to be roasted, ground, and packaged.

vested by hand, for only those which are fully ripened are picked. Robusta cherries remain on the tree after they ripen. Ripe arabica cherries fall to the ground and spoil. Arabica trees must therefore be carefully watched and picked over several times—which increases the cost of producing the richer-flavored arabica beans.

After harvesting, the cherries may be dried and the pulp around the beans removed. Or, in wet climates or for particular types of coffee, the harvested cherries may be washed and then pulped to separate the beans. The dry and wet methods of preparation produce distinctive flavors in the beans and, along with the differences between varieties, account for the subtle flavor distinctions between beans from the various growing areas. The beans are gray green. When they have been thoroughly dried, they are sorted, bagged, graded according to type and quality, and shipped to processors.

Processing Coffee. The flavor of coffee is determined not only by the variety, but also by the length of time the green beans are roasted. In continuous roasting, hot air is forced through small quantities of beans for a 5-minute period; in batch roasting, much larger quantities of beans are roasted for a longer time. Dark-roasted coffees (French or espresso roasts) are stronger and mellower than lightly roasted beans.

Instant coffee is prepared by forcing an atomized spray of very strong coffee extract through a jet of hot air; this evaporates the water in the extract and leaves the dried coffee particles. Another method of producing instant coffee is FREEZE-DRYING. To make decaffeinated coffee, the green bean is processed in a steam or chemical bath to remove the CAFFEINE, the substance that produces coffee's stimulating effect.

Coffee Consumption. Native to Ethiopia and cultivated and brewed in Arab countries for centuries, coffee was introduced into Europe in the mid-17th century. Plantations established in Indonesia, the West Indies, and Brazil made coffee cultivation an important element in colonial economies. Today, Latin America and Africa produce most of the world's coffee. The United States is the largest importer.

Coffin, Henry Sloane   Henry Sloane Coffin, b. New York City, Jan. 5, 1877, d. Nov. 25, 1954, an American Presbyterian minister, was president of Union Theological Seminary from 1926 to 1945. He called for a reexamination of Christian doctrine in the light of modern science, urged Christians to try to remake society, and promoted the ecumenical movement. His nephew, William Sloane Coffin, Jr., was chaplain at Yale University (1958–75) and prominent during the 1960s in the civil rights and antiwar movements.

Coggan, Donald   Frederick Donald Coggan, b. Oct. 9, 1909, was archbishop of Canterbury from 1974 to 1980. Principal of the London College of Divinity from 1944 to 1956, he became bishop of Bradford (1956) and archbishop of York (1961). He was raised to a life peerage as Lord Coggan of Canterbury in 1980.

cognitive psychology   Cognition is the act of knowing, and cognitive psychology is the study of all human activities related to knowledge. These activities include attention, creativity, MEMORY, PERCEPTION, PROBLEM SOLVING, thinking, and the use of language.

Until about 1970 the cognitive approach had little impact outside the experimental laboratory, but the subsequent appearance of cognitively oriented therapies, information-processing analyses of intelligence tests, and cognitive theories of personality suggest that its influence is increasing.

Differences from Behaviorism. Cognitive psychology arose partly as a reaction to BEHAVIORISM. The behaviorist insistence that only stimuli and responses lay within the scope of science had long prevented the effective study of higher mental processes; the establishment of cognitive psychology broke this taboo.

Characteristic Methods. In cognitive psychology the human mind is conceived of as a structured system for handling information. According to most cognitive theories, information picked up by the senses is analyzed, stored, recoded, and subsequently used in various ways; these activities are called information processes. They need not be represented in consciousness; cognitive psychology relies very little on conscious introspection. Instead, experiments are designed to take advantage of various objective indicators of information processing: reaction-time measurement, response selection, performance in memory tests, and so on. Mathematical and logical analyses of such data are used to construct models of the underlying processes. These models are not intended to represent actual brain mechanisms. Although it is assumed that all mental activity has some physiological basis, it is hoped that the program of mental information-processing can be understood without regard to the machinery of the brain.

The analogy between brain and computer, or mind and program, has influenced cognitive psychology in many ways. Concepts such as code, INFORMATION STORAGE AND RETRIEVAL, buffer, and executive routine frequently appear in cognitive theories. Moreover, there has been a trend to regard cognitive psychology and ARTIFICIAL INTELLIGENCE as coordinate sciences, each borrowing concepts from the other. Not all cognitive psychologists subscribe to this view, however; some feel that the differences between human and artificial intelligence are so great that the analogy is misleading.

Topics of Investigation. Although the historical roots of cognitive psychology go back to introspective psychology and associationism, Donald Eric BROADBENT's *Perception and Communication* (1958) was the first book entirely devoted to human information processing. It introduced the notion of several distinct kinds of storage systems (memories) of limited capacity and of attention as a mechanism for filtering incoming information. A wide range of new techniques for the study of information processing were soon devised and led to a number of important discoveries. For example, a short-term memory of sharply limited capacity, which is primarily verbal and shows rapid forgetting, has been distinguished from a long-term memory that shows little evidence of any limitations at all. Special kinds of memory for visual material have also been postulated, and techniques now permit the objective study of visual imagery. Recent research has dealt not only with episodic memory for personal experiences but also with semantic memory, which is essentially one's store of knowledge. Reaction-time methods have been used to explore the structure of semantic memory, and there have been a number of attempts to model that structure with computer programs. The success of these attempts remains controversial.

Several other areas of interest have concerned cognitive psychologists from the first. One of these is PATTERN RECOGNITION: how does the information-processing system categorize and distinguish among objects? Another is attention: how and at what level does the individual select among the available alternative sources of information? There has also been continued work on the higher mental processes: decision making, problem solving, and thinking. The field of PSYCHOLINGUISTICS, for example, was created by applying experimental methods to the study of language. It has been heavily influenced by concurrent developments in linguistics itself, especially the work of Noam CHOMSKY.

The development of cognitive processes in the growing child has also become a subfield in its own right, strongly affected by the work of Jean PIAGET and his students. The perceptual theories of James and Eleanor Gibson use a different definition of information and reject the concept of information processing entirely.

Cohan, George M.

George Michael Cohan, b. Providence, R.I., July 3, 1878, d. Nov. 5, 1942, was an actor, singer, dancer, playwright, composer, director, and producer. He dominated the American theater at the beginning of the 20th century.

His first full-length play, *The Governor's Son*, opened in New York in 1901. This fast-paced mixture of popular song, comedy, and melodrama set the standard for subsequent Cohan productions. *Little Johnny Jones* (1904) introduced two of Cohan's most enduring songs, "I'm a Yankee Doodle Dandy" and "Give My Regards to Broadway."

In 1923, Cohan took on a serious role as a second-rate variety performer in *The Song and Dance Man*. Ten years later he gave what many critics considered the finest performance of his career as Nat Miller in Eugene O'Neill's *Ah, Wilderness!* Cohan also appeared as Franklin Roosevelt in *I'd Rather Be Right* (1937).

coherent light   see INTERFERENCE; LASER

cohesion

Cohesion is the tendency of matter to hold itself together, a result of intermolecular attractive forces. As two molecules or atoms of a body approach each other, their potential energy reaches a minimum value at a certain equilibrium distance. Work is then required, either to push them closer together or to pull them farther

apart. Any force tending to decrease the distance meets with a rapidly increasing reaction of compressive elasticity, whereas any force tending to increase this distance is opposed by cohesion. Cohesion is great in solids, much less in liquids, and practically nonexistent in gases. The cohesive property of some materials is diluted by the adhesive properties of their parts (see ADHESION).

Coimbra

[kweem'-bruh] Coimbra (1981 pop., 74,600) is the capital of Coimbra district and of Beira Litoral province in west central Portugal. Located on the Mondego River, about 224 km (139 mi) northeast of Lisbon, Coimbra is a distribution center for the surrounding agricultural region, and industries include ceramics, textiles, wine, and beer. The University of Coimbra is Portugal's oldest university; it was founded in Lisbon in 1290 and permanently moved to Coimbra in 1537. Other historic landmarks include the Old Cathedral, a 12th-century Romanesque structure, and the 16th-century church of Santa Cruz. Nearby are the extensive remains of the ancient Roman town of Conimbriga, from which Coimbra takes its name. Coimbra itself was called Aeminium in Roman times. It was a Moorish stronghold in the 8th and 9th centuries, and after Ferdinand I of Castile captured the area in 1064, it was a headquarters for the reconquest of Portugal from the Moors. It later served (1139–1260) as the capital of Portugal.

coin collecting   see NUMISMATICS

coke

Coke is the residue formed when COAL is heated in the absence of air. It is primarily carbon with mineral matter and some residual volatile material. In manufacturing coke, as temperature increases, free water evaporates and tar and gas evolve; coal becomes coke above 550° C (1,022° F).

Beginning in the 17th century, coke was produced in the type of beehive ovens developed earlier for CHARCOAL production. Modern rectangular coke ovens can hold far larger charges—up to 33 metric tons (36 U.S. tons) of coal—and also permit the recovery of a number of coal by-products. One metric ton of coal produces 0.7 metric tons of coke. The largest plants can discharge 5 to 10 million metric tons of coke annually.

Coke is about 90 percent carbon and has considerable mechanical strength. It is thus an excellent fuel for the BLAST FURNACE: it burns easily, acts as a reducing agent for the iron ore, and is strong enough to support the column of ore, coke, and stone.

Coke, Sir Edward

[kuk] Edward Coke, b. Feb. 1, 1552, d. Sept. 3, 1634, was an English jurist and politician best remembered for his defense of the COMMON LAW against royal prerogative. Educated at Trinity College, Cambridge, Coke read law at the Inner Temple in London and in 1578 pleaded his first case. In 1592 he was named solicitor general and in 1594 attorney general,

winning the latter office over Francis BACON. At that time Coke was a vigorous spokesman for the prerogative of the crown. He became known as a severe prosecutor for his trials of such well-known men as the earl of ESSEX and Sir Walter RALEIGH.

Three years after the accession of JAMES I in 1603, Coke became chief justice of the common pleas and in 1613 was made chief justice of the King's Bench. During this period of time, he emerged as a staunch defender of the common law.

Coke opposed the king's assertion of his right to decide cases outside the common-law courts, contending that such decisions were null and void. His frequent disputes with the king, as well as the zeal with which he prosecuted (1616) the king's favorite, Robert Carr, earl of Somerset, and his wife for the murder of Sir Thomas Overbury, made numerous enemies for Coke. In 1616, Coke was removed as chief justice, but through influence regained his position on the privy council in 1617. Elected to Parliament in 1620, he led the opposition to James and to CHARLES I, who succeeded to the throne in 1625. Coke's most significant writing is his *Institutes of the Laws of England* (1628).

Jean Baptiste Colbert, the French minister of finance under Louis XIV, was a leading exponent of French mercantilism.

Coke, Thomas [kohk]   Thomas Coke, b. Sept. 9, 1747, d. May 3, 1814, was a Welsh-born Methodist leader and the first bishop of the Methodist Episcopal church in the United States. Educated at Oxford and ordained (1772) an Anglican priest, he later developed an interest in Methodism. In 1784, John WESLEY appointed him superintendent of the U.S. Methodist movement but disapproved when Coke adopted the title of bishop later that year. The resulting Christmas Conference of 1784 brought Coke and Francis ASBURY to episcopal leadership of the Methodist Episcopal church.

Colbert, Claudette [kohl-bair']   Claudette Colbert is the stage name of Lily Claudette Chauchoin, b. Paris, Sept. 13, 1903, an American stage and screen actress. Her film comedies of the 1930s and '40s include *It Happened One Night* (1934; Academy Award). Colbert appeared on the stage in *Marriage-Go-Round* (1958), *The Kingfisher* (1978), *A Talent for Murder* (1981), and *Aren't We All?* (1985).

Colbert, Jean Baptiste   Jean Baptiste Colbert, known as the Great Colbert, b. Reims, France, Aug. 29, 1619, d. Sept. 6, 1683, was the most prominent member of a distinguished family of French administrators under LOUIS XIV, directing France's internal affairs from 1661 to 1683. Best known for Colbertism (also called MERCANTILISM), a thorough application of government controls over the economy, he was also a codifier of laws and an initiator of state cultural and scientific undertakings.

Born to a merchant family, Colbert began (1640) his career in the ministry of war. He became (1651) the personal and financial confidant of Cardinal MAZARIN and in

1661 helped Louis XIV convict the corrupt superintendent of finances, Nicolas FOUQUET. Colbert became superintendent of public buildings in 1664, controller general of finances in 1665, and secretary of state for the royal household in 1668 and for the navy in 1669.

Colbert's mercantilist policies included governmental subsidization and inspection of industries; establishment of new East and West Indies companies (see EAST INDIA COMPANY, FRENCH); reduction of tariffs internally and their increase against Dutch competitors; and a more equitable and efficient tax administration. Colbert also established an excellent navy and was responsible for the famous Code of Civil Procedure (1667) and Code of Criminal Procedure (1670).

Colbert founded academies for the fine arts, music, and science, and the Academy of France in Rome. He also established triumphal arches, the Louvre's classical colonnade, the Hôtel des Invalides (a hospital for war veterans), and the Tuileries Gardens, all in Paris. As a hardworking state servant he combined the fostering of cultural grandeur with healthy, financial administration, yet when he died he was not well liked.

Colchester   Colchester (1985 est. pop., 143,100) is a municipal borough situated on the Colne River, in Essex, England. It is a port, trade center, and the location of the University of Essex (1961). It was the site of the first Roman colony in Britain, Camulodunum, which was founded in AD 43. Some Roman walls and gateways survive as ruins. Colchester's massive Norman castle houses a museum of Roman antiquities. In the 16th century Flemish weavers were settled in Colchester to develop the British wool industry.

Colchis [kahl'-kis]   Colchis was a historical region on the eastern shore of the Black Sea south of the Caucasus mountains; it now forms part of the Georgian Soviet Socialist Republic. In Greek mythology, it was the home of MEDEA and the destination of JASON and the Argonauts. The Greeks, who established trading posts on the coast, found Colchis inhabited by many different peoples. Under nominal Persian rule from the 6th century BC, Colchis was briefly conquered (89–65 BC) by MITHRADATES VI of Pontus and thereafter ruled by Rome.

cold, common   The common cold, or acute coryza, is an infection of the upper respiratory tract that can be caused by any one of more than 200 viruses. When infection occurs, the walls of the respiratory tract swell and produce excess mucus, giving rise to the typical cold symptoms of stuffy or runny nose, throat discomfort, malaise, and occasional coughing. Colds can produce fevers of up to 39° C (102° F) in infants and children, but such fevers in adults indicate that the infection is probably influenza. Most colds run their course in three to ten days, but infants and elderly persons are susceptible to complications such as sinusitis, ear inflammations, and pneumonia.

Because of the number of viruses involved, people do not develop immunity to colds as they do to many other viral diseases. Among the cold-causing viruses are paramyxoviruses (parainfluenza and respiratory syncytial virus), picornaviruses (rhino-, echo-, and coxsackievirus), coronavirus, adenovirus, and influenza type C virus. Each virus also has numerous subsets; for example, the parainfluenza virus appears in four distinct forms, the fourth of which seems to cause only colds whereas the other three can cause croup, bronchiolitis, or pneumonia. More than 100 rhinoviruses have also been identified. Studies suggest that rhinoviruses trigger the release of natural proteins called kinins into the blood, causing vessels to expand and plasma to leak into other tissues. This irritates nerve endings and produces cold symptoms. All cold viruses are spread by direct contact or by airborne particles.

Colds are treated with rest and fluids, in addition to antihistamines, decongestants, and cough medicines as needed. Aspirin is recommended only when symptoms are severe, because it increases viral shedding and makes the sufferer more contagious. Vaccines are of little use in prevention because so many kinds of viruses are involved. Vitamin C, despite claims, does not prevent colds, but large doses may lessen symptoms.

cold-blooded animal   see BODY TEMPERATURE

cold war   The term *cold war* refers to the strategic and political struggle that developed after World War II between the United States and its Western European allies, on one hand, and the USSR and Communist countries, on the other. The cold war initially centered on the use of USSR military forces to install Communist governments in Eastern Europe. These Soviet actions ran counter to the U.S. government's insistence upon the right of self-determination for the peoples of Eastern Europe and raised fears that the USSR would also try to communize Western Europe. The USSR had suffered enormous losses in the war against Nazi Germany and looked upon Eastern Europe as a bulwark against another invasion from the West. The Soviet leaders considered U.S. objections to Soviet actions in Poland, Hungary, and Romania a betrayal of wartime understandings about spheres of influence in Europe. Thus they placed Eastern Europe behind a military and political barrier known in the West as the IRON CURTAIN.

Political differences were exacerbated by ideological conflict. The Marxist-Leninist Soviet leaders believed that capitalism would inevitably seek the destruction of the Soviet system. In the United States, a long-standing suspicion and dislike of communism strengthened the view that the USSR was intent on expansion and world conquest.

The Struggle over Germany.   Meanwhile, competition began for control of Germany and other strategic points such as the Dardanelles, the straits linking the Black Sea

(Below) *U.S. Secretary of State Dulles* (left) *greets Soviet leader Nikita Khrushchev* (right) *and Nikolai Bulganin* (center) *at a 1955 summit conference in Geneva.* (Right) *Children of West Berlin await evacuation by plane to West Germany during the Soviet blockade of 1948–49.*

(Left) *An East German who has attempted to escape into West Berlin is shot dead by guards at the base of the Berlin Wall.* (Right) *The cylindrical objects stored on the deck of this Soviet vessel bound for Cuba are fuselage assemblies of ballistic missiles. The crisis precipitated by the installation of nuclear weapons in Cuba in 1962 was resolved when Soviet premier Nikita Khrushchev acceded to U.S. President John F. Kennedy's demand that the missiles be withdrawn.*

with the Aegean and the Mediterranean. Soviet pressures on Greece and Turkey led President Harry TRUMAN to declare in March 1947 that the United States would give economic and military aid to those countries and would also "support free peoples who are resisting attempted subjugation by armed minorities or by outside pressures." The announcement in June 1947 of the U.S. MARSHALL PLAN to restore the faltering economies of Western Europe—including that of West Germany—prompted a series of ripostes from the Kremlin.

In February 1948 the democratic government of Czechoslovakia was overturned by a Communist coup; in May 1948 Soviet authorities severed all Western land-access routes to BERLIN. Only the success of air cargo planes in supplying West Berlin, isolated within the Soviet zone of occupation that later became East Germany, permitted the United States to resist the Soviet pressure.

In 1949 the Western powers entered into a military agreement that led to the formation of the NORTH ATLANTIC TREATY ORGANIZATION (NATO), designed to establish a military counterweight to the Soviet forces in Europe. Meanwhile, in China, a long civil war ended with the victory of Communist forces under Mao Zedong in 1949.

War in Korea. The first phase of the cold war culminated in the North Korean invasion of South Korea on June 26, 1950, resulting in U.S. involvement in a land war in Asia (see KOREAN WAR) and creating a state of hostility among Americans that made normal relations with any Communist government impossible.

Competing Strategies. To meet these challenges, each side fashioned a strategy. The U.S. strategy was called "containment," a term first used by the U.S. diplomat and Soviet expert George KENNAN in arguing that Soviet expansionism might be contained by a strategy of responding to Soviet pressures and probes wherever they occurred. The Kremlin adopted a strategy of retaliation against U.S. containment. During the 1950s the United States sought to anticipate and prevent further Communist gains by maintaining overwhelming military superiority, by forming new alliances in Asia (the SOUTHEAST ASIA TREATY ORGANIZATION) and in the Middle East (the CENTRAL TREATY ORGANIZATION), and by extending economic and military assistance to any country thought to be in danger of Communist attack or subversion.

Relations between the two powers improved somewhat following Joseph STALIN's death in 1953. The wars in Korea and French Indochina were brought to an end, and the first postwar summit meeting of Soviet and Western leaders was held in Geneva in July 1955. But no more than a surface thaw was achieved. After Nikita KHRUSHCHEV's consolidation of power in 1956, the USSR embarked on two new strategies. The first involved economic and military competition with the United States for influence with Arab and Third World countries. This strategy evolved into Soviet support for colonial revolutions, or "wars of national liberation," and for left-wing governments in Guatemala and Cuba. The second strategy, based upon Soviet development of intercontinental ballistic missiles, was to divide the Western powers by renewing Soviet pressure to eject the West from Berlin. In 1955 the WARSAW TREATY ORGANIZATION was established as a response to the rearming of West Germany. A new round of Soviet–American confrontations ensued, all the riskier because now both sides possessed nuclear weapons. The risks were underscored by the Berlin crisis of 1961 and by the CUBAN MISSILE CRISIS of 1962.

Détente. The Nuclear Test Ban Treaty of 1963 was a turning point in the cold war. It seemed to signify that U.S. and Soviet leaders wanted to end a costly and risky struggle that increased the danger of a real war. (See ARMS CONTROL.) Nevertheless, ideological rivalry, competition for influence, and the arms race continued between the two superpowers. U.S. involvement in the VIETNAM WAR, for example, was at its height during the late 1960s. East and West were able, however, to negotiate in a spirit of détente. U.S. rapprochement with China occurred in the 1970s, and the arms race was slowed by the Strategic Arms Limitation (SALT) agreements of 1972 and 1974.

Estrangement and Reconciliation. Relations between the United States and the USSR deteriorated in the late 1970s, especially after the Soviet invasion of Afghanistan in 1979. This revival of the cold war continued in the early years of the Reagan administration, fueled by Soviet support for the Sandinista government of Nicaragua and by America's declared intention to develop an antinuclear STRATEGIC DEFENSE INITIATIVE. With the rise to power of Soviet leader Mikhail Gorbachev in 1985, however, the situation began to change dramatically. Gorbachev's policy of reconciliation with the West, which led to self-determination for the satellite countries of Eastern Europe and the symbolic abandonment (1989) of the BERLIN WALL, finally brought the cold war to an end.

Cole, Nat King   The pianist and singer Nat King Cole, originally named Nathaniel Adams Coles, b. Montgomery, Ala., Mar. 17, 1919, d. Feb. 15, 1965, was the first black singer of popular ballads who was successful with white audiences. Beginning in the 1940s, Cole made numerous hit records with his jazz trio. In 1956–57 he was the only black with a television series, and in the 1960s his film, nightclub, and concert appearances were internationally popular. The soul singer Natalie Cole is his daughter.

Cole, Thomas   Thomas Cole, b. Bolton-le-Moors, England, Feb. 1, 1801, d. Feb. 11, 1848, was the first important landscape painter in the United States and the founder of the HUDSON RIVER SCHOOL. Cole sought to record accurately, although romantically, the forests, mountains, and rivers of the American Northeast. He traveled up the Hudson River and—like the Hudson River school artists after him, including his pupil Frederick Church—was captivated by the scenery, which ranged from the primitive and wild to soft, cultivated fields.

The influences of the English artists Joseph Mallord William Turner and John Martin are evident in such early works as *View near Ticonderoga* (1826; Fort Ticonderoga Museum, Ticonderoga, N.Y.), with its tiny Indian figure standing in a storm beside great rocky cliffs and gnarled trees. Other views are more lyrical yet remain grand in scope and content. After trips (1829–32 and 1841–42)

Thomas Cole's Kaaterskill Falls *(1827) is one of several paintings of the scenic Catskill region of New York State. The work exemplifies the idyllic beauty of the wilderness as depicted by Cole and the other members of the Hudson River school. (Lee B. Anderson Collection, New York City.)*

to Italy and England, the artist turned increasingly to allegorical landscape series, including *The Course of Empire* (1835–36; New York Historical Society, New York City) and *The Voyage of Life* (1840; Munson-Williams-Proctor Institute, Utica, N.Y.). Cole's fine reputation rests on his fresh and original transcriptions of real settings; his allegorical series now seem slightly ponderous.

Cole, Timothy   Timothy Cole, b. London, Apr. 6, 1852, d. May 17, 1931, was an important 19th-century American wood engraver. He worked as an engraver-illustrator for New York periodicals, notably *Scribner's* and *Century Magazine*; in 1883 the latter commissioned his best-known work, a series of wood engravings of European master paintings. Later Cole specialized in wood engravings of paintings in American public and private collections and in developing new techniques of wood engraving.

Coleman, Ornette   Ornette Coleman, b. Fort Worth, Tex., Mar. 9, 1930, is a saxophonist and composer whose ideas have opened new avenues for avant-garde jazz musicians. Largely self-taught, Coleman began playing alto sax in his early teens. His recording *Free Jazz* (1960), a 37-minute improvisation for jazz octet on Coleman-composed themes, set the tone for much of his later work. He has also written completely scored compositions: a 21-movement suite for orchestra (*Skies of America*, 1972), for example.

Coleoptera   see BEETLE

Coleridge, Samuel Taylor   Samuel Taylor Coleridge, b. Oct. 21, 1772, d. July 25, 1834, was a major English romantic poet and essayist. He was associated with William WORDSWORTH, with whom he wrote the LYRICAL BALLADS, an extremely influential collection of poems. He was also a major philosopher and literary critic, opposing the empiricism of 18th-century British philosophy with an idealist system, partly derived from German thinkers, that regarded the mind as active rather than passive in its ability to create through imagination.

The son of a clergyman, Coleridge attended Christ's Hospital in London before entering Cambridge. Dreamy and bookish, he soon wearied of college life and enlisted in the dragoons. In 1794, Coleridge met the equally radical and idealistic poet Robert Southey, and together the two planned a utopian community, or pantisocracy, to be founded on the banks of the Susquehanna River in the United States. In preparation for the community, Coleridge proposed to the sister of Southey's fiancée; when the scheme collapsed he went through with the marriage.

The couple moved to Nether Stowey, Somerset, in 1797 and became friendly with Wordsworth and his sister Dorothy. There the two men composed *Lyrical Ballads* (1798); Coleridge contributed the RIME OF THE ANCIENT MARINER, which, together with his two other magical poems, *Christabel* and "Kubla Khan," established his reputation as a poet and articulated the mysterious, demonic side of British romanticism. In 1798, Coleridge and the Wordsworths traveled to Germany, where Coleridge began his study of German philosophy; in 1800 they settled in England's lake district.

Unhappy with his wife, Coleridge fell in love with Sara Hutchinson, whose sister Wordsworth later married. Coleridge's marital difficulties added to other miseries, for he was by then addicted to laudanum (opium dissolved in alcohol). In 1802, Coleridge published "Dejection: An Ode," the last of his great poems. Thereafter he turned mainly to politics, religion, philosophy, and literary criticism.

From 1816 until his death Coleridge lived at Highgate, in London, where his home became a center for admirers and literary aspirants. In 1817 he published *Biographia Literaria*, a classic of criticism, in which he put forward his ideas on the unifying and synthesizing power of poetry and his theory of the primary and secondary imaginations. Coleridge's influence on poetry, philosophy, and literary criticism is great and undisputed, but the extent of his debt to German philosophy is still debated.

Colette   Sidonie Gabrielle Colette, b. Jan. 28, 1873, d. Aug. 3, 1954, one of the most famous French writers of her day, is known for her insight into human psychology and her ability to convey vivid sensory images. Noted for their style, Colette's novels are characterized by a representation of erotic instinct and sensuous experience and a sympathy with nature, especially flowers and animals.

Colette's insight into character was enhanced by three marriages, numerous love affairs, and experience as a music-hall mime. Her first husband was a music critic and novelist, and her first works, the Claudine novels, were written in collaboration with him and published under his pen name, Willy.

Colette established her reputation as a novelist with *Chéri* (1920; Eng. trans., 1929), which traces the disintegration of an adolescent's affair with an aging courtesan. In its sequel, *The Last of Chéri* (1926; Eng. trans., 1932), the youth commits suicide. *Sido* (1929; Eng. trans., 1953) recalls Colette's childhood. Later works include *The Cat* (1933; Eng. trans., 1936); *Gigi* (1944–45; Eng. trans., 1952), on which Vincente Minnelli based a musical film of the same name in 1958; and *L'Étoile vesper* (The Evening Star, 1947), a reminiscence.

Samuel Taylor Coleridge wrote most of his enduring poetry during six years of close friendship with William Wordsworth. Their collaboration resulted in the Lyrical Ballads *(1798), the poetic manifesto of the English romantic movement. (National Portrait Gallery, London.)*

The French writer Sidonie Gabrielle Colette, known as Colette, reveals sensitivity to and appreciation of nature, sensuality, and human experience in such works as La Vagabonde *(1910),* Chéri *(1920),* Sido *(1929), and* Gigi *(1944–45).*

Colfax, Schuyler   Schuyler Colfax, b. New York City, Mar. 23, 1823, d. Jan. 13, 1885, served (1869–73) as vice-president of the United States under President Ulysses S. GRANT and was disgraced by his involvement with CRÉDIT MOBILIER OF AMERICA. A founder of the Republican party in Indiana, Colfax was elected to the U.S. House of Representatives in 1854. While serving (1863–69) as speaker, Colfax apparently accepted stock in the Crédit Mobilier company, revealed when the Crédit Mobilier scandal broke in 1872; Colfax's political career was ruined.

Colgate University   Colgate University was established in 1819 by Baptists. It is a private nonsectarian liberal arts school for men and women in Hamilton, N.Y., and offers master's degrees in several subjects.

colic [kah'-lik]   Colic is an acute pain resulting from an irritation in such organs as the stomach, intestines, gallbladder, and the ureter duct. It commonly strikes infants who eat too rapidly and swallow air. It also results from emotional stress and overeating and can be a symptom of appendicitis, passage of a gallstone or a kidney stone, bowel or ureter obstruction, or lead or zinc poisoning. Treatment, directed at the cause of the irritation, may include pain relievers.

Coligny, Gaspard de, Seigneur de Châtillon [kohl-een-yee', gahs-pahr' duh, shah-tee-yohn']   Gaspard de Coligny, b. Feb. 16, 1519, d. Aug. 24, 1572, was a leader of the HUGUENOTS in the French Wars of Religion. Coligny was appointed admiral of France in 1552 and subsequently sent expeditions to Brazil and Florida. He earned a military reputation in the wars against the Habsburgs and disputed the honors of victory at Renty (1554) with his rival, François, 2d duc de Guise (see GUISE family).

Coligny converted to Calvinism after his capture in the Battle of St. Quentin in 1557. When the religious wars began in 1562, he joined Louis I, prince de Condé, whom he succeeded as commander of the Huguenot forces in 1569. Although defeated at Moncontour, Coligny led a march across France to defeat the royal army at Arnay-le-Duc in June 1570. Later he won the confidence of Charles IX and advocated a policy of war with Spain. In the SAINT BARTHOLOMEW'S DAY MASSACRE, Coligny was murdered under the supervision of Henri, 3d duc de Guise.

See also: RELIGION, WARS OF.

Colima (state)   Colima (1989 est. pop., 426,225) is a state in west central Mexico on the Pacific coast that includes the Revillagigedo Islands. Its capital is the city of Colima. The state's 5,191-km^2 (2,004-mi^2) area chiefly comprises a coastal plain that rises to the foothills of the Sierra Madre Occidental. The principal economic activities are raising livestock and cultivating rice, sugarcane, coffee, cotton, and maize. Iron, copper, lead, and gold are mined. The state was part of the Aztec kingdom of Colima and was conquered by the Spanish in 1523.

colitis [koh-ly'-tis]   Colitis is a general term for disorders involving the lower INTESTINE, or colon. The most severe, ulcerative colitis, is also called inflammatory bowel disease, a name also applied to CROHN'S DISEASE. Ulcerative colitis produces ulcers in the colon's inner lining, and it can eventually lead to arthritis and liver, skin, and eye damage. It may increase the risk of developing colon and rectal cancers, as well. The condition was once blamed on psychological causes, but evidence now indicates a physiological cause. This cause remains uncertain, but suggestions range from an autoimmune response to microbial agents to environmental and genetic linkages. Symptoms include abdominal pain, a frequent and urgent need to move the bowels, fever, muscle aches, and appetite loss. Drugs used in treatment include steroids and sulfasalazine.

A more common, less severe condition called irritable bowel syndrome (IBS) was once known as mucous colitis and spastic colon. Symptoms can include both DIARRHEA and CONSTIPATION, but the colon does not become inflamed. IBS was once also thought to be psychological in origin, but medical evidence now places blame on hypersensitivity of intestinal nerves. Treatment is mainly through changes in diet and life-style, but drugs may sometimes be used.

For amoeba-caused colitis, see amoebic DYSENTERY.

collage [kuh-lahzh']   Collage, a term derived from the French verb *coller* ("to paste"), is the technique of incorporating such materials as paper, cloth, foil, rope, newspaper, and other printed matter in an oil painting. Related to collage are the *papiers collés* (pasted paper) in which similar materials are combined in drawings. Pablo PICASSO created the first collage in May 1912 (*Still Life*

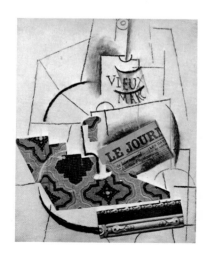

Picasso's Bouteille de vieux marc *(1912) juxtaposed fragments of reality—newspaper and fabric—to evoke the environment of a café. From 1912 to 1914, Picasso and Braque generated an avant-garde movement among French cubist painters, eschewing traditional composition in favor of experimentation with collage. (Musée National d'Art Moderne, Paris.)*

with a *Caned Chair*; Picasso Collection, France), and in September 1912 Georges BRAQUE produced the first *papier collé*; (*The Fruit Dish*; private collection, France). Containing nontraditional and intrinsically worthless materials, collages and *papiers collés* were intentional repudiations of the classical tradition of *belle peinture*, the definition of fine art as one consisting of fine materials. Although Picasso and Braque regarded their collages and *papiers collés* as independent art forms, these immediately proved to be the sources of major stylistic inventions in the development of CUBISM.

During World War I the Dadaists (see DADA) advanced the concept of collage: in 1915 Jean ARP dropped pieces of paper onto a large sheet and pasted these pieces exactly where they fell. This first collage per se (without the addition of painting or drawing) became known as abstract collage.

Concurrent with their first experiments in collage and *papiers collés*, Braque and Picasso began to create sculptures called assemblages, consisting of cardboard, string, wood, wire, and sheet metal. The Italian futurists (see FUTURISM) advocated the use of as many as 20 materials in a single construction. Related to both collage and assemblage is decoupage, the decoration of generally utilitarian objects by completely covering them with cutout paper figures or patterns.

collagen [kahl'-uh-jen]   Collagen, a protein, is the major fibrous constituent of BONE, CARTILAGE, LIGAMENTS, SKIN, TENDONS, and other CONNECTIVE TISSUES. It comprises a group of white inelastic fibers with the tensile strength of wire. The collagen molecule is a group of three coiled polypeptide chains, each composed of about 1,000 amino acid units. Four types of collagen, with differing polypeptide chains, have been identified: collagen found in skin, bone, and tendon; in cartilage; in fetal tissue; and in basement membranes. Biosynthesis within cells leads to the formation of procollagens, followed by cleavage to collagen, and assembly, outside the cell, into the fibril.

collagen disease   Collagen disease is a term applied to a group of diseases that involve abnormalities of the immune system and inflammation of connective tissue and blood vessels. Collagen fibers are a major component of connective tissue. The name rheumatic disease is often used because the most common of all such diseases, rheumatoid arthritis, shows all of the characteristics of this group of diseases. The blood plasma of many patients with collagen disease shows significant levels of autoantibodies (antibodies against the body's own proteins or cells); the resulting antigen-antibody reaction leads to inflammation in many body tissues. Collagen diseases include rheumatoid ARTHRITIS, RHEUMATIC FEVER, LUPUS ERYTHEMATOSUS, dermatomyositis, polyarteritis nodosa, and scleroderma.

Both rheumatoid arthritis and rheumatic fever are characterized by widespread joint pain; rheumatic fever may also result in permanent heart damage. Lupus ery-

thematosis is an autoimmune disease that affects the brain, joints, kidneys, skin, and membranes lining body cavities. Dermatomyositis is most commonly seen as a rash accompanied by muscular pain. In polyarteritis nodosa the walls of arteries are damaged, and in scleroderma thick layers of collagen fibers are deposited; both diseases result in impaired organ function.

Although no satisfactory treatment yet exists for scleroderma, the other collagen diseases may be dealt with medically.

See also: BONE DISEASES.

collard [kahl'-urd]   A nonheading cabbagelike vegetable, collard is grown for its large, edible leaves. Collard, with cabbage, cauliflower, broccoli, Brussels sprouts, and kohlrabi, belongs to the cole crops of the Cruciferae family. All are derived from wild cabbage. Collard is a biennial (but perennial in continuously warm areas) that produces a stout stalk 30–60 cm (11–24 in) tall.

Collard is also called tree cabbage because it has a long stem of up to 60 cm (24 in) that has a crown of cabbagelike, edible greens.

collective bargaining   see LABOR UNION

collective farm   Collective farms are large, state-owned agricultural units found primarily in Communist countries, especially in the Soviet Union, where they were forcibly introduced in the late 1920s, replacing privately owned farms. The collective, or *kolkhoz*, is controlled by the state, which sets production targets and prices for crops—usually grain—and pays workers according to their output. The *kolkhoz* has proved to be an inefficient agricultural system, and supplies of vegetables, poultry, and the like often come from the private plots that individual collective members are now allowed to cultivate.

The People's Republic of China has established huge collective farms, called communes, that often comprise thousands of people living in many villages within a region. Reforms, beginning in the post-Mao era, to allow individual households to contract with their commune to supply a certain quantity of a crop or of such farm animals as poultry or rabbits have been overwhelmingly successful.

See also: COOPERATIVE; KIBBUTZ.

college   see UNIVERSITY

college entrance examinations   see EDUCATION-AL MEASUREMENT AND TESTING

collie   The collie is a herding dog that originated in Scotland. The two varieties of collies are the rough (long-haired) and the smooth (shorthaired). The rough collie was used as a shepherd's dog, whereas the smooth variety probably worked as a drover, guiding cattle and sheep to market. The name *collie* is possibly derived from *colley dog*, a dog used to herd the now-extinct Scottish breed of colley sheep.

The collie has a slender but muscular body; a deep chest; a characteristic long, smooth muzzle; and erect ears, which bend forward near the tips. The tail is moderately long, with a slight upward curve at the end. In the rough collie, the heavy coat forms a mane around the forequarters, with feathering on the legs. There are four color-types: sable and white (brown and white), tricolor (black, white, and brown), blue merle (mottled blue gray and black with white), and white (predominantly white). Collies range from 60 to 66 cm (22 to 26 in) high at the shoulders and weigh from 23 to 34 kg (50 to 75 lb).

The rough-coated collie is a working dog that was used to herd sheep. The smooth collie was used to guide livestock to market.

Collins, Eddie   Hall of Fame baseball player Edward Trowbridge Collins, b. Millerton, N.Y., May 2, 1887, d. Mar. 25, 1951, has long been considered one of his sport's finest 2d basemen. Collins's 25-year American League career (Philadelphia Athletics, 1906–14, 1927–30; Chicago White Sox, 1915–26) yielded 3,311 hits, a .333 batting average, and 743 stolen bases. He hit over .340 in 4 different decades, had 10 seasons with 40 or more stolen bases, and had an on-base percentage of at least .400 in 13 different seasons—a high level of performance over a remarkably long time. Collins stole 14 bases in World Series play, a record shared with Lou Brock.

Collins, Judy   Singer-songwriter Judy Marjorie Collins, b. Seattle, Wash., May 1, 1939, began her career during the FOLK MUSIC revival of the late 1950s. By the mid-1960s Collins was singing her own compositions—protest songs and lyrical romantic ballads—as well as folk songs. She was actively involved in voter drives in the South and in the Vietnam War protest movement. In 1974 she produced and codirected the award-winning film *Antonia: Portrait of a Woman*, about the career of her childhood piano teacher, conductor Antonia Brico. *Trust Your Heart*, her autobiography, was published in 1987.

Collins, Michael (astronaut)   The American astronaut Michael Collins, b. Rome, Italy, Oct. 31, 1930, flew as command-module pilot of APOLLO *11*, the first manned lunar-landing mission. Collins served as an air force test pilot and was selected as an astronaut in 1963. His first mission in space was as pilot of GEMINI *10* (1966) with commander John YOUNG. Following an around-the-world tour and an appearance before a joint session of Congress in the wake of his 1969 moon mission, Collins resigned from the air force and NASA to become assistant secretary of state for public affairs in 1970. In 1971 he was named director of the National Air and Space Museum of the Smithsonian Institution, Washington, D.C., and was responsible for developing exhibits for the $40-million museum's opening in 1976. From 1978 to 1980 he was undersecretary of the Smithsonian. Collins's autobiography, *Carrying the Fire* (1974), provides an inside view of the astronaut corps.

Michael Collins, pilot of the command module Columbia *during the first lunar landing, walked in space at what was then a record altitude in 1966. Following the dramatic Apollo 11 flight in 1969, Collins resigned from the military and NASA.*

Collins, Michael   (Irish revolutionary statesman) Michael Collins, b. Oct. 16, 1890, d. Aug. 22, 1922, was one of the founders of the Irish Free State. He participated in the EASTER RISING of 1916, and after the founding (1919) of Dáil Éireann, the revolutionary assembly, he served as minister of finance in the revolutionary government and as one of the leaders of the IRISH REPUBLICAN

ARMY. In 1921 he participated at the conference that negotiated the treaty creating the Irish Free State. Together with Arthur GRIFFITH, he led the pro-treaty side when SINN FEIN split over acceptance of the treaty. During the ensuing civil war, Collins was killed in an ambush.

Collins, Wilkie   Wilkie Collins, b. Jan. 8, 1824, d. Sept. 23, 1889, is usually considered to be the first English detective novelist. His early novels appeared in the magazine *Household Words,* published by his friend Charles Dickens. A brilliant though melodramatic storyteller, Collins wrote 25 novels. The most noteworthy are *The Woman in White* (1860) and the popular *The Moonstone* (1868).

Collins, William   William Collins, b. Dec. 25, 1721, d. June 12, 1759, is often deemed the greatest English lyric poet of the 18th century and a precursor of the romantics. In his lifetime his reputation rested on his *Persian Eclogues* (1742), but his later fame derives from such odes as "To the Evening" and "To Simplicity," poems admired for their concise language and imaginative qualities. In about 1750, after suffering from mental illness, Collins gave up writing.

Collodi, Carlo   [kohl-loh'-dee]   Carlo Collodi was the pseudonym of Carlo Lorenzini, b. Nov. 24, 1826, d. Oct. 26, 1890, an Italian journalist and author of the children's book *The Adventures of Pinocchio,* first published in 1880 as a magazine serial (see PINOCCHIO). Collodi wrote political satire during the campaigns for the unification of Italy. He turned to children's literature in 1875, translating the fairy tales of Charles Perrault, and publishing his first story, "Giannettino," in 1876.

colloidal state   [kuh-loyd'-ul]   A colloidal state is a condition in which one substance is dispersed in another. Colloids are distinguished from suspensions essentially by the size of the dispersed particles: colloidal particulate size is approximately 1 to 500×10^{-7} cm. Colloidal particles do not settle and cannot be filtered by ordinary techniques (in contrast to suspensions). Colloids differ from solutions (in which the particles are of molecular size) as well, in that the dispersed particles of colloids cannot pass through the fine pores of membranes and cannot therefore be separated out by the technique known as DIALYSIS. Because of their size, colloid particles diffuse slowly.

Colloids may be classified according to the original phases of their constituents. A solid dispersed in a liquid is called a sol; a solid or semisolid colloidal system is a gel. An emulsion consists of one liquid dispersed in another; an aerosol, such as smoke or mist, consists of a solid or liquid dispersed in a gas. Some alloys are solid-in-solid colloids.

Collor de Mello, Fernando   [coh'-yohr deh meh'-yoh]   Fernando Affonso Collor de Mello, b. Aug. 12, 1949, was inaugurated as Brazil's first popularly elected president in 29 years on Mar. 15, 1990. He studied economics at the University of Brasília, became president of his family's media group in 1978, served (1982–86) in the national legislature, and was elected governor of Alagoas state in 1986. He formed the National Reconstruction party in 1989 and campaigned on a populist platform. The youngest president in Brazilian history, he pledged to cut inflation and government bureaucracy.

collotype   Collotype is a photomechanical, lithographic printing process that can reproduce continuous variations of tone without using any form of mechanical screening. (Normally, a screen is used for a halftone reproduction.) The collotype process is especially suitable for short-run reproduction of works of art or book inserts in one or more colors. The process involves the action of light on a gelatin film placed on a plate-glass base. Light passing through a negative onto the plate hardens the gelatin; the hardened parts retain ink, whereas the soft parts repel ink.

Colman, Ronald   British actor Ronald Colman, b. Feb. 9, 1891, d. May 19, 1958, was a romantic leading man in silent and sound films during the 1920s, '30s, and '40s. His films include *Beau Geste* (1926), *A Tale of Two Cities* (1935), *Lost Horizon* (1937), *Random Harvest* (1942), and *A Double Life* (1948; Academy Award).

Colmar   Colmar (1982 pop., 62,483) is the capital of Haut-Rhin department of northeastern France. It is situated on the Lauch River about 25 km (16 mi) west of the German border. A road and rail hub located on the Logelbach Canal, the city is also an important textile manufacturing center. Tourists are attracted by the many medieval buildings, including a 13th-century Dominican convent, now an art museum, which houses the famous Isenheim altar (c.1512–15) by Matthias GRÜNEWALD. First mentioned in written sources in the 9th century, Colmar became a free city of the Holy Roman Empire in 1226. It became the capital of French Alsace in 1673, but it was held by Germany from 1871 to 1919 and again during World War II.

Cologne   Cologne (German: Köln) is a city in northwestern Germany in the state of North Rhine–Westphalia. Located on the west bank of the RHINE RIVER, it has a population of 927,500 (1987 est.). The surrounding area is fertile and intensively cultivated. To the west are brown coal deposits that supply much of the city's energy demands; the steel works of the Ruhr to the north produce materials for the city's metal industries. The site has long

The Cologne Cathedral, with its soaring twin spires, dominates other buildings nearby. A fine example of Gothic architecture, the cathedral sustained only partial damage during World War II, when the city was heavily bombed.

been a crossroads of trade and travel north-south along the Rhine and over the belt of open country extending west into Belgium and east across Germany into Poland.

Contemporary City. Heavily damaged by bombing during World War II, Cologne has been rebuilt and is again an important manufacturing center noted for metalworking, mechanical engineering, chemicals, and glassworking. It also continues to make Kölnisches Wasser (eau de cologne), although perfume is no longer among its most important products. The Gothic Cologne Cathedral, large and impressive, was begun in 1248 and completed in 1880. The University of Cologne was founded in 1388.

History. Cologne originated in about AD 50 as a small, fortified town (Colonia Agrippina) on the frontier of the Roman Empire. The site is occupied today by the inner city. The medieval town grew around this nucleus and became one of the most important centers of commerce in Western Europe. It formed part of the lands of the archbishop of Cologne but freed itself from his direct control in 1288. It exercised jurisdiction over the river, and all passing ships were required to stop and offer their cargoes for sale. The city suffered severely during the Thirty Years' War and the later conflicts of the 17th and 18th centuries, and its importance declined. In 1794 the French conquered the area, but after the Napoleonic Wars, Cologne was handed over to Prussia (1815). Its economic growth dates from this time, and it was especially strong between 1870 and 1920.

Colombia   Colombia is a republic located in northwestern South America. Bordered by Ecuador and Peru on the south, Brazil and Venezuela on the east, and Panama on the northwest, it has extensive coastlines on both the Pacific (about 1,300 km/800 mi) and the Caribbean (1,600 km/1,000 mi). Colombia is the fourth largest country in Latin America; approximately 13% of the nation's total population live in the capital city of BOGOTÁ. In the early 1970s, industry surpassed agriculture as the major contributor to the gross domestic product, but agriculture, particularly coffee, continues to be Colombia's basic source of wealth. By the 1990s, however, the illegal trade in drugs was thought to exceed legal exports and threatened the nation's stability.

Land

A country of contrasts, Colombia has both snowcapped peaks and tropical regions. Its topography is dominated by three Andean ranges that cross the country from southwest to northeast. The Western Cordillera has five peaks over 4,000 m (13,000 ft) high, but the Central Cordillera is higher, with six snowcapped peaks over 4,900 m (16,000 ft). The Eastern Cordillera, longest of the three, branches off into Venezuela, and its highest elevations are above 5,000 m (17,000 ft). Pico Cristóbal Colón, the highest point (5,775 m/18,947 ft), lies to the north. Two major rivers, the Cauca and Magdalena, run through the valleys on each side of the Central Cordillera. The mountains divide Colombia into three major regions—the highland core, the coastal lowlands, and the eastern plains.

In the highlands, the Magdalena Valley includes important basins of settlements, most notably Cundinamarca, where Bogotá is located. Set in the Central Cordillera to the west of the Magdalena are two of Colombia's most important cities, MEDELLÍN (the second largest) and Manizales. Farther to the south in the Cauca Valley, Colombia's richest farmland, is CALI. The Pacific lowlands are a sparsely populated, swampy strip served by the port of Buenaventura. Of greater importance are the Caribbean lowlands, where the bulk of the nation's commerce moves through the ports of SANTA MARTA, BARRANQUILLA, and CARTAGENA. The lightly populated *llanos* ("plains") in the east constitute nearly 60% of the country's total area and give way to unexplored tropical jungle in the southeast.

Climate. As with most countries near the equator, elevation is the decisive climatic factor. Areas under 915 m (3,000 ft) constitute the hot zone (*tierra caliente*), and from 915 to 2,000 m (3,000 to 6,500 ft) above sea level is the temperate zone (*tierra templada*). Regions extending to 3,000 m (10,000 ft) are the cold zone (*tierra fría*); the bleak and treeless zone called the *páramos* continues to 4,500 m (15,000 ft), above which is the zone of eternal snow (*nevado*). The hot zone is marked by heavy annual rainfall (over 7,600 mm/300 in) along the Pacific; the temperate zone—in which 40% of the population live—has moderate rainfall and a mean annual temperature of 18°–24° C (65°–75° F). Temperature range in the cold zone is 10°–18° C (50°–65° F), and there is heavier

REPUBLIC OF COLOMBIA

Land: Area: 1,138,914 km^2 (439,737 mi^2). Capital and largest city: Bogota (1985 pop., 3,982,941).

People: Population (1990 est.): 31,800,000. Density: 27.9 persons per km^2 (72.3 per mi^2). Distribution (1989): 67% urban, 33% rural. Official language: Spanish. Major religion: Roman Catholicism

Government: Type: republic. Legislature: Senate, House of Representatives. Political subdivisions: 23 departments, 24 intendancies, 5 commissariats, 1 special district.

Economy: GNP (1988): $37.2 billion; $1,240 per capita. Labor distribution (1981): services—53%; agriculture—26%; industry—21%. Foreign trade (1987): imports—$4.3 billion; exports—$4.6 billion. Currency: 1 Colombian peso = 100 centavos.

Education and Health: Literacy (1987 est.): 88% of adult population. Universities (1987): 34. Hospital beds (1983): 46,651. Physicians (1984) 23,250. Life expectancy (1989): women—68; men—64. Infant mortality (1989): 54 per 1,000 live births.

rainfall there during the two wet seasons (April to June and September to December).

Resources. Almost 95% of the world's emeralds come from Colombia, which is also Latin America's most important gold producer. The petroleum reserves were bolstered by a major find in 1984. Coal deposits are the largest in Latin America. Colombia is also rich in platinum.

People

Most Colombians are mestizos (of mixed Indian and Spanish descent) or mulattoes (a mixture of black and white). Whites constitute an estimated 20% of the population, blacks 4%, Indians 1%. Historically, whites have held most positions of power. Descent from an important family remains a crucial qualification for membership in the traditional socioeconomic elite, which dominates national life. However, social mobility, particularly movement into the middle class, has increased in recent times. Most people speak Spanish, and 95% of the population are Roman Catholic.

Patterns of settlement have changed since World War II. Urbanization has continued: a solid majority of Colombians now live in cities. The rate of population growth increased from 2% annually in the 1940s to over 3% by the end of the 1970s. Through the decade of the 1980s a decline in the birthrate indicated that growth, at least in the near future, will be smaller. Illegal migration into bordering Venezuela has been heavy, with many thousands of Colombians employed there.

Although primary education is free, educational facilities are limited, and 20% of urban children and 40% of rural children do not attend primary schools. Although Colombia has a large intellectual community concentrated in the urban centers, it suffers from a shortage of skilled technicians.

The best-known Colombian writer is Gabriel GARCÍA MÁRQUEZ, who received the Nobel Prize in 1982. (See also LATIN AMERICAN LITERATURE.)

Economic Activity

Colombia's steady economic growth was interrupted in the mid-1980s, particularly by a large foreign debt and a negative trade balance. Subsequently, however, despite internal violence, the economic picture brightened for the 1990s; the country reached agreement on the debt and again attained a trade surplus.

Colombia is the world's second largest producer of coffee (after Brazil), and coffee regularly accounts for more than half of export revenues. Following coffee in agricultural economic importance are sugarcane, cotton, and rice. Bananas are raised along the coasts; corn is the most widely grown crop.

Although industry employs somewhat less of the labor force than agriculture, it now makes a larger contribution to the national income. The manufacture of consumer goods has become particularly important. Textiles are the leading industrial export. The major industrial centers are Bogotá, Medellín, and Cali. Tourism declined during the

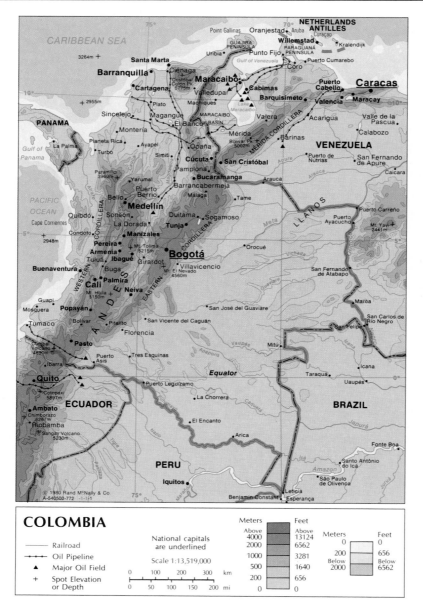

COLOMBIA

———	Railroad		National capitals are underlined
•+•+•	Oil Pipeline		
▲	Major Oil Field		Scale 1:13,519,000
+	Spot Elevation or Depth		

Meters	Feet
Above 4000	Above 13124
2000	6562
1000	3281
500	1640
200	656
0	0

Meters	Feet
0	0
200 Below 2000	656 Below 6562

0   100   200   300 km
0   50 100 150   200 mi

© 1980 Rand McNally & Co
A-540500-772 -1-1/-1

1980s. Despite relatively high unemployment and inflation (and domestic violence from right and left), Colombia had one of the most dynamic economies in Latin America during the 1980s. It also suffered severely from the terrorist activities of international drug traffickers.

Government

Colombia is a republic headed by a president elected every four years by universal adult (18 or older) suffrage. The president heads the cabinet. The bicameral congress consists of a senate and chamber of representatives, both of whose members serve four-year terms. The two leading political parties are the Liberals and Conservatives.

History

Precolonial Colombia was home to a variety of Indian cultures, notably the Chibcha, dominant in the east-central highlands. The first Spanish settlements were established in 1509, and in 1538, after the interior had been conquered, Bogotá was established. The area became the Spanish colony of NEW GRANADA, which in 1717 became a viceroyalty.

In 1810 the struggle for independence began. After 1812, it was led by Simón BOLÍVAR. The movement was successful, and in 1819 the independent republic of Gran Colombia was declared. Ruled by Bolívar and Francisco SANTANDER, it included the present-day states of Colombia, Ecuador, Panama, and Venezuela. By 1830, however, this republic had disintegrated, and Colombia (with Panama), Ecuador, and Venezuela became independent nations. During this period the Liberal and Conservative political parties were founded, composed of the followers of Bolívar and Santander, respectively.

The rest of the 19th century was characterized by rivalry between the Liberal and Conservative factions, resulting in a series of armed struggles. It culminated in a

(Above) *Farm workers tend pineapples on a plantation in Colombia, where agriculture is a principal source of employment.* (Left) *Cartagena's cobbled streets wind through the old section of the city, founded as a Spanish port more than 400 years ago.*

Bogotá lies at the eastern edge of a sloping plateau about 2,600 m (8,530 ft) above sea level and is flanked by two peaks of the Eastern Cordillera of the Andes. Air travel to this long hard-to-reach city has stimulated growth and modernization.

bloody civil war from 1899 to 1903, during which Panama rebelled and achieved its independence with aid from the United States. Conflict between the two parties continued, this time resulting in *la violencia* from 1948 to 1957, in which more than 250,000 persons died. In 1953 a military coup occurred, and Gen. Gustavo Rojas Pinilla became dictator. His repressive policies failed to halt the strife, but the warring parties finally came together in opposition to his corrupt regime.

In 1957, after the overthrow of Rojas Pinilla by the military, the Liberals and Conservatives agreed to the formation of a National Front government. In the ensuing period the presidency alternated between the two parties, and all other public offices were divided equally. In 1974 the National Front ended, and fully competitive elections were held. In 1978, Dr. Turbay Ayala, a Liberal, was elected president. His government imposed tough security laws, which, however, failed to stem a tide of Marxist guerrilla activity and terrorism, allegedly abetted by Cuba. In the 1982 elections the Liberals won a majority in Congress, but a rift in the party allowed the election of a Conservative, Belisario Betancur Cuartas, as president. He faced two disparate crises in November 1985: guerrillas seized the national courts building in Bogotá and about 100 persons died as government forces recaptured it, and a volcanic eruption in the north unleashed mud slides and floods that killed over 20,000. Virgilio Barco Vargas, a Liberal, was elected president in 1986. In 1989, as drug-related violence escalated, he declared war on the drug traffickers. He seized assets, detained thousands, and reinstated the U.S.-Colombian extradition treaty (Colombian cartels controlled about 80% of the cocaine smuggled into the United States). Barco's successor, the Liberal César Gavira Trujillo, assumed office in August 1990. He offered lenient treatment to drug traffickers, and several important drug ringleaders had surrendered by early 1991.

Colombo

Colombo, the capital, largest city, and chief port of Sri Lanka, is located near the mouth of the Kelani River on Sri Lanka's southwest coast. The population is 683,000 (1986 est.). Colombo has one of the largest artificial harbors in the world; tea, cocoa, rubber, and coconuts are exported. There are steel mills and oil refineries in Colombo, which is also a center for gem merchants.

The oldest section of Colombo is the Pettah, or native market. Along the western edge of the city is the Galle Face, a park and promenade. Government buildings are near the port section, and the residential areas stretch inland. The Colombo campus of the University of Sri Lanka was built in 1967; there are also two Buddhist universities and a technical college.

Colombo's original Sinhalese name, *Kalanotto* (for "Kelani Ferry"), was corrupted by Arabs to Kolambu and by the Portuguese to Colombo. Settled as early as 543 BC, Colombo had a long succession of colonial rulers. The Portuguese arrived in 1517, followed by the Dutch (1658) and English (1796).

Colón

[koh-lohn'] Colón is the capital city of Colón province in north central Panama. Situated on Manzanillo Island at the north (Atlantic) entrance to the Panama Canal, it has a population of 58,749 (1989 est.), making it Panama's third largest city. Founded in 1850 as Aspinwall, for one of the builders of the Panama Railroad, it was named Colón (for Columbus) in 1890. It remained a small settlement until construction of the canal began in 1904. It has a tropical climate, and the economy is based on trading fruit and hardwoods.

colon

see INTESTINE

colonial styles in North America

The term *colonial style* is properly applied to the fine and decorative arts produced between 1620 and 1776 in the English and French colonies of North America. It is not used to describe the art of the Spanish and Portuguese colonies of the New World. This art is discussed elsewhere in the encyclopedia under LATIN AMERICAN ART AND ARCHITECTURE and SPANISH MISSIONS. *Colonial style* evokes an image of houses, objects, and paintings that are technologically primitive, unsophisticated in design, and plain in appearance. This popular misconception has its roots in the Victorian centennial (1876) search for a native style rooted in an imaginary golden age of economic honesty, political virtue, and careful craftsmanship. The revival of "colonial" design was greatly influenced by the contemporaneous ARTS AND CRAFTS MOVEMENT and was more a creation suited to contemporary tastes than it was an authentic re-creation of a past aesthetic.

Many of the buildings and objects made during the colonial period in North America indeed were plain and

The Governor's Palace in Williamsburg, Va., originally constructed between 1706 and 1720, was destroyed by fire in 1780. The colonial Georgian structure was reconstructed during the 1920s.

This teakettle and stand, designed by the Philadelphia silversmith Joseph Richardson, exemplifies rococo style in colonial North America. (c.1750; Garvan Collection, Yale University Art Gallery, New Haven, Conn.)

utilitarian, but those which were prized at the time of their creation and which have been preserved are often elaborate and ambitious. The effort was clearly not to produce plainness but to create an effect of richness with an emphasis on pure form and pleasing and correct proportions. Imported raw materials such as silver and mahogany, imported finished materials such as textiles and ceramics, and imported design books such as James GIBBS's *Book of Architecture* (1728) and Thomas CHIPPENDALE's *The Gentleman and Cabinet Maker's Director* (1754) reveal the desire for things suited to the taste, ambitions, and self-image of a wealthy mercantile gentry that was aesthetically as well as economically tied to Europe, especially to England.

American design in the 17th and 18th centuries, however, was not mere aping of foreign forms and motifs. Craftsmen and artists recombined elements in distinctively American ways, composing designs that were often highly original and successful. Differences in patronage, social needs, craft practices, and materials created strong regional schools with recognizably local forms and aesthetic vocabularies.

The South. Most closely following the social and topographical model of rural England, the southern colonies eschewed urban development and built country houses after the practice and, in some cases, the designs of the British squirearchy and their architects. The wealthy planters even furnished their homes with London-made articles. About 100 southern homes from the pre-Revolutionary period survive. Mount Airy (1758–62; Richmond County, Va.), built by John Ariss for the Tayloe family and a fine example of its type, is a symmetrical, rectangular sandstone block with framing dependencies. Its facade and plan are based on a plate from Gibbs's *Book of Architecture*.

The Middle Colonies. In the middle colonies social, economic, and topographical factors contributed to the early development of cities and to the concentration of

craftsmen and patrons in a manner that encouraged the rapid development of the arts. As in the South, the gentry built stately Palladian buildings such as Christ Church (1727–54) in Philadelphia, based on Gibbs's Church of Saint Martin-in-the-Fields (1726) in London and Mount Pleasant (1761–62; Fairmount Park, Philadelphia).

The interiors of such houses were modestly proportioned but richly adorned with furnishings provided by skilled cabinetmakers and silversmiths. Characteristic of late BAROQUE or Queen Anne design is the faceted teapot (c.1730; Yale University Art Gallery, New Haven, Conn.) by Peter van Dyck of New York. Emphasis is placed on elegant form, also a primary design element of a contemporary Philadelphia armchair (c.1740; Winterthur Museum, Winterthur, Del.). The succeeding ROCOCO period is exemplified by the teakettle on a stand (c.1750; Yale University Art Gallery, New Haven, Conn.) made by Joseph Richardson in Philadelphia; its inverted "double bellied" form and asymmetrical rocaille ornament epitomize the style and the high level of technical design achieved by colonial artisans. Its counterpart in furniture is the rococo Philadelphia highboy (c.1770; Metropolitan Museum of Art, New York City), with pleasing architectural proportions and fashionable rococo Chippendale ornament.

In painting, Pennsylvania nurtured young Benjamin WEST, who later distinguished himself in London as a history painter and as president of the Royal Academy. The native strain is best represented by the graceful portraits of Charles Willson Peale (see PEALE FAMILY).

New England. The arts flourished with great vigor in New England. Even the earliest period produced such extraordinary examples as the portraits *Capt. John Freake* and *Mrs. Elizabeth Freake and Baby Mary* (c.1674; Worcester Art Museum, Worcester, Mass.). Full of color and elegant surface pattern, these paintings, based on

This elegant covered glass goblet, designed and engraved by John Frederick Amelung, reveals the technical expertise of the early American craftsman. Although glassware was manufactured in North America during the 17th century, it was not until the mid-18th century that American wares attained a high level of artistry. (1788; Metropolitan Museum of Art, New York.)

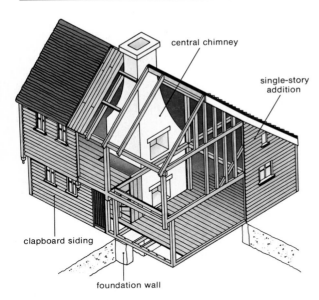

The saltbox house, a standard architectural design of 17th-century New England, was derived from the colonial two-story home with a lean-to-addition. Employing the heavy-timber construction common in England, the house was framed with heavy oak beams and filled in with plaster, brick or other material and sheathed with clapboards. The typical colonial house was built about a central chimney, with four large rooms in the two-story block and a kitchen, pantry, and extra sleeping area located in the single-story addition.

(Right) This mahogany highboy, crafted in Philadelphia by an unknown cabinetmaker, has the graceful proportions and exquisite ornamentation that made Philadelphia's furniture among the finest in the colonies. (c.1770; Metropolitan Museum of Art, New York.)

(Below) The portrait Mrs. Elizabeth Freake and Baby Mary was painted by the artist known only as the Freake master, in the flat, linear style of Elizabethan portraits. (c.1674; Worcester Art Museum, Worcester, Mass.)

the Elizabethan court style, were by an anonymous artist called the Freake master.

The bold undulating surfaces of the baroque period remained popular in 18th-century America, developing into such native designs as the desk and bookcase (1765–85; Yale University Art Gallery, New Haven, Conn.) made in the Townsend-Goddard workshops of Newport, R.I., one of the most original and urbane designs in colonial art. Similarly baroque in inspiration is the covered goblet (1784–95; Metropolitan Museum, New York) made in the glasshouse of John F. Amelung in New Bremen, Md., in finely etched, clear lead glass. The bold patterns and bright primary colors of baroque taste are also evident in crewelwork (linen embroidered with colored woolen threads). As in most 18th-century design, the elements are drawn from tradition, design books, and fancy, but rarely from nature.

John Singleton COPLEY, the largely self-taught Boston artist, was able to paint portraits as fine as those produced in London. *Mary and Elizabeth Royall* (c.1758; Museum of Fine Arts, Boston) demonstrates the full range of his talents.

Canada. Settled by the French and by clerics (until its conquest by Britain in 1759), Canada produced primarily ecclesiastical-related art of continental European derivation during the colonial period. Congruent with the mission to convert the inhabitants, the church imported

skilled artisans, primarily woodcarvers and gilders, to decorate their churches. The most significant example is Noël Levasseur's baroque altar wall (1680–1740) in the Ursuline Convent in Quebec City, composed of carefully proportioned architectural elements and statuettes and given a dramatic effect by the contrasts of black on white with decorative gilding.

Although all of these colonial art objects are basically useful, the aesthetic element is as strong as the utilitarian element in overall design and choice of materials. Rooted in basic needs, the style of these objects points to a self-conscious and accomplished—if pragmatic—culture.

colonialism   Colonialism is a system of control by a country over a dependent area or people outside its borders. Some colonies have been established by the migration of settlers from the colonizing country, as in the British colonies in North America, Australia, and New Zealand. Some colonies have been founded by religious groups fleeing persecution, such as the PILGRIMS who settled in Massachusetts. Other colonies were organized by groups of merchants or businessmen, such as the British, Dutch, and French EAST INDIA COMPANIES. European colonialism from the 15th to the 19th century was usually associated with economic aims; it was linked with the IMPERIALISM of the new nation-states and governed by the economic policies of MERCANTILISM.

Colonialism began with the ancient Phoenicians, who established colonies around the shores of the Mediterranean as early as the 10th century BC. The ancient Greeks and Romans were energetic colonizers. In the Middle Ages Venice and Genoa had colonies on the banks of the Black Sea and on islands in the Aegean. Modern colonialism is thought of as beginning after the discovery of America and of the sea route to the Far East, when the new European states began to found colonies abroad (see BRITISH EMPIRE; FRENCH COLONIAL EMPIRE).

Early Modern Colonialism. During the early modern period two distinct types of colonialism occurred in the Atlantic zone and in Asia. In the Atlantic zone, including North and South America and southern Africa, colonies of people were established. In Central and South America, which were colonized by Spain and Portugal, Europeans settled in the midst of indigenous populations. In North America, the native population was far less numerous than in Latin America. As the English and French (and to a lesser extent, Spanish, Dutch, and Swedish) colonists moved in, the native Americans were pushed aside or eliminated. In southern Africa in the 18th century, Dutch colonists (later called Afrikaners) drove the Khoikhoi and San back toward the desert zones, but were not able to prevent the more numerous Bantus from occupying a great part of what is now the Republic of South Africa.

In its early phases, colonialism in India and Indonesia was different from that of the Atlantic area. There was no massive immigration of European colonists. The colonial powers—first Portugal, then Holland and England—established commercial agencies on the coasts, and the civilizations of India and Indonesia felt little impact from

Europe. In China and Japan, where the Portuguese and Dutch established some agencies, there was even less European influence.

19th-Century Colonialism. In America the colonial empires began to disintegrate at the end of the 18th century. The American Revolution ended British rule in what is now the United States, and revolts in Latin America established the independence of most of that area by 1825. Britain and other European nations entered a new colonial era in the 19th century. To replace its losses in North America, Britain soon acquired Australia and New Zealand, which, with Canada (the British North American provinces that remained loyal during the American Revolution), became Britain's chief colonies of settlement. In the course of the 19th century these colonies became self-governing, and in the 20th century they were recognized as dominions (autonomous units with status equal to Britain) within the COMMONWEALTH OF NATIONS.

The Industrial Revolution of the 19th century greatly increased the military and technological power of the European countries, enabling them to extend their rule over areas with large indigenous populations. To regions in Asia and Africa where previously there had been only commercial posts, the European nations now sent troops along with commercial agents, officials, and Christian missionaries. These areas were turned into markets for Europe's industrial products and suppliers of its raw materials. By mid-century the British controlled virtually all of India; the Dutch asserted similar control over Indonesia, then known as the Netherlands East Indies; and the French controlled Indochina. The entire continent of Africa, except for Ethiopia and Liberia, was parceled out among the European powers after the Conference of Berlin in 1885.

The colonial powers abolished slavery in the regions they controlled and laid the basis for economic development. The administration of both the economy and the government, however, remained in European hands.

The Coming of Independence. The weakening of the European imperial powers during World War II brought about the end of colonialism in Africa and Asia. The local elites sought to take power into their own hands and succeeded in doing so after political struggle and revolution that was sometimes, as in Algeria and Indochina, quite prolonged and bloody. The new states all wanted to industrialize and looked to other countries to furnish the necessary technology. The United States and the USSR offered large-scale economic assistance. Some former colonial powers also extended aid. The new relationship between the developing countries and those providing aid meant a degree of continued dependence even though the old political bonds had been severed. Sometimes aid was accompanied by strong political and military influence. This new state of affairs has been called neocolonialism, usually by left-wing groups in the former colonies.

color   Color is a sensation that is aroused when light falls on the retina of the eye. Light may be perceived either as originating directly from a light source or as re-

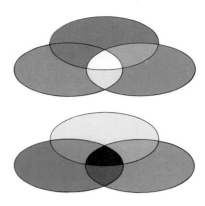

Combining colored lights is called additive mixing (top). *Depending on the proportions used, the three primary colors of light—red, green, and blue—combine to yield any color, including white. Subtractive mixing occurs when artists' pigments are combined* (bottom). *Here the primary pigments—red, yellow, and blue—can also be mixed to produce different colors.*

flected light. White light is perceived as colorless because the eye is completely attuned to the characteristics of such light, and only a neutral color sensation is aroused by it. Color perception depends on the different degrees to which various wavelengths of light stimulate the eye.

Spectral Colors. White light can be dispersed by a prism, which resolves a beam of white light into its colored components, the SPECTRUM. Visible LIGHT is ELECTROMAGNETIC RADIATION within a wavelength range of about 410 nm (nanometers) to about 770 nm. The various spectral colors may be characterized by their wavelengths within this range.

An object that reflects only the part of white light between 540 nm and 600 nm will appear yellow. Yellow light may also be generated by combining green and orange red light (the colors adjacent to yellow in the spectrum) or by combining all colors except blue. Blue is called the complementary color of yellow; the other colors also have complements. Colored light mixed with light of its complementary color appears white. The actual color sensation produced by an object is determined by a combination of the composition of the incident light and the object's reflective properties. An object illuminated by blue light can, of course, reflect only blue light. The color of the object will then be observed only as shades of blue or black. For example, yellow and orange objects reflect almost no blue light and, under these circumstances, will appear black.

Definition and Classification. Color has so many meanings for different observers that a strict definition is difficult, if not impossible. The chemist is conscious of color as a quality concerning a pigment or a dye; the psychologist describes color in terms of visual perception; and the physicist may define color in terms of qualities such as the wavelength of light and its intensity.

A description of color has its foundations in attempts to classify colors. The basic distinction is made between those colors with hue and those without it. The members of the first group—red, orange, yellow, green, blue, and so on—are termed chromatic colors; those of the second group—black, gray, and white—are called achromatic colors.

The next classification divides the chromatic colors into groups by hue, that is, all reds are together, all blues are together, and so on. In doing so a continuous circle of overlapping hues is formed, ranging from red through orange to yellow, and then through green to blue and violet. Violet overlaps red, thus completing the circle.

Achromatic colors are arranged in a single series from black through the grays to white. Some of the chromatic colors of a single hue are darker or lighter, and it is possible to match each degree of lightness to gray of the achromatic colors. This classification is known as brightness, or luminance.

If a particularly vivid hue is mixed with an achromatic color of the same brightness, the resulting stimulus depends on the relative amounts of these two components. This characteristic of color is called saturation. The achromatic colors have zero saturation; the saturation of chromatic colors has a value between zero and one.

All the colors can be classified to form a color tree by placing colors of the same brightness on a disk, with the hues placed consecutively around the disk and with the saturation increasing outwardly from the center.

Primary Colors. The human eye is not a selective instrument; it cannot distinguish two superimposed colors as such. Taking advantage of this fact, in 1801 Thomas YOUNG, and later Hermann von HELMHOLTZ, found that it

The Munsell color system (A) *describes colors in terms of value, hue, and chroma. The value scale denotes a color's degree of darkness. It is measured along a cylinder* (1) *in steps ranging from perfect black to perfect white. Hues are indicated on a band* (2). *Chroma, the extent to which a color differs from gray, is represented by its distance from the cylinder* (3). *The band* (2) *shows different hues with the same value and chroma. Wedges* (4) *show the same hue with two different values and varying chroma. Ten colors represent the basic hues* (B).

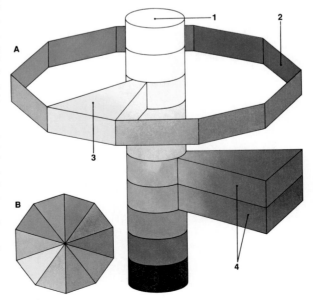

was possible to match any given colored light, using a combination of three primary light sources. Occasionally one color was found that could not be matched by direct addition of the three primaries. It was always found, however, that if one of the primaries was added to the given color, the other two primaries could produce a color match with the combination of the sample and the third primary. The selection of the three primaries is arbitrary, and the primaries need not be monochromatic sources. Artists choose red, blue, and yellow pigments as their three primary colors, but red, blue, and green light is used in color television.

color blindness   Color blindness is the inability to recognize the colors red, green, blue-violet, or some combination of these. Anomalopia is partial color blindness, in which both red and green are poorly recognized. Color blindness is almost always an inherited disorder linked to the X chromosome, which contains the genes that determine male sex characteristics. Thus, the problem occurs primarily in males, with approximately 8 percent of all men (only 0.44 percent of women) being color-deficient (see EYE DISEASES).

Degenerative diseases or injury to the optic nerve or retina may also result in color blindness. Color-vision testing cards, such as the Ishihara, and disks, such as the Farnsworth D-15, determine the type and severity of the color defect.

Color-blind people must take certain precautions; for example, special attention must be given in determining traffic signals. Many branches of the armed forces do not recruit people who have color blindness, and certain occupations are not practical for them, such as fashion designing.

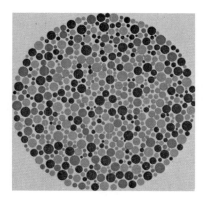

Color blindness may be diagnosed, using special test pictures composed of colored dots. This test is used to determine a person's ability to recognize reds and greens. People with normal color vision can see the number 29, but those with red-green blindness, or anomalopia, see the number 70.

color-field painting   Color-field painting was one of two mainstreams in American ABSTRACT EXPRESSIONISM of the late 1940s and early 1950s. It developed concurrently with gestural abstraction, represented by Jackson POLLOCK, and was propounded by three major figures,

Clyford STILL, Mark ROTHKO, and Barnett NEWMAN. To maximize the visual impact and immediacy of color, they applied colors over large areas, which entailed the elimination of figuration and its symbolism, the simplification of drawing and gesture, and the suppression of contrasts of light and dark. The effect—of vastness and overwhelming emotional impact—was further enhanced by canvases of monumental dimensions.

color index   A color index is a quantitative measure of the color, and thus the spectral type, of a STAR. It is derived from the difference in the apparent stellar MAGNITUDE as measured, using two photometric systems of different and accurately known color sensitivity. A commonly used set of three bands, defined by filters and by the color sensitivity of the detectors, is the UBV (ultraviolet blue visual) system. In this system the color index is found by subtracting the visual magnitude from the blue (B minus V) or from the ultraviolet (U minus V) magnitude. Other multicolor systems extending into the infrared have also been found useful (see HERTZSPRUNG-RUSSELL DIAGRAM).

Because the magnitude of a hot star will be greater in the blue region of the spectrum than in the visual, blue, or hot, stars have more negative color-index values than cooler, redder stars. The actual values of the B minus V color index range from about -0.3 for the hottest young supergiants at 50,000 K, to about +2.0 for the coolest observable main sequence dwarf stars. The B minus V color index of the Sun is +0.62.

Colorado   Colorado, one of the Mountain states of the United States, is a landlocked, rectangular territory. It is bordered by six states: Wyoming and Nebraska on the north, Utah on the west, New Mexico and Oklahoma on the south, and Kansas on the east. Permanent human occupation of the area dates back at least 10,000 years. Spanish exploratory expeditions beginning in the early 16th century left no settlements, and it was not until the discovery of gold in 1858 that Colorado received its first modern permanent settlement. The name *Colorado* was chosen in 1861 by the first territorial governor, William Gilpin, because the region contains the source of the Colorado River; the word is Spanish for "red." Since World War II, Colorado has been one of the fastest-growing states.

Land and Resources

Colorado has a higher average elevation (2,070 m/6,790 ft) than any other U.S. state, with about 1,000 peaks higher than 3,048 m (10,000 ft). Of the country's 80 peaks over 4,267 m (14,000 ft), Colorado has 53. The state's lowest point, in the southeast, is nearly two-thirds of a mile high (1,021 m/ 3,350 ft), and the highest is Mount ELBERT at 4,399 m (14,433 ft).

Physiographic Regions. Portions of three great physiographic regions of the continental United States dominate the topography of Colorado: the GREAT PLAINS, the ROCKY MOUNTAINS, and the COLORADO PLATEAU.

COLORADO

Land: Area: 269,594 km² (104,091 mi²); rank: 8th. Capital and largest city: Denver (1990 pop., 467,610). Counties: 63. Elevations: highest—4,399 m (14,433 ft), at Mount Elbert; lowest—1,021 m (3,350 ft), at the Arkansas River.

People: Population (1990): 3,307,912; rank: 26th; density: 12.3 persons per km² (31.8 per mi²). Distribution (1988 est.): 81.7% metropolitan, 18.3% nonmetropolitan. Average annual change (1980–90): +1.45%.

Government: (1991). Governor: Ray Romer, Democrat. U.S. Congress: Senate—1 Democrat, 1 Republican; House—3 Democrats, 3 Republicans. Electoral college votes: 8. State legislature: 35 senators, 65 representatives.

Economy: State personal income (1988): $54.4 billion: rank: 22d. Median family income (1979): $21,279; rank: 12th. Agriculture: income (1988)—$3.7 billion. Forestry: sawtimber volume (1987)—67.1 billion board feet. Mining: value (1987)—$1.5 billion. Manufacturing: value added (1987)—$15.1 billion.

Miscellany: Statehood: Aug. 1, 1876; the 38th state. Nickname: Centennial State; tree: Colorado blue spruce; motto: *Nil Sine Numine* ("Nothing without Providence"); song: "Where the Columbines Grow."

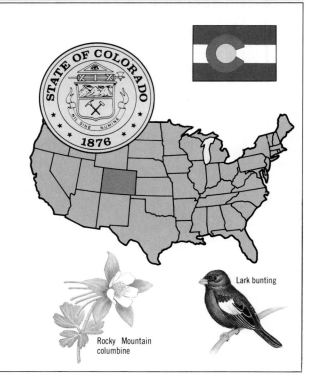

Lark bunting

Rocky Mountain columbine

The Great Plains, covering slightly more than one-third of the state, constitute a relatively flat sweep of unglaciated, plateaulike land. Rising to the west the plains abruptly give way to the Rocky Mountains, which cover the central third of the state. The Rockies comprise several north-south trending ranges: the Front Range (the easternmost range and including PIKES PEAK), the Sangre de Cristo (Blood of Christ) Mountains, the Park Range, the Sawatch Range, and the San Juan Mountains. The western third of the state is part of the Colorado Plateau. This region is characterized by valleys, deep canyons, and mesas. The soils of the mountain and plateau regions are thin, and those of the plains are poorly developed, low in organic material, and high in alkalinity but respond well to irrigation and fertilization. Some areas of alluvial deposits along the major rivers are relatively fertile.

Rivers and Lakes. Six major rivers, the COLORADO, ARKANSAS, South and North Platte, Republican, and Rio Grande, rise in Colorado and supply water to 18 other states. Canyons have been carved by many of the state's rivers, including the 300-m-deep (1,000-ft) ROYAL GORGE on the Arkansas River and the Black Canyon on the Gunnison, a tributary of the Colorado. The only natural lake of any size is Grand Lake, but more than 1,900 reservoirs (artificial lakes) have been constructed. More than 27 transmountain diversion projects deliver water from the mountains to the populous and drier East Slope of the Rockies. Groundwater resources are most important in the relatively dry Great Plains province.

Climate. Colorado has a semiarid continental climate that is strongly influenced by the terrain, with marked zonation in the mountains. The mean annual temperature is 7° C (45° F) with a range from an average low in January of -3° C (26° F) to a high in July of 23° C (73° F). A significant factor for human comfort is the low humidity.

Generally, precipitation increases with elevation, the western slopes of the Rockies receiving the most. Almost all lower elevations record less than 254 mm (10 in) with the minimum of 178 mm (7 in) at Alamosa (elevation, 2,297 m/7,535 ft). The state's maximum precipitation is 1,067 mm (42 in), recorded at Wolf Creek Pass (elevation, 3,307 m/10,850 ft). The greater precipitation at high elevations (stored in a snowpack of several meters on the high peaks) is critical in overcoming the problems of low moisture in populated areas. A hazard exacerbated by climate and topography is air pollution. Denver, with 177 bad air days/year, is ranked second in the United States only to Los Angeles, with 318.

Vegetation and Animal Life. Colorado has five distinct life zones, which are associated with climate and topog-

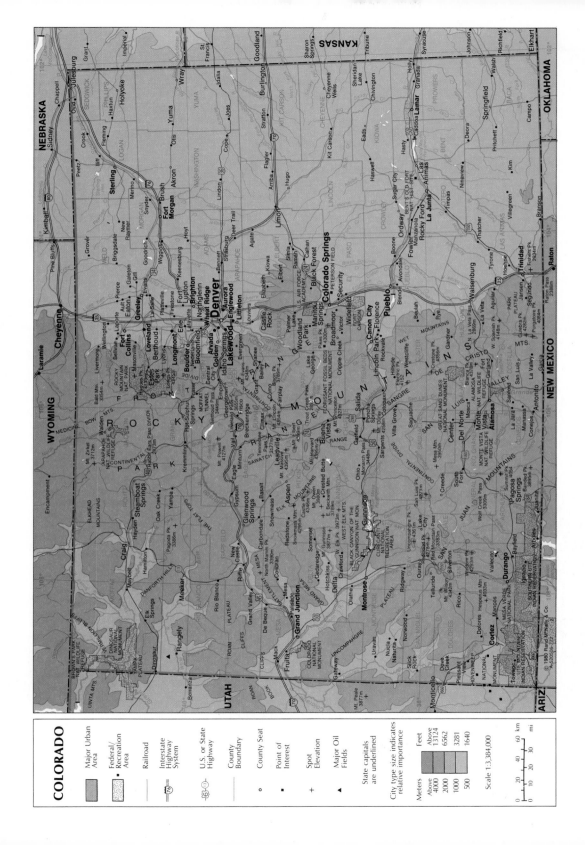

COLORADO

Major Urban Area

Federal / Recreation Area

Railroad

Interstate Highway System

U.S. or State Highway

County Boundary

○ County Seat

■ Point of Interest

+ Spot Elevation

▲ Major Oil Fields

State capitals are underlined

City type size indicates relative importance

Meters	Feet
Above 4000	Above 13124
2000	6562
1000	3281
500	1640

Scale 1:3,384,000

km 0   20   40   60
mi 0 10 20 30

© 1980 Rand McNally & Co.
A-520506-772-2-2

raphy and provide habitat for a wide variety of plant and animal life. The eastern plains up to an elevation of 1,830 m (6,000 ft) are a zone of open grassland and wildflowers inhabited typically by pronghorn antelope (in decreasing numbers), jackrabbits, and burrowing mammals. Trees occur naturally only along river banks. The transition foothills zone up to an elevation of 2,440 m (8,000 ft) is a brushland of juniper, sagebrush, mountain mahogany, scrub oak, pinion pine, berry shrubs, grasses, and wildflowers. It is inhabited by gray fox, skunks, and raccoons. The montane zone (up to 3,050 m/10,000 ft) has varied plants dominated by ponderosa pine and Douglas fir along with aspen, lodgepole pine, and limber pine. The subalpine zone (up to 3,500 m/11,500 ft) has homogeneous forests of Englemann spruce and fir. Above the timberline in the alpine zone are found wildflowers, mosses, and lichens.

Wildlife in the mountains includes bighorn sheep, pika, marmot, mountain lion, red fox, pine marten, and porcupine. Coyotes, mule deer, and small mammals such as beaver and deer mice are ubiquitous, but several once-numerous species, including grizzly bears, bison, wolverines, lynx, wolves, and otter, are now either rare or extinct.

Natural Resources. Colorado has known deposits of more than 250 economically useful minerals, including coal, petroleum, natural gas, molybdenum, vanadium, zinc, and uranium, with about 35 minerals actively mined. Gold and silver, once important, are now of minor significance, but Colorado's oil-shale deposits contain the country's largest (although unexploited) reserves of oil. Parks and forests are managed by several federal agencies on 36% of the total land, and the state's scenic beauty attracts increasing numbers of tourists.

People

Colorado's population, which is 81.7% urban, is concentrated in the corridor along the eastern slope of the Rockies, especially the Front Range. Western Colorado is, with few local exceptions, very sparsely populated. The population of the state–3,307,912 in 1990–is growing rapidly, showing increases of 30.8% between 1970 and 1980 and 14.5% between 1980 and 1990. Only DENVER (the capital), COLORADO SPRINGS, and Aurora exceed 200,000, and of 24 other places over 10,000, 14 are in the Denver area and only 2, DURANGO and Grand Junction, are in the west. Blacks make up about 3.4% of the population, people of Spanish origin 11.2%, and Indians less than 1%. Religious affiliation is predominantly Protestant (65 to 70%), with more than 100 recognized sects.

Education. Colorado began publicly supported primary education in 1862, more than a decade before statehood. Public education is today administered through 181 local school districts. The University of Colorado (1876), a public university with campuses at Boulder, Colorado Springs, and Denver, provides professional and graduate programs, as does Colorado State University (1870). Other public institutions are the Colorado School of Mines (1874), the University of Northern Colorado (1889), the University of Southern Colorado (1933), and Metropolitan State College (1963). The United States Air Force Academy (1954) is located near Colorado Springs. Among the state's ten private colleges are the University of Denver (1864), Colorado Women's College (1888), Colorado College (1874), and Loretto Heights College (1891).

Cultural Institutions. Denver is the locus for the state's cultural activities with its Colorado Heritage Center, Li-

The slope of Sam's Knob provides an excellent downhill skiing site in Snowmass-at-Aspen, a planned recreational development opened in 1967. The nearby city of Aspen, an internationally famous resort community, lies on the western slopes of the Rocky Mountains.

(Above) *The Garden of the Gods, a park northwest of Colorado Springs, is famous for its multicolored limestone formations.* (Right) *Denver, a former mining settlement in central Colorado, is the state's capital and largest city. The dome of the capitol* (right foreground) *is finished with gold extracted from Colorado's mines.*

brary, Museum of Natural History, Art Museum, Symphony Orchestra, and Civic Theatre Group. Boettcher Concert Hall opened in Denver in 1978 and is the first structure of a planned performing arts complex. The Colorado Springs Fine Arts Museum is a fine regional facility, and the University of Colorado Shakespeare Festival in BOULDER and the Aspen Music School and Festival in ASPEN have become important permanent institutions. The Denver Public Library is one of the largest in the American West.

Historical Sites and Recreation. Colorado has two national parks: Rocky Mountain National Park, containing some of the mountain range's highest peaks, and MESA VERDE NATIONAL PARK, containing the most extensive Indian cliff dwellings in the United States. Other points of interest are the DINOSAUR NATIONAL MONUMENT, with its well-preserved fossils, and the dramatic rock formations of the Garden of the Gods, a park near Colorado Springs. Central City, a former gold-rush boom town, is now a summer resort. Aspen and Vail are two of the country's best-known ski resorts.

Communications. Colorado's major newspaper, and the major regional newspaper of the Mountain states, is the Denver *Post.* Second in circulation is the *Rocky Mountain News;* founded in 1859, it was Colorado's first newspaper. The state has 27 daily newspapers, more than 100 radio stations (mostly local), and 12 television stations.

Economy

Colorado's economy has historically focused on primary products, such as buffalo hides, gold, and silver, with the more recent addition of services, such as ski resorts and real-estate sales. Today manufacturing has replaced mining and agriculture in importance and accounts for more than half the total value of goods produced. Tourism, with an estimated 8 million visitors a year, now produces more revenue than mining.

Manufacturing. The state's leading manufacturing industries produce metals, food products, machinery, clay and glass products, electronic instruments, chemicals and chemical products, and transport equipment. Manufacturing is heavily concentrated in the Denver metropolitan area.

Agriculture. Livestock and livestock products contribute 70% of Colorado's farm receipts. Cattle and sheep are raised in both the mountains and on the plains, with the heaviest concentration in the northeastern part of the state. Wheat, alfalfa, corn (maize), and sugar beets are the principal crops. Colorado has large tracts of irrigated farmland.

Mining. Mining plays a diminishing role in the Colorado economy. The principal mining products are petroleum, molybdenum, and coal. Sand and gravel are also important, as are various kinds of stone and, to a lesser extent, uranium.

Transportation. Colorado has 121,819 km (76,697 mi) of U.S., state, and county highways. Seven major freight railroads and eight scheduled airlines serve the state.

Government and Politics

Government is by a bicameral legislature and governor, elected for a 4-year term, under the constitution approved July 1, 1876. The separate judiciary includes a 7-member Supreme Court, district courts, and various local courts. The constitution is generally conceded to be so detailed as to inhibit effective governance, although recent amendments have allowed flexibility. The General Assembly consists of 35 senators serving 4-year terms and 65 representatives serving 2-year terms. Colorado is represented in the U.S. Congress by 2 senators and 6 representatives. It has 8 electoral votes in national presidential elections.

Over the years Colorado has exhibited an almost even division between the Democratic party and the Republican party in electing both its state and federal officials. This reflects the balance of voting trends between the

The world's highest bridge spans Royal Gorge, a spectacular chasm cut in granite by the Arkansas River in south-central Colorado. The Royal Gorge Suspension Bridge, constructed in 1929, is 321 m (1,053 ft) above the river's level.

predominantly Democratic south and cities (Denver, Colorado Springs, Pueblo) and the Republican suburbs and rural northeast.

History

Occupancy of the area that is now Colorado was established by nomadic hunters more than 10,000 years ago. By the 1st century AD, Indians known as Basket Makers had come to the mesa country of southwest Colorado. By AD 800 these people had been absorbed by the CLIFF DWELLERS and their pueblo culture, which was based on agriculture and flourished between the 10th and 13th centuries (see ANASAZI). At the time of European exploration and settlement, Colorado was inhabited by various nomadic tribes on the plains and by the UTES in the mountain valleys.

Exploration and Acquisition by the United States. The early explorers of Colorado were Spaniards. The first expedition to penetrate the area was probably that of Francisco CORONADO in 1541. Spanish expeditions continued through the 18th century, but their influence was negligible. The region was not claimed for Spain until 1706. The Spanish, however, introduced the horse, which provided the Indians with a mobility that both threatened European interests and inhibited the Indians' shift from nomadic hunting to agriculture. Intertribal warfare and conflict between the Spanish and the French continued through the 18th century.

With the LOUISIANA PURCHASE (1803), the United States obtained from France the eastern and central parts of Colorado. American exploration of the region began soon after. An army officer, Zebulon Montgomery PIKE, led a party into Colorado in 1806. Other expeditions in-

cluded those of Stephen H. LONG (1820) and John C. FRÉMONT (1842–43, 1845). The area's first semipermanent white inhabitants were the so-called MOUNTAIN MEN, who were trappers and fur traders.

The remainder of Colorado's territory passed from Spain to Mexico following Mexico's independence in 1821. The Treaty of Guadalupe Hidalgo (1848), which ended the MEXICAN WAR, gave this area to the United States. The discovery of gold in 1858 near present-day Denver caused a sudden influx of settlers. Mining camps, such as Auraria, Central City, Gold Hill, Boulder, and Cripple Creek, sprung into existence. Ignoring Indian claims to the land, the settlers proclaimed it the Territory of Jefferson, a move not recognized by the U.S. Congress. The Colorado Territory was organized in 1861.

Statehood. Colorado was admitted as the 38th U.S. state in 1876. The Indian wars (with the Arapaho, Cheyenne, and later the Utes), which had continued through the 1860s and '70s, came to an end in 1880 when a treaty was signed with the Ute chief Ouray. In 1881 the Indians were deported to reservations. The gold boom had subsided by the end of the 1860s only to be replaced by a silver boom in the 1870s. Silver magnate and Colorado politician Horace TABOR was a leading figure of this era. After 1893, however, silver prices dropped, and many of the mines closed.

By the beginning of the 20th century Colorado had become a predominantly agricultural state. Denver, which had been connected to the Union Pacific Railroad in 1870, became a shipping and distribution point for ranches and farms. Mineral resources other than precious metals, such as coal, oil, and molybdenum, were exploited in the early 1900s.

Economic Depression and Recovery. The Great Depression, combined with the Dust Bowl droughts of 1935 and 1937, caused a severe setback to the Colorado economy. World War II, however, brought a renewed demand for Colorado's mineral production, and military spending in the state gave a further boost to the economy. Following the war manufacturing continued to expand until, by the mid-1950s, it had replaced agriculture as the leading sector of the economy. Tourism experienced a similar growth.

Since the end of World War II Colorado's rate of growth has been among the highest in the nation. People came to the state for a variety of reasons: among them, to find employment in the expanding industries and to escape the problems and crowding of older urban areas. The rapid increase in Colorado's urban population, however, created a situation not unfamiliar to the nation's other cities. The population increase also put a severe burden on the state's modest water supplies, which are also necessary for irrigated agriculture. Since the early 1950s a series of water storage and regulation projects have carefully budgeted nearly all of the state's water supply. Today Colorado faces the challenge of resolving conflicts of interest between environmentalists wishing to preserve Colorado's scenic beauty and recreational resources, and mining and industrial interests attempting to exploit Colorado's mineral resources.

Colorado (Indian tribe)   The Colorado are an Indian people who live in the coastal lowlands of northwestern Ecuador. They received the name *Colorado* (Spanish for "red") from the red pigment with which they paint their bodies. They speak a dialect of Chibchan and call themselves Tatchila or Tsatchela. In the 18th century there were about 3,000 Colorado, but they are rapidly disappearing, numbering fewer than 300 today.

The Colorado are tropical-forest dwellers with a well-developed slash-and-burn agriculture. Fishing is intensively practiced. Living in scattered homesteads, they have no true villages; the single-family household is the basic socioeconomic unit. SHAMANS exercise both civil and spiritual authority.

Colorado Desert   The Colorado Desert is a dry basin and range area extending from San Gorgonio Pass in Riverside County, Calif., 264 km (164 mi) southward to the Gulf of California in Mexico west of the Colorado River. At its northern apex is Palm Springs, Calif. Much of the area to the south, including the Salton Sea, lies below sea level.

Before the Colorado River delta built up to its present level, the southern desert was under the waters of the Gulf of California. The Coachella and IMPERIAL VALLEYS were left with rich sedimentary deposits and have become highly productive farmland.

Colorado Plateau   The Colorado Plateau is an arid, upland region in Arizona, Utah, Colorado, and New Mexico. Covering an area of more than 130,000 km^2 (50,000 mi^2), and ranging from 1,524 to 3,962 km (5,000 to 13,000 ft) high, it is bounded on the east by the southern Rocky Mountains and the Rio Grande Valley and on the west by the Great Basin. The Colorado River flows from north to south through the plateau and has formed its main feature—the GRAND CANYON. Other major features are Bryce Canyon, MESA VERDE, PAINTED DESERT, PETRIFIED FOREST, and Zion national parks. The area is mainly desert.

Colorado River (Colorado)   The Colorado River is a major river of the southwestern United States. Created by rain and melting snow in the humid forest of the Rocky Mountains in north central Colorado, it falls steeply about 2,300 km (1,430 mi) southwest and south through spectacular canyons (including the GRAND CANYON), and through the desert where annual precipitation may be less than 250 mm (10 in) and evaporation more than 2,000 mm (80 in). It finally flows quietly into the Gulf of California. Its main tributaries are the Gunnison, Dolores, Green, San Juan, Little Colorado, Gila, and Virgin rivers. The drainage area, which includes parts of seven states, is 632,000 km^2 (244,000 mi^2). The largest cities on the river are YUMA, Ariz., and Grand Junction, Colo.

Several Indian tribes, including the Navajo and Pueb-

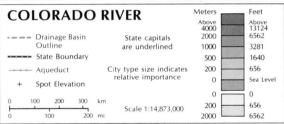

COLORADO RIVER

- ‒ ‒ ‒ Drainage Basin Outline
- ━━━ State Boundary
- ⊢━━━⊣ Aqueduct
- + Spot Elevation

State capitals are underlined

City type size indicates relative importance

Meters	Feet
Above 4000	Above 13124
2000	6562
1000	3281
500	1640
200	656
0	Sea Level
0	0
200	656
2000	6562

Scale 1:14,873,000

lo, populated the area when the Spanish arrived in 1540, and named the river for its reddish color. River development began in the 1920s and continued for 50 years until slowed by environmental concerns and diminishing returns.

The many dams, including HOOVER and Glen Canyon, have largely regulated the seasonal and annual discharge fluctuations, and 21 billion m^3 (741 billion ft^3) are available each year for power generation, recreation, irrigation, and municipal use. Vast areas of previously unproductive but fertile soil are now irrigated—the largest such area is the IMPERIAL VALLEY of California. Much water is withdrawn for municipal consumption, most notably for the Los Angeles–San Diego area, and considerable quantities from the upper Colorado are diverted for municipal and agricultural use east of the Rockies. Proper allocation of water to the seven contiguous states and to Mexico has been a continual problem. Arizona realized a larger share when the long-term Central Arizona Project, to carry water eastward from the Colorado, connected with Phoenix in 1985; it was scheduled to reach Tucson in 1991. Further hydroelectric development is not expected because reservoir evaporation losses, already great, would become unacceptable. Salinity in the lower course has been so increased by reservoir evaporation and the return flow of irrigation waters that when the river reaches Mexico it is too saline for some uses.

Colorado River (Texas)   The Colorado River of Texas, the longest river wholly within Texas, rises in the Llano Estacado in the west central part of the state. It flows southeast for 965 km (600 mi) to Matagorda Bay of the Gulf of Mexico. Among its tributaries are the Concho, Pedernales, and San Saba rivers, Pecan Bayou, and Beals Creek. The Colorado is navigable as far as Austin, the state capital, 240 km (150 mi) from its mouth. The Marshall Ford Dam northwest of Austin is the most important of a number of flood-control dams built along the Colorado's course.

Colorado Springs   Colorado Springs, the seat of El Paso County, is located on a 1,830-m-high (6,000-ft) mesa in central Colorado. The population of the city is 281,140 (1990), and that of the metropolitan area is 397,014. Colorado College, the U.S. Air Force Academy, Fort Carson, and Ent Air Force Base are located there. The Combat Operations Center of the North American Air Defense Command is located just south of the city. Local industries include printing and electronics. Tourists are attracted by nearby mineral springs, Pike National Forest, and Pikes Peak. The city was founded in 1871 and consolidated with Colorado City in 1917.

Colorado tick fever   Colorado tick fever is a viral disease transmitted to humans by the wood tick, *Dermacentor andersoni*, from small mammals. It occurs in the Rocky Mountain area and in eastern California and Oregon. The symptoms, which usually appear within a week of a tick bite, include high fever, nausea, malaise, loss of appetite, and muscle and joint aches. Symptoms last about two days, disappear, and recur, usually more severely. Fatalities are rare.

coloration, biological   Animals often have distinctive COLOR patterns for protection, to attract mates or members of the group, or to warn away enemies; plants use color to aid pollination.

Cryptic coloration, or general resemblance to surroundings, may conceal both predator and prey. Warning coloration (usually in insects and fish) consists of bold markings that warn predators away from inedible or poisonous animals. Species with neither cryptic nor warning coloration may resemble, or mimic, a warning-colored animal or predator. Such deceptive coloration is called Batesian MIMICRY.

Albinos are plants or animals that have no color when it is normal for their species to have color. True ALBINISM is

Both the ringed plover chick and its egg are cryptically colored. Plovers are shore birds that dig shallow nests in the open ground; the coloration acts as camouflage, helping the young blend with their surroundings as protection against predators.

The striking coloration of the monarch butterfly (right) warns birds that it is unpalatable and poisonous. The viceroy butterfly (left) mimics the color pattern of the monarch; thus birds avoid the viceroy, although it is a member of a different family and is harmless.

inherited. Albino plants lack CHLOROPHYLL, the green substance necessary for the manufacture of food by photosynthesis; they are unable to live unless supplied with special nutrients.

Cryptic Coloration. Cryptic coloration depends on the animal's living place, habits, means of defense, and enemies. Fawns have spotted coats that aid in their concealment when they lie motionless. Some nesting birds such as the woodcock nest in the open, but their coloration blends in so well with the grassy background that they are rendered virtually invisible. Plains animals depend less on coloration than on speed for survival, but they often have bold, disruptive markings to disguise their shapes and throw off an attacking predator.

Animals are generally darker on their backs than on their undersides. Since light falls mostly from above, the back is colored darker so that the overall hue corresponds to that of the underside, which is in shadow and therefore darker.

Seasonal Changes. Many animals and plants change color with the season. The snowshoe hare, for example, is brown in summer and autumn and turns white in winter. It is thus able to blend with its surroundings in all seasons. In the breeding season, many birds and fish change

The male stickleback develops special coloration to attract its mate. During most of the year both the male and the female are grayish green (top). During the breeding season, however, the male's belly becomes red and its back, bluish white (bottom).

Certain flowers have color markings called honey guides, which attract pollinating insects. The markings of the primrose (left), the stripes in the center of the violet (center), and the dots leading into the foxglove (right) guide insects to pollen sites.

color to attract mates. In spring the usually dull-colored male stickleback has a bright red belly that attracts females ready to spawn.

Sudden Changes. Some fish, reptiles, amphibians and mollusks can rapidly change colors to match their background or to express anger or fright. The best-known animal capable of this is the chameleon. Flounder are uniform in color on a uniformly colored background but become spotted on a spotted background. Sudden color changes are caused by the movement of PIGMENT within cells called chromatophores.

Mimicry. Hoverflies are harmless and not protected by distasteful qualities, but many are marked and colored like wasps. Birds, deceived by this mimicry, do not attack. The North American monarch butterfly is poisonous and distasteful and protected by warning coloration. This coloration is mimicked by the viceroy butterfly, which is palatable.

Flowers. Colors and shapes attract insects to the center of a flower, where the nectar and pollen are located. While taking this food, the insect inadvertently carries pollen from flower to flower. Bees, active during the day, are attracted by brightly colored flowers; moths, most active at dusk or at night, pollinate mostly white flowers.

Some orchids resemble in color and shape the females of certain wasps or bees; the male insect becomes covered with pollen as it tries to copulate with the flower.

Cause of Color. Some colors originate from pigments. Others are caused by structures of the surface tissues or feathers that reflect certain light rays and eliminate others. Birds, for example, do not have a true blue pigment. The brilliant blue of blue jays and other birds results from the reflections of light by highly specialized feathers.

coloratura   see SOPRANO

colorpoint shorthair cat   Colorpoint shorthair cats are recognized by some registries as a separate breed and by others as a variety of Siamese. Colorpoint shorthairs include red-points, tortie-points (tortoiseshell-points), and lynx-points (tabby-points). The red-point has reddish gold points—mask, ears, paws, and tail—on a white coat. The tortie-point, always female, is cream-colored, with brown and red points. The lynx-point has silvery striped points on a pale cream coat.

The lynx-point, or tabby-point, shorthaired cat is one of three varieties of colorpoints. The colorpoint cat was developed from the Siamese and the domestic cats.

Colosseum [kahl-uh-see'-uhm]   The Colosseum is the popular name for the Flavian Amphitheater in Rome. Situated between the Esquiline and Palatine hills, near the southeast end of the Forum, it was so named because the amphitheater stood next to a colossal, 37.2-m high (120-ft) statue (now demolished) of Nero. Construction of the Colosseum was started by Vespasian in AD 69. When inaugurated (AD 80) by his son Titus, the immense oval superstructure stood 49 m high (160 ft) and covered an

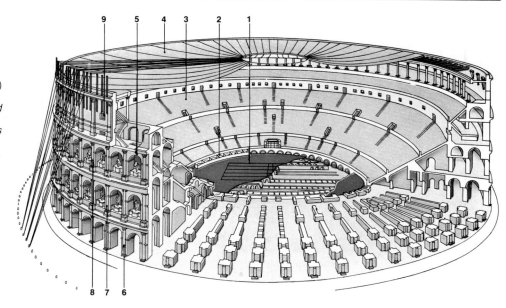

The Roman Colosseum, built by the Flavian emperors AD c.69–80, served as a model for later amphitheaters throughout the Roman Empire. An oval arena (1) covered the cages of the animals. A wall protected the spectators in the podium (2) and tiered seats (3), and a movable awning, the velarium *(4), sheltered them from the weather. The arcaded facade (5) was embellished with Ionic, Doric, and Corinthian columns (6–8). The attic story, pierced by rectangular openings (9), featured Corinthian pilasters.*

area 615 m long (118 ft) by 156 m wide (510 ft). The exterior walls were of travertine, the inner walls of tufa, and the vaulting of the ramped seating area of monolithic concrete. Seventy-six of the 80 bays served as entryways, so that circulation was easy. Marble and wooden seats accommodated up to about 50,000 spectators.

Chambers below the floor housed animals for the games. The ravenous beasts were passed from these chambers to the arena by means of special corridors and counterbalanced elevators. On occasion, the flooring was removed and the entire area flooded for mock naval battles.

Although the Colosseum has been damaged in several earthquakes, much of it is still standing. Only a portion of its masonry remains, however, because it served as a handy quarry during the Middle Ages; much of the travertine for Saint Peter's Basilica came from the Colosseum.

Colossians, Epistle to the   The Epistle to the Colossians is a book of the New Testament of the Bible. Scholars are divided on whether it was written by Saint PAUL during one of his imprisonments after AD 60 or by a later follower of Paul who further developed some of his ideas. The author confronts a type of GNOSTICISM that taught that angelic powers rule the cosmos and that various ascetic and ritual practices are required of Christians. Against these teachings, the epistle shows that since Christ is ruler of the whole cosmos and has saved believers, neither fear nor extreme practices are appropriate. Colossians has many passages in common with the Epistle to the EPHESIANS, especially the passages that describe the church as a body, with Christ as its head.

Colossus of Rhodes   see SEVEN WONDERS OF THE WORLD

Coloureds   see SOUTH AFRICA

Colt, Samuel   Samuel Colt, b. Hartford, Conn., July 19, 1814, d. Jan. 10, 1862, was the American inventor of the revolver, or six-shooter. He conceived of a gun with revolving chambers before he was 20 and in 1836 established a company to mass-produce the revolvers, as they came to be called. Westerners, particularly Texans, liked the guns, but Colt was unable to interest the U.S. Army until the outbreak of the Mexican War.

Colt became enormously wealthy from Colt's Patent Fire-Arms Manufacturing Company, which brought mass production by means of interchangeable parts to new heights. He also laid a submarine electrical cable from New York City to Coney Island in 1843.

Samuel Colt, a 19th-century American inventor, is best known for his revolving-breech pistol, or "six-shooter."

Colter, John John Colter, b. near Staunton, Va., c.1775, d. Nov. 1813, was an American fur trader and guide who in 1807–08 traveled through the then-unexplored area that is now YELLOWSTONE NATIONAL PARK. He had previously participated in the Lewis and Clark Expedition (1803–06). Joining Manuel Lisa's fur-trapping group in 1807, Colter was sent into northwestern Wyoming and returned with tales not only of a dramatic escape from the Blackfoot Indians but of steaming geysers. He guided another trading party from St. Louis to the Three Forks of the Missouri in 1809–10.

Coltrane, John John William Coltrane, b. Hamlet, N.C., Sept. 23, 1926, d. July 17, 1967, is considered one of the major innovators of contemporary jazz. A saxophonist (tenor and soprano) and composer, Coltrane began his career in big bands, played with Miles Davis in the late 1950s, and formed his own quartet in 1960. He became one of the leaders of a jazz movement, called the New Wave, that sought greater freedom from harmonic and thematic restrictions in improvisation.

colubrid [kahl'-uh-brid]   Colubrids are the largest family (Colubridae) of living snakes, comprising about 300 genera and more than 1,400 species. Members of this family are found on every continent except Antarctica and have adapted to almost every terrestrial habitat. Typically, colubrids have belly scales as wide as the body, and the upper and lower jaws bear teeth. The teeth are not hollowed to serve as poison fangs, but in some species (rear-fanged snakes) the teeth at the back of the upper jaw are enlarged and grooved along the front to conduct venom.

Most colubrids are harmless to humans. Exceptions exist, however, such as the BOOMSLANG, *Dispholidus typus*, of Africa; the mangrove snake, *Boiga dendrophila*, of southeast Asia; and the false water cobra, *Hydrodynastes gigas*, of Brazil.

Food and feeding habits of colubrids vary greatly. Smaller forms may feed on earthworms and insects; larger species feed on small vertebrates, including other snakes. Some species poison their prey; others constrict and suffocate their victims; still others simply seize and swallow their prey alive. The majority of colubrids reproduce by laying eggs, but the young of many species are born alive.

Commonly, the colubrids are divided into five subfamilies: Colubrinae, Natricinae, Homolopsinae, Lycodontinae, and Xenodontinae. The largest and most diverse of these is the Colubrinae, distributed throughout the world. Most North American snakes belong to this subfamily. Members range from the small insectivorous genera, such as the ringneck snakes, *Diadophis*, to the large rat snakes, *Elaphe*, king snakes, *Lampropeltis*, and whip snakes, *Masticophis*.

The Natricinae, also distributed worldwide, contain

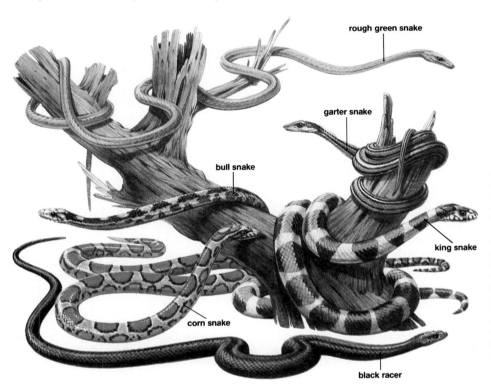

rough green snake

garter snake

bull snake

king snake

corn snake

black racer

Colubrids constitute the largest snake family in the world. Mostly harmless, these snakes move quickly and have well developed eyes and slender tails. The rough green snake is a small, docile snake sometimes kept as a pet. The common garter snake gives birth to live young. The bull snake is a constrictor that raids birds' nests and rodent burrows. The corn snake is frequently found in corncribs, searching for rodents. The king snake eats other snakes, including venomous species. The black racer is a swiftly moving snake of the meadows.

the familiar watersnakes, *Natrix*, and garter snakes, *Thamnophis*. The homolopsines are aquatic snakes, found from Southeast Asia to Australia in fresh or salt water. The Lycodontinae, mostly African, contain some highly specialized forms such as the egg-eating snake, *Dasypeltis*. The Xenodontinae include most of the tropical American species, such as the slug-eating snakes, *Dipsas*, and the racerlike *Alsophis*.

colugo [kuh-loo'-goh] Colugos, or flying LEMURS, *Cynocephalus*, are primitive gliding mammals belonging to the family Cynocephalidae, order Dermoptera. They are about 41 cm (16 in) long, weigh 1 to 2 kg (2 to 4 lb), and have a 25-cm (10-in) tail. A broad gliding membrane extends from the neck and body to the tips of fingers, toes, and tail. The head and lower-incisor comb teeth resemble those of a true lemur; the comb teeth may be used for grooming. The fur is mottled brown or gray. There are two species: *C. volans* lives in the Philippines and *C. variegatus* in the East Indies. Colugos eat fruit, buds, flowers, and leaves. They are slow climbers and do not walk on the ground.

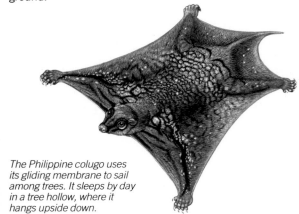

The Philippine colugo uses its gliding membrane to sail among trees. It sleeps by day in a tree hollow, where it hangs upside down.

Colum, Padraic [kahl'-uhm, pad'-rik] The Irish-American poet Padraic Colum, b. Dec. 8, 1881, d. Jan. 11, 1972, was a leading figure in the Irish Literary Renaissance. His poetry is collected in such volumes as *Wild Earth* (1909) and *Collected Poems* (1952). In 1911 he helped found the *Irish Review*. He also wrote such plays as *Broken Soil* (1903) for the Irish National Theatre, as well as novels, and prepared collections of Irish folktales, which influenced his work. After 1914 he lived in the United States.

Columba, Saint Saint Columba, b. *c.*521, d. June 9, 597, was an Irish abbot and missionary to whom is attributed the conversion of Scotland to Christianity. A member of a noble family of Donegal, he was trained at the monasteries of Moville and Clonard. After preaching

and founding churches and monasteries in Ireland for 15 years, he went (563) with 12 companions to the island of Iona off the coast of Scotland. There he founded a monastery that became the center of spiritual life for Ireland, Scotland, and Northumbria. It was from Iona that Columba evangelized the Scottish mainland. Feast day: June 9.

Columban, Saint Saint Columban, *c.*543–615, was an Irish monk and scholar who brought to Europe both the Irish cultural traditions of the monks and the confessional practices that were to affect the church throughout the Middle Ages and beyond. In 591, he and 12 companions were sent as missionaries to the continent of Europe. He founded the monastery of Luxeuil, which became a famous center of learning; during the Middle Ages its abbots were counted as princes of the Holy Roman Empire. Columban introduced the strict system of private penance from Ireland and wrote penitentials for this purpose. The later system of confession developed from this practice. Feast Day: Nov. 23.

Columbia The capital of South Carolina and the seat of Richland County, Columbia is the largest city in the state, with a population of 98,052 (1990). It is located in the center of the state on the Congaree River.

Long the market city for the surrounding agricultural region, Columbia is now also the heart of an industrial belt, with a number of cotton textile and fiber processing factories as well as electronics and plastics plants. Fort Jackson, a major army installation, is nearby. The University of South Carolina (1801) and several other smaller colleges are there.

Founded in 1786, Columbia replaced Charleston as the capital city. The city was almost completely destroyed on Feb. 17, 1865, by the Union army under Gen. William Tecumseh Sherman. It was rebuilt after the Civil War.

Columbia Broadcasting System see RADIO AND TELEVISION BROADCASTING

Columbia Icefield The Columbia Icefield is a large sheet of glacial ice in Canada, southeast of Mount Columbia in Jasper National Park on the Alberta–British Columbia border. Covering an area of some 518 km^2 (200 mi^2) and at an altitude of 2,438 to 3,048 m (8,000 to 10,000 ft), it is the largest glacial ice sheet in North America outside the Arctic Circle. The main surface of the icefield drops off steeply from the plateau into deep canyons. Crevasses in the lower glaciers may measure up to 160 m (100 ft) deep.

The icefield forms a three-way oceanic divide, with water from the icefield flowing to the Atlantic, Pacific, and Arctic oceans. The Saskatchewan, Columbia, and Athabasca glaciers extending from the icefield are major sources of these three rivers. Because of its accessibility, the Columbia Icefield is the site of extensive systematic study; since 1945, measurements show a consistent thinning of the icefield. The main areas below the late-summer snow line have been mapped every two to three years. Today tourists can drive near the icefield on the scenic 317-km (197-mi) Icefields Parkway.

Columbia River

The Columbia River is a major waterway of the northwestern United States and southwestern Canada. Fed by rain and snow from the mountains of British Columbia, Canada, it rises in Columbia Lake, British Columbia, and flows 1,950 km (1,210 mi), first northwestward and then south, entering the United States in northeastern Washington. It follows a generally southward course through the state and then turns west, forming part of the border between Oregon and Washington in its final 480 km (300 mi) to the Pacific Ocean. The river drains an area of 668,000 km^2 (258,000 mi^2), 85% of it in four northwestern U.S. states and 15% in Canada. The headwaters include several large glacial lakes. Important tributaries are the Kootenay, Snake, and Willamette rivers.

The Columbia was discovered by a Boston trader, Robert GRAY, in 1792 and named for his ship. It was explored by Lewis and Clark in 1805, and the river gorge through the CASCADE RANGE became an early transportation route. Improvements now permit commercial navigation more than 650 km (400 mi) above the mouth. The lower river has always been navigable to PORTLAND, Oreg. (a short way up the Willamette), and Vancouver, Wash., which are the major ports.

The most powerful river in the United States, the Columbia and its tributaries account for one-third of all U.S. hydroelectric potential. It has a fall of 820 m (2,700 ft) and an annual discharge of 222 billion m^3 (about 93 trillion ft^3) near the mouth. Hydroelectric development has proceeded rapidly since the 1930s, and most of the mainstream potential is now used. The Dalles, John Day, Chief Joseph, and GRAND COULEE are the largest of the mainstream dams. Commercial fishing, recreation, and energy-intensive industry, such as aluminum refining, are important.

Columbia University

Established in 1754 as King's College, Columbia University is an independent, coeducational IVY LEAGUE institution in New York City. Columbia College was the university's undergraduate college for men until 1983, when enrollment was opened to women. BARNARD COLLEGE (1889), an independent undergraduate college for women, has been affiliated with the university since 1900. Among Columbia's graduate divisions are the world's oldest library school (1926), a school of journalism founded (1912) by Joseph PULITZER, and TEACHERS COLLEGE.

columbine

Columbine is the common name for the genus *Aquilegia*, perennials belonging to the buttercup family, Ranunculaceae. Columbines are valued for their dainty flowers of many colors, usually with the petals extending backward to form hollow tubes called spurs. The common European columbine, *A. vulgaris*, the source of numerous horticultural varieties and wild plants, reaches about 60 cm (2 ft) in height and bears drooping blue, purple, pink, or white flowers.

The columbine is a member of the buttercup family. Three varieties of columbines are the long spurred (1), short spurred (2), and spurless (3).

columbium   see NIOBIUM

Columbus (Georgia) Columbus, a city in western Georgia, is the seat of Muscogee County and also the second largest textile center in the South. The city has a population of 179,278 (1990). Situated on the Chatahoochee River below a series of falls, it is an important shipping center and a large hydroelectric-power producer. Industries manufacture iron and steel, machinery, chemicals, processed foods, beverages, wood, concrete, and rubber. Columbus College is in the city, as is the Confederate Naval Museum. Fort Benning, the large army infantry base, and Lawson Air Force Base are nearby.

Founded in 1827 on the site of a Creek Indian village, Columbus quickly became an important inland cotton port. During the Civil War it was an important arms-manufacture and supply center for the Confederacy. On Apr. 16, 1865, a week after Gen. Robert E. Lee had surrendered, it was captured by Union forces led by Gen. James H. Wilson.

Columbus (Ohio) Columbus is the capital of Ohio and the seat of Franklin County. Located in the center of the state on the banks of the Scioto River, it was laid out as the state capital in 1812 and named for Christopher Columbus. It was the first U.S. city that was planned and built as a state capital, and it was incorporated as a city in 1834.

Columbus is the largest city in Ohio, with a population of 632,910 (1990). It's metropolitan-area population is 1,377,419.

The economy of Columbus is oriented toward service occupations, such as insurance, finance, education, and government. Some important large industries are located in the city, including machinery manufacturing, metal fabricating, printing, and publishing.

The following major higher educational institutions are located in Columbus: Ohio State University (1870), one of the largest in the United States; Capital University (1850); Franklin University (1902); Otterbein College (1847); and Columbus Technical Institute (1952).

Columbus has important cultural and recreational attractions, including the Center of Science and Industry Museum, Columbus Gallery of Fine Arts, and Ohio Theater, where the Columbus Symphony Orchestra and other fine arts groups perform. Among its historic landmarks are the Greek Revival capitol building and the Camp Chase Confederate Cemetery. Downtown Columbus has a beautiful riverfront civic center on the Scioto.

Columbus developed in the 19th century as a stagecoach center and was connected to canal (1831) and railroad (1850) systems. It grew quickly as an aircraft construction center during World War II.

Columbus, Christopher Christopher Columbus, an Italian-born navigator who sailed in the service of Spain, is commonly described as the discoverer of the New

Christopher Columbus's voyages to the New World began a new era of European discovery and conquest. (Metropolitan Museum of Art, New York City.)

World—America. Although Columbus was in search of a westward route to Asia by sea, the discoveries he did make were more important and valuable than the route he failed to find. It is certain, however, that Columbus was not the first European to cross the Atlantic. Documentary evidence supports claims that the Vikings reached the New World about AD 1000. And there is circumstantial evidence to suggest that both Portuguese and English fishing vessels made the crossing during the 14th century, probably landing in Newfoundland and Labrador.

Columbus's Early Life. The best available evidence suggests that Christopher Columbus (Cristoforo Colombo in Italian; Cristóbal Colón in Spanish) was born in Genoa in 1451. Christopher had little education and learned to read and write only as an adult. He went to sea, as did many Genoese boys, and voyaged in the Mediterranean. In 1476 he was shipwrecked off Portugal, found his way ashore, and went to Lisbon; he apparently traveled to Ireland and England and later claimed to have gone as far as Iceland. He was in Genoa in 1479, returned to Portugal, and married. His wife, Dona Felipa, died soon after his son, Diego, was born (c.1480).

By this time Columbus had become interested in westward voyages. Acquiring books and maps, he accepted Marco Polo's erroneous location for Japan—2,400 km (1,500 mi) east of China—and Ptolemy's underestimation of the circumference of the Earth and overestimation of the size of the Eurasian landmass. He came to believe

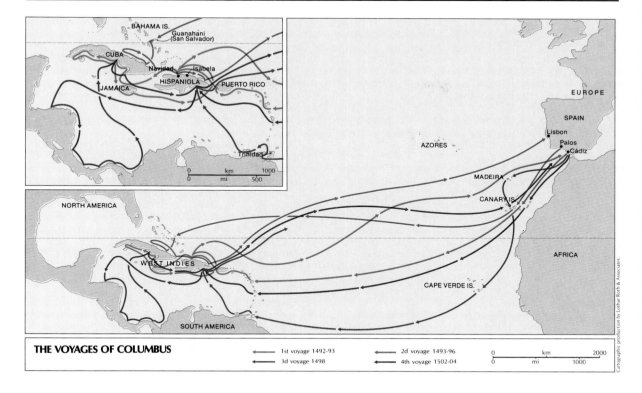

THE VOYAGES OF COLUMBUS

← 1st voyage 1492-93   ← 2d voyage 1493-96
← 3d voyage 1498   ← 4th voyage 1502-04

that Japan was about 4,800 km (3,000 mi) to the west of Portugal—a distance that could be sailed in existing vessels. In 1484, Columbus sought support for an exploratory voyage from King John II of Portugal, but he was refused. In 1485, Columbus took his son Diego and went to Spain, where, after almost seven years of effort, he gained the support of ISABELLA I of Castile in 1492.

The First Voyage. The *Pinta*, the *Niña*, and the *Santa María* were outfitted in the minor port of Palos. Columbus was aided in recruiting a crew by two brothers—Martín Alonzo PINZÓN, who received command of the *Pinta*, and his younger brother Vicente Yáñez Pinzón, who commanded the *Niña*. They left Palos on Aug. 3, 1492, rerigged the *Niña* in the Canaries, and sailed to the west. A landfall was made on the morning of Oct. 12, 1492, at an island in the Bahamas, which Columbus named San Salvador, and historians later identified as Watling Island (which was then renamed San Salvador). In 1986 a group of scholars claimed that the true landfall was Samana Cay, 105 km (65 mi) to the south.

The landing was met by Arawak, a friendly local population that Columbus called Indians. Some days later the expedition sailed on to Cuba, where delegations were landed to seek the court of the Mongol emperor of China and gold. In December they sailed east to Hispaniola, where, at Christmas, the *Santa María* was wrecked near Cap-Haïtien. Columbus got his men ashore. The Indians seemed friendly; so 39 men were left on the island at the settlement of Navidad while Columbus returned to Spain

on the *Niña*. Martín Alonzo Pinzón, who had explored on his own with the *Pinta*, rejoined Columbus, but the ships were separated at sea. Columbus finally landed (March 1493) in Lisbon and made his way across Spain to Barcelona, where he was welcomed by Isabella and her husband, Ferdinand II of Aragon. Columbus claimed to have reached islands just off the coast of Asia and brought with him artifacts, Indians, and some gold.

The Second Voyage. Portuguese claims to Columbus's discoveries led Pope Alexander VI to issue papal bulls in 1493 that divided the world into areas open to colonization by Spain and Portugal. The two nations moved the line of demarcation to 370 leagues west of the Cape Verde Islands by the Treaty of Tordesillas (1494) and undertook colonization.

Funded by Ferdinand and Isabella, Columbus set sail from Cádiz on his second voyage on Sept. 25, 1493. This time he had 17 ships and almost 1,500 men. Again they stopped in the Canary Islands and then made landfall on Nov. 3, 1493, near Dominica among the Lesser Antilles. The expedition then sailed through the Lesser Antilles, past Puerto Rico, and reached the site of Navidad on Nov. 27–28, 1493. The encampment had been destroyed, and the Spaniards, who had seized gold and women, had been killed.

Columbus set up a new colony, named Isabela, about 113 km (70 mi) to the east of Navidad's site. He left in April 1494, explored the southern coast of Cuba, discovered and circumnavigated Jamaica, and returned to Isabela after 5 months. Columbus tried to govern the colony until he returned to Spain in 1496, but he was not a good administrator. He left his brother Bartolomé in charge with instructions to move the settlement to the south coast of Hispaniola. This was done in 1496, and this settlement, named Santo Domingo, became the first permanent European settlement in the New World.

Columbus reached Cádiz in June 1496. He was coolly received at court. He had not found the rich Asian mainland, and his efforts to get gold from the Indians on Hispaniola had been only moderately successful. The Spanish settlers were unruly and would not work, and some had returned to Spain with complaints about Columbus.

The Third Voyage. Columbus was finally authorized to make a third voyage. He departed in May 1498 with six ships and made landfall on Trinidad on July 31, 1498. The next day he reached the mainland and thus discovered South America. The expedition then sailed across the Caribbean to Santo Domingo. The colonists there were in revolt, and Columbus soon had to face a royal commissioner, Francisco de Bobadilla, who arrived from Spain in 1500 with full powers. Bobadilla removed the Columbus brothers from the government and sent them back to Spain in chains.

Fourth Voyage. Freed by royal command after arrival in Cádiz in November 1500, Columbus soon mounted a fourth expedition, which left Spain in May 1502, made a landfall at Martinique, and sailed to Santo Domingo. There he was denied permission to land. His ships sailed west, reached Honduras in Central America, and sailed along the coast past Panama, finally heading again for Santo Domingo. His vessels, rotted by shipworm, were abandoned in Jamaica, where Columbus was marooned for a year. Finally rescued, he reached Spain in November 1504.

Christopher Columbus died in Valladolid on May 20, 1506, still believing that he had reached Asia. Columbus's real greatness lies in the fact that having found the West Indies—making major errors in his navigational computations and location in doing so—he was able to find his way back to Europe and return to the Indies. It is as a result of Columbus's "discovery" that the New World became part of the European world.

column   see ARCHITECTURE

coma   (optics) see ABERRATION, OPTICAL

___

coma   (unconscious state)   Coma is a deep state of unconsciousness. The patient feels no pain and exhibits only minimal reflex responses to stimuli, a fact confirmed by radiological studies of the BRAIN. Consciousness depends on the interaction of the brain's two cerebral hemispheres and on parts of the upper brainstem where mechanisms are located for activation of the hemispheres. A coma can occur when either the hemispheres or the activating centers are damaged. Damage may be caused by pressures on brain tissue (from bleeding or edema), tumors, shock, lack of oxygen, poisoning, infections, epilepsy, or concussion.

A person in terminal coma may lack all reflexes, including those involved in breathing. In such cases a mechanical respirator is necessary to keep the patient alive. Difficult ethical questions arise concerning the continuing maintenance of such patients on life-support systems when they have no hope of recovery (see DEATH AND DYING; EUTHANASIA). When patients continue in a comatose state for much longer than a month, the condition is described as a persistent vegetative state and is usually considered irreversible.

Patients in reversible coma may be aided by large doses of barbiturates. Recovery proceeds by stages, each of which may vary in duration by several days. In general, a patient first enters stupor, a state of unconsciousness that can be only temporarily interrupted. The next phase is a state of delirium and extreme agitation. Eventually the patient becomes quieter but is in a state of mental confusion. Later—in the automatism phase—the patient responds to questions but performs only simple tasks in an automatic way. Gradually, as recovery progresses, the highest brain functions return.

___

Comanche   [kuh-man'-chee]   The Comanche are a North American Indian tribe belonging to the Shoshonean division of the Uto-Aztecan linguistic stock. Early in possession of horses, by about 1700 the Comanche left a semidesert homeland west of the Rockies and moved into the southern plains. In sweeping south and eastward they drove out various APACHE groups, including the Jicarilla and Lipan. Their historic territory extended from the Arkansas River in southeastern Colorado along the flanks of the Rockies south to the Pecos River in Texas and north through western Oklahoma and southwest Kansas. They were organized into at least 11 independent bands, each with its own chief and territory.

Expert horsemen, the Comanche supplemented their buffalo-hunting economy with trade in horses, mules, and captives obtained in raids against white settlements in Texas and New Mexico. During the 18th century, the Comanche effectively prevented French and Spanish expan-

George Catlin's portrait of a Comanche warrior, Little Spaniard (1834), reflects the legging and breechclout attire typical of the Plains Indians. At the height of their power, the Comanche ruled much of the southwestern plains of the United States. (National Collection of Fine Arts, Washington, D.C.)

sion into the southern plains. The Medicine Lodge Treaty of 1867 restricted the Comanche and their close allies the KIOWA and Kiowa Apache to 3 million acres (1.2 million ha) of land in southwestern Oklahoma. War resulted, culminating (1874) in a combined Comanche, Kiowa, Kiowa Apache, and Southern Cheyenne attack on Adobe Walls, Tex. General Mackenzie penetrated their stronghold in Palo Duro Canyon, Tex., in the winter of 1874. With their camps destroyed, the destitute Indians drifted back to Fort Sill in Oklahoma and to reservation life the following year.

It is estimated that the Comanche may have numbered 20,000 in the 18th century, but by 1910 the population had shrunk to 1,500. In 1987 an estimated 4,650 Comanche were on or near the Oklahoma reservation.

Comaneci, Nadia [koh-mahn-eech', nahd'-yah]

Nadia Comaneci, b. Nov. 12, 1961, is a Romanian gymnast who was the heroine of the 1976 Olympic Games at Montreal. She won gold medals for performances in the balance beam, uneven parallel bars, and the all-around event, plus a silver medal in the team event and a bronze medal in the floor exercises. She was only 14 years of age and a mere 39 kg (86 lb); her popularity was such that she was elected Female Athlete of the Year by the Associated Press. Comaneci also competed at the 1980 Olympics in Moscow, where she won 2 more gold medals (balance beam, floor exercises) and a silver (all-around). In 1989 she made a daring escape from Romania into Hungary and subsequently defected to the United States.

Nadia Comaneci's expression mirrors her intense concentration during a routine on the balance beam. The Romanian gymnast was awarded a score of 10 for her initial exercise on the uneven parallel bars at the 1976 Olympics, marking the first perfect score recorded in Olympic competition. Comaneci earned six subsequent perfect marks in Montreal and won three of Romania's four gold medals.

comb jelly

Comb jellies are about 80 species of transparent, usually small marine INVERTEBRATES constituting the phylum Ctenophora, which means "comb-bearing." The bodies bear eight rows of parallel "combs," each comb consisting of a series of fused cilia (see FLAGELLA). The combs are used for locomotion.

A common comb jelly propels itself through water by the action of hairlike combs, arranged in eight rows on its body. The comb jelly can paralyze a fish with its long tentacles.

Comb jellies resemble jellyfish in that both animals have bodies consisting of a gelatinous mass between an inner and outer layer of tissue, with the mass surrounding a central gastric cavity. Unlike jellyfish, comb jellies have combs and mesodermal tissue powering the combs. They also have canals leading from the gastric cavity to pores at the opposite end of the body from the mouth; jellyfish can eject waste only from the mouth. Ctenophores also have a balancing organ, or statocyst. They reproduce sexually and are hermaphroditic.

Several comb jelly species are named for their shapes, such as the sea walnut and sea gooseberry. The ribbon-like Venus's girdle may reach 1.5 m (4.9 ft) in length.

combination see PERMUTATION AND COMBINATION

combine

In agriculture, a combine is a composite harvesting machine that reaps and threshes grain such as wheat, barley, rye, and oats. With adaptations, combines can also harvest sorghum, soybeans, and other crops.

Motor-powered combines were first used in the U.S. Great Plains during the 1920s and were originally trailers pulled by tractors. Most machines are now self-propelled.

Combine operations include the cutting operation, where the grain is cut just below the heads. A reel pushes the grain headfirst up an elevator belt into the thresher, which threshes, or separates, the grain from its stalks. The mix passes another moving belt. The straw walker then carries the straw to the rear of the machine, where it drops to the ground. The grain, being heavier and smaller, drops through the straw and walker to screens and a conveyor below.

The screens permit the grain to fall through while a blast of air from a fan comes up through the screens and carries chaff and lighter weed-seeds out to the rear of the machine. A separate conveyor at the end of the screens picks up unthreshed heads, which are returned to the thresher. Cleaned grain is moved by a conveyor to an attached storage bin. (See art on page 118.)

See also: GRAIN; McCORMICK, CYRUS HALL.

combustion

Combustion, the burning of any substance, is a process that evolves light and heat. If the latter two are not present the process is called oxidation. Oxygen is generally required for combustion; although oxygen itself does not burn, it reacts chemically with the fuel to liberate the CHEMICAL ENERGY stored in the molecular bonds. The oxygen may be in the form of a compound, such as nitric acid (HNO_3) or hydrogen peroxide (H_2O_2) in

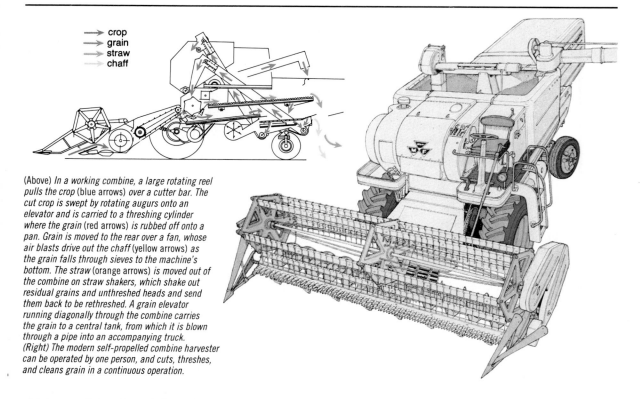

crop
grain
straw
chaff

(Above) *In a working combine, a large rotating reel pulls the crop (blue arrows) over a cutter bar. The cut crop is swept by rotating augurs onto an elevator and is carried to a threshing cylinder where the grain (red arrows) is rubbed off onto a pan. Grain is moved to the rear over a fan, whose air blasts drive out the chaff (yellow arrows) as the grain falls through sieves to the machine's bottom. The straw (orange arrows) is moved out of the combine on straw shakers, which shake out residual grains and unthreshed heads and send them back to be rethreshed. A grain elevator running diagonally through the combine carries the grain to a central tank, from which it is blown through a pipe into an accompanying truck.*
(Right) *The modern self-propelled combine harvester can be operated by one person, and cuts, threshes, and cleans grain in a continuous operation.*

which case it is released through a series of chemical steps. Other materials may support combustion, such as the gases fluorine and chlorine.

On a molecular basis, combustion supposedly originates by the formation of radicals and spreads by a CHAIN REACTION that increases the supply of radicals. Flame-retardant chemicals function by their ability to "soak up" radicals, thus terminating the chain reaction. Extremely rapid combustion is called an explosion. This can occur if the production of radicals greatly exceeds the rate of chain termination, or if heat buildup is great enough to accelerate the reactions of very rapid rates. (See also FLAME; SPONTANEOUS COMBUSTION.)

Comecon   see COUNCIL FOR MUTUAL ECONOMIC ASSISTANCE

Comédie Française, La [koh-may-dee' frahn-sez', lah]   La Comédie Française or le Théâtre Français, the French national theater, was founded in 1680 in Paris by merging three existing companies: the Hôtel de Bourgogne, le Théâtre du Marais, and MOLIÈRE's troupe. It is organized cooperatively, according to the original charter granted by Louis XIV and revised by Napoleon. During the French Revolution it split into two rival factions; in 1803 it was reconstituted. It is still noted for its productions of classical French drama.

comedy   All literary forms contain comic elements, but *comedy* is here used to describe a genre of humorous plays that deal with ordinary or domestic events and end happily. In the *Poetics*, Aristotle said that comedy depicts "people as worse than they are," tragedy as "better." Tragedy represented the sufferings of noble characters in order to stir pity in the audience; comedy, inferior people whose actions arouse laughter without causing pain. Comedy may involve laughter *at* a character who is a fool, coward, miser, or zany, or laughter *with* the rogue or trickster who upsets the normal order. Henri Bergson suggested in *Laughter* (1900; Eng. trans., 1956) that comedy substitutes mechanical and predictable events for natural and spontaneous ones. Sigmund Freud's *Jokes and Their Relationship to the Unconscious* (1905; Eng. trans., 1953) states that humor provides infantile gratification by disrupting the adult world and is frequently a means of unconscious sexual release.

Ancient Greek Comedy. Comedy may have developed from the playful celebrations (Greek *komos* means "revels") honoring the god Dionysus (see GREEK LITERATURE, ANCIENT). Greek old comedy survives in the satirical plays of ARISTOPHANES. In *Lysistrata* women protest against the prolonged war between Athens and Sparta by staging a sex strike; *The Clouds* mocks Socrates and other philosophers; *The Frogs* and *The Birds* contain animal choruses that PARODY tragic language and themes. Middle comedy is thought to have softened this satire by turning to a fantasy world of gods and heroes, but no examples have survived. New comedy is known only from some fragments of MENANDER's plays; it concerned contemporary manners, domestic themes, and romance.

Ancient Roman Comedy. The comedies of TERENCE and PLAUTUS, modeled on Greek new comedy, almost invariably concern the attempts of young lovers to overcome obstacles posed by an old father or some rich and corrupt person. They are often aided by a wily slave who outwits such stock characters as the pimp and the braggart soldier. These plays contain no social satire; the characters are practical in their desire for wealth and pleasure, and the happy ending neutralizes any hint of moral blame.

Renaissance Comedy. Comedy disappeared during the Middle Ages, although MEDIEVAL DRAMA contained comic scenes. During the Renaissance the plays of Plautus and Terence were frequently imitated; Machiavelli's *Mandragola* (1518; Eng. trans., 1927) is a well-known example. The Italian COMMEDIA DELL'ARTE, popular entertainments perhaps descended from Roman comedy, were an important factor in the development of later comedy. The actors wore masks and played stock roles in improvised scenes of FARCE and slapstick.

Elizabethan Comedy. William SHAKESPEARE's *The Comedy of Errors* (1590) is based on Plautus's *The Menaechmus Twins*, but his other comedies extend and vary classical plots. *As You Like It*, The MERCHANT OF VENICE, and A MIDSUMMER NIGHT'S DREAM add serious themes to romantic plot. *Measure for Measure* (1604) is darkly satirical, and The TEMPEST is a play in which love and forgiveness reestablish morality. Ben Jonson's "comedy of humours" is satirical: *Every Man in His Humor* (1598) and *The Alchemist* (1610) focus on obsessive characters.

Shakespeare's tragedies and histories include comic scenes and represent a Renaissance innovation, TRAGICOMEDY. His greatest comic character, Falstaff, is a version of the braggart soldier depicted by Plautus. A similar mixture appears in the subplots of the so-called cloak-and-sword comedies of Lope de VEGA and Pedro CALDERÓN DE LA BARCA.

17th- and 18th-Century Comedy. Seventeenth-century French drama kept tragedy and comedy strictly separate. MOLIÈRE's *Tartuffe* and *The Misanthrope* are comedies of manners that ridicule hypocrites and imposters, fools who ignore common sense. English RESTORATION DRAMA produced brilliant, albeit less elegant, comedies of this kind. William WYCHERLEY's *The Country Wife* (1675) resembles Roman comedy in its frank sexual humor and a plot that depends on disguise and trickery; William CONGREVE's *The Way of the World* is the stylish high point (see WIT).

In the 18th century the comedy of manners gave way to more prudish "sentimental comedy," such as Richard STEELE's *The Conscious Lovers* (1772) and Pierre MARIVAUX's *Le Jeu de l'amour et du hasard* (The Game of Love and Chance, 1730). In Oliver GOLDSMITH's *She Stoops to Conquer* (1773) and Richard Brinsley SHERIDAN's *The Rivals* (1775), comedy returned to Roman plots in which

love is an excuse for humorous misunderstandings. Caron de BEAUMARCHAIS's *The Barber of Seville* (1775; Eng. trans., 1818) and *The Marriage of Figaro* are also witty versions of Roman comedy, with Figaro the barber as the wily slave.

Modern Comedy. Nineteenth- and twentieth-century comedy lacks a dominant pattern. Oscar WILDE's *The Importance of Being Earnest* (1899) is a comedy of manners that satirizes middle-class respectability but makes fun of its own aristocratic dandyism. George Bernard SHAW's *Man and Superman* (1905) is a comedy of ideas in which middle-class notions are demolished, but whose hero is undercut by his own self-satisfaction. Comedy has again combined with tragedy in Samuel BECKETT's WAITING FOR GODOT and Eugène IONESCO's *The Bald Soprano* (1950; Eng. trans., 1965), which treat spiritual emptiness and pessimism with comic absurdity.

Comenius, John Amos [koh-meen'-ee-uhs] John Amos Comenius, a Czechoslovakian religious leader, b. Mar. 28, 1592, d. Nov. 15, 1670, developed the philosophy of pansophism and was a major figure in the humanistic tradition of education. A member, and eventually bishop, of the Moravian Brethren, a pietistic Protestant sect, Comenius became a refugee after the onset of the Thirty Years' War and persecution by the Habsburgs. His wanderings brought him into contact with intellectual leaders in Germany, Poland, Sweden, England, and Holland.

From his experience of hardship, he forged a philosophy that emphasized political unity, religious reconciliation, and educational cooperation. Comenius envisaged educated people as those who sought knowledge from all sources in order to become more like God—omniscient and universally compassionate. Comenius's major work was *The Great Didactic* (1628–32; Eng. trans., 1896), in which he set forth his educational theories. His other writings include *The Gate of Languages Unlocked* (1631; Eng. trans., 1659), and *The Visible World* (1658; Eng. trans., 1659), the forerunner of illustrated schoolbooks.

---

comet Comets are celestial bodies of small mass that travel around the Sun (see SOLAR SYSTEM), usually in elongated orbits. They become visible as they near the Sun, and sometimes they form a visible tail.

For centuries, comets have been considered harbingers of catastrophe. Their appearances, and sometimes their motions, were accurately chronicled. In the 17th century Sir Isaac Newton discovered a method of deriving the true orbit of a comet from its observed trajectory in the sky, and he determined that the comet of December 1680 followed a very elongated, parabolic orbit. Edmond HALLEY, a contemporary of Newton's, found that the orbits of the comets of 1531, 1607, and 1682 were almost identical, a discovery that led him to conclude that they were in reality a single comet, whose return in 1758 he correctly predicted. Since then it has been called HAL-

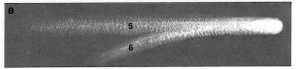

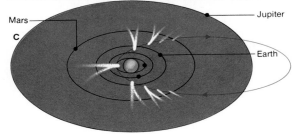

Although all comets are part of the solar system, most orbit far from the Sun. A comet (A) in the Sun's vicinity consists of a bright, starlike nucleus (2) and a hazy, luminous coma (1), which together form the head (3) of the comet. In addition, a tail (4) usually forms, often reaching lengths comparable to the distance from the Earth to the Sun. As comets approach the Sun (B), they often develop both a straight, ionized gas tail (5) and a curved, dusty tail (6). Throughout the comet's orbit (C), these tails point away from the Sun.

LEY'S COMET. It has been observed 20 times since 239 BC, its most recent swing around the Sun having occurred in 1985–86.

A newly discovered comet is provisionally designated by the year of discovery and a letter indicating its order in comet sightings that year. Once the date at which the comet reaches perihelion (closest approach to the Sun) is determined, the comet is officially designated by the calendar year followed by a Roman numeral specifying the chronological order of the perihelion passages in that year (for example, 1882 II). Some comets are named for their discoverers.

At present, comets are sought both with visual telescopes and with telescopes that can photograph extensive areas of the sky. About ten comets are discovered each year, and on the average one comet every three years is visible without a telescope. In 1985 the U.S. *Interplanetary Sun-Earth Explorer* (*ISEE*) *3* was maneuvered into an encounter with comet P/Giacobini-Zinner, and in 1986 the European Space Agency, Japan, and the Soviet Union all obtained closer views of Halley's comet with their separate spacecraft.

Comet Orbits

All comet orbits that have been established are elliptical. Short-period comets have periods of less than 200 years, and their orbits are mostly inclined at a small angle to the orbital plane of the Earth (the ecliptic). The comet with

the shortest known period is Encke's comet (3.3 years). Long-period comets have periods that may reach several thousand years, and their orbital planes may lie at various angles to the ecliptic. Some comets observed only once appear to have parabolic or hyperbolic orbits that would bring them near the Sun only once.

Physical Nature of Comets

Nucleus and Coma. Almost the entire mass of a comet is concentrated in its nucleus. The diameter of the nucleus is on the order of a few kilometers. The density, between 0.1 and 1 g/cm^3 (6 and 60 lb/ft^3), indicates that the nucleus is very tenuous. According to Fred L. Whipple's "dirty snowball" model—confirmed by recent observations—the nucleus consists of a conglomerate of such compounds as water, carbon dioxide, ammonia, and methane, all frozen and mixed with grit and dust. When the comet approaches the Sun, this frozen matter sublimes and forms a cloud of gas and grit—called the coma—around the nucleus. Closer to the Sun, the production of gases increases. The gas and dust particles are repelled from the nucleus by the solar radiation pressure and the SOLAR WIND (a stream of charged particles), forming the tail. The average diameter of the coma is about 100,000 km (62,000 mi), but its mass and density are small.

The apparent brightness of a comet depends on its distance from the Sun (and from the Earth). In addition, a comet not only reflects light but also absorbs and then itself emits light. Consequently, the brightness may increase quite rapidly upon approach to the Sun.

Tail. When a bright comet becomes visible, the most noticeable feature is the tail. At the appearance of Halley's comet in 1910, the tail stretched for more than 90° over the celestial sphere. During Halley's most recent appearance in 1985–86, however, this elongation took place while the comet was on the far side of the Sun, so that the show made in Earth's night sky was undramatic.

This scene from the Bayeux Tapestry, which records the Norman Conquest, depicts the appearance of Halley's comet in AD 1066. The comet was regarded as an evil omen by King Harold of England and his subjects.

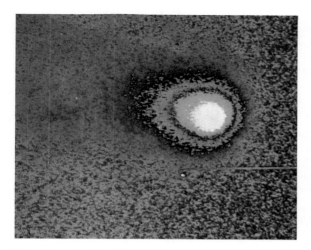

Different wavelengths of ultraviolet light were used in this photograph of the head of the comet Kohoutek, taken from the U.S. space station Skylab *on Dec. 25, 1973. Each color indicates a different temperature region.*

The length of the tail ranges from 1 to 100 million km (0.62 to 62.14 million mi). It is formed of gas from the coma and always points away from the Sun because of the solar wind.

A comet may have one of two types of tail, and many comets have both types—a double tail. One is elongated and almost straight, has a fibrous structure, and consists of ionized gases. This type of tail is called a Type I tail, a gas tail, or a plasma tail. Type II tails, or dust tails, are more strongly curved and hazier; they consist of dust repelled by sunlight. A comet may possess several dust tails in addition to a gas tail. Some comets have an anomalous tail, or antitail, which points toward the Sun (for example, the Arend-Roland comet, 1957 III). The antitail is actually a very thin layer of dust lying along the orbit of the comet, having been expelled at an earlier stage.

Disintegration of Comets

Many comets, especially short-period ones, slowly disintegrate, mainly under the influence of the Sun's gravitational force, and a few have also been observed plunging into the Sun. A regular decrease in the brightness of short-period comets is often observed. Comets also leave waste products behind in their orbits, in the form of millions of meteoroids. When the Earth crosses such an orbit, METEOR showers are frequently observed.

Scientists speculate that collisions of comets—or cometary fragments—with the Earth may occasionally occur, with devastating results. In one hypothetical scenario, past cometary collisions are thought to have thrown enough dust into the Earth's atmosphere to have caused the extinctions of some species of plants and animals (see EXTINCTION). Also, the impact of a comet, or piece of a comet, remains one of the more plausible explanations for a tremendous blast that occurred in the Tunguska region of Russia in June 1908.

Origin of Comets

Various theories have been developed in recent centuries to account for comets, but the one most widely accepted at present is that comets were formed at the same time as the rest of the solar system. In 1950 the Dutch astronomer Jan OORT proposed that the Sun is surrounded by an enormous "cloud" of comet material at a distance about 1,000 times that of the radius of the known solar system. This theory was followed in 1951 by Dutch-American astronomer Gerard KUIPER's proposal that a ring of cometary material lies in the plane of the solar system, several hundred times as far from the Sun as the Earth is. Both proposals have been widely accepted, with some astronomers suggesting that the Oort and Kuiper clouds actually merge along the Oort cloud's much denser inner boundary. Perturbations by interstellar clouds or passing stars would cause some of the comet materials to dislodge and enter the inner solar system in the form of comets, with short period comets more likely arising from the Kuiper belt.

comic opera   Developing from the French Opéra-Comique, which had spoken rather than sung dialogue, comic opera has also been influenced by Italian opera buffa and English ballad opera. In France the form became *opéra-bouffe*, related to operetta. Treating amusing characters in often ludicrous situations, comic opera is musically less demanding than opera but requires more skill than musical comedy. Gilbert and Sullivan are the best-known creators of comic opera in English.

comic strip   Comic strips are a popular art form dating from the 1890s, when they were introduced into the Sunday color supplements of American newspapers as a means of promoting readership. A strip usually consists of a series of cartoons depicting humorous or adventurous incidents and involving a recurring cast of characters.

James Swinnerton's cartoon strip "The Little Bears and Tigers," run by the *San Francisco Examiner* in 1892, was the first newspaper comic strip. The first successful comic series was Richard Outcault's "Down in Hogan's Alley," which first appeared July 7, 1895, in Joseph PULITZER's *New York World* as a single picture, or tableau, of life in an 1890s urban slum. Its central character, "The Kid," was a bald, impish tyke with a knowing grin; when, in 1896, the printer applied yellow ink to his nightshirt, he became widely known as "The Yellow Kid."

William Randolph HEARST, publisher of the *New York Journal* and Pulitzer's chief rival, noted the success of "The Yellow Kid" and hired Outcault away from Pulitzer. Pulitzer retaliated by employing George LUKS, later a leading ASHCAN SCHOOL painter, to carry on the same cartoon; as a result "Hogan's Alley" appeared in both papers simultaneously. The term *yellow journalism*, referring to sensational journalistic practices, was inspired by this rivalry.

The first strip to make regular use of speech balloons was Rudolph DIRKS's "The Katzenjammer Kids," which first appeared in 1897. In 1906, the graphic artist Lyonel

(Above) *"The Yellow Kid"* (left), *created by Richard Outcault in 1896, is considered the first successful comic strip.* (Center) *"The Katzenjammer Kids," created by Rudolph Dirks in 1897, is the longest continuously running comic strip still in publication.* (Right) *The first daily comic strip, Bud Fisher's "Mutt and Jeff," debuted in 1907.*

(Above) *"Blondie," introduced in 1930 by Chic Young, established its popularity through the humorous portrayal of domestic relationships. It became the most widely syndicated comic strip in the world, appearing in about 1,600 newspapers in more than 50 countries.* (Right) *"Dick Tracy," Chester Gould's police adventure strip, debuted in 1931 and was enthusiastically received, perhaps because of the public's concern over the gangsterism of that era.*

FEININGER created two strips, "Wee Willie Winkie's World" and "The Kinder Kids," in a style that lay somewhere between Art Nouveau and expressionism. George Herriman's "Krazy Kat" (1911), a comic drama of love and rejection in the manner of a surreal commedia dell'arte, proved a hit with intellectuals because of its wit and advanced style. More typical of the cartoonist's hatched drawing style were Rube GOLDBERG's ingenious mechanical inventions.

George McManus pioneered the domestic comic strip in "Newlyweds" (1904) and "Bringing Up Father" (1913). In brilliant calligraphic lines he satirized the pretentious settings and absurd fashions of the newly rich Maggie and Jiggs.

In 1908, Ham Fisher's "Mutt and Jeff" became one of the first strips to appear in a daily paper. After 1914 various syndicates distributed the funnies to papers throughout the country. New comics abounded, but they lacked some of the inventive draftsmanship and robust humor of the pioneer cartoonists. Harold Gray's "Little Orphan Annie" and Chic YOUNG's "Blondie" are survivors of that era.

The 1930s depression created a public ready and willing to escape realities. The freaky characters of Chester GOULD's "Dick Tracy," begun in 1931, were on a par

with such exotic adventure strips as "Tarzan," "Terry and the Pirates," and "Prince Valiant." These and the science-fiction series "Buck Rogers" and "Flash Gordon" created an appetite for further adventure heroes: "Superman," "Batman," and "Wonder Woman." Superadventure was rendered in a superrealistic style, an approach introduced by cartoonists Harold Foster and Alex Raymond. In another vein the hillbillies in Al CAPP's "L'il Abner" satirized politics and social conventions.

The violence and eroticism common to many comic strips was attacked in the 1950s, and the industry agreed (1954) to eliminate such material. The new strips were characterized by a breezy and original drawing style. Walt Kelly had already created (1949) "Pogo," a strip in which animals parodied the political scene. Most strips dealt with less controversial matter. The kids in Charles SCHULZ's still popular "Peanuts," begun in 1950, spoke to the aspirations and frustrations of adults through the actions of children, while the satirical *Mad* magazine (1952) appealed to people of all ages.

The youth revolution of the 1960s brought forth the uninhibited "underground" comics, of which the most popular was by Robert Crumb. At the same time, the terse style and mechanical quality of comics inspired POP

© 1949, Edgar Rice Burroughs, Inc.

© 1982, DC Comics, Inc.

(Above left) "Tarzan" was introduced by the artist Harold Foster in 1929. (Above, right) Bob Kane's "Batman" first appeared in 1939. (Below) Charles Schulz's "Peanuts" uses children and animal characters to lampoon the behavior of adults.

© 1959, United Features Syndicate, Inc.

ARTISTS such as Roy LICHTENSTEIN and Andy WARHOL. The blithe political satirizing in Garry TRUDEAU's popular "Doonesbury" (begun 1970) won for its creator the 1975 Pulitzer Prize for political cartooning.

Comic books, begun as compilations of newspaper comic strips, took on a life of their own in the mid-1930s as new heroic characters were created who lived only in the books. The favorite reading matter of several generations of children, the most popular comic books dealt luridly with crime or terror. When criticism of the industry brought on the 1954 Comics Code, comic-book sales declined somewhat.

A new breed of comic-book superheroes emerged in the 1960s. Though endowed with superhuman powers, characters such as Steve Ditko's "Spiderman" (1962) and Jack Kirby's "Hulk" (1962) expressed the same basic emotional needs that their more human counterparts did. Superhuman characters with human problems have remained popular.

By the 1980s, comic-book sales had become robust again, and a variety of small publishing houses had sprung up to challenge the traditional comic book giants DC Comics and Marvel Comics. Cross-marketing techniques linked comic-book characters to television cartoons, movies, video games, and toy lines. Meanwhile, comic books gained in popularity among American adults, reflecting a long-standing trend seen in Europe and Japan. More mature subject matter, such as Art Spiegelman's treatment of his father's Holocaust experiences in "Maus" (collected in book form, 1987), was seen. Comic books now enjoy a wider readership than ever.

Comintern   The Comintern, or Communist International, was a world organization of Communist parties under the leadership of the Communist party of the USSR. It was founded in Moscow in 1919 to guide the European revolution that Vladimir Ilich Lenin believed was soon to come. It dictated policies to the Communist parties in other countries, deploying them in the service of the Soviet state, and concerned itself with party discipline, propaganda, and the organizing of pro-Communist groups. In May 1943, when the USSR was allied with capitalist countries against Germany, Moscow dissolved the Comintern. It was replaced in 1947 by the Cominform, a European organization of Communist parties, which was abolished in 1956.

See also: INTERNATIONAL, SOCIALIST.

Commager, Henry Steele   Henry Steele Commager, b. Pittsburgh, Pa., Oct. 25, 1902, a versatile American historian who is concerned with social and constitutional issues, has taught at New York University (1926–38), Columbia University (1939–56), and Amherst College (1956–72). With Samuel Eliot MORISON he wrote *The Growth of the American Republic* (1930), which, in revised editions, remains a standard textbook of U.S. history. Commager's constitutional works include *Majority Rule and Minority Rights* (1944). Other writings focus on intellectual history, for example, *The American Mind* (1950) and *The Empire of Reason* (1978).

Commandments, Ten   see TEN COMMANDMENTS

commando   A member of a small military force used to raid enemy territory, a commando is trained in GUERRILLA warfare and hand-to-hand combat. The term originated among the Boers (Afrikaners) in South Africa, who originally applied it to the men "commandeered" by law to fight against the indigenous Africans. In the SOUTH AFRICAN WAR (1899–1902) the commandos were the local Boer militia units.

During World War II the British adopted the name for troops trained in guerrilla warfare. The first British commando unit was created in 1940 to raid the coasts of German-held territory. Commando units later were introduced as part of the Royal Marines and have been used in special actions. The U.S. Army's RANGERS, originally formed in 1755 to fight Indians, performed as commandos during World War II. They have since been replaced by various SPECIAL FORCES units.

Stock characters of the Italian commedia dell'arte *included Harlequin, the witty servant. The later English harlequinade was based on the escapades of this and other characters.*

commedia dell'arte [kohm-may'-dee-ah del ahr'-tay] The *commedia dell'arte* ("professional comedy") emerged in Italy in the mid-16th century and flourished in western Europe into the 18th century. The name was given to traveling companies who played in European theaters and marketplaces, before both royalty and commoners. Actors, generally wearing masks, improvised dialogue. The typical scenario of stock characters included the braggart captain, lecherous old men, young lovers, young women, Arlecchino or HARLEQUIN, and other *zanni*, or comic servants. The *commedia* was unique in its improvisational style, lively wit, obscene action, and overall vitality. It was quite unlike the staid and decorous literary comedy (*commedia erudita*) written in five acts.

Possible origins of the *commedia* are Roman Atellan farces, whose characters resemble those of the *commedia*; the mimes and farces of the medieval theater; and Eastern mimes and PUPPET drama from Constantinople. More recent scholarship suggests that it emerged from early 16th-century folk drama, carnivals, festivals, and mountebank shows. Ruzzante (Angelo Beolco; 1502–42), whose troupe performed partially improvised plays, has been considered the father of the *commedia*.

Vigorous, free, and broadly satirical in its treatment of hypocrisy and social class, the *commedia dell'arte* had extensive theatrical influence. The plays of Carlo GOLDONI and Carlo GOZZI brought the form to an end. At first they improvised and used *commedia* characters and masks, but they later developed written comedies, literary in style, dispensing with masks and reducing the number of *commedia* characters. The *commedia dell'arte* continues its influence in Charlie CHAPLIN's comedies, Marcel MARCEAU's mimes, PUNCH AND JUDY shows, English Christmas pantomimes, and the *Théâtre du Soleil*, a contemporary leftist acting company in France.

Commerce, U.S. Department of A business-oriented arm of the U.S. government, the U.S. Department of Commerce was established to promote economic growth and technological advancement. It provides business people with information on markets abroad, negotiates trade agreements with other countries, makes loans to businesses in depressed areas, subsidizes the merchant marine, makes weather reports, explores the oceans and atmosphere, issues patents, and compiles population statistics.

The department was first set up as the Department of Commerce and Labor in 1903; it was reorganized as the Department of Commerce in 1913. Among its bureaus is the Bureau of Economic Analysis, which compiles statistics of national income, gross national product, and other economic activity. The Bureau of the Census conducts censuses of population, housing, agriculture, and industry and provides other periodic surveys. Other agencies include the Patent and Trademark Office, the National Bureau of Standards, the Economic Development Administration, the Minority Business Development Agency, the National Oceanic and Atmospheric Administration, the United States Travel and Tourism Administration, and the Maritime Administration, which operates the UNITED STATES MERCHANT MARINE ACADEMY.

commercial art SEE GRAPHIC ARTS; INDUSTRIAL DESIGN

commercial law SEE BUSINESS LAW

commodity market SEE FUTURES

Commodus, Roman Emperor [kahm'-uh-duhs] Lucius Aelius Aurelius Commodus, 161–192, the son of MARCUS AURELIUS, ruled as coemperor of Rome from 177 and sole emperor from 180. Abandoning his father's military campaign against the German tribes (a move that many Romans considered treasonable), Commodus returned to Rome, where he persecuted the Senate and endowed his cronies with enormous power. Apparently mad, he identified himself as the personification of Hercules and displayed himself in gladiatorial contests. His advisors had him throttled to death by a wrestler.

common carrier A common carrier is a company that undertakes to transport goods and passengers for the general public. It may be a railroad, airline, trucking company, shipping line, bus company, taxicab company, mover, freight forwarder, or pipeline. Telephone and telegraph companies are also classed as common carriers if they serve all who wish to use them.

A common carrier is distinguished from contract carriers and private carriers in that it is committed to serving the general public at a preannounced schedule of rates. A contract carrier, on the other hand, limits its service to particular individuals; a private carrier is engaged in carrying its own goods. The common carrier is required by law to accept business from anyone who wishes to hire it, although it can refuse to transport perishable or dangerous goods.

Common carriers are regulated by public authorities as to the rates they may charge and the services they must offer. They are liable for loss of life, injury, and damage to property, except when they can show that the loss or damage resulted from certain specific causes.

Federal regulation of common carriers in the United States began with the Interstate Commerce Act of 1887, which established the INTERSTATE COMMERCE COMMISSION (ICC). Today the ICC regulates railroads, interstate truckers, and domestic carriers by water. The FEDERAL COMMUNICATIONS COMMISSION regulates interstate and foreign telephone and telegraph communication.

States and municipalities regulate such common carriers as local bus lines, taxicab companies, and interurban railroads.

Common Cause   Common Cause is a nonpartisan citizens' lobby founded in 1970 by John W. GARDNER, former U.S. secretary of health, education, and welfare. Its stated aim is to make politicians and government bureaucracies more responsive to the people and to bring the public's business into the open from behind closed doors, at both the national and state levels. Common Cause hires professional lobbyists to work for it in Washington, D.C., engages in lawsuits, and seeks to arouse the public in its fight against the undue influence of SPECIAL-INTEREST GROUPS.

common law   Two great systems of law have spread over the Western world. CIVIL LAW, descended from the laws of the Roman Empire, is used by most European countries. Common law, descended from the common law of England, is used in the United States and most of the Commonwealth countries. Both systems of law resist simple definition. Unlike civil law, common law was not embodied in a text or code: it evolved case after case in court decisions; the common-law judge did not consult an official text before rendering his judgment, but drew instead upon precedents established by other court decisions. Jurists eventually wrote treatises and commentaries on the common law and although these commanded the respect of the legal profession, they did not constitute law, and judges were not compelled to follow them when deciding cases.

Development of Common Law

Common law developed in England after the introduction of FEUDALISM following the Norman Conquest (1066). In feudalism the monarch was the supreme landlord. All title to real property was ultimately traced to the crown. The king made land grants to the great barons, who in turn made grants to their own retainers, or vassals. Each grant created certain obligations for both tenant and landlord, and private courts were created to oversee the performance of these duties. On the lowest level, every manor had a manorial court with jurisdiction over the manor's serfs (see MANORIALISM). On a higher level, the great barons provided honorial courts to settle disputes among their vassals, or KNIGHTS. The principal concern of such courts was the land grants that the vassals received in return for military service: the courts oversaw the rules of inheritance, marriage, and other matters that pertained to the land grants.

The King's Court. At the head of the system of courts was the king's court, *curia regis,* founded at Westminster by WILLIAM I (r. 1066–87). Originally an advisory body of the barons, it developed legislative and judicial functions. From the former emerged Parliament; from the latter, the royal court system.

As the power of the king gradually increased, the great barons played a lesser role in the *curia regis.* The king relied instead on a smaller, more specialized set of advisors within the *curia.* With the help of these advisors the monarchs, especially HENRY II (r. 1154–89), sought to curb the power of the great barons by replacing local private law with a common law for the entire country, namely, the king's law. In extending royal justice the *curia regis* was aided by the continued existence from Anglo-Saxon times of the shire, or county, courts. Beginning in the 12th century, these local communal courts were visited at roughly 7-year intervals by royal judges sent from Westminster on a set route or *eyre* (from the Old French *eire,* a circuit). Royal justice was made available to a vast new segment of the population, and at these hearings, as well as at the court sessions in Westminster, began the court decisions, or precedents, that form the basis of common law.

The Jury. One of the tools of royal justice was the JURY, which could be summoned by royal authority only. In 1166, Henry issued the Assize of Clarendon, initiating a procedure by which jurors were commanded to appear before a royal judge and relate any knowledge they had of crimes or criminals in a given area. This sort of presentment jury became widespread thereafter. Later Henry instituted a procedure called the grand assize to determine which of two or more claimants had the better right to a piece of land. Four knights elected twelve jurors who were acquainted with the facts of the case and who, after visiting the site, informed the court which claimant had the better right. Such procedures proved popular as an alternative to judicial combat, or ordeal by battle, which was then used in the feudal courts.

Writs. The royal court exerted its authority by issuing WRITS, or written orders in the king's name, requiring some action to be taken by a defendant or a local court.

The king's court had become three courts by the 13th century: Common Pleas, King's Bench, and the Exchequer. During the 12th and 13th centuries, the justices issued literally scores of new writs to settle issues before the court. A plaintiff at one of the local assize courts could present to an itinerant justice his plaint or grievance as a "bill in General Eyre." If successful, he could obtain a trial of his case.

Actions. In addition to new writs, principally in common pleas concerning land, new personal actions appeared, such as the action of account, which was used at first by a lord to compel his bailiff to account for the manor's profits. Later the action of account was used against a person who had received money to be used for the benefit of the plaintiff. Another important action was trespass, which called upon a defendant to show why he had caused damage to the plaintiff. The action of trespass developed into several actions including trespass to the person, to goods, and to land. Leaseholders acquired their own version of trespass, called ejectment; a tenant could demand to know why he had been ejected from his lease or term before it expired.

Society is always changing, and sooner or later law must change to provide new rules and remedies. A more or less standard example of the manuscript collections of writs was printed in 1531, and thereafter printed editions of the register guided lawyers in the drafting of writs until 1833, when forms of action were largely abolished; by 1875 they were completely abolished.

The common law was not entirely confined to writs. The king in council might also issue statutes restating or amending the decisions of the courts. EDWARD I is remembered for his Statutes of Westminster (1275 and 1285) and the Statute of Gloucester (1278). The second Statute of Westminster dealt at length with land and inheritance; it also encouraged the creation of new writs to provide remedies in cases where no law existed. "Whensoever from henceforth it shall fortune in the Chancery, that in one case a writ is found, and in like case falling under like law, and requiring like remedy is found none, the clerks in Chancery shall agree in making the writ. . . ."

Records of Cases

The records of actual cases tried in the courts of Common Pleas and King's Bench are the best evidence of the activity and continuity of the common-law courts. The case records contain details about the cause of action, the names of the litigants, and the decision of the court. The records show that as common law became more technical in the 14th century, a body of professional lawyers arose, trained in the complexities of pleading cases in court (see INNS OF COURT).

The first steps toward reporting cases were made in puzzling compilations called Year Books (1292–1536). They usually stated the grievance of the plaintiff and the answer of the defendant, followed by the arguments of counsel and, sometimes, the court judgment. Before the invention of printing in the mid-15th century, it was not unusual for lawyers to cite several cases to try to establish the traditional use of a certain rule in like cases. A ruling in a single case, however, was not an authority binding the court. The appearance of Burrow's Reports about 1750 marked the advent of something like the modern form of a court report. These reports made a clear distinction between the facts of a case, the arguments of counsel, and the judgment of the court, and provided at least an outline of the reasoning upon which a decision was based.

Equity

The common law administered in Common Pleas and King's Bench lost its flexibility at the end of the 13th century. Plaintiffs began to petition the king for remedies, and the chancellor had the task of properly disposing of their requests. By the end of the 14th century, the chancellor was presiding as a judge in his own court of Chancery, and a branch of the law called EQUITY began to grow as a supplement to common law. The work of a court of equity was easily justified by the argument that rules of law must of necessity be general, but that circumstances are infinitely variable and require that in some cases the strict letter of the law be set aside to avoid injustice or a result contrary to reason.

In various ways Chancery developed a character of its own. A brief comment on the final decree in Chancery may illustrate a difference between common law and equity. The judgment of a common-law court was either for the plaintiff or for the defendant: one party won, the other lost. But in an equity court the plaintiff might secure a general relief recognizing his or her rights and at the same time be asked to fulfill some obligation to the defendant. A decree in equity could be drafted to secure the relative duties and rights of the parties in line with the maxim, "He who seeks equity must do equity."

At times the coexistence of courts of law and equity seemed to give English subjects two kinds of justice, and from the 17th century onward reformers urged that English law and courts be simplified. This finally came about in 1875, when a single high court of justice was created. Other reforms abolished the writ system. In the United States during the 19th century, the majority of state constitutions provided for one action at law and equity.

Expansion of the Common Law

Common law crossed the Atlantic with the English language and served English colonial settlements whenever conditions permitted. Occasionally it had to yield in favor of religious beliefs or local customs. Judges in early America often lacked professional knowledge of the law; to be a man of property respected in his own community was sufficient qualification for the bench.

Prior to 1776 a few colonists went to England for legal education at the Inns of Court. The victory of the colonies in the American Revolution did not result in a rejection of English common law; however, the attitudes of individual Americans toward common law were full of contradictions. At one extreme were men like John Dudley, associate justice of the Supreme Court of New Hampshire (1785–97), who believed that "common sense is a much safer guide for us than common law." He boasted that he had never read the treatises of either Thomas Littleton or Sir William BLACKSTONE and never would. At the other extreme was George WYTHE, law tutor to Thomas JEFFERSON and the first professor of law at the College of William and Mary. Among his students were John Marshall, James MONROE, Edmund Randolph (see RANDOLPH family), and Henry CLAY. Wythe used Blackstone as a textbook, and his lectures compared English with Virginia law.

In the United States in the early 19th century, lawyers faced considerable hostility and suspicion. On one hand, the public demanded codification of the law as a means of achieving simplicity and certainty. On the other hand, it sought to democratize the profession of law by removing educational requirements for a license to practice. The latter proposal was actually put into effect in New Hampshire (1842), Maine (1843), Wisconsin (1849), and Indiana (1851). In these states any person could practice law who was a citizen more than 21 years of age, or a resident of the state, or a voter "of good moral character." It was argued that a citizen had the natural right to earn a living in any business, profession, or calling. Moreover, the abundance of open land profoundly affected American society, producing a fairly equal distribution among many landowners. On the frontier it was easy to conclude that common sense was enough.

Inevitably, the development of law in the United States came to reflect much that was distinctive in the American environment. For example, very early in the history of the United States, American jurists favored the recognition of so-called common-law marriages. James Kent stated, in *Fenton* v. *Reed* (1809), that "A contract of marriage *per verba de presenti* [words in the present tense, for example, "I do."] amounts to an actual marriage, and is as valid as if made *in facie ecclesiae* [in church]." Free consent, the meeting of minds, made a valid contract. Kent's opinion was almost universally accepted. On the frontier, where churches were few and ordained ministers scarce, common-law marriage was expedient.

American legal reformers also sought to replace laws created by judges with legislation in broad areas. The 19th-century jurist David Dudley FIELD drafted a civil procedure code, a penal code, and a criminal procedure code that were adopted by New York State and widely copied elsewhere. A Uniform Commercial Code has been adopted by every state except Louisiana, which has a civil-law system reflecting its French tradition.

Although there are many differences between English common law and American variations on it, the legal system of the United States bears many important marks of the common law. The professional language used by American lawyers is understood in Great Britain. Printed reports of U.S. cases show that courts have applied and still apply the doctrine of precedent (*Stare decisis*) associated with common law. Rules of equity supplement the common law in Great Britain, and an action at law and equity is used in the United States. In the United States, persons who fear that they may be deprived of their rights will demand "due process of law" and an observance of "the rule of law," principles essential to common law, and juries are judges of the facts in important cases. The United States thus remains one of the common-law countries.

Common Market   see EUROPEAN COMMUNITY

Common Prayer, Book of   see BOOK OF COMMON PRAYER

Common Sense   *Common Sense,* a political pamphlet by Thomas PAINE, had a profound effect on the thinking of Americans during the early stages of the American Revolution. Published in January 1776 and distributed throughout the colonies in an edition of well over 100,000 copies, *Common Sense* brought into sharp focus the rising revolutionary sentiment by placing blame for the suffering of the colonies directly on the reigning British monarch, George III. The spirit of Paine's argument was echoed in the American Declaration of Independence.

Commons, House of   see PARLIAMENT

Commonwealth Games   The Commonwealth Games, originally called the British Empire Games, were first held in 1930 at Hamilton, Ont., Canada, to provide competition for the member nations of the British Commonwealth 2 years after each Olympic Games competition. They have been held every four years, except for 1942 and 1946, in London (1934), Sydney (1938), Auckland, New Zealand (1950), Vancouver, British Columbia (1954), Cardiff, Wales (1958), Perth, Australia (1962), Kingston, Jamaica (1966), Edinburgh, Scotland (1970), Christchurch, New Zealand (1974), Edmonton, Alberta (1978), Brisbane, Australia (1982), Edinburgh (1986), and Auckland (1990). Although several sports are staged, the Commonwealth Games are best known for their world-class competition and records in track and field and swimming. At the 1954 gathering, Roger Bannister of Great Britain and John Landy of Australia—the only two men who had run the mile in less than 4 minutes—met for the first time, with Bannister winning in his best time ever, 3:58.8.

Commonwealth of Nations   The Commonwealth of Nations, usually called simply the Commonwealth, is an association of Great Britain and independent countries that were formerly part of the BRITISH EMPIRE, together with their dependencies. The stated purpose of the Commonwealth is consultation and cooperation. Heads of Commonwealth governments meet at intervals of one to three years, but their decisions are not binding on each other. A state may withdraw from the Commonwealth, as did Ireland (1949), South Africa (1961), and Pakistan (1972), though Pakistan rejoined in 1989. Fiji's membership lapsed in 1987.

The founding document of the Commonwealth was the Statute of Westminster of 1931, in which the dominions of Australia, Canada, New Zealand, and South Africa were described as "autonomous communities within the British Empire, equal in status" to the United Kingdom. As other British dependencies gained independence, some becoming republics, the Commonwealth dropped the requirement that members hold allegiance to the British monarch. Instead, members recognize the monarch as the Commonwealth's symbolic head.

The Commonwealth has a secretariat in London that arranges meetings and conferences, disseminates information, and provides various technical services. There have long been economic ties between Britain and other members of the Commonwealth, and members formerly received preferential tariff treatment for goods they sold in Britain. When Britain joined the European Economic Community in 1973, the tariff preferences had to be abandoned.

communal living   Communal living is a term that describes the practice of several unrelated persons living together to pursue their vision of the good life. Most communitarians have utopian goals, the pursuit of which gives participants an elevated sense of collective- and self-worth. Communal life provides a feeling of certitude that is often difficult to maintain in the larger, more complex society, and a degree of social support found in few other kinds of human relationships.

Early communal movements in the United States were constituted of Christian sectarian groups, such as the Mennonites, Moravians, and Shakers. After 1825, European socialist ideas found expression in such utopian communes as Robert OWEN's NEW HARMONY, Ind., group (see also UTOPIAS). With later waves of immigration came such new communal groups as the Hutterites, Theosophists, Bohemians, and anarchists.

The mid-1960s signaled a new phenomenon. Thousands of primarily middle- to upper-middle-class youth renounced the materialism of the their parents and headed for rural communes. The term COUNTERCULTURE characterizes these new communards. Subsequently, communal groups with religious orientation reappeared. One of the most infamous modern communes, a religious-political cult headed by the Rev. Jim Jones, ended with a mass suicide in JONESTOWN, Guyana. (See also RELIGIOUS CULTS.)

A few communal groups that last beyond five years tend to demand high commitment from their members. Members are expected to renounce the outside world completely, to give all personal belongings to the group, and to engage in practices that demonstrate total allegiance. The high degree of social control exercised in these groups has elicited charges of "brainwashing."

commune   The commune was a self-governing municipality in the MIDDLE AGES that guaranteed to its population personal liberty, the right to regulate trade and collect taxes, and the right to its own system of justice within the town walls. In northern Europe, especially in England, France, and the Low Countries, communes were recognized through charters granted usually from the royal government or the local count.

In Italy communes were sworn associations of townsmen that arose during the 11th century to overthrow the rule of the local bishop or feudal magnates. At first, these communes were ruled by consuls elected from the

wealthy merchant class and, hence, were really oligarchies. In the 13th century, the Italian communes created the office of *podestà*, a foreigner who served as chief magistrate, usually for a year or 6 months.

With the rise of the *popolo*—the small merchants and retailers of the Italian cities—the communes became more broadly based democracies. In the late 13th and early 14th centuries, civil strife and threat of conquest often forced the communes to hand over dictatorial powers to a single strong leader, called the *signore* ("lord").

Commune of Paris   The Commune of Paris was the revolutionary municipal government of Paris established from Mar. 18 to May 28, 1871.

In March 1871, Parisians, irritated by the national government's surrender to Germany in the FRANCO-PRUSSIAN WAR, reacted to seemingly anti-Parisian acts of the government by establishing an independent municipal government of Paris. The national government reassembled the scattered French armies and invested Paris, which had already endured a 4-month siege by the Germans. In May the city fell, and the Commune was suppressed. The battle for the city left about 33,000 dead and parts of the city in ruins.

During la semaine sanglante *("bloody week") of May 21–28, 1871, the Parisian communards resisted the troops of the Versailles government by barricading the streets and burning several buildings, including the Tuileries Palace* (shown) *and the Hôtel de Ville.*

Although the Commune was only marginally socialist in membership or actions, it has occupied an important place in socialist and communist doctrine as the earliest example of a proletarian government. Its brutal repression alienated much of the French working class from parliamentary government and turned it toward revolutionary SYNDICALISM.

communicable diseases   see INFECTIOUS DISEASES

communication

Communication embraces the variety of behaviors, processes, and technologies by which meaning is transmitted or derived from information. The term is used to describe diverse activities: conversation; data exchange between computers; courting behavior of birds (see ANIMAL COMMUNICATION); the emotional impact of a work of art; the course of a rumor; and the network of nervous and metabolic subsystems that make up the body's immune system. This article focuses on human communication, including interpersonal communication, language and verbal behavior, and the anthropological aspects of communication in society.

History

Until the 20th century, theories of communication were the province of writers on philosophy, language, and rhetoric (see RHETORIC AND ORATORY). Aristotle taught that rhetoric was a search for all the available means of persuasion and that one had to examine the speaker, the message, and the audience to understand the effect of rhetoric and how that effect was achieved. That concept endured to the 20th century. Descartes and Leibniz recognized mathematics as a universal language for the description of physical systems and phenomena, and they speculated about the development of artificial languages (see LANGUAGES, ARTIFICIAL) to improve the precision of communication. Psychologists studying behavior and its antecedents in various stimuli explored some aspects of communication behavior in the first half of the 20th century, but it was not until the publication of two enormously influential works in 1948 that a comprehensive theory of communication emerged. In that year, both Claude SHANNON's monograph *The Mathematical Theory of Communication* and Norbert WIENER's *Cybernetics: or Control and Communication in the Animal and the Machine* were published to wide acclaim.

Communication Models

Shannon's model included six elements: an information source (usually a person), a transmitter, a communication channel, a noise source, a receiver, and a destination (usually another person). His and Warren Weaver's revised model, published the same year, includes a source (the speaker), an encoder (the vocal system), a message (language and visual cues), a channel (sound waves in the air), a decoder (the listener's ears), and a receiver (the listener). The noise source (static on a radio; background noise in face-to-face communication) in later formulations came to be known as ENTROPY.

Norbert Wiener, also a mathematician, introduced the concept of FEEDBACK, a construct he deduced from observations about interactions between humans, animals, and the physical environment. Wiener described the many ways in which organisms modify their own behavior to correct for adverse reactions to some other aspect of their behavior. In communication, feedback is a verbal or visual cue that indicates whether the message has been received and correctly interpreted; it may be a nod of the head, a slap in the face, or a question. Wiener used the term HOMEOSTASIS to describe the ability to detect a deviation from a desired state and a feedback mechanism by which the discrepancy is noted and fed back for the purpose of modifying behavior. Such a system more closely approximates actual interpersonal communication, and few theoretical models today fail to incorporate the concept.

Later models present a range of specific theories that pertain to various communication situations. In the social sciences, these theories have modified the Shannon-Weaver and cybernetic models to include greater emphasis on the nature of the next interaction, the response to the message, and the context within which the interaction occurs. An extreme model put forth by Marshall McLUHAN holds that the communication medium exerts so strong an influence on the communication process that it virtually controls what is communicated.

Noam CHOMSKY, in *Syntactic Structures* (1957), rejected some of the mathematical assumptions of Shannon and Weaver as inadequate for describing the ways in which people use English grammar; this in turn influenced psychologist George A. Miller to experiment with human responses to language and meaning. Social psychology and anthropology have also developed elaborate models, which treat such factors as predispositional personality variables, the credibility of the source, states of cognitive consistency of the receiver, the nature and role of attitudes, and selected message variables.

Interpersonal Communication

Two basic approaches have been used to define interpersonal communication. One approach includes all the ways in which people influence each other, even unintentionally. Anthropologist Edward T. Hall's popular book *The Silent Language* (1959) described the ways in which such NONVERBAL COMMUNICATION as the physical proximity between two people communicated much about their

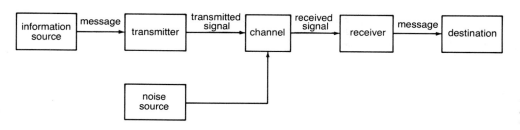

Shannon's diagram of a syntactic communication chain, although representative of technical systems, can be applied to all forms of communication.

cultural background or personal relationship. This approach defines communication by referring to the response of the receiver and therefore includes the total environment of social behavior, not just specific acts or utterances.

Other scholars believe that communication should be limited to only those intentional interactions that occur by means of symbols. This view assumes that although the attempt to communicate with another may fail in the sense that the speaker may not evoke the desired response, *intention* nevertheless defines the communication act. This orientation has produced research into persuasibility factors of personality; the importance of the order of presentation of arguments; and the role of selective perception, source credibility, and pressures to conform to group norms.

Language and Verbal Behavior

A second major area of human communication focuses on language and verbal behavior. Today this field is dominated by linguistics, anthropology, and psychology. The common concern is the potential of language to transmit meaning. Language is not the only system of communication. Others are gestures, representational arts, and other symbol systems such as traffic signs; but language has much greater communicative power.

Two phenomena indicate the kinds of questions addressed in this field of study. First, when people speak they do not transmit their thoughts to another; rather they transmit sounds and visual cues, which must be interpreted in order for communication to occur. The American philosopher Charles Sanders PEIRCE pointed out that meaning was not inherent in these sounds and cues but was the product of the relationship between them and the item referred to by the speaker (and the listener). Conventions among speakers of the same language allow a certain sound to represent a word that another convention agrees is the name of an object. Peirce used the term SEMIOTICS to refer to language and communication. Charles Morris, following Peirce, divided the field into three parts: SEMANTICS, the study of the relationship between signs (sounds and visual cues, for example) and meaning; syntactics, the rules governing the combination of signs without regard for their meaning; and pragmatics, the various uses and effects of signs by individuals.

The second phenomenon is that any concept, idea, or object, no matter how sophisticated or culture bound, can be expressed in any other language. Furthermore, in any language an infinite number of sentence possibilities exist, and yet even a relatively young child can produce and understand sentences he or she has never heard before. To explain these facts, Chomsky, concentrating on the syntactic aspects of language, has postulated that innate grammatical principles are programmed into the human brain as part of a human being's genetic heritage. Apart from the fact that there is no independent evidence in favor of this, Chomsky deemphasizes the most important function of language—communication. SPEECH DEVELOPMENT and cognitive development, both directly related to this aspect of communication, have been the subject of intense investigation by Jean PIAGET, Jerome Bruner, and Roger Brown.

Communication and Culture

Anthropologists looking at human communication tend to focus on its central role in the continuance of a society—the preservation and transmittal of the unformulated aspects of a culture. Society arises and continues to exist through the communication of significant symbols. The concepts of honor, bravery, love, cooperation, and honesty, for example, are embodied in language and other symbolic behaviors that create and sustain belief in ways of acting because they function as names signifying proper, dubious, or improper ways of expressing relationships.

Communication has another importance for anthropologists. Edward SAPIR pointed out that language is not only a means of providing a systematic inventory of the various items of experience (through naming); it also defines that experience because of the way in which language itself imposes its thought patterns on human perception. Benjamin Lee Whorf took this hypothesis even further, arguing that the world is differently experienced and conceived in different linguistic communities because each language embodies and perpetuates a different worldview. Few authorities today accept that strong a relationship between language and culture. Nonetheless, anthropology clearly takes the broadest view of communication, seeing it as the mechanism through which human relations exist and develop.

---

communications satellite A communications satellite is an artificial SATELLITE placed into orbit around the Earth to facilitate communications on Earth. Most long-distance radio communication across land is sent via MICROWAVE relay towers. In effect, a satellite serves as a tall microwave tower to permit direct transmission between stations, but it can interconnect any number of stations that are included within the antenna beams of the satellite rather than simply the two ends of the microwave link.

Intelsat satellites orbit above the equator over the Pacific (1), Atlantic (2), and Indian (3) oceans. Each satellite's orbital velocity is synchronized with the rotation of the Earth. They thus remain in fixed positions relative to the surface and can relay messages among most of the world's inhabited areas.

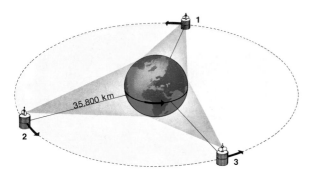

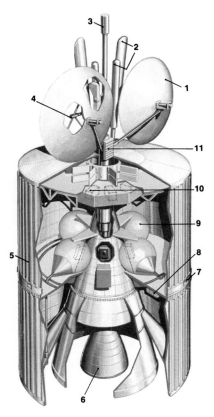

The Intelsat IV series of communications satellites, first launched in 1971, were 528 cm (17 ft) high and could relay more than 4,000 two-way telephone calls or 12 television programs simultaneously. Among the satellite's major components were a spot-beam communications antenna (1), wide-beam transmitting and receiving antenna (2), telemetry and command antenna (3), antenna-positioner mechanism (4), solar panels (5), apogee motor for the satellite's final placement in orbit (6), sun sensor (7), battery pack (8), hydrazine fuel tanks for the jets that stabilized the satellite's orientation in space (9), electronics compartments (10), and planar-array antenna (11).

History. The concept of using a satellite repeater was first proposed by Arthur C. Clarke in the October 1945 issue of *Wireless World*. The development of powerful rockets in the mid-1950s and the simultaneous development of sensitive low-noise receiving equipment made communications satellites a realistic consideration.

The period from 1958 to 1963 was one of experimentation with both active satellites, those with electronic instrumentation, and passive satellites, those which simply reflected signals. On Dec. 18, 1958, the U.S. Army placed *Score* in a low-altitude orbit. It had only one voice channel and could retransmit messages directly or store them for later playback. On Aug. 12, 1960, NASA launched Echo, a passive aluminized plastic balloon, 30 m (100 ft) in diameter, into an orbit 1,600 km (1,000 mi) above the Earth. In 1962 experiments were conducted on TELSTAR and RELAY, medium-altitude active satellites with the capacity of one television channel or several hundred voice channels. In 1963, SYNCOM *2* became the first synchronous satellite with a period matching the Earth's rotation rate. These satellites proved the basic concepts and were the basis of later commercial satellite designs.

The Communications Satellite Corporation (COMSAT) was incorporated on Feb. 1, 1963, as a private U.S. company to establish, in conjunction with the telecommunications administrations of other countries, a commercial communications satellite system. In mid-1964 the International Telecommunications Satellite Consortium (INTELSAT) was formed with 12 countries; membership had increased by the late 1980s to 110. Starting with EARLY BIRD (*Intelsat I*), in 1965, the system evolved through five generations of satellites with ever-increasing capacity to the *Intelsat VI* series in 1989, each capable of conveying 33,000 and perhaps eventually 100,000 conversations. The rapid growth of the system required increased capacity, and advances in technology and launch capability supplied the means to build and launch higher-capacity satellites. The global Intelsat system now carries the major portion of the world's long-distance international telecommunications traffic.

The success of communications satellites for international use resulted in their use for domestic service as well. The largest-capacity satellite launched thus far is *Comstar*, leased by Comsat General Corporation to American Telephone and Telegraph. Its capacity is 18,000 two-way telephone circuits, or 24 television channels.

Stucture and Operation. A communications satellite is a platform that houses radio receivers and their antennae, receives signals from the Earth stations, and amplifies and passes the signals to a transmitter and antenna, with sufficient power to reach Earth. Such a satellite also requires solar cells to supply power to the amplifiers; fuel to periodically adjust the satellite's position to offset forces caused by the Sun and the Moon; and attitude control equipment to keep the satellite antennae pointed properly at the Earth, using either the Sun, the edge of the Earth, or a radio beacon on Earth as a reference point. Telemetry encoders and transmitters measure voltages, currents, temperatures, and other parameters describing the condition of the satellite and transmit this information to Earth. Finally, a structure must house all this equipment. For example, an *Intelsat V* weighs more than 1,950 kg (4,300 lb).

The major Earth stations that communicate with these satellites typically comprise an antenna about 30 m (100 ft) in diameter, a receiver that is cooled to 14 K in order to reduce its noise; and a radio transmitter with a power output in the range of several hundred to several thousand watts to send signals to the satellite. Smaller Earth stations—even portable receivers—are also used, but on a more restrictive basis because of their greater demands on satellite capacity.

In order to meet the needs of increased communications traffic, projected at more than 100,000 circuits in the 1990s, all speech will be converted to digital bits, a method already used to a great extent in communications networks. Additional capacity is obtained by using the same frequency band several times over multiple narrow beams from the satellite, and by extending the frequency band. Private business satellites for a wide variety of services are becoming common, and the availability of higher-powered satellites permits smaller antennae for Earth stations with modest traffic demands. Satellites are coming into routine use for communications to ships and planes. The trend will be toward higher capacity at lower cost for each circuit. In some areas of the world, satellites can broadcast directly to individual homes.

Communion   see EUCHARIST; MASS

—

communism   Communism, as understood today, refers to the political and socioeconomic doctrines of the USSR and of those governments and political parties in Eastern Europe, China, and elsewhere that have shared those doctrines. Communism also means the traditionally centralized political system of the Soviet Union and other countries in which Communist parties have held power. This system is associated with collective ownership of the means of production, central economic planning, and rule by a single political party. Its ideology is MARXISM, as interpreted by leaders such as V. I. LENIN and MAO ZEDONG. Once a dynamic, expansive movement, world Communism had undergone startling transformations by the early 1990s.

Communism is an outgrowth of 19th-century SOCIALISM. It became a distinct movement after the RUSSIAN REVOLUTIONS OF 1917, when a group of revolutionary socialists seized power and adopted the name Communist party of the USSR. Mongolia became a Communist state in 1921. After World War II other Communist states were established in the Eastern European countries of Poland, East Germany, Czechoslovakia, Hungary, Romania, Bulgaria, Yugoslavia, and Albania, and in the Asian countries of China and North Korea. Communist regimes were subsequently established in Cuba, in the Southeast Asian countries of Vietnam, Laos, and Kampuchea (Cambodia), and in Afghanistan. Pro-Soviet revolutionary governments came into existence in South Yemen (1970–90) and several African states, notably Angola, Mozambique, and Ethiopia. In the Western Hemisphere the leftist Sandinista regime (1979–90) in Nicaragua was under substantial Soviet and Cuban influence.

Early Forms of Communism. Originally, the term *communism* signified an ideal society in which property would be owned in common and the necessities of life shared by members of the community according to their needs. Communism in this sense dates back to classical antiquity. PLATO proposed a kind of aristocratic communism in his *Republic*. Some of the early Christian groups held property in common. The idea of common ownership figured in Sir Thomas More's UTOPIA (1516), and was espoused by such religious groups as the ANABAPTISTS in 16th-century Germany. It inspired numerous religious and social reformers of the 19th century, including Étienne CABET, Charles FOURIER, Robert OWEN, Pierre Joseph PROUDHON, and the comte de SAINT-SIMON. Their theories contributed to the 19th-century socialist movement aimed at replacing the system of private property with one in which property would be owned by society as a whole. Stronger revolutionary socialist theories were expressed by François BABEUF during the French Revolution and by Louis BLANC and Auguste BLANQUI later in France (see REVOLUTIONS OF 1848).

Karl Marx, a German social theorist, collaborated with Friedrich Engels in 1848 to produce the Communist Manifesto, *a 40-page pamphlet written for a group of European revolutionaries. The principles outlined in the* Communist Manifesto, *which Marx elaborated in* Das Kapital *(1867) and later writings, form the ideological basis of scientific socialism.*

The Rise of Marxism. In their COMMUNIST MANIFESTO (1848), Karl MARX and Friedrich ENGELS applied the term *communism* to a final stage of socialism in which all class differences would disappear and humankind would live in harmony. Marx and Engels declared that the course of history was determined by the clash of opposing forces rooted in the economic system and the ownership of property. Just as the feudal system had given way to CAPITALISM, so in time capitalism would give way to socialism. The class struggle of the future would be between the bourgeoisie, or capitalist employers, and the proletariat, or workers. The struggle would end, according to Marx, in the socialist revolution and the attainment of full communism.

Marxism became the dominant body of thought in European socialism in the 19th century. Within the socialist parties, controversy raged between those who felt the need for a revolutionary overthrow of capitalism and those who held that socialism might be achieved through gradual reforms.

European Marxists were strongly international in their outlook. They proclaimed their opposition to imperialism and militarism and declared that the workers had no fatherland. However, the outbreak of World War I in 1914 demonstrated that nationalism still had a strong grip on the socialist parties. Except for a few radicals such as Karl LIEBKNECHT and Rosa LUXEMBURG in Germany and Lenin in Russia, the party leaders and most members supported the war policies of their governments. The Russian Revolutions of 1917, which enabled Lenin and his followers to seize power, divided world socialism into competing groups of parties—those which opted for the Russian path and those which kept to the democratic tradition.

Communism in the USSR

Two Russian revolutions took place in 1917. The first, in February (O.S.; March, N.S.), brought the collapse of the tsarist regime and its replacement by a weak provisional government. A jostling for power began among various parties and groups, including two factions, called BOL-

SHEVIKS AND MENSHEVIKS, of the Russian Social Democratic Workers' party, a Marxist party founded in 1898. The Mensheviks, led by, among others, the party's founder, Georgy PLEKHANOV, believed that "feudal" Russia would have to pass through the capitalist phase under a bourgeois democratic regime before it would be ripe for socialism. The Bolsheviks, led by Lenin, called for the overthrow of the provisional government in favor of immediate rule by workers and peasants.

Leninism. Lenin was not only a revolutionist but a prolific writer who made important additions to the theory of Marxism and created a doctrine for professional revolutionists that gained considerable influence in the economically backward areas of the world. In his pamphlet *What Is To Be Done?* (1902) he called for an elitist, disciplined party of professional revolutionists to lead the working class toward communism. Lenin espoused an almost military organizational discipline within the party. His forceful insistence upon his own point of view caused the Russian socialists to divide into Bolshevik and Menshevik factions in 1903.

In October (O.S.; November, N.S.) 1917, Lenin led the Bolsheviks in a successful coup d'état against the provisional government of Russia. The initial period of Lenin's Soviet government (1917–21) was characterized by trial and error in the midst of economic dislocation, social chaos, domestic civil war, and foreign intervention. Lenin soon abandoned the notion that the government could function as a "democratic dictatorship of workers and peasants." He dissolved the Constituent Assembly that had been elected after the Bolshevik seizure of pow-

Joseph Stalin, a minor Communist party bureaucrat, emerged as the undisputed ruler of the Soviet Union following the death of Lenin. Convinced that it was unrealistic to expect the immediate overthrow of capitalism in the West, Stalin advocated "socialism in one country," which contradicted the internationalist theories of Marx and Lenin.

er, outlawed all other parties, and made the internal discipline of the ruling Bolshevik, or Communist, party even stricter.

Lenin also laid the basis for the domination of other Communist parties by the USSR. He insisted that foreign parties break with the existing Second (Socialist) INTERNATIONAL and form a Third, or Communist, International, which came to be known as the COMINTERN. Every party was required to impose Leninist discipline on its members and on the world Communist movement as a whole. As a result of this, the Comintern, with its headquarters in Moscow and controlling Communist parties in other countries, eventually became little more than an instrument of Soviet foreign policy.

A second phase began in 1921, when Lenin recognized that priority must be given to economic reconstruction. The NEW ECONOMIC POLICY (NEP) legalized private trade, encouraged small-scale private enterprise, and loosened the state's grip on agricultural production, all in sharp contrast to the radical social and economic experimentation of the preceding period. The NEP, however, was no more than a strategic retreat. The party took the offensive again in 1928 by introducing centralized economic planning through the First Five-Year Plan, which called for forced-draft industrialization and the collectivization of agriculture. By means of these programs, implemented at terrible human cost, the Communist party attempted to create the kind of industrial system that already existed in the capitalist countries of the West, but with state ownership of the means of production.

Stalinism. The Soviet leader by this time was Joseph STALIN. Following Lenin's death in 1924, Stalin skillfully used his position as general secretary of the Communist party to obtain a monopoly of power. He overcame the opposition of Leon TROTSKY, who had been Lenin's chief lieutenant during the revolution. Lenin and Trotsky had justified their seizure of power as being only the beginning of international revolution that would soon overthrow capitalism in advanced industrial countries such as Germany. They had believed that they would have to wait for

V. I. Lenin proclaims the success of the October Revolution of 1917, which brought the Bolsheviks to power in Russia. Lenin's writings and political practices profoundly influenced the Communist movement in the 20th century.

Chairman Mao Zedong confers with Soviet leader Nikita Khrushchev at a meeting in Moscow in 1957. Relations between the People's Republic of China and the Soviet Union deteriorated during the 1960s, and the two communist giants remained at odds until the 1980s.

the revolution to happen elsewhere before they could successfully build socialism in Russia. Stalin, however, enunciated the doctrine of "socialism in one country," maintaining that the USSR could build socialism by itself. Stalin ruthlessly carried out the policies of industrialization and collectivization. Between 1936 and 1940, most of the Old Bolsheviks (the leaders of the 1917 revolution) were executed. At the same time Stalin systematically eliminated most of the officer corps of the Red Army, purged the government bureaucracy, and unleashed indiscriminate mass terror against the population as a whole. (See GREAT PURGE.)

Under Stalin the party strove to control every aspect of Soviet life. His policy decisions, made arbitrarily, were enforced as much by the secret police as by the party. The pervasive controls were relaxed somewhat during World War II, in order to gain popular support for the war effort against the invading Germans, but at the end of the war they were quickly reestablished. The Soviet population was once again forced to endure economic privation and political repression so that the Soviet leadership could expand the domestic base of heavy industry.

Stalin died in 1953, and Soviet leadership was eventually taken over by Nikita KHRUSHCHEV. At the 20th Congress of the Communist party in February 1956, Khrushchev denounced Stalin's political methods and disclosed some of the crimes Stalin had committed to protect his rule. Under Khrushchev the party cautiously loosened its grip on the country without permitting any basic criticism of Communist policies. Many of the labor camps in the GULAG system, to which millions of people had been sentenced under Stalin's regime, were closed, and a degree of dissent was tolerated. Khrushchev also sought to raise living standards. In October 1964, Khrushchev was unseated by his associates and replaced by Leonid BREZHNEV as general secretary and Aleksei KOSYGIN as premier.

Although it did not return to the terror of Stalin's time, the Brezhnev regime cracked down on domestic dissidence. Under Brezhnev, the Soviet Union undertook a major arms buildup and sought to expand its influence abroad in ways that damaged relations with the United States and threatened East-West détente. At home the Soviet system suffered from widespread bureaucratic stagnation and rampant corruption. Brezhnev, who died in 1982, was succeeded by two short-lived successors, Yuri ANDROPOV and Konstantin CHERNENKO.

The Gorbachev Revolution. In March 1985 a new leader, Mikhail GORBACHEV, took over in the Kremlin. Seeking to revitalize the Soviet system, Gorbachev advocated GLASNOST, or openness in public affairs, and called for PERESTROIKA, a restructuring of economic organization and political life. Among other institutional changes was the creation of the powerful new office of Soviet president, to which Gorbachev himself was duly elected.

The Soviet leader's espousal of more friendly relations with the West won him much popularity abroad. Within the Soviet Union, however, Gorbachev's reform program encountered political opposition and bureaucratic obstruction. At his behest the Soviet Communist party gave up its Leninist claim to a monopoly of political power, grudgingly accepting a degree of political pluralism and the prospect of genuine parliamentary democracy. This alienated Communist hardliners without satisfying radical reformers. Gorbachev's program was also threatened by a host of socioeconomic problems, including strikes and food shortages. Most dangerous of all was the outbreak of ethnic tensions and separatism, especially in the Caucasus, Central Asia, and the Baltic republics. By 1990 the longer-term survival of the USSR as a multinational state could no longer be taken for granted.

Communism in Eastern Europe

When the Soviet armies moved into Eastern Europe at the end of World War II, they installed Communist govern-

During the Hungarian Revolution of 1956, Hungarians celebrated the capture of a Soviet tank by unfurling a flag emblazoned with the cross of Saint Stephen, a historical symbol of Hungarian nationalism. This moment of triumph was short-lived: Soviet troops brutally put down the revolution, whose champion, Prime Minister Imre Nagy, was eventually executed (1958).

ments in Poland, East Germany, Czechoslovakia, Hungary, Romania, and Bulgaria. Stalin soon moved to reduce these new "people's democracies" to the status of Soviet satellites. Because the Comintern had been dissolved during the war, another international organization, the Communist Information Bureau (Cominform), was founded in 1947 to coordinate the policies of Communist parties.

Yugoslavia. Communist regimes were also established in Yugoslavia and Albania after the war. In these countries, however, the Communists came to power largely through their own efforts, after fighting a successful struggle for national liberation from German occupation. When the Yugoslav leader, TITO, resisted Stalin's efforts to control him, the Yugoslav party was expelled (1948) by the Cominform. Stalin them purged the other East European parties of so-called Titoists, national Communists, and other deviationists. Throughout the area under his power, Stalin imposed the same political and economic regimentation with which he ruled the USSR.

The Crises of 1956. Stalin's imperialistic system received a series of shocks after his death, in March 1953. Those who succeeded him in the Kremlin had to establish their own policies, including a rapprochement with Tito, partial easing of the Soviet grip on the East European satellites, and some half-hearted domestic reforms. After Khrushchev's denunciation of Stalin in 1956, a crisis of authority occurred in Eastern Europe. It was most severe in Poland and Hungary. In Poland the Communists were able to survive the crisis after Moscow allowed the return to power of Władysław GOMUŁKA, a former leader who had been ousted as a national Communist in 1948. In Hungary the unrest exploded into open rebellion (October 1956). Because of popular pressure, certain Communist leaders permitted the reintroduction of a genuine multiparty system and declared Hungary's neutrality in international politics. The HUNGARIAN REVOLUTION was put down by Soviet troops. In the aftermath of the 1956 upheaval, Khrushchev sought to tie the Soviet-bloc countries together by fostering the development of such institutions as the WARSAW TREATY ORGANIZATION and the COUNCIL FOR MUTUAL ECONOMIC ASSISTANCE.

Later Developments. The decay of Soviet authority over other Communist governments could also be seen elsewhere. Yugoslavia had been the first to take a different road after 1948, giving up the attempt to collectivize agriculture and turning over industrial enterprises to workers' councils. Its leaders held to this path after Tito's death, in 1980.

In 1968 economic and political liberalization led by Alexander DUBČEK threatened to undermine the Communist party's control of Czechoslovakia and set off repercussions in other East European countries. Moscow denounced the trend as "creeping counterrevolution." In August 1968, Czechoslovakia was invaded by armies of the Warsaw Treaty Organization, and orthodox leadership reinstated.

To justify its intervention in Czechoslovakia, the USSR asserted the right and duty of Communist countries to render "fraternal assistance against counterrevolution," which was known in the West as the Brezhnev Doctrine.

In 1979 the doctrine was exercised in Afghanistan, which was occupied by Soviet troops to prop up the pro-Soviet regime there.

In 1980 a wave of strikes in Poland led to the legalization of an independent trade union movement, SOLIDARITY, and the promise of further liberalization. In December 1981, however, the Polish government, pressured by Moscow, declared a "state of war" against its own society and suppressed Solidarity. Although martial law was officially lifted in 1983, the Polish Communist regime under Gen. Wojciech JARUZELSKI ruled with a heavy hand.

The Overthrow of the System. In 1989, with the tacit endorsement of the Gorbachev regime, negotiations with Solidarity led to Poland's first partially free elections in 40 years and produced a major defeat for the Polish Communist party. Jaruzelski then called on a Solidarity leader to head a coalition government that included both Communists and anti-Communists. The new Solidarity-led government soon introduced a package of sweeping economic reforms designed to replace Poland's defunct command economy with the free market.

Throughout Eastern Europe, 1989–90 was a time of major upheaval. East Germany, amid widespread popular protests, changed its leadership, and in November 1989 it opened its border with West Germany for the first time in decades. In March 1990 free elections in East Germany produced a non-Communist government. This marked the beginning of the end of a separate East German state, which in a rapid succession of moves merged with West Germany. Demands for reform supported by Moscow toppled the Czechoslovak regime in November 1989, leading quickly to a freely elected non-Communist government there. In 1990, Hungary also held free elections. Hungary's reformist Communist party had reconstituted itself and campaigned under a new name; nonetheless, it was voted out of office. In December 1989 the Romanians overthrew the brutally repressive dictatorship of Nicolae CEAUŞESCU. Romania's new leaders renounced Marxism, but many of them were former Communists, and they used strong-arm methods in dealing with dissidents. Bulgaria also underwent a change in top leadership, but its first steps toward democracy were hesitant. In Yugoslavia the authority of the Communist party crumbled as the country experienced a revival of separatism and ethnic strife. Even Albania, long a bastion of rigid orthodoxy, experienced violent upheavals.

Communism in China

In 1949 a Communist movement won power in China under the leadership of Mao Zedong. Founded in 1921, the Chinese Communist party allied with the KUOMINTANG (Nationalists) in 1923, under orders from the Comintern. By 1927, however, the Nationalists had turned on the Communists, and a long civil war began. Forced to retreat into the interior (the LONG MARCH of 1934–35), the Chinese Communists built their party on peasant support. During the Second Sino-Japanese War, which began in 1937 and eventually became part of World War II, the party provided more effective resistance to the Japanese

In China during the Great Proletarian Cultural Revolution (1966–69), militant students, organized as Red Guards, rallied under banners and photographs of Chairman Mao to attack "bad elements" and "revisionists." After Mao's death (1976), the leaders known collectively as the Gang of Four lost their bid to retain power; subsequently, they were blamed for the excesses of the Cultural Revolution.

than did the Kuomintang, and by the end (1945) of the war controlled large areas. By 1949 it had defeated the discredited Kuomintang and established control over the country.

Maoism. Although the Chinese Communist party gave lip service to the doctrines of Lenin and Stalin, its Marxism was shaped by its own unique experience and blended with the ideas of Mao. Mao saw humans as engaged in a permanent struggle against nature. Society was riven by contradictions between classes and between groups. The class struggle could be solved by revolution, but after the revolution it was necessary to work out the conflicts that existed among groups of people and even within the party. Mao also believed that the revolution did not end when the Communists came to power; it had to be waged continually against vestiges of the old culture and against bureaucratic habits.

The Sino-Soviet Split. Under Stalin, Sino-Soviet relations were correct but not close. Khrushchev initially improved relations with Beijing by recognizing China's autonomy in the world Communist movement. Political and ideological differences soon emerged, however, particularly after Khrushchev's denunciation of Stalin and his espousal of the goal of "peaceful coexistence" with the West. The Chinese showed no interest in reducing COLD WAR tensions. In 1960 the USSR discontinued military and technical aid to China. After the USSR signed (1963) a treaty with the United States and Great Britain banning most tests of nuclear weapons, the Chinese accused the USSR of joining with China's enemies. Thereafter, both sides waged a bitter propaganda war.

The Sino-Soviet dispute destroyed the unity of Marxism-Leninism as a world view and weakened the pretension of the USSR to be the leader of the world Communist movement. When Khrushchev's successors tried to improve relations with Beijing, they were rebuffed by Mao Zedong. The Chinese, who were struggling to maintain revolutionary militance in a vast peasant country, refused to accept Soviet leadership. They had collectivized agriculture and socialized industry during the 1950s but then had turned away from Soviet-style economic planning. They announced a GREAT LEAP FORWARD that was to carry China into the Communist era ahead of other countries.

The aim was to speed up economic progress by using China's human reserves in place of scarce capital, but the acceleration resulted in a seriously disorganized economy, and the attempt was abandoned.

A struggle continued in China between those who wanted to follow the Soviet approach to industrialization and those who thought of the Soviets as another bourgeois society. Mao himself declared that the Soviet Communists had betrayed the revolution. In 1966, Mao launched the CULTURAL REVOLUTION, in which millions of young Communists, organized as Red Guards, went through the country denouncing senior officials and establishing revolutionary committees in place of local government bodies. The Cultural Revolution ended in 1969, and the leaders set about rebuilding new party and state organs. The power struggle finally ended after Mao's death in 1976 with the moderates in control, led by DENG XIAOPING. China then embarked on a program of technological modernization. China established diplomatic relations with the United States in 1979 and subsequently encouraged increased interaction with Western nations. It also improved relations with the USSR. The end of the Sino-Soviet conflict was symbolized by Gorbachev's visit to Beijing in 1989.

Chinese Contradictions. Deng's initial, ideologically ambiguous call for the "four modernizations" developed into a concerted program for economic reform, featuring various market incentives and the establishment of special economic zones with considerable latitude for private enterprise. Opponents of the party's dictatorship asked for more, a "fifth modernization"—that is, the renunciation of the party's leading role and the introduction of democracy. This was rejected by most of China's aging Communist elite. Deng and his entourage wanted economic reform without political change. They were determined to crush their critics by force, if necessary, and did so in the June 1989 massacre of students and others in Beijing's Tiananmen Square where up to one million pro-democracy protesters had gathered for weeks on end.

Communism Elsewhere

Communist movements developed in a number of countries in Asia, Africa, Latin America, and Europe. In some

In May 1989, as Soviet leader Mikhail Gorbachev, with his wife Raisa, met with Chinese leader Deng Xiaoping, students were demonstrating for democracy in Beijing's Tiananmen Square. A short time later Chinese army troops and vehicles brutally suppressed the protesters, killing several hundred of them.

cases, notably in Asia and Africa, they have been associated with NATIONALISM and anticolonialism. In Latin America, Communists identified themselves with the struggle against poverty and economic imperialism. In Western Europe they became major parliamentary parties in France and Italy and won control of many municipal governments.

North Korea. The Democratic People's Republic of [North] Korea was established (1948) under Soviet occupation forces after World War II. The state survived the KOREAN WAR (1950–53), and its first leader, KIM IL SUNG, remained in power more than 35 years later, even as his son, Kim-Jong Il, moved to the fore. When the Sino-Soviet conflict developed, Kim and his party had to maneuver between the two great powers. In domestic affairs the Korean Communists followed orthodox patterns emphasizing strict political control and giving continued priority to heavy industry.

Southeast Asia. Communism in Vietnam became intertwined with the long struggle for national liberation from French colonial rule. The well-organized Communist party became the most effective faction in the liberation movement (VIET MINH) during World War II, and by the end of the war it was the strongest political force in Vietnam. The French, seeking to reestablish their colonial rule after the Japanese withdrew, were forced to fight a long war that ended in their defeat at DIEN BIEN PHU in 1954 and in the division of Vietnam into a Communist state in the north and an anti-Communist state in the south. In 1957 a Communist-led insurrection began in the south, leading to the VIETNAM WAR, in which the United States became heavily involved. After U.S. withdrawal in 1973, the armies of North Vietnam soon conquered (1975) South Vietnam, and a unified Socialist Republic of Vietnam was established on July 2, 1976.

The Vietnamese Communists followed the Soviet model in their internal policies, including a single-party regime, state-owned industry, and collectivized agriculture. In foreign affairs they aligned themselves with the USSR and set out to establish hegemony over the other Indochinese countries of Laos and Cambodia. The Laotian Communists (PATHET LAO) had consolidated their power in 1975 after years of military and political struggle. Cambodia (renamed Kampuchea) had been taken over by a harsh Communist (KHMER ROUGE) regime in the same year; the regime depopulated the cities and killed large numbers of Cambodians. In 1977 fighting erupted between Kampuchea, which received military aid from China, and Vietnam, which was backed by the USSR. This culminated in 1979 in the Vietnamese conquest of Kampuchea, which in turn provoked a brief punitive invasion of Vietnam by China. A decade later Vietnam's economy was in a shambles, and the search for a peaceful settlement of the civil war in Kampuchea still remained elusive.

Cuba. Communism came to Cuba after a revolution that brought Fidel CASTRO to power in January 1959. While at first he seemed to have only a pragmatic socialist program, Castro gradually moved leftward, expropriating the property of U.S. business firms and turning to the USSR for economic assistance. The U.S. government tried unsuccessfully to overthrow Castro through the BAY OF PIGS INVASION in 1961. Subsequently, the USSR placed nuclear missiles in Cuba, and the ensuing CUBAN MISSILE CRISIS (1962) seemed to bring the United States and the USSR to the brink of war. In 1965, Castro merged his political movement with the Communist party of Cuba and followed Soviet guidance thereafter.

For a time Castro sought to extend his revolution to other countries of Latin America, but the death (1967) of his former associate Che GUEVARA in Bolivia, where Guevara had gone to organize a guerrilla movement, marked the end of that effort. In the 1970s, detachments of Cuban troops and military advisors appeared in Africa, where they played a part in the civil war in Angola and assisted Ethiopia against Somalia. Despite a substantial annual subsidy from the Soviet Union, Cuba's economy has stagnated as the result of rigid central planning and excessive bureaucratization.

Western Europe. France and Italy emerged from World War II with large Communist parties. The French party had won popular support because of the part it played in the wartime resistance movement. In the first three decades after the war it regularly received between 20 and 26 percent of the votes cast in national elections, giving it a large bloc of seats in the National Assembly. It had strong support among industrial workers and some of the peasantry. Until the 1960s the French party supported Moscow's positions faithfully, but after the Soviet invasion of Czechoslovakia in 1968 it assumed more critical positions. In 1976 it adopted a policy of "socialism in the colors of France," and in 1981, Communists were appointed to the cabinet. Nonetheless, during the 1980s the party suffered a major erosion of electoral strength, and its role in French politics became increasingly marginal.

The Italian Communist party was long known for its critical attitude toward Moscow. Under the leadership (1944–64) of Palmiro TOGLIATTI, it put forward a doctrine of "polycentrism"—meaning that there should be room for a diversity of views among Communist parties. Later, under Enrico Berlinguer (1972–84), it became politically and ideologically moderate, favoring alliances with non-Communist parties. Its political fortunes waned after 1980.

Eurocommunism. During the 1970s leaders of the Italian, French, and Spanish Communist parties began to act together as a political bloc on the basis of common reformist concepts known as Eurocommunism. This regional unity did not last very long. Eurocommunism lost most of its political appeal and disintegrated along national lines.

Problems and Prospects

Communism today is in flux everywhere. International Communist unity has not existed for decades. Under Gorbachev, the Soviet party all but abandoned the goal of overall Communist conferences, emphasizing instead multilateral relations with a wide variety of "progressive forces" throughout the world. Clearly, the world Communist movement no longer exists, having fallen victim to national rivalries and general ideological disorientation.

Communist ideology offers no ready solutions to the many pressing practical problems that now confront Communist governments. Foremost among these is the challenge of economic reform. No one knows for certain how to dismantle command economies without causing socioeconomic chaos. Will a limited degree of marketization and partial measures of agricultural decollectivization prove adequate to achieve the desired economic rejuvenation? Even more basically, can there be really effective economic reform without prior political change of

a fairly fundamental sort, transforming dictatorships into democracies? There are good reasons to doubt that there can be. Once widely regarded as the proverbial "wave of the future," communism now appears headed for eventual extinction as a major political force.

See also: CHINA, HISTORY OF; COMMUNIST PARTY, U.S.A.; RUSSIA/ UNION OF SOVIET SOCIALIST REPUBLICS, HISTORY OF; UTOPIAS.

Communism Peak Communism Peak (formerly Stalin Peak), in southeastern Tadzhikistan, is the highest mountain (7,495 m/24,590 ft) in the USSR. Located in the Pamirs, it was first identified as the USSR's tallest peak in 1932 and first scaled in 1933.

Communist Manifesto The *Communist Manifesto* (1848), a political pamphlet written by Karl MARX in association with Friedrich ENGELS, is one of the most famous documents in the history of MARXISM and COMMUNISM. Intended as a platform statement for a small international workers' party, the Communist League, and published during the REVOLUTIONS OF 1848, the brief work sketches Marx's evolving philosophy of "scientific socialism," a philosophy he fully expounded in *Das Kapital* (see KAPITAL, DAS).

Communist Party, U.S.A. The Communist party of the United States is a left-wing Marxist party dedicated to revolutionary socialism and to support of the Communist movement throughout the world. After the victory of the Communists (Bolsheviks) in Russia in October (O.S.; November, N.S.) 1917, and the establishment of the Communist International (COMINTERN) in Moscow in March 1919, new Communist parties were founded in many countries, including the United States.

From the beginning, the American Communist movement, with about 40,000 members, was plagued with internal divisions, government repression, and Comintern intervention. In 1923 the Communists emerged from underground. Led by Charles E. Ruthenberg, they took the name Workers (Communist) Party of America in 1925. The name was changed in 1929 to Communist Party of the United States (CPUSA). After Ruthenberg's death in 1927, Jay Lovestone became the secretary of the party, but he soon came into conflict with the Soviet leader Joseph Stalin and was expelled from the party in 1929.

In the mid-1930s, the CPUSA, under the leadership of Earl BROWDER, became an important political force, its members increasing from only 7,500 in 1930 to 75,000 in 1939. This last figure understates the party's influence, for it operated through many front organizations that the party controlled but whose members and sympathizers were largely non-Communists. The NAZI-SOVIET PACT of August 1939, which the CPUSA supported, was politically embarrassing to the Communists. Germany's attack on the USSR in June 1941, however, enabled the party to regain its influence. Browder then tried to Americanize the CPUSA, toning down revolutionary appeals and insisting on the necessity of integrating the party into American democratic life. In February 1946 he was expelled from the CPUSA.

The CPUSA played a significant role in supporting Henry A. WALLACE, who ran as a third-party Progressive in the 1948 presidential elections. Thereafter, the party steadily lost ground as the COLD WAR developed. Eleven of its leaders were convicted in 1949 under the SMITH ACT of conspiring to advocate the overthrow of the U.S. government and were sentenced to jail. The MCCARRAN ACT of 1950, which required the registration of all party members, and the "witchhunt" investigations of Sen. Joseph R. MCCARTHY and the House Committee on UN-AMERICAN ACTIVITIES drove the CPUSA virtually underground in the 1950s. It reemerged in the more liberal atmosphere of the mid-1960s but was much weakened. Revelations of Stalin's crimes and the Soviet suppression of the Hungarian Revolution (both in 1956) had caused many to leave the party.

━

community and junior colleges The community or junior college—an American educational innovation—offers two-year programs of study leading to associate degrees and certificates. Such colleges do not offer bachelor's, graduate, or professional degrees. Most U.S. community colleges are public institutions, receiving funds from a state, a local school district within a state, or other public sources. Private two-year colleges receive most of their income from student tuition.

Two-year colleges in general have six distinguishing characteristics: OPEN ADMISSION, a local service region, low cost, a comprehensive educational program, diversified learners, and ties with community organizations. Community colleges offer education geared to the needs of the learners and their communities and provide a more direct link between preparatory education and the workplace than do four-year institutions.

History. The junior college was originally conceived as an extension of secondary education and as a way to enable universities to focus on advanced work. William Rainey HARPER, president of the University of Chicago, was the most successful proponent of the idea. Two of the earliest private junior colleges were Stephens College (Columbia, Mo., 1833) and Lasell Junior College (Newton, Mass., 1852).

In 1917 there were 5 accredited U.S. junior colleges; in 1920 there were more than 200, whose primary focus was on general and college-transfer education. Transformation of other types of institutions, such as business schools, into two-year colleges and the addition of junior colleges as part of universities spurred further growth.

In 1947, President Harry Truman's Commission on Higher Education called for more tuition-free, public, two-year community colleges. Since then public two-year colleges have evolved through state action and local initiatives into comprehensive institutions offering a wide range of programs. In the late 1980s more than 50% of entering U.S. college students and 40% of all undergrad-

uate students were enrolled in a community college. There are more than 1,450 two-year colleges in the United States.

Organization and Curriculum. Common practices distinguish these two-year colleges' relations with other educational institutions. They have built strong alliances with high schools in joint efforts to serve minorities and gifted students and to provide early access to community-college courses. They have also forged transfer agreements and joint-service compacts with four-year colleges and universities.

Academic curricula are organized into five basic functions: collegiate, career, general, compensatory or remedial, and community education. Although institutions vary in emphasis, most colleges offer some form of all of them.

The collegiate function, also known as the college parallel or transfer program, offers the same type of courses as do four-year colleges.

CAREER EDUCATION is intended to prepare students for employment or to improve job skills. Known also as vocational, terminal, technical, or occupational education, career programs attract two out of three students attending community colleges.

General education emphasizes critical thinking, developing values, understanding traditions, respecting diverse cultures and opinions, and putting knowledge to use throughout life.

The guiding and teaching of students unprepared for college-level study is one of the most difficult challenges facing community colleges. Remedial or COMPENSATORY EDUCATION is the most common term used for courses designed to teach underprepared students. Students usually enroll in such courses voluntarily, based on test scores and high school records.

Community education embraces adult basic education, continuing education, and community-based education. Offerings may include classes for credit or not for credit and may vary in duration from an hour to an entire term. Television, newspapers, radio, and videotape may be used to reach students off campus as well as on. Courses may center on education or recreation, on programs of personal interest, or on benefits for the entire community. Community colleges find these courses an excellent way to cement ties with the community and to encourage people to be lifelong learners.

━

community property Community property is property held mutually by husband and wife and treated by law as belonging to both of them. It is based on the principle that because spouses work for their mutual benefit, they should share equally in the fruits of their labor. The only assets not considered community property are those which one party owned before marriage or received as a gift or inheritance after marriage. All states in the United States permit wives to control their own property, but only community-property states provide the wife with a legally protected interest in her husband's earnings or assets.

The community-property system, which evolved from

French and Spanish civil law, exists in eight states: Arizona, California, Idaho, Louisiana, Nevada, New Mexico, Texas, and Washington. In the case of divorce, most states require spouses to divide community property evenly. In some of these states all community property goes to the surviving spouse; in others it is divided equally between the surviving spouse and the deceased spouse's estate. A number of court rulings have held that community-property rights do not apply to unmarried couples living together, although the partners may have other legal claims on each other's property.

Como [koh'-moh]   Como (1984 est. pop., 94,634) is the capital and chief city of Como province, in the Lombardy region of northern Italy. Primarily a resort city, it lies at the southwestern tip of Lake Como amid the Italian Alps. Since the 14th century Como has been famous for its silk-manufacturing industry and today produces synthetic fibers as well. In 196 BC, Como became a Roman colony, and it was the birthplace of both Plinys. In 1127, Como became a free commune, but it was soon dominated successively by Milan, Spain, France, and Austria until 1859, when it was liberated by Giuseppe Garibaldi.

Como, Lake   Lake Como, part of Italy's scenic Lake District, is located in Lombardy, in northern Italy. Covering 145 km² (56 mi²), Como—Italy's third largest lake—is about 50 km (30 mi) long but only 5 km (3 mi) wide.

The lake is of glacial origin and is nestled in a basin surrounded by Alpine ranges. The southern half of Como splits into two arms separated by Bellagio Promontory. Como is fed principally by the Adda River, which enters from the northeast. Long famous as a tourist center, the lake is ringed by resorts including Como and Lecco.

Comoros [kahm'-uh-rohz]   The island nation of Comoros is situated in the Mozambique Channel between Madagascar and the African mainland. It comprises three main islands—Grande Comore, Anjouan, and Moheli (renamed Njazidja, Nzwani, and Mwali, respectively, in 1977)—and numerous islets and reefs. MORONI, the capital, is on Grande Comore. A fourth island in the Comoros archipelago, MAYOTTE, is considered by the Comoran government to be part of the country; its status is unsettled.

Land, People, and Economy

The rugged islands are volcanic in origin and have a few resources. Flora and fauna are similar to those of Madagascar. The climate is tropical, with a monsoon season extending from November to April. Annual rainfall ranges from 109 to 551 cm (43 to 217 in); cyclones are frequent.

The Comoran people are of mixed African, Malagasy, and Arab descent. Although Arabic is the official language, a dialect of Swahili is the primary spoken tongue.

The economy of Comoros is extremely underdeveloped. As many as 100,000 Comorans live abroad, and

---

AT A GLANCE

FEDERAL ISLAMIC REPUBLIC OF THE COMOROS

Land: Area: 1,862 km² (719 mi²), excluding Mayotte (375 km²/145 mi²). Capital and largest city: Moroni (1986 est. pop., 21,000).

People: Population (1990 est.): 460,188. Density: 247 persons per km² (640 per mi²). Distribution (1986): 25.7% urban, 74.3% rural. Official languages: Arabic, French. Major religion: Islam.

Government: Type: republic. Legislature: Federal Assembly. Political subdivisions: 3 islands (excluding Mayotte, administered by France as a territorial community).

Economy: GNP (1988 est.): $207 million; $475 per capita. Labor distribution (1982): agriculture—80%; government—3%. Foreign trade (1987): imports—$52 million; exports—$12 million. Currency 1 Comoros franc = 100 centimes.

Education and Health: Literacy (1980 est.): 15% of adult population. Universities (1990): none. Hospital beds (1982): 813. Physicians (1984): 31. Life expectancy (1990): women—58; men—54. Infant mortality (1990): 89 per 1,000 live births.

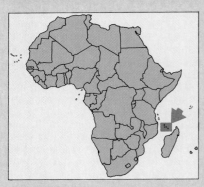

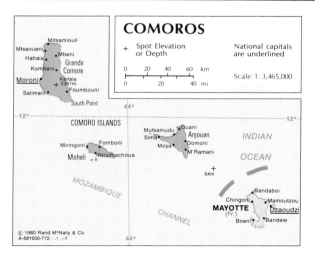

COMOROS

+ Spot Elevation or Depth

National capitals are underlined

| 0 | 20 | 40 | 60 | km |
Scale 1 : 3,465,000
| 0 | 20 | 40 | mi |

Mitsamiouli

Mtsaoueni • Mbeni
Hahaia • Grande
Kombani • Comore
Moroni • Kartala
2361m
Salimani • Foumbouni

South Point

COMORO ISLANDS

44°
−12°

Mutsamudu • Quani
Sima • Anjouan
Moya • Domoni
M'Ramani

INDIAN

Miringoni • Fomboni
Moheli • Nioumachoua

OCEAN

MOZAMBIQUE

+
54m

Chingoni • Bandaboi
MAYOTTE • Mamoutzou
(Fr.) • Dzaoudzi
Boeni • Bandele

CHANNEL

© 1980 Rand McNally & Co.
A-581000-772-1-1-1-1

44°

12°

population pressures have led to severe soil erosion and deforestation in places. Most people are engaged in subsistence agriculture, but much of the best land is used for cash crops such as vanilla and cloves. Many foodstuffs must be imported, and the government is heavily dependent on foreign aid.

History and Government

The Comoros were peopled initially from Polynesia, then later from East Africa and the Arab world. The islands came under French control between 1843 and 1886 and were administered jointly with Madagascar from 1912 to 1946. After gradually winning greater internal autonomy, a large majority of the population on all islands but Mayotte voted in favor of independence in 1974. In July 1975, Comoros unilaterally declared its independence; in 1976 the primarily French-speaking inhabitants of Mayotte chose to remain under French rule.

Ahmed Abdallah, the first president of Comoros, was overthrown in August 1975 but returned to power in a 1978 coup led by foreign mercenaries. Later that year voters approved a constitution making Comoros a federal Islamic republic. The constitution was amended in 1982 to strengthen the powers of the president and make Comoros a one-party state. Abdallah was elected to a second term in 1984, but he was assassinated in November 1989. French and South African pressure led to the mercenaries' departure, and multiparty presidential elections were held in March 1990.

compact disc A compact disc (CD) is a laser-read (also termed optically read) data-storage device on which audio, video, or textual material can be stored. To date, it has been used mostly to record stereophonic sound, differing from the conventional phonograph record primarily in that it stores information in digital, rather than analog, form (see DIGITAL TECHNOLOGY; VIDEO TECHNOLOGY). Stereophonic (two-channel) sound signals are digitally sampled at a rate of 44,100 times per second per channel. Each

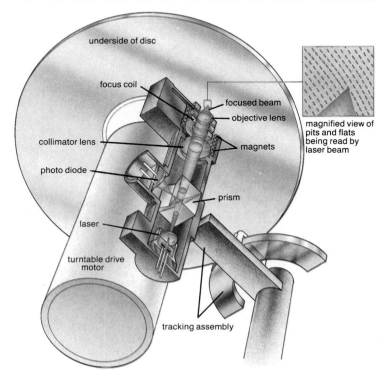

underside of disc

focus coil

focused beam

objective lens

collimator lens

magnets

photo diode

prism

magnified view of pits and flats being read by laser beam

laser

turntable drive motor

tracking assembly

In a compact disc player, light from a laser replaces the tone arm and cartridge used in a conventional record player. The laser beam focuses on the tiny pits and flats engraved in grooves around the disc, and "reads" them as a digital code—a series of zeroes and ones. When the laser beam is reflected back from the mirrored underside of the disc, a prism deflects it onto the photo diode, which converts the signal from digital to analog. The lenses help to maintain the beam in correct focus. Compact discs are read from the center to the outer edge. The rotation at the center begins at about 500 revolutions per minute (rpm) and slows to about 200 rpm as the laser beam scans outward. In effect, the disc is read at a constant speed of about four feet (1.22 m) per second. Because the pits are microscopic in size (about 0.1 micrometer deep, 0.5 micrometers wide, and between 1 and 3 micrometers in length), and because the space between the grooves is only 1.6 micrometers, a typical compact disc can hold up to 74 minutes of music on its single playing side. Much of the circuitry within the playback system is concerned with the detection and correction of errors. Several types of systems are used, so that the player can identify small mistakes within the digital code and correct them, and is capable of replacing small parts of the code if they are destroyed by a scratch or a defect in the disc.

sample is expressed as a binary number value consisting of 16 binary digits, or bits. The sampled digital values, along with error-correction data, tracking codes, and cuing data, are recorded on a master digital tape, which, after a series of intermediate steps, is used to make compression-molded plastic discs 12 cm (4.72 in) in diameter, each covered by a thin, reflective metallic layer and protected by a clear plastic coating. During playback, a low-powered laser beam, mounted in a movable assembly, reads the digital data through the reflective rear surface of the disk by differentiating between the presence and absence of "pits" beneath the clear, transparent surface of the CD. Changes in reflectivity caused by the pits are translated, via a photodiode (see DIODE), into electrical signals that are converted back into an analog signal for reproduction by conventional amplifiers and loudspeakers.

Another application for the CD is called CD-ROM (Compact Disc Read-Only Memory), used for the storage of computer text or programs. Typically, a CD-ROM can store in excess of 500 megabytes (millions of bytes) of data, as compared with the capacity of hard disks for home computers, whose maximum storage capacity is about 30 megabytes.

New uses of CDs include devices that play the discs through a television set. Using a special electronic interface between CD player and TV, the CD-V will play 20 minutes of sound and show 5 minutes of sound-with-picture. Laser videodiscs, with CD-quality sound, can show entire movies on a TV screen. CD-interface (CD-I), still in development, will allow the viewer to stop play, request more information, and get it in the form of sound with graphics, a film clip, or a body of text scrolled on the screen.

comparative anatomy   see ANATOMY

—

comparative psychology   Comparative psychology is the study of ANIMAL BEHAVIOR, focusing on the similarities and differences among species with a view to explaining the evolution of human behavioral abilities and tendencies. Cross-species generalizations, however, are now made only with great caution. Psychologists tend to rely more on interventions and experiments than do ethologists.

See also: BEHAVIORAL GENETICS; ETHOLOGY; SOCIOBIOLOGY.

—

compass, navigational   The compass is a device that indicates direction on the Earth's surface, relative to magnetic north. It is the principal instrument of NAVIGATION; without it, a navigator would have difficulty in setting the course for a ship or airplane. There are two basic types of compass, the magnetic and the gyroscopic. The magnetic compass derives its directional property from the Earth's magnetism, whereas the gyroscopic compass is a mechanical device that employs a spinning wheel and senses the Earth's rotation.

This liquid compass, made about 1775 by Joseph Rou, comprises a card with Italian compass markings to which magnets are attached that float on a liquid in a sealed globe. The compass card remains level on a swaying ship because liquid in a container, no matter how it is tilted, always remains horizontal.

Magnetic Compass

It appears that Mediterranean seamen of the 12th century were the first to use a magnetic compass at sea. There are two types of magnetic compass, the dry card and the liquid. The dry-card compass used on ships consists of a system of magnetized needles suspended by silk threads from a graduated compass card about 25 cm (10 in) in diameter. In a liquid compass the card is mounted in a

A typical, liquid magnetic compass consists of a liquid-filled bowl in which a floating, graduated card, usually made of mica or aluminum, is attached to a hemispherical float supported by a pivoted, jewel-bearing cap. A ring magnet is mounted beneath the card, with its magnetic axis parallel to the north-south markings on the card. A reference pointer, or lubber, within the bowl is fixed in line with the ship's bow. Because the magnet always remains parallel to the Earth's magnetic field, any turn of the ship results in a turning of the card with respect to the lubber, and indicates the ship's heading.

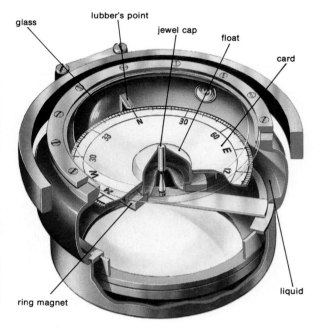

glass
lubber's point
jewel cap
float
card
liquid
ring magnet

sealed bowl filled with a liquid of low freezing point.

A magnetic compass mounted on a steel ship is influenced by the ship's magnetism. Magnetic correctors, therefore, are used to neutralize this magnetism at the compass position so that the needle system is influenced by the Earth's magnetism only. In aircraft the magnetic compass is often located at a position outside the cockpit, where the magnetism of the craft has the least effect. From this location, compass directions are transmitted electrically to the cockpit, and the system is known as a transmitting compass.

Gyroscopic Compass

The magnetic compass for ships and aircraft is now being superseded by the gyroscopic compass, or gyrocompass. When it became possible to spin a wheel electrically, serious attention was given to the possibility of using a spinning wheel—the axis of which tends to maintain a fixed direction in space—for directional purposes. A spinning wheel that is free to move about three axes is known as a free GYROSCOPE. In a meridian-seeking gyroscope the Earth's force of gravity causes the spin axis of the gyroscope to oscillate horizontally around the vertical plane of the meridian, an oscillation that is continually reduced in amplitude by a damping device. Through the agency of this device, the spin axis settles horizontally in the vertical plane of the meridian, thereby acting as an efficient compass.

William Thomson (later Lord Kelvin) made an attempt to design a gyrocompass in 1883, but credit for inventing the first practical gyrocompass belongs to Hermann Anschütz-Kaempfe, whose first successful compass appeared in 1907. The first American gyrocompass, designed by Elmer A. SPERRY, was produced in 1911; the first English design, by S. G. Brown and J. Perry, is dated 1917.

compensation laws   see UNEMPLOYMENT INSURANCE; WORKERS' COMPENSATION

compensatory education   Compensatory education is a form of remedial education designed to assist persons, usually children, to overcome the negative effects of social and economic deprivation. It is based on the assumption that such disadvantaged persons interact less with adults than do persons from more affluent homes and are less exposed to concepts basic to the development of language and intellect. Compensatory education programs, such as HEAD START (1964) in the United States, attempt to introduce basic concepts to disadvantaged children before they reach school in order to avoid a cycle of failure later on. The ELEMENTARY AND SECONDARY EDUCATION ACT OF 1965 (subsequently extended and amended) provided a major impetus to compensatory education programs in the United States.

compiler   see COMPUTER; COMPUTER LANGUAGES

complex (chemistry)   see COORDINATION COMPOUNDS

complex (psychology)   In PSYCHOANALYSIS a complex is a pattern of ideas and impulses that are emotionally charged and partly or wholly repressed. The term was coined by Carl JUNG in 1906 as part of his analysis of schizophrenic thinking and behavior. The pattern usually originates during early childhood, but it continues to exert a determining influence on a person's adult experiences and conduct.

A well-known example of a complex is Alfred ADLER's concept of the inferiority complex. According to Adler, a small child tends to measure himself or herself against others, particularly parents, and to feel puny and inadequate by comparison. Sigmund FREUD held that complexes arise as a result of the maturation of the child's innate sexual and aggressive instincts. For example, the so-called Oedipus and Electra complexes emerge when a child develops a wish for an exclusive, vaguely sexual union with the parent of the opposite sex and feels a hostile rivalry toward the parent of the same sex.

complex number   A complex number is any number that can be written in the form $a + bi$, where a and b are real numbers and i is defined to be $\sqrt{-1}$, the so-called imaginary unit. An understanding of complex numbers is essential in many branches of engineering and physics, especially for solving the many differential equations encountered in these areas.

The need for complex numbers first arose in the study of the solution of algebraic equations. Negative numbers are needed to solve such equations as $x + 4 = 3$, with its solution -1; fractions to solve such equations as $2x = 3$, with its solution $3/2$; and irrational numbers to solve such equations as $x^2 = 2$, with its solutions $\sqrt{2}$ and $-\sqrt{2}$. Similarly, complex numbers are needed to solve such equations as $x^2 + 1 = 0$ because there is no solution in real numbers to such an equation. In this particular example, $x^2 \geq 0$ for all real numbers x, so that $x^2 + 1 \geq 1$ for all real numbers x. Because there is no solution in real numbers, a new number, i, is invented for which $i^2 = -1$ and thus $i^2 + 1 = 0$. Because the equation $x^2 = 2$ has the solution $x = \sqrt{2}$, by analogy, the solution of $i^2 = -1$ is written $i = \sqrt{-1}$. If b is set equal to zero, the complex number $a + bi$ reduces to the real number a; thus, real numbers are special cases of complex numbers. On the other hand, setting a equal to 0 in $a + bi$ produces complex numbers of the form $0 + bi$, or bi, which are sometimes referred to as pure imaginary numbers, the name dating back to the time when complex numbers were not generally accepted.

composite material   see CERAMICS; MATERIALS TECHNOLOGY

compost   Compost is a soil conditioner and fertilizer, the product of the decomposition of animal and plant matter. Gardeners use it to replenish the humus, or organic component, in soil. Compost is made by building a pile consisting of alternate layers of soil, manure, and such vegetable materials as weeds, grass clippings, leaves, and garbage. If the pile is kept moist, microorganisms in the manure and soil digest the plant matter. This process eventually transforms the whole pile into humus. Chemicals are sometimes added to quicken composting, and the addition of lime increases the calcium content of the compost and reduces its acidity. Some sewage systems now manufacture a compost from treated sludge.

compound, chemical   A chemical compound is a substance in which two or more ELEMENTS are joined by CHEMICAL BONDS. A compound can be created or broken down by means of a chemical reaction (see REACTION, CHEMICAL) but not by mechanical or physical separation techniques. A compound's smallest units may be molecules or ions. (See ION AND IONIZATION.)

Elements lose their individual properties upon formation into a particular compound; for instance, the highly reactive metallic element sodium (Na) and the poisonous gas chlorine (Cl) form a compound, common table salt (NaCl), which has a white crystalline structure. Elements in compounds always are combined in definite proportion (see CHEMICAL COMBINATION, LAWS OF); for example, a molecule of water (H_2O) is always made up of two hydrogen atoms and one oxygen atom. In contrast, a mixture has substances present in variable proportions, and each substance retains its identity.

The field of chemistry that involves defining and measuring the ways elements combine to form compounds is known as STOICHIOMETRY. Standard forms of CHEMICAL SYMBOLISM AND NOTATION are used to represent the structure of compounds; the subdiscipline of STEREOCHEMISTRY defines their possible three-dimensional arrangement. The phenomenon of creating and breaking down chemical compounds in living organisms is known as METABOLISM.

compressed air   see PNEUMATIC SYSTEMS

Compromise of 1850   Five laws enacted (Sept. 9–20, 1850) by the U.S. Congress aimed at ending sectional disputes that threatened the Union are known collectively as the Compromise of 1850. During the late 1840s the long-slumbering conflict between congressional representatives of the North and South awakened with renewed vehemence over the question of the extension of slavery into the newly acquired western territories. Northerners generally favored the WILMOT PROVISO (1846), which would have excluded slavery from these lands. Southerners, on the other hand, opposed this provision. When California sought admission to the Union as a free state in 1849, a grave crisis approached. Also causing conflict at the time were disputes over Texas boundary claims; the existence of slavery and the slave trade in Washington, D.C.; and, for Southerners, the unenforceability of the FUGITIVE SLAVE LAWS.

In an attempt to preserve the Union, Henry CLAY, early

Henry Clay proposed to the U.S. Senate what was later called the Compromise of 1850—a series of five measures intended to resolve disputes over the extension of slavery into southwestern U.S. territories.

in 1850, proposed a series of measures intended to satisfy both North and South. After lengthy, heated debate most of Clay's program passed. The five acts making up the Compromise provided for the admission of California to the Union as a free state; organization of New Mexico and Utah as territories that could enter the Union with or without slavery; the settlement of the Texas boundary claims with the federal government assuming $10 million in debts contracted by the Republic of Texas; the prohibition of the slave trade—though not slavery—in the District of Columbia; and a more stringent Fugitive Slave Law.

Many politicians viewed the Compromise of 1850 as the final solution to the slavery controversy; Daniel WEBSTER, whose eloquence helped secure passage of the five laws, declared them the most important legislation in 30 years. In fact, the Compromise simply postponed the conflict that the continued existence of slavery made inevitable. The issue of slavery in the territories reemerged in 1854 with the KANSAS-NEBRASKA ACT.

Compsognathus   [kahmp-sahg'-nuh-thuhs]   *Compsognathus* (Greek *kompsos*, "elegant"; *gnathos*, "jaw"), the smallest known DINOSAUR, was only 50 to 60 cm (about 2 ft) long and weighed no more than 4 kg (8.8 lb). Two finely preserved skeletons have been found in Upper Jurassic limestones in Germany and France (see FOSSIL RECORD).

Compsognathus belonged to a group of fleet-footed theropod dinosaurs called coelurosaurs. It was a lightly built biped with an unusually long, slender tail, which it used to balance and steer itself when running. It had some hollow bones, like those of birds, and its delicate jaws contained many sharp, backwardly curved teeth. The forelimbs were half as long as the legs, which had long, slender, birdlike feet. The animal was carnivorous; within the skeleton found in Germany are remains of a smaller reptile, apparently remnants of a last meal.

Remarkably birdlike in many features, *Compsognathus* may have possessed feathers and may have been close to the actual ancestry of birds.

Compton, Arthur Holly   Arthur Holly Compton, b. Wooster, Ohio, Sept. 10, 1892, d. Mar. 15, 1962, was an American experimental physicist who received the 1927 Nobel Prize for physics for discovering the COMPTON EFFECT. From 1920 to 1923, Compton performed and interpreted his famous X-ray scattering experiments, which showed that radiation existed as photons, or particles, as well as waves. He continued his X-ray work as professor (1923–45) at the University of Chicago, and during the war he directed the research in Chicago that led to the atomic bomb.

Compton-Burnett, Ivy   English novelist Ivy Compton-Burnett, b. June 5, 1884, d. Aug. 27, 1969, claimed that her knowledge of life extended in time no later than 1910, when she was 26. She stubbornly produced novels—19 of them—whose milieu was always the same: the enclosed and claustrophobic middle-class family of Victorian and Edwardian times, whose dramas are played out almost entirely through brilliant, stylized, and elliptical conversation rather than conventional description and narrative. Among her novels are *Men and Wives* (1931), *More Women than Men* (1933), *A Family and a Fortune* (1939), *Manservant and Maidservant* (1947), *A Heritage and Its History* (1960), and *The Last and the First*, published posthumously in 1971.

Compton effect   Scattered radiation is normally of the same wavelength as the incident beam. According to the generally accepted, classical viewpoint that prevailed at the beginning of the 20th century, electromagnetic radiation of a particular wavelength or frequency could be regarded as a continuous, periodic oscillation of electromagnetic forces. When such radiation interacts with an electron or other charged particle subject to no other significant forces, the free particle would oscillate and produce a reradiating, or scattering, of electromagnetic radiation. The oscillations, and therefore the scattered radiation, would have a frequency identical to that of the incident radiation. This theory, formulated by Sir Joseph John THOMSON, seemed to be in accord with experimental observations of relatively long-wavelength X rays.

In the 1920s, Arthur Holly Compton confirmed what others had earlier indicated, that some scattered radiation could be of longer wavelength. This Compton effect is in violation of classical theory and could be accounted for only in terms of QUANTUM MECHANICS, for which it provided a strong confirmation. Compton's systematic studies of the phenomenon led to an equation expressing the Compton effect quantitatively. This result was readily derived from modern theories, using the assumption that the process involves a collision of a single photon. Subsequent

CLOUD CHAMBER studies of individual scattering events, in which the motion of the electron was also observed, fully confirmed the individual-photon interpretation.

Comptroller of the Currency, Office of the   The Office of the Comptroller of the Currency is an agency of the U.S. government responsible for administering the system of national banks. A bank wishing to affiliate with the system must be chartered by the Office of the Comptroller and abide by its regulations. Each bank is examined periodically. The Office of the Comptroller is under the jurisdiction of the Treasury Department. It has a large staff of bank examiners. The comptroller, who is appointed by the president of the United States, also serves as one of three board members of the FEDERAL DEPOSIT INSURANCE CORPORATION (FDIC).

compulsive behavior   see OBSESSIVE-COMPULSIVE DISORDER

computer   A computer is an apparatus built to perform routine calculations with speed, reliability, and ease. Three important types are digital computers, which function internally and perform operations exclusively with digital (discrete) numbers (a type on which most recent progress has centered and that is the focus of much of this article); analog computers, which use continuously variable parts exclusively for internal representation of magnitudes and to accomplish their built-in operations;

The first practical adding machine was built in 1642 by Blaise Pascal. It consisted of a series of gears that were turned by dials representing the numbers to be added. The answer was displayed on drums rotated in sequence by the gears.

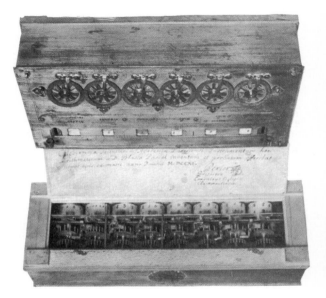

This elaborate device, built in 1833, is part of a calculating machine designed by Charles Babbage, an English mathematician. Known as a difference engine, it was designed for performing the long computations needed for mathematical and astronomical tables.

and the less-common HYBRID COMPUTERS, which use both continuously variable techniques and discrete digital techniques in their operation.

Digital, analog, and hybrid computers are conceptually similar in that they all depend on outside instructions; in practice, however, they differ most noticeably in the means they provide for receiving new programs to do new calculating jobs. Digital computers receive new programs rather easily via manual instructions or, in modern versions, via automatic means. For analog or hybrid computers, however, reprogramming is likely to involve partial disassembly and reconnection of mechanisms and components.

History of Computers

The most important early computing instrument is the ABACUS, which has been known and widely used for more than 2,000 years. It is simply a wooden rack holding parallel wires on which beads are strung. Another computing instrument, the ASTROLABE, was also in use about 2,000 years ago for navigation.

Blaise PASCAL is widely credited with building the first "digital calculating machine" in 1642. It performed only additions of numbers entered by means of dials and was intended to help Pascal's father, who was a tax collector. In 1671, Gottfried Wilhelm von LEIBNIZ invented a computer that was built in 1694; it could add and, by successive adding and shifting, multiply. Leibniz invented a special "stepped gear" mechanism for introducing the addend digits, and this mechanism is still in use. In 1820, Tomas of Colmar (Charles Xavier Thomas) developed the first commercially successful mechanical calculator that could add, subtract, multiply, and divide. By about 1890 the available built-in operations included accumulation of partial results, storage and reintroduction of past results, and printing of results, each requiring manual initiation.

Babbage. While Tomas of Colmar was developing the desktop calculator, a series of very remarkable developments in computers was initiated in Cambridge, England, by Charles BABBAGE. Babbage realized (1812) that many long computations, especially those needed to prepare mathematical tables, consisted of routine operations that were regularly repeated; from this he surmised that it ought to be possible to do these operations automatically. He began to design an automatic mechanical calculating machine, which he called a "difference engine," and by 1822 he had built a small working model for demonstration. With financial help from the British government, Babbage started construction of a full-scale difference engine in 1823.

The difference engine, although of limited flexibility and applicability, was conceptually a great advance. Babbage continued work on it for 10 years, but in 1833 he shifted his attention to what today would be described as a general-purpose, fully program-controlled, automatic mechanical digital computer. Babbage called his machine an "analytical engine." The plans for the analytical engine specified a parallel decimal computer operating on numbers (words) of 50 decimal digits and provided with a storage capacity (memory) of 1,000 such numbers. Built-in operations were to include the all-important "conditional control transfer" capability, which would allow instructions to be executed in any order, not just in numerical sequence. The analytical engine was to use punched cards, which were to be read into the machine from any of several reading stations.

Babbage's computers were never completed. Between 1850 and 1900 great advances were made in mathematical physics, and it came to be understood that most observable dynamic phenomena can be characterized by differential equations, so that ready means for their solution and for the solution of other problems of calculus would be helpful. The designing of railroads and the construction of steamships, textile mills, and bridges required differential calculus to determine such quantities as centers of gravity, centers of buoyancy, moments of inertia, and stress distributions.

Use of Punched Cards by Hollerith. A step toward automated computation was the introduction of punched cards, which were first successfully used in connection with computing in 1890 by Herman HOLLERITH and James Powers, working for the U.S. Census Bureau. They developed devices that could automatically read the information that had been punched into cards, without human intermediation.

The many advantages of punched cards were noted by commercial interests and soon led to the development of improved punched-card business-machine systems. These systems used electromechanical devices for such operations as turning the wheels of an adding machine.

Automatic Digital Computers. By the late 1930s punched-card machine techniques had become well established and reliable, and several research groups strove to build automatic digital computers. One promising machine, constructed of standard electromechanical parts, was built by an International Business Machines (IBM) team led by Howard Hathaway AIKEN. Aiken's machine, called the Harvard Mark I, handled 23-decimal-place numbers (words) and could perform all four arithmetic operations as well as trigonometric functions. The Mark I was originally controlled from prepunched paper tape without provision for reversal, so that automatic "transfer of control" instructions could not be programmed. Output was by card punch and electric typewriter.

Electronic Digital Computers. The outbreak of World War II produced a desperate need for computing capability, especially for the military. New weapons systems were produced for which trajectory tables and other essential data were lacking. In 1942, John W. MAUCHLY, John Presper Eckert, Jr., and their associates at the Moore School of Electrical Engineering of the University of Pennsylvania decided to build a high-speed electronic computer to do the job. This machine became known as ENIAC, for Electronic Numerical Integrator and Computer (or Calculator). The size of its numerical word was 10 decimal digits, and it could multiply two such numbers at the rate of 300 products per second.

ENIAC used 18,000 standard vacuum tubes, occupied 167.3 m^2 (1,800 ft^2) of floor space, and consumed about 180,000 watts of electrical power. It had punched-card input and output and arithmetically had 1 multiplier, 1 divider–square rooter, and 20 adders employing decimal "ring counters," which served as adders and also as quick-access (0.0002 seconds) read-write register storage. The executable instructions composing a program were embodied in the separate units of ENIAC, which were plugged together to form a route through the machine for the flow of computations. ENIAC is generally acknowledged to be the first successful high-speed electronic digital computer (EDC) and was productively used from 1946 to 1955.

The Modern "Stored Program" EDC. Intrigued by the success of ENIAC, the mathematician John VON NEUMANN undertook (1945) a theoretical study of computation that demonstrated that a computer could have a very simple, fixed physical structure and yet be able to execute any kind of computation effectively by means of proper programmed control without the need for changes in hardware. Von Neumann contributed a new understanding of how practical fast computers should be organized and built; these ideas, often referred to as the stored-program technique, became fundamental for future generations of high-speed digital computers.

The machine had an all-purpose COMPUTER MEMORY, which became the assembly place in which parts of a long computation were stored, worked on piecewise, and assembled to form the final results.

The first generation of modern programmed electronic computers to take advantage of these improvements appeared in 1947. This group included computers using random-access memory (RAM), which is a memory designed to give almost constant access to any particular piece of information. These machines had punched-card or punched-tape input and output devices and RAMs of 1,000-word capacity with an access time of 0.5 μsec (0.5 × 10^{-6} sec). Physically, they were much more com-

pact than ENIAC. This group of machines included EDVAC and UNIVAC (see UNIVAC), the first commercially available computers.

Advances in the 1950s. Early in the 1950s two important engineering discoveries changed the image of the electronic-computer field, from one of fast but often unreliable hardware to an image of relatively high reliability and even greater capability. These discoveries were the magnetic-core memory and the transistor-circuit element.

These new technical discoveries rapidly found their way into new models of digital computers; RAM capacities increased from 8,000 to 64,000 words in commercially available machines by the early 1960s, with access times of 2 or 3 μsec. These machines were very expensive to purchase or to rent and were especially expensive to operate. This situation led to modes of operation enabling the sharing of the high capability available; one such mode is batch processing, in which problems are prepared and then held ready for computation on a relatively inexpensive storage medium, such as magnetic drums, magnetic-disk packs, or magnetic tapes. Another mode of use for fast, powerful machines is called TIME-SHARING. In time-sharing the computer processes many waiting jobs in such rapid succession that each job progresses as quickly as if the other jobs did not exist.

Advances in the 1960s. In the 1960s efforts to design and develop the fastest possible computers with the greatest capacity reached a turning point with the completion of the LARC machine for Livermore Radiation Laboratories of the University of California by the Sperry-Rand Corporation. The LARC had a core memory of 98,000 words and multiplied in 10 μsec.

During this period the major computer manufacturers began to offer a range of computer capabilities and costs, as well as various peripheral equipment—such input means as consoles and card feeders; such output means as page printers, cathode-ray-tube displays, and graphing devices; and optional magnetic-tape and magnetic-disk

ENIAC, the first high-speed electronic computer, was designed by J. P. Eckert and J. W. Mauchly (foreground). The computer had to be rewired to handle different types of computations.

The evolution of the electronic computer—from a slow calculating machine to a programmable, high-speed data processor—has been made possible by the miniaturization of electronic logic gates. Shown here are a single-gate vacuum tube (back), a single-gate, solid-state transistor (left), and a modern silicon wafer containing thousands of gates (front).

file storage. These found wide use in business for such applications as accounting, payroll, inventory control, ordering supplies, and billing. Central processing units (CPUs) for such purposes did not need to be very fast arithmetically and were primarily used to access large amounts of records on file, keeping these up to date. By far the greatest number of computer systems were delivered for the more modest applications, such as in hospitals for keeping track of patient records, medications, and treatments given. They are also used in automated library systems.

Recent Advances. The trend during the 1970s was, to some extent, away from extremely powerful, centralized computational centers and toward a broader range of applications for less costly computer systems. Most continuous-process manufacturing, such as petroleum refining and electrical-power distribution systems, now use computers of relatively modest capability for controlling and regulating their activities. Moreover, a new revolution in computer hardware came about, involving miniaturization of computer-logic circuitry and of component manufacture by what are called large-scale integration, or LSI, techniques. About 1960 photoprinting of conductive circuit boards to eliminate wiring became highly developed. Then it became possible to build resistors and capacitors into the circuitry by photographic means (see PRINTED CIRCUIT). In the 1970s vacuum deposition of transistors became common, and entire assemblies, such as adders, shifting registers, and counters, became available on tiny "chips." In the 1980s very large-scale integration (VLSI), in which hundreds of thousands of transistors are placed on a single chip, became increasingly common. Many companies, some new to the computer field, introduced in the 1970s programmable minicomputers supplied with software packages. The size-reduction trend continued with the introduction of personal computers (see COMPUTER, PERSONAL). Many companies such as Apple

Computer and Radio Shack introduced very successful personal computers in the 1970s, spurred on in part by a fad in VIDEO GAMES.

By the late 1980s some personal computers were run by microprocessors that, handling 32 bits of data at a time, could process about 4 million instructions per second.

Microprocessors equipped with read-only memory (ROM), which stores fixed programs, now perform an increasing number of process-control, testing, monitoring, and diagnosing functions, as in automobile ignition systems and production-line inspection tasks.

The U.S. firms of Cray Research and Control Data Inc. dominated the field of supercomputers, or the most powerful computer systems, through the 1970s and '80s. In the early 1980s, however, the Japanese government announced a massive plan to design and build a new generation of supercomputers. This new generation—the so-called fifth generation—will employ new technologies in very large-scale integration, along with the programming language PROLOG, and will be capable of advances in the area of artificial intelligence, such as voice recognition and parallel processing.

Progress in the area of software has not matched the great strides in hardware. Software has become the major cost of many systems because programming productivity has not increased very rapidly. New languages, such as ADA, have been developed to help alleviate this problem.

The computer field continues to experience tremendous growth. Computer networking, computer mail, and electronic publishing are just a few of the applications that are still in the early stages of development and use.

How a Digital Computer Works

Digital Encoding and Processing. In order to process numbers and data electronically, it is necessary to represent information as electrical quantities. In order to represent the ten digits of the decimal number system, one might choose a set of ten electrical values and assign one value to each of the ten digits. While this arrangement is

Supercomputers have the highest processing speeds and the largest primary memories, and they are required for modeling very complex phenomena such as the weather. The semicircular arrangement of processors in this Cray supercomputer is meant to keep interconnecting wire lengths at a minimum and the speed of signal transfers at a maximum.

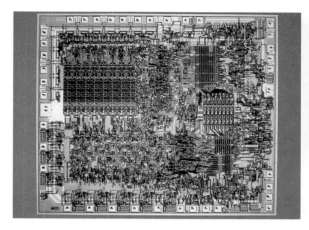

All electronic computers contain processors, such as the Intel 8080 seen above and, magnified, at left. The miniaturization of processors has been made possible by microscopic engineering, including photomasking, laser etching, and epitaxy.

straightforward, it is not employed in computers because the broad range of values needed makes practical circuits impossible to build. In addition, when characters other than numbers are included in the list of items to be processed, the increased number of distinct values becomes unworkable.

To solve the problem, all data is coded as BINARY NUMBERS. The most reliable distinction that can be realized in electrical systems occurs when only two possible values exist. A light bulb that may be either on or off is an example; the two possibilities are distinct and unmistakable. The two binary values zero (0) and one (1) are used to represent the electrical ideas off and on. These individual digits are usually referred to as binary digits, or bits. A way of extending the set of possible representations beyond two is also required. If a string of zeros and ones is allowed to represent a digit or character, then the number of possible representations becomes the value of 2 to the power of the number of bits. For example, if 4 bits are used, then there are 2^4, or 16, possible 4-bit sequences that can be built. The set of sequences can, of course, be used to represent 16 characters and digits rather than only 10. If 6-bit sequences are used, then 64-four possible characters and digits can be represented. This binary coding of items is the principal means for representing all data in electronic computers. Typically, the 10 digits of decimal arithmetic are represented by the first 10 sequences in the 4-bit strings listed above. This is called the binary-coded-decimal representation.

Inside the computer, electronic on and off states are realized using basic logic units called gates. As the required operations of a computer became more complex, switches were developed that have a variety of ways in which they can be turned on or off. In order to systematically describe these ways, two elementary functions are defined. These are the AND function and the OR function, which operate in the following manners. The result of the AND function with any number of binary values is truth if all the values are true; otherwise, it is false. Generally, a 1 corresponds to a true value, and a 0 corresponds to a false value. The result of the OR function with any number of binary values is truth if any one (or more) of the values is true. By applying these two functions along with the inverse function, which takes any value and produces the opposite value, one can describe any required activity in digital processing.

In modern electronic computers the TRANSISTOR is the device that acts as a switch. When computers using transistors were first built, the size of each transistor was about ⅛ square-inch. Today, hundreds of transistors can reside in a comparable space when integrated in a SEMICONDUCTOR chip (see INTEGRATED CIRCUIT). The technologies and processes that are used to make microscopic integrated circuits—such as masking, etching, and EPITAXY—are themselves made possible by computers (see COMPUTER-AIDED DESIGN AND COMPUTER-AIDED MANUFACTURING).

Components of a Digital Computer. Any digital computer contains four basic elements: an arithmetic and logic unit, a memory unit, a control unit, and input-output units.

The arithmetic and logic unit is that part of the computer where data values are manipulated and calculations performed. This section of the computer usually contains numerous registers and paths between these registers. Registers are collections of memory devices that can save particular values.

Not all computers are built to perform calculations with values. Some are designed to sort out lists of items or select items having a certain property. For example, a library may have its entire card catalog stored in a computer. When a borrower is seeking a particular title, the computer is given the task of searching the library booklist and comparing the desired title with the list. This is not an arithmetic problem, but a logic problem. Logic problems involve examining values for certain properties and making decisions based on those properties. All logic problems can be described as a collection of AND, OR, and inverse (NOT) functions.

Because all the operands needed for execution of arithmetic and logic functions cannot be stored in registers, another means is provided: the memory unit. The memory unit stores data that are not currently being pro-

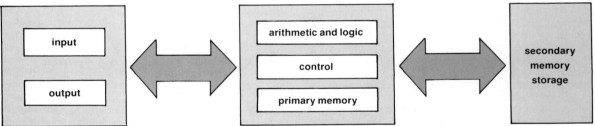

A modern mainframe computer is shown with its complex of units. The heart of the system is the central processing unit, or CPU (1), which performs all arithmetic and logic functions. It is linked with the other units through the processor controller (2). The CPU contains a limited primary memory, but the major drive and data storage systems are found in the magnetic tape subsystem (3) and other secondary subsystems (4). In front are the terminals (5) that operators use to communicate with the computer. At the left are printing subsystems for output of hard data, including a large system printer (6), a subsystem (7), and a printer terminal (8). Also seen here are the communications controller (9) for modem and other outside linkages, the system's power unit (10), and a coolant distribution unit (11).

cessed. The operation of a computer requires a list of procedural instructions, which are also stored in the memory.

The process of summoning content from the memory is referred to as a fetch operation. The process of saving a value in memory is called a store, or sometimes write, operation. When contents stored in memory are needed often, as in the case of procedural instructions, the computer must fetch the information quickly and not necessarily in sequential order. Primary memory is employed for this task. Secondary memory is sometimes referred to as bulk memory. It is ordinarily stored on magnetic tapes or disks and segmented into files.

The process of getting information into and out of the computer is handled by an input-output unit. INPUT-OUTPUT DEVICES bridge the gap between data in the form used by the computer and data in the form used with a particular access device. A computer keyboard is such a device. It is also the job of an input-output unit to manage problems of timing. For example, the rates at which typists can press keys varies greatly. Also, it is wasteful for the computer to wait for all the necessary characters to be entered before beginning a processing sequence, and input-output devices can alleviate this problem. Similar timing problems arise when the computer has completed operations and then must display results.

Each of the computer parts described so far—arithmetic and logic, memory, and input-output—is able to perform its own functions and communicate results. For these parts to work together effectively, however, it is necessary to have a control unit that coordinates the actions. To perform this job, a time frame of reference is established by the control unit. Generally, time within a computer is divided into moments whose length is determined by a basic rate at which the components in the control unit can react. This rate is fixed by a precision clock.

The control unit initiates an operation by first fetching an instruction from a list of instructions, called the program. The program is stored in the primary memory. Each instruction is an exact description of how the hardware units are to respond at a given moment in the time scheme of the computer. The control unit of a computer is made to proceed through a list of directions describing how to manipulate certain data. The arithmetic and logic unit, control unit, and primary memory constitute what is usually called the CENTRAL PROCESSING UNIT, or CPU.

Computer Operation and Programming. As has been said, all computers require a program, or list of instructions, to guide their activity. Sometimes the program is designed, or resides, within the hardware of the computer and cannot be changed without redesigning the hardware. More often, the program is entered as software into memory and may be easily removed or altered.

Processor elements interact in a way that is largely determined by the hardware design, and they are controlled by operating systems, of which there may be many suitable kinds. The operation of secondary memory and a variety of input-output devices, however, introduces requirements that reduce the number of suitable operating systems. An operating system must be chosen so that it can manage the interactions of particular types of keyboards, modems, disk drives, printers, video output systems, and so on.

Computer programs are referred to as software, and they reside in either read-only memory, ROM, which is usually unchangeable, or random-access memory, RAM, which can be altered more easily. Programs are written for a number of different levels within the computer and in a number of different programming languages (see COMPUTER LANGUAGES). A computer is capable of performing a particular function once given a signal, and there are often several ways in which it can perform the function. Therefore it must be further instructed to use a certain method. An enumeration of the functions of a computer, along with its methods for performing the functions, is called the instruction set of the computer.

The instruction set can be viewed from the programmer's perspective or the machine's perspective. For the machine, any instructions must be encoded in terms of ones and zeros. From the programmer's perspective, pages filled with ones and zeros are tedious and difficult to interpret. For this reason acronyms are assigned to each instruction in the set, making them more readable. As an example, adding two numbers that are stored in two registers might be given the label ADD A,B. The language of ones and zeros is called machine language. The language that uses labels to simplify matters is called ASSEMBLY LANGUAGE. Every program must eventually be converted into machine language in order to be executed.

Assembly language, although much easier to deal with than machine language, is nevertheless difficult to use,

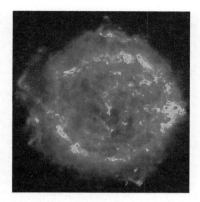

A powerful Cray supercomputer constructed this detailed, false-color picture of supernova remnant Cassiopeia A. Using radio data gathered by the Very Large Array telescope installation, the computer analyzed and pieced together over 4 million discrete picture elements.

especially in large and complex instruction sets. Therefore, instructions in high-level languages are given in terms that are more readily understandable than those of assembly-language programs, and such high-level-language instructions are relatively independent of the particular computer on which they run. A high-level instruction can be broken down into several assembly-level instructions. Examples of common high-level languages are FORTRAN, BASIC, and Pascal.

Successful programming requires that a task be broken down into methodical steps, or, in other words, an ALGORITHM, that can be understood not only by the computer, but also by other programmers. After a program is written, it must be checked thoroughly in order to remove errors. This process is often as time-consuming as the program writing. Difficulties with programs are of two types: logic errors and programming errors. The use of an incorrect series of steps in the design of an algorithm is called a logic error. Incorrect use of the programming language is called a programming error. The process of locating these errors is called debugging.

Computer Applications. The direct or indirect influence of computers is now nearly universal. Science is a field in which computers have been widely applied from the start. In order to solve scientific problems it is inevitable that researchers must deal with the language of science: mathematics. In attempting to understand more deeply complex natural phenomena, the scientist must use mathematical relationships that become increasingly difficult, as well as data that become more voluminous. It would be impossible to manage many of the studies of complex scientific phenomena without the aid of computers.

Businesses now use computers extensively and on a worldwide basis. A well-known example is the banking industry, which is heavily dependent on computers. Automated bank tellers are now ubiquitous and are little more than input-output devices for a bank's computer. They are also an example of the powerful system called COMPUTER NETWORKING, in which computers, databases, and input-output devices are connected by means of cable, sometimes over great distances.

A relatively new area for computers is that of communications (see TELECOMMUNICATIONS). Communications

This four-legged robot is able to climb and descend stairs smoothly, equipped with whiskerlike sensors in its feet and connected by an umbilical to a controlling computer.

consist of the flow and control of information. This is part of what a computer does as it manages the data moving among the elements within itself. By expanding the concept of a computer to include networks of input-output devices rather than a single, complete device, the result is a communications system. If the memory unit and arithmetic and logic unit of a computer are both relatively small but control many input-output devices, then the computer will act more like a message-handling system than a computational device (see ELECTRONIC MAIL).

Small, powerful, and low-cost personal computers for the home have been made possible by progress in microelectronics. These desktop machines are now capable of performing many of the functions of larger computers. Initially used in home applications such as video games and recordkeeping, by the late 1970s personal computers were proving useful in business and education as well. The development of more powerful microprocessors and advances in computer networking in the mid- to late-1980s enhanced the power of personal computers so much that they are now widely used even in large corporations. (See COMPUTER, PERSONAL; COMPUTERS IN EDUCATION.)

An important application of personal computers is desktop publishing (see PUBLISHING, DESKTOP). In this growing technology, software programs and inexpensive printers are used to produce text and graphics that are camera ready for publication.

Modern Concerns. Researchers continually seek new ways to build better computers. The goals of their efforts are usually in one or more of the following areas: reducing costs, increasing processing speeds, increasing capabilities, and making computers easier to use. This last quality—ease of use—is commonly referred to as "friendliness." Sometimes improvements involve new devices; at other times they are brought about by new methods of integrating hardware or software elements.

Memory, both primary and secondary, is one part of the computer that has received considerable attention over the years. Semiconductor chips have become the mainstays of primary memories, with magnetic tapes and disks handling secondary-memory storage. Other phenomena continue to be experimented with as possible forms of memory technologies. These include magnetic bubble devices, electron tunneling devices, and COMPACT DISCS. In the area of magnetic storage, considerable effort has been applied to find ways of storing information more densely.

Progress in semiconductor technologies continues, producing increased processing speeds and the fitting of more circuitry into less space. Very large-scale integration (VLSI), the integration of hundreds of thousands of circuits on a silicon wafer, was achieved by the late 1980s.

The use of optical means to store information has always been attractive, primarily because the inherent high frequency of light implies that it should provide high densities. Unfortunately, the human eye is more tolerant of informational errors than is a computer. For this reason, as well as the difficulty of creating a material that can be written on repeatedly using laser light, the appearance of optical storage media has been slow. Other laser-optical technologies are being developed, however, with optical fibers already used to transmit information in some networks. One day computers may have, in addition to optical memories, optical processors (see OPTICAL COMPUTING).

Another area of experimentation is in the organization of computer parts. Most memory is organized so that a location is given an address, and contents are found by locating that address. Content-addressable memory, CAM, is a newer arrangement style, in which information is located according to its value content. With this method a computer can search for one item in a group to quickly find the whole group. Another change in computer organization—one that is now used in a small percentage of computers—is the use of fewer instructions in order to maximize processing speeds. This is the basis of so-called reduced instruction set computers (RISC).

A significant amount of interest exists in the field of ARTIFICIAL INTELLIGENCE. The technologies and benefits that will derive from this area of study will undoubtedly filter down to all areas of computer science. Much work in artificial-intelligence research involves programs built to perform in ways similar to the way in which humans think.

A GLOSSARY OF COMPUTER TERMS

Note: terms followed by an asterisk have separate entries in the set.

algorithm* A procedure or set of rules that can be followed in order to solve a well-defined problem.

analog Referring to an ability to change continuously and in direct proportion to a dynamic phenomenon, thereby imitating it.

artificial intelligence* The simulation of human intelligence by a machine; this is more a goal than a fact.

assembly language* A low-level computer language composed of symbolic representations of machine language.

baud A unit of information-transmission speed equal to one signal per second.

bit From *binary digit*; the smallest piece of information in a digital system—a 0 or 1, or a physical representation of either.

byte A basic unit of computer information, often composed of 8 bits. A kilobyte (K) equals 1,024 (2^{10}) bytes, a megabyte (M) equals 1,024K (2^{20} bytes), and a gigabyte equals 1,024M (2^{30} bytes).

CD-ROM Compact Disc*—Read-Only Memory; a laser-read disk that stores read-only memory.

compiler A program that translates a particular high-level language into low-level language that can be processed by a particular CPU.

CPU Central Processing (or Processor) Unit*; the part of a computer that executes the functions of arithmetic and logic, interprets instructions, and maintains control over hardware.

cursor A movable mark (usually an underline) on a display screen that indicates where the next entered instruction will be displayed.

debug To search for and eliminate errors in a software program.

desktop publishing (publishing, desktop*) Generating and producing high-quality printed matter with a personal computer and an electronic printer.

digital (digital technology*) Composed of, or employing, discrete, binary representations of information.

disk drive The hardware that places information on, or retrieves information from, floppy disks or hard disks.

doping The treatment of silicon with foreign atoms in order to make specific regions electron rich or electron poor.

DOS Disk Operating System; a popular operating system designed for IBM computers.

DRAM Dynamic Random Access Memory; a semiconductor memory chip that stores information on a very short-term basis and that is constantly recharged.

epitaxy* The deposition of thin chemical layers on a semiconductor chip.

EPROM Erasable Programmed Read-Only Memory; a read-only memory that can be reprogrammed from time to time.

expert system* A computer program that acts like an expert by employing a specific-knowledge database and rules of inference.

floppy disk A flexible, magnetic disk, used for external memory storage.

FLOPS Floating Point Operations Per Second; a speed of computation in the CPU.

flowchart* a graphic description of the scheme of logic operations, used as an aid in programming.

gate A basic circuit element; the locus of a logic operation within a chip, producing either an AND, OR, or NOT function.

graphics tablet An input device in which graphical information can be drawn on a flat surface.

hard disk A hard, magnetic disk, used for external memory storage.

hardware The tangible features of a computer system: CPU, disk drive, printer, and so on.

high-level language A symbolic programming language that is readily understood by the user, such as BASIC, FORTRAN, or COBOL.

input; input device (input-output device*) Information that is entered into a computer, and any of various methods for doing this, such as a keyboard, mouse, or graphics tablet.

integrated circuit* An organized array of microelectronic elements interconnected on a single semiconductor chip.

interface A boundary where different computer media or devices are connected.

interpreter A program that translates a particular high-level language into a machine's low-level language in a piece-by-piece manner.

joystick An input device in which directional pushes on a lever impart specific commands to the computer.

keyboard A tactile input device consisting of an array of keys arranged somewhat like those of an ordinary typewriter.

LAN Local-Area Network; in computer networking, a network generally contained inside one building or complex.

language (computer languages*) An encoding of computer commands, required for all programmable computers.

laser disc Also called optical disc, a small disk on which digital data are stored as minute pits and bumps, and which is read by a laser beam. This can be an audio compact disc*, a CD-ROM, or a CD/I (compact disc/interactive), which provides both audio and video information.

light pen An input device; a photosensitive pen that, when placed against a video screen and moved about, responds to light images that are present.

mainframe A very large and powerful computer, with enormous memory capacity and the ability to handle multiple input-output units.

machine language The lowest-level computer language, consisting of strings of binary digits and readable by the CPU.

mask In chip manufacture, a microscopic template that fits over a chip, protecting specific regions from chemical treatment during an etching process.

memory (computer memory*) The capacity to store data; primary memory resides within the CPU and is easily accessed, whereas secondary memory is made possible by external units such as magnetic tapes or disks.

menu A list of routine or command options that appears on a screen in an interactive program.

microcomputer A miniaturized computer based on a microprocessor; a personal computer is an example.

microprocessor An ultracompact CPU in which circuits for arithmetic and logic functions, control functions, and ROM are contained on a single chip.

minicomputer A compact computer, sometimes only slightly larger than a microcomputer, but more powerful, and usually suited to a particular application.

MIPS   Million Instructions Per Second; used to describe speeds at which a CPU can process instructions.

model   (computer modeling˙) Object or process simulated by a computer.

modem*   A device that converts digital data into analog signals (and vice versa) for transmission over telephone lines.

mouse   A cable-connected input device consisting of a palm-sized box with a button on top. The mouse is moved across a tabletop, causing a movable pointer on the screen to choose from a list of items or commands.

multitasking   In a computer, the process of performing, concurrently, two or more tasks.

networking   (computer networking˙) The interconnecting of computer systems in order to share CPUs, databases, and input-output devices.

on-line   Connected to a usually distant CPU, and ready to initiate the processes of input and output.

operating system   A program that coordinates the variety of ongoing computer processes: loading, storing, and executing programs; input-output; timesharing; networking.

optical computing*   A still-experimental technology in which a computer processes digital data in the form of light pulses.

output; output device   Information that is given out by a computer, and any of various methods for doing this, such as a printer, video screen, or speech synthesizer.

parallel processing*   Processing in which instructions are broken down into smaller instructions that are executed simultaneously.

peripherals   Add-on hardware devices that are controlled by the CPU, such as printers, modems, and disk drives.

personal computer   (computer, personal˙) A general-purpose microcomputer designed to be used by one person.

pixel   From picture element; a small, discrete unit of visual information on a video screen.

plotter   Output device that places graphic images on paper.

printer*   Any of a number of machiners used for placing output (usually in text form) on paper.

program   A list of instrucitons, written in a programming language, to be followed by a computer.

prompt   A message given by the operating system to the computer user, usually asking for the next entry.

RAM   Random-Access Memory; a memory unit to which data can be constantly added or from which data can be constantly removed, in a random manner (as opposed to sequentially).

register   A primary memory in the CPU that acts as a temporary storage unit for data that is actually being used.

RISC   Reduced Instruction Set Computer; a computer that employs a CPU that is governed by a smaller set of basic instructions, thereby limiting or narrowing its applicability but speeding up its operations.

ROM   Read-Only Memory; a memory unit containing unchanging data or instructions that can be accessed randomly.

semiconductor*   A substance, such as silicon, having an electrical resistance somewhere between that of an insulator and a true conductor.

software   (computer software˙) Instructions or programs that reside in a computer's memory.

spreadsheet*   An applications program designed for the easy manipulation of data in the form of words, numbers, or graphical elements.

SRAM   Static Random-Access Memory; a semiconductor memory chip that stores information on a short-term basis and does not have to be constantly recharged.

supercomputer   The fastest, most powerful, and most expensive computers, with processing speeds over 10^9 FLOPS.

timesharing*   The simultaneous use of a central computer by independent stations, made possible by an operating system that allocates computer time.

transphasor   In optical computing, the analog of the transistor: a switch, or gate for light pulses.

VDT   Video Display Terminal; a video output device that can employ a CRT, a liquid crystal display, or an array of light-emitting diodes.

VLSI   Very Large Scale Integration; the integration of thousands of circuit elements on a single silicon wafer.

voice recognition   The ability of a computer (actually its input device) to translate spoken words into digital signals.

word processor   (word processing˙) A program designed for manipulating written text, used for writing, editing, and rewriting.

---

computer, personal   A personal computer is a computer that is based on a microprocessor, a small SEMICONDUCTOR chip that performs the operations of a CENTRAL PROCESSING UNIT. The general class of microcomputers comprises computers based on microprocessors. The personal computer is a microcomputer.

Personal computers are single-user machines, whereas larger computers generally have multiple users. The first generation of personal computers was distinguishable from minicomputers and mainframe computers by a small memory capacity, typically in the 16–64 kilobyte range (a kilobyte, or K, is 1,024 bytes). Models available from the mid-1980s on, however, had memories in the megabyte to gigabyte range (a megabyte, or M, is 1,024K, and a gigabyte is 1,024M); this increased memory capacity equaled and even surpassed the power of earlier minicomputers and mainframe computers.

Basic Structure. A computer system consists of three parts: the central processing unit (CPU), INPUT-OUTPUT DEVICES, and memory. A CPU performs arithmetic and logic operations. The microprocessors of personal computers process data in 8-bit, 16-bit, or 32-bit chunks.

The most common input-output devices are keyboards and cathode-ray tube (CRT) displays, which can provide both graphic and text modes.

Primary memory refers to memory that is directly accessible by the CPU. Many older CPUs have primary memories with 64-kilobyte capacities. Newer processors can handle 1 megabyte or more. Personal computers are often packaged with less primary memory than the CPU can handle. A wide range of add-on memory devices, therefore, is available. Secondary memory refers to external memory required for storing data that will not fit into the computer's primary memory.

Applications. The usefulness of the personal computer has grown steadily with the introduction of powerful computer-software programs that can be used by the individ-

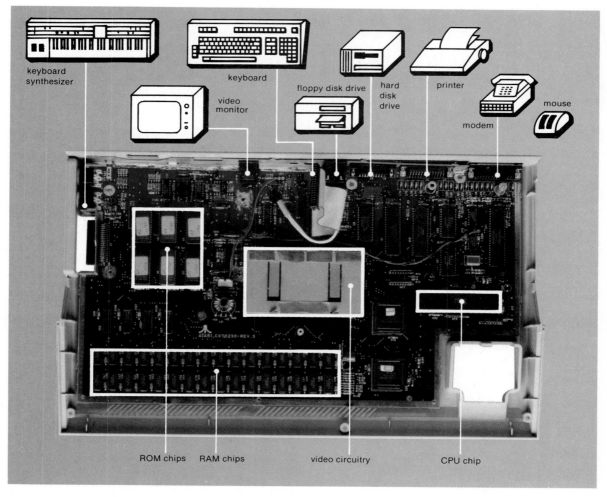

keyboard synthesizer

keyboard

video monitor

floppy disk drive

hard disk drive

printer

modem

mouse

ROM chips   RAM chips   video circuitry   CPU chip

Inside a personal computer, the central processing unit (CPU) lies on a single chip. Primary memory is provided by random-access-memory (RAM) and read-only-memory (ROM) chips, while a variety of other chips control the many functions of the computer. The many input and output devices that can be plugged into the computer include a keyboard for manual input, a hard-disk drive and a soft-disk drive for input and output of secondary memory, a modem for telephone input and output, a printer for output of hard data, and even a sound synthesizer for the translation of musical information (both input and output). An additional input device, called a mouse, plugs into the keyboard. At the center of the computer shown resides the complex circuitry that controls video output.

ual. WORD PROCESSING, SPREADSHEET, and DATABASE programs are all versatile software programs. Home entertainment programs (some modeled after VIDEO GAMES) and instructional software, both for use at home and in school, are plentiful (see COMPUTERS IN EDUCATION).

The ever-increasing power of personal computers gives them wider applications for both business and science. Software that relies on large memory, such as EXPERT SYSTEMS and computer-aided design programs, can now be run on personal computers. The powers of personal computers are also being greatly increased by their interconnections in networks (see COMPUTER NETWORKING). One problem that the computer industry must address, however, is the continuing high cost of developing software.

computer-aided design and computer-aided manufacturing   Computer-aided design and computer-aided manufacturing (CAD/CAM) has been called the "new industrial revolution." It is the integration of two technologies—computer-aided design (CAD) and computer-aided manufacturing (CAM). Computer-integrated manufacturing (CIM) also refers to this concept. In CAD, engineers use specialized COMPUTER SOFTWARE to create models (see COMPUTER MODELING) that represent the geometry and other characteristics of objects. Such models are analyzed by computer and redesigned as necessary. This allows for flexibility in studying different and daring designs without the high costs of building and testing

physical prototypes. In CAM, engineers use computers for planning manufacturing processes, controlling manufacturing operations, testing finished parts, and managing entire plants (see PROCESS CONTROL). CAD is linked with CAM through a database shared by design and manufacturing engineers.

A trend in mechanical CAD/CAM is toward further integration of design and manufacturing. "Desktop manufacturing," a relatively new process, enables a designer to fabricate a plastic model directly from data stored in computer memory. One such system uses a laser to fuse plastic granules together layer by layer until the model is achieved. EXPERT SYSTEMS will help designers to consider not only function but also manufacturing consequences at early stages when designs can be easily modified. With sophisticated software, design engineers will be capable of doing much of the work of manufacturing engineers. Advances in electronic CAD/CAM will also allow nonspecialists to design integrated circuits.

(Above) *Computers now aid in the design of machinery, such as the disk-brake assembly displayed on the screen. With its memory a computer can convert rough sketches, written on the screen with an electronic pen, into detailed drawings.* (Below) *In the design stage of a CAD/CAM program, a model is displayed on a monitor along with a menu of options available to the design engineer. To make changes, the engineer may use a keyboard, mouse, or light pen.*

(Below) *Robots are extremely valuable for applications that involve danger, repetition, tedium, or great precision. Thus, one of the most common applications of robots is in machine welding.*

(Below) *A computer-controlled robot, equipped with a laser, is used in the manufacture of semiconductor chips. As computers continue to grow in complexity, further developments have come to depend increasingly on the use of computers themselves.*

computer art   see COMPUTER GRAPHICS; PAINTBOX; VIDEO ART

computer-assisted instruction   see COMPUTERS IN EDUCATION

computer crime   Computer crime is generally defined as any crime accomplished through special knowledge of computer technology. Increasing instances of WHITE-COLLAR CRIME involve computers as more businesses automate and information becomes an important asset. Computers are objects of crime when they or their contents are damaged, as when terrorists attack computer centers with explosives or gasoline, or when a "computer virus"—a program capable of altering or erasing computer memory—is introduced into a computer system. As subjects of crime, computers represent the electronic environment in which frauds are programmed and executed; an example is the transfer of money balances in accounts to perpetrators' accounts for withdrawal. Computers are instruments of crime when used to plan or control such criminal acts as complex embezzlements over long periods of time, or when a computer operator uses a computer to steal valuable information from an employer.

Computers have been used for most kinds of crime, including fraud, theft, larceny, embezzlement, burglary, sabotage, espionage, murder, and forgery, since the first cases were reported in 1958. One study of 1,500 computer crimes established that most of them were committed by trusted computer users within businesses. Much of known computer crime has consisted of entering false data into computers, which is simpler and safer than the complex process of writing a program to change data already in the computer. With the advent of personal computers to manipulate information and access computers by telephone, increasing numbers of crimes—mostly simple but costly electronic trespassing, piracy of copyrighted information, and vandalism—have been perpetrated by computer hobbyists, known as "hackers," who display a high level of technical expertise. Organized professional criminals have been attacking and using computer systems as they find their old activities automated.

There are no valid statistics about the extent of computer crime. Victims often resist reporting suspected cases, because they can lose more from the embarrassment, lost reputation, litigation, and other consequential losses than from the acts themselves. The largest recorded computer crimes involving insurance, banking, product inventories, and securities have resulted in losses of tens of millions to billions of dollars.

Recent U.S. legislation, including laws concerning privacy, credit card fraud, and racketeering, provides criminal-justice agencies with tools to fight business crime. As of 1988 all but two states had specific computer-crime laws, and a federal computer-crime law (1986) deals with certain crimes involving computers in different states and in government activities.

computer graphics   Computer graphics is the use of computers to produce pictorial representations of information, whether a video-game maze, a graph of a company's yearly earnings, or a full-blown simulation of dogfighting jet planes. Computer-graphics technology has advanced to the point where almost any pictorial image

Three-dimensional computer graphics programs can present data in a number of ways that reveal complex and subtle trends. The programs are flexible and accommodate new data easily.

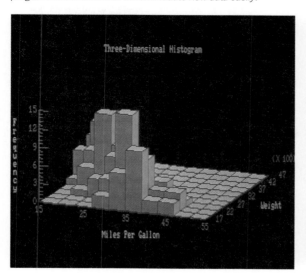

Computer-produced designs such as this "Mandelbrot dragon," named for the mathematician Benoit Mandelbrot, can be built up by repeating geometrical figures or processes known as fractals.

The imaginative use of computer graphics is seen in an increasing number of modern films. The computer-generated knightly figure in this sequence from Stephen Spielberg's The Young Sherlock Holmes (1985) was integrated with real camera footage so that it appeared to step down from a stained glass window and attack a man.

may be stored in a computer and manipulated and rendered according to the user's wishes.

Most computers may be used to generate pictorial images. All that is required is a graphics software program (see COMPUTER SOFTWARE) and INPUT-OUTPUT DEVICES adapted to the nature of the images. For example, a basic personal-computer system, with a keyboard and color monitor, can execute fairly complicated graphics programs, such as one that simulates a flying airplane. Other input-output devices, such as printers, color plotters, electronic sketch pads, and video cameras, can enhance the computer's graphics capabilities.

Sophisticated graphics require a great deal of computer memory and expensive input-output devices. A pictorial image may contain an enormous amount of informa-

This apparently real scene is actually the product of the computer manipulation of patterns generated from fractals.

tion, each piece of which must be translated by the computer into a digital code and stored in memory. If that image is part of a long string of related images, such as an animated cartoon or a simulated airplane in flight, then the amount of information that must be stored and manipulated may be vast, requiring the kind of power that only supercomputers can provide. Because most computers have comparatively small internal memories and operating speeds, graphics programs typically show only essential pictorial details.

Computer graphics often employs specialized hardware and software technologies. On the hardware side, a great deal of effort has been devoted to perfecting video displays. Most computer graphics are shown on monitors, or cathode-ray tubes (CRTs). Two types are typically used: raster-scan CRTs and vector CRTs. In the more common raster-scan CRT, an electron beam sweeps the screen horizontally many times per second, creating an image that consists of a two-dimensional grid of dots; each of these dots, or pixels (for picture elements), may be manipulated in color and intensity. In vector CRTs, the electron beam sweeps back and forth between two or more points on the screen, creating an image composed of lines. Vector CRTs are commonly employed in drafting, for which line drawings are adequate.

On the software side, graphics programs employ a wide variety of special display ALGORITHMS, or internal data-processing procedures, to create realistic images. For example, FRACTAL algorithms (see GEOMETRY, FRACTAL) produce random images that can reveal an infinite amount of texture and are ideal for illustrating mountains and oceans. Fuzzy sets, or algorithms based on statistical probabilities, are useful for generating images of fire, smoke, and other natural phenomena. An iterative algorithm can reproduce the same image countless times, making tiny changes in each one. Hidden-surface removal algorithms can erase lines and surfaces from unseen portions of an image, such as the underside of a cube. Pseudocoloring, or "colorizing," can endow a colorless image with a wide range of hues. Modeling some complicated images, such as a human face, is still difficult to achieve because of the complex algorithms involved.

Few industries have taken as thorough advantage of the computer's ability to generate and manipulate images as the VIDEO GAME business. However, computer graphics also plays an important role in many other industries. For example, computer-aided design (CAD) systems have replaced drafting boards in thousands of engineering and architectural firms. Cartographers, seismologists, geologists, astronomers, and chemists are also heavy users of graphic-oriented computer systems. Military applications, such as realistic flight simulators for pilot training, are growing. The computer's imaging ability has also found a home in Hollywood, where elaborate special effects are often fashioned by computer.

See also: COMPUTER-AIDED DESIGN AND COMPUTER-AIDED MANUFACTURING; COMPUTER MODELING; PAINTBOX; VIDEO ART.

▬

computer industry   Since the end of World War II, the COMPUTER industry has grown from a standing start into one of the biggest and most profitable industries in the United States. It now comprises thousands of companies, making everything from multimillion-dollar high-speed supercomputers to printout paper and floppy disks. It employs millions of people and generates tens of billions of dollars in sales every year.

The computer industry has three major historical roots: the American inventor and entrepreneur Herman HOLLERITH, who devised a punch-card tabulator and sorter in the late 19th century; the mechanical-calculator and cash-register manufacturers of the late 19th century; and a small group at the University of Pennsylvania, who, during World War II, conceived of and built the first high-speed computer.

By all rights, the mechanical-calculator and cash-register makers were the computer's most logical parents. The impetus to build computers came from an entirely different source, however: the military needs of World War II. In 1942, John W. MAUCHLY, a physicist at the Moore School of Engineering of the University of Pennsylvania, proposed the construction of a giant digital electronic calculator to be used for the computation of ballistic firing tables for the military. The army gave the Moore School a contract to build Mauchly's calculator, and the result was the creation of ENIAC (for Electronic Numerical Integrator and Computer) in 1945.

In 1946, Mauchly and John Presper Eckert, Jr., the engineer who had supervised ENIAC's design and construction, left the Moore School to develop a general-purpose computer system.

In 1950, with their company short on cash, Eckert and Mauchly sold out to Remington Rand. Drawing on Rand's substantial financial resources, Eckert and

Mauchly finally completed their project; the first UNIVAC (Universal Automatic Computer) was delivered to the Census Bureau in March 1951.

In 1911, Hollerith's small tabulating-machine company had merged with three other firms to form the Computing-Tabulating-Recording Corporation, which changed its name to the International Business Machines (IBM) Corporation in 1924. IBM became one of the most respected and profitable companies in the country, making most of its money by manufacturing and leasing punch-card tabulating equipment, which was fast, reliable, and well suited to the counting and analysis of large amounts of statistical data.

IBM dominated the tabulator business and for a time had no real interest in computers, but president Thomas J. Watson appreciated the value of good publicity. In 1939, Howard AIKEN, an engineering professor at Harvard University, approached Watson with an idea for building a huge electromechanical calculator. Watson decided to fund Aiken's project, and IBM built the Mark I, donating it, with much fanfare, to Harvard in 1943.

IBM finally undertook a crash program to build a computer system of its own. Called the IBM 701, the machine rolled off the assembly line in 1953. Other models, including the relatively inexpensive, medium-sized 650, followed during the next few years. In 1964, IBM consolidated its position with the introduction of the System/360, the first compatible family of computers, which was an enormous success.

The first computers were made with vacuum tubes; by the late 1950s, computers were being made out of transistors. In 1959, Robert NOYCE, a physicist at the Fairchild Semiconductor Corporation, in Mountain View, Calif., invented the integrated circuit, a tiny chip of silicon that contained an entire electronic circuit.

The invention of the integrated circuit led to the development of small, rugged, efficient, and relatively inexpensive minicomputers, which were first produced by the Digital Equipment Corporation in 1963.

In 1971, Marcian E. Hoff, Jr., an engineer at the Intel Corporation, invented the microprocessor, which was a central processor on a chip that enabled computer designers to further shrink the size and cost of computers. This paved the way for the development of personal computers (see COMPUTER, PERSONAL).

The first widely used personal computer was introduced in 1975. The personal-computer industry has come a long way in a very short time. The growing demand for personal-computer hardware (MODEMS, monitors, and printers) and software (SPREADSHEETS, WORD PROCESSING EQUIPMENT, desktop publishing, and instructional programs) gave rise to dozens of ancillary industries.

▬

computer languages   The power of a digital computer lies in the rapidity with which it can execute many instructions. Each instruction executed by the CENTRAL PROCESSING UNIT (CPU) of a computer performs a small part of a much larger task. In the early days of electronic computers it was recognized that the computer itself

THREE EXAMPLES OF COMPUTER LANGUAGES

Below are computer programs written in three languages—BASIC, FORTRAN, and C language. They each calculate the average of a series of numbers. In each case the program begins by setting variables called SUM (the sum of numbers entered up to a given point) and NUMBER (the number of numbers entered up to a given point) to zero. The program then asks the user if there is additional input. If "Y" or "y" is typed, a new value is asked for and accepted. It is then added to the ongoing SUM, and the value of NUMBER is increased by one. Any response other than "Y" causes the average to be calculated. Because division by zero is not possible, a check for no inputs at all is made. Many remarks are written into the BASIC and FORTRAN programs, but C language employs simple characters that outline steps.

BASIC

```
10   REM Averaging Program ASW
     5/30/86
15   REM BASIC version (Microsoft)
20   REM Initialize variables
30   LET SUM=0
40   LET NUMBER=0
50   REM Main loop begins here
60   INPUT "More input (Y/N)?"; Q$
70   IF Q$="y" THEN LET Q$="Y"
80   IF Q$<>"Y" THEN 140
90   INPUT N
100  LET SUM=SUM+N
110  LET NUMBER=NUMBER+1
120  GOTO 60
130  REM Continue here to finish
140  IF NUMBER=0 THEN END
150  REM Calculate results
160  LET AVERAGE=SUM/NUMBER
170  REM Report results
180  PRINT "Total="; SUM
190  PRINT "Number="; NUMBER
200  PRINT "Average="; AVERAGE
210  END
```

FORTRAN

```
C Averaging Program ASW 5/30/86
C FORTRAN version
C
C Initialize variables
      SUM=0
      NUMBER=0
C Main loop begins here
10    WRITE (6,*) 'More input <Y/N>? '
      READ (6,20) Q
20    FORMAT (A1)
      IF (Q .NE. 'y')GOTO 30
      Q='Y'
30    IF (Q .NE. 'Y')GOTO 40
      READ (6,*) N
      SUM=SUM+N
      NUMBER=NUMBER+1
      GOTO 10
C Continue here to finish
40    IF (NUMBER .EQ. 0)GOTO 50
C Calculate results
      AVERAG=SUM/NUMBER
C Report results
      WRITE(6,*) 'Total=', SUM
      WRITE(6,*) 'Number=', NUMBER
      WRITE(6,*) 'Average=', AVERAG
50    CONTINUE
      END
```

C

```
/* Averaging Program ASW 5/30/86 */
/* C version (VAX) */
#include      <stdio.h>
main()
{
    char q;
    int number;
    float n, sum;
    sum = 0; number = 0;
        while ((q = query()) = = 'Y')
    {  scanf("%f", &n); printf("\n");
       sum = sum + n; number+ + ;
    }
    if (number)
    {  printf("Total=%f\n", sum);
       printf("Number=%d\n", num-
          ber);
       printf("Average=%f\n", sum/num-
          ber);
    }
}
query()
{  char c[2];
   printf("Another?");
   scanf("% 1s", c); printf(" ?");
   return(toupper(c[0]));
}
```

could be used to translate powerful instructions automatically into sequences of elementary instructions. Thus the concept of computer languages was born.

Machine and Assembly Languages. A CPU operates by responding to differences in electrical voltages. Higher and lower voltages are represented in the most basic computer language—machine language—by the binary digits zero and one. Machine-language programs are composed of long strings of BINARY NUMBERS and are difficult to understand. ASSEMBLY LANGUAGE is a step up from machine language. It allows the computer programmer to think in terms of cumulative operations, such as addition and subtraction, rather than the more basic electrical modulations (see COMPUTER PROGRAMMING). An assembler program translates such operations into a machine-language program. Machine and assembly languages are called low-level languages.

High-Level Languages. Computer programmers need to express problems in a form that is independent of the design of the CPU. They also prefer not to specify every detail of an operation when writing COMPUTER SOFTWARE. As a result, high level, or symbolic, computer languages have been developed. With a high-level language a user can obtain the sum of two numbers by giving the computer a command such as "PRINT 512+637." For this to happen, high-level languages must be translated into low-level languages. This is accomplished, within the computer, by either a compiler or an interpreter.

A compiler program translates a source program into machine language and executes it. An interpreter program reads individual words of a source program, causing the consecutive executions of partial segments of a machine-language program. A compiler program runs more quickly but is more difficult to write than an interpreter program. Personal computers (see COMPUTER, PERSONAL) tend to use interpreted languages such as BASIC. Minicomputers and mainframe computers often used compiled languages such as FORTRAN.

History. The first electronic digital computers were built in the 1940s and were programmed in machine language. Assembly languages were then developed, reducing somewhat the time required for programming. In 1956 the first widely used high-level programming language was introduced. Called FORTRAN (from FORmula TRANslator), it was designed for dealing with the complicated calculations of scientists and engineers. COBOL (from COmmon Business-Oriented Language) was introduced soon after and was designed to aid in business data processing. ALGOL (for ALGOrithmic Language) was introduced in 1960; it was designed as a tool for computer scientists to use for finding solutions to mathematical or programming problems. LISP (from LISt Processor) was also developed in the late 1950s by computer scientists. In particular, LISP was designed for working on problems of artificial intelligence, as in attempts to make computers translate human languages.

The confusion of many different types of languages led to an attempt in the 1960s to produce a language that could serve both the business and the scientific-engineering communities. This project produced the language PL/1 (from Programming Language One). Nevertheless, newer languages continued to emerge. BASIC (from Beginner's All-purpose Symbolic Instruction Code) was developed in the 1960s to give computer novices a readily understandable programming tool. This was a time when time-sharing operating systems were making computers more available, particularly in grade schools and colleges. APL (from A Programming Language) was also developed for time-sharing systems, but in this case the goal was to provide a very powerful language for sophisticated mathematical and scientific calculations.

Newer Languages. In the 1970s a number of new general-purpose computer languages emerged. Pascal, named for the 17th-century mathematician and philosopher who invented a mechanical calculating machine, was designed to be a teaching language and to encourage good programming habits in students. Pascal has now largely replaced ALGOL as the language used by computer scientists for the formal descriptions of algorithms. The economical C language is similar to Pascal in many ways, and it allows the experienced programmer to write programs that make more efficient use of computer hardware. The language Ada is named in honor of Lady Ada Lovelace, the programmer for English inventor Charles Babbage's never-completed mechanical computer. Commissioned by the U.S. Department of Defense, Ada has a purpose similar to PL/1: it is meant to be a universal language. Like PL/1, Ada is complicated, but because its use is required in U.S. defense projects, its industrial employment is ensured.

Other specialized languages include FORTH, a creative language designed for use in scientific and industrial control and measurement applications; PILOT (from Programmed Instruction, Learning, Or Testing), designed

for use in writing instructional software; and LOGO, a sophisticated offspring of LISP, originally developed to help very young children learn about computers. Japanese researchers recently chose a newer language, PROLOG (from PROgramming LOGic), to be used with their next generation of powerful supercomputers. The structure of PROLOG makes it convenient for programming logical processes and for making deductions automatically. PROLOG is considered the language that will be used in artificial-intelligence systems of the future. Parallel processors, computers that perform many operations simultaneously, require programming that breaks instructions into smaller parts to be executed concurrently (see PARALLEL PROCESSING). Occam, a nonsequential language capable of running on such computers, enhances the speed at which parallel processors work.

computer memory A digital computer memory is the component of a computer system that provides storage for the computer program instructions and for data. The internal, or primary, memory is an essential feature of computers. Many computer operations involve reading instructions from memory and executing them by reading data from memory, performing an operation, and writing results back into memory. Because there is room to store only a limited amount of information in the primary memory of a computer, permanent storage of large amounts of information must be accommodated by external, or secondary, memories such as magnetic tapes (see INFORMATION STORAGE AND RETRIEVAL).

Structure. A primary memory component consists of many storage locations, each of which is uniquely identified by a number called an address. To read from memory, the address of the desired information must be supplied to the memory along with a command to "read." The content of the specified location is then produced as output. To write into memory, the address of the location and the information to be written must be supplied to the memory along with a "write" command.

Each read or write operation is called an access. Sequential access memories, such as magnetic tape, are usually used for secondary storage. To move from one address to another in such memories, it is necessary to proceed sequentially through all locations between the two addresses—for example, by winding a tape. In random-access memories (RAMs), on the other hand, all locations can be accessed directly by electronic switching. RAMs are used in primary memories because of their speed.

Memory units that are frequently read from but never written into, such as the control programs in hand calculators, are known as read-only memories (ROMs). ROMs have permanent information placed in them during manufacture. Programmable ROMs (PROMs) may be manufactured as standard units and then have permanent information implanted in them. Erasable programmable ROMs (EPROMs), on the other hand, may have new information implanted in them by the user.

Properties. The *size* of a computer memory refers to the amount of information that may be stored; the smallest unit of information in digital computer systems is the bit, or binary digit, a unit with one of two values, 0 or 1, used in the BINARY NUMBER system. An addressable unit is the group of bits that constitute the information in an addressable storage location. Common sizes for the addressable unit are 8, 16, 32, and 64 bits. The memory size is specified by the addressable unit size and by the number of addresses. Modern computers have from 64,000 to more than 4 billion addressable locations.

The rate of information transfer between the CENTRAL PROCESSING UNIT (CPU) and memory is determined by the memory cycle time and the path width, or number of bits moved in each cycle. Memory cycle time is the time required by the memory system to carry out a read or write operation.

Types. Until the 1970s most large primary memories used ferrite cores—rings of magnetized material about a millimeter in diameter, strung like beads on a wire grid. The direction of magnetization of each core in the memory determines the binary value it carries. Ferrite-core memories are "nonvolatile"; that is, they retain their store of information even after power has been removed from the system.

Most primary memories now are made up of small INTEGRATED CIRCUIT chips, each of which can hold up to one million bits of information. The information is stored electrically in arrays of tiny semiconductor capacitors, which can be either uncharged or charged, corresponding to binary values of 0 and 1. Such memories are "volatile"—their information is lost when power is removed. The most widely used RAM is the DRAM, or dynamic RAM, which must be constantly recharged during its operation. Another type, the static RAM, or SRAM, does not require constant "refreshing" but uses more circuitry and space.

Performance Improvement. Several design methods are available to improve primary memory performance. In one technique, called interleaved memory, two memory modules are built, and each can be accessed independently to provide instructions and data to the CPU. A second performance-improvement method is the insertion of a higher-performance, small memory between the primary memory and the CPU.

computer modeling   Computer modeling is the use of computers to model objects and to simulate processes. Computer models are valuable because they allow a person to study the response of a system to conditions that are not easily or safely applied in a real situation. With a computer model a process can be speeded up or slowed down. A model can also allow an observer to study how the functioning of an entire system can be altered by changing individual components of the system.

A computer model is usually defined in mathematical terms with a computer program (see COMPUTER PROGRAMMING). Mathematical equations are constructed that represent functional relationships within a system. When the program is running, the mathematical dynamics become analogous to dynamics of the real system. Results are given in the form of data. Another type of model involves a COMPUTER GRAPHICS representation of an object, which can be manipulated on a video-display terminal in much the same way that a three-dimensional clay or wood model might be manipulated. This is the basis of computer-aided design (see COMPUTER-AIDED DESIGN AND COMPUTER-AIDED MANUFACTURING).

SPREADSHEET programs are simple and inexpensive computer models that are widely applicable to business

These three-dimensional computer models of the human brain were developed from a computer program containing detailed information on the cross-sectional appearance of the brain. Used for educational purposes, the models can show the brain from a number of angles. Sections of the brain can be highlighted or eliminated, and the entire model can be rotated on the screen.

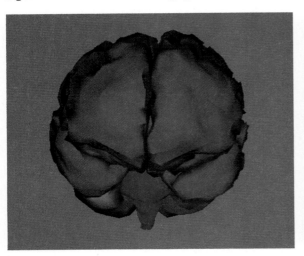
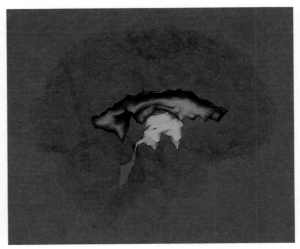

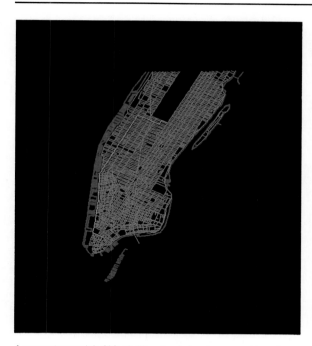

A computer model of Manhattan streets has been used here to find the most direct route between selected points and to display it on the computer's monitor screen.

concerns. They can be used, for example, to study how changes in levels of sales and prices affect a company's profits.

computer music Computer music is any music in which computers are used to transmit musical instructions to electronic instruments or live performers. These instructions are transmitted in the form of electrical impulses, which are, in turn, reproduced as sounds.

Max V. Mathews, an electrical engineer, established the pioneering computer music project at Bell Laboratories, Murray Hill, N.J., in 1957. Mathews was inspired by the relationship between number and tone in Arnold Schoenberg's twelve-tone piano music. Twenty years after the inception of the Bell Laboratories project, Pierre BOULEZ's Institut de Recherche et de Coordination Acoustique/Musique (IRCAM) was inaugurated in Paris. Significant work in computerized music is also being done at many U.S. universities, including Princeton, Stanford, Illinois, and the University of California at San Diego. Some composers of computer music are Milton BABBITT, John CAGE, Yannis XENAKIS, Herbert Brün, John Chowning, Emmanuel Ghent, Julia Morrison, Dika Newlin, Laurie Spiegel, Morton Subotnick, and James Tenney.

computer networking Computer networking is the interconnecting of many computers for the purposes of sharing CENTRAL PROCESSING UNITS (CPUs), DATABASES, and INPUT-OUTPUT DEVICES. In a computer network, individual stations, which can consist of any of these units, are called "nodes." Nodes are connected by coaxial cables, optical fibers, or standard telephone lines. Networks that are set up for individual businesses and schools, and that are usually contained within a single building, are called local-area networks, or LANs. Wider networks, however, can use telephone lines to span states, countries, or the entire globe.

computer programming Computer programming is the process or activity of developing programs, or lists of instructions, that control the operation of a computer. A number of essential types of programs exist: operating-system programs control the most fundamental operations of the computer, such as language interpretation and input and output; applications programs tailor the computer's powers to performing specific tasks, such as figuring payrolls, creating mechanical designs, and processing texts.

Computer programs are expressed in precise notations called programming languages (see COMPUTER LANGUAGES). The programs for elementary computer processes are written in low-level languages that are cumbersome and difficult for the ordinary user to follow. High-level languages strike a compromise between the precise meanings required by the machine and the spoken language of the user.

The programming of a computer may be broken down into the following stages: requirements definition, design specification, coding, testing, and maintenance. The requirements stage involves quantifying the necessary operations to be performed by the program. In the design-specification stage, directions are provided for meeting the requirements by quantifying the processing steps and the data-storage structures in greater detail. For this, an ALGORITHM, or step-by-step procedure, is devised. Coding is the stage in which the design is turned into steps expressed in a chosen programming language. Testing is the stage in which the program is verified as being correct with respect to the requirements and design specification. After the program is tested and found to be correct, it is released to its users. The final stage is maintenance, in which enhancements and corrections are made.

Because maintenance is the most expensive stage in programming, recent work has emphasized design, coding, and testing techniques that accommodate changes in the original program. Many new programming techniques have been developed under the title CASE (Computer-Aided Software Engineering). CASE programs automate the various phases of computer programming.

computer software Computer software consists of the programs, or lists of instructions, that control the operation of a computer. The term can refer to the sum of all programs that may be used with a certain computer, or it can refer to a single program (see COMPUTER PROGRAMMING).

Software is intangible information stored as electrical impulses in the memory of a computer, in contrast to the hardware components of a computer system. These electrical impulses are decoded by the hardware and interpreted as instructions, with each instruction guiding or controlling the hardware for a brief time.

A wide variety of software is used in a computer system, and it is classified by the layers of operation within the system. The lowest layer is nearest to the machine hardware; the highest layer is nearest to the human operator. A compiler is a software program whose purpose is to convert programs written in a high-level, or user, language into the low-level form that can be interpreted by the electrical circuits of the hardware (see COMPUTER LANGUAGES). Interpreter programs perform a similar task. An operating system is a software program that controls the computer system itself. It organizes hardware functions such as reading and writing input and output data (from a keyboard, screen, or disk-drive unit; to a screen, printer, or disk-drive unit), and intercepting commands from the user.

Applications software adapts the computer to the performance of specific tasks, such as figuring a payroll or modeling a machine part. Applications software is written in any of a variety of high-level computer languages, such as FORTRAN, COBOL, or Pascal, each of which is appropriate for certain applications. These languages must be used in conjunction with an appropriate compiler.

Applications software is rather diverse. A horizontal program can cut across many application areas; examples are SPREADSHEETS and DATABASE programs. Vertical applications programs are tailored to narrow and specific tasks, such as medical billing or the design of an airplane. Other common software programs include WORD PROCESSING PROGRAMS, VIDEO GAMES, and desktop publishing programs (see PUBLISHING, DESKTOP).

Popular software is usually distributed on magnetic disks (see INFORMATION STORAGE AND RETRIEVAL). When a disk is read by a computer's disk-drive unit, the software is recorded in the main memory of the computer. With tremendous advances in microelectronics, which have led to powerful memory chips, even microcomputers can now accommodate sophisticated software programs.

Although the costs of computer hardware have decreased dramatically over the years, the cost of software has not. This is mainly because techniques for developing software have not improved dramatically, but it is also related to the problem of unauthorized software copying, or piracy. The expanding roles of personal computers in homes and businesses have increased the importance of software (see COMPUTER, PERSONAL).

computer terminal A computer terminal (also called a data terminal or data communication terminal) is a device that allows a user to interact with a central COMPUTER. Terminals, which are generally connected to the CENTRAL PROCESSING UNIT (CPU) by direct wiring or telephone lines, are the most commonly seen components of a computer system. The typewriterlike devices used for making airline and motel reservations are computer terminals, as are the devices resembling cash registers used in automated checkout counters. Terminals typically contain some form of keyboard for input to the computer and either a printing mechanism or video screen for presenting output. Transmission between terminal and computer is in a coded form of electrical signals such as ASCII, the American Standard Code for Information Interchange.

computer virus A computer virus is a portion of computer code designed to insert itself into an existing computer program, alter or destroy data, and copy itself into other programs in the same computer or into programs in other computers. Its name was coined from its ability to "replicate" and "infect" other computers. A computer virus can spread through shared COMPUTER SOFTWARE, through an on-line service (see DATABASE), or through a network (see COMPUTER NETWORKING). Often, programmers who design computer viruses are "hackers" who do so as a prank. Their typical virus might cause a humorous message to appear on a computer's video screen. Others, however, design viruses with the deliberate intent to destroy data.

computers in education The 1980s witnessed the introduction and widespread use of personal computers (see COMPUTER, PERSONAL) at all levels of schooling. During the decade the number of computers used in U.S. elementary and secondary schools increased from less than 100,000 to more than 2.5 million. A majority of students now use computers and COMPUTER SOFTWARE at some time during the school year—either to learn about computers or as a tool for learning other subjects. The typical school has 1 computer per 20 students.

Some critics see computer education as merely the latest in a series of unsuccessful attempts to revolutionize education through the use of audio- and visually oriented nonprint media. For example, motion pictures, broadcast television, filmstrips, audio recorders, and videotapes were all initially heralded for their instructional potential, but each of these ultimately became minor classroom tools alongside conventional methods. (See also PROGRAMMED LEARNING; TEACHING MACHINES.)

Supporters believe that computers are a much more powerful learning medium than these others. They cite the essential interactive nature of using computers programmed to provoke decision making and manipulations of visual environments. Also, each computer is controlled by one student or pair of students. Learning tasks can become more individualized, enabling students to receive immediate feedback. Some experts say that having students work collaboratively on computers leads to greater initiative and more autonomous learning. Proponents also argue that because computers are so pervasive in U.S. society, "computer literacy" is essential.

Computers in elementary and secondary schools are used in two major contexts. The first is computer-education instruction—whereby students learn how to type on

 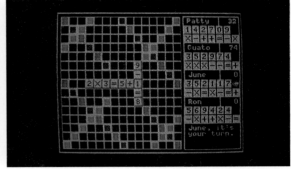

(Left) *Using computers, students can conduct a simulated dissection of a frog.* (Right) *Math skills are developed in computer games such as this, in which equations are built by using operating symbols.*

computer keyboards (keyboarding); how to use WORD PRO-CESSING programs; how to program computers in languages such as BASIC, Pascal, and LOGO; and how to use other computer applications such as database programs and spreadsheets. One-half of computer use by secondary students and one-third of its use by elementary students is of this kind.

The other major computer-based activity is computer-assisted instruction (CAI). CAI programs are specifically written for teaching individual students in school settings. They present students with a question and compare the student's answer with the single correct answer. Typically, the program responds to a correct answer with praise and to wrong answers with an explanation and another, similar problem. Sometimes CAI programs are embedded in a gamelike context, and most provide audio and video embellishments. Most CAI programs cover limited material, but some large-scale, multiyear reading and mathematics curricula have been developed.

Studies of the effects of CAI on how well children learn basic skills have generally been supportive of CAI, although critics claim that CAI's effects may be mainly limited to the early grades, to more routine skills, to students from disadvantaged backgrounds, and to learning-disabled students.

Yet there are good reasons for the dominance of CAI. Its activities are relatively easy to program, it is compatible with traditional methods of instruction, and it requires relatively little effort to organize computer use. Also, CAI activities can be kept distinct from other classroom learning activities by being located in centrally based "laboratories."

Non-CAI programs have made some inroads. Several types of software are in widespread use: programs that give students practice in applying logic and solving puzzles; programs for making posters, newspapers, and other classroom projects; word-processing programs for individual student reports; and programs for vocational preparation. Other types of educational computer programs include simulations (programs that let classes explore controversial issues or complex environments by involving them in simpler "models") and microcomputer-based

laboratories with materials and software enabling classes to conduct scientific investigations.

In writing, schools use word-processing programs designed specially for younger writers, but programs are also available for outlining and other "prewriting" tasks and collaborative writing and peer editing. Programs are also available to support and encourage student creativity in the arts and in technical education.

These programs are more difficult to implement than CAI. Many require a change in educational goals and basic practices. All require substantial preparation by teachers and more effort on the part of the software manufacturers. Another factor retarding the spread of more powerful software is the nature of the computers that schools purchased in the late 1970s and early 1980s, when the only computers available were somewhat limited. Because schools need computers in large numbers, and computers that work with the software they already have, they have continued to buy the older, less powerful computers. The high cost of computers is also an inhibiting factor.

Comsat   see COMMUNICATIONS SATELLITE

Comstock Lode   The Comstock Lode, a 5.6-km (3.5-mi) stretch of the Sierra Nevadas in far western Nevada, was the richest silver-mining region of its size in the history of the United States. The lode took its name from Henry T. P. Comstock, an investor who sold out early with only a small profit. Developed with capital from California, the eastern states, and Europe, the area around Virginia City, Nev., yielded almost $300 million in silver and gold ore before production severely declined after 1882. Equally important, innovations there in ore processing and in timbering, ventilation, and drainage of extremely deep mines encouraged other exploration and discoveries in California, Idaho, Montana, and the Southwest after 1880.

Comtat   Comtat (also called Comtat-Venaissin) is a historic region and former papal enclave in southeastern

France, surrounding but not including the city of Avignon. Its capital was Carpentras. Comtat was held by a succession of rulers until about 1000, when it passed to the counts of Toulouse, who held it as a fief of the Holy Roman Empire. During the 13th century Comtat was ceded to Pope Gregory X by Philip III. It remained under papal rule until 1791, when it became part of France. The area is now in the Vaucluse department.

Comte, Auguste

Comte, Auguste [kohnt]   Auguste Comte, b. Jan. 19, 1798, d. Sept. 5, 1857, was a French philosopher and a leading figure in 19th-century POSITIVISM. Comte's scientific courses at the École Polytechnique convinced him that the scientific method should be applied to social problems. He later devoted himself to SOCIOLOGY, a word he coined to describe the science of society.

Comte believed his main contribution to be the theory that humanity has passed through three stages of intellectual development: the theological, the metaphysical, and the positive. In the first stage, the universe was explained in terms of gods, demons, and mythological beings. In the second stage, reality was explained in terms of abstractions such as essence, existence, substance, and accident. According to Comte, the metaphysical stage was just ending, giving way to the scientific, or positive, stage. In this final stage, explanations could be based only on scientific laws discovered through experimentation, observation, or logic. Mathematics, astronomy, physics, chemistry, and biology—classified by Comte on the basis of increasing complexity—were already scientific; Comte sought to complete the positive stage by making sociology, the most complex of all, a science.

In *A General View of Positivism* (1848; Eng. trans., 1957), Comte proposed a positive religion, in which metaphysics was eliminated and humanity was the object of worship—an idea much criticized by contemporaries. Although his law of three stages soon ceased to be convincing, his approach to sociology greatly influenced later theorists.

Conable, Barber B.

Conable, Barber B.   Barber Benjamin Conable, Jr., b. Warsaw, N.Y., Nov. 2, 1922, became the seventh president of the World Bank on July 1, 1986. Between 1965 and 1985 he served as a Republican U.S. representative from New York and thereafter as a professor at the University of Rochester. A graduate of Cornell University, Conable trained in the law. He was in the U.S. Marine Corps during World War II and the Korean War and served one term in the New York State Senate (1963–65). In Congress he developed a reputation as an economics expert.

Conakry

Conakry [kahn'-uh-kree]   Conakry (1983 est. pop., 656,000) is the capital and largest city of Guinea. It is located on Tombo Island and is connected by a causeway to the mainland. Its fine port on the Atlantic Ocean is partially sheltered by the Los Islands, an important source of bauxite. Conakry is the administrative, transportation, and commercial center of Guinea, with a variety of light industries. Chief exports are bananas, alumina (treated bauxite), oranges, coffee, fish, and palm products. The city was conquered by the French in 1884. Its economic development began after World War II.

Conant, James Bryant

Conant, James Bryant [kohn'-uhnt]   James Bryant Conant, b. Dorchester, Mass., Mar. 26, 1893, d. Feb. 11, 1978, was a chemist, president of Harvard University, and an influential critic of American schools. He was educated at Harvard (B.A., 1913; Ph.D., 1916), taught (1919–33) chemistry there, and was president from 1933 to 1953, when he was appointed U.S. high commissioner for West Germany. Made ambassador in 1955, he resigned in 1957.

In 1957 Conant began studying American high schools. He suggested changes in teacher training, decentralized control of education, and increased funding for inner-city schools. He advocated large comprehensive high schools that would be responsible for educational and vocational guidance of youth up to the age of 21. Among his works in this field are *Slums and Suburbs* (1961) and *The Comprehensive High School: A Second Report to Interested Citizens* (1967).

concentration

concentration   The concentration of a SOLUTION expresses the relative amounts of the substances constituting the solution. Different means of expressing concentration are used by chemists to emphasize various aspects of solutions.

Molarity. Molarity is perhaps the most widely used measurement of concentration. It is the number of moles of solute per liter of solution. (A mole of a substance weighs, in grams, the same as its molecular weight. A mole of a substance contains the same number of molecules as a mole of any other substance.) The symbol for molarity is M. A $0.5M$ solution, for example, is prepared by weighing out one-half mole of the solute and dissolving it in some solvent; pure solvent is then added until the total quantity is one liter. The concept of molarity is useful because, as the quantity of solute in a given volume of solution is known, amounts may be dispensed rapidly and accurately by volume.

Molality. The molality (m) of a solution is the number of moles of solute per kilogram of solvent. Molality expresses the ratio of solute to solvent; for a given solvent, two different solutions of equal molality have the same ratio of solute to solvent molecules. It is a useful unit of concentration in treating the colligative properties (those which depend only on the number or ratio of molecules) of a solution.

Weight Percent. When the molecular weight of a solute is unknown or irrelevant, its concentration may be expressed in terms of its weight relative to the weight of the solution.

Normality. The normality (*N*) of a solution expresses the number of equivalents (see EQUIVALENT WEIGHT) of solute for each liter of solution. Equivalents are the quantities of substances that have the same combining capacity in chemical reactions. Equivalents are either identical to moles or are simple fractions of them.

---

concentration camp Concentration camps are places of detention for civilians considered political enemies; imprisonment usually takes place without trial. Concentration camps have been established several times in modern history. The best-known examples of concentration camps were those used by the British to contain the noncombatant Boer population during the SOUTH AFRICAN WAR of 1899–1902 and those in which the German Nazi regime (1933–45) interned political enemies, housed slave labor, and eventually exterminated millions of Jews and others (see HOLOCAUST). Concentration camps were also used on a large scale by the Spanish general Valeriano Weyler (1838–1930) in suppressing the Cuban rebellion that began in 1895. In the United States during World War II, more than 100,000 Japanese and Japanese-Americans (NISEI) on the West Coast were removed to relocation camps in the interior. The USSR has maintained corrective labor camps, in which, during the time of Joseph Stalin, millions of citizens died (see GULAG).

Concepción [kohn-sep-see-ohn'] Concepción is the third largest city in Chile and has a population of 294,400 (1987 est.). Situated in the south central part of the country, on the Río Bío-Bío, 10 km (6 mi) from its mouth, the city is the capital of Bío-Bío region and an important industrial center. Through its port, Talcahuano, the city ships agricultural and forest products from the surrounding region. Most of Chile's coal comes from the area around Concepción. Founded in 1550 by Pedro de Valdivia on the site of the Indian village of Penco, Concepción was twice sacked and burned by the Araucanian Indians in the 1550s. It was destroyed by earthquakes in 1570, 1730, and 1751. In 1754 it was moved to its present site where it was leveled by earthquakes in 1835 and 1939.

Concertgebouw Orchestra [kuhn-sairt'-kuh-bow] The Concertgebouw Orchestra of Amsterdam is recognized as one of the world's finest symphonic organizations. Founded in 1883 by the Concertgebouw Gezelschap (Concert Hall Society), it has occupied its present home, the Concertgebouw, since 1888. The orchestra is supported by both government and public funds. In 1895, Willem Mengelberg was appointed principal conductor. He was barred from conducting in Holland in 1945 because he had collaborated with the Nazis. That year, Eduard van Beinum succeeded Mengelberg as principal conductor and led the orchestra until his death in 1959. From 1961 to 1964, Eugen JOCHUM and Bernard HAITINK were co-conductors of the orchestra. Since 1964, Haitink has been the orchestra's permanent conductor and artistic director.

---

concertina [kahn-sur-tee'-nuh] An improved small ACCORDION, but without the accordion keyboard, the concertina was patented in England in 1829. Its hexagonal end pieces are fitted with studs for selecting the various pitches from its reeds. Fully chromatic and capable of various tonal effects, it has been used in solo and chamber music. Tchaikovsky used four concertinas in his second orchestral suite. A popular instrument for informal occasions during the 19th century, the concertina is still widely used, especially in England.

The concertina is a portable, free-reed instrument similar to the accordian. The keyboards on either end are connected by bellows whose compression and expansion do not vary the note sounded.

---

concerto [kuhn-chairt'-oh] The concerto is a musical form in which two or more dissimilar musical forces are used. For example, one or more soloists may play opposite an orchestra. The term literally means a "getting together" of several voices or of voices accompanied by instruments. The first publication (1587) of works titled *Concerti* was a collection of church music and madrigals by Andrea and Giovanni Gabrieli (see GABRIELI family).

In the early 17th century, the concerto became largely an orchestral form. Three types are distinguished: the orchestral concerto, in which differences in texture or treatment marked the opposing groups of instruments; the concerto grosso, in which a small group called the concertino (usually two violins and a basso continuo played by a keyboard instrument and cello) competed against the main force, called the *tutti* or *ripieno* ("remainder" or "filling"); and the solo concerto for one instrument and orchestra.

As the dominant concerto form of the late 18th and 19th centuries, the solo concerto took on a three-movement form (fast, slow, fast), a modified SONATA form as the first movement, and often a RONDO as the last. In the 20th century the concerto grosso and orchestral concerto have been revived.

---

conch [kahnch] Conch is the common name for certain marine snails, usually in the family Strombidae.

Conchs have a shell with overlapping whorls—the outermost whorl being broad and triangular—and a wide, flattened lip along its opening. They are MOLLUSKS of the gastropod order Mesogastropoda, possessing one gill, auricle, and kidney, all on one side of the body. The operculum, or covering of the shell opening, has been modified into a clawlike structure that is used to dig into the sand and provide an anchor against which the conch pushes to propel itself. The queen conch, *Strombus gigas*, found in the Atlantic Ocean from Florida to Brazil, is a plant-eater reaching a length of about 30 cm (1 ft) and a weight of 2.3 kg (5 lb). Some WHELKS are also called conchs.

conciliarism [kuhn-sil'-ee-ur-izm] Conciliarism is both a theory and a movement in the history of the Roman Catholic church. As a theory, it holds that an ecumenical council (see COUNCIL, ECUMENICAL) is superior in authority to the papacy. In this view, the pope is like a constitutional ruler who receives his authority from the entire church membership, and whose decisions may be reviewed by the church community through an ecumenical council. As a movement, conciliarism originated with various canonists of the 12th and 13th centuries and was enunciated by the Council of Constance (1414–18). It later appeared in other forms, mostly nationalistic movements such as GALLICANISM. Conciliarism was condemned by the First VATICAN COUNCIL (1869–70).

Concord (Massachusetts) Concord is a town in northeastern Massachusetts, 30 km (19 mi) northwest of Boston. Founded in 1635, it is noted as the birthplace of the American Revolution. Concord retains a semirural character and has a population of 17,076 (1990). On Apr. 19, 1775, at a bridge spanning the Concord River, American farmers fired on British soldiers who had been sent from Boston to destroy military supplies (see LEXINGTON AND CONCORD, BATTLES OF). The site of the battle is marked by *Minuteman*, a sculpture by the local 19th-century artist Daniel Chester FRENCH. Concord was the locale for a circle of American writers, including Louisa May Alcott, Ralph Waldo Emerson, Nathaniel Hawthorne, and Henry David Thoreau. Walden Pond, made famous by Thoreau, is south of the town.

Concord (New Hampshire) Concord is the capital of and the third largest city in New Hampshire, with a population of 36,006 (1990). It is located in the south central portion of the state on the Merrimack River and is the seat of Merrimack County. The economy relies on the manufacture of electrical equipment, textiles, and leather and wood products, as well as on insurance, granite quarrying, and state governmental operations.

Settlement began as early as 1659, and in 1733 the village was incorporated as Rumford by Massachusetts. After years of dispute, it was determined in 1762 that the area lay within New Hampshire, and in 1765 it was reincorporated as Concord. The state capital was moved there in 1808. Concord was the birthplace of President Franklin Pierce.

concordat [kahn-kor'-dat] A concordat is a formal agreement or convention between the Roman Catholic church, almost always represented by the papacy, and a sovereign state in which questions of mutual concern are regulated. Usually concordats have been concluded in order to terminate preexisting friction or hostilities between church and state. Concordats have taken the form of an international treaty, a papal BULL, or of separate, simultaneous declarations by the two parties involved.

A total of 148 concordats have been made, 15 since World War I. The Concordat of Worms (1122), which settled the INVESTITURE CONTROVERSY between the pope and the Holy Roman emperor, is usually cited as the first true concordat. Other important examples are the Concordat of Bologna (1516) with the French king Francis I and the Concordat of 1801 between Napoléon I and Pope PIUS VII. The treaty of 1801 ended more than 10 years of hostility and violence between the church and the French Revolution by reestablishing Roman Catholicism as a state-supported religion and effecting a compromise between the status of the church under the Old Regime and the Civil Constitution of the Clergy of 1790. The Concordat of 1801 served as a model for agreements with various emerging national states throughout the 19th century. In 1984 a new concordat between the Vatican and Italy curtailed church privileges in that country.

Concorde [kahn'-kord] The Concorde is the best-known SUPERSONIC TRANSPORT (SST), the result of a November 1962 agreement between the governments of Great Britain and France to build a civil transport airplane that could fly at twice the speed of sound—Mach 2, which is about 2,125 km/h (1,320 mph). The Concorde is made of a special aluminum alloy and is shaped like a tailless delta with a long but narrow wing of so-called ogival form, with subtly curved leading edges and elevons (airfoil control surfaces) on the trailing edge to control both pitch (dive and climb) and roll.

The prototype flew on Mar. 2, 1969, and a refined model entered service with British Airways and Air France on Jan. 21, 1976. London and Paris are now linked by supersonic transport to eight other cities. The establishment of Concorde service in the United States caused a wave of opposition. Protesters contended that the Concorde damages the environment because of the noise it generates and also because of its effect on the ozone content of the upper atmosphere. Regular Concorde service to New York City finally began on Aug. 1, 1978.

concrete see CEMENT AND CONCRETE

concretion [kahn-kree'-shuhn] A concretion is a mineral segregation found in SEDIMENTARY ROCK. Generally spheroidal, concretions range in size from minute to 3 m

(10 ft). They are formed when water precipitates silica, calcite, or an iron compound around a body that differs from adjacent rock. Such bodies include plant fossils, which are sometimes found well preserved in concretions (known as coal balls) in or just above coal beds. Differences in hardness, mineralogy, color, and weathering characteristics aid in the identification of concretions.

concubinage [kahn-kue'-bin-ij] Concubinage is the state of cohabitation of a man and a woman in which they live as if they are married persons although they are not legally married. The female partner is the concubine, and she has recognized status in the man's household—even legally recognized status—although that status is less than that of a wife. Concubinage does not differ very much from some forms of polygyny (see POLYGAMY), the form of plural MARRIAGE in which a man takes more than one wife. When concubinage is found in monogamous societies, it may be an evasion of law or of prevailing custom, or both, concerning marriage to only one spouse at a time. When practiced in polygamous societies, it may be an evasion of other customs relating to marriage. In either kind of society, it may be a way of displaying affluence.

The idea of concubinage was particularly well developed in traditional China, although the actual practice was not widespread, being limited to a small portion of the elite.

concussion [kuhn-kuhsh'-uhn] Concussion is a temporary state of brain dysfunction caused by a blow to the head. The symptoms may include temporary loss of consciousness, headaches, and amnesia, or memory lapses. The recovery period lasts from a few hours to weeks, depending on the severity of the symptoms, and requires complete bedrest. Brain injury is not readily apparent, although lasting injury may occur from a bruise or a tearing of the brain, or from bleeding between the brain and the skull.

Condé (family) [kohn-day'] A junior line of the French royal dynasty of BOURBON, the house of Condé began its history by leading the revolt of the HUGUENOTS against the crown. **Louis I, prince de Condé,** b. May 7, 1530, d. Mar. 13, 1569, was the uncle of Henry of Navarre, later king as HENRY IV. Louis was killed at the Battle of Jarnac. His son, **Henri I de Condé,** b. Dec. 29, 1552, d. Mar. 5, 1588, vied with Henry of Navarre for the Huguenot leadership. In the next generation **Henri II,** b. Sept. 1, 1588, d. Dec. 26, 1646, was brought up a Roman Catholic. He opposed the regency of MARIE DE MÉDICIS but later was loyal to LOUIS XIII.

The fourth and most distinguished prince was **Louis II de Condé,** b. Sept. 8, 1621, d. Dec. 11, 1686, known as the Great Condé. Except for his rival the vicomte de TURENNE, he was the most celebrated general of the age. After early victories against Spain, notably Rocroi (1643) and Lens (1648), he opposed the regent, ANNE OF AUS-

TRIA, and Cardinal MAZARIN in the civil wars of the FRONDE. When his party was defeated in 1653, he fought for Spain against France until 1659.

condensed-matter physics Condensed-matter physics is a branch of PHYSICS dealing with properties of condensed materials—solids, semisolids, and liquids. In dealing with such properties as conductivity, superconductivity, and surface phenomena, condensed-matter physics includes the concerns of SOLID-STATE PHYSICS (a term that it is superseding) while extending to studies of noncrystalline states.

condenser see HEAT EXCHANGER; REFRIGERATION

Condillac, Étienne Bonnot de [kohn-dee-yahk'] The French philosopher Étienne Condillac, b. Sept. 30, 1715, d. Aug. 2, 1780, was a leading advocate of the ideas of John LOCKE. After studying theology he became (1740) a priest. He was elected to the French Academy in 1767. His main works include *Essai sur l'origine des connaissances humaines* (Essay on the Origin of Human Knowledge, 1746), *Traité des systèmes* (Treatise on Systems, 1749), and *Traité des sensations* (Treatise on Sensations, 1754).

Condillac's primary philosophical interest was the explanation of human knowledge and experience. His starting point was provided by Locke, who had argued that all genuine human knowledge has its origins in sense experience. Locke assumed, however, that the contents provided by experience were acted upon by various faculties of the mind. Condillac undertook to show that the faculties of the mind were themselves the result of sense experience. In this respect, his EMPIRICISM was more consistent and rigorous than Locke's. The writings of Condillac were a significant contribution to SENSATIONALISM, a theory that says all knowledge comes from the senses.

conditioning see BEHAVIOR MODIFICATION; LEARNING THEORY

condominium [kahn-doh-min'-ee-uhm] In property law, a condominium is the ownership of a dwelling in a multioccupant building, with an undivided ownership interest in the land and the components of the building used in common by all the owners, such as halls, elevators, and heating equipment. The maintenance of the common facilities is usually provided by an association of the owner-tenants. Some of the more elaborate condominiums in suburban areas have outdoor recreational facilities, such as golf courses; their prices approximate those of single houses. A condominium differs from an apartment cooperative in that a cooperative is owned by a corporation in which the tenants of the apartments hold shares. The owner of a condominium unit has the right to sell it or lease it.

The California condor, largest North American bird of prey, is now nearly extinct. Hopes for its survival lie in the breeding programs run by the San Diego and Los Angeles zoos.

condor   Condors are large, extremely rare VULTURES in the family Cathartidae, order Falconiformes. They usually feed on dead animals. The Andean condor, *Vultur gryphus*, of western and southern South America, is the world's heaviest flying bird of prey, averaging 9 to 11.25 kg (20 to 25 lb) in weight. It reaches a length of 1.4 m (54 in), has a wingspan of 3 m (10 ft), and is mostly black. The California condor, *Gymnogyps californianus*, native to the coastal mountains at the southern end of the San Joaquin Valley, is slightly smaller and is dark grayish brown, with an orange head.

To save the California condor from extinction, a rescue program was initiated in 1979 that involved taking eggs from nests in the wild and incubating and breeding the young birds. In the mid-1980s all wild California condors were captured and brought into captivity. Condors have been bred in captivity, and it is hoped that some birds may eventually be returned to the wild.

Condorcet, Marie Jean Antoine Nicolas Caritat, Marquis de [kohn-dohr-say']   The marquis de Condorcet, b. Sept. 17, 1743, d. Mar. 29, 1794, was a French philosopher and mathematician. He wrote a notable essay (1785) on the theory of probability and became a prominent member of the Legislative Assembly during the French Revolution. Condorcet's opposition to the excesses of the Jacobins, however, caused him to be accused of conspiracy. He died in his cell, presumably a victim of suicide. While in hiding he wrote *Sketch for a Historical Picture of the Progress of the Human Mind* (1795; Eng. trans., 1955).

More than any other writer of the Enlightenment, Condorcet was a prophet of progress. In stating the conditions for realizing the continuity of human progress, he focused on the importance of education, the free exchange of ideas, a republican form of government, a guided economy, the emancipation of women, and a language with one clear meaning for each word.

condottieri [kohn-doht-tyair'-ee]   Leaders of mercenary armies during the wars in Italy from the early 14th to the 16th century, the condottieri took their name from the *condotta*, or "contract," by which they agreed to serve a lord or city. Mercenaries were used because of the inefficiency of the communal militia and the desire of the merchant class to avoid personal military service. By the middle of the 14th century most condottieri were Germans and Hungarians.

During a lull in the Hundred Years' War, the English captain Sir John HAWKWOOD led (*c*.1360) his White Company into Italy, fighting at times for Milan, Florence, and the papacy. Italian soldiers, for example, members of the Malatesta and SFORZA families, also fought for pay and often became the rulers of Italian cities. Venice hired its generals on long-term contracts and thus created loyal standing armies led by famous condottieri, such as Erasmo da Narni (*c*.1370–1443) and Bartolomeo Colleoni (1400–75). Often criticized for their treachery, the condottieri were replaced by more reliable national armies at the close of the Italian Wars.

conducting   Conducting is the art of directing and controlling the performance of a musical composition by means of gestures. Usually a sizable ensemble is involved, such as an orchestra, band, or chorus, or mixed voices and instruments. The conductor is responsible for setting and maintaining or varying the tempo of the piece being played, regulating the dynamics (gradations of volume), determining the balance between the performing groups, and cuing important solo entrances. In order to achieve the desired performance the conductor must above all be a leader who, by force of personality or demonstration of superior musicianship, can persuade the musicians to accept his or her interpretation of the music.

A conductor must be able to read a full score, which may consist of more than a dozen staves with different clefs and transpositions, and be able to hear the music mentally. Many conductors memorize a score and conduct it from memory. In addition, a conductor should be thoroughly familiar with both instrumental and vocal technique. A profound knowledge of the history of musical style is also essential to a conductor who wishes to convey the composer's intentions faithfully.

Originally, the primary purpose of conducting was simply to keep the performers together. The ancient Egyptians, however, used a sign language (called cheironomy, or chironomy) involving special positions of the fingers and angles of the arms not only to indicate beat but also to teach and control melody. Such techniques were later common among medieval choir directors. The ancient Greeks used the *kroúpalon*, a wooden clapper attached to the right heel of the conductor, to keep time. Silent indication of tempo did not become widespread until the late 17th century, when ensembles were kept together by the gestures of the keyboard continuo player or by the movements of the first violinist's bow.

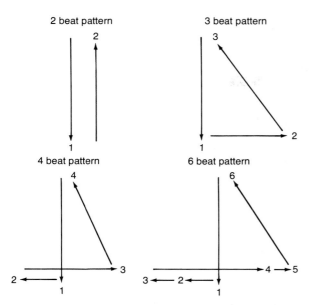

2 beat pattern   3 beat pattern

4 beat pattern   6 beat pattern

The basic gestures for beating time are given above. The first beat of each measure is indicated by a downward motion of the right hand, the final beat by an upward motion. The left hand is used primarily to indicate dynamics and important entrances (by pointing).

The evolution of conducting into a full-time position was a concomitant of the development of and emphasis on the ORCHESTRA in the second half of the 18th and the early 19th century. The baton came into use as a means of giving greater clarity to conducting. Many choral conductors, however, still prefer to conduct without a baton.

Important conductors include Hans von Bülow, Gustav Mahler, and Arthur Nikisch in the 19th century; Arturo Toscanini, Serge Koussevitzky, Leopold Stokowski, and Bruno Walter in the early 20th century; and more recently, Herbert von Karajan, Bernard Haitink, Leonard Bernstein, and Seiji Ozawa.

conduction, electric Electric conduction is the transportation of electric charge through matter. Moving charges of a given sign, with an overall net drift in one direction, set up a current (see CIRCUIT, ELECTRIC).

Materials are commonly divided into three basic electrical classes: conductors (which include most metals), SEMICONDUCTORS, and INSULATORS. The external feature that distinguishes these three classes is the conductivity, or RESISTIVITY, of the materials. The unit measure of resistivity is the OHM.

In metals the current is carried by electrons (the VALENCE electrons). The ions are tied to the crystal structure. The direction of current flow is by convention taken to be in the direction of positive charge carrier flow; that is, it is opposite to the direction of electron flow. In other materials, such as electrolytes, the current can be carried by both positive and negative ions traveling in opposite directions. In ionized gases (plasmas) the current is carried by both electrons and ions, but the electrons are so much more mobile that their effect usually dominates. If an equal number of positive and negative charges passes a given reference point in the same direction, then the net current is zero.

Copper is one of the best and most commonly used metallic conductors, but its conductivity is extremely sensitive to the presence of impurities in the metal. Another common conductor is aluminum, which has the primary advantage of light weight. For electric heating filaments, a material with low conductance and high resistance to oxidation in air is ideal. A material commonly used for this purpose is nichrome, a chromium-nickel alloy.

conduction, heat See HEAT AND HEAT TRANSFER

cone A cone is a three-dimensional geometric surface generated by a family of line segments, each segment containing as endpoints a point of a closed plane curve and a fixed point not in the plane of the curve. The fixed point is called the vertex, the closed curve is the directrix, the area bounded by the directrix is the base, and the line segments are the elements, or generators, of the cone. Cones are distinguished according to the form of the directrix.

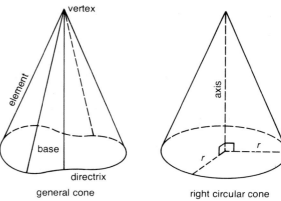

general cone   right circular cone

The perpendicular distance from the vertex to the base is called the altitude of the cone, and the length of any element is the slant height of the cone. The volume of a cone is one-third the product of its altitude and the area of its base.

A conical surface is generated by lines called generators that pass through a fixed point (the vertex) and each point of a fixed curve (the directrix). The various curves that are formed by the intersection of conical surfaces and planes are called CONIC SECTIONS.

coneflower Coneflower is a common name given to plants in the genera *Rudbeckia*, *Ratibida*, and *Echinacea*, belonging to the composite family, Compositae.

The perennial purple coneflower (also called Rudbeckia purpurea) has 10-cm-wide (4-in) flowers that open in late summer or early autumn. It grows to a height of 1 m (3 ft).

Coneflower, *Rudbeckia amplexicaulis,* has ligules of the ray flowers, which are 1.3 to 3.2 cm (0.5 to 1.25 in) long and often purplish brown at the base. It is found from Kansas to Texas and southeast to Georgia. Another species is *R. hirta* (BLACK-EYED SUSAN). The prairie coneflower, *Ratibida columnifera,* has a flower head with blunt-toothed, yellow, ray flowers and a conical disk of brown flowers; it blooms throughout the summer.

Conestoga [kahn-eh-stoh'-guh]   The original Conestogas were a type of covered WAGON. The name was taken from the region in which, in the 18th century, they were first built—Conestoga, Pennsylvania. Conestogas were primarily used to carry heavy loads of freight across the prairies of the United States; their large, broad wheels enabled them to pass over the ruts and through the mud of the prairie roads. A large canvas cover was used for protection against bad weather.

A later development of the Conestoga was the prairie schooner, so called because its white top gave it the appearance of a sailing ship; this type was also known simply as the covered wagon. It had lower sides and a flat floor, and it was thus simpler and cheaper to build than the Conestoga. Most prairie schooners had a canvas cover spread over arched hoops; a variant had the sides sloping out toward the top, giving a V-shaped appearance, and a flat canvas roof.

Large numbers of prairie schooners, hauled by mules, oxen, and horses, made up the wagon trains that carried American pioneers to Oregon, Utah, and California in the late 1840s.

Coney Island   Coney Island is a section of Brooklyn, N.Y., on the Atlantic Ocean. It was formerly separated from the mainland by a channel that silting filled in. A popular tourist resort since the mid-19th century, it was reached by subway in 1920. Coney Island is known for its amusement facilities, boardwalk, beaches, and the New York Aquarium.

Confederate States of America   The Confederate States of America was the name adopted by the states that seceded from the United States in 1860–61 to form an independent nation. By 1860 many white Southerners believed that preservation of their way of life required perpetuation of the system of SLAVERY, which, in turn, necessitated adding more slave states to the Union. Finding the Republican party unalterably opposed to the expansion of slavery, Southerners felt threatened by the election of the Republican Abraham Lincoln to the presidency in November 1860. Many concluded that only independence could safeguard their way of life.

By April 1861, the seven states of the Deep South had declared themselves independent and had organized a

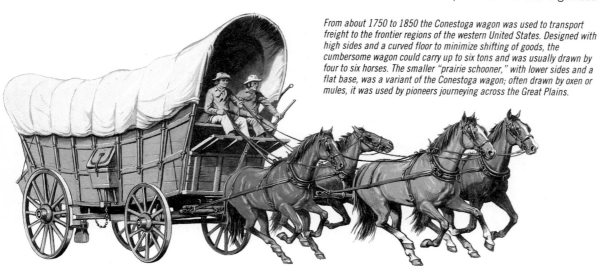

From about 1750 to 1850 the Conestoga wagon was used to transport freight to the frontier regions of the western United States. Designed with high sides and a curved floor to minimize shifting of goods, the cumbersome wagon could carry up to six tons and was usually drawn by four to six horses. The smaller "prairie schooner," with lower sides and a flat base, was a variant of the Conestoga wagon; often drawn by oxen or mules, it was used by pioneers journeying across the Great Plains.

Representatives from the seceding states convened in Montgomery, Ala., in February 1861, to create an administration and constitution for the Confederacy. On Feb. 18, 1861, Jefferson Davis was inaugurated as president at Montgomery's capitol building.

new government. After the U.S. CIVIL WAR began in April 1861, four more states joined the Confederacy.

Although the constitution of the new government specifically protected the system of slavery, in most other ways it resembled closely that of the U.S. government. The Confederate president, however, served a single 6-year term and had the authority to veto individual items in appropriations bills. Jefferson DAVIS was the only Confederate president. Judah P. BENJAMIN, who served successively as attorney general, secretary of war, and secretary of state, was the ablest member of Davis's cabinet. RICHMOND, Va., became the capital of the Confederacy.

Southerners hoped that the U.S. government would acquiesce in their independence, but Northerners proved unwilling to accept the dissolution of the Union. The story of the Confederacy thus became that of the Civil War as the young nation sought to win freedom from a stronger foe.

Most of the problems that beset a nation at war afflicted the Confederacy. Military invasion isolated sections of the country. Most serious was the loss in 1863 of the Mississippi River, which divided the Confederacy almost in half. Battles and marching armies devastated many towns, ruined crops, and wrecked bridges and railroads. Although the South was able to buy ships and supplies abroad, the foreign recognition and aid that it had

hoped for did not materialize. Because the South had so little industry, an increasingly effective Union naval blockade began to cause shortages of nearly everything—transportation equipment, medicine, clothing, coffee, salt. Families fleeing before advancing Northern armies created refugee problems and exacerbated shortages.

The key to the Confederacy's survival was the army; a total of about 750,000 men served during the 4 years of the Confederacy, their courage and devotion often wasted under the poor leadership of their generals. Most were volunteers, although in 1862 a shortage of recruits compelled the government to conscript men. Casualties, disease, and desertion caused a gradual decline in the army's strength, a decline that became more serious as the war continued.

The Confederate government's munitions plants were a respectable success, and its navy was remarkable. Southerners were not seafaring people, yet they built the first submarine to sink an enemy vessel in combat and equipped one of the first successful iron warships. Confederate raiders strongly challenged Union naval might and inflicted heavy damage on Northern maritime commerce.

The Confederacy attempted to meet the cost of the war through bonded indebtedness and taxation. When the public resisted heavy taxes and the government could not sell enough bonds, it began to print money. The resulting inflation intensified as the war went on, increasing the suffering of civilians and undermining the South's will to fight.

Confederate efforts to win independence were also hampered by differences between President Davis and his critics. From early in the war, Davis quarreled with Gener-

By February 1861, when the Confederacy was formed, seven slave states had seceded from the United States. After the attack on Fort Sumter (April 12-13), four more states joined the Confederacy.

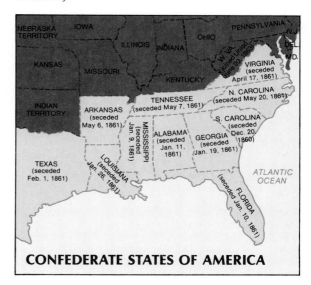

CONFEDERATE STATES OF AMERICA

als Joseph E. JOHNSTON and P. G. T. BEAUREGARD. The president also engaged in squabbles with members of the Congress and some of the state governors. Newspaper criticism of Davis grew harsh.

In the spring of 1865, Robert E. LEE, general in chief of all the Confederate armies, surrendered, and organized resistance to the U.S. government ceased. After a dozen years of RECONSTRUCTION, the last federal troops were withdrawn (1877) from the South. The Confederate States of America passed into American mythology as the "Lost Cause."

Confederation, Articles of   see ARTICLES OF CONFEDERATION

---

confession (law)   A confession, in criminal law, is a statement made by a person charged with the commission of a crime, acknowledging guilt of the offense charged. For the confession to be considered competent evidence of guilt, the person making it usually must disclose mental intent, along with his or her physical acts. Most jurisdictions, however, require that a confession be corroborated by other evidence before a person may be convicted. Under common law and U.S. constitutional law, a confession must be voluntary—that is, freely made and not coerced by duress (threats or violence) or fraud (raising hopes or making promises). In MIRANDA V. ARIZONA (1966), the Supreme Court required that officers must advise a suspect in custody that he or she may remain silent and may consult an attorney.

---

confession (religion)   Confession is the popular name for the Christian SACRAMENT of Penance or Reconciliation recognized by the Roman Catholic and Orthodox churches. The rite consists in the acknowledgment of sins to a priest, who grants absolution in the name of God. Its biblical basis is found in the action of Jesus forgiving sins (Mark 2) and his commissioning of the Apostles to forgive sins (John 20:22–23).

Essential to every confession is an inner conversion of the heart, with sorrow for sin and intent to lead a new life. In the Orthodox Church, confession is usually required before the reception of Communion. Since 1215, Roman Catholics have been required to confess their sins annually if they are in serious SIN. Individual confession directly to God in private is more characteristic of Protestantism.

confessional literature   see AUTOBIOGRAPHY

Confessions, Les   Jean Jacques ROUSSEAU began his famous autobiography, *Les Confessions*, while living in England near his friend, the philosopher David Hume, between 1765 and 1767. He continued it in France after their quarrel. Although published posthumously in 1782 (Part I) and 1789 (Part II), it was read aloud by him in salons. A landmark in literature, *Les Confessions* breaks with the standard 18th-century autobiography, primarily a record of public achievements, and instead probes thoughts, emotions, and hidden motives.

---

confessions of faith   The official Protestant statements of belief issued as standards of doctrine during the 16th and 17th centuries are called confessions of faith. The result of dogmatic controversy, they are generally polemical and reflect the historical situations from which they arose. A list of the major confessions of faith issued by the Lutheran, Calvinist, or Reformed churches includes the AUGSBURG CONFESSION (1530), Helvetic Confessions (1536 and 1566), Gallican Confession (1559), Belgic Confession (1561), Scottish Confessions (1560 and 1581), Heidelberg Catechism (1562), and Westminster Confession (1647). Since the 17th century, other confessions have been issued by the Congregationalists, Baptists, Presbyterians, and Quakers. Some Reformation statements were called articles of religion, for example, the THIRTY-NINE ARTICLES. The ancient professions of faith are usually called CREEDS.

Confessions of St. Augustine, The   see AUGUSTINE, SAINT

---

configuration   In chemistry, the configuration of a compound refers to its three-dimensional form. Many physical and chemical properties of a compound are a result of the arrangement in space of the atoms in its molecules.

Stereoisomers (see STEREOCHEMISTRY), for instance, are compounds that have the same molecular formula but vary in the three-dimensional structure of the atoms within the molecule. The lactic acid that is found in sour milk, for example, has the same physical properties as the lactic acid obtained from living muscle with the exception that the two optically rotate plane-polarized light in opposite directions (see OPTICAL ACTIVITY). The two compounds are not superimposable on each other, just as a right hand is not superimposable on a left hand. Such compounds are known as optical isomers. Geometric ISOMERS also have different configurations of atoms within the molecule but have no optical activity.

configuration, electronic   see ELECTRON CONFIGURATION

---

confirmation   A Christian rite that follows BAPTISM, confirmation is considered the second SACRAMENT of initiation by the Roman Catholic, Eastern Orthodox, and Anglican churches. In the Roman Catholic church it is normally conferred by a bishop by anointing with holy oil (chrism) on the forehead. In the Orthodox church, the rite is called chrismation and is administered by a priest at the time of baptism. Episcopalians describe confirmation as a sacramental rite and consider it a time for mature, public affirmation of baptismal vows, accompanied by the laying on of hands by the bishop.

conflict theory

conflict theory   In the social sciences, *conflict theory* refers to the theoretical approach that views social phenomena as the result of conflict between individuals or groups. Conflict theory has developed at both micro and macro levels. The micro level studies the individual and from his or her behavior seeks to draw inferences about collective behavior. Psychologists, social psychologists, and sociobiologists locate the cause of conflict behavior in human nature—either in the imperatives of survival that have programmed forms of AGGRESSION and defensive response, or in individual aggressive impulses triggered by personality dynamics.

Sociologists, anthropologists, political scientists, and organization and communications theorists adopt the macro approach to conflict. They hold that collective conflict behavior is not the product of individual behavior but behavior socially induced either by a sense of collective grievance or by national leaders for purposes of defending the national territory or defeating another nation. This school defines conflict as a condition in which one identifiable group engages in conscious opposition to another identifiable group, in what the American sociologist Lewis Coser has called "a struggle over values and claims to scarce status, power and resources."

Conflict may, according to some theorists, have a positive social function. It may be the only means by which an exploited group can assert its rights, and it may be an unavoidable characteristic of international politics in that the threat of violence is essential to creating stability and maintaining peace, war being one means by which states adjust their competitive interests.

Because conflict theory investigates the process by which nations develop their national strategies and decide upon war, it has become germane to the study of international politics. Conflict theory must take account of the motivations and perceptions of individual leaders and decision makers—and to the extent that individual citizens are engaged in the conflict by conscious appeals to their beliefs and patriotism, the micro-level approach to conflict theory remains important.

conformity

conformity   Conformity is behavior in accord with the expectations of a social group, expressing acquiescence to the norms of that group (see NORM, SOCIAL). The term, however, is used differently in psychology and sociology.

Psychology.   In social psychology, the term refers to an individual's compliance with a group judgment, perhaps counter to his or her own judgment. Conformity is usually analyzed at an individual or small-group level, in contrast to the more general, societal focus of sociology.

Classical experiments by social psychologists Muzafer and Carolyn Sherif and Solomon Asch treated conformity as an aspect of group dynamics. They found that an individual tends to conform to a unanimous group judgment even when that judgment is obviously in error (Asch); that

the more eager an individual is to become a member of a group, the more that person tends to orient his or her behavior to the norms of the group (Sherif); and that the more ambiguous the situation, the greater the group's influence on the individual (Asch). When the group's judgment reflects personal or aesthetic preference, however, the individual feels little pressure to conform.

There is some evidence to indicate that first-born children show a greater tendency than later-born children to conform to unanimously expressed judgments of the group; that there is a relationship between self-confidence and resistance to group pressures to conform; and that females tend to yield to group pressure more readily than do males.

Sociology.   In sociology, the term *conformity* refers to adherence to societal and cultural norms. Nonconformity, or DEVIANCE, results when norms are not observed. Although deviance within society can become so great that the society dissolves, deviance may, in fact, be conformity to the norms of a particular subculture.

Social scientists often examine conformity in the context of deviance. Deviant behavior varies in some way from the normative rules of a social system. The functioning of society, however, is a mixture of conformity and deviance. A social system is a complex network of social relations that acts to draw the behavior of its members toward the core values of the group. Because the range of behavior is so wide, social groups try to regulate behavior, or establish boundaries. These boundaries are maintained by the interaction between behavior that deviates from the norm and agents that work to control behavior. A norm remains valid only if it is used regularly as a basis of judgment. Deviance (in limited quantities) and conformity help to preserve social stability.

Confucianism

Confucianism [kuhn-fue'-shuhn-izm]   Confucianism, the philosophical system founded on the teaching of Confucius (551–479 BC), dominated Chinese sociopolitical life for most of Chinese history and largely influenced the cultures of Korea, Japan, and Indochina. The Confucian school functioned as a recruiting ground for government positions, which were filled by those scoring highest on examinations in the Confucian classics. It also blend-

The symbolic representation of the yin-yang theme pervades Chinese cosmology. The circle incorporates the duality of the feminine (Yin) and the masculine (Yang) elements, which maintain a balance in their union of opposites from which all things originate.

The Chinese philosopher Confucius formulated an ethical system that has influenced Chinese culture for some 2,000 years. The Analects, *a collection of his sayings, emphasizes the development of a collective moral unity that would create a peaceful way of life.*

ed with popular and imported religions and became the vehicle for articulating Chinese mores to the peasants. The school's doctrines supported political authority using the theory of the mandate of heaven. It sought to help the rulers maintain domestic order, preserve tradition, and maintain a constant standard of living for the taxpaying peasants. It trained its adherents in benevolence, traditional rituals, filial piety, loyalty, respect for superiors and for the aged, and principled flexibility in advising rulers.

Confucius. Westerners use *Confucius* as the spelling for Kong Fuzi—Master Kong—China's first and most famous philosopher. Confucius had a traditional personal name (Qiu) and a formal name (Zhongni). Confucius's father died shortly after Confucius's birth. His family fell into relative poverty, and Confucius joined a growing class of impoverished descendants of aristocrats who made their careers by acquiring knowledge of feudal ritual and taking positions of influence serving the rulers of the fragmented states of ancient China. Confucius devoted himself to learning. At age 30, however, when his short-lived official career floundered, he turned to teaching others. Confucius himself never wrote down his own philosophy, although tradition credits him with editing some of the historical classics that were used as texts in his school. He apparently made an enormous impact on the lives and attitudes of his disciples, however. The book known as the *Analects,* which records all the "Confucius said. . . ." aphorisms, was compiled by his students after his death. Because the *Analects* was not written as a systematic philosophy, it contains frequent contradictions and many of the philosophical doctrines are ambiguous. The *Analects* became the basis of the Chinese social lifestyle and the fundamental religious and philosophical point of view of most traditionalist Chinese intellectuals throughout history. The collection reveals Confucius as a person dedicated to the preservation of traditional ritual practices with a spiritual delight in performing them.

Doctrine. Confucianism combines a political theory and a theory of human nature to yield a *dao*—a prescriptive doctrine or way. The political theory starts with a doctrine of political authority based on the mandate of heaven. The legitimate ruler derives authority from heaven's command. The ruler bears responsibility for the well-being of the people and therefore for peace and order in the empire.

Confucian philosophy presupposes a view of human nature in which humans are essentially social animals whose mode of social interaction is shaped by *li* (convention or ritual), which establishes value distinctions and prescribes activities in response to those distinctions. Education in *li*, or social rituals, is based on the natural behavioral propensity to imitate models. Sages, or superior people—those who have mastered the *li*—are the models of behavior from which the mass of people learn. Ideally, the ruler should himself be such a model and should appoint only those who are models of *de* (virtue) to positions of prominence. People are naturally inclined to emulate virtuous models; hence a hierarchy of merit results in widespread natural moral education.

Then, with practice, all people can in principle be like the sages, by acting in accordance with *li* without conscious effort. At that point they have acquired *ren* (humanity), the highest level of moral development; their natural inclinations are all in harmony with *dao* (way). The world is at peace, order abounds, and the harmony between the natural and the social sphere results in material well-being for everyone. This is Confucius's utopian vision, which he regards as modeled on the practice of the ancient sage kings.

Historical Development. Confucianism emerged as a more coherent philosophy when faced with intellectual competition from other schools that were growing in the fertile social upheavals of preimperial China (c.400–c.200 BC). DAOISM, Mohism, and Legalism all attacked Confucianism. A common theme of these attacks was that Confucianism assumed that tradition or convention (*li*) was correct. MENCIUS (c.372–c.289 BC) developed a more idealistic version of Confucianism stressing *ren* as an innate inclination to good behavior that does not require education. Xun Zi (c.313–c.238 BC), on the contrary, argued that all inclinations are shaped by acquired language and other social forms.

Confucianism rose to the position of an official orthodoxy during the HAN dynasty (206 BC–AD 220). It absorbed the metaphysical doctrines of Yin (the female principle) and Yang (the male principle) found in the I CHING (Book of Changes) and other speculative metaphysical notions. With the fall of the Han, the dynastic model, Confucianism fell into severe decline. Except for the residual effects of its official status, Confucianism lay philosophically dormant for approximately 600 years.

With the reestablishment of Chinese dynastic power in the TANG dynasty (618–906) and the introduction of the Chan (Zen Buddhist) premise that "there is nothing much to Buddhist teaching," Confucianism began to revive. The SONG dynasty (960–1279) produced Neo-Confucianism—an interpretation of classical Confucian doctrine (principally that of Mencius) that addressed Buddhist and Daoist issues. Its development was due mainly to Zhengho (1032–85) and Zhengyi (1033–1107), but for the orthodox statement of Neo-Confucianism, one turns to ZHU XI (1130–1200). His commentaries on the four scriptures of Confucianism were required study for the imperial civil service examinations.

Neo-Confucianism focuses on the term *li*, which here means "lane" or "pattern." Correct behavior is held to follow a natural pattern (*li*) that is apprehended by *Xin* (heart-mind). Mencius's theory of the innate goodness of man is a theory of the innate ability of this heart-mind to apprehend *li* in situations and to follow it. To become a sage, one must study *li* and develop the ability to "see" it by a kind of intuition. Later, in the MING dynasty (1368–1644), WANG YANGMING claimed that the heart projects *li* on things rather than just noticing external *li*. To become a sage, one cannot just study situations, one must act before *li* becomes manifest. Thus the heart-mind, which guides the action, is the source of *li* (moral patterns).

After the disastrous conflicts with Western military technology at the dawn of the 20th century, Chinese intellectuals blamed Confucianism for the scientific and political backwardness of China. Chinese Marxism, nonetheless, differs from Western Marxism in ways that reveal the persistence of Confucian attitudes toward politics, metaphysics, and theories of human psychology. Anti-Confucianism has been a theme in various political campaigns in modern China—most notably during and just after the CULTURAL REVOLUTION. Increased toleration for all religions since Mao Zedong's death may lead to a moderate revival of Confucianism, although the interest seems to be mostly in historical issues.

In Taiwan, by contrast, Confucian orthodoxy has survived and serves to underpin an anti-Marxist, traditional authoritarianism. Serious, ongoing Confucian philosophy, however, is found mainly in Hong Kong and among Chinese scholars working in the West.

––

conglomerate (business)   A conglomerate is a large corporation that, by a process known as MERGER, acquires subsidiaries in widely divergent fields. The merger process involves either acquiring a controlling share of a company's stock or buying the company outright. Large businesses began to diversify when antitrust laws prevented their growth within a single field. Since the 1960s in the United States, however, the merger and what is called a "hostile takeover" (the acquiring of a company that wishes to remain independent but cannot prevent the sale of its stock to a corporate buyer) have become standard methods of corporate enlargement. Rather than invest in the building of a new company—with the necessary and often risky expense of erecting a factory, buying machinery, penetrating a new market, and so on—a CORPORATION may find it cheaper to purchase an existing business, especially when it can do so by acquiring stock whose total cost is often far below the actual value of the company. There is concern that such mergers may be fundamentally negative in their effect on the economy,

for they usually represent merely a shifting of, rather than an addition to, industrial assets.

––

conglomerate (geology)   Conglomerates, as well as sedimentary breccias, are coarse-grained SEDIMENTARY ROCKS formed by the consolidation and hardening of rounded or angular GRAVEL deposited on the CONTINENTAL SHELF (see SEDIMENT, MARINE). More than 30 percent of the large particles of these rocks are themselves rock fragments exceeding 2 mm (0.08 in) in diameter. Such fragments may be pebbles, COBBLES, or boulders, or mixtures of these sizes. Both conglomerates and sedimentary breccias may be named and classified by the proportion of gravel-sized particles, the type of matrix, and the types of gravel-sized particles.

Conglomerates, such as this colorful polymictic specimen, are composed of broken fragments of rock that have been carried from their point of origin, rounded into pebbles by water, and set in materials such as silt, sand, or clay.

––

Congo   The Congo, also called the Congo-Brazzaville—to distinguish it from Congo-Léopoldville, now Zaire—is an independent state on the equator in western Africa. It is bounded by the Central African Republic and Cameroon to the north, Zaire to the east, the Atlantic Ocean and Cabinda to the southwest, and Gabon to the west. The Congo was a French colony until 1960, when independence was granted.

Land and Resources

The Congo is composed of five topographic regions: a narrow plain along the Atlantic coast; the adjoining Mayombé Highlands with their rocky hills and valleys; the 320-km-wide (200-mi) Niari River valley in the southwest; an area of plateaus and river valleys formed by the northern tributaries of the Congo River; and a floodplain formed by the western section of the Congo River basin in the northeast.

The climate is tropical; the year is evenly divided into a rainy season (November–April) and a dry season (May–October). Average annual temperatures range between

AT A GLANCE

PEOPLE'S REPUBLIC OF THE CONGO

Land: Area: 342,000 km² (132,047 mi²). Capital and largest city: Brazzaville (1985 est. pop., 596,200).

People: Population (1990 est.): 2,242,274. Density: 6.6 persons per km² (17.0 per mi²). Distribution (1985): 39.5% urban, 60.5% rural. Official language: French. Major religions: traditional religions, Roman Catholicism, Protestantism.

Government: Type: republic. Legislature: People's National Assembly. Political subdivisions: 9 regions.

Economy: GDP (1988 est.): $2.2 billion; $1,000 per capita. Labor distribution (1985): agriculture—75%; commerce, industry, and government—25%. Foreign trade (1987): imports—$494.4 million; exports—$912 million. Currency: 1 C.F.A. franc = 100 centimes.

Education and Health: Literacy (1985): 62.9% of adult population. Universities (1990): 1. Hospital beds (1988): 3,787. Physicians (1988) 500. Life expectancy (1990): women—55; men—52. Infant mortality (1990): 110 per 1,000 live births.

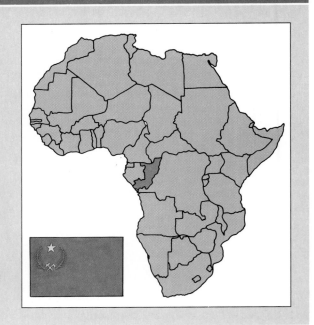

20° and 27° C (68° and 81° F). Rainfall is abundant—a minimum of 1,220 mm (48 in) annually. Vegetation includes great stretches of tropical rain forest, coastal and swampy areas of mangrove trees and water grasses, and savanna grasslands. Coconut palms and plantain trees are also common.

People

The people of the Congo belong to five major ethnic groups. The Kongo peoples constituted 48% of the population in the mid-1980s, the Téké constituted 17%, and the Sanga 20%. Small minorities of Binga Pygmies and Europeans, mostly French who live in the cities, are also

Brazzaville, which lies directly across the Congo River from the Zairian capital of Kinshasa, is the capital and largest city of the Congo. The city was named for its founder, the French explorer Pierre Savorgnan de Brazza.

found there. All these groups have their own language, but French is the official national language, and Lingala and Kituba, two patois dialects intelligible to most tribes, are used widely as trade languages.

About half of the Congo's people still adhere to animistic religions; the rest are Christians. Many traditional arts—sculpture, dancing, and oral literature—survive, but the colonial experience produced new cultural forms. A popular school of painting uses European techniques to express traditional African themes; musical groups playing electric guitars and a fledgling recording industry have created a Brazzaville sound known throughout Equatorial Africa.

Compared to its neighbors, the Congo is an urbanized country, with nearly half of the population living in the four major cities: BRAZZAVILLE, the capital; Pointe-Noire; Kayes; and Loubomo. The southern third of the country contains 70% of the population, and this concentration has facilitated the development of education and medical services.

More than 90% of the children attend free, compulsory primary schools run by the state. Regional health centers augment large hospitals in Brazzaville and Pointe-Noire.

Economic Activity

Agriculture has traditionally employed the bulk of the Congolese labor force, although only 2% of the land is cultivated. Most farmers grow cassava (manioc), plantains, and other food crops on small plots for local consumption; cash crops (sugarcane, oil palms, coffee, and cacao) are cultivated on large holdings, many of which are state owned. About 60% of the Congo is forested. Timber was the leading export until the early 1970s, when it was surpassed by petroleum. Since 1980 petroleum has provided more than 90% of all export earnings. Oil revenues have been used to finance development projects and to purchase raw materials and machinery for the nation's factories and foodstuffs and consumer goods for the growing urban population. After 1983, however, low world oil prices and a large foreign debt forced austerity measures. The Congo is one of the most industrialized nations in sub-Saharan Africa. Manufactures include timber and agricultural products, textiles, chemicals, and paper.

Although the climate and terrain make it difficult to build and maintain roads, the Congo's waterways and railroads are vital to Central Africa's transportation network. Waterways link the country with the Central African Republic, Zaire, and Chad; railroads join Brazzaville to Pointe-Noire and Gabon.

History and Government

The southern region of the Congo formed part of the kingdom of KONGO, a state that flourished during the 16th century. Its king received the first Portuguese expeditions and subsequently signed a cultural exchange treaty and welcomed missionaries. Slave trading by the Portuguese destroyed the state. In the late 19th century a French party led by Pierre Savorgnan de Brazza (for whom the capital is named) penetrated the area. In 1883 part of

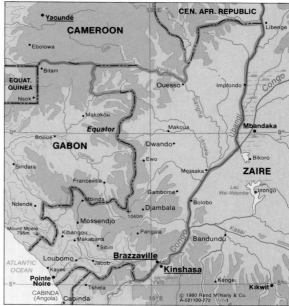

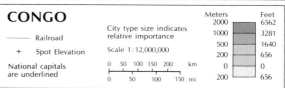

the Congo became a French protectorate, and in 1910 the Congo joined French Equatorial Africa (FEA), which, with its capital at Brazzaville, also included Chad, the Central African Republic, and Gabon.

In 1960 the Congo won independence, and the FEA was dismantled. The nation has not yet adjusted to the loss of this hinterland. A labor uprising overturned the government in 1963, and in 1968 a military coup was staged. The Congo, declared a Communist state in 1969, moved to the left ideologically while maintaining economic ties with France and other Western European nations.

In 1979 a new constitution was approved, and the National People's Congress, the main legislative body, was reestablished. In the 1980s the government moved away from its former close relationship with the USSR and improved its ties with France, China, and the United States. The Congolese Workers' party was once the sole legal political party and elected the president. After a wave of labor union unrest, constitutional revisions effective in January 1991 legalized a multiparty system and a transitional government headed by a prime minister was installed.

Congo crisis see ZAIRE

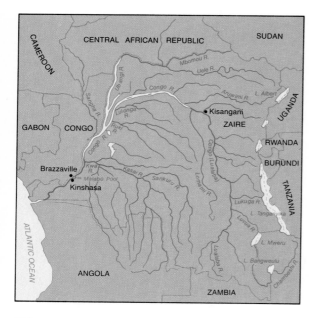

Congo River   The Congo (or Zaire) River flows 4,670 km (2,900 mi), from headwaters in Zambia, northwest through Zaire and then southwest to the Atlantic. It is the second longest river in Africa. Although most of its course is through Zaire, the river and its tributaries drain parts of the Central African Republic, Cameroon, the Congo, Angola, and northern Zambia—a basin of 3,458,000 km^2 (1,335,000 mi^2). Called the Zaire by Europeans during the 15th century, a corruption of a word meaning "river" in Bantu languages of the region, it was referred to by later visitors as the Congo, after the great precolonial

Dugout canoes are still used as vehicles of transportation along the Congo (Zaire) River in west-central Africa. This stretch of the Congo forms the boundary between Zaire and the Congo.

kingdom (Kongo) located near its mouth.

The river system may be divided into three sections: The Upper Congo consists of the southeast headwaters, notably the Lualaba, along with the Luvua and Lukuga west of Lake Tanganyika. These streams widen in several places to form lakes such as Bangweulu and Mweru; at other points, the watercourse narrows and drops, creating rapids and waterfalls that hinder navigation. The Middle Congo begins at Kisangani and flows more than 1,600 km (1,000 mi) to the Chenal, a narrow channel located 35 km (22 mi) northeast of Kinshasa. This stretch of the river is navigable, and its flow is increased by waters from the UBANGI, Sangha, and Kwa tributaries. The Lower Congo begins at the Chenal, where the river separates into two branches to form a large, swampy lake called Malebo Pool (formerly Stanley Pool). Immediately downstream, the Congo narrows and is punctuated by rapids and waterfalls. The river's elevation drops 275 m (900 ft) in about 320 km (200 mi), making long-distance navigation impossible between the pool and the Atlantic. There is a major hydroelectric complex at Inga, near the coast. In central Zaire, the river system drains dense tropical forest. The northern and southern parts of the basin are characterized by open grasslands and scattered trees. Wildlife is abundant, and the stream harbors more than 200 species of fish.

Most of the peoples living along the Congo and its tributaries are fishermen who supplement their diet either by cultivating root crops or by exchanging some of their catch for foodstuffs produced by neighbors. The Congo is also an important avenue of trade. In the late 19th century, explorers such as Henry Morton STANLEY penetrated the interior by following the river trade routes.

Congregationalism [kahn-gruh-gay'-shuhnul-izm] Congregationalism, a form of Protestant church organization based on the autonomy of each congregation, emerged as part of the liberal wing of PURITANISM in the English REFORMATION. By 1600, many clergymen were calling for reform in the Church of England, arguing that the key to adequate change was to grant local congregations autonomy. These congregationalists opposed Presbyterians, who wished to manage churches by means of district assemblies, and Anglicans, who wanted bishops for the same purpose.

Those who agreed on the democratic principle of congregational self-government, however, differed among themselves about what to do. Some were called Separatists because they refused to associate with the national church; a notable example was the PILGRIM group, which established (1620) the PLYMOUTH COLONY in North America. Although others, the non-Separatists, did not openly break with the Church of England, increasing persecution led many to emigrate to New England under the auspices of the MASSACHUSETTS BAY COMPANY. The Separatists who remained in England, where they were called Independents, achieved substantial political influence in the period following the ENGLISH CIVIL WAR (the Commonwealth and Protectorate). The Restoration in 1660 brought renewed repression, but the Toleration Act of 1689 allowed freedom of worship.

In New England, Congregationalist churches worked so closely with civil governments in every colony except Rhode Island that no other type of church was allowed in the area until 1690, when English authorities forced them to tolerate other religious groups. State government support for Congregationalist churches did not end until 1818 in Connecticut and not until 1834 in Massachusetts.

In 1790, Congregationalists formed the largest, strongest church in America. In 1957 the U.S. Congregationalists merged with the Evangelical and Reformed Church to form the UNITED CHURCH OF CHRIST.

Congress, Library of   see LIBRARY OF CONGRESS

Congress of Racial Equality   The Congress of Racial Equality (CORE) was founded in Chicago in 1942 to combat discrimination against black people by means of interracial, nonviolent, direct action. The organization expanded rapidly under the leadership of James Farmer in the mid-1950s. In the early 1960s, CORE organized the Freedom Rides, in which mixed racial groups rode buses throughout the South in an eventually successful effort to force desegregation of interstate buses and their terminals and restaurants. In the mid-1960s, Floyd B. McKissick led CORE in endorsing black nationalism. Since 1968, Roy Innis has headed CORE.

Congress of the United States   The Congress of the United States, the nation's lawmaking body, is made up of two houses, the HOUSE OF REPRESENTATIVES and the SENATE. The main power of Congress, as set forth in the CONSTITUTION OF THE UNITED STATES, is to make laws that, when signed by the PRESIDENT, become the law of the land, governing American life. Congress also has the responsibility to determine that public policies are being administered by the government in accordance with the law and as efficiently and effectively as possible. Moreover, because Congress is intended to represent the nation's citizens, its members are expected to provide assistance and services to their constituents—the people back home in their states and districts. Congress sometimes is required to perform specialized judicial and electoral functions. It acts as a judicial body in the process of impeachment and removal of the president, and it has the power to choose the president and vice-president should no candidate gain a majority of electoral votes following a presidential election.

Membership

The Constitution restricts the membership of Congress by requiring House members to be 25 years of age and senators 30. House members must have been U.S. citizens for at least 7 years, and senators for 9. Although members of the House are required only to be inhabitants of

The United States Congress, shown here in a joint session of the House of Representatives and the Senate, receives an address by President Ronald Reagan.

their states, and not necessarily residents of the districts from which they are elected, in fact local residency has become an unwritten, or customary, requirement for success at the polls.

Congressional Elections

Each state gets one House member regardless of its population. Beyond that, the states are given representation in the House of Representatives on the basis of their population. The House is reapportioned every 10 years, after the federal census. Within states, congressional district boundary lines are drawn by the state legislatures. All House members are elected in single-member districts, the total number of which has been set by Congress at 435. Today, each House member has about half a million constituents. House members are elected every 2 years. The Constitution awards each state two senators. Senators are elected to 6-year terms, and one-third of the seats come up for election every 2 years.

Congressional Organization

Congress is organized in three notable ways: its party organization and leadership; its committee structure; and its staff.

The United States Senate meets in the north wing of the Capitol building. The vice-president traditionally presides over the Senate, although the vice-president's senatorial power is limited to breaking a tie vote. Unlike representatives, senators have assigned seats and sit by seniority from front to rear. The gallery on the right is reserved for the press, and the other three may be used by visitors.

Party Leadership. Both houses of Congress are organized into majority and minority political parties, each with its own leadership, but the House and the Senate are organized differently. In the House, the leader of the majority party serves as the Speaker, who is the presiding officer of the House. Because the Speaker controls debate in the House, has an important role in the selection of committee members and chairpersons, and can influence the scheduling and dispensation of legislation, the Speaker possesses substantial power. The majority party organization is provided by the majority leader and his or her assistants (called whips), along with specialized party committees. They are chosen by the majority party caucus, made up of all the party members in the House. Similarly, the minority party chooses a minority leader, party whips, and members of its own party committees.

In the Senate, the presiding officer is not an important leader and does not exercise influence over proceedings under most circumstances. Although the VICE-PRESIDENT OF THE UNITED STATES may preside over the Senate, that person is not, in practice, required to do so. Usually, senators take turns presiding over the body in a nominal and routine way. The leadership of the Senate is provided by the majority leader, who is selected by the majority party caucus. In turn, the minority party chooses its minority leader. Although the majority leader manages the business of the Senate, he or she does so in consultation with the leader of the minority party.

Committees and Subcommittees. The most important organizational feature of the House and Senate is the structure of their committees, which provide the locus of most congressional work. Congressional committees generally correspond to the major departments of the executive branch. Thus both the House and the Senate have created committees concerned with agriculture, defense,

housing, commerce, science and technology, education, government operations, international relations, judiciary affairs, and service veterans. The work of each committee is further subdivided so that it can be considered by subcommittees. Almost all the important legislative work of the Congress is done in its subcommittees.

The most powerful committees of Congress are those concerned specifically with government finance. Both houses have budget committees whose job it is to set expenditure targets for each fiscal year and to establish the authorized level of the national debt. In addition, both houses have appropriations committees that consider the budget requests of executive agencies in detail and recommend budget legislation to their respective houses for approval. Moreover, both houses have committees on taxation—the House Ways and Means Committee and the Senate Finance Committee. These two committees are concerned with government revenues and recommend the tax bills to their own houses. Because the power of the purse is the most formidable of congressional powers, these committees exercise great influence; hence membership on them is much sought after.

Membership on House and Senate committees is ultimately determined by party caucuses in the two houses. The partisan composition of committees are roughly equivalent to the party makeup of the houses themselves. The Senate has 16 permanent, standing committees, and the House has 22, with about 260 subcommittees.

Staff. About 7,500 staff employees work for House members and about 3,600 for senators. House and Senate committees together employ more than 3,000 in staff. Congress receives research and information services from major agencies. The Congressional Research Service, an arm of the LIBRARY OF CONGRESS, provides wide-ranging research services for members and committees.

The GENERAL ACCOUNTING OFFICE supplies reviews of the economy, efficiency, and effectiveness of government programs. The Office of Technology Assessment provides policy analysis in science and technology. Finally, the Congressional Budget Office, working with the House and Senate budget committees, furnishes fiscal and economic research for Congress. Altogether, more than 23,000 staff employees work for the Congress.

The Legislative Process in Congress

The legislative work of Congress begins when a bill is introduced by a member. A bill is merely a document drawn up to specify the details of a proposal of law. Public bills concern general questions of policy and become public laws if they are passed by Congress and signed by the president. Private bills are concerned with such individual matters as claims against the government or cases having to do with immigration and naturalization.

House members introduce bills simply by dropping them in the hopper at the clerk's desk in the House chamber. Senators introduce bills by making a statement offering a bill for introduction and sending it to the desk of the secretary of the Senate. Once introduced, bills are referred to committees and, in turn, to subcommittees. After subcommittees complete their review of bills, they are returned to the full committees for recommendation as to their passage by the full house. When a committee sends a bill to the full house membership for consideration, it sends along a report, or written explanation of its action.

After a bill is reported from the committee that has considered it, it is placed on a calendar, the agenda for floor consideration of bills. Most House bills are funneled to the floor for debate and voting by special rules worked out by the House Rules Committee. In the Senate, bills are normally taken up on the floor by requests for unanimous consent to do so. Debate on bills in the House is regulated by a number of rules that place limitations on the number and duration of members' speeches. In contrast, the Senate normally practices unlimited debate on bills, although a procedure called CLOTURE exists for putting an end to prolonged speechmaking, or filibustering (see FILIBUSTER). During floor debate, amendments may be offered that change or add to the bill.

After debate on a bill is concluded, and voting has taken place on all amendments offered, the bill is up for final passage. In the House, voting on amendments and final passage may occur by a voice vote, although a roll-call vote is the normal procedure on major bills. House members vote during roll calls by using the electronic voting system in the House chamber. Forty-four voting stations are located throughout the chamber. Members cast their votes by inserting special identification cards in a slot on the voting device and pushing the yea or nay buttons. With this system, the 435 members of the House can cast all their votes in a short time. The Senate has no similar system; senators respond to roll calls by answering yea or nay when the clerk calls their names in alphabetical order.

Bills passed by a majority vote of the members of the House and Senate are sent to the president for approval. If the president vetoes a bill, the disapproval may be overridden by a two-thirds vote of both houses. If the House and the Senate pass bills in different forms, a joint conference committee consisting of representatives and senators is appointed to work out the differences. Agreements of a conference committee must, in turn, be approved by both houses.

The House of Representatives is at present composed of 435 members elected for two-year terms. The leaders of the minority party sit to the left of the Speaker of the House, and the leaders of the majority party to the right. Joint sessions of Congress are held in this chamber.

Congress and the Executive

The legislative and executive branches of government are separate and independent, but Congress and the executive do not work in isolation from each other. Only members of Congress may introduce legislation, but the president provides leadership to Congress by recommending a legislative program. He thus influences both Congress's agenda and the substantive content of its day-to-day policy decisions.

Congress, however, is not simply a rubber stamp for presidential policy initiatives; it scrutinizes presidential proposals and often changes them substantially. Moreover, Congress itself initiates legislation—much of the important legislation dealing with urban problems, civil rights, social security, and welfare programs enacted in recent decades originated in Congress.

The most important leverage the Congress has over the executive stems from its fiscal powers. Executive agencies may not spend money unless the expenditure has been authorized and appropriated by Congress. Congress greatly strengthened its budgetary powers by the Budget and Impoundment Control Act of 1974, which provided for a congressional budget, created new committees to consider overall budget outlays, and established the Congressional Budget Office. The new law also limited the president's power to rescind or delay (impound) the spending of money appropriated by Congress.

Initiatives in foreign policy usually are taken by the president, but Congress is also involved in the making of foreign policy through its power to tax and spend, to finance foreign policies, to declare war, and to ratify treaties (which require the approval of two-thirds of the Senate). Congress placed unusual limitations on the presidential conduct of foreign relations in 1973 when it passed the War Powers Act, restricting the president's authority to commit U.S. troops abroad.

In various other ways, Congress influences the work of the executive branch. Senate confirmation is required for presidential nominations of cabinet officials, ambassadors, federal judges, and certain other officials. Congressional committees investigate executive agencies and officials and regularly review the administrative implementation of congressionally enacted programs. Ultimately, Congress has the power to remove the president from office through IMPEACHMENT, a process in which the House investigates alleged presidential wrongdoing and votes on the charges, and the Senate tries the president on these charges.

From time to time Congress sets up special committees to investigate subjects that do not fall directly in the jurisdiction of its standing committees. Special committees have been created to investigate criminal charges against members, to study social and economic problems, to probe into unethical political activities, and to publicize controversial issues. Famous special committees were the House Committee on Un-American Activities, set up in 1938 to investigate fascist, Communist, and other extremist political organizations, the Senate Select Committee on Presidential Campaign Activities (commonly known as the Watergate committee), set up in 1973, and the House and Senate select committees investigating the Iran-contra affair in 1987.

In the 1970s Congress accelerated its use of the legislative veto, a device originated in the 1930s by which provisions were written into a law requiring the executive to seek congressional approval before taking actions authorized under that law. In 1983 the U.S. Supreme Court ruled that the legislative veto was an unconstitutional intrusion by the legislature into the executive sphere (see Immigration and Naturalization Service v. Chadha).

Congress and the Public

Members of Congress live and work under great pressure. House members, whose terms are only 2 years, must start planning for their next campaign as soon as they are elected to the first one. Members commonly travel weekly to their districts, maintain staff and offices there, send newsletters to their constituents, and campaign vigorously for reelection even when their districts are considered "safe" seats. They make extensive use of free postal services and the printed reports of the Congressional Record to show their constituents that they are active in their behalf.

Members are constantly being canvassed by representatives of the numerous special-interest groups among the electorate, who solicit their votes for or against proposed legislation. These lobbyists are influential because their organizations can mobilize voters and contributors at election time.

Congressional Medal of Honor   see MEDALS AND DECORATIONS

Congressional Record

Since its inaugural issue on Mar. 4, 1873, the *Congressional Record* has recorded the daily proceedings of the Senate and the House of Representatives of the United States. The *Record* is not a transcript, however; before publication, members of Congress may edit their remarks made on the floor and insert material that has not figured in sessions. *The Daily Digest,* a supplement at the back of each issue, summarizes the day's activities in both houses, as well as the work of the committees and subcommittees. The *Record* is available to the public on the day following the proceedings it covers.

Congreve, William [kahn'-greev]

The English dramatist William Congreve, b. Jan. 24, 1670, d. Jan. 19, 1729, was one of the most polished comic stylists of Restoration drama. Educated in Ireland at Kilkenny School and Trinity College, Dublin, Congreve returned to England in 1688, ostensibly to study law. He first published a novel, *Incognita* (1692). His first play, *The Old Bachelor* (1693), was highly successful. It was followed the same year by *The Double Dealer,* a darker comedy of

William Congreve was one of England's most notable playwrights of the late 17th century. Although he wrote several dramatic works, he is better known for sophisticated comedy. When a production of his major work, The Way of the World, *was unenthusiastically received in 1700, Congreve abandoned the theater for a government position.*

intrigue; *Love for Love* (1695), his most popular comedy; and *The Mourning Bride* (1697), his only tragedy. The lukewarm reception of Congreve's last and greatest play, *The Way of the World* (1700), may have prompted his retirement from the stage.

Congreve's plays, which were written at the close of the era of Restoration comedy, represent as much a revival as a continuation of Restoration traditions. His greatest achievement was the perfection of a sophisticated comic style, in which character and witty dialogue are emphasized, and which is consistent with a larger, humane sensibility—as the verbal battles of Millamant and Mirabell in *The Way of the World* brilliantly demonstrate. Yet the plays have darker and more cynical undercurrents. In his last two comedies Congreve attempted to balance the tolerant norms of social comedy with a satiric condemnation of man's failings.

conic sections [kahn'-ik]   A conic section (or simply, a conic) is a curve formed by the intersection of a plane with a right circular CONE, or conical surface. When

Conic sections are generated when a cone is cut by a plane at various angles. A horizontal cutting plane generates a circle. When the plane is tilted, the circle first becomes an ellipse; when the intersecting plane is parallel to the conic surface, a parabola is obtained. A plane that is tilted even further toward the vertical forms a hyperbola.

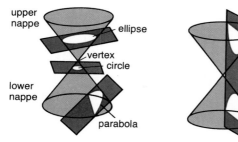

the intersecting plane is perpendicular to the axis of the conical surface, the conic formed is a CIRCLE. When the plane is parallel to an element of the cone (or generator of the surface), the conic is a PARABOLA. Planes that are oblique (neither parallel nor perpendicular) to the axis and not parallel to an element describe two types of curves: an ELLIPSE (if the plane intersects only one nappe, or sheet, of the cone) or a HYPERBOLA (if both nappes are intersected).

The type of conic section may also be determined in another way. A conic section is generated by a point that moves so that the ratio of its distance from a fixed point (called a focus) to its distance from a fixed line (called a directrix) is constant. This ratio is called the ECCENTRICITY (e) of the curve. For $e = 1$, the conic is a parabola; for $e < 1$, it is an ellipse (the circle is a special case); and for $e > 1$, it is a hyperbola.

conifer [kahn'-ih-fur]   Conifers are the largest group of GYMNOSPERMS (nonflowering seed plants), including such familiar examples as PINES, SPRUCES, and FIRS. Most members of this group bear separate POLLEN CONES (male) and SEED CONES (female), usually on the same tree, and have simple evergreen leaves that are needlelike or scalelike. Along with the gnetums, they are considered more advanced than the other two living gymnosperm groups, CYCADS and GINKGOS, because nonmotile rather than swimming sperm are involved in their fertilization.

The map shows the nearly worldwide distribution of conifers, as represented by four genera. The Scotch pine (bottom left) bears separate seed (female) cones and clusters of pollen (male) cones on the same tree (top left). The seed cone grows large after fertilization. The male and female cones of the monkey-puzzle tree (bottom right) grow on separate trees.

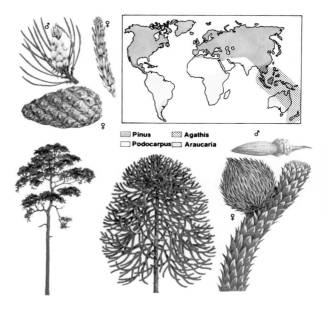

Conifers usually have needle-shaped leaves, which efficiently reduce water loss because of their low surface-area-to-volume ratio. The seeds grow in cones (flowers) that are unisexual. The tree may be mono- or dioecious (of one or both sexes). The large, distinctive woody cones are the female inflorescences. Male flowers are also in cones (strobili) but are normally insignificant. Most conifers are evergreens, although species of Larix *are deciduous, shedding their leaves seasonally.*

Distribution. Conifers are distributed from the Arctic to the Antarctic circles, with a number of representatives in the tropics. Even though many genera and species have become extinct, conifers are still the dominant forest trees of the world in terms of numbers of individuals. Authorities disagree as to the exact number of kinds, but conifers probably constitute close to 500 native species in approximately 45 genera. The largest genera are *Pinus* (about 100 species, according to some classification systems), *Podocarpus* (about 75 species), and *Juniperus* (about 65 species). In contrast, some other genera are represented by only one species.

Traditionally, the conifers have been divided into several families. Some families, especially Araucariaceae and Podocarpaceae, are confined mostly to the Southern Hemisphere, whereas Pinaceae and Taxaceae are distributed primarily in the Northern Hemisphere. Certain species have a limited geographical distribution. Coastal redwood, *Sequoia sempervirens,* follows the fog belt along the California coast north of San Francisco to southern Oregon; giant redwood, *Sequoiadendron giganteum,* is restricted mainly to the Sierra Nevada from central California to southern Oregon; and dawn redwood, *Metasequoia glyptostroboides,* discovered in the early 1940s as a "living fossil," is found only in a limited area of central China, in the province of Sichuan.

Coniferous forests extend as a broad band across North America and Eurasia south of the Arctic tundra at sea level and below alpine tundra in the high mountains. The dominant life forms there are mostly needle-leaf evergreen trees, mainly spruces, firs, and pines. In the United States, at higher elevations in the northern Appalachians, southern Appalachians, and Rockies, the two dominant genera of conifers are *Picea* (spruce) and *Abies* (fir). In fact, different species of each genus occur in each of the three mountain ranges.

In the Rockies, ponderosa pine, *Pinus ponderosa*, and Douglas fir, *Pseudotsuga menziesii,* are usually the dominants at intermediate elevations, with lodgepole pine, *Pinus contorta,* coming in after lumbering and fire. In the foothills, the most conspicuous conifers are piñon, *P. edulis,* and western juniper, *Juniperus scopulorum.* Many conifers are important in the Sierra Nevada. At higher elevations, red fir, *Abies magnifica,* is dominant, whereas various species of pines and other conifers are common at lower altitudes. At middle elevations in northern California, giant redwood is a conspicuous element of the vegetation. The Pacific conifer forest extends from central California to Alaska, along the coast. The coastal redwood was common from San Francisco to southern Oregon, but it has been considerably reduced in numbers due to lum-

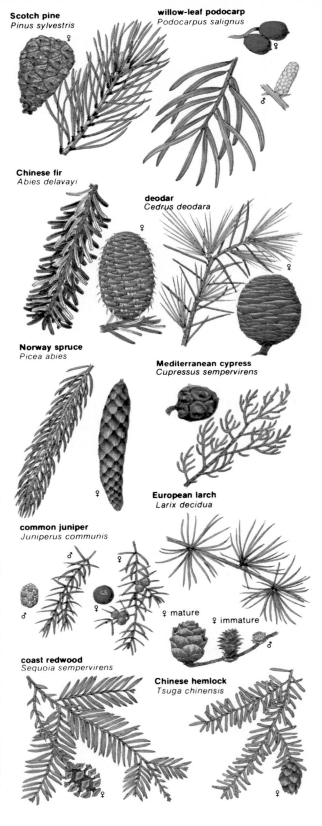

Scotch pine
Pinus sylvestris
♀

willow-leaf podocarp
Podocarpus salignus
♀
♂

Chinese fir
Abies delavayi
♀

deodar
Cedrus deodara
♀

Norway spruce
Picea abies
♀

Mediterranean cypress
Cupressus sempervirens

common juniper
Juniperus communis
♂
♀
♂
♀

European larch
Larix decidua
♀ mature   ♀ immature
♂

coast redwood
Sequoia sempervirens
♀

Chinese hemlock
Tsuga chinensis
♀

bering. Some of the most interesting conifers occur in the temperate rain forest—with an annual rainfall of about 3,810 mm (150 in)—on the Olympic Peninsula of Washington. Western hemlock, *Tsuga heterophylla,* western arborvitae, *Thuja plicata,* and giant fir, *Abies grandis,* are some of the more common species. North of this area and extending to Alaska, the dominant tree is Sitka spruce, *Picea sitchensis.*

Conifers are also conspicuous elements of the vegetation in deciduous forest regions. Eastern hemlock, *Tsuga canadensis,* is an important tree in the transition zone between coniferous and deciduous forests in the northern United States, and also in deciduous forests of the southern Appalachians; stands of white pine, *Pinus strobus,* and red pine, *P. resinosa,* are still fairly common in sand dune areas around Lake Michigan; short leaf pine, *P. echinata,* and loblolly pine, *P. taeda,* important dominants of pine forests in the southeastern United States, are perpetuated by burning and lumbering; bald cypresses, *Taxodium distichum,* follow the Mississippi embayment from about southern Illinois to Louisiana and extend to Florida; and tamarack, *Larix laricina,* black spruce, *Picea mariana,* and arborvitae, *Thuja occidentalis,* are major components of bogs in the northern United States.

In the Southern Hemisphere, some of the important conifers that contribute to extensive forest formations are *Podocarpus, Araucaria,* and *Agathis.*

Height and Age. Some conifers are among the world's tallest trees. Several coastal redwoods in northern California are between 107.3 and 111.9 m (352 and 367 ft) tall, and a Douglas fir in Ryderwood, Wash., measures 98.8 m (324 ft). Perhaps the world's thickest tree is the famous cypress, *Taxodium mucronatum,* from Santa Maria del Tule, near Oaxaca, Mexico, which measures about 16.2 m (53 ft) in diameter; and some giant redwoods attain a diameter of 11.3 m (37 ft).

Some conifers live to exceptionally old ages. Some giant redwoods reach an incredible age of more than 4,000 years. The oldest known specimen is a California bristle-cone pine, *Pinus aristata,* in which 4,900 annual rings have been counted. A specimen of *Taiwania cryptomerioides* from China is reputed to be about 1,600 years old. Some coastal redwoods are at least 1,000 years old, including one specimen that is estimated to be 2,200 years of age.

Adaptability. Many conifers adapt easily to cultivation in foreign countries. Monterey cypress, *Cupressus macrocarpa,* confined naturally to the Monterey Peninsula of southern California, grows well in New Zealand; Douglas fir, native to the western United States, is used for reforestation in Japan, Australia, and South Africa; and the Australian *Araucaria bidwillii* is used for reforestation in South Africa.

In many countries, conifers are valuable lumber trees. Douglas fir is one of the chief sources in North America; monkey puzzle tree, *Araucaria araucana,* is the principal lumber tree of Chile; kauri pine, *Agathis australis,* is one of the main trees in New Zealand; and *Cryptomeria japonica* is an important source of lumber in Japan.

Fossil Conifers. Conifers first appeared in the geological record during the latter part of the Pennsylvanian Period of the Paleozoic Era, about 300 million years ago, and as a group they reached their developmental climax in the late Jurassic or early Cretaceous periods of the Mesozoic Era, about 120 million years ago. Toward the end of the Cretaceous Period they began to decline, probably as a result of competition from ANGIOSPERMS (flowering plants), which evolved rapidly and rose to dominance by the end of this period. From the end of the Cretaceous to the present, the decline in the number of species has continued slowly but steadily.

The conifers are thought possibly to have evolved from the Cordaitales, an extinct group of gymnosperms. It is believed that the conifers developed rapidly during the Triassic and Jurassic periods, when some of the modern families became segregated. It is difficult, however, to identify any modern genera in rocks older than the lower Cretaceous, because many of the generic types are a maze of intermediate forms called transition conifers. Some of the most abundant fossils, in the form of petrified wood, have been found in the family Araucariaceae. One of the best sources of this material is from the Petrified Forest National Monument in Arizona, which contains thousands of silicified logs from the Triassic (about 200 million years ago).

conjugation (biology)   In biology, conjugation is a simple form of REPRODUCTION, occurring in some bacteria, algae, and Protozoa, in which there is an exchange of genetic material between two organisms, but no true sex cells (sperm and egg) are involved. In some species of bacteria, two cells of different mating type position themselves close to one another. A cytoplasmic bridge forms between the two cells, and genetic material is passed from one cell (the positive, or male, type) to the other cell (the minus, or female, type). The bacteria then separate and undergo normal fission reproduction. The green freshwater alga *Spirogyra* also conjugates. Two filaments line up next to each other, form cytoplasmic bridges, and pass genetic material between the cells. Paramecia also exhibit conjugation. Two cells attach themselves along their oral grooves and pass genetic material through a cytoplasmic, or conjugation, tube. They then separate and typically undergo normal binary fission.

conjugation (chemistry)   In organic chemistry, conjugation is a property of bonding systems in which two double bonds are separated by a single bond: $C{=}C{-}C{=}$ C. Compounds with conjugated double-bond systems are unusually stable and show anomalous behavior in the course of reactions. The two sets of double bonds tend to function as a unit because the electrons of the double bonds delocalize, or shift and spread out, throughout the system. Among the commercially important compounds with conjugated double-bond systems are isoprene (the basic chemical unit of natural rubber) and butadiene, both of which are important in the manufacture of synthetic rubber.

conjunction In astronomy, two or more bodies in the solar system are in conjuction when they have the same longitude, that is, when their positions are aligned when seen from the Earth. The term *conjunction* may be distinguished from opposition, but it is often used loosely to describe any close planetary alignment.

conjunctivitis [kuhn-juhnk-tiv-y'-tis] Conjunctivitis is an inflammation of the conjunctiva, the transparent mucous membrane lining the inside of the eyelids and the white of the eyeball. Normally the white, or sclera, is clearly visible through the conjunctiva, but when the conjunctiva is inflamed, its normally invisible blood vessels become engorged, making the eye appear red. Conjunctivitis may be caused by many types of infectious agents, as well as by toxic, chemical, and allergenic irritants. The inflammation is generally associated with a scratchy or itching sensation and an exudate of mucus or pus. A form of conjunctivitis that may result in blindness is caused by gonorrhea. Silver nitrate or penicillin eyedrops are routinely administered to newborn infants to treat possible gonorrheal infection.

Conkling, Roscoe Roscoe Conkling, a U.S. senator, exemplified the power of state politicians in the era of congressional dominance after 1865. Conkling, b. Albany, N.Y., Oct. 30, 1829, d. Apr. 19, 1888, entered Congress in 1859, became a senator in 1867, and left office in 1881. As the head of the Stalwart wing of the Republicans during the 1870s, Conkling lost power in patronage fights with Presidents Rutherford B. HAYES and James A. GARFIELD. His defeat in 1881 represented an important gain in presidential power. As a lawyer he told the Supreme Court in 1882 that the due-process clause of the 14th Amendment applied to corporations as well as individuals. Known as "the curled darling of Utica," Conkling faded from prominence when politics became more issue-oriented in the 1880s.

Connacht [kahn'-uhkt] Connacht (or Connaught) is a historical region that was one of five ancient kingdoms of Ireland. The influence of Connacht's kings and of later Norman lords has left this the most Gaelic and Norman part of Ireland. Situated in the northwest, it comprises the modern counties of Galway, Mayo, Roscommon, Sligo, and Leitrim. The area is 17,120 km^2 (6,610 mi^2), and the population is 431,409 (1986). Towns, with locally based industries, are little more than villages. Galway, with a population of 47,104 (1986), is the largest.

Connally, John B. American politician and government official John Bowden Connally, b. Floresville, Tex., Feb. 27, 1917, served as President Richard M. Nixon's secretary of the treasury (1971–72) and as a special advisor to the president (1973). Originally a Democrat, he was an administrative assistant to Sen. Lyndon Johnson in 1949, served briefly as President John F. Kennedy's secretary of the navy in 1961, and was governor of Texas from 1963 to 1969. He was riding in the same car with President Kennedy in Dallas in 1963 when Kennedy was assassinated; Connally was seriously wounded. In 1972 he worked for the reelection of President Nixon and shortly afterward became a Republican.

Connally, Tom Thomas Terry Connally, b. McLennan County, Tex., Aug. 19, 1877, d. Oct. 28, 1963, was chairman of the Senate Foreign Relations Committee (1941–46, 1949–53) during the Roosevelt and Truman administrations. After serving two terms (1901–04) in the Texas legislature, he was elected to the U.S. House of Representatives in 1916 and to the Senate in 1928 as a Democrat. As chairman of the Foreign Relations Committee, he sponsored (1943) the Connally Resolution, which provided for Senate approval of any treaty related to the creation of the UNITED NATIONS. Connally was vice-chairman of the U.S. delegation to the San Francisco Conference (1945) and U.S. representative to the UN General Assembly in 1946.

Connecticut The New England state of Connecticut is a vital part of the industrial and transportation corridor of the northeastern United States. One of the smallest U.S. states, it is bordered by Massachusetts on the north, Rhode Island on the east, Long Island Sound (an arm of the Atlantic Ocean) on the south, and New York on the west. Connecticut was first explored by Europeans in 1614, and the earliest white settlements were established in the 1630s. Manufacturing has dominated the economy since the middle of the 19th century. Connecticut is the chief producer of submarines, aircraft engines, and helicopters in the United States. Several major insurance companies are headquartered in the state, mainly in and around Hartford, the state capital. The word *Connecticut* is derived from the Algonquian Indian *quinnehtukqut*, meaning "beside the long tidal river."

Land and Resources

Connecticut is a scenic state, with many streams and extensive woodlands. It has 994 km (618 mi) of tidal shoreline.

Physiographic Regions. Almost all of Connecticut lies within the geomorphic region known as the New England Upland (a low, dissected plateau sloping southward from Maine to Long Island Sound). It may be divided into three major physiographic regions—the Western Highlands, the Central Lowlands, and the Eastern Highlands.

The Western Highlands, a rugged region of strong relief, rises to 598 m (1,962 ft) at Haystack Mountain and has the state's highest point at Mount Frissell (725 m/2,380 ft) in the Taconic section of the northwest. The Central Lowlands, about 32 km (20 mi) wide, are fertile.

CONNECTICUT

Land: Area: 12,997 km^2 (5,018 mi^2); rank: 48th. Capital: Hartford (1990 pop., 139,739). Largest city: Bridgeport (1990 pop., 141,686). Counties: 8. Elevations: highest—725 m (2,380 ft), at Mount Frissell; lowest—sea level, Long Island Sound.

People: Population (1990): 3,295,669; rank: 27th; density: 253.6 persons per km^2 (656.8 per mi^2). Distribution (1988 est.): 92.6% metropolitan, 7.4% nonmetropolitan. Average annual change (1980–90): +0.6%.

Government: (1991). Governor: Lowell P. Weicker, Jr., Independent. U.S. Congress: Senate—2 Democrats; House—3 Democrats, 3 Republicans. Electoral college votes: 8. State legislature: 36 senators, 151 representatives.

Economy: State personal income (1988): $74.6 billion; rank: 19th. Median family income (1979): $23,149; rank: 2nd. Agriculture: income (1988)—$382 million. Fishing: value (1988) 17 million. Forestry: sawtimber volume (1987)—7.6 billion board feet. Mining: value (1987)—$122 million. Manufacturing: value added (1987)—$22.3 billion. Services: value (1987)—$16.9 billion.

State Facts: Statehood: Jan. 9, 1788; the 5th state. Nickname: Constitution State; tree: white oak; motto: *Qui transtulit sustinet* ("He who transplanted still sustains"); song: "Yankee Doodle."

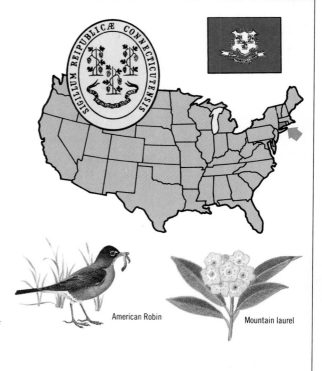

American Robin

Mountain laurel

The Eastern Highlands are less elevated than their western counterpart, and most of the region consists of rolling terrain.

The Coastal Lowlands, a narrow strip along Long Island Sound, includes an indented shoreline where low, rocky headlands alternate with smooth, sandy beaches and broad, flat tidal marshes. Several small islands lie off the coast.

Rivers and Lakes. The valleys of Connecticut contain more than 13,000 km (8,075 mi) of rivers and streams. The state's principal waterway is the CONNECTICUT RIVER, which flows through parts of the Central Lowlands and the Eastern Highlands before entering Long Island Sound; its chief tributary in the state is the Farmington River.

The major stream in western Connecticut is the HOUSATONIC RIVER, which receives the Naugatuck River shortly before flowing into the Sound. The Eastern Highlands are drained by the extensive network of the Shetucket and Quinebaug rivers, whose waters combine a short distance before joining with the Yantic River to form the Thames, a broad river that empties into Long Island Sound.

Connecticut has numerous small natural lakes, the largest of which is Bantam Lake, near Litchfield. The state also has numerous artificial lakes, which are used for power production, flood control, and irrigation. The largest, Lake Candlewood, is near DANBURY.

Climate. Connecticut has a moderate climate, with four well-defined seasons. The state as a whole receives ample precipitation, which is distributed more or less evenly throughout the year. Hurricanes occasionally strike along the shore, usually during August or September. BRIDGEPORT, on the coast, has a mean January temperature of -1° C (30° F) and an average July temperature of 23° C (74° F); it receives about 991 mm (39 in) of precipitation per year. HARTFORD, in the central part of the state, has a mean January temperature of -4° C (25° F) and an average July temperature of 23° C (74° F); it receives about 1,092 mm (43 in) of precipitation yearly.

Vegetation and Animal Life. Nearly 60% of Connecticut's total area is covered by forestland. Most of the trees are hardwoods, including white oak, hickory, ash, maple, beech, birch, and elm; softwoods include such evergreens as white pine, red pine, and hemlock. Among the numerous flowering plants found are mountain laurel, pink dog-

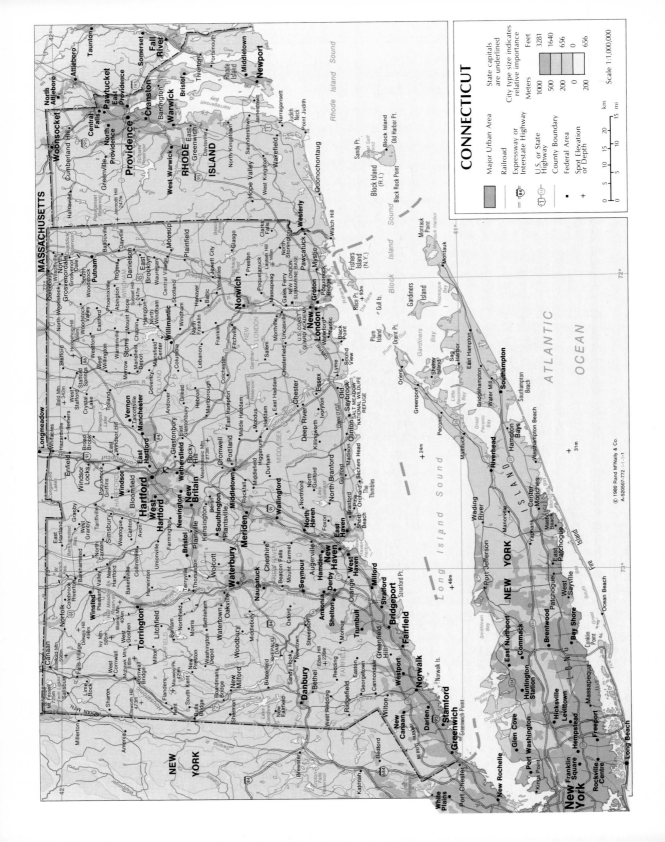

Hartford, the state capital, has been headquarters for large insurance companies since 1795. The gold-domed state capitol stands in the center of Bushnell Park. Between the park and the Connecticut River is Constitution Plaza, a major urban renewal complex that helped revitalize the downtown area in the 1960s.

wood, white dogwood, azaleas, hepatica, jack-in-the-pulpits, and cowslips.

Connecticut has few large animals other than the white-tailed deer. Wild animals commonly found include rabbits, skunks, opossums, raccoons, beavers, squirrels, and foxes. Large numbers of game birds, such as ducks, ruffed grouse, pheasants, and quail, are found. The state's many streams and lakes harbor large numbers of fish, notably bass, perch, pickerel, trout, and shad. Although the marine life in Long Island Sound near the shoreline has suffered because of pollution, flounder, smelt, porgy, clams, and mussels are still found.

Mineral Resources. Only a few deposits of minerals occur in quantities large enough for commercial exploitation. The principal minerals are stone, sand and gravel, and clay, with some feldspar, lime, and mica.

People

The 1990 population census of Connecticut was 3,295,669, an increase of about 6% over 1980. This low rate of increase, far below the state's 20% growth rate of 1960–70, was due largely to out-migration. The state's population is identified as mostly urban, with the main concentrations occurring along Long Island Sound (especially in the southwest) and in the central part of the state. In terms of population, the chief cities are Bridgeport, Hartford, NEW HAVEN, WATERBURY, STAMFORD, NORWALK, New Britain, Danbury, Bristol, and West Hartford. The state has a large Italian-American community, as well as many who trace their ancestry to Poland and other countries of Eastern Europe, Greece, and French-speaking Canada. About 7% of the state's population are black. Bridgeport and Stamford have substantial minorities of

Hispanic, notably Puerto Rican, background. About 4,500 American Indians also live in Connecticut. Roman Catholics constitute the largest religious body in the state. The largest Protestant groups are the United Church of Christ, Episcopalians, Methodists, and Baptists. The state also has substantial communities of Jews and Greek Orthodox.

Education and Cultural Activity. Connecticut has a long tradition of public education. In 1642 a free school was opened in New Haven, and in 1650 a law was enacted in Connecticut Colony requiring townships with 50 or more families to establish a public elementary school. The best known institution of higher education in Connecticut is YALE UNIVERSITY (founded 1701), in New Haven. The University of Connecticut (1881) has campuses at Storrs, Groton, Stamford, and Waterbury. Other units of the state university system are Central Connecticut (1849), Eastern Connecticut (1889), Western Connecticut (1903), and Southern Connecticut (1893).

Cultural Institutions. Connecticut has a wide array of cultural institutions: the Wadsworth Atheneum in Hartford, with a large collection of European and American paintings; the New Britain Museum of American Art; the Yale University Art Gallery, the Yale Center for British Art, and the Peabody Museum of Natural History, all in New Haven; and the American Clock and Watch Museum in Bristol. Well-known theaters are the American Shakespeare Festival Theatre in Stratford; the Hartford Stage Company; and the Long Wharf and Yale Repertory theaters (both in New Haven).

Historical Sites. Notable among Connecticut's colonial structures are the Henry Whitfield house (built in 1639, now containing a museum) in Guilford, one of the oldest

The northwestern corner of Connecticut is a predominantly rural area. Its scenic hills, valleys, streams, and forests have made this part of the state a popular recreation area.

stone dwellings in New England. The Old State House (built in 1706 and now including a museum) and the Mark Twain Memorial (the writer's residence during the 1870s) are in Hartford. Mystic Seaport, in Mystic, has been rebuilt as a facsimile of a 19th-century whaling town. The town of Litchfield has many well-preserved colonial buildings.

Sports and Recreation. A section of the APPALACHIAN TRAIL is found in Connecticut, as well as many beaches along Long Island Sound. A well-known automobile racetrack is located at Lime Rock.

Communications. In 1984 Connecticut had 9 television and more than 75 radio stations, in addition to 24 daily newspapers with a combined circulation of 907,000 copies. The *Hartford Courant* is considered the most influential daily paper.

Economy

The leading sector of Connecticut's economy is manufacturing. The state also has a large insurance industry; a substantial number of national firms have their home offices there. The headquarters of many large industrial corporations are located in Greenwich, Stamford, Danbury, and other communities of Fairfield County. The state's per capita income is among the highest in the nation.

Agriculture. Connecticut has a small agricultural sector of limited economic importance to the state. The chief commodities are dairy products, especially whole milk, and poultry products, notably eggs and broilers. Significant numbers of cattle and hogs are marketed. The most valuable crop is shade tobacco, the leaves of which are used in the outer wrapping of cigars.

Mining. The yearly value of Connecticut's mineral out-

put is relatively small. Although feldspar, stone, sand and gravel, lime, and clay are produced, the state is ranked among the lowest of U.S. states in nonfuel mineral production.

Manufacturing. Connecticut is the nation's leading producer of submarines, helicopters, and jet engines for aircraft. Other major, manufactured goods are nonelectric machinery, fabricated metals, electrical and electronic items, precision instruments, firearms, chemicals, textiles, and cutlery and silverware. The principal manufacturing centers are Hartford, Bridgeport, New London, New Haven, Norwalk, and Waterbury.

Tourism. Connecticut has a sizable tourist industry and attracts vacationers both to its varied beaches and to the pleasant, wooded hills in its western regions. More than 100 state parks and state forests are open to visitors.

Transportation. Extensive transportation facilities are available, with most land and inland-water routes following a generally north-south direction. The leading seaports are Bridgeport, New Haven, and New London; ocean-going vessels navigate the Connecticut River as far north as Hartford. The state also has more than 100 airports.

Energy. In the late 1980s, Connecticut had an electricity-generating capacity of 7.4 million kilowatts; the annual production was 36.4 billion kilowatt hours. More than 90% of this electric power is produced in thermal plants using coal or refined petroleum.

Shade-grown tobacco, Connecticut's leading field crop, yields a high-quality tobacco leaf used as the outer wrapping of cigars. The leaves are protected from direct sunlight and heavy rain by a shade tent of open mesh cloth.

Government and Politics

Connecticut is governed under a constitution of 1965, as amended. The chief executive of the state is a governor, popularly elected to a 4-year term; no restrictions are placed on the number of terms the governor may serve. Connecticut's legislature, called the General Assembly, consists of a 36-member senate and 151-member house of representatives; all the legislators are popularly elected to 2-year terms. The highest tribunal is the state supreme court consisting of a chief justice and five associate justices; the court only hears appeals. The highest trial court is the superior court. Members of the supreme court and the superior court are appointed to 8-year terms by the General Assembly.

The main units of local government are the state's 169 towns; the Connecticut town is similar to the township in other states and may contain villages, boroughs, and cities. Connecticut has eight electoral votes in national presidential elections and is represented in the U.S. Congress by two senators and six representatives.

Politics. The Republicans dominated the governorship of Connecticut from the 1830s to 1931; since then, Democrats have usually held the office, including Ella GRASSO, who in 1974 became the first U.S. woman elected governor in her own right. During the 1970s the state's major cities usually voted Democratic, and the small towns voted Republican; the growing suburban areas, however, were fairly evenly divided between supporters of the two parties. More recently, despite a larger Democratic registration, the Republicans have won a significant number of congressional and presidential elections.

History

When, early in the 17th century, the first Europeans arrived in present-day Connecticut, the area was sparsely inhabited by 6,000 Algonquian-speaking Indians. Other Indian groups were the PEQUOT and the closely related MOHEGAN (written about by James Fenimore COOPER in *The Last of the Mohicans*); the Niantic; the Quinnipiac; and the Wangunk.

Adriaen BLOCK, a Dutch navigator, discovered the Connecticut River in 1614 and claimed the region for the Dutch. A small Dutch trading fort was built in 1633 on the site of modern Hartford, but was soon abandoned. Meanwhile, English settlers from the Plymouth Colony and the Massachusetts Bay Colony established settlements at Wethersfield, Hartford, New Haven, New London, Guilford, Milford, Saybrook, Windsor, and other places. The Pequot Indians tried to prevent white settlement, but they were soundly defeated in the PEQUOT WAR (1637). The settlements of Hartford, Wethersfield, and Windsor joined together to form the Connecticut (or River) Colony, which adopted (1639) the FUNDAMENTAL ORDERS, a constitution based on democratic principles. In 1662 John Winthrop, Jr., governor of the Connecticut Colony (see WINTHROP family), obtained a royal charter that gave the colony considerable self-government and control of New Haven Colony. The latter reluctantly agreed to unite with the Connecticut Colony in 1665. Between 1685 and 1689, James II attempted to organize New England under one government; Connecticut, however, resisted and refused to turn over its charter. Colonists are believed to have hidden (1687) the document in the CHARTER OAK tree in Hartford. By the early 18th century, Connecticut farmers were producing agricultural products for export to the other American colonies, and the coastal towns traded with the West Indies. Connecticut also became known for its clocks, silverware, tinware, and shipbuilding.

By the 1770s the state had a population of nearly 200,000. During the AMERICAN REVOLUTION, about 30,000 state troops joined the Continental Army, and large amounts of food and provisions were contributed. A few battles were fought in Connecticut, among them skirmishes at Danbury (1777), New Haven (1779), and New London (1781).

Representatives from Connecticut played an important role at the CONSTITUTIONAL CONVENTION of 1787, especially in promoting the so-called Connecticut Compromise, which helped establish the present method of apportioning representation in the U.S. Congress among the states. On Jan. 9, 1788, Connecticut became the fifth state to ratify the U.S. Constitution. Most of the state's residents opposed the War of 1812, and New England representatives who opposed the war met at the HARTFORD CONVENTION in 1814–15.

During the first half of the 19th century, Connecticut's economy grew considerably, with manufacturing overtaking agriculture by mid-century. The state was known for its textiles (including silk), clocks, firearms (notably the repeating revolver manufactured in Hartford by Samuel COLT), shipbuilding, and rubber products. Commerce, shipping, and insurance were also important.

Most residents of Connecticut opposed slavery, which was abolished in the state in 1848. During the Civil War the state sent more than 57,000 men to the Union army and supplied firearms, ammunition, and numerous ships. Industry in Connecticut continued to expand after the war; meanwhile, the state's cities grew as immigrants arrived from Europe and Canada, many of them around the turn of the century.

Numerous industries were founded during World War I, when Connecticut was a major producer of war matériel, especially munitions. A U.S. naval base (now a submarine station) was established at Groton in 1917. The Depression of the 1930s seriously affected the state. Industrial output declined markedly, and the unemployment rate rose considerably. The economy revived again during World War II, when Connecticut produced submarines, aircraft engines, firearms, and other items crucial to the war effort.

Despite relative prosperity in the postwar period, Connecticut saw some older cities, such as Danbury and Bridgeport, decline as manufacturers closed or moved to other parts of the country. Newer, diversified industries took hold, however, and Connecticut prospered; by the late 1980s its per-capita income was among the nation's highest.

Connecticut River   The Connecticut River, which is 655 km (407 mi) long, is the longest river in New England. It rises in the Connecticut Lakes in northern New Hampshire, near the Canadian border, and flows south. The river marks the boundary between New Hampshire and Vermont, crosses central Massachusetts and Connecticut, and enters Long Island Sound. With its many small tributaries, it drains an area of 28,710 km^2 (11,085 mi^2). The Connecticut River valley is a rich agriculture region.

Major industrial cities on the river's course include Springfield, Mass., and Hartford, Conn. Many dams supply power and flood control, and at Haddam Neck, near the mouth of the river, is a nuclear power plant. For 97 km (60 mi) below Hartford, the river is tidal and navigable. It was discovered in 1614 by a Dutch captain named Adriaen Block. The first settlers came from the Boston area to the Massachusetts part of the river valley in the early 17th century.

connective tissue   Connective tissue supports and gives form to the body and its organs. Connective tissues differ in appearance, consistency, and composition in different regions of the body, depending on local functional requirements. They include BONE, CARTILAGE, LIGAMENTS, TENDONS, fibrous membranes, and a loose network of fibers that permeate all the tissues of the body.

The fibers, which are produced by specialized cells in the tissues, are of two kinds: inelastic fibers, which provide support to the surrounding tissue; and elastic fibers, which provide elasticity. As the body ages, inelastic fibers tend to become tougher and less flexible. The underlying process is the spontaneous tendency of COLLAGEN, the major protein of inelastic fibers, to form chemical cross-links between its molecules, thus forming a more rigid structure. The perfect recoil of the elastic fibers may be reduced by calcification with age.

Connell, Evan S., Jr.   The writer Evan Shelby Connell, Jr., b. Kansas City, Mo., Aug. 17, 1924, is known chiefly for his companion novels *Mrs. Bridge* (1959) and *Mr. Bridge* (1969), which explore the moral ambiguities of the American middle class. Among his other novels are *The Patriot* (1960); *The Diary of a Rapist* (1966), a powerful study of a man at war with society; and *Double Honeymoon* (1976). *A Long Desire* (1979) and *The White Lantern* (1980) are personal reflections.

Connelly, Cornelia   Cornelia Augusta Peacock Connelly, b. Philadelphia, Jan. 15, 1809, d. Apr. 18, 1879, was the American founder of the Society of the Holy Child. She married an Episcopal minister in 1831; both she and her husband, Pierce Connelly, converted to Roman Catholicism, however, and the marriage was suspended (1844) so that Pierce might enter the priesthood. Cornelia became a nun and settled in England, where she

founded (1846) the society, a teaching order. The order spread to Europe, Africa, and the United States. In 1959 the process for her beatification was begun.

Connelly, Marc   Marc Connelly, b. McKeesport, Pa., Dec. 13, 1890, d. Dec. 21, 1980, was a playwright whose collaboration with George S. KAUFMAN produced some of the wittiest plays of the Broadway stage during the 1920s. Among their joint successes were *Dulcy* (1921), written for Lynn Fontanne; *To the Ladies* (1922), written for Helen Hayes; the satirical *Merton of the Movies* (1922); *Beggar on Horseback* (1924), a satire of middle-class values; and the musical *Be Yourself* (1924). Connelly's own play, *The Green Pastures* (1930; film, 1936), based on Roark Bradford's folk rendering of Old Testament stories, won the Pulitzer Prize. He also wrote fiction, film scripts, and *Voices Offstage: A Book of Memoirs* (1968).

Connolly, Maureen   Maureen Catherine Connolly, b. San Diego, Calif., Sept. 17, 1934, d. June 21, 1969, was an American tennis player who, at the age of 16, became the youngest woman (until Tracy Austin in 1979) to win the U.S. National Championship. She won that title three times (1951–53), the French title twice (1953–54), and the Wimbledon championship three times (1952–54). Connolly was also one of only a few players in history to win (1953) the Grand Slam. Despite her size (1 m 65 cm/5 ft 5 in), she played with great power, earning the nickname "Little Mo." A horse-riding accident cut short her career when she was 19 years old.

Connors, Jimmy   James Scott Connors, b. Belleville, Ill., Sept. 2, 1952, is an American tennis champion. A left-hander with a powerful return of service, he dominated tennis in 1974 when he won 99 of 103 matches, including the Australian, Wimbledon, and U.S. Open titles. Connors played for U.C.L.A. in 1971 and became the first freshman to win the national collegiate singles title.

Jimmy Connors, an American tennis player noted for his powerful game and mercurial temperament, enjoyed his finest year in 1974, when he won the Wimbledon, U.S. Open, and Australian Open titles. Connors again achieved the world's number one ranking in 1982, winning Wimbledon and the U.S. Open.

In the summer of 1973, he won the U.S. Professional Championships. From 1974 to 1978, he was the most consistent player in men's tennis, winning more than 50 tournaments. In 1984 he became the first player to win 100 singles titles.

Using his most effective weapon—a flat, two-handed backhand—Connors won at Wimbledon in 1974 and 1982 and reached the finals in 1975, 1977, 1978, and 1984. He also won the U.S. Open five times, in 1974, 1976, 1978, 1982, and 1983. He is considered one of the top U.S. players in history.

conodont [kohn'-uh-dahnt] Conodonts are minute fossils resembling tiny teeth or a jaw and teeth that occur in marine rocks ranging in age from Cambrian to Triassic (see GEOLOGIC TIME). Less than 0.5 mm to somewhat more than 2 mm (.02 to .08 in) in length, they are composed mostly of the calcium phosphate mineral APATITE. The biological affinities of conodonts are unknown, although some paleontologists suggest that they are the hard parts of extinct fish. Widespread distribution and resistance to decomposition make them valuable guide fossils for stratigraphic correlation.

See also: FOSSIL RECORD.

conquistadors [kuhn-kees'-tuh-dorz] The conquistadors were the military adventurers who led the Spanish exploration and conquest of the New World during the 16th century. Mostly of common stock, they frequently ravaged the Indian population and the lands of the Americas. They were fierce and often ruthless fighters, motivated by both missionary zeal and greed for gold and other riches. Among the most famous conquistadors were Vasco Núñez de BALBOA, who discovered the Pacific Ocean; Hernán CORTÉS, who defeated the Aztecs; Francisco PIZARRO, who sacked the Inca kingdom; Hernando DE SOTO, who discovered the Mississippi River; and Francisco Vásquez de CORONADO, who explored the western United States.

Conrad, Joseph A unique figure in English literature, not only because of his genius as a writer of novels, short stories, and essays but also because of the variety of his experience, Joseph Conrad, b. Berdyczów, Poland, Dec. 3, 1857, d. Aug. 3, 1924, came from the nobility of Russian-dominated Poland and was christened Jósef Teodor Konrad Korzeniowski.

In 1861 his father, Apollo Korzeniowski, a writer and translator, was arrested for political activity against Russia and exiled to a remote Russian province with his wife and son. Conrad's mother died in exile, and in 1867, Apollo, suffering from tuberculosis, was permitted to return to Poland, where he died in 1869. Conrad was then brought up by his maternal uncle, Thaddeus Bobrowski.

Conrad announced when he was 15 that he wanted to go to sea, but he did not win Bobrowski's approval until October 1874. He made several voyages from Marseille,

The Polish-born British writer Joseph Conrad created novels and short stories admired equally for their symbolism, psychological depth, and skillful evocation of atmosphere.

took part in some gunrunning to Spain, and enjoyed Marseille's waterfront society. He got into debt, however, and in 1878 he shot himself, the bullet lodging near his heart. Conrad recovered, settled his debts with his uncle's assistance, and left Marseille in a British freighter, the *Mavis*, intending to join the British merchant navy. He left the *Mavis* in June 1878 and then resumed his dissolute life in London. A sharp rebuke from his uncle sent him back to his career. With, as he said, only six words of English, he sailed first in a coaster carrying coal on the east coast of England and then as an ordinary seaman on a wool-clipper, *The Duke of Sutherland*, bound for Australia. Conrad worked for 16 years as a seaman, rising through the ranks of the British merchant navy and obtaining his master's certificate in 1886. In the same year he became a British subject.

Between 1882 and 1889, Conrad sailed on the bark *Palestine*, the S.S. *Vidar*, and the bark *Otago*. As second mate of the *Palestine*, which had to be abandoned off the coast of Sumatra in March 1883, he first visited the Far East. Having recovered in a Singapore hospital from a back injury received in 1887, he became mate of the local trading ship the S.S. *Vidar*. In 1888 he obtained his first and only command, the *Otago*, which he joined at Bangkok and sailed on a difficult, fever-ridden passage to Singapore and Australia. During 1890 Conrad traveled on the Congo River in West Africa. There he contracted malaria, which impaired his health for the rest of his life. He returned to England in 1891.

Conrad's four-month stay in the Congo interrupted his work on *Almayer's Folly*, a novel based on the character of a trader whom he had met in Borneo. When this was published in 1895, Joseph Conrad, as he now called himself, gave up the sea for the equally precarious life of a writer. In 1896 he married Jessie George, and his second novel, *An Outcast of the Islands*, also set in Borneo, was published. From then until his death, Conrad moved restlessly from one home to another in England. Although he was tormented by the difficulties of creation and lack of money, his work did bring him critical recognition and the friendship of many fellow writers, including Ford Madox Ford, John Galsworthy, Henry James, and H. G. Wells. It was not until 1913, when his novel *Chance* appeared, that he became a best-selling writer.

Although Conrad objected to being typed as a writer of sea stories, much of his work is derived from his maritime experience: *Lord Jim* (1900), inspired by a story he heard of the desertion of the pilgrim ship *Jeddah* by her crew; *The Nigger of the "Narcissus"* (1897), based on his journey from Bombay to England in 1884; and the long short stories "The Secret Sharer" (1912) and "The Shadow-Line" (1917), both based on the *Otago*'s passage from Bangkok to Singapore.

HEART OF DARKNESS (1902), a fictionalized account of his experiences on the Congo, bridges the gap between sea fiction and land fiction, and in *Nostromo* (1904), an account of a South American republic, he deals with the individual as a social and political being. *The Secret Agent* (1907) concerns an anarchist bomb plot that took place in London in 1894. *Under Western Eyes* (1911) describes a Russian student, Razumov, unwillingly drawn into the betrayal of a fellow student involved in an assassination attempt. Conrad is buried in Canterbury.

Conrad, Paul   The American cartoonist Paul Conrad, b. Cedar Rapids, Iowa, June 27, 1924, has twice won (1964 and 1971) the Pulitzer Prize for editorial cartooning. Upon graduation (1950) from the University of Iowa, he became a cartoonist for the *Denver Post*, moving in 1964 to the *Los Angeles Times*, which syndicates his work. His books include *The King and Us* (1974), *Pro and Conrad* (1979), and *Drawn and Quartered* (1985).

Conrad II, King of Germany and Holy Roman Emperor   Conrad II, b. *c.*990, d. June 4, 1039, king of the Germans (1024–39) and Holy Roman emperor (1027–39), founded the Salian, or Franconian, dynasty. An obscure nobleman, he owed his election to his descent from Otto I's daughter Liutgard, because his predecessor, HENRY II, left no heirs.

Conrad was a firm, ruthless ruler who reestablished the empire's prestige in Burgundy, Italy, and Poland. He favored the *ministeriales*, lay officials of servile origin, and the petty nobles who benefited from his decree making fiefs heritable. This law ensured the growth of FEUDALISM in the empire. Lacking sympathy for ecclesiastical reform, he dominated the church through lay investiture and simony.

Conrad III, King of Germany and Holy Roman Emperor   Conrad III, b. *c.*1093, d. Feb. 15, 1152, was the first of the HOHENSTAUFENS to rule (1138–52) the Holy Roman Empire. Even before his election as king, Conrad had feuded with the WELF family of Bavaria and Saxony whom his predecessor, LOTHAIR II, had favored; they remained his persistent foes. The death of Duke

Henry the Proud, who had refused to recognize Conrad, and the accession of his 10-year-old son, HENRY THE LION, enabled Conrad to win a partial victory in 1142 by depriving the Welfs of the Bavarian duchy. At the urging of BERNARD OF CLAIRVAUX, Conrad participated in the Second Crusade (1147–49), and his contacts with the Byzantine emperor MANUEL I COMNENUS during this expedition led to an alliance against ROGER II of Sicily, his rival in the Italian peninsula. Conrad's Italian policy was generally weak, and his reign proved little more than a prelude to the great Hohenstaufens. He was succeeded by his nephew, FREDERICK I Barbarossa.

See also: GUELPHS AND GHIBELLINES.

Conrad IV, King of Germany   Conrad IV, b. Apr. 26, 1228, d. May 21, 1254, king of Germany and of Sicily, was the son of Holy Roman emperor FREDERICK II of the HOHENSTAUFEN dynasty. He was elected German king in 1237, in the midst of the struggle between his father and the papacy. In 1245, Pope INNOCENT IV declared both Frederick and Conrad deposed, and Henry Raspe, landgrave of Thuringia (d. 1247), and William, count of Holland (d. 1256), were recognized as successive German antikings. After Frederick's death (1250), Conrad went to Sicily to assume his father's crown. He died in Italy just after Innocent had found a rival candidate for the crown in Edmund, younger son of Henry III of England.

conscience   Conscience is the capacity for moral judgment. Appeals to conscience to determine right from wrong have been adopted by all religious traditions, in which conscience is always related to the acceptance of the divine will. As such, conscience has been explained popularly as the voice of God inwardly directing a person to do right.

Conscience has been variously explained by philosophers. In one conception, conscience is a kind of intuitive perception. Francis HUTCHESON and the 3d earl of SHAFTESBURY, for example, thought conscience could be described as a moral sense, an intuitive faculty that operates through feelings of right and wrong. In another conception, conscience is reason applied to moral principles. Proponents of EMPIRICISM have suggested that conscience is the cumulative and subjective inference from past experience giving direction to the choices made by an individual.

According to the depth psychology of Sigmund FREUD, a form of conscience, the superego, is a product of unconscious activity. Some psychologists have identified conscience with an expression of values or guilt feelings. Others regard conscience as learned reaction to stimuli.

conscientious objector   A conscientious objector is one who on religious, philosophic, or political grounds objects to CONSCRIPTION into military service. The earliest known conscientious objectors in Europe were Christians who refused to bear arms in the Roman legions. This refusal reemerged among many pacifistic dissenting sects after the Reformation, notably among the Quakers (Society of FRIENDS) in England, the BRETHREN and MENNONITES in Germany, and the DOUKHOBORS and Molokans in Russia.

Recognition of the rights of conscientious objectors was unusual until recent times. Exemptions were made during the U.S. Civil War. In both world wars the United States granted exemption or noncombatant service only to members of recognized pacifist religious sects. Philosophical and political objectors were not usually exempted, and many of those who refused the draft were imprisoned. In Britain, also, during World War I many objectors were imprisoned, but in World War II a more liberal attitude prevailed, three kinds of exemption being allowed.

The United States dropped the religious requirement in 1970, recognizing objection based on strong ethical principles but refusing to allow objection to a particular war such as that in Vietnam. Many draft-age men left the country rather than serve in that war.

Since World War II the Scandinavian countries, the Netherlands, West Germany, France, and Belgium have all passed laws recognizing religious and philosophic objectors and providing a variety of alternatives in noncombatant and civilian service.

consciousness The terms *conscious* and *consciousness* are used in different ways. In one sense, a person is conscious when awake, but unconscious when asleep, knocked out, or comatose. Yet people also do things unconsciously even when they are awake.

The term *consciousness* is most often used by philosophers and psychologists as meaning "attention to the contents or workings of one's own mind." This notion was articulated and emphasized in the 17th century by John LOCKE and René DESCARTES. They held that consciousness accompanies every waking mental state—that no mental state goes unscanned by its owner. In this view the mind is transparent to itself—that is, it can perceive its own activity—and is known infallibly by its own inner aspect, or "feel." Indeed, such self-transparency was taken for nearly 300 years to be the defining feature of the mind. That conception culminated in the psychological theories of Wilhelm WUNDT and Edward Titchener, who advocated a science of introspection.

Early in the 20th century the transparency doctrine came to grief for three separate reasons. The first reason was Sigmund FREUD's compelling evidence that some very important mental activity is not only subconscious, but firmly resists conscious access through the mechanism of repression. At first Freud's idea of the UNCONSCIOUS was greeted with consternation as being virtually self-contradictory, but whatever the fates of particular Freudian explanations, it has since won acceptance as being useful and entirely feasible.

The second difficulty for the transparency doctrine was that it made the mind inscrutable to objective science. What is known introspectively to a single person would be utterly private to that person.

The behaviorists John B. WATSON and B. F. SKINNER

and the philosopher Gilbert RYLE rebelled against the idea of an intractably private inner sense and its equally private objects, and they denied the very existence of consciousness in the strong sense promulgated by Locke, Descartes, and the introspective psychologists. Ryle insisted that *mind* is an illusory concept, and that it is really nothing more than a collection of observable behaviors. Similarly, the behaviorists argued that behavioral responses to environmental stimuli are merely responses to the stimuli, and do not inherently represent hidden mental states or events; accordingly, psychology should be the science of behavior, not of introspection (see BEHAVIORISM).

The third difficulty for the transparency doctrine was COGNITIVE PSYCHOLOGY's comparatively recent discovery that everyone does a great deal of mental processing, reasoning, and analysis of many sorts without being able to introspect it at all. Perhaps the closest thing to a cognitive theory of consciousness is D. C. Dennett's hierarchical organization theory—based on earlier work by Ulric Neisser—according to which high-level brain centers selectively command lower-level components during mental activity.

conscription Conscription, the compulsory enrollment of persons into military service, has been employed at one time or another by almost every government. Conscription has been the chief means of staffing European armies since the time of Napoleon, who turned the citizen army that had risen to the defense of the French Revolution into an army composed mainly of conscripts. Population growth and the longer training required to use modern military technology have helped shift the emphasis from universal conscription to selective methods mixed with voluntary recruitment of long-service professionals.

Early American colonial laws requiring universal MILITIA service had eroded considerably by the time of the American Revolution. The revolutionary armies depended on a variety of procedures for recruiting, supplemented by short-term conscription. During the U.S. Civil War, both sides employed limited conscription, the Confederacy a little more successfully than the Union. The Draft Act of 1863 met with widespread resistance, and in such large Northern cities as New York, violent riots occurred (see DRAFT RIOTS).

The first successful U.S. conscription policy, the World War I Selective Service Act of 1917, created a separate agency, not part of the military services, with a wide network of local draft boards. Civic leaders were thus used to select local youths to meet national military draft quotas and simultaneously to reserve manpower for essential production and services. This procedure was revived and refined in 1940.

After a brief lapse following World War II, the Selective Service System was revived in 1948. As the military-age population grew and military demands became stabilized, the Selective Service System broadened its grounds for deferring and effectively excusing registrants from active military service. Thus, while stimulating military enlistments, active and reserve, the system also encouraged early marriage and fatherhood and enrollment for college and graduate education.

These inequities were only partially reversed during the Vietnam War. Pressures for reform led to a lottery system in 1969, but this proved only a partial answer to growing criticism, and the system was discontinued in 1973. Beginning in 1980, however, young men were obliged to register for a possible future draft.

See also: CONSCIENTIOUS OBJECTOR.

conservation   Conservation is the philosophy and policy of managing the environment to assure adequate supplies of natural resources for future as well as present generations. In the late 1800s and early 1900s, *conservation* usually referred to management of a single, economically valuable resource such as forests, soils, or wildlife. Today, reflecting an increasing understanding of ECOLOGY—the science of the interrelationships between living things and their environment—the use of the term *conservation* has been extended to consider the environment as a whole.

Natural resources traditionally have been classified as renewable and nonrenewable. Renewable resources are those which, under proper management, regenerate and even improve their resource values, but which when misused can be depleted or lost entirely. They include plants and animals and other resources such as soils and inland waters. Nonrenewable resources are minerals and fossil and nuclear fuels, which are present on the Earth in fixed amounts and, once used, do not regenerate. Increasingly, elements of the environment, such as oceans, tidal lands, and the air itself, are also being recognized as natural resources.

The goals of resource conservation are (1) the maintenance of essential ecological processes—globally, the CARBON CYCLE, the NITROGEN CYCLE, and the HYDROLOGIC CYCLE; locally, the regeneration of SOIL, recycling of nutrients, and cleansing of waters and air—and life-support systems, such as agricultural systems, coastal and freshwater systems, and forests; (2) the preservation of genetic diversity; and (3) the assurance that utilization of species and ecosystems such as forests and grazing lands is sustainable. The consumption of nonrenewable resources should insure that scarce minerals are used conservatively and recycled where possible, and that their mining and use have the least possible adverse impact on other resources, and on environmental quality.

History: The Role of the United States

The conservation movement began in the United States largely in response to the unparalleled damage the settlers had inflicted on natural resources. Individuals and organizations, appalled by this destruction, arose to champion conservation. In 1875 the American Forestry Association was founded, followed in 1883 by the American Ornithologists' Union, the Boone and Crockett Club in 1887, the SIERRA CLUB in 1892, and the New York Zoological Society in 1895. These were pioneers among

Pollution from industrial, agricultural, and domestic sources threatens the balance of life in many rivers and lakes. This infrared aerial photograph, taken over Toledo, Ohio, shows the flow of effluent into Lake Erie.

the nongovernmental organizations that have played a vital role in the development of conservation.

The Beginnings of Federal Involvement. In 1864, Congress gave the state of California Yosemite Valley for a public park and recreation area, effectively making it the precursor of today's national park system; in 1872, it established Yellowstone as America's first true national park (see NATIONAL PARKS). The Division of Forestry, now the U.S. Forest Service, was created in 1876. The Geological Survey was established in 1879, and its first director, John Wesley POWELL, publicized the agricultural possibilities and limitations of the West. The U.S. Biological Survey, precursor of the Fish and Wildlife Service, was founded in 1885. In 1897, Gifford PINCHOT was appointed chief of the reorganized Division of Forestry. Pinchot became a key architect of the conservation policies that developed under President Theodore Roosevelt.

The Roosevelt Administrations. Conservation of natural resources was firmly established as an important concern and priority of the federal government under Teddy Roosevelt's administration (1901–09). The establishment of national parks, national forests, and WILDLIFE REFUGES (the first in 1903) set out the conservation principle that public lands must be held in trust by the federal government and managed for the good of the country as a whole.

The catastrophe known as the DUST BOWL occurred in the early 1930s, when a series of dry years coincided with the extension of agriculture to unsuitable lands, and when poor agricultural practices had caused grossly deteriorated conditions on vast areas of midwestern and western farm lands. Dry and denuded lands simply blew away, and the clouds of dust reached as far east as Washington, D.C., dramatizing the severity of the crisis. With the establishment (1933) of the Soil Erosion Service, the country began to accept the principle that it was appropriate for the government to intervene to assist private landowners, especially in the areas of soil and water conservation. The year 1933 also saw the creation of the CIVILIAN CONSERVATION CORPS and the TENNESSEE VALLEY AUTHORITY.

Post World War II. In the period following World War II, growing populations, advanced technological capabilities, and increased emphasis on economic development put new stresses on the environment and its resources. For example, DDT and other synthetic PESTICIDES were developed in an attempt to reduce insect-borne diseases in humans and to increase food production. The initial results were dramatically successful. DDT was heavily used virtually worldwide, and in many areas malaria, carried by the anopheles mosquito, practically disappeared. Particularly in the United States, the new pesticides helped to produce bumper crops. Nevertheless, it became apparent that these substances were producing severe environmental effects, and in many cases creating problems that were worse than those the pesticides were intended to cure. The publication in 1962 of Rachel CARSON's *Silent Spring* alerted Americans to the dangers of unwise pesticide applications, and eventually the use of DDT and related pesticides was severely restricted.

The Emergence of Environmentalism. As pollution increased throughout the 1950s and '60s, conservation problems were forcibly brought to public attention via television. People saw the ghastly effects of mercury poisoning at Minimata Bay in Japan in the 1950s, the Torrey Canyon OIL SPILL (1967) in the English Channel, and the killer smog episodes in Los Angeles and London. One result was an unprecedented growth of public concern and the emergence of citizen conservation organizations. Many came to recognize that the narrow approaches to conservation that had marked earlier efforts were no longer appropriate, and that a more comprehensive environmental approach was needed. Conservationists began to become environmentalists.

Public environmental concerns led Congress to develop the National Environmental Policy Act of 1969 (NEPA), and to pass it unanimously over President Richard M. Nixon's objections. In the process of developing NEPA, Congress found that there were over 80 government units whose activities affected the environment, yet there was no governmental mechanism to develop environmental policy, maintain an overview of governmental actions, or provide environmental coordination. To fill these needs, NEPA established the Council on Environmental Quality and mandated the ENVIRONMENTAL IMPACT STATEMENT in an attempt to assure that environmental factors received due consideration in any federal actions. Today, most states, and many foreign countries, have adopted somewhat similar mechanisms to assess the environmental effects of proposed actions.

The 1970s represent the high point in the passage of U.S. conservation-related legislation. Following NEPA and the establishment of the ENVIRONMENTAL PROTECTION AGENCY in 1970, a series of important pollution-related measures were legislated: the Clean Air Act of 1970, the Water Pollution Control Act of 1972, the Toxic Substances Control Act of 1976, and the Clean Water Act of 1987.

International Conservation

The most effective early international conservation efforts involved agreements on migratory species, such as the 1911 treaty for the conservation of the northern fur seal (signed by Canada, Japan, Russia, and the United States) and the 1916 U.S.-Canadian treaty for the conservation

Tuareg herds are watered at a well in the Sahel, a semiarid region south of the Sahara that is rapidly turning into desert.

of migratory waterfowl. Only since World War II, however, has public awareness led to increasing international cooperation on such conservation issues as ENDANGERED SPECIES, national parks, conservation education, and conservation law. The UN Conference on the Human Environment, held in Sweden in 1972, firmly established conservation of natural resources as an important concern of governments throughout the world.

Today, conservation is concerned with a small number of major global issues. Each of these affects the others, and all are basic to human survival. Although not strictly conservation issues, population growth and economic factors underlie virtually all conservation problems.

Deforestation. Tropical forests are being destroyed at an ever-increasing rate. Estimates of the extent and rate of loss vary, but it appears that nearly half of the world's tropical forests already have been lost, and the remainder will all but disappear in the next two to three decades. The loss is incalculable. These forests provide habitat for an estimated half of the world's plant and animal species, provide water and fuel for much of the world's population, and influence regional and global climate. Commercial logging, clearance for agriculture, ranching, and fuel gathering are all responsible for the destruction. Solutions include the development of alternative fuelwood supplies through fuelwood plantations, the regulation of logging, and a consensus as to the value of forest conservation over commercial development.

In contrast, temperate-zone forests have actually increased in recent decades. Their greatest threat is ACID RAIN pollution, which is already severely affecting large areas of the conifer forests of northeast North America and Europe.

Loss of Agricultural Land. As the world's population increases, the lands needed to produce its food are disappearing, covered by buildings and roads, their topsoil lost through erosion, and their productivity destroyed by the salinization caused by irrigation. Large-scale commercial agriculture in parts of the United States results in severe and unsustainable rates of erosion soil loss. Overgrazing and firewood gathering denude vast areas of arid lands, resulting in the inexorable spread of deserts and desertlike conditions. Much of the problem in the developing countries is caused by unsound or ineffective development-assistance efforts. The United Nations estimates that, at present rates of loss, by the year 2000 about one-third of the world's arable land will be nonproductive.

Loss of Biological Diversity. The ever-increasing loss of plant and animal species represents a major conservation concern. Habitat loss, especially in tropical forest areas, is the greatest threat. Overexploitation threatens some species, such as whales and the rhinoceros. The Convention on Trade in Endangered Species of Flora and Fauna has worked well to control trade in most threatened species. A more fundamental solution, however, must be the establishment of a global network of areas that protect and maintain representative samples of the world's ecosystems.

Conservation as a Political and Economic Issue

The benefits of conservation are often long-term and may accrue to future as well as present generations. Many of the benefits (environmental quality, for example) do not neatly fit in conventional cost-benefit economic calculations. Thus, conservation efforts nearly always run counter to the objectives of short-term economic gain.

In developed countries, conservation issues are often clear-cut economic ones. From the start, the concept of public-trust management of U.S. public lands has provided a major focus for conflict between conservationists and the economic interests of loggers, ranchers, and miners, who virtually without cease have sought control over the resources of public lands and, particularly in recent years, have received generous access to timber, minerals, and grazing privileges. Recreational use of public lands has increased dramatically, and while this has created a larger constituency for public-trust management, it has also caused new problems. Increased numbers of hikers, cyclists, horseback riders, and campers are overusing many fragile park and wilderness areas, and future access probably must be limited. Presently, off-road vehicles pose the greatest immediate problem because of their impact on wild country ecosystems.

In developing countries it has become clear that conservation and sound development are mutually interdependent. Increasingly, conservation is being incorporated into economic development—through environmental assessments of development projects, for example, or national conservation strategies and environmental action plans. Some countries, such as Bolivia, Costa Rica, and the Philippines, have made "debt-for-nature" swaps, in which conservation organizations assume a portion of a country's foreign debt in return for the establishment of conservation programs.

See also: POLLUTANTS, CHEMICAL; POLLUTION, ENVIRONMENTAL; POLLUTION CONTROL; RECYCLING OF MATERIALS.

conservation, laws of   In physics, conservation laws are statements that overall amounts of certain physical quantities remain the same in the course of a given isolated process. Among the most fundamental laws are those for MASS, ENERGY, linear MOMENTUM, ANGULAR MOMENTUM, and electric charge. For example, the law of conservation of mass applies to chemical reactions. It states that the total mass of an isolated reaction does not change from beginning to end. The conservation law for linear momentum states that both the overall direction and the magnitude of the momentum remain unchanged, because linear momentum is a vector quantity (see VECTOR ANALYSIS). The conservation law for electric charge is fundamental, there being no known exceptions. This conservation law applies to the algebraic sum, or total charge, of a system.

The law of conservation of energy is now one of the most important and firmly established conservation laws of nature, although it has been necessary to recognize that energy may occur in many different forms and is also equivalent to mass. In macroscopic systems characterized by temperature, pressure, and volume, the law of conservation of energy is known as the first law of THERMODYNAMICS, in which heat is recognized as a form of energy (see HEAT AND HEAT TRANSFER).

There appears to be a connection between conservation laws and symmetry in nature (see SYMMETRY, physics). Every conservation law apparently corresponds to a particular symmetry. For example, in nuclear reactions, the total baryon number—the difference between the number of baryons (neutrons and protons being the most common) and antibaryons—is believed to be an exactly conserved quantity. Finally, there are processes in which some quantities are approximately conserved, and there are quantities that appear to be conserved for one kind of process but not for another. The laws of conservation and symmetry have been used to predict the existence of undiscovered particles and forces, as in the case of the ELECTROWEAK THEORY.

conservatism   In the political sense, conservatism means a belief in the importance of maintaining established values and institutions. Conservatives feel that rapid change is likely to bring more ills than benefits, especially when it attacks ways of life that have developed over a long period of time. They tend to be pessimistic about the chances of improving people's behavior through social change and are often skeptical of popular democracy and what they see as an excess of personal freedom.

Conservatives usually favor traditional religion, and in capitalist countries they tend to be probusiness and antigovernment. In Communist societies, however, they are likely to be opposed to those who desire change in party and state institutions. In nonindustrial societies conservatives are likely to favor agrarian policies.

Modern conservatism traces its roots to the French Revolution (1789) and the reaction against the excesses that occurred among many who had sympathized with its aims. The English statesman Edmund BURKE made an eloquent statement of the conservative view in his *Reflections on the Revolution in France* (1790). Burke strongly rejected what he considered the inevitable violence, arbitrariness, and radical destructiveness of the Revolution. He saw government as a contract between generations past, present, and future; the political inheritance, in his view, was not to be squandered with experimentation. The conservatism of the 19th century was also a reaction against the Industrial Revolution and the often associated assumption that reason could improve, if not perfect, all social interactions and institutions.

Conservatism in the United States was initially represented by the Federalist framers of the U.S. Constitution, who sought to avoid direct popular election of the president; they distrusted democracy with its factions and sentiments. To the aristocracies of Europe, however, they appeared quite radical because they proposed to do away with the monarchy and inherited privileges. Alexander HAMILTON and other Federalists favored a strong central government and a strong president, interpreted the Constitution very freely, and wanted the government to play a decisive role in the economy.

Under the impact of industrialization, American conservatism became more identified with agrarian, populist views and a distrust of the central government. By the 20th century, however, the mainstream of conservatism was represented by business interests who had generally secured their political and economic position and were concerned about maintaining the rights of property and the free-enterprise system both out of self-interest and out of a belief that the system that had allowed them to advance would allow others to do the same. They opposed the extension of governmental authority in regulating the economy and providing social services. Modern conservatism has thus adopted many of the laissez-faire views of 19th-century liberalism.

Conservative parties

Political parties classified as conservative exist in several countries. Traditionally supported by businesspeople, they have also appealed to workers and other segments of the population. In the United States, conservatives usually join one of the two major parties.

British Conservative Party The Conservative party of Great Britain came into being in the 1830s, a time when the primary policies of the TORY PARTY were support of the crown and protection of agriculture. In an effort to appeal to a wider electorate, Tory leader Sir Robert PEEL adopted the name *Conservative* and set out to broaden the Tory program. Benjamin DISRAELI, who assumed leadership of the Conservatives in the mid-century, however, gave new formulation to the party's principles: to preserve the nation's institutions, especially the crown; to maintain the empire; to secure peace with honor; and to ameliorate the condition of the people.

Conservative reform measures attracted the votes of many middle-class people, and in 1886 the party was strengthened by the accession to its ranks of the Liberal Unionists, those Liberals who opposed home rule for Ireland. From 1886 to 1905, the Conservatives were in office for all but three years. They were returned to office in 1915 as part of a wartime coalition, and from 1922 to 1945 they were in power almost continuously. Later they held office from 1951 to 1964 and from 1970 to 1974 and were returned again in 1979. Their devotion to the principles of Disraeli has been reasserted by such 20th-century leaders as Sir Winston CHURCHILL, Anthony EDEN, and Harold MACMILLAN. Under the leadership of Edward HEATH and Margaret THATCHER from the 1960s through the 1980s, the party negotiated (1973) British entry into the European Economic Community and advanced strong antiunion measures to fight inflation. Thatcher, who was prime minister for over 11 years (1979–90), was succeeded by John MAJOR.

Canadian Conservative Party. The Conservative party in Canada, first known as the Liberal-Conservative party, has modeled itself on the Conservative party of Great Britain. The Canadian party held power throughout most of the period from 1854 to 1894 under the leadership of Sir John A. MACDONALD. After confederation in 1867, it set out to be the party of national reconciliation and construction. Its later leaders have included Robert BORDEN, who led it to power in 1911; Richard Bedford BENNETT, in the 1930s; John BRACKEN, under whom it reached out to attract the populist prairie vote and changed its name to Progressive Conservative in 1942; John DIEFENBAKER, who served as prime minister from 1957 to 1963; Joseph CLARK, who was prime minister for nine months in 1979–80; and Brian MULRONEY, who became prime minister in 1984.

consonance   see DISSONANCE (music)

---

conspicuous consumption   Conspicuous consumption is the ostentatious display of wealth or nonessential goods and services. Such goods are purchased, not for their inherent utility, but for the status they confer on the buyer and user, especially among the newly rich or those who wish to be considered wealthy. The term was introduced by Thorstein VEBLEN in *The Theory of Leisure Class* (1899) and later expanded upon by John Kenneth GALBRAITH in *The Affluent Society* (1958).

---

conspiracy   A conspiracy, in Anglo-American common law, is a combination of two or more persons formed for the purpose of committing some unlawful or criminal act or for the purpose of using unlawful or criminal means to commit an act not in itself unlawful. The essence of the crime is the agreement and, in some jurisdictions, the taking of steps to effect the plan. Where actual damage is sustained by one or more victims, conspirators are also subject to civil suit. In 1981 the U.S. Supreme Court permitted the application of the triple-damages provision of the RICO Act to groups identified as "criminal enterprises," in an effort to combat organized crime and drug gangs.

Anglo-American statute law and the law of continental Europe do not recognize conspiracy as a crime when the purpose itself is legal. In the 19th century the common-law definition of conspiracy was sometimes used against labor unions: courts held that whereas it was legal for individual workers to withhold their labor from an employer, an agreement among workers to strike was a conspiracy.

Under U.S. federal statutes, it is a crime to conspire to commit an offense against the federal government or to conspire to interfere with, harm, threaten, or intimidate a federal officer. Conspiracy by businesses in restraint of trade has been punishable since 1890 under the Sherman Anti-Trust Act. Although most legal actions under the Sherman Act have been brought against corporations, there has been a trend recently toward including individual corporate officers as defendants in such cases.

Constable, John   The English artist John Constable, b. June 11, 1776, d. Mar. 31, 1837, has been called the father of modern landscape painting. The first major English artist to concentrate exclusively on the depiction of rural scenes, without classicizing or historical associations, Constable was also the first to paint such scenes on the scale usually reserved for recording important events in history. He devoted his life to painting a small portion of the English countryside, especially the area around the River Stour in East Anglia. When he decided to concentrate on observed nature, Constable was accordingly forced to invent a new, freer manner of working that permitted him to express the transient effects of light and shade on the landscape. The specks and strokes of white paint that often lie on the surface of his landscapes are one of the means by which he tried to capture the sparkle and freshness that fascinated him.

Determined to paint the objective facts of rural England—its well-tilled fields and modest houses, its cloud-filled skies and changeable weather—Constable, almost despite himself, infused his paintings with his innermost feelings. Over the span of his working life, these feelings ranged from a joyful participation in the alternating seasons of the year, as in his 1.8-m-wide (6-ft) *The Hay Wain* (1821; National Gallery, London), to his sorrow following the death of his wife in 1828. His inner torment is revealed in *Hadleigh Castle*, exhibited in 1829 (Yale Center for British Art, New Haven, Conn.).

Constable had little success in England during his lifetime. Because landscape painting was considered a minor genre, he was not admitted to full membership in the Royal Academy until 1829, when he was more than 50 years of age. He was, however, greatly admired in France, where three of his works, including *The Hay Wain* and *View on the Stour near Dedham* (1822; Huntington Art Gallery, San Marino, Calif.), were shown at the Paris Salon of 1824. The rising generation of French romantic painters was impressed by his free handling of paint and lively rendering of light and shade in high-key colors. Eugène Delacroix repainted parts of his *Scenes from the*

John Constable's affection for his native East Anglia countryside is displayed in Boatbuilding near Flatford Mill *(1815), one of his earlier works. Although Constable, who has been called "the father of modern landscape painting," received little recognition in his own country while alive, he was widely admired by his contemporaries in France, where his work had great influence. (Victoria and Albert Museum, London.)*

Massacre at Chios (1824) after seeing the Constable paintings at a Paris dealer's. More significantly for the future, Constable was also a major force in the regeneration of French landscape painting effected by the Barbizon school.

Today, Constable's finished, exhibited paintings are sometimes distinguished from his sketches or studies, which are often preferred for their greater spontaneity. Excellent examples of the finished works are located in the Metropolitan Museum of Art, New York City, whereas the sketches can best be seen in the Victoria and Albert Museum, London, and in the Yale Center for British Art (New Haven, Conn.).

Constance, Lake

Lake Constance (German: Bodensee) lies on the borders of Switzerland, Austria, and Germany. The lake covers 540 km^2 (210 mi^2) and is more than 67 km (about 42 mi) long and about 12 km (8 mi) wide. Its maximum depth is 252 m (827 ft). Located at the edge of the Alps, the lake is fed by the RHINE RIVER, which enters at the eastern end and leaves at the western end. The lake divides at the northwestern end, and the southern arm (the outlet) is the Untersee; the northern arm is the Überlinger See. The two largest cities on the lake are Konstanz (Constance) and Friedrichshafen.

constant

A constant is a quantity whose value, under specified conditions, does not change. Some constants remain fixed under all conditions. Much of modern science, and physics in particular, is based on the assumption that certain physical quantities are constants. The velocity of light, the gravitational constant, PLANCK'S CONSTANT, and the BOLTZMANN CONSTANT are all examples of fundamental constants.

Constant, Benjamin

The French writer Benjamin Constant, b. Oct. 25, 1767, d. Dec. 8, 1830, is best known for his brief semiautobiographical novel *Adolphe* (1816; Eng. trans., 1817), notable for its style and psychological complexity. He was instrumental in the development of the French romantic sensibility but also wrote on government and comparative religion.

Educated in Germany, England, and Scotland, Constant pursued a diplomatic and political career, espousing the republican ideals of the French Revolution. His long affair with Madame de STAËL, the celebrated aesthetician and novelist, had a great influence on his ideas.

Constanţa

[kawn-stahnt'-sah]   Constanţa is a port city in southeastern Romania, on the Black Sea. It has a population of 327,676 (1986 est.). Capital of the Constanţa district, it is a trade center, serving the USSR, Turkey, and the Mediterranean area. A pipeline from the Ploiesti oilfields brings petroleum to Constanţa for distribution. Pulp and paper products and prefabricated concrete are manufactured in the city. Several theaters and museums

are located there, and the resort area of Mamaia is nearby.

Constanţa was once the site of Tomis, a city settled by Greeks in the 7th century BC. It came under Roman rule in 72 BC and was renamed Constantiana after Constantine I had the city rebuilt during the 4th century AD.

Constantine

[kahn'-stuhn-teen]   Constantine (ancient Cirta), the capital of Constantine province in northeast Algeria, is cut off from a surrounding plateau on three sides by the precipitous Rhumel River gorge. It has a population of 438,000 (1987 est.).

Constantine is a center of the grain trade, and woolen and leather goods are manufactured there. The University of Constantine was established in 1961.

Probably settled in prehistoric times, the town was the prosperous capital of Numidia by the 3d century BC. In AD 313 it was renamed for the Roman emperor Constantine I, who rebuilt it. Frequently contested by various Muslim dynasties, it fell in the 16th century to the Turks and to the French in 1837.

Constantine V, Byzantine Emperor

Constantine V, b. 718, d. Sept. 14, 775, ruled the Byzantine Empire from 741. He continued and intensified the policy of ICONOCLASM (prohibition of religious images) begun by his father Leo III, convening a synod of bishops for the purpose in 754. This further weakened ties between Byzantium and Italy, which opposed iconoclasm. Constantine strengthened the empire in the east, winning (747) a naval victory over the Arabs and leading (763–75) expeditions against the Bulgars.

Constantine I, King of Greece

Constantine I, b. Aug. 2, 1868, d. Jan. 11, 1923, became king of Greece in March 1913 after the assassination of his father, GEORGE I. During World War I he advocated the maintenance of Greece's neutrality and was accused of pro-German sentiments by his political critics, led by Eleuthérios VENIZELOS. In June 1917, Britain and France forced Constantine to abandon his throne to his son, Alexander. Venizelos was reinstated as prime minister, and Greece soon entered the war on the Allied side.

After the death of Alexander in October 1920 and the unexpected electoral defeat of Venizelos in November 1920, a plebiscite on December 5 restored Constantine to the throne. Greece's defeat by Turkey in Anatolia forced him to abdicate in September 1922.

Constantine II, King of Greece

Constantine II of Greece, b. June 2, 1940, succeeded to the throne on Mar. 6, 1964, upon the death of his father, King PAUL. After a military junta seized power in 1967, Constantine attempted a countercoup. His effort failed, and he went into exile. In 1973 the military government deposed him and abolished the monarchy.

Constantine I, called the Great, profoundly influenced the history of both the Roman Empire and the Christian church by his adoption of Christianity. Because he established Constantinople (Byzantium) as the capital of the empire, he is sometimes considered the first Byzantine emperor. (National Museum, Belgrade.)

Constantine I, Roman Emperor (Constantine the Great)   Flavius Valerius Constantinus was the first Roman emperor to adopt Christianity. He was born at Naissus (modern Niš, Yugoslavia) about AD 280, the son of CONSTANTIUS I, who in 305 became senior emperor (augustus) in the West. When on his father's death in 306 the Roman army in Britain proclaimed Constantine augustus in his place, the Eastern emperor GALERIUS refused to recognize the claim.

Constantine survived the civil war that disrupted the western half of the empire during the next five years and by 312 was in a position to challenge Maxentius, who controlled Italy and Africa. Constantine's defeat (Oct. 28, 312) of Maxentius at the Milvian Bridge outside Rome not only removed a dangerous rival but also secured his share in the new government formed by Licinius, whom Galerius had appointed augustus of the West in 308.

The nature of Constantine's conversion to Christianity has long been disputed. Before 312, Constantine seems to have been a tolerant pagan, not committed to any one deity. Between 312 and 324, however, he gradually adopted the Christian God as his protector and on several occasions granted special privileges to individual churches and bishops. His alliance with Christianity was strengthened by the political quarrel with Licinius. The death of Galerius in 311—and that of his successor in the East, Maximinus Daia, in 313—left Constantine and Licinius in control of both halves of the empire. The two rulers were soon at odds. In the ensuing civil war, politics and religion became so entangled that contemporaries described Constantine's conflict with Licinius (a pagan) as a crusade against paganism. Soon after his victory over Licinius at Chrysopolis (Sept. 18, 324), Constantine openly embraced Christianity.

The following year, Constantine assembled the bishops in a council at Nicaea (see NICAEA, COUNCILS OF) to debate the doctrines of Arius, a presbyter of Alexandria in Egypt, who argued that Christ was a created being and

therefore not divine. Although this was not Constantine's first attempt to reconcile orthodox and heretical factions in Christianity, it was the first time he had used the imperial office to impose a settlement. Following a lengthy and heated debate, the bishops condemned ARIANISM and adopted a CREED (the Nicene Creed) that affirmed the divinity of Christ.

More important to the pagan majority in the empire, whose beliefs Constantine rejected but continued to tolerate, were the secular problems that required new and vigorous solutions: meeting the invasions of the GOTHS and other tribal groups along the western frontiers; securing the provinces by dividing the army, increasingly recruited from the barbarian population of the empire, into stationary frontier units and a more mobile reserve; reforming the coinage to prevent further inflation; and expanding the bureaucracy to meet the needs of an increasingly centralized government. In his own day Constantine's reputation rested more on his handling of these issues than on his arbitration of Christian disputes. In historical terms, though, these actions were less influential than his unexpected adoption of Christianity. Even the founding in 324 of Constantinople (modern ISTANBUL), the "new Rome" that survived the collapse of the Western empire, was a less important innovation. Embellished with monuments pirated from pagan sanctuaries, Constantinople itself was not only the new capital of the empire but also the symbol of the Christian triumph.

The civil war following Constantine's death on May 22, 337, did not destroy the new order he had created. The victor, his son CONSTANTIUS II, was an Arian, but he was no less committed to the Christianization of the empire. Paganism survived, but only during the short reign (360–63) of JULIAN THE APOSTATE was it again represented on the imperial throne.

Constantinople   see ISTANBUL

Constantinople, councils of [kahn'-stan-tih-nohp'-ul]   The councils of Constantinople were four ecumenical COUNCILS of the Christian church, held between the 4th and the 9th centuries. Constantinople I was called in 381 by THEODOSIUS I, then Roman emperor of the East, primarily to confront ARIANISM, the heresy that had been subdued only temporarily by the First Council of NICAEA (325). More than 150 bishops, all from the Eastern empire, met to reaffirm the doctrines of the Nicene CREED and to depose Maximus, the Arian patriarch of Constantinople. They also condemned Apollinarianism, a position that denied the full humanity of Christ. The council defined the position of the HOLY SPIRIT within the TRINITY as proceeding from God the Father, coequal and consubstantial with him.

Constantinople II was convoked by JUSTINIAN I in 553, to condemn NESTORIANISM and reconfirm the doctrine that Christ's two natures, one human and one divine, are perfectly united in one person. Constantinople III was summoned by Constantine IV in 680–81 with the consent of Pope Agatho. It condemned MONOTHELITISM and affirmed that Christ has two wills, one human and one divine, but that these are without division or confusion.

The Roman Catholic church considers Constantinople IV to have met in 869–70. The principal action of that council was to depose PHOTIUS, the patriarch of Constantinople. Later, Photius was restored to his see, and he held another council (879–80), which is considered ecumenical by the Orthodox church.

—

Constantinople, Latin Empire of The Latin Empire of Constantinople came into existence on Apr. 13, 1204, when the Fourth CRUSADE (primarily composed of Frenchmen, Venetians, and other Italians, collectively called Franks or Latins) conquered and sacked Constantinople, the capital of the BYZANTINE EMPIRE. It ended on July 25, 1261, when troops from the Byzantine rulers' place of exile, NICAEA, reoccupied the city. At its greatest extent (c.1216), the Latin Empire included territories in northwest Anatolia adjacent to the Sea of Marmara and the Dardanelles and eastern Thrace as far as Adrianople and the lower Maritza. The Latin emperors also claimed suzerainty over the kingdom of Thessalonica, the principality of Achaea, and the duchy of Athens.

The Crusaders elected (1204) Baldwin IX (1171–1205), count of Flanders, as Emperor Baldwin I. From the beginning, the Latin emperor was hampered by constitutional restrictions. The Venetians enjoyed self-government in Constantinople, as well as complete control over the former Byzantine lands they had taken—Crete and the Aegean islands, Corfu, and other Ionian islands. The emperor could not act without the consent of a council of Frankish barons and Venetians.

Baldwin I was captured (1205) by a Vlach-Bulgarian army and died in prison in Bulgaria. His brother Henry (c.1174–1216), who succeeded him, fought successfully

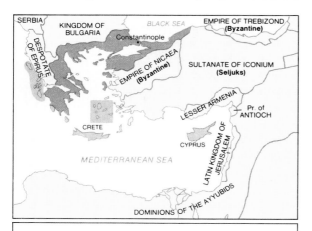

LATIN EMPIRE OF CONSTANTINOPLE, 1204–61

Latin Empire　　Venetian Possessions

against the empire's enemies—the exiled Byzantines at Nicaea and in EPIRUS and the Vlach-Bulgarian kings. His successors—Peter of Courtenay (r. 1216–17), Robert of Courtenay (r. 1217–28), John of Brienne (coemperor 1231–37), and Baldwin II (r. 1228–61)—were weak and incapable. The empire in its final years depended on the Venetian navy and financial aid from Louis IX of France and from Venice; Baldwin II, who repeatedly visited western Europe in quest of aid, was even forced to mortgage his son for a loan from Venice. After 1240 his authority scarcely extended beyond the city walls.

—

Constantius I, Roman Emperor [kahn-stan'shee-uhs] Constantius I, AD 250–306, Roman emperor from 305 to 306, was the father of CONSTANTINE I. He served in the western empire as caesar under MAXIMIAN, whose stepdaughter he married, thereby abandoning Constantine's mother, Saint HELENA. Constantius won a reputation for military brilliance and energy by restoring (296) Roman rule in Britain and defeating (298) the Alemanni in Gaul. When DIOCLETIAN and Maximian abdicated in 305, Constantius succeeded as ruler of the West, and GALERIUS became emperor in the East. Constantius died in Britain, having just defeated the Picts with Constantine's help.

—

Constantius II, Roman Emperor The Roman emperor Constantius II, b. Aug. 7, 317, d. Nov. 3, 361, was the third son of CONSTANTINE I. He was appointed caesar by his father in 324 and shared the throne with his brothers, Constantine II and Constans, following Constantine's death in 337. Educated as Christians, the brothers attempted to Christianize their pagan subjects and used their authority to settle doctrinal disputes in favor of ARIANISM. After the death of Constans in 350, Constantius ruled alone and directed his attention to the war against the Persians. Civil war threatened in 360, however, when his cousin JULIAN THE APOSTATE, caesar since 335, refused to supply troops for the campaign. En route to confront Julian, Constantius died in Cilicia.

—

Constellation The *Constellation*, a 36-gun frigate, was launched in 1797, one of the first six ships built for the U.S. Navy. On Feb. 9, 1799, during the undeclared naval war with France (1798–1800), the ship, under the command of Thomas Truxton, captured the 40-gun French frigate *L'Insurgente*. A year later the *Constellation* engaged another French frigate, the *Vengeance*. After being rebuilt, the *Constellation* was used against Confederate commerce raiders during the Civil War and served as a flagship of the Atlantic fleet during World War II. Designated a national historical landmark in 1964, the ship is now anchored at Baltimore, Md.

—

constellation Constellations are groupings of the brighter visible stars in the night sky. Many of these

**THE NORTHERN
CONSTELLATIONS**

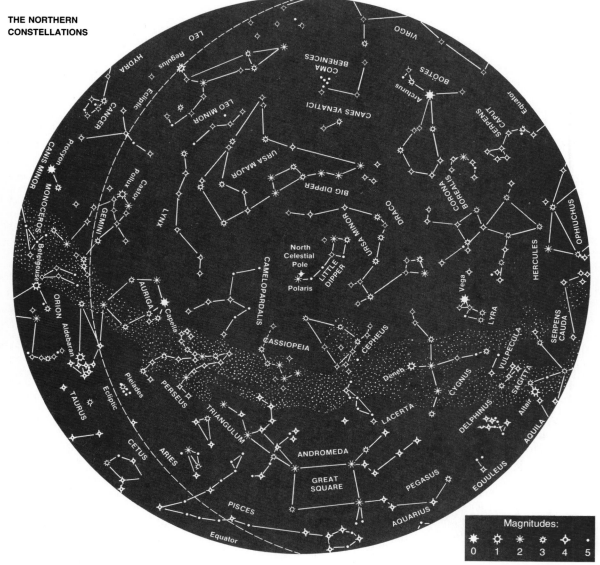

THE CONSTELLATIONS*

Name	Hemisphere
Andromeda	N
Antlia (Air Pump) [1]	S
Apus (Bird of Paradise) [2]	S
Aquarius (Water Carrier)	N/S
Aquila (Eagle)	N/S
Ara (Altar)	S
Aries (Ram)	N
Auriga (Charioteer)	N
Boötes (Herdsman)	N
Caelum (Graving Tool) [1]	S
Camelopardalis (Giraffe) [3]	N
Cancer (Crab)	N
Canes Venatici (Hunting Dogs) [4]	N
Canis Major (Larger Dog)	S
Canis Minor (Smaller Dog)	N
Capricornus (Sea Goat)	S

Name	Hemisphere
Carina (Keel) [1]	S
Cassiopeia	N
Centaurus (Centaur)	S
Cepheus	N
Cetus (Whale)	N/S
Chamaeleon [2]	S
Circinus (Compasses) [1]	S
Columba (Dove) [2]	S
Coma Berenices (Berenice's Hair) [5]	N
Corona Australis (Southern Crown)	S
Corona Borealis (Northern Crown)	N
Corvus (Crow)	S
Crater (Cup)	S
Crux (Southern Cross) [6]	S
Cygnus (Swan)	N
Delphinus (Dolphin)	N

Name	Hemisphere
Dorado (Goldfish) [2]	S
Draco (Dragon)	N
Equuleus (Colt)	N
Eridanus (River)	S
Fornax (Furnace) [1]	S
Gemini (Twins)	N
Grus (Crane) [2]	S
Hercules	N
Horologium (Clock) [1]	S
Hydra (Sea Serpent)	N/S
Hydrus (Water Snake) [2]	S
Indus (Indian) [2]	S
Lacerta (Lizard) [4]	N
Leo (Lion)	N
Leo Minor (Smaller Lion) [4]	N
Lepus (Hare)	S

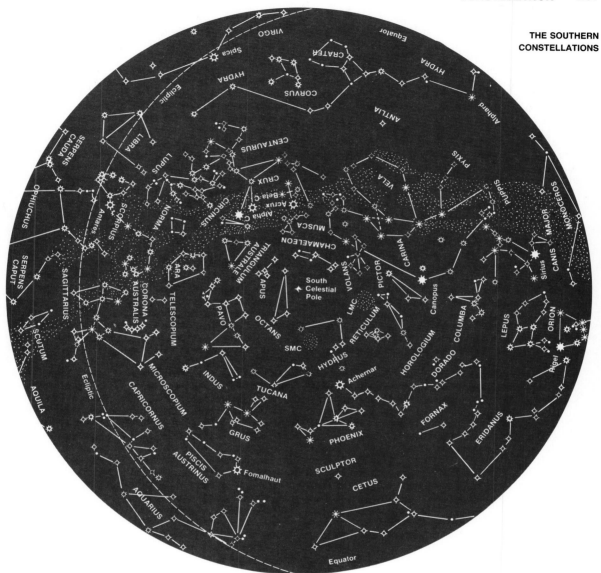

THE CONSTELLATIONS* (continued)

Name	Hemisphere
Libra (Scales)	S
Lupus (Wolf)	S
Lynx [4]	N
Lyra (Lyre)	N
Mensa (Table Mountain) [1]	S
Microscopium (Microscope) [1]	S
Monoceros (Unicorn) [7]	N/S
Musca (Fly) [2]	S
Norma (Level) [1]	S
Octans (Octant) [1]	S
Ophiuchus (Serpent Holder)	N/S
Orion (Hunter)	N/S
Pavo (Peacock) [2]	S
Pegasus (Winged Horse)	N
Perseus	N
Phoenix [2]	S

Name	Hemisphere
Pictor (Easel) [1]	S
Pisces (Fishes)	N
Piscis Austrinus (Southern Fish)	S
Puppis (Stern) [1]	S
Pyxis (Mariner's Compass) [1]	S
Reticulum (Net) [1]	S
Sagitta (Arrow)	N
Sagittarius (Archer)	S
Scorpius (Scorpion)	S
Sculptor (Sculptor's Apparatus) [1]	S
Scutum (Shield) [4]	S
Serpens (Serpent): Cauda and Caput (Tail and Head)	N/S
Sextans (Sextant) [4]	N/S
Taurus (Bull)	N
Telescopium (Telescope) [1]	S

Name	Hemisphere
Triangulum (Triangle)	N
Triangulum Australe (Southern Triangle) [2]	S
Tucana (Toucan) [2]	S
Ursa Major (Larger Bear)	N
Ursa Minor (Smaller Bear)	N
Vela (Sails) [1]	S
Virgo (Virgin)	N/S
Volans (Flying Fish) [2]	S
Vulpecula (Little Fox) [4]	N

*Many of the constellations were listed by Ptolemy (2d century). The others were formulated by the following: [1]Nicolas Louis de Lacaille; [2]Johann Bayer; [3]Jakob Bartsch; [4]Johannes Hevelius; [5]Tycho Brahe; [6]unknown; [7]Augustin Royer (fl. 1679).

groupings are based on imaginary figures formed by the stars. In astronomy it is useful to imagine that the figures are seen on the inner surface of a huge sphere surrounding the Earth—the so-called CELESTIAL SPHERE.

The celestial sphere is divided into 88 constellations, 47 of which date from ancient times and were listed by the Alexandrian astronomer PTOLEMY. More than a century after the first attempt to designate constellation areas by formalized boundaries, such boundaries were established by the International Astronomical Union in 1930. The boundaries are often complex, but all segments of the boundaries lie east-west or north-south on the celestial sphere.

Constellations are used today to indicate general directions in the sky, whereas COORDINATE SYSTEMS are used for the precise location of celestial objects. Constellations also continue to serve as orientation guides at night for navigators and for sky observers. The constellations may be divided into three groups: (1) the equatorial constellations, which lie on each side of the celestial EQUATOR, the projection onto the sky of the Earth's equator; (2) the north circumpolar constellations, which never set for observers at northern mid-latitudes; and (3) the south circumpolar constellations, which never set for observers at southern mid-latitudes. The ZODIAC, widely used in ASTROLOGY, consists of 12 constellations through which the Sun appears to move because of the Earth's yearly orbital motion. The Sun's yearly path is called the ECLIPTIC.

The times when given constellations rise and set depend on the time of year and on the observer's position on the Earth's surface. Constellations also slowly shift on the celestial sphere's coordinates because of the PRECESSION OF THE EQUINOXES and other movements. The star patterns themselves slowly change because of the relative motions of the stars, but such changes are observable only over immense periods of time.

constipation Constipation is difficulty or infrequency in evacuating the bowels. The retention of FECES in the colon and rectum allows too much water to be absorbed from the material, which then dries and hardens, making defecation more difficult. When the bowel is continually overloaded with feces, its muscles lose their tone and constipation becomes chronic, which may in turn lead to HEMORRHOIDS.

Constipation may be a symptom of an underlying disorder, such as an obstruction of the bowel by a tumor or a structural deformity. Several other conditions can cause bowel muscles to lose their normal propulsive ability. Constipation is also caused by a diet lacking in the plant fiber needed to form fecal bulk or by ignoring the urge to defecate. The mistaken belief that defecation should occur daily, at a regular time, and in large amounts, however, causes some people to believe they are constipated when they are not.

Constitution The *Constitution*—called "Old Ironsides" because bullets could not penetrate its tough oak sides—was one of the first of the original six frigates that made up the U.S. Navy. Launched in 1797, the ship carried 50 guns and a crew of more than 450. The ship served in the Tripolitan War (1801–05) and made its name in the War of 1812, when it won every battle in which it engaged. Most famous were battles with the British frigates *Guerriere*, 1,200 km (750 mi) off the coast of Massachusetts (Aug. 19, 1812), and *Java*, off the Brazilian coast (Dec. 29, 1812). The ship was scheduled to be scrapped in 1830, but Oliver Wendell Holmes's poem "Old Ironsides" inspired a public movement to save it. Restored in 1925, the *Constitution* is now moored in Boston.

constitution A constitution is the body of rules or precedents governing the affairs of a nation, state, or other organized group. It may be a written document, as in the United States, or it may be unwritten, consisting of laws and customs that have evolved over time, as in Great Britain. The difference is one of degree. Even a written constitution incorporates an evolving body of legally binding custom and interpretation; conversely, large parts of any unwritten constitution are written down as laws.

Written constitutions, which first became widespread during the 18th and 19th centuries, generally set out a framework by which laws are made and enforced. A more specific constitution would be inflexible and would quickly grow obsolete. No constitution reflects all the political practices of a country. The U.S. Constitution does not mention the cabinet or political parties. The Soviet constitution guarantees free speech and political liberty, but actual practice has not conformed.

Practices for amending constitutions vary. Usually, however, amendment is made relatively difficult. Constitutions may be discarded when governments are overthrown by force or when new constitutions are adopted by legal means.

Constitution Act The Canadian constitution is enshrined in the Constitution Act, which came into effect on Apr. 17, 1982. It incorporates the BRITISH NORTH AMERICA ACT of 1867, as amended, other pertinent laws, and a BILL OF RIGHTS known as the Canadian Charter of Rights and Freedoms. The Constitution Act, passed by the British Parliament as part of the Canada Act in 1982, patriated the constitution, granting Canada the right to amend its own constitution, a right reserved, heretofore, to the British Parliament. The amending formula requires the consent of the Canadian Parliament and seven provincial legislatures representing 50% of the population. Dissenting provinces may be exempted from the amended provisions. In some cases, the consent of all ten provincial legislatures is required. Quebec remains outside of the constitution. By the Meech Lake agreement of 1987, Quebec acceded to the act on condition that certain amendments be added, recognizing Quebec as a "distinct society." Those amendments failed in 1990 to gain ratification.

Constitution of the United States

Constitution of the United States The Constitution of the United States comprises the nation's fundamental law, providing the framework for its governance and the principles under which it must operate. Judicial reinterpretation has given the Constitution the flexibility to accommodate changes in the specific laws subject to its authority. As Chief Justice John MARSHALL pointed out early in the 19th century, the Constitution was "intended to endure for ages to come, and, consequently, to be adapted to the various *crises* of human affairs. To have prescribed the means by which government should, in all future times, execute its powers, would have been to change entirely, the character of the instrument, and give it the properties of a legal code."

The distinction Marshall made between the Constitution and other law was in keeping with the framers' provision for the supremacy of the Constitution in Article VI, which states: "This Constitution, and the Laws of the United States which shall be made in pursuance thereof; and all Treaties made, or which shall be made, under the Authority of the United States, shall be the supreme Law of the Land...."

Genesis of the Constitution

The first constitution of the United States was the ARTICLES OF CONFEDERATION ratified in 1781. Because this document left too much sovereignty to the states, it was defective as an instrument of government. Some leaders felt that the individual states suffered economically from the lack of a strong central authority; commercial barriers between the states seemed particularly onerous. They also felt that the lack of unity among the states was causing serious problems in international relations and the defense of the nation. The weakness of the central government was dramatized by such events as SHAYS'S REBELLION (1786–87) in western Massachusetts, and by the ability of one state to block legislation desired by the other twelve. The ANNAPOLIS CONVENTION of 1786 called for a general CONSTITUTIONAL CONVENTION, which met in Philadelphia in May 1787.

Twelve states (all but Rhode Island) named 73 delegates to the Constitutional Convention. Of these, 55 came but only 39 signed the Constitution on Sept. 17, 1787. The leaders of the convention were statesmen who in modern parlance would be called middle-of-the-road: George WASHINGTON, Alexander HAMILTON, James MADISON, John JAY, and Benjamin FRANKLIN. Conspicuous by their absence were the firebrands of democracy, Patrick HENRY and Sam ADAMS, and the author of the Declaration of Independence, Thomas JEFFERSON.

The prevailing political philosophy of the framers of the Constitution would later be articulated as follows by Madison in *The Federalist*:

George Washington addresses the Constitutional Convention of 1787. The delegates from 12 states attending this convention drafted a new federal constitution to replace the Articles of Confederation. (Virginia Museum of Fine Arts.)

It may be a reflection on human nature, that such devices [checks and balances] should be necessary to control the abuses of government. But what is government itself, but the greatest of all reflections on human nature? If men were angels, no government would be necessary. If angels were to govern men, neither external nor internal controls on government would be necessary. In framing a government which is to be administered by men over men, the great difficulty lies in this: you must first enable the government to control the governed; and in the next place oblige it to control itself. A dependence upon the people is, no doubt, the primary control on the government; but experience has taught mankind the necessity of auxiliary precautions.

What they sought was a balance that Madison called "mixed government" and "free government," a compromise between monarchy and democracy as they knew them.

Despite the consensus among the framers on the objectives of the Constitution, the controversy over the means by which those objectives could be achieved was lively. Controversy developed over the presidency and the way in which the PRESIDENT was to be elected; the relationship of the states to the national government; the relationship of the national government to the people; and the relationship of state to state. The latter conflict was partially resolved through the great compromise that gave small states equal representation with the large states in the SENATE but apportioned representation according to population in the HOUSE OF REPRESENTATIVES. Other compromises involved the slavery issue; each slave was to be counted as three-fifths of a person in determining representation and in apportioning direct taxes, and the migration or importation of slaves was allowed to continue until 1808. Generally, sectional interests were also protected by compromise. Northern interests were upheld by giving the new government the power to regulate trade and commerce, and the South was protected against export taxes and the immediate prohibition of the slave trade. Southern and Western border interests were reassured that their territorial rights would be protected by the requirement that treaties be ratified by two-thirds of the Senate.

After it was signed, the Constitution was offered for ratification. By its own terms, "the Ratification of the Conventions of nine States" was required. This was achieved on June 21, 1788, and by 1790 all 13 of the original states had ratified it. Ratification was vigorously opposed by the ANTI-FEDERALISTS, who feared that a powerful central government would minimize the role of the people in governance and threaten individual rights and local interests. The effort to counter the arguments of the Anti-Federalists led to intense campaigning, including the writing of *The Federalist* by Madison, Hamilton, and Jay (see FEDERALIST, THE). The significant and lasting accomplishment of the opponents was to get the BILL OF RIGHTS added to the Constitution.

Framework

The framework of government established in the Constitution emphasizes four overriding concepts: popular control without majority rule; the limitation of governmental power; federalism; and a tripartite government.

Popular Control but not Majority Rule. The framers provided for ultimate control of the government by the people through the electoral process. Such control, however, was not to be exercised either easily or immediately, except perhaps over the House of Representatives. Originally, senators were to be chosen by the state legislatures and the president by the electors in the ELECTORAL COLLEGE. Since the state legislatures controlled the selection of senators, and presidential electors and seats in the state legislature were won in popular elections, it was assumed that the popular will would eventually have an effect on the choice of senators and presidents. It could also be argued that the people would have a voice in the choice of federal officials appointed by the president, with the advice and consent of the Senate, but this could be true of federal judges only in the long run, since they were given virtually lifetime tenure.

The framers, with their complex views on government, felt that the popular majority must be represented in the federal legislature. At the same time, they felt that they must not give over all legislative power to a popular majority. Consequently, they approved an arrangement by which one house of the legislature represented majority will and another house served as a check on the first.

Power Limited and Circumscribed. Despite the framers' anxiety over governmental power, their experience with the Articles of Confederation taught them that the national government must have the power needed to achieve the purposes for which it was to be established. In *The Federalist*, Hamilton described these purposes:

The principal purposes to be answered by union are these—the common defence of the members; the preservation of the public peace, as well against internal convulsions as external attacks; the regulation of commerce with other nations and between the States; the superintendence of our intercourse, political and commercial, with foreign countries.

The first objective, then, was to spell out and grant the power necessary for what Hamilton called "energetic" government, while at the same time making explicit the limits of that power and creating safeguards to ensure that the new government did not exceed those limits.

The framers granted 18 specific powers to Congress, but in Article I, Section 9, listed a rather large number of things that Congress was not allowed to do. Evidently the framers wanted to make it clear that certain powers were emphatically denied to Congress.

The specific powers of the president were enumerated in Article II, Sections 2 and 3. Several presidents have interpreted the clause in Article II, Section 1, "the executive Power shall be rested in a President," to mean that they had much broader substantive powers, and the courts have sometimes supported these claims. The phrase *executive power*, however, had a more exact and limited meaning for the framers, as Hamilton explained in *The Federalist*:

> The essence of the legislative authority is to enact laws, or, in other words, to prescribe rules for the regulation of society; while the execution of the laws, and the employment of the common strength, either for this purpose or for the common defence, seem to comprise all the functions of the executive magistrate.

Presidential power was limited in other ways. The 4-year term, thought of primarily as a term long enough to ensure presidential independence, was also viewed as a limiting device. In addition, the president was made liable to IMPEACHMENT proceedings.

The framers believed they had granted ample but fairly well-defined, limited power to the judiciary. They wrote in Article III, "The judicial power of the United States, shall be vested in one supreme court, and in such inferior courts as the Congress may from time to time ordain and establish." Judicial power as such was understood by the framers to mean the power to decide cases and controversies. Nothing was said about judicial review of acts of Congress, and it is doubtful that any of the framers foresaw how important judicial review could and would become.

The framers were aware that the aggregate of powers granted to all the branches of the national government was enormous. The Constitution incorporated ways of circumscribing the power that it granted. What the framers dreaded most, and were most concerned to guard against, was the concentration of power in one person's hands. Thus they provided for a separation of powers and a system of checks and balances. They felt that these principles involved different ideas and that, although they were to some extent complementary, they were also, to some extent, contradictory. Separation was intended to diffuse power, to divide it up systematically so that legislative, executive, and judicial powers would be in separate hands and would be exercised separately.

In short, the framers did not rely on parchment alone to limit the power granted the new government. They further circumscribed it by diffusing it among branches designed to be independent and capable of retaining their independence, and by granting some specific powers as a check by one branch on the power of another. The framers also emphasized that the power of the states would serve as a check on the power of the new national government.

Federalism as a Basis. Despite their common heritage, background, and homogeneity, the original states were 13 different and distinct political entities, each commanding considerable loyalty from its citizenry. However much the framers wanted a strong central government, they knew that they could establish one only by allowing the states to retain power or by making it appear that they

did. They realized, or at least Hamilton did, that, as a practical matter, there could not be a double sovereignty; the framers persuaded the public to accept the Constitution by claiming that sovereignty was indeed divisible. Under the federal system they devised, the national government was given the authority to exercise only the enumerated powers granted it, but it had supreme authority in those areas. State sovereignty was therefore largely a fiction; it was destined to have a stormy future, involving a bloody civil war.

Three Coordinate Branches of Government. Throughout U.S. history, the power relationship among the three branches of the federal government has been difficult to define. Woodrow WILSON complained in 1884 that presidential "power has waned; and its power has waned because the power of Congress has become predominant." Although Wilson later changed his mind, at the time he wrote these words he felt that congressional predominance was inherent in the system. At other times the SUPREME COURT has appeared to be the most powerful branch of the government; even as powerful a president as Franklin D. ROOSEVELT felt that the Court had wrested inordinate power from the other two branches. And later, especially during the presidencies of Lyndon JOHNSON and Richard NIXON, many people feared that governmental power had become concentrated in an "imperial presidency."

The framers felt that the legislative branch might tend to predominate. Thus they wanted a strong executive, for they believed, as Hamilton wrote in *The Federalist*, that "energy in the executive is a leading character in the definition of good government." They hoped to establish a government in which the three branches would be coordinate in power, but they felt that in fact the judiciary, though not subordinate, did not actually share in the exercise of real power.

THE CONSTITUTION OF THE UNITED STATES

The text of the Constitution is printed below in regular type, retaining the original spelling and capitalization. Comments by Harold W. Chase on its provisions are printed in italic type.

We the People of the United States, in Order to form a more perfect Union, establish Justice, insure domestic Tranquility, provide for the common defence, promote the general Welfare, and secure the Blessings of Liberty to ourselves and our Posterity, do ordain and establish this Constitution for the United States of America.

These stated objectives make clear the framers' commitment to the proposition that government should serve to enhance the value and dignity of the individual, as opposed to the proposition to which authoritarian governments have traditionally adhered, that the individual's highest duty is to serve the state.

ARTICLE I

Section 1. All legislative Powers herein granted shall be vested in a Congress of the United States, which shall consist of a Senate and House of Representatives.

Section 2. The House of Representatives shall be composed of Members chosen every second Year by the People of the several States, and the Electors in each State shall have the Qualifications requisite for Electors of the most numerous Branch of the State Legislature.

No Person shall be a Representative who shall not have attained to the age of twenty five Years, and been seven Years a Citizen of the United States, and who shall not, when elected, be an Inhabitant of that State in which he shall be chosen.

Representatives and direct Taxes shall be apportioned among the several States which may be included within this Union, according to their respective Numbers, which shall be determined by adding to the whole Number of free Persons, including those bound to Service for a Term of Years, and excluding Indians not taxed, three fifths of all other Persons. The actual Enumeration shall be made within three Years after the first Meeting of the Congress of the United States, and within every subsequent Term of ten Years, in such Manner as they shall by Law direct. The Number of Representatives shall not exceed one for every thirty Thousand, but each State shall have at Least one Representative; and until such enumeration shall be made, the State of New Hampshire shall be entitled to chuse three, Massachusetts eight, Rhode-Island and Providence Plantations one, Connecticut five, New-York six, New Jersey four, Pennsylvania eight, Delaware one, Maryland six, Virginia ten, North Carolina five, South Carolina five, and Georgia three.

When vacancies happen in the Representation from any State, the Executive Authority thereof shall issue Writs of Election to fill such Vacancies.

The House of Representatives shall chuse their Speaker and other Officers; and shall have the sole Power of Impeachment.

Section 3. The Senate of the United States shall be composed of two Senators from each State, chosen by the Legislature thereof, for six Years; and each Senator shall have one Vote.

Immediately after they shall be assembled in Consequence of the first Election, they shall be divided as equally as may be into three Classes. The Seats of the Senators of the first Class shall be vacated at the Expiration of the second Year, of the second Class at the Expiration of the fourth Year, and the third Class at the Expiration of the sixth Year, so that one third may be chosen every second Year; and if Vacancies happen by Resignation, or otherwise, during the Recess of the Legislature of any State, the Executive thereof may make temporary Appointments until the next Meeting of the Legislature, which shall then fill such Vacancies.

No Person shall be a Senator who shall not have attained to the Age of thirty Years, and been nine Years a Citizen of the United States and who shall not, when elected, be an Inhabitant of that State for which he shall be chosen.

The Vice President of the United States shall be President of the Senate, but shall have no Vote, unless they be equally divided.

The Senate shall chuse their other Officers, and also a President pro tempore, in the Absence of the Vice President, or when he shall exercise the Office of President of the United States.

The Senate shall have the sole Power to try all Impeachments. When sitting for that Purpose, they shall be on Oath of Affirmation. When the President of the United States is tried, the Chief Justice shall preside: And no Person shall be convicted without the Concurrence of two thirds of the Members present.

Judgment in Cases of Impeachment shall not extend further than to removal from Office, and disqualification to hold and enjoy any Office of Honor, Trust or Profit under the United States: but the Party convicted shall nevertheless be liable and subject to Indictment, Trial, Judgment and Punishment, according to Law.

Section 4. The Times, Places and Manner of holding Elections for Senators and Representatives, shall be prescribed in each State by the Legislature thereof; but the Congress may at any time by Law make or alter such Regulations, except as to the Places of chusing Senators.

The Congress shall assemble at least once in every Year, and such Meeting shall be on the first Monday in December, unless they shall by Law appoint a different Day.

Section 5. Each House shall be the Judge of the Elections, Returns and Qualifications of its own Members, and a Majority of each shall constitute a Quorum to do Business; but a smaller Number may adjourn from day to day, and may be authorized to compel the Attendance of absent Members, in such Manner, and under such Penalties as each House may provide.

Each House may determine the Rules of its Proceedings, punish its Members for disorderly Behaviour, and, with the Concurrence of two thirds, expel a Member.

Each House shall keep a Journal of its Proceedings, and from time to time publish the same, excepting such Parts as may in their Judgment require Secrecy; and the Yeas and Nays of the Members of either House on any question shall, at the Desire of one fifth of those Present, be entered on the Journal.

Neither House, during the Session of Congress, shall, without the Consent of the other, adjourn for more than three days, nor to any other Place than that in which the two Houses shall be sitting.

Section 6. The Senators and Representatives shall receive a Compensation for their Services, to be ascertained by Law, and paid out of the Treasury of the United States. They shall in all Cases, except Treason, Felony and Breach of the Peace, be privileged from Arrest during their Attendance at the Session of their respective Houses, and in going to and returning from the same; and for any Speech or Debate in either House, they shall not be questioned in any other Place.

No Senator or Representative shall, during the Time for which he was elected, be appointed to any civil Office under the Authority of the United States, which shall have been created, or the Emoluments whereof shall have been encreased during such time: and no Person holding any Office under the United States, shall be a Member of either House during his Continuance in Office.

Section 7. All Bills for raising Revenue shall originate in the House of Representatives; but the Senate may propose or concur with Amendments as on other Bills.

Every Bill which shall have passed the House of Representatives and the Senate, shall, before it become a Law, be presented to the President of the United States; if he approve he shall sign it, but if not he shall return it, with his Objections to that House in which it shall have originated, who shall enter the Objections at large on their Journal, and proceed to reconsider it. If after such Reconsideration two thirds of that House shall agree to pass the Bill, it shall be sent, together with the Objections, to the other House, by which it shall likewise be reconsidered, and if approved by two thirds of that House, it shall become a Law. But in all such Cases the Votes of both Houses shall be determined by Yeas and Nays, and the Names of the Persons voting for and against the Bill shall be entered on the Journal of each House respectively. If any Bill shall not be returned by the President within ten Days (Sundays excepted) after it shall have been presented to him, the Same shall be a Law, in like Manner as if he had signed it, unless the Congress by their Adjournment prevent its Return, in which Case it shall not be a Law.

Every Order, Resolution, or Vote to which the Concurrence of the Senate and House of Representatives may be necessary (except on a question of Adjournment) shall be presented to the President of the United States; and before the Same shall take Effect, shall be approved by him, or being disapproved by him, shall be repassed by two thirds of the Senate and House of Representatives, according to the Rules and Limitations prescribed in the Case of a Bill.

Sections 1 to 7 of Article I define the composition of the Congress, the qualifications of its members, and the manner in which it will conduct its business.

No absolute limit was placed on the number of members of the House, but in 1913 Congress limited the membership to 435. The clause requiring that senators be chosen by their respective state legislatures was superseded by the 17th Amendment (1913), which requires the popular election of senators.

The Senate is entrusted with the power of trying all impeachments; specific directions are given as to how the trial shall be conducted and as to the impact of its judgment. The House alone has the power to impeach, however.

Significantly, there have been few impeachments, giving some credence to Thomas Jefferson's view that "experience has already shown that the impeachment the Constitution has provided is not even a scarecrow. It is a cumbersome, archaic process. . . ." The later experience of President Nixon, however, showed the threat of impeachment to be more than a scarecrow.

Although each house is to be the judge of the elections and qualifications of its members, the Supreme Court has held, in a case involving the seating of Adam Clayton POWELL in 1969, that "the Constitution leaves the House without authority to exclude any person, duly elected by his constituents, who meets all the requirements for membership expressly prescribed" in the Constitution.

The privileges and immunities of members of Congress detailed in Section 6 have come under close judicial scrutiny in recent years. The Supreme Court has supported a broad view of congressional immunity, particularly with respect to the speech or debate clause:

The speech, or debate, clause was designed to assure a coequal branch of the government wide freedom of speech, debate and deliberation without intimidation or threats from the executive branch. It thus protects members against prosecutions that directly impinge upon or threaten the legislative process.

The provision of Section 7, paragraph 3, that every resolution be presented to the president before it takes effect, has permitted the growth of a special use of the "concurrent resolution." It is now commonly accepted that the constitutional provision requires the president's approval only to give a resolution the force of law. Consequently, the concurrent resolution has been employed as a means of controlling or recovering power delegated by Congress to the president. For example, Congress has delegated power to the president to reorganize executive agencies on the condition that his orders may be vetoed within a prescribed time by a concurrent resolution.

Section 8. The Congress shall have Power To lay and collect Taxes, Duties, Imposts and Excises, to pay the Debts and provide for the common Defence and general Welfare of the United States; but all Duties, Imposts and Excises shall be uniform throughout the United States;

To borrow Money on the credit of the United States;

To regulate Commerce with foreign Nations, and among the several States, and with the Indian Tribes;

To establish an uniform Rule of Naturalization, and uniform Laws on the subject of Bankruptcies throughout the United States;

To coin Money, regulate the Value thereof, and of foreign Coin, and fix the Standard of Weights and Measures;

To provide for the Punishment of counterfeiting the Securities and current Coin of the United States;

To establish Post Offices and post Roads;

To promote the Progress of Science and useful Arts, by securing for limited Times to Authors and Inventors the exclusive Right to their respective Writings and Discoveries;

To constitute Tribunals inferior to the supreme Court;

To define and punish Piracies and Felonies committed on the high Seas, and Offences against the Law of Nations;

To declare War, grant Letters of Marque and Reprisal, and make Rules concerning Captures on Land and Water;

To raise and support Armies, but no Appropriation of Money to that Use shall be for a longer Term than two Years;

To provide and maintain a Navy;

To make Rules for the Government and Regulation of the land and naval Forces;

To provide for calling forth the Militia to execute the Laws of the Union, suppress Insurrections and repel Invasions;

To provide for organizing, arming, and disciplining, the Militia, and for governing such Part of them as may be employed in the Service of the United States, reserving to the States respectively, the Appointment of the Officers, and the Authority of training the Militia according to the discipline prescribed by Congress;

To exercise exclusive Legislation in all Cases whatsoever, over such District (not exceeding ten Miles square) as may, by Cession of particular States, and the Acceptance of Congress, become the Seat of the Government of the United States, and to exercise like Authority over all Places purchased by the Consent of the Legislature of the State in which the Same shall be, for the Erection of Forts, Magazines, Arsenals, dock-Yards, and other needful Buildings;—And

To make all Laws which shall be necessary and proper for carrying into Execution the foregoing Powers, and all other Powers vested by this Constitution in the Government of the United States, or in any Department or Officer thereof.

The framers of the Constitution undoubtedly believed that the legislative power of Congress was originally limited to the 17 specific areas listed in Article I, Section 8, plus whatever was necessary and proper for carrying them out. As John Marshall wrote for the Supreme Court in 1819,

This government is acknowledged by all to be one of enumerated powers. The principle, that it can exercise only the power granted to it, would seem too apparent to have required to be enforced by all those arguments, which its enlightened friends, while it was depending before the people, found it necessary to urge. That principle is now universally admitted.

Marshall, however, added two important corollaries to constitutional doctrine, both of which have markedly influenced constitutional interpretation. The first corollary is that "the government of the Union, though limited to its powers, is supreme within its sphere of action." In other words, where Congress has the power to act, its actions take precedence over state actions. The second corollary is that the "necessary and proper" clause in paragraph 18 should be broadly construed to provide Congress "some choice of means of legislation, not strained and compressed within the narrow limits for which gentlemen contend." In practice, these corollaries have given Congress clear advantages in the continuing struggle for power between the national and state governments.

Experience has shown that the enumerated powers of Section 8 do not include all matters in which congressional action might be needed. Congress has been granted other specific powers in several amendments. For example, the 13th, 14th, and 15th amendments assure citizens of several basic rights, and all three provide that "Congress shall have power to enforce this article by appropriate legislation."

For the most part, however, the power of the national government has been expanded not by breaching the doctrine of enumerated powers as it pertains to Congress, but rather by broad interpretation of those specific powers, notably the power to regulate commerce, and by a liberal interpretation of the "necessary and proper" clause.

A common misconception about the U.S. political system is that Congress has the constitutional power to legislate virtually anything it deems to be for the general welfare. It is true that the Constitution gives Congress "the power to lay and collect Taxes, Duties, Imposts and excises, to pay the Debts and provide for the common Defence and general Welfare of the United States," but this is different from giving Congress the power to legislate freely for the general welfare. Indeed, if Congress did have such a power, there would be no need to grant other enumerated powers. Congress's power to provide for the general welfare is limited to taxing and spending. Whereas these powers are considerable, clearly a great difference exists between the power to compel and the power to entice by the offer of money. Congress may try to entice the states to do something in, for example, the field of education by means of subsidies or grants, but it cannot compel them to accept the enticements.

One of the great controversies about the exercise of congressional power has been over the extent to which Congress may delegate its powers to the president and others. In the days of the NEW DEAL, in the 1930s, the Supreme Court put some checks on Congress's growing proclivity to delegate power. It held that Congress could only delegate power if it circumscribed the delegation "within prescribed limits and the determination of facts to which the policy as declared by the legislature is to apply." The question is no longer hotly discussed on the national level, partly because Congress is now careful to set standards when it delegates power, and partly because the Court has grown more permissive. On the state and municipal levels, however, delegation remains a lively issue, probably because judges feel uneasy about delegating power to government officials of less than national stature.

The question of Congress's power to investigate has also aroused considerable controversy. The Supreme Court has held that this power is inherent in Congress's power to legislate and to oversee the executive branch. From time to time the Court has limited the power, when it determined that the congressional investigation served no legitimate legislative purpose, or encroached on 1st Amendment rights of witnesses, or was tantamount to punishment without judicial trial.

Section 9. The Migration or Importation of such Persons as any of the States now existing shall think proper to admit, shall not be prohibited by the Congress prior to the Year one thousand eight hundred and eight, but a Tax or duty may be imposed on such Importation, not exceeding ten dollars for each Person.

The Privilege of the Writ of Habeas Corpus shall not be suspended, unless when in Cases of Rebellion or Invasion the public Safety may require it.

No Bill of Attainder or ex post facto Law shall be passed.

No Capitation, or other direct, Tax shall be laid, unless in Proportion to the Census or Enumeration herein before directed to be taken.

No Tax or Duty shall be laid on Articles exported from any State.

No Preference shall be given by any Regulation of Commerce or Revenue to the Ports of one State over those of another: nor shall Vessels bound to, or from, one State, be obliged to enter, clear or pay Duties in another.

No Money shall be drawn from the Treasury, but in Consequence of Appropriations made by Law; and a regular Statement and Account of Receipts and Expenditures of all public Money shall be published from time to time.

No Title of Nobility shall be granted by the United States: And no Person holding any Office of Profit or Trust under them, shall, without the Consent of the Congress, accept of any present, Emolument, Office, or Title, of any kind whatever, from any King, Prince, or foreign State.

Section 10. No State shall enter into any Treaty, Alliance, or Confederation; grant Letters of Marque and Reprisal; coin Money; emit Bills of Credit; make any Thing but gold and silver Coin a Tender in Payment of Debts; pass any Bill of Attainder, ex post facto Law, or Law impairing the Obligation of Contracts, or grant any Title of Nobility.

No State shall, without the Consent of the Congress, lay any Imposts or Duties on Imports or Exports, except what may be absolutely necessary for executing it's inspection Laws: and the net Produce of all Duties and Imposts, laid by any State on Imports or Exports, shall be for the Use of the Treasury of the United States; and all such Laws shall be subject to the Revision and Controul of the Congress.

No State shall, without the Consent of Congress, lay any Duty of Tonnage, keep Troops, or Ships of War in time of Peace, enter into any Agreement or Compact with another State, or with a foreign Power, or engage in War, unless actually invaded, or in such imminent Danger as will not admit of delay.

Besides enumerating the powers granted to Congress, the framers wanted to make clear what Congress was expressly forbidden to do. The prohibitions they selected reflect the high value they placed on civil liberty and private property. It is no exaggeration to say that the writt of HABEAS CORPUS is the most important single safeguard of personal liberty known to Anglo-American law; here, the Constitution explicitly permits its suspension only in "Cases of Rebellion or Invasion [when] the public Safety may require it."

Although the ex post facto law prohibition was later interpreted to apply only to criminal law, it was once seen as a means of protecting property holders from arbitrary government seizure of their property. Similarly, the prohibition against bills of attainder and the requirement that capitation and direct taxes be apportioned were seen as protections of property rights.

Limiting Congress to enumerated powers entailed the corollary that "the powers not delegated to the United States... are reserved to the States respectively, or to the people," in the words of the 10th Amendment. Consequently, if in the interest of maintaining a viable federal system it was necessary to forbid the states to exercise certain powers, these had to be spelled out; Section 10 does so.

It is noteworthy that the prohibition against bills of attainder and ex post facto laws is extended to the states. The prohibition of laws "impairing the Obligation of Contracts" is even more significant. By extending the meaning of the word contract to include public grants of land, exemptions from taxation, and charters of corporations, the Supreme Court once provided property owners with a barrier against the power of states to protect public health, safety, and morals. Later, the Court decided that a state had no right to bargain away this power. Consequently, the contract clause may no longer be used to protect vested interests.

ARTICLE II

Section 1. The executive Power shall be vested in a President of the United States of America. He shall hold his Office during the Term of four Years, and, together with the Vice President, chosen for the same Term, be elected, as follows:

Each State shall appoint, in such Manner as the Legislature thereof may direct, a Number of Electors, equal to the whole Number of Senators and Representatives to which the State may be entitled in the Congress: but no Senator or Representative, or Person holding an Office of Trust or Profit under the United States, shall be appointed an Elector.

The Electors shall meet in their respective States, and vote by Ballot for two Persons, of whom one at least shall not be an Inhabitant of the same State with themselves. And they shall make a List of all the Persons voted for, and of the Number of Votes for each; which List they shall sign and certify, and transmit sealed to the Seat of the Government of the United States, directed to the President of the Senate. The President of the Senate shall, in the Presence of the Senate and House of Representatives, open all the Certificates, and the Votes shall then be counted. The Person having the greatest Number of Votes shall be the President, if such Number be a Majority of the whole Number of Electors appointed; and if there be more than one who have such Majority, and have an equal Number of Votes, then the House of Representatives shall immediately chuse by Ballot one of them for President; and if no Person have a Majority, then from the five highest on the List the said House shall in like Manner chuse the President. But in chusing the President, the Votes shall be taken by States, the Representation from each State having one Vote; A quorum for this Purpose shall consist of a Member or Members from two thirds of the States, and a Majority of all the States shall be necessary to a Choice. In every Case, after the Choice of the President, the Person having the greatest Number of Votes of the Electors shall be the Vice President. But if there should remain two or more who have equal Votes, the Senate shall chuse from them by Ballot the Vice President.

The Congress may determine the Time of chusing the Electors, and the Day on which they shall give their Votes; which Day shall be the same throughout the United States.

No Person except a natural born Citizen, or a Citizen of the United States, at the time of the Adoption of this Constitution, shall be eligible to the Office of President; neither shall any Person be eligible to that Office who shall not have attained to the Age of thirty five Years, and been fourteen Years a Resident within the United States.

In Case of the Removal of the President from Office, or of his Death, Resignation, or Inability to discharge the Powers and Duties of the said Office, the Same shall devolve on the Vice President, and the Congress may by Law provide for the Case of Removal, Death, Resignation or Inability, both of the President and Vice President, declaring what Officer shall then act as President, and such Officer shall act accordingly, until the Disability be removed, or a President shall be elected.

The President shall, at stated Times, receive for his Services, a Compensation, which shall neither be encreased nor diminished during the Period for which he shall have been elected, and he shall not receive within that Period any other Emolument from the United States, or any of them.

Before he enter on the Execution of his Office, he shall take the following Oath or Affirmation:—"I do solemnly swear (or affirm) that I will faithfully execute the Office of President of the United States, and will to the best of my Ability, preserve, protect and defend the Constitution of the United States."

A perennial difficulty in the constitutional interpretation of presidential power is the meaning of the first sentence of Article II: "The executive Power shall be vested in a President of the United States of America." What is executive power? Presidents have held differing views of the powers inherent in their office. William Howard Taft took the view that the president had only the powers expressly given him in the other sections of Article II. In contrast, Theodore Roosevelt held that by virtue of the opening sentence of Article II the president, as steward of all the people, could do anything on behalf of the people that was not expressly denied him in the Constitution. On several momentous occasions Franklin D. Roosevelt asserted the power to do things expressly forbidden by the Constitution. For example, before the United States entered World War II, he traded some old destroyers to Britain in exchange for military bases, although Article IV, Section 3 of the Constitution gives Congress the exclusive power to dispose of property belonging to the United States. Abraham Lincoln also suggested that a president must occasionally suspend part of the Constitution to preserve the whole.

Section 1 of Article II describes the electoral college system for electing the president. Paragraph 3 was superseded by the 12th Amendment. Paragraph 6 suggests that a president who is unable to discharge his powers and duties may be removed from office. The inadequacies of this provision became a matter of concern in the 20th century; both Woodrow Wilson and Dwight Eisenhower were ill and clearly unable to function for a time. The 25th Amendment, passed in 1967, spells out a procedure for relieving a disabled president.

Section 2. The President shall be Commander in Chief of the Army and Navy of the United States, and of the Militia of the several States, when called into the actual Service of the United States; he may require the Opinion, in writing, of the principal Officer in each of the executive Departments, upon any Subject relating to the Duties of their respective Offices, and he shall have Power to grant Reprieves and Pardons for Offences against the United States, except in Cases of Impeachment.

He shall have Power, by and with the Advice and Consent of the Senate, to make Treaties, provided two thirds of the Senators present concur; and he shall nominate, and by and with the Advice and Consent of the Senate, shall appoint Ambassadors, other public Ministers and Consuls, Judges of the supreme Court, and all other Officers of the United States, whose Appointments are not herein otherwise provided for, and which shall be established by Law: but the Congress may by Law vest the Appointment of such inferior Officers, as they think proper, in the President alone, in the Courts of Law, or in the Heads of Departments.

The President shall have Power to fill up all Vacancies that may happen during the Recess of the Senate, by granting Commissions which shall expire at the End of their next Session.

Section 3. He shall from time to time give to the Congress Information of the State of the Union, and recommend to their Consideration such Measures as he shall judge necessary and expedient; he may, on extraordinary Occasions, convene both Houses, or either of them, and in Case of Disagreement between them, with Respect to the Time of Adjournment, he may adjourn them to such Time as he shall think proper; he shall receive Ambassadors and other public Ministers; he shall take Care that the Laws be faithfully executed, and shall Commission all the Officers of the United States.

Section 4. The President, Vice President and all civil Officers of the United States, shall be removed from Office on Impeachment for, and Conviction of, Treason, Bribery, or other high Crimes and Misdemeanors.

Part of the controversy over presidential power turns on the question of what additional powers, if any, are inherent in the president's role as commander in chief. This issue becomes even more complicated when presidents take extraordinary actions in time of war or contend that they may legitimately claim extra power by combining the powers of the chief executive and the commander in chief. The Supreme Court scrutinized this question in YOUNGSTOWN SHEET AND TUBE CO. V. SAWYER (1952) and decided that the Korean War emergency did not give President Harry S. Truman the right to seize steel companies that were on strike.

Greater controversy has arisen over whether the president may commit the nation's armed forces to war without a congressional declaration of war, although the Constitution states that "the congress shall have Power ... To declare War." Many have argued that the United States should not have become involved in hostilities in Korea and Vietnam without a declaration of war. In 1973, Congress passed the War Powers Resolution over President Nixon's veto. With some qualifications, the resolution permits the president to commit the armed forces "into hostilities or into situations where imminent involvement in hostilities is clearly indicated by the circumstances" in specified emergencies for a period of 60 days without specific authorization from Congress. Congress reserves the power to terminate the action earlier if it sees fit to do so.

The Constitution gives the president the power to make treaties with the advice and consent of the Senate. It is important to note that the president frequently negotiates agreements with other governments that are not referred to the Senate for its advice and consent. Two kinds of executive agreements are made: those which the president is authorized by Congress to make, or which he lays before Congress for approval and implementation; and those which he enters into simply by virtue of his diplomatic powers and his powers as commander in chief. The line between executive agreements and treaties is difficult to define. Congress has often been uneasy about what many conceive to be a presidential method of avoiding advice and consent.

Although the president is endowed by the Constitution with considerable power to appoint officials, nothing is explicitly said about his power to remove them. Arguably, the power to remove may be considered part of the power to appoint, although Supreme Court decisions have narrowed the president's removal power to "purely executive officers," not including commissioners of independent regulatory commissions or the War Claims Commission.

Presidents have long asserted EXECUTIVE PRIVILEGE, that is, the privilege of withholding testimony about confidential conversations between a president and his close advisers. In UNITED STATES V. RICHARD M. NIXON *(1974), the Supreme Court held that executive privilege does exist but that it is not absolute. In cases where "the legitimate needs of the judicial process outweigh presidential privilege," the privilege must give way. The Court did not speak to the question of whether or not the privilege would have to give way in a congressional hearing; it spoke only of the judicial process.*

ARTICLE III

Section 1. The judicial Power of the United States, shall be vested in one supreme Court, and in such inferior Courts as the Congress may from time to time ordain and establish. The Judges, both of the supreme and inferior Courts, shall hold their Offices during good Behaviour, and shall, at stated Times, receive for their Services, a Compensation, which shall not be diminished during their Continuance in Office.

Nowhere in the Constitution is the Supreme Court explicitly granted the power of judicial review, that is, the power to declare acts of Congress and state legislatures and the actions of national and state officials unconstitutional and to reverse the decisions of state courts on constitutional questions. The power accorded to the Supreme Court is tersely described in Article III as "the judicial Power"; the institution of judicial review has grown out of the interpretation of that power. The initiative was seized by Chief Justice Marshall in MARBURY V. MADISON *(1803), who took upon himself the power to interpret the Constitution as necessary to reach a decision in the case.*

Judicial review has become an integral part of the U.S. political system, and it would take nothing less than a constitutional amendment to do away with it. A lively dispute, however, has been going on throughout U.S. history about the extent to which the power should be exercised. Some believe in judicial self-restraint—that is, that the Court should assume that the acts and actions of coordinate departments of the national government and of state governments are constitutional unless it is convincingly demonstrated that they are not. Others, who are often called judicial activists, feel that the Court should be quick to exercise the power of review. They assert that they too believe in judicial self-restraint as a general proposition, but they maintain that when it comes to important rights, the Constitution itself requires that the acts and actions of others should not be assumed constitutional.

Section 2. The judicial Power shall extend to all Cases, in Law and Equity, arising under this Constitution, the Laws of the United States, and Treaties made, or which shall be made, under their Authority;—to all Cases affecting Ambassadors, other public Ministers and Consuls;—to all Cases of admiralty and maritime Jurisdiction;—to Controversies to which the United States shall be a Party;—to Controversies between two or more States;—between a State and Citizens of another State;—between Citizens of different States;—between Citizens of the same State claiming Lands under Grants of different States, and between a State, or the Citizens thereof, and foreign States, Citizens or Subjects.

In all Cases affecting Ambassadors, other public Ministers

and Consuls, and those in which a State shall be Party, the supreme Court shall have original Jurisdiction. In all the other Cases before mentioned, the supreme Court shall have appellate Jurisdiction, both as to Law and Fact, with such Exceptions, and under such Regulations as the Congress shall make.

The Trial of all Crimes, except in Cases of Impeachment, shall be by Jury; and such Trial shall be held in the State where the said Crimes shall have been committed; but when not committed within any State, the Trial shall be at such Place or Places as the Congress may by Law have directed.

Section 3. Treason against the United States, shall consist only in levying War against them, or in adhering to their Enemies, giving them Aid and Comfort. No Person shall be convicted of Treason unless on the Testimony of two Witnesses to the same overt Act, or on Confession in open Court.

The Congress shall have Power to declare the Punishment of Treason, but no Attainder of Treason shall work Corruption of Blood, or Forfeiture except during the Life of the Person attainted.

Section 2 of Article III concerns jurisdiction of the courts. Jurisdiction is the authority of a court to exercise judicial power in a particular case. As indicated earlier, Congress may not enlarge or diminish the power that the Constitution vests in the courts. But Congress is granted vast power in Section 2 with respect to the jurisdiction of the Supreme Court. Paragraph 2 of that section indicates the relatively few cases in which the Supreme Court shall have original jurisdiction (the power to be the first court to hear a case), but provides that "in all other Cases before mentioned, the Supreme Court shall have appellate Jurisdiction, both as to Law and Fact, with such Exceptions, and under such Regulations as the Congress shall make."

Thus, there is no doubt that Congress has the constitutional authority to enlarge or diminish the Court's appellate jurisdiction (its power to review decisions of lower courts). Congress sometimes tries to curtail the appellate jurisdiction of the Court, especially when it is unhappy with recent Court decisions. Such efforts may be unwise, but they are not unconstitutional.

ARTICLE IV

Section 1. Full Faith and Credit shall be given in each State to the public Acts, Records, and judicial Proceedings of every other State. And the Congress may by general Laws prescribe the Manner in which such Acts, Records, and Proceedings shall be proved, and the Effect thereof.

Despite the apparent simplicity and clarity of this provision, it has been the source of an enormous amount of litigation on highly technical grounds, so much so that Justice Robert H. Jackson, in writing about it, called it "the Lawyer's Clause of the Constitution."

This clause is invoked most often today in divorce cases in which one of the spouses goes to another state to obtain the divorce, and in workers' compensation cases in which the employment contract is drawn up in one state and the employee is injured in another state. Not only is there a question of which state's court has jurisdiction and what credit the other state's court should give to the first one's judgment, a question also exists about which state's law should take precedence when laws conflict.

Section 2. The Citizens of each State shall be entitled to all Privileges and Immunities of Citizens in the several States.

A Person charged in any State with Treason, Felony, or other Crime, who shall flee from Justice, and be found in another State, shall on Demand of the executive Authority of the State from which he fled, be delivered up, to be removed to the State having Jurisdiction of the Crime.

No Person held to Service or Labour in one State, under the Laws thereof, escaping into another, shall, in Consequence of any Law or Regulation therein, be discharged from such Service or Labour, but shall be delivered up on Claim of the Party to whom such Service or Labour may be due.

Section 3. New States may be admitted by the Congress into this Union; but no new States shall be formed or erected within the Jurisdiction of any other State; nor any State be formed by the Junction of two or more States, or Parts of States, without the Consent of the Legislatures of the States concerned as well as of the Congress.

The Congress shall have Power to dispose of and make all needful Rules and Regulations respecting the Territory or other Property belonging to the United States; and nothing in this Constitution shall be so construed as to Prejudice any Claims of the United States, or of any particular State.

Section 4. The United States shall guarantee to every State in this Union a Republican Form of Government, and shall protect each of them against Invasion; and on Application of the Legislature, or of the Executive (when the Legislature cannot be convened) against domestic Violence.

Although theories have conflicted about the privileges and immunities clause of Section 2, paragraph 1 (plus another in the 14th Amendment), it has become settled doctrine that the clause only forbids a state from discriminating against citizens of other states in favor of its own. But there are certain privileges and immunities for which a state, as parens patriae, may require a previous residence, such as the right to fish in its streams, to hunt game in its fields and forests, to divert its waters, or even to engage in certain businesses of a quasi-public nature, such as insurance.

Paragraph 2 deals with extradition. By a 1793 act of Congress, this responsibility was delegated to the governors of the states. But the Supreme Court later ruled that while the duty is a legal one, its performance cannot be compelled by writ of mandamus. Consequently, governors of states have often refused compliance when, in their opinion, substantial justice required such refusal. Section 3, paragraph 2, clearly gives Congress the sole power to dispose of and make rules respecting territory or other properties, a provision that Franklin D. Roosevelt ignored when he exchanged U.S. destroyers for British military bases.

ARTICLE V

The Congress, whenever two thirds of both Houses shall deem it necessary, shall propose Amendments to this Constitution, or, on the Application of the Legislatures of two thirds of the several States, shall call a Convention for proposing Amendments, which, in either Case, shall be valid to all Intents and Purposes, as Part of this Constitution, when ratified by the Legislatures of three fourths of the several States, or by Conventions in three fourths thereof, as the one or the other Mode of Ratification may be proposed by the Congress; Provided that no Amendment which may be made prior to the Year One thousand eight hundred and eight shall in any Manner affect the first and fourth Clauses in the Ninth Section of the first Article; and that no State, without its Consent, shall be deprived of its equal Suffrage in the Senate.

Although a movement to call a constitutional convention to approve an amendment requiring a balanced federal budget gained temporary momentum in 1979, only the first method of proposing amendments has ever been applied successfully.

All proposals, except the one to repeal the 18th Amendment, have been referred to state legislatures. In that one instance, Congress prescribed that the proposal should be ratified by popularly elected conventions chosen especially for the purpose, but it left the details of their summoning to the several state legislatures. What resulted in most states was a popular referendum; the conventions were made up almost entirely of delegates previously pledged to vote for or against the proposed amendment.

During the controversy in the 1970s over ratification of the proposed Equal Rights Amendment, the perennial question arose as to whether a state legislature that has ratified an amendment may later reconsider its vote before the amendment is ratified by three-fourths of the state legislatures. This question has not been definitively settled. In passing a resolution in 1978 to extend the deadline for ratification of the amendment, however, the Senate specifically rejected an amendment to allow the states to rescind earlier ERA ratification.

The first of the two exceptions to the amending power became obsolete in 1808. The second, that "no State, without its Consent, shall be deprived of its equal Suffrage in the Senate," explains why the Senate is the only legislative body in the United States whose composition is exempt from the Supreme Court's one-man, one-vote ruling in Reynolds v. Sims (1964).

ARTICLE VI

All Debts contracted and Engagements entered into, before the Adoption of this Constitution, shall be as valid against the United States under this Constitution, as under the Confederation.

This Constitution, and the Laws of the United States which shall be made in Pursuance thereof; and all Treaties made, or which shall be made, under the Authority of the United States, shall be the supreme Law of the Land; and the Judges in every State shall be bound thereby, any Thing in the Constitution or Laws of any State to the Contrary notwithstanding.

The Senators and Representatives before mentioned, and the Members of the several State Legislatures, and all executive and judicial Officers, both of the United States and of the several States, shall be bound by Oath or Affirmation, to support this Constitution; but no religious Test shall ever be required as a Qualification to any Office or public Trust under the United States.

The paragraph containing the supremacy clause has been called the linchpin of the Constitution because it combines the national government and the states into one governmental system, one federal state. It indicates that although the powers of the national government may be strictly enumerated, they are supreme over any conflicting state powers whatsoever.

Accordingly, when a conflict occurs between national and state law, the only question to be answered is, ordinarily, whether the former represents a fair exercise of Congress's power.

ARTICLE VII

The Ratification of the Conventions of nine States, shall be sufficient for the Establishment of this Constitution between the States so ratifying the Same.

Done in Convention by the Unanimous Consent of the States present the Seventeenth Day of September in the Year of our Lord one thousand seven hundred and Eighty seven and of the Independence of the United States of America the Twelfth

In witness whereof We have hereunto subscribed our Names,

G. Washington–Presidt. and deputy from Virginia
New Hampshire: John Langdon, Nicholas Gilman
Massachusetts: Nathaniel Gorham, Rufus King
Connecticut: Wm: Saml. Johnson, Roger Sherman
New York: Alexander Hamilton
New Jersey: Wil: Livingston, David Brearly, Wm. Paterson, Jona: Dayton
Pennsylvania: B. Franklin, Thomas Mifflin, Robt. Morris, Geo. Clymer, Thos. FitzSimons, Jared Ingersoll, James Wilson, Gouv Morris
Delaware: Geo: Read, Gunning Bedford jun, John Dickinson, Richard Bassett, Jaco: Broom
Maryland: James McHenry, Dan of St Thos. Jenifer, Danl Carroll
Virginia: John Blair—, James Madison Jr.
North Carolina: Wm. Blount, Richd. Dobbs Spaight, Hu Williamson
South Carolina: J. Rutledge, Charles Cotesworth Pinckney, Charles Pinckney, Pierce Butler
Georgia: William Few, Abr Baldwin

The Articles of Confederation provided for their own amendment only by the unanimous consent of the 13-state legislature. The Constitution, however, was to take effect upon being ratified by conventions in only nine states. In the legal sense, this was an act of revolution.

AMENDMENTS TO THE CONSTITUTION OF THE UNITED STATES

AMENDMENT I

Congress shall make no law respecting an establishment of religion, or prohibiting the free exercise thereof; or abridging the freedom of speech, or of the press; or the right of the people peaceably to assemble, and to petition the Government for a redress of grievances.

AMENDMENT II

A well regulated Militia, being necessary to the security of a free State, the right of the people to keep and bear Arms, shall not be infringed.

AMENDMENT III

No Soldier shall, in time of peace be quartered in any house, without the consent of the Owner, nor in time of war, but in a manner to be prescribed by law.

AMENDMENT IV

The right of the people to be secure in their persons, houses, papers, and effects, against unreasonable searches and seizures, shall not be violated, and no Warrants shall issue, but upon probable cause, supported by Oath or affirmation, and particularly describing the place to be searched, and the persons or things to be seized.

AMENDMENT V

No person shall be held to answer for a capital, or otherwise infamous crime, unless on a presentment or indictment of a Grand Jury, except in cases arising in the land or naval forces, or in the Militia, when in actual service in time of War or public danger; nor shall any person be subject for the same offence to be twice put in jeopardy of life or limb; nor shall be compelled in any criminal case to be a witness against himself, nor be deprived of life, liberty, or property, without due process of law; nor shall private property be taken for public use, without just compensation.

AMENDMENT VI

In all criminal prosecutions, the accused shall enjoy the right to a speedy and public trial, by an impartial jury of the State and district wherein the crime shall have been committed, which district shall have been previously ascertained by law, and to be informed of the nature and cause of the accusation; to be confronted with the witnesses against him; to have compulsory process for obtaining witnesses in his favor, and to have the Assistance of Counsel for his defence.

AMENDMENT VII

In Suits at common law, where the value in controversy shall exceed twenty dollars, the right of trial by jury shall be preserved, and no fact tried by a jury, shall be otherwise re-examined in any Court of the United States, than according to the rules of the common law.

AMENDMENT VIII

Excessive bail shall not be required, nor excessive fines imposed, nor cruel and unusual punishments inflicted.

AMENDMENT IX

The enumeration in the Constitution, of certain rights, shall not be construed to deny or disparage others retained by the people.

AMENDMENT X

The powers not delegated to the United States by the Constitution, nor prohibited by it to the States, are reserved to the States respectively, or to the people.

The first ten amendments, which make up the so-called Bill of Rights, were designed to calm the fears of the mild opponents of the Constitution in its original form. The amendments were proposed to the state legislatures by the first Congress that assembled under the Constitution in 1789 and were ratified in 1791. Some of the framers had argued that the Bill of Rights was not necessary since the national government did not in any case have the power to do what was expressly forbidden in the proposed amendments.

AMENDMENT XI

The Judicial power of the United States shall not be construed to extend to any suit in law or equity, commenced or prosecuted against one of the United States by Citizens of another State, or by Citizens or Subjects of any Foreign State.

The Supreme Court's acceptance of jurisdiction in a suit against a state by a citizen of another state in 1793 provoked such angry reactions in Georgia and such anxieties in other states that, at the first meeting of Congress after this decision, what became the 11th Amendment was proposed by an overwhelming vote and quickly ratified (1798). The amendment has afforded the states protection against suits for debts, but in other respects it has proved comparatively ineffective in protecting states' rights against federal judicial power. The Supreme Court has held that a suit is not "commenced or prosecuted" against a state by the appeal of a case that was instituted by the state itself against a defendant who claims rights under the Constitution, laws, or treaties of the United States. This permits a person to sue a state in a federal court by appealing a decision in a state court.

AMENDMENT XII

The Electors shall meet in their respective states and vote by ballot for President and Vice-President, one of whom, at least, shall not be an inhabitant of the same state with themselves; they shall name in their ballots the person voted for as President, and in distinct ballots the person voted for as Vice-President, and they shall make distinct lists of all persons voted for as President, and of all persons voted for as Vice-President, and of the number of votes for each, which lists they shall sign and certify, and transmit sealed to the seat of the government of the United States, directed to the President of the Senate;—The President of the Senate shall, in the presence of the Senate and House of Representatives, open all the certificates and the votes shall then be counted;—the person having the greatest number of votes for President, shall be the President, if such number be a majority of the whole number of Electors appointed; and if no person have such majority, then from the persons having the highest numbers not exceeding three on the list of those voted for as President, the House of Representatives shall choose immediately, by ballot, the President. But in choosing the President, the votes shall be taken by states, the representation from each state having one vote; a quorum for this purpose shall consist of a member

or members from two-thirds of the states, and a majority of all the states shall be necessary to a choice. And if the House of Representatives shall not choose a President whenever the right of choice shall devolve upon them, before the fourth day of March next following, then the Vice-President shall act as President, as in the case of the death or other constitutional disability of the President.—The person having the greatest number of votes as Vice-President, shall be the Vice-President, if such number be a majority of the whole number of Electors appointed, and if no person have a majority, then from the two highest numbers on the list, the Senate shall choose the Vice-President; a quorum for the purpose shall consist of two-thirds of the whole number of Senators, and a majority of the whole number shall be necessary to a choice. But no person constitutionally ineligible to the office of President shall be eligible to that of Vice-President of the United States.

This amendment, ratified in 1804, supersedes Article II, Section 1, paragraph 3, prescribing the operation of the Electoral College. Of particular interest is the spelling out of the process to be used in the event that no candidate receives a majority of the electoral votes.

AMENDMENT XIII

Section 1. Neither slavery nor involuntary servitude, except as a punishment for crime whereof the party shall have been duly convicted, shall exist within the United States, or any place subject to their jurisdiction.

Section 2. Congress shall have power to enforce this article by appropriate legislation.

AMENDMENT XIV

Section 1. All persons born or naturalized in the United States, and subject to the jurisdiction thereof, are citizens of the United States and of the State wherein they reside. No State shall make or enforce any law which shall abridge the privileges or immunities of citizens of the United States; nor shall any State deprive any person of life, liberty, or property, without due process of law; nor deny to any person within its jurisdiction the equal protection of the laws.

Section 2. Representatives shall be apportioned among the several States according to their respective numbers, counting the whole number of persons in each State, excluding Indians not taxed. But when the right to vote at any election for the choice of electors for President and Vice President of the United States, Representatives in Congress, the Executive and Judicial officers of a State, or the members of the Legislature thereof, is denied to any of the male inhabitants of such State, being twenty-one years of age, and citizens of the United States, or in any way abridged, except for participation in rebellion, or other crime, the basis of representation therein shall be reduced in the proportion which the number of such male citizens shall bear to the whole number of male citizens twenty-one years of age in such State.

Section 3. No person shall be a Senator or Representative in Congress, or elector of President and Vice President, or hold any office, civil or military, under the United States, or under any State, who, having previously taken an oath, as a member of Congress, or as an officer of the United States, or as a member of any State legislature, or as an executive or judicial officer of any State, to support the Constitution of the United States, shall have engaged in insurrection or rebellion against the same, or given aid or comfort to the enemies thereof. But Congress may by a vote of two-thirds of each House, remove such disability.

Section 4. The validity of the public debt of the United States, authorized by law, including debts incurred for payment of pensions and bounties for services in suppressing insurrection or rebellion, shall not be questioned. But neither the United States nor any State shall assume or pay any debt or obligation incurred in aid of insurrection or rebellion against the United States, or any claim for the loss or emancipation of any slave; but all such debts, obligations and claims shall be held illegal and void.

Section 5. The Congress shall have power to enforce, by appropriate legislation, the provisions of this article.

AMENDMENT XV

Section 1. The right of citizens of the United States to vote shall not be denied or abridged by the United States or by any State on account of race, color, or previous condition of servitude.

Section 2. The Congress shall have power to enforce this article by appropriate legislation.

The 13th, 14th, and 15th amendments are known as the RECONSTRUCTION *amendments. They were passed in the years following the Civil War in order to end slavery and guarantee blacks the right to vote and other important rights. Over the last century, however, the 14th Amendment has been gradually broadened by judicial interpretation to become an important weapon in the continuing defense of the civil rights and individual liberties of all Americans. Its "due process" clause is generally regarded as protecting almost all rights guaranteed in the Bill of Rights from state invasion. The "equal protection" clause similarly has been invoked to integrate schools, to reapportion electoral districts more equitably, and to outlaw a multitude of invidious discriminatory acts and actions.*

AMENDMENT XVI

The Congress shall have power to lay and collect taxes on incomes, from whatever source derived, without apportionment among the several States, and without regard to any census of enumeration.

AMENDMENT XVII

The Senate of the United States shall be composed of two Senators from each State, elected by the people thereof, for six years; and each Senator shall have one vote. The electors in each State shall have the qualifications requisite for electors of the most numerous branch of the State legislatures.

When vacancies happen in the representation of any State in the Senate, the executive authority of such State shall issue writs of election to fill such vacancies: *Provided,* That the legislature of any State may empower the executive thereof to make temporary appointments until the people fill the vacancies by election as the legislature may direct.

This amendment shall not be so construed as to affect the election or term of any Senator chosen before it becomes valid as part of the Constitution.

AMENDMENT XVIII

Section 1. After one year from the ratification of this article the manufacture, sale, or transportation of intoxicating liquors within, the importation thereof into, or the exportation thereof from the United States and all territory subject to the jurisdiction thereof for beverage purposes is hereby prohibited.

Section 2. The Congress and the several States shall have concurrent power to enforce this article by appropriate legislation.

Section 3. This article shall be inoperative unless it shall have been ratified as an amendment to the Constitution by the legislatures of the several States, as provided in the Constitution, within seven years from the date of the submission hereof to the States by the Congress.

AMENDMENT XIX

The right of citizens of the United States to vote shall not be denied or abridged by the United States or by any State on account of sex.

Congress shall have power to enforce this article by appropriate legislation.

AMENDMENT XX

Section 1. The terms of the President and Vice President shall end at noon on the 20th day of January, and the terms of Senators and Representatives at noon on the 3d day of January, of the years in which such terms would have ended if this article had not been ratified; and the terms of their successors shall then begin.

Section 2. The Congress shall assemble at least once in every year, and such meeting shall begin at noon on the 3d day of January, unless they shall by law appoint a different day.

Section 3. If, at the time fixed for the beginning of the term of the President, the President elect shall have died, the Vice President elect shall become President. If a President shall not have been chosen before the time fixed for the beginning of his term, or if the President elect shall have failed to qualify, then the Vice President elect shall act as President until a President shall have qualified; and the Congress may by law provide for the case wherein neither a President elect nor a Vice President elect shall have qualified, declaring who shall then act as President, or the manner in which one who is to act shall be selected, and such person shall act accordingly until a President or Vice President shall have qualified.

Section 4. The Congress may by law provide for the case of the death of any of the persons from whom the House of Representatives may choose a President whenever the right of choice shall have devolved upon them, and for the case of the death of any of the persons from whom the Senate may choose a Vice President whenever the right of choice shall have devolved upon them.

Section 5. Sections 1 and 2 shall take effect on the 15th day of October following the ratification of this article.

Section 6. This article shall be inoperative unless it shall have been ratified as an amendment to the Constitution by the legislatures of three-fourths of the several States within seven years from the date of its submission.

AMENDMENT XXI

Section 1. The eighteenth article of amendment to the Constitution of the United States is hereby repealed.

Section 2. The transportation or importation into any State, Territory, or possession of the United States for delivery or use therein of intoxicating liquors, in violation of the laws thereof, is hereby prohibited.

Section 3. This article shall be inoperative unless it shall have been ratified as an amendment to the Constitution by conventions in the several States, as provided in the Constitution, within seven years from the date of the submission hereof to the States by the Congress.

AMENDMENT XXII

Section 1. No person shall be elected to the office of the President more than twice, and no person who has held the office of President, or acted as President, for more than two years of a term to which some other person was elected President shall be elected to the office of the President more than once. But this Article shall not apply to any person holding the office of President when this Article was proposed by the Congress, and shall not prevent any person who may be holding the office of President, or acting as President, during the term within which this Article becomes operative from holding the office of President or acting as President during the remainder of such term.

Section 2. This article shall be inoperative unless it shall have been ratified as an amendment to the Constitution by the legislatures of three-fourths of the several States within seven years from the date of its submission to the States by the Congress.

AMENDMENT XXIII

Section 1. The District constituting the seat of Government of the United States shall appoint in such manner as the Congress may direct:

A number of electors of President and Vice President equal to the whole number of Senators and Representatives in Congress to which the District would be entitled if it were a State, but in no event more than the least populous State; they shall be in addition to those appointed by the States, but they shall be considered, for the purposes of the election of President and Vice President, to be electors appointed by a State; and they shall meet in the District and perform such duties as provided by the twelfth article of amendment.

Section 2. The Congress shall have power to enforce this article by appropriate legislation.

AMENDMENT XXIV

Section 1. The right of citizens of the United States to vote in any primary or other election for President or Vice President, for electors for President or Vice President, or for Senator or Representative in Congress, shall not be denied or abridged by the United States or any State by reason of failure to pay any poll tax or other tax.

Section 2. The Congress shall have power to enforce this article by appropriate legislation.

AMENDMENT XXV

Section 1. In case of the removal of the President from of-

fice or of his death or resignation, the Vice President shall become President.

Section 2. Whenever there is a vacancy in the office of the Vice President, the President shall nominate a Vice President who shall take office upon confirmation by a majority vote of both Houses of Congress.

Section 3. Whenever the President transmits to the President pro tempore of the Senate and the Speaker of the House of Representatives his written declaration that he is unable to discharge the powers and duties of his office, and until he transmits to them a written declaration to the contrary, such powers and duties shall be discharged by the Vice President as Acting President.

Section 4. Whenever the Vice President and a majority of either the principal officers of the executive departments or of such other body as Congress may by law provide, transmit to the President pro tempore of the Senate and the Speaker of the House of Representatives their written declaration that the President is unable to discharge the powers and duties of his office, the Vice President shall immediately assume the powers and duties of the office as Acting President.

Thereafter, when the President transmits to the President pro tempore of the Senate and the Speaker of the House of Representatives his written declaration that no inability exists, he shall resume the powers and duties of his office unless the Vice President and a majority of either the principal officers of the executive department or of such other body as Congress may by law provide, transmit within four days to the President pro tempore of the Senate and the Speaker of the House of Representatives their written declaration that the President is unable to discharge the powers and duties of his office. Thereupon Congress shall decide the issue, assembling within forty-eight hours for that purpose if not in session. If the Congress, within twenty-one days after receipt of the latter written declaration, or, if Congress is not in session, within twenty-one days after Congress is required to assemble, determines by two-thirds vote of both Houses that the President is unable to discharge the powers and duties of his office, the Vice President shall continue to discharge the same as Acting President; otherwise, the President shall resume the powers and duties of his office.

AMENDMENT XXVI

Section 1. The right of citizens of the United States, who are 18 years of age or older, to vote shall not be denied or abridged by the United States or any State on account of age.

Section 2. The Congress shall have the power to enforce this article by appropriate legislation.

Of the last 11 amendments to the Constitution (the 16th through the 26th), 6 deal with elections and voting. The 17th Amendment (1913) requires popular election of United States senators; the 19th (1920) gives women the right to vote; the 22d (1951) limits presidents to two terms in office; the 23d (1961) permits residents of the District of Columbia to vote for president and vice-president; the 24th (1964) prevents anyone from being denied the right to vote for failing to pay a poll tax; and the 26th (1971) extends the franchise to 18-year-olds.

Two amendments concern the prohibition of intoxicating

liquors. The 18th (1920) instituted prohibition, and the 21st (1933) repealed it.

The 16th Amendment (1913) was the direct result of an 1895 Supreme Court decision that a tax on incomes derived from property was a "direct tax" and could only be imposed by the rule of apportionment according to population. Accordingly, a constitutional amendment was required to permit a practical national income tax.

The 20th Amendment (1933) eliminated the "lame duck" problem. After every election, defeated members of Congress ("lame ducks") participated in a short session of Congress before newly elected members took office in March. This was thought to be disadvantageous. A constitutional amendment was required to change the dates on which presidents, vice-presidents, and members of Congress took office, for such a change would shorten the terms of those currently serving.

The 25th Amendment (1967) provided for removal of an incapacitated president and for filling a vacancy in the office of vice-president. The latter provision was invoked upon the resignation of Vice-President Spiro Agnew in 1973 and upon the elevation of Gerald Ford to the presidency in 1974.

PROPOSED CONSTITUTIONAL AMENDMENTS
EQUAL RIGHTS AMENDMENT

Section 1. Equality of rights under the law shall not be denied or abridged by the United States or by any State on account of sex.

Section 2. The Congress shall have the power to enforce, by appropriate legislation, the provisions of this article.

Section 3. This amendment shall take effect two years after the date of ratification.

A resolution proposing the so-called Equal Rights Amendment was passed by the Congress on Mar. 22, 1972, and submitted to the states for ratification. In 1978 the deadline for ratification was extended until June 30, 1982, at which time the amendment lacked ratification by 3 of a needed 38 states. On July 14, 1982, the amendment was reintroduced into Congress; it was defeated by the House in November 1983.

DISTRICT OF COLUMBIA AMENDMENT

Section 1. For purposes of representation in Congress, election of the President and Vice President, and Article V of this Constitution the District constituting the seat of government of the United States shall be treated as though it were a state.

Section 2. The exercise of the rights and powers conferred under this article shall be by the people of the District constituting the seat of government and as shall be provided by Congress.

Section 3. The Twenty-third Amendment to the Constitution is hereby repealed.

Section 4. This article shall be inoperative, unless it shall have been ratified as an amendment to the constitution by the legislators of three-fourths of the several states within seven years from the date of its submission.

In August 1978, Congress sent this proposed amendment to the states for ratification, calling for treating the District of Columbia as though it were a state. The amendment died in August 1985, having been ratified by only 16 of the needed 38 states.

Constitutional Convention
The Constitutional Convention, which wrote the Constitution of the United States, convened in Philadelphia on May 25, 1787. It was called by the Continental Congress and several states in response to the impending bankruptcy of Congress and a sense of emergency arising from an armed revolt—SHAYS'S REBELLION—in New England. The convention's assigned task, following proposals made at the ANNAPOLIS CONVENTION the previous September, was to formulate amendments to the ARTICLES OF CONFEDERATION. The delegates, however, immediately set about writing a new constitution.

Fifty-five delegates representing 12 states attended at least part of the sessions. Thirty-four of them were lawyers; most of the others were planters or merchants. Although George WASHINGTON, who presided, was 55, and John DICKINSON was 54, Benjamin FRANKLIN, 81, and Roger SHERMAN, 66, most of the delegates were young men in their twenties and thirties. Conspicuously absent were the radical leaders of the drive for independence in 1775–76, such as John ADAMS, Patrick HENRY, and Thomas JEFFERSON. The delegates' knowledge concerning government, both theoretical and practical, made the convention perhaps the most brilliant such gathering ever assembled.

During the first phase (May 23–July 26) the delegates developed the general outlines of a national government. They readily agreed to create a three-branch government (legislative, executive, and judicial), but the delegates were sharply divided over the basis of representation. Edmund Randolph (see RANDOLPH family) presented the so-called Virginia Plan, drawn up mainly by James MADISON, that called for a bicameral legislature with representation proportional to population, the upper house to be elected by the lower. This proposal, which clearly favored the larger states, was countered by the so-called New Jersey Plan of William Paterson (1745–1806), which provided for a unicameral legislature in which all the states were equally represented. The issue was settled by a compromise proposed by Roger Sherman and Oliver ELLSWORTH of Connecticut. A bicameral legislature was finally approved, giving the states equal representation in the upper house and basing representation in the lower on population.

During the second phase (July 27–August 6) the convention recessed while a five-man Committee of Detail organized its resolutions into the rough draft of a constitution. During the third phase (August 6–September 6) the delegates debated the committee's draft and fought over conflicting interests such as those between commerce and agriculture and between slaveholders and others. The most controversial issue was the composition of the executive branch and the means of electing the executive; this was settled on September 6 with the adoption of the ELECTORAL COLLEGE suggested by Franklin. The last phase was mainly the work of the Committee on Style, which put the document in finished form. On September 17 the Constitution was signed by 39 of the 42 delegates present.

Constitutional Union party　The Constitutional Union party was founded in 1860 by U.S. politicians trying to stem the movement toward civil war. One of the four parties fielding candidates in that year's election, it nominated John BELL for president and Edward EVERETT for vice-president. Although the party carried only Kentucky, Tennessee, and Virginia, the votes it won in other states indicated the widespread strength of sentiment to preserve the Union

constructivism　Constructivism is one of several idealist, ABSTRACT ART movements that arose in Europe and Russia between 1913 and 1920. It stressed total acceptance of technological, scientific society and the possibility of an ideal world based on the perfect functionalism of the machine.

Constructivism's main antecedent is the COLLAGE cubism of PICASSO and BRAQUE, which helped overturn conventional modes of representation. The two main currents of constructivism are represented in the works of Vladimir TATLIN and in those of the brothers Naum GABO and Antoine PEVSNER. In 1913, Tatlin made his first purely abstract relief construction of wood, metal, and glass.

After the outbreak of the Russian Revolution in 1917, Tatlin, Gabo, and Pevsner, along with Aleksandr RODCHENKO and Kasimir MALEVICH, who had founded (1915) the related school of SUPREMATISM, taught at the First State Art School in Moscow, and the new art found temporary official approval as the "true" style of the proletarian revolution. Tatlin, turning toward engineering and architecture, designed (1919) his famous *Monument to the Third International*, a leaning steel tower about 400 m (1,300 ft) high. The project was carried as far as a huge timber model in 1920. The same year, Gabo wrote and published the *Realistic Manifesto*, the chief document of constructivist art and ideas, which was also signed by Pevsner. In 1923 the principles of constructivism were introduced at the Weimar BAUHAUS by El LISSITZKY and László MOHOLY-NAGY, and exerted a lasting effect on 20th-century art.

Russian constructivist literature was related to the more prominent Western art movement called FUTURISM. Such literary constructivists as Vladimir MAYAKOVSKY wrote political poetry and set it in wild, eccentric type, while other writers experimented with documentary descriptions they called factographs, in the belief that these compendiums would replace the novel.

In the postrevolutionary Russian theater such directors as Vsevolod MEYERHOLD and Sergei EISENSTEIN created new, efficient systems (biomechanics) of acting and training based on machinelike movements. Using nonrepresentational sets, they staged mechanized, often comic, performances that suggested huge functioning machines. Meyerhold's staging of *The Magnificent Cuckold* in 1922 became world famous.

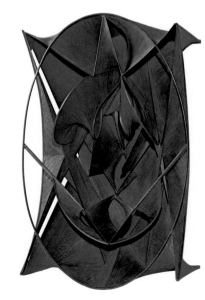

Antoine Pevsner's Oval Fresco (1945), an abstract assemblage of bronze and oxidized tin, is typical of his constructivist works. The precise manipulation of free and enclosed space illustrates the two major characteristics of constructivism. (Stedelijk Museum, Amsterdam.)

consul (ancient Roman history) [kahn'-sul]　The consuls, in Roman history, were the two principal magistrates of Rome under the republic, equal in power and holding supreme authority in all civil and military matters. Elected by the *comitia centuriata* for one year, they could not be reelected for ten years. Both were chosen from among the PATRICIANS until 367 BC, after which one was elected from the PLEBEIANS. They had usually served previously as quaestor, aedile, and praetor. The office is thought to have been instituted on the expulsion of the kings in 510 BC. It survived under the Roman Empire but without real power.

consul (modern government official)　A consul is a civil servant who represents his or her country in a foreign nation. The customary consular ranks are: consul general, consul, vice consul, and consular agent. The honorary consul is usually a businessperson residing in the host country who is often a citizen of that nation rather than of the country represented. A consul's primary duty is handling commercial matters involving the country served, although such tasks as issuing visas and renewing passports come within a consul's purview. In the United States, the consular service is part of the FOREIGN SERVICE. Consuls general and consuls are appointed by the president, subject to the approval of the Senate.

Consulate [kahn'-sul-uht]　In French history, the Consulate was the system of government established by

Napoléon Bonaparte after the overthrow of the DIRECTORY in the coup of 18 Brumaire (Nov. 9, 1799). The governmental form of three consuls was originally devised by Emmanuel Joseph SIEYÈS, who envisioned the consuls' having equal power. Bonaparte as first consul soon modified this plan, however, reducing the second and third consuls to mere ciphers under his dictatorship. In 1802 he was made first consul for life. The Consulate ended 2 years later, when he crowned himself emperor as NAPOLEON I.

consumer price index A consumer price index is a device for measuring the aggregate change in the prices of retail goods and services that people buy. One of the best-known indexes is the Consumer Price Index (CPI) of the U.S. Bureau of Labor Statistics. The CPI measures changes in the cost of a typical market basket of goods purchased in a U.S. metropolitan area. Thus, if the average cost of a market basket of goods was $15 in the period 1982–84 (as the reference point 1982–84 = 100), and if the average cost of the same basket was $20 in 1989, the price increased by one-third, or 33.3%, and the index would be 133.3 in 1989. The market basket used by the CPI includes many things not sold in stores, such as housing, medical care, transportation, and entertainment. The components are revised periodically to reflect changes in buying habits and new products. Research for the 1987 revision of the market basket revealed that, for the first time, urban Americans were spending more on services than on goods and commodities.

Consumer Product Safety Commission The Consumer Product Safety Commission (CPSC) is an independent federal regulatory agency established in 1972 by the Congress of the United States. Its purposes are to protect the public against unreasonable risks of injury from manufactured products, to help consumers evaluate products for safety, to develop uniform national safety standards for consumer products, and to promote research that will increase the safety of such products. The five commissioners, one of whom serves as chairperson, are appointed by the president, subject to Senate approval, for terms of 7 years. The CPSC is empowered to establish mandatory safety standards where they are appropriate and to ban products that it considers hazardous.

consumer protection Consumer protection comprises all the activities of government, business, and consumer organizations designed to ensure consumers' rights in the marketplace. The following are generally considered consumers' rights: (1) the right to safety from product-related hazards; (2) the right to information about products, including the facts consumers need in order to protect themselves from fraud and misleading product claims; (3) the right to redress, that is, the right to reject unsatisfactory products and services and to ob-tain satisfaction when the complaint is justified; (4) the right to choose among a variety of products in a marketplace free from control by one or a few sellers; (5) the right to be heard in governmental decision making that affects consumers, including representation in governmental policy making on such matters as import quotas and tariffs and representation in regulatory decisions involving such issues as food-safety regulations.

The Development of Consumer Protection. The U.S. government first became involved in controlling misleading information when a mail-fraud law was passed in 1872. The first legislation concerning product safety was the Federal Food and Drug Act of 1906, which forbade the adulteration of food and drugs and misbranding, that is, using false or misleading claims (see PURE FOOD AND DRUG LAWS).

The Sherman Act, the first legislative attempt to control monopoly power (see MONOPOLY AND COMPETITION), was passed in 1890, and in 1914 the FEDERAL TRADE COMMISSION (FTC) was created to control unfair methods of competition. The need to protect consumers from unfair methods of competition was recognized in 1938 in the Wheeler-Lea Amendment to the Federal Trade Commission Act.

In 1938 the Federal Food and Drugs Act was updated by the Federal Food, Drug, and Cosmetic Act. It empowered the FOOD AND DRUG ADMINISTRATION (FDA) to test the safety of new drugs before they are placed on the market. During the 1950s and '60s, new legislation authorized the setting of safety standards for several other products, including flammable fabrics, household chemicals, toys, and motor vehicles. In the 1960s, Ralph NADER rose to prominence as a crusader on behalf of consumers. In order to regulate the safety requirements for a wider range of products, the CONSUMER PRODUCT SAFETY COMMISSION was established in 1972.

Government Programs to Protect Consumer Rights. Federal and state governments in the United States now set product standards, regulate the product information that is available, encourage consumer education, help consumers obtain redress, take antitrust action, and ensure consumer representation in government. Federal standards delineate the rules against which product composition, performance, and safety can be judged. The FDA establishes the ingredients that must be in a product before it can be called macaroni, for example.

The government assists consumers in obtaining redress in several ways. The law and the courts hold manufacturers liable for the safety of their products and for assuring that a product's performance corresponds reasonably to the claims made for it. Groups of consumers who have experienced similar problems may band together in a CLASS ACTION to sue a seller. The power of government agencies to force sellers to make restitution to consumers is limited; in most cases, government regulatory efforts are focused on preventing the sale of products that injure consumers or of activities that adversely affect them. The Consumer Product Safety Commission's power to require the repurchase, repair, or replacement of banned products is one exception. The Office of Consumer Affairs in the Department of Commerce serves as a clearinghouse for consumer complaints. Some manufacturers have voluntarily recalled products after their sale to correct defects that had been discovered.

Private Consumer Programs. Various business organizations provide consumers with information about products, and many corporations have consumer-affairs offices. Supported by local businesses, the BETTER BUSINESS BUREAU works to prevent misleading advertising claims. Consumers Union, the consumer-supported, product-testing organization, provides comparative brand ratings in its magazine, *Consumer Reports.*

The Consumer Federation of America, a national federation of about 220 organizations, and the group of organizations headed by Ralph Nader have played an important part in representing consumer interests before the Congress and government agencies.

contact lens   Contact lenses are glass or plastic devices that float on the eyeball and are used to correct vision (see EYE; EYEGLASSES). They may also be used for cosmetic reasons (to hide a disfiguring eye or to change eye color) or for medical purposes (to measure the electrical output of the eye, or to study or treat certain eye diseases).

Although crude glass lenses had been used occasionally in the late 19th century, it was only in the 1940s, with the invention of the first plastic lens, that contact lenses began to come into popular use. Initially, only scleral lenses in glass or plastic were produced. These covered almost the entire surface of the eye and, because they prevented the movement of tears over the eyeball, required frequent use of an artificial tear solution. Scleral lenses are rarely used today.

Corneal lenses, which cover a much smaller portion of the eye surface and float on the eye's own layer of tears, were introduced in the late 1940s. They were originally made of hard plastic and had to be removed and sterilized daily. In the 1970s, thinner, softer plastics were introduced. Water-absorbent for greater flexibility, they were also highly gas-permeable, allowing sufficient oxygen to reach the cornea (which, because it has no blood vessels, must get all its oxygen from the air) so that they could be worn for long periods of time. The newest class of lens is the extended-wear lens, which is extremely thin and can be worn comfortably for several weeks or longer before it needs to be removed for cleaning.

Like soft daily-wear lenses, extended-wear lenses conform so well to the surface of the cornea that they do not correct corneal astigmatism, an abnormality related to the shape of the cornea. "Toric" lenses, however, a new class of soft lens, can now correct mild to moderate astigmatism. Bifocal soft lenses are available for those who need correction for near as well as for distant vision.

contagious diseases   see INFECTIOUS DISEASES

contempt   Contempt, in law, is an intentional disregard of a public authority, most commonly with respect to judicial and legislative proceedings. An action that obstructs a legislative body, such as refusing to answer questions within the scope of a legislative investigation, is contempt of the legislature.

Contempt of court may be direct or constructive (indirect). Direct contempt is committed in the presence of the court and results in obstructing the judicial proceedings. Constructive contempt occurs outside of court and tends to obstruct the administration of justice. It is usually a willful refusal to obey a lawful order.

Contempt of court may also be classified as civil or criminal. Civil contempt consists of failing to obey a court order designed to benefit another person. An act in disrespect of the court or obstructing the administration of justice is criminal contempt. Both types of offenses may be punished by fines or imprisonment. A person imprisoned for civil contempt is released after complying with the court order; criminal contempt is punishable by a fixed jail term.

continental climate   Continental climates, characterized by great extremes in temperature and relative dryness, are typical of the interior of large landmasses. Land surfaces heat more quickly and reach higher temperatures than water surfaces; they also cool more rapidly and reach lower temperatures. Unlike the seas, which can absorb considerable amounts of solar energy, landmasses store the energy they receive during the day in a very shallow layer and quickly release it at night. This gives continental areas large daily and seasonal temperature extremes, and ensures that the warmest and coldest periods of the year follow the times of maximum and minimum solar radiation (summer and winter solstices) with a lag of only a few weeks.

Continental climates typically are relatively dry during at least part of the year. The great distance from the ocean results in low relative HUMIDITY, reduced cloudiness, and low annual PRECIPITATION. This is, however, highly seasonal, because the high summer temperatures increase the capacity of air to hold water, resulting in a marked predominance of summer precipitation and thunderstorms. In its extreme form, a continental climate results in a DESERT.

Continental Congress   The Continental Congress, made up of delegates from the 13 original American states (initially colonies), was the government of the United States in one form or another for 15 years (1774–89).

The First Continental Congress (September–October 1774) was an extralegal body called to protest certain measures of the British Parliament, especially the INTOLERABLE ACTS and the QUEBEC ACT. This congress, however, also urged the colonies to arm themselves for defense of

Delegates to the Continental Congress bow their heads in prayer. The Congress first met in 1774 as an advisory body representing intercolonial interests; during the Revolutionary War it functioned under the Articles of Confederation as a central government.

their rights. By the time the Second Congress convened (May 1775), the battles of Lexington and Concord had taken place, and the AMERICAN REVOLUTION had begun. The Second Congress adopted the DECLARATION OF INDEPENDENCE in July 1776 and drafted the ARTICLES OF CONFEDERATION (completed in November 1777), giving itself a constitutional basis. The Articles, however, were not finally ratified until Mar. 1, 1781; thus Congress carried on the direction of the Revolution on a makeshift, ad hoc basis.

Throughout its existence, the Continental Congress, in which each state had only one vote, tended to be politically polarized: state-oriented "republicans," distrusting central authority, usually represented the upper South and New England; and nationally minded conservatives usually represented the Middle States and South Carolina. The first group dominated Congress from the spring of 1776 until the end of 1780. It organized the Continental Army, negotiated an alliance with France, and kept the army in the field by borrowing and issuing unsecured paper money. By December 1780, however, Congress was bankrupt and mutiny was threatening just as the war was coming to a climax. The republicans, discredited, were supplanted by a nationalist majority, which dominated Congress until 1783. When peace came that year, popular support for national measures ended, the army was disbanded, and locally minded politicians resumed control of Congress.

After the war, Congress functioned with great difficulty. It did arrange for auditing most of the war debts and for surveying and beginning the sale and governance of the immense public domain of western lands; by the Northwest Ordinance of 1787, it created the NORTHWEST TERRITORY. Congress also maintained diplomatic establishments in Paris and London. Although its ministers negotiated treaties with several minor powers, they were wholly unsuccessful in settling differences with France and Britain. At home, hamstrung by the Articles of Confederation, Congress was equally impotent in paying its debts and coping with commercial disruptions and armed revolts such as SHAYS'S REBELLION in Massachusetts. The Continental Congress was finally displaced under the terms of the Constitution adopted in 1787. It transferred power to the new federal government in 1789, and its small administrative machinery became the core of President Washington's administration.

See also: CONSTITUTION OF THE UNITED STATES.

Continental Divide　In the United States the Continental Divide, sometimes called the Great Divide, is the geologic line separating areas that drain into the Atlantic Ocean or its arms (east-flowing streams) from those draining into the Pacific Ocean (west-flowing streams). The divide generally follows the crest of the Rocky Mountains, although in parts of Wyoming and Arizona it is marked only by low elevations. The Continental Divide runs through Glacier, Yellowstone, and Rocky Mountain national parks.

---

continental drift　The idea that continents move laterally with respect to each other was considered highly revolutionary when the German meteorologist, A. L. WEGENER, began to formulate it as an integrated theory in 1912. Wegener postulated that, beginning in the Mesozoic Era of GEOLOGIC TIME, a huge primeval supercontinent that he called *Pangaea* (or *Pangea*; Greek, "all land") had fragmented and that the pieces had drifted apart to form the present continents. He supported his hypothesis with evidence from various fields. The "jigsaw fit" of Africa and South America was merely suggestive; much more convincing was the geographic distribution of fossils that indicated ancient land connections between the southern

According to the theory of plate tectonics, the Earth's surface consists of lithosphere (1) made up of large rigid slabs, or tectonic plates, that drift about on an underlying plastic zone, or asthenosphere (2). Three types of boundaries may be formed by the movement of tectonic plates (A, B, C, D). Where plates move apart, a mid-oceanic ridge (3) of new crust is created by magma pushing up from the hot mantle below. An oceanic trench (4) is produced where two plates converge and one slides beneath the other. Where two plates move in parallel but opposite directions, a fracture zone, or transform fault, is formed that may link two trenches (5) or two offset ridges (6).

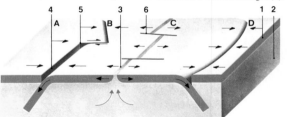

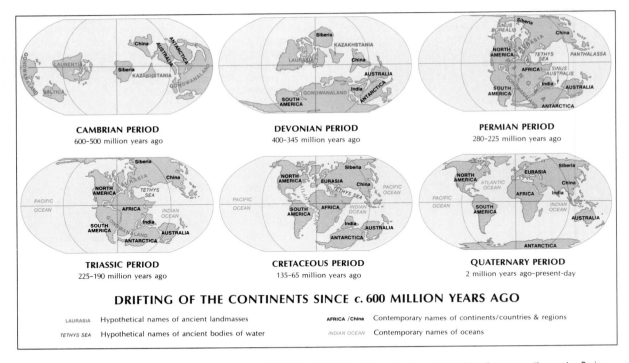

CAMBRIAN PERIOD
600–500 million years ago

DEVONIAN PERIOD
400–345 million years ago

PERMIAN PERIOD
280–225 million years ago

TRIASSIC PERIOD
225–190 million years ago

CRETACEOUS PERIOD
135–65 million years ago

QUATERNARY PERIOD
2 million years ago–present-day

DRIFTING OF THE CONTINENTS SINCE c. 600 MILLION YEARS AGO

LAURASIA	Hypothetical names of ancient landmasses	**AFRICA** /China	Contemporary names of continents/countries & regions
TETHYS SEA	Hypothetical names of ancient bodies of water	INDIAN OCEAN	Contemporary names of oceans

Geologists believe that more than 500 million years ago, during the Cambrian Period, six major continents were spread out along or near the equator. During the Devonian Period, the continents had begun to cluster as a result of continental drift. At the end of the Permian Period, a single supercontinent, Pangea, had formed and had begun to break apart. The fragmentation into new continents and drifting continued through the Triassic, Cretaceous, and Quaternary periods, leading to Earth's present geography.

continents. The conventional "stabilist" interpretation rejected continental drift and favored transoceanic land bridges that had sunk, such as the fabled Atlantis, since the Mesozoic Era. Wegener showed, however, that this interpretation was geophysically untenable.

Other evidence supporting Wegener's hypothesis came from a comparison of the rocks on both sides of the Atlantic, which seems to indicate that the continents had been closely connected in the past, and from a study of ancient climatic zones. Thus the distribution of a series of late Paleozoic ICE AGE deposits known as tillites in South Africa, South America, India, and Australia could best be accounted for by supposing that the continents had once been arranged to form Gondwanaland, the southern part of Pangea, and that Gondwanaland had been superimposed on the former position of the South Pole. The distribution of Mesozoic coal deposits also indicated that Europe and the United States had been situated in an equatorial belt at the time the tillites were deposited farther south.

Wegener's hypothesis did not offer a plausible explanation of what could have caused continental drift, and it was generally dismissed. Critics pointed to apparent contradictions in some of his arguments and disputed the validity of the evidence he cited. Geophysical evidence since then, however, has strongly supported the hypothesis of drifting continents (see PLATE TECTONICS).

continental shelf and slope   The continental shelf and slope constitute the continental terrace, the submerged seaward margin of a continent. The shelf itself is an underwater platform that dips gently seaward and extends from the shoreline to a break in slope, generally at a depth of about 120 m (400 ft), where it joins the continental slope. The shelf ranges in width from only a few to hundreds of kilometers; the depth at its outer limit ranges from 35 to 250 m (115 to 820 ft), and the worldwide mean depth is 128 m (420 ft). Topographic relief is caused mainly by reefs, glaciated channels, and MORAINES. The great economic importance of the shelf, stemming from its seafood and mineral resources, has made it the most thoroughly studied ocean area. The continental slope plunges to ocean depths; typically standing 4 km (2.5 mi) high, the slope marks the edge of the continental block and is the Earth's most impressive escarpment. Resembling a great mountain front, such as the south-facing rampart of the Himalayas, the continental slope generally is straight, rugged, and deeply furrowed by SUBMARINE CANYONS.

continental shield A continental shield is a broad area of ancient crystalline rock that has remained structurally stable for a long period of GEOLOGIC TIME. Most shield areas are relatively low-lying, with subdued topography; the inner reaches of some, however, may rise to more than 1,000 m (3,300 ft). At the margins, the rocks continue beneath younger overlapping strata to form a bordering platform.

Most shields consist of METAMORPHIC ROCKS, mainly gneiss, transected by belts of greenstone, a slightly altered rock similar to basalt in composition. Shield rocks were formed by the upward transfer of lighter elements from deeper levels of the crust and mantle during earlier periods of mountain building. The younger greenstone belts originated as volcanic chains along later rifts or sags in the gneiss. Virtually all shields were formed early in Precambrian time, more than 2.5 billion years ago. The CANADIAN SHIELD, a vast area underlying the eastern half of Canada, is typical. Except for uplift and deep erosion, it has remained largely undisturbed since it formed 2.6 billion years ago.

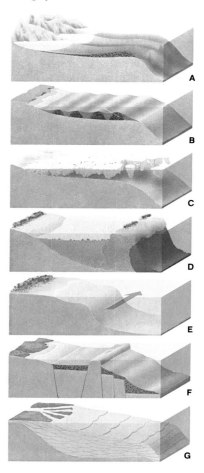

Structural features of continental shelves and slopes vary according to climate, oceanographic conditions, and the nature of adjacent land masses. A shelf gouged out by glaciers consists of deep troughs at right angles to the coastline (A). A shelf near a glacier-free area generally has a series of low sand ridges parallel to the coast (B). The grinding action of floating ice forms smooth, flat, shallow shelves (C). Shelves in tropical seas may be composed of land sediment deposited between the shore and a damlike coral reef at the edge of the continental slope (D). Shelves with steeper than normal slopes (E) are found in areas where strong currents constantly erode the seafloor. Fault-controlled shelves (F) are formed from sedimentation behind offshore fault barriers. Wide-layered shelves (G) are the result of river-discharged sediment that accumulates near large delta areas.

continuing education see ADULT EDUCATION

continuity In mathematics, continuity is the idea of a changing quantity that produces no sudden interruptions, breaks, or jumps. A FUNCTION f is continuous at a point a if the values of $f(x)$ are close to $f(a)$ when x is close to a.

A. L. CAUCHY, a French mathematician of the early 19th century, gave the first modern definition of continuity. According to Cauchy, a function $f(x)$, involving the set of real numbers, is continuous at point a if it is defined at a and if for every value $e > 0$ (however small e may be), there is a value $s > 0$ (depending on e) such that $|f(a) - f(x)| < e$ whenever $|a - x| < s$. In addition, $f(x)$ is continuous for a set I if it is continuous at every point of I. The concept of continuity is closely related to the mathematical concept of a LIMIT.

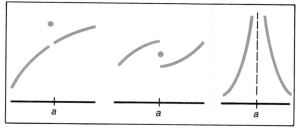

types of discontinuities

If a function is not continuous at point a, it is called discontinuous at a. Apart from discontinuities where $f(a)$ is not defined (as in the right-hand diagram), there are two main kinds of discontinuities: removable discontinuities, in which the function may be redefined at a point or points to make it continuous (as in the left-hand diagram), and jump discontinuities, where the function approaches different values from different directions, and thus cannot be made continuous (as in the center diagram).

contra see IRAN-CONTRA AFFAIR; NICARAGUA

contraband Contraband consists of goods imported into or exported from a nation in violation of its laws or treaties. The term is also used in international law, under which a nation at war may seize military supplies being shipped to an enemy. The Declaration of London—the product of the international Naval Conference of 1909—distinguished three main classes of goods: absolute contraband (military equipment); conditional contraband (food, clothing, vehicles); and free goods. In practice, however, belligerents tend to abide by their own rules as to what trade they will or will not allow in the areas under their control.

See also: BLOCKADE; SMUGGLING.

contrabassoon [kahn'-truh-buh-soon'] The contrabassoon, also known as the double bassoon, is the lowest wind instrument of the orchestra. Pitched an octave lower than the BASSOON, its range extends to an octave below the B-flat below the bass staff. The contrabassoon sounds an octave lower than written. Developed about 1880, the modern contrabassoon has a tube more than 5 m (16 ft) long that is doubled up on itself three times; the bell points down. The tone is fluent and flexible, but the lowest and highest notes are somewhat unsatisfactory and are therefore not used as frequently. Moreover, the tone lacks sufficient volume for proper balance in fortissimo orchestral passages.

contraception   see BIRTH CONTROL

contract A contract is an agreement, enforceable by law, that arises when an offer to make such an agreement is accepted. An offer contains a promise (for example, "I will pay $1,000") and a request for something in return (a person's car). The acceptance consists of sincere assent by the party to whom the offer is made, showing that the person agrees to the terms offered. The offer may be terminated in a number of ways. For example, the party making the offer may cancel it (a revocation), or the party to whom the offer is made may reject it. When the party to whom the offer is made responds with a different offer, called a counteroffer, the original offer is terminated. Then the counteroffer may be accepted by the party making the original offer.

Requirements of a Valid Contract

A contract results from a bargain. This implies that each party to the contract gives up something, or promises to do so, in exchange for something given up or promised by the other party. This is called consideration. In the example given above, the consideration on one side is the promise to pay $1,000, and on the other, the promise to deliver a car. With rare exceptions, a promise by one party, without some form of consideration being extended by the other party, does not result in a contract or other enforceable obligation, regardless of the sincerity of the promise. Although each party must extend consideration to the other in order to form a contract, the value of the consideration need not be equal.

Competence. For a contract to be enforceable it must be between competent parties. A contract with a person who has been adjudicated insane is likely to be declared void. A contract involving a minor—in most states of the United States a minor is now a person under 18—may be enforced or voided by the minor, unless the contract is for necessities such as food, lodging, or medical services, in which case he or she may be held responsible for the reasonable value of what was purchased. Persons suffering from a disability such as intoxication from drugs or liquor, or insane persons not adjudicated insane, usually may void a contract if the other party knows or should have

known of the disability and if the consideration received is returnable.

Legality. The last requirement of a valid contract is that its provisions be legal. If a purported contract requires an illegal act, the result is a void contract. Parties to an illegal contract have no standing in court. Not only are contracts requiring criminal acts illegal, but so are those requiring commission of a TORT (a breach of civil law such as misrepresentation or trespass) or those in breach of public policy.

It is commonly assumed that an enforceable contract must be in writing. This is usually untrue. Most oral contracts are enforceable, but written contracts are easier to prove. Some types of contracts must be in writing—for example, contracts for the purchase or sale of any interest in real property, contracts to pay debts of others, and contracts that require more than a year to perform. Contracts for the sale of personal property, that is, movable property, as distinguished from land, at a price above a specified sum set by law must be in writing unless payment or delivery has been made or unless the goods were especially manufactured. Although only a few types of contract must be in writing, the terms of a written contract ordinarily may not be contradicted in court by oral testimony.

Remedies for Breach of Contract

In the event of a breach of contract, the injured party usually sues for money damages (the award of a sum of money designed to compensate for losses stemming from the breach). Damages are measured by what may reasonably be foreseen as financial losses; unforeseeable losses may not be collected. If an award of money is not compensatory because something about the promised performance was unique, the party who breaks a contract may be ordered by the court to perform as agreed. This is called specific performance. For example, real estate is always considered unique. Therefore, when a party has contracted to sell real estate but changes his or her mind, the court may grant specific performance and order that the deed for the real estate be delivered to the agreed buyer.

Most contracts are formed with an implicit understanding that neither party need perform unless the other has completed his or her promised performance. An exception to this understanding occurs when a party has performed most of his or her obligation and the part not performed is relatively immaterial. The doctrine of substantial performance provides that in such a case the opposite party must perform, although he or she may secure money damages to the extent that he or she was damaged by lack of complete performance.

contralto The contralto is the lowest female voice, with a range of about two and a half octaves upward from about E in the bass clef. The voice is called alto when employed in a chorus. The term *alto* may also denote a male singer of the same range (see COUNTERTENOR). Female contraltos have a dark, rich sound in their lower register, and they often have a considerable upward range, although with less brightness at the top than the other female voices. True contraltos are rare, and composers have written relatively little for them.

Contreras, Battle of   see MEXICAN WAR

control systems   see AUTOMATION; FEEDBACK

---

convection

Convection is the movement of gases or liquids in response to a nonuniform temperature distribution. Heat applied to a fluid generally causes an expansion of the fluid in the region closest to the source of heat. This region now has a lesser density (is lighter than) its surrounding regions and, under the influence of gravity, travels upward. Similarly, a region of fluid that has been cooled becomes more dense and travels downward. In either case, a convection current is established that travels through the body of the fluid, tranferring heat and causing a temperature redistribution.

An important exception to the principle that warmth creates an upward flow is water. Water that is at or near its freezing point of 0° C (32° F) contracts when heated until it reaches its maximum density at 4° C (39° F). Within this range the warmer regions flow downward. Above 4° C, water behaves normally.

Convection currents permit buildings to be heated without the use of circulatory devices. The heated air moves solely by gravity. In the atmosphere, convection causes the wind to blow.

---

convection cell

A convection cell, or heat-transfer cell, is a circulation pattern that is established within a mass of material—whether solid, liquid, or gas—because of temperature differences in the material. For example, convection cells are seen on the SUN. In the Earth's atmosphere, cells form as warmed air rises and spreads out laterally, cooling and then sinking around the central region of rising air. It has been proposed that convection patterns in the Earth's mantle, between the core and the rigid outer crust, are related to large-scale surface features and processes such as CONTINENTAL DRIFT, geosynclines, island arcs, and deep-sea trenches. Scientists doubt that these patterns take the form of simple convection cells that involve a complete circulation and mixing of mantle material; convection currents of different sizes and shapes and rates of flow are known to exist, however, in the mantle. Some coincide with ocean ridges where new crustal material appears and is involved in SEAFLOOR SPREADING. Others are the likely cause of the Earth's so-called hot spots, or major volcanic centers, such as Hawaii and Iceland. In addition, convection cells almost certainly exist in the Earth's liquid nickel-iron core. Circulation of this electrically conductive material gives rise to the Earth's magnetic field (see EARTH, GEOMAGNETIC FIELD OF).

---

convent

The word *convent* was first used by the mendicant friars of the 13th century, in place of "abbey" or "monastery," to signify the building in which members of RELIGIOUS ORDER shared a common life. Today, however, the word is applied almost exclusively to the domiciles of religious women, or nuns, although it is also frequently used to refer to convent life in general. Roman Catholic canon law requires a minimum of three members to establish a convent.

Both general and specific requirements are imposed on a person wishing to join a convent. They include normal intelligence, sound mental and physical health, and a desire to serve God in a life dedicated to the work of the church. Specific requirements are set according to the makeup and work of a particular religious group. Cloistered religious orders are called to a life of prayer and contemplation, whereas missionary orders are called to a life of service. Still others are called to teach and do nursing work.

The Second VATICAN COUNCIL called for a renewal of convent life, with adaptation of rules and constitutions in a manner appropriate to the needs of the church and world today.

convention, political   see POLITICAL CONVENTION

---

convergence

In mathematics, convergence refers to a situation in which one quantity approaches a second quantity. An infinite SEQUENCE, or ordered set of numbers,

$$a_1, a_2, \ldots, a_n, \ldots$$

is convergent if it approaches a LIMIT. That is, it converges if the nth number, or term, a_n in the sequence can be made arbitrarily close to some quantity a (the limit) as n approaches infinity.

Convergence of an infinite SERIES, or sum of the terms of an infinite sequence, can be discussed by considering the sequence formed from the partial sums of the series. If the sequence of partial sums converges to the limit S as the number of terms n in the series approaches infinity, then the original infinite series is said to converge and have the limit (or sum) S.

Converse, Frederick Shepherd

Frederick Shepherd Converse, b. Newton, Mass., Jan. 5, 1871, d. June 8, 1940, was the first American composer to have an opera produced at the Metropolitan Opera. *The Pipe of Desire* was performed there in 1910, although it had its premiere in Boston in 1906. Converse was an influential teacher at the New England Conservatory from 1899 to 1901 and at Harvard from 1901 to 1907. He was dean of the New England Conservatory from 1930 to 1938. Converse composed orchestral works (including seven symphonies), choral works, chamber music (including three string quartets), piano pieces, and songs.

conveyor A conveyor is a mechanical device used to move materials and objects from one location to another. Conveyors may exist in many forms, depending on their intended use.

The belt conveyor is used to move solid objects, such as packages, and bulk materials, such as grains, sand, gravel, earth, coal, and fragmented ores. The bucket conveyor consists of a series of buckets attached to an endless belt or to chains mounted on a rigid frame, and is powered by a drive system. It is generally used to move bulk material vertically. The screw conveyor consists of a rotating shaft, with continuous spiral flighting attached, that operates inside a trough or a tube to move bulk material from one location to another. (See ARCHIMEDES' SCREW.)

The pneumatic conveyor consists of a tube or a duct through which bulk materials, such as grain, cement, pulverized coal, and other particles, are moved by a current of air furnished by a fan or a blower.

A hydraulic conveyor consists of a tube or a pipe through which pulverized materials, such as sand, silt, coal, or ores, are suspended in water and are pumped or allowed to flow by gravity. The discharge pipe from a hydraulic dredge is an example of this conveyor.

Among these types, the belt conveyor is the most important. Its first recorded use in the United States came in 1785, but its most dramatic application occurred in 1914, when Henry Ford incorporated power-driven conveyors in his assembly-line production of automobiles.

convulsion A convulsion is a violent, involuntary muscular contraction, or spasm. The term *seizure* is sometimes used instead of convulsion, but a seizure is, more accurately, any sudden attack of symptoms. A convulsion may be caused by any damage or biochemical abnormality in the brain that leads to uncoordinated electrical activity in motor or sensory portions of the central nervous system. Convulsions may occur in connection with high fever, UREMIA, cardiac arrest, alcohol or drug withdrawal, eclampsia, liver damage, or EPILEPSY.

Convulsions are often preceded by a so-called aura, which may consist of sensations such as abdominal pain, seeing things get smaller (looking-glass phenomenon), or smelling the odor of burning. The aura may last seconds, minutes, or hours. During a grand mal convulsion there is sudden loss of consciousness; falling to the ground; massive contraction of muscles, with thrashing, tongue biting, and loss of bladder control; and foaming at the mouth. The brain is in a state of total disorder and the body is exhausted. When the motor activity stops, the patient may be in a coma for up to 30 minutes and will awake confused, drowsy, and with a headache.

Medication is available both to treat and to prevent most attacks. Many patients outgrow their disorder as they enter or pass through puberty.

Conway Cabal [kahn'-way kuh-bahl'] The Conway Cabal was a group of officers that attempted to oust George WASHINGTON as commander in chief of the Continental Army during the American Revolution. It was named for Thomas Conway (1735–1800?), an Irish-born officer previously in the French army. Encouraged by a faction in the Continental Congress, Conway, along with Thomas MIFFLIN, Benjamin RUSH, and others, maneuvered to replace Washington with Horatio GATES. They backed down when Washington discovered their plans in November 1777.

Coogan, Jackie The American actor Jack Leslie Coogan, b. Los Angeles, Oct. 26, 1914, d. Mar. 1, 1984, achieved international fame as a child star in 1920, when he appeared as the endearing moppet in Charles Chaplin's *The Kid*. Roles in *Peck's Bad Boy* and *Oliver Twist* followed a year later. Coogan's career as a star ended toward the end of the 1920s, as he grew older; a celebrated court battle over custody of his film earnings also contributed to his decline. He remained in Hollywood but in later life found himself limited to smaller, less important roles. In the 1960s he played Uncle Fester on the television series "The Addams Family."

Cook, James The English navigator James Cook, the greatest explorer of the 18th century, is known for his voyages to the Pacific Ocean and his application of scientific methods to exploration and to cartography. Born on Oct. 27, 1728, Cook went to sea as a youth and made several voyages to the Baltic Sea. He joined the Royal Navy in 1755 as an able-bodied seaman, soon became a mate, and within four years became a master. In 1759, during the SEVEN YEARS' WAR, Cook was given command of the *Mercury,* sailing to Canada and up the St. Lawrence River, where he participated in naval operations against Quebec.

After the war ended in 1763, Cook, commanding the schooner *Grenville,* spent four years surveying the coasts of Labrador, Newfoundland, and Nova Scotia. He also studied mathematics in order to master the science of navigation. Cook had observed a solar eclipse in 1766

In the course of three voyages to the Pacific Ocean, Captain James Cook, an 18th-century British navigator, explored the coasts of New Zealand and eastern Australia and discovered the Hawaiian Islands.

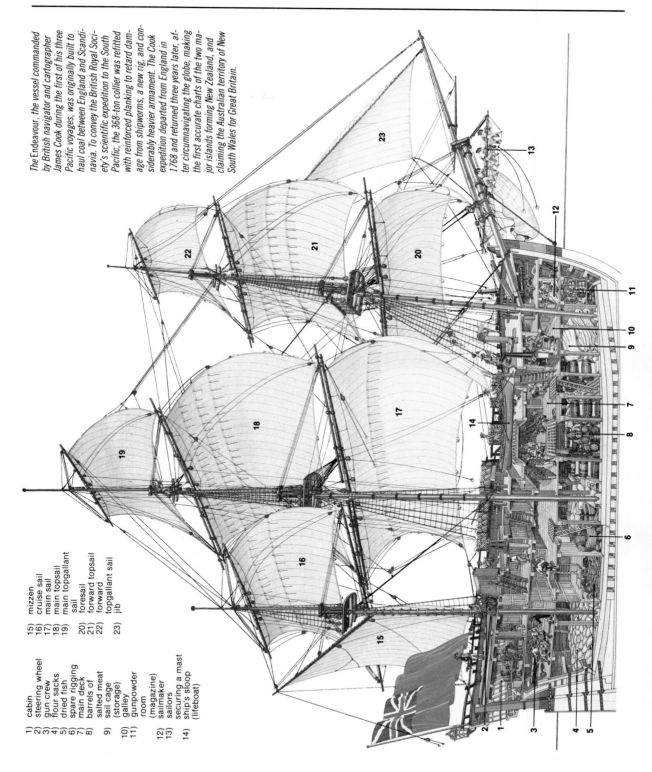

The Endeavour, the vessel commanded by British navigator and cartographer James Cook during the first of his three Pacific voyages, was originally built to haul coal between England and Scandinavia. To convey the British Royal Society's scientific expedition to the South Pacific, the 368-ton collier was refitted with reinforced planking to retard damage from shipworms, a new rig, and considerably heavier armament. The Cook expedition departed from England in 1768 and returned three years later, after circumnavigating the globe, making the first accurate charts of the two major islands forming New Zealand, and claiming the Australian territory of New South Wales for Great Britain.

1) cabin
2) steering wheel
3) gun crew
4) flour sacks
5) dried fish
6) spare rigging
7) main deck
8) barrels of salted meat
9) sail cage (storage)
10) galley
11) gunpowder room (magazine)
12) sailmaker
13) sailors
14) securing a mast
   ship's sloop (lifeboat)
15) mizzen
16) cruise sail
17) main sail
18) main topsail
19) main topgallant sail
20) foresail
21) forward topsail
22) forward topgallant sail
23) jib

VOYAGES OF JAMES COOK

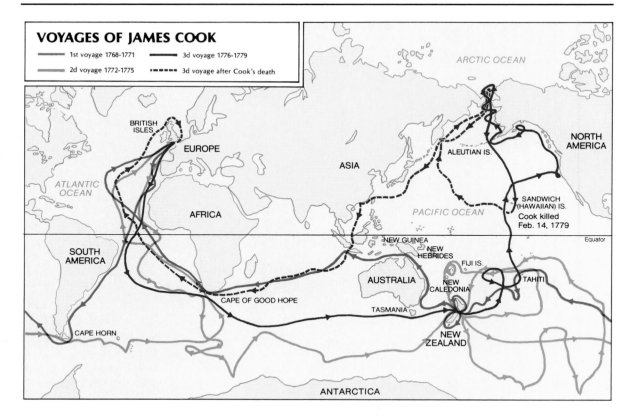

—— 1st voyage 1768-1771	—— 3d voyage 1776-1779
—— 2d voyage 1772-1775	∎∎∎∎ 3d voyage after Cook's death

and used it to determine the longitude of Newfoundland. After his return to England in 1767, Cook was commissioned a lieutenant in the Royal Navy.

Voyage of the Endeavour. In 1768 the Royal Society requested the Admiralty's aid in observing the transit of Venus at Tahiti, to occur in June 1769, and Cook was given command of the expedition. Secret instructions made clear that Cook also was to search for *terra australis incognita,* the "unknown southern land." Cook and the *Endeavour* left Plymouth on Aug. 26, 1768, carrying in addition to the crew an astronomer, two botanists—Joseph BANKS and Daniel Solander—and artists.

The *Endeavour* traveled by way of the Madeira, Canary, and Cape Verde islands and Rio de Janeiro and rounded Cape Horn into the Pacific. The ship reached Tahiti in April 1769. During their three months on the island, the scientists examined it thoroughly and observed the transit of Venus on June 3. They sailed west through the Society Islands and then southward, finally reaching New Zealand, which had been discovered by Abel Tasman in 1642. The expedition then sailed west, reached the unexplored eastern coast of Australia, and sailed north along it. Cook surveyed about 3,200 km (2,000 mi) of Australian coast, and confirmed the existence of a passage between Australia and New Guinea (the Torres Strait). The expedition sailed on, refitted at Batavia in Java, and returned by way of the Indian Ocean and the Cape of

Good Hope. It reached England on July 13, 1771.

Voyages of the Resolution. The Admiralty soon authorized a new expedition. Cook commanded the *Resolution,* which was accompanied by the *Adventure,* and again took scientists and artists. They left Plymouth on July 13, 1772, and headed for the Cape of Good Hope. Then they traveled south, crossing the Antarctic Circle in January 1773. Finding no continent, they went on to New Zealand and from there explored the South Pacific.

The *Resolution* and *Adventure* lost contact, and the latter returned to England, becoming the first vessel to circumnavigate the world from west to east. The *Resolution,* again crossed the Antarctic Circle, stopped at Easter Island and Tonga, and explored the New Hebrides, New Caledonia, and Norfolk Island. Finally it crossed the South Pacific again, rounded Cape Horn, crossed the South Atlantic to the Cape of Good Hope, and then sailed north to reach England in July 1775. Cook had proved that no great continent existed in the temperate region of the Pacific, but he had become convinced that there was an Antarctic continent. As a result of his expeditions, Cook was elected a fellow of the Royal Society.

Promoted to captain, Cook sailed again on the *Resolution* on July 12, 1776, this time to search for the Northwest Passage from the Pacific side. At the Cape of Good Hope he was joined by the *Discovery.* The two ships visited Tahiti. They discovered Christmas Island and then the Hawaiian Islands, which Cook called the Sandwich Islands, in January 1778. Sailing onward to North America, the expedition landed near Vancouver and then went through the Bering Strait into the Arctic Ocean but was blocked by ice. The ships returned to Hawaii, where Cook was killed by the Polynesian inhabitants on Feb. 14, 1779. The expedition then returned to England.

James Cook had surveyed and charted thousands of kilometers of coast and had solved many mysteries of the Pacific Ocean area. He had also opened the northwest American coast to trade and colonization. Cook handled ships and crews extraordinarily well, avoided scurvy—hitherto the scourge of long sea voyages—and conducted all of his explorations in a remarkably peaceful fashion.

Cook Islands   The Cook Islands are a group of islands in the southeast Pacific Ocean, west of French Polynesia and 3,220 km (2,000 mi) northeast of New Zealand, of which they are a dependency. They are widely scattered, with a total land area of 234 km² (93 mi²) and a population, largely Polynesian, of 17,185 (1986). The islands are divided into the southern, or lower, Cooks—which consist of volcanic islands and raised coral atolls—and the northern Cooks—which are low coral atolls. The center of government is on Rarotonga in the southern group. Exports include citrus, copra, and mother-of-pearl. The islands were explored by the Spanish in 1595 and by the Portuguese in 1606. Capt. James Cook made three trips to the islands in the 1770s. They were declared a British protectorate in 1888 and became part of New Zealand in 1901. Since 1965 the Cooks have been self-governing in free association with New Zealand.

Cooke, Alistair   Alfred Alistair Cooke, b. England, Nov. 20, 1908, is a journalist and broadcaster long known as Britain's interpreter of America and, since 1971—when he became host of the television series "Masterpiece Theater"—as the explicator of the British to Americans. From 1938, Cooke covered U.S. news for

Alistair Cooke, known in Britain and the United States for his journalism and broadcasting, is also the author of many books, including A Generation on Trial: U.S.A. vs. Alger Hiss *(1950; 2d enlarged ed., 1968);* Six Men *(1977), portraits of celebrated men personally known to Cooke; and* The Patient Has the Floor *(1986), a sampling of his speeches.*

British newspapers, most notably for the *Manchester Guardian* (1945–72), and also broadcast a weekly program, "Letter from America," to BBC radio. From 1952 to 1959 he was host and narrator on the esteemed American television program "Omnibus." Many of his books (*One Man's America*, 1952; *The Americans*, 1979) are adaptations of his broadcast scripts.

Cooke, Jay   Jay Cooke, b. Sandusky, Ohio, Aug. 10, 1821, d. Feb. 18, 1905, was an American financier and investment banker. At age 14 he became a store clerk, and by age 21 he was a partner in a Philadelphia banking firm. In 1861 he started his own banking house, Jay Cooke & Company, and floated a war loan for the state of Pennsylvania. During the Civil War, Cooke successfully marketed federal bonds nationwide. He established banks in several cities, but in 1873 his company failed after investing heavily in the construction of the Northern Pacific Railway. Subsequently, he repaid his creditors and acquired a new fortune in western mining.

Cooke, Terence J.   An American Roman Catholic bishop and cardinal, Terence James Cooke, b. March 1, 1921, d. Oct. 6, 1983, became auxiliary bishop of New York (1965), Francis J. Spellman's successor as bishop (1968), and a cardinal in March 1969. In addition to his duties as archbishop of New York, Cooke served as chairman of the National Conference of Catholic Bishops' committee on pro-life activities. He was also the U.S. military vicar.

cooking   Cooking is the art and science of preparing food for eating by the application of heat. The term also includes the full range of culinary techniques: preparing raw and cooked foods for the table; final dressing of meats, fish, and fowl; cleaning and cutting fruits and vegetables; preparing salads; garnishing dishes; decorating desserts; and planning meals.

Earliest Types of Cooking

The origins of cooking are obscure. Primitive humans may first have savored roast meat by chance, when the flesh of a beast killed in a forest fire was found to be more palatable and easier to chew and digest than the customary raw meat. They probably did not deliberately cook food, though, until long after they had learned to use fire for light and warmth. From whenever it began, roasting spitted meats over fires remained virtually the sole culinary technique until the Paleolithic Period, when the Aurignacian people of southern France began to steam food over hot embers by wrapping it in wet leaves. Aside from such crude procedures as toasting wild grains on flat rocks and using shells, skulls, or hollowed stones to heat liquids, no further culinary advances were made until the introduction of pottery during the Neolithic Period.

The earliest compound dish was a crude paste (the prototype of the *pulmentum* of the Roman legions and the po-

A late archaic terra-cotta figurine from the town of Tanagra, Greece, portrays a woman tending her oven.

lenta of later Italians) made by mixing water with the cracked kernels of wild grasses. This paste, toasted to crustiness when dropped on a hot stone, made the first bread.

Advances in Cooking Techniques. Culinary techniques improved with the introduction of earthenware, the domestication of livestock, and the cultivation of edible plants. A more dependable supply of foodstuffs, including milk and its derivatives, was now assured. The roasting spit was augmented by fired-clay vessels and the cooking techniques of boiling, stewing, and braising, and perhaps even incipient forms of pickling, frying, and oven baking were added. Early cooks probably had already learned to preserve meats and fish by smoking, salting, air-drying, or chilling.

Cooking in Ancient Societies. Although the diets of peoples of the ancient world are well documented, little is known about their cooking techniques. In the Sumerian capital of Ur, street vendors hawked fried fish and grilled meats to passersby. In Egypt, small, raw birds were pickled in brine and eaten cold in the 3d millennium BC, but excavations from the same period indicate that more sophisticated cooking methods were in use and that the rich particularly liked elaborate stews. Leavened BREAD seems to have first appeared in Egypt.

Greek warriors of the 12th century BC feasted mostly on plain, spit-roasted meats and raw onions. In the succeeding centuries, however, deforestation and the subsequent erosion of the soil (the results of widespread timbering and overcultivation of the olive) radically altered the Greek diet and, consequently, Greek cooking techniques. Fish, which does not lend itself to spit-roasting, largely supplanted meat, and a scarcity of timber limited the use of open fires. The Homeric heroes had butchered, salted, and roasted their own meats alfresco, while female slaves ground corn for their bread; but the *mageiros,* a high-ranking slave and baker-chef, supervised the cooking in later times, when foods were prepared in indoor kitchens. Under the mageiros's direction sophisticated kitchen equipment evolved, ranging from simple earthenware pots to elaborately decorated metal casseroles, kettles, cauldrons, and gridirons, and including amphorae that functioned in much the same manner as the modern bain-marie, or double boiler. Archestratus, a Greek, wrote the first cookbook, *Hedypathia* (Pleasant Living), in the 4th century BC.

Development of Modern Cuisines

Modern European cooking was shaped in large part by the conditions existing during the early Middle Ages. In the north, where abundant timber and a relatively cold climate favored the use of open fires, the rotating spit and suspended cauldron gave rise to a cuisine that consisted of thick roasts and long-simmered soups, stews, and sauces. Because trade access to other regions was limited, homegrown raw materials were used almost exclusively. Abundant pasturage permitted large dairy herds. Dairy products were thus major components of the cuisine, and butter was the principal cooking fat.

Along the Mediterranean, where olives were abundant, fuel scarce, and the climate warm, an oil-based cuisine developed. This cuisine comprised mainly light dishes that could be cooked quickly over enclosed charcoal fires and small cuts of meat that did not require prolonged exposure to heat. The spit and cauldron, which evolved into the roasting oven and stockpot, were the chief utensils of the north, but the south relied on the skillet and saucepan. These contrasting approaches are reflected today in dishes as different as the French *tripes à la mode de Caen,* which requires up to ten hours of slow cooking, and the typically Italian *saltimbocca alla romana,* a light veal dish that can be sautéed in minutes.

A medieval feast is set before Jean, duc de Berry, in this miniature (1413–16) by the Limbourg brothers. The earliest books of European court cuisine, dating from the late 14th century, prescribe heavily seasoned soups, stews, and roasts. (Musée Condé, Chantilly, France.)

The kitchen in colonial New England was dominated by a huge fireplace, which supplied heat to the room and was used for the daily food preparation. A smaller oven was heated with coals for weekly baking of breads and pastries.

Medieval Cookery. By all accounts, the medieval cookery of northern Europe would not have pleased a modern palate. Sauces were merely bread-thickened broths, and such dishes as browets and hotchpots were hashes distinguishable only by their relative degrees of wetness or dryness. Spices, for the few who could afford them, were used indiscriminately to mask the pervasive odor of spoiled meat. Few culinary niceties were possible in kitchens where cooks were kept at arm's length from their pots by the heat of blazing log fires.

South of the Alps, however, the Italians were able to draw on culinary legacies from the Greeks, Etruscans, and Saracens and to develop regional cuisines that were both simple and balanced. Green vegetables, rare in transalpine Europe, were an essential part of the cuisine. Fish stews were both nutritious and delectable and required little cooking time. Pastas, polenta, and rice lent themselves to many sauces and garnishes that barely resembled the soggy sauces and bland stews of France, England, and Germany. By the early Renaissance, Italians of reasonable means cooked and ate much as most Italians do today.

In 1533, Catherine de Médicis arrived in France from Florence with a retinue of master chefs. She brought Italian staples: milk-fed veal, baby peas, artichokes, broccoli, and various pastas. The French court tasted, for the first time, such delicacies as quenelles (fish dumplings),

The gas-burning stove, which came into use during the late 19th century, made possible careful regulation of both stove-top and oven temperatures.

zabaglione (a rich egg-yolk and wine custard), and scaloppine. With her arrival, French cookery embarked on a course that produced the most complex and refined cuisine in the Western world.

Emergence of the French Cuisine. Professional chefs had existed in Europe at least since the emergence of Athens as the cultural center of the classical world, but no single individual's impact on a national cuisine even remotely approached that of Antonin Carême, who revolutionized French cooking (and northern European cooking in general) during a career spent in the kitchens of Europe's social and political leaders. Stressing "delicacy, order, and economy," Carême systematized and codified French cooking, brought symmetry and logical progression to the service of meals, and introduced a new awareness of freshness and sanitation into the French kitchen.

Carême wrought culinary miracles with the inadequate equipment at his disposal. The charcoal-burning stoves with which he worked brought his delicately constructed dishes into direct contact with live embers, often scorching or setting them ablaze. Ovens had to be stoked and emptied of ashes repeatedly, and with no effective means of temperature control, armies of cooks were required to give their undivided attention to individual dishes. In 1795, however, the American-born physicist and adventurer Count Rumford (Benjamin Thompson) produced the first of a series of devices that ultimately evolved into the closed-top cooking range. By means of an ingenious system of flues and dampers, the range made adjustable heat possible and enormously expanded the scope of culinary activities.

The Chinese Influence. The rice-based cooking of China has exerted the most pervasive influence on world cookery. Like the Italians, the Chinese faced a chronic fuel shortage early in their history that necessitated achieving maximal results from minimal means. Chinese cooks expended their working time on advance preparation of ingredients, which they ingeniously cut and hacked into morsels small enough to be cooked in seconds. The basic utensil was the wok.

The wok is a thin, unfooted metal bowl that conducts heat evenly and quickly and can be used for a wide variety of basic culinary techniques: stir-frying, deep-fat frying, braising, sautéing, and, with the addition of a bamboo basket and cover, steaming. Using the wok, a Chinese cook can produce an astonishingly complex, hot, one-dish meal in two minutes or less by using precut ingredients in a rapid succession determined by the cooking time each requires. Chinese cooking is characterized by a harmony of contrasting colors, flavors, and textures; by the crispness and brightness of its vegetables and the appropriateness of its sauces; by its eschewal of dairy products; and by its unusual—to Western taste—ingredients.

Japan, perennially overpopulated and short of both food and fuel, further refined Chinese cooking techniques, creating an exquisite cuisine composed primarily of raw and very lightly cooked foods. In Indian cultures the potential monotony of a vegetarian cuisine was relieved by the imaginative use of indigenous spices. In the Near East, nomads and their descendants continued to cook much as the Homeric warriors had when meat was plentiful. When it was relatively scarce, they combined meat with grain to produce such dishes as couscous, grains of wheat cooked soft in the steam of a stew. In the Americas, native cooking depended chiefly on tomatoes, corn, various peppers, gourds, and squashes.

American Cuisines. Neither the contemporary United States nor Canada has a clearly defined national cuisine, and that of Mexico has been influenced heavily by the cooking of Spain. Nonetheless, New World cooking has profoundly influenced worldwide cooking by its use of chocolate, vanilla, tomatoes, corn, potatoes, peppers, and many other foods unknown elsewhere before the late 15th century. More recently, American food technology increasingly has shaped the course of cooking throughout the world. At the same time, jet travel has exposed Americans to Old World dishes and techniques.

Technological advances notwithstanding (see FOOD INDUSTRY), cookery today is basically what it has been since Neolithic times. People still roast, grill, and bake their foods, using dry-heat techniques known, at least in rudimentary form, for countless millennia. They still sauté food in small amounts of fat, fry food in deep fat, boil food in liquids, and stew and braise food in lesser amounts of liquid, as people have done since the invention of pottery.

Cooley, Denton A.   Denton Arthur Cooley, b. Houston, Tex., Aug. 22, 1920, an American surgeon and educator, is known for his pioneering work in heart surgery. He distinguished himself by his surgical talents in infantile heart disease and by his heart transplant operations. In April 1969 he became the first to implant an artificial heart into a human. He inserted a silicone heart into a 47-year-old man who kept it for 65 hours, until a human heart was available for transplant. A professor of surgery (1962–69) at Baylor University School of Medicine, Cooley founded (1962) the Texas Heart Institute in Houston and has been chief of surgery there since 1969.

Cooley's anemia   Cooley's anemia, or beta-thalassemia major, results from an inherited deficiency that causes the red blood cells to be small, low in hemoglobin, and short-lived. The frequent transfusions required to prevent profound anemia produce excessive amounts of iron, which greatly tax the heart. Death occurs in the teens or early twenties because of anemia or heart failure. Persons with Cooley's anemia have inherited two genes that produce insufficient beta-hemoglobin chains (see GENETIC DISEASES). Persons who have one normal gene and one beta-thalassemia gene have only minor symptoms and a normal life span. Researchers have hypothesized that thalassemia and a related disease, SICKLE-CELL DISEASE, are caused by a genetic mechanism that prevents malaria. Cooley's anemia occurs primarily in peoples originating in Mediterranean and Southeast Asian regions; its incidence is high among Italians.

Coolidge, Calvin   Calvin Coolidge was the 30th president of the United States, achieving the office upon the death of Warren G. HARDING in 1923. He was elected president in 1924 and retired from public life in 1929. During his more than 5 years in the White House, Coolidge kept a deliberately low presidential profile. He favored a minimum of government intervention in domestic affairs; foreign policy he left in the hands of Secretary of State Frank B. KELLOGG.

Early Political Career. John Calvin Coolidge was born on July 4, 1872, in Plymouth Notch, Vt., the son of a merchant. After graduating from Amherst College, he studied law and began practicing in the small town of Northampton, Mass. His law practice and his political activities were routine until 1910. As a Republican, he served in a variety of local offices and was elected to the state legislature in 1907. His work there attracted little notice. After being elected mayor of Northampton in 1909 and 1910, Coolidge devoted himself fully to his political career. In 1911 he went to the state senate, where his thorough work earned him leadership positions. In 1913 he became president of the senate.

Coolidge was a taciturn, frugal, and industrious man who admired businesspeople and corporations, and he used his influence in the senate to caution against reform measures that might discourage individuals from investing their capital in new projects. As to governmental activity, he said that administration should have "a chance to catch up with legislation." In 1915, Coolidge was elected lieutenant governor. His friendship with party leaders and his ability to voice the interests of Massachusetts earned him popularity in his party and brought him the governorship in 1918.

As governor, Coolidge had to deal only with minor matters until the dramatic Boston police strike of 1919. This strike developed out of the inflation that followed World War I, as police officers saw their wages hold steady while the cost of living and the incomes of other groups rose. Although it was illegal for police officers to form a labor union, they did so anyway. When Boston authorities threatened disciplinary action against the union leaders, the police officers countered with a strike. During the strike, criminal elements roamed the city; there was

CALVIN COOLIDGE
30th President of the United States (1923–1929)

Nickname: "Silent Cal"

Born: July 4, 1872, Plymouth Notch, Vt.

Education: Amherst College (graduated 1895)

Profession: Lawyer

Religious Affiliation: Congregationalist

Marriage: Oct. 4, 1905, to Grace Anna Goodhue (1879–1957)

Children: John Coolidge (1906–   ); Calvin Coolidge (1908–1924).

Political Affiliation: Republican

Writings: *The Autobiography of Calvin Coolidge* (1929)

Died: Jan. 5, 1933, Northampton, Mass.

Buried: Plymouth Notch, Vt.

Vice President: Charles G. Dawes (1925–29)

rioting, violence, and property damage. On the second day, Governor Coolidge called out the state militia to restore order. In a public exchange of letters with Samuel Gompers, president of the American Federation of Labor, Coolidge made the statement, "There is no right to strike against the public safety by anybody, anywhere, anytime."

His popular action in the Boston police strike earned Coolidge the Republican vice-presidential nomination in 1920. Party leaders had selected Senator Lenroot of Wisconsin for the post, but the delegates chose Coolidge instead. He and Warren G. Harding won election easily. As vice-president, Coolidge remained in the background. The presidency came to him upon the death of Harding on Aug. 2, 1923.

Coolidge as President. As president, Coolidge kept a slack rein, believing that the nation needed to focus attention on private affairs rather than be pressed to follow bold new public policies. His outlook paralleled that of the business community. One of his sayings was that "the business of America is business." After commercial farmers had lobbied in Congress for relief from depressed conditions, Coolidge vetoed the resulting McNary-Haugen bill. When the farmers argued that manufacturers received substantial federal help from the high protective tariff and that the government ought to do something for agriculture, the president replied that the farmers were also aided by the tariff. His vetoes prevailed over the farm

bloc in Congress. During his administration the economy prospered and the stock market boomed, but the prosperity did not benefit all sections of the nation equally. Industries such as coal mining remained depressed, and some cities had unemployment rates surpassing 10 percent.

In 1928, Coolidge announced that he would not seek reelection. He retired to Northampton, Mass., wrote his autobiography, and died there on Jan. 5, 1933. He was buried in the family plot in Plymouth Notch, Vt.

cooling tower A cooling tower is a device that cools large quantities of water carrying waste heat from power-generating stations, industrial plants, or on a smaller scale, central-air-conditioning systems. To be cooled, water usually is sprayed into air passing through the tower. As evaporation occurs, the temperature of the remaining water decreases.

To aid evaporation, the water spray falls onto a series of decks or baffles inside the tower. These devices increase the surface area of the water exposed for evaporation. The cooled water then falls into a catch basin, or pond, at the bottom of the tower. In a steam plant, this water is then circulated from the cooling tower to the condenser. Industrial cooling towers are usually tall structures with a hyperbolic shape.

coonhound see BLACK-AND-TAN COONHOUND

Cooper, Gary Gary Cooper, b. Helena, Mont., May 7, 1901, d. May 13, 1961, was the stage name of Frank James Cooper, one of the most famous of Hollywood's film stars. Known especially for his portrayals of strong, silent heroes, he won Academy Awards for two such characterizations in *Sergeant York* (1941) and *High Noon* (1952).

Cooper played variations on this role in such films as *The Virginians* (1929), *A Farewell to Arms* (1933), *The Plainsman* (1937), *Beau Geste* (1939), *For Whom the Bell Tolls* (1943), and *The Court Martial of Billy Mitchell* (1955). His lighter comic and romantic films include *Mr. Deeds Goes to Town* (1936) and *Love in the Afternoon* (1957).

Gary Cooper (center) *appears in a scene from the 1941 film* Sergeant York. *Cooper achieved stardom as the strong, silent hero of Westerns and adventure movies.*

Cooper, James Fenimore James Fenimore Cooper, b. Burlington, N.J., Sept. 15, 1789, d. Sept. 14, 1851, the most significant American novelist before Nathaniel Hawthorne and a member of the Knickerbocker group, was an author of international stature and continuing influence. His works have been widely translated; some, such as his LEATHERSTOCKING TALES, are considered world classics. Cooper invented the modern sea novel; his wilderness novels were the first significant examples of their type, and many of their elements have become standard in today's Western stories and films.

Life. Cooper grew up in Cooperstown, N.Y., an area developed from wilderness by his father. He attended Yale University for two years; served for another few years in the navy; married Susan De Lancey, from an influential New York family; and tried gentleman farming. His first novel, *Precaution* (1820), was moderately received, but *The Spy* (1821) was an immediate success. In 1822 the Coopers moved to New York City, where he became a pro-

James Fenimore Cooper was one of the first American writers to achieve a wide international audience. He is best remembered for the five novels known collectively as The Leatherstocking Tales. *That saga, which includes* The Last of the Mohicans *(1826) and* The Deerslayer *(1841), recounts the adventures of the backwoodsman Natty Bumppo and his Indian comrades.*

fessional writer and a leader of the city's intellectuals. From 1826 to 1833, Cooper lived abroad in England, France, Switzerland, and Italy. After returning to the United States he settled in Cooperstown.

Works. Cooper's novels are generally classified in six overlapping groups. Included among the historical romances are *The Leatherstocking Tales* (1823–41), *The Spy,* and *The Wept of Wish-ton-Wish* (1829). *The Leatherstocking Tales* are also grouped among the wilderness novels, which include such works as *Wyandotte* (1843). The best known of the sea novels are *The Pilot* (1823), his first novel of this type, *The Red Rover* (1828), and *The Water-Witch* (1831). Cooper's relatively minor fiction falls into the last three groups: novels with European settings, such as *The Bravo* (1831); sociopolitical novels, such as *Home as Found* (1838); and the so-called Littlepage Manuscripts, such as *Satanstoe* (1845), most of which were written late in his career. Cooper's nonfiction includes travel books, a history of the U.S. Navy, and social critiques, particularly criticism of what he felt to be Europeans' false notion of American democracy.

Cooper, Leroy Gordon, Jr. The American astronaut Leroy Gordon Cooper, Jr., b. Shawnee, Okla., Mar. 6, 1927, was the fourth American to orbit the Earth. He joined the air force in 1949, later earned a bachelor of science degree in aeronautical engineering from the Air Force Institute of Technology, and was assigned to test-pilot training.

Cooper was chosen in 1959 to be one of America's first seven astronauts. His first mission in space as part of Project Mercury (see MERCURY PROGRAM) took him around the Earth 22 times in 1963. His second mission in space was as commander of GEMINI 5 (1965), which lasted just under eight days in space.

Cooper, Peter An American businessman, inventor, and philanthropist, Peter Cooper, b. New York City, Feb.

12, 1791, d. Apr. 4, 1883, is remembered as the builder of the first U.S. steam locomotive *Tom Thumb*. He also established (1859) Cooper Union, a New York City college devoted to free adult education in technology, science, and art. Always active in municipal affairs, Cooper supported public schools and sought better police and fire protection. Apprenticed to a coach maker at 17, Cooper eventually increased his business holdings to include a glue company, iron mines, and several foundries. He introduced (1856) the Bessemer process into U.S. steelmaking and was president of the first transatlantic cable company. At the age of 85 he ran for president as the Greenback party nominee.

Cooper Union   see COOPER, PETER

---

cooperative   A cooperative is a voluntary form of business organization owned by its patrons and run for the benefit of those who use its services. Cooperatives are found in most countries of the world today. They operate on a break-even basis, distributing profits to the members in proportion to the volume of business each member has done with the cooperative.

Principles of Cooperatives. Most cooperatives follow principles that originated with the Rochdale Society of Equitable Pioneers in Rochdale, England. In 1844, a group of 28 flannel weavers and other workers opened a cooperative store that purchased groceries, sold them for cash at the prevailing price, and distributed profits to the members on the basis of their patronage.

Today's basic cooperative principles, known as the Rochdale principles, include the following: (1) Open membership—anyone may become a member by purchasing one or more shares of stock and doing business with the cooperative. (2) One member, one vote—each member has only one vote in the cooperative regardless of the number of shares of stock the member owns. This principle is sometimes modified to allow voting in proportion to patronage. (3) No price cutting—cooperatives normally sell goods at the prevailing market price. (4) Service at cost—all profits are allocated to the members on the basis of percentage. (5) Limited dividends—cooperative dividends in the United States are generally limited by law to 8 percent. This ensures that the benefits are returned to patrons in the form of patronage refunds. (6) Quality products—because cooperatives are owned by their patrons, they generally provide the quality of products and services most generally needed and desired. (7) Education—new patrons are indoctrinated both in the need for cooperatives and in their principles of operation.

Types. The five major types of cooperatives are supply, marketing, consumer, credit, and those providing services.

Supply cooperatives are operated primarily by farmers. Local supply cooperatives owned by farmers provide feed, seed, fertilizer, oil, chemicals, and other materials needed on the farm. These local cooperatives generally own regional and national cooperatives that produce the goods sold by the local cooperatives. There are approximately 2,000 U.S. farm supply cooperatives; they supply U.S.

agriculture with about 26 percent of its requirements.

Marketing cooperatives engage in the collection, processing, sale, and distribution of farm products. The right of U.S. farmers to form marketing cooperatives was guaranteed by Congress in the Capper-Volstead Act of 1922. Marketing cooperatives handle about 28 percent of total U.S. agricultural production.

Consumer cooperatives have been much less successful in the United States than supply and marketing cooperatives. Interest expanded rapidly in the early 1970s, however, when many small food-purchasing cooperatives were formed in large cities. These cooperatives seek to lower food costs through direct-to-consumer purchases of a relatively small number of grocery items.

Credit unions and the various components of the cooperative farm credit system are numerous in the United States. In a CREDIT UNION, members pool their savings. These savings in turn become a source of funds for those who want to borrow. Farm credit cooperatives, including the federal land banks, production credit associations, and banks for cooperatives, are the largest single source of credit for American farmers and ranchers.

Cooperatives throughout the World. From their beginnings in Rochdale, cooperatives expanded throughout the world. Cooperative activities in Canada developed along the same general lines as in the United States. In Europe they range from the strong consumer and producer cooperatives of Scandinavia to employee cooperatives in France that own industrial plants.

In Africa, Asia, and South America, cooperatives are increasingly used as tools of economic development. In areas where landholdings have been fragmented into small units, cooperatives provide a means of access to credit and supplies and a channel through which products can be marketed.

So-called cooperatives are also prominent in Communist countries, especially the Soviet Union, where agriculture is organized in large COLLECTIVE FARMS. Membership is usually compulsory, and the government determines production goals. Any surplus may be sold on the free market.

Cooperstown   Cooperstown (1990 pop., 2,180), a resort village and the seat of Otsego County, is located in eastern New York. Noted primarily, but erroneously, as the birthplace of baseball (1839), Cooperstown is the home of the National Baseball Hall of Fame and Museum.

---

coordinate systems (astronomy)   Coordinate systems are used in astronomy to designate the locations of celestial objects in the sky. Because a direction can be conveniently specified by using two angles, the basic coordinate systems in astronomy are what would be called spherical polar coordinates in geometry. In describing the coordinate systems used in astronomy it is convenient to adopt the model of the CELESTIAL SPHERE, which has the "fixed" stars on its surface and the observer at its center, the origin O. The angles used to specify positions on the celestial sphere are similar to the longitude and latitude of a point on the surface of the Earth. It is necessary to define a reference plane (equivalent to a great circle on the celestial sphere) through the origin, and a reference direction in that plane. Four principal reference systems are used.

The Equatorial System

The reference circle of the equatorial system is the equator, and the reference direction from which angular distances on this circle are measured is the vernal EQUINOX. A great circle passing through a star and the celestial poles is called an hour circle. The angle measured from the equator to the star along the hour circle is the star's declination, δ, measured in degrees, with positive as north and negative as south. The angle measured from the vernal equinox in the west-to-east direction, which is opposite to the apparent rotation of the celestial sphere, is the star's right ascension, α, measured in hours, such that 360 degrees is equivalent to 24 hours. An observer's local meridian is the great circle passing through the observer's zenith and the celestial poles. The angle measured westward from this meridian to the hour circle is called the hour angle (HA) of the star. Since the vernal equinox and equator are not fixed, because of PRECESSION, it is necessary to specify at what date or epoch the coordinates were measured.

The Horizontal System

The reference plane of the horizontal system is the observer's horizon, and the reference direction from which angular distances on this plane are measured is north. The coordinates are altitude, h, measured from the horizon to the star along the vertical circle containing the zenith and the star (positive above the horizon and negative below it); and azimuth, A, measured eastward from the north to that vertical circle. The zenith distance, ζ, sometimes used instead of h, is the angle from the zenith to the star.

The Ecliptic System

The reference circle of the ecliptic system is the ECLIPTIC, and the reference direction is the vernal equinox, with the epoch specified. Celestial latitude, β, is measured from the ecliptic along the latitude circle (passing through a star and the ecliptic north pole), with positive as north and negative as south. Celestial longitude, λ, is measured from the vernal equinox to the latitude circle in the same sense as right ascension. This is convenient when referring to bodies in the solar system.

The Galactic System

The reference plane of the galactic system is the mean plane of our galaxy (the Milky Way), called the galactic equator, and the reference direction is the galactic center. Galactic latitude, b, is measured from the galactic equator along the great circle passing through the star and the galactic poles, with positive as north and negative as south. Galactic longitude, l, is measured eastward from the galactic center.

coordinate systems (mathematics)   A coordinate system is a method by which a set of numbers is used to locate the position of a point. The numbers are called the point's coordinates. In a coordinate system, a single point corresponds to each set of coordinates. Coordinate systems are used in ANALYTIC GEOMETRY to study properties of geometric objects with algebraic techniques.

When an object having a finite number of degrees of freedom is considered among all the objects of that kind, the object in question can be conveniently characterized and distinguished from the other objects by a set of coordinates, that is, a set of numbers, one for each degree of freedom. For example, a point in a plane has two degrees of freedom, so that the point has two coordinates with respect to any coordinate system of the plane.

Common coordinate systems are Cartesian coordinates and polar coordinates in two-dimensional space, and Cartesian, spherical, and cylindrical coordinates in three-dimensional space.

Coordinate Systems in Two Dimensions. Through an arbitrary point O in the plane, two mutually perpendicular lines, usually horizontal and vertical, are drawn. The x-axis is taken to be horizontal, the y-axis is vertical, and point O is called the origin. The portion of the x-axis to the right of the origin is the positive x-axis, and the part of the y-axis above the origin is called the positive y-axis. The two axes (coordinate axes) divide the plane into four quadrants: the upper right (first), the upper left (second), the lower left (third), and the lower right (fourth). The x-coordinate, or abscissa, of a point P in the plane is the perpendicular distance of P from the y-axis. It is positive if P is to the right of the y-axis, negative if P is to the left, and zero if P is on the y-axis. The y-coordinate, or ordinate, of P is analogously the perpendicular distance of P from the x-axis. It is, respectively, positive, negative, or zero if P is above, below, or on the x-axis. The ordered pair (x, y) represents the coordinates of P in the coordinate system thus defined. The point P with coordinates (x, y) is symbolically represented as P (x, y). This system is called a two-dimensional, or plane, Cartesian coordi-

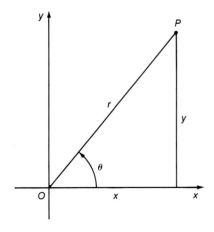

nate system (named for René DESCARTES).

A polar coordinate system in two dimensions is a system determined by a fixed point O, called the pole, and an axis through it, called the initial line. A point P in the plane can then be fixed by specifying two quantities: (1) the angle Θ through which the axis must be rotated in the counterclockwise direction so as to pass through P, and (2) the positive distance r of the point P from the pole. The notation $P(r, \Theta)$ is used to represent P in polar coordinates r and Θ.

Coordinate Systems in Three Dimensions. Three mutually perpendicular lines (the coordinate axes) are drawn through an arbitrary point O, the origin, in space. The axes are called the x-axis, y-axis, and z-axis. The plane containing the x-axis and the y-axis is the xy-plane (a coordinate plane) and the z-axis is a normal (line that is perpendicular) to this plane. The other two coordinate planes are defined likewise. The x-coordinate of a point P is the perpendicular distance of P from the yz-plane. The y-coordinate and the z-coordinate are defined similarly. The three coordinate planes divide all space into octants. If P is a point in the first octant, all the coordinates of P are positive.

The spherical coordinate system in space is a system that locates a point P by its distance from a fixed point O (the pole), and by two angles that describe the orientation of the segment OP. The coordinate system is fixed by two perpendicular half-lines through O. One of these is the polar axis, and the plane that contains the two half-lines is called the initial meridian plane. A coordinate system consisting of a plane with polar coordinates and a z-axis through the pole, or origin, perpendicular to the plane is called a cylindrical polar coordinate system.

coordination compounds Coordination compounds are chemical substances formed by the union of two or more compounds that can exist independently. They are called coordination complexes or complex compounds. The chemical linkage between the two substances is usually a covalent bond (see CHEMICAL BOND) characterized by the sharing of a pair of electrons donated by an atom from one of the combining substances. This type of bond is called a coordinate covalent bond and forms most readily between a metallic element and a nonmetallic element. The atoms, ions, or molecules of nonmetallic elements that furnish the pairs of electrons to a central metal atom and thereby become bonded or linked to it are known as ligands, and the central atom or center of coordination is usually a transition metal such as copper, nickel, or cobalt.

Coordination compounds exist as solids, liquids, or gases. For example, nickel forms a gaseous nickel tetracarbonyl compound, which is useful in metal purification by the Mond process. Coordination compounds form readily in aqueous solution, and applications have been developed for refining silver and gold from their ores through water-soluble cyanide complexes.

In 1893, Alfred Werner proposed the first theory that successfully explained the properties of coordination compounds. Werner described the aggregate of the central metal atom and its convalently held ligands as a coordination sphere. The number of donor atoms bonded to the metal atom is called its coordination number. Coordination numbers of 6, 4, and 2, in that order, most frequently occur. For example, in $Ag(NH_3)_2Cl$, silver chloride (AgCl) is combined with two molecules of ammonia (NH_3) and Ag has coordination number 2.

Metals, ligands, and ions can combine in many ways, forming coordination compounds that are ISOMERS of all types, that is, compounds that have identical composition but different arragements of their parts. Coordination compounds may be geometric isomers, stereoisomers (see STEREOCHEMISTRY), isomers with OPTICAL ACTIVITY, and isomers that differ in how ligands and ions are associated.

coot Coot is the common name for ducklike aquatic birds that belong to the genus *Fulica*. They are related to the rails and gallinules. Coots have plump bodies, short tails, and lobed toes. They are strong swimmers and divers, and feed chiefly on vegetation. The American coot, *F. americana*, is slate gray with a white bill and has a white patch under the tail; it is the only U.S. species. The common coot, *F. atra*, of the Old World lacks the white tail patch. Some sea ducks, especially the scoters, are colloquially called coots.

Coover, Robert The novels of the American writer Robert Lowell Coover, b. Charles City, Iowa, Feb. 4, 1932, often transmute ordinary events into the unlikely and bizarre. His early work includes *The Origin of the Brunists* (1966; William Faulkner Award) and *The Public Burning* (1977), a satirical, panoramic tale that ends with the public execution of Julius and Ethel Rosenberg. Among more recent novels are *Gerald's Party* (1986), a rather heavy-handed social satire, and *A Night at the Movies* (1987), a series of brilliant parodies of popular cinematic myths. Coover's other works include plays and short stories.

Copán [koh-pahn'] Copán, in northwest Honduras, was the most southern of MAYA cities in the Classic period (AD 250–900). At least 16 Maya kings ruled in succession; the last king, Yax Pac ("Rising Sun"), commissioned many of the constructions visible today.

Copán royalty emphasized the arts and writing, and even members of the royal family appear to have been scribes and priests. Kings were commemorated by lifelike portraits on stelae (stone shafts). Long texts on sides and backs of stelae were sometimes inscribed in unusual fashion, with glyphs (ideograms) made into full human, supernatural, or animal figures. The Main Acropolis, a royal palace, overlooks the Hieroglyphic Stairway, a funerary pyramid whose steps are inscribed with 2,500 glyphs, the longest Maya text known. Excavations in the 1970s and '80s revealed living quarters of both the rich and poor at Copán as well as tombs and treasures of the elite.

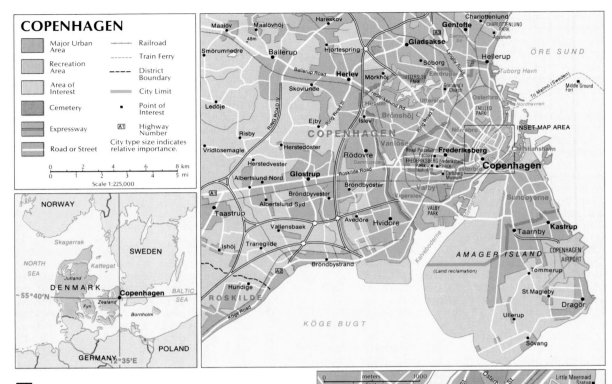

COPENHAGEN

▨	Major Urban Area	—+—	Railroad
▨	Recreation Area	-----	Train Ferry
▨	Area of Interest	- - -	District Boundary
▨	Cemetery	▬	City Limit
▨	Expressway	■	Point of Interest
▨	Road or Street	A1	Highway Number

City type size indicates relative importance.

Scale 1:225,000

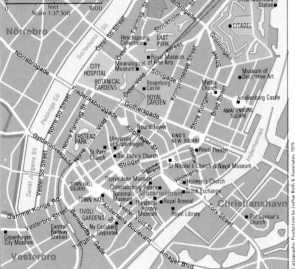

Scale 1:37,500

Cartographic Production by Lothar Roth & Associates, 1979

Copenhagen [koh'-pen-hah-gen]   Copenhagen (Danish: København; or the "merchants' harbor") is the capital and largest city of Denmark. It has a population of 476,810 (1988 est.), and its metropolitan area is the home of 1,340,618 people, about 26% of Denmark's total population. The city lies on the eastern shore of the island of Sjaelland, or Zealand, at the southern end of Øresund (The Sound), the waterway that separates Denmark from Sweden and links the Baltic with the North Sea.

Contemporary City. The nucleus of the city is Slotsholmen, or Castle Isle, where a fortification was built in 1167. Its site is now occupied by Christiansborg Palace, constructed between 1907 and 1915 as a home for the legislature and government ministries. Nearby is the Thorvaldsen Museum and the Exchange (Børsen), built from 1619 to 1640, with a twisting spire made up of the interwoven tails of four sculptured dragons. North of the old city is Frederikstad, a planned suburb built in the 18th century. In it is the Amalienborg Palace, since 1794 the residence of the Danish sovereign. Rosenborg Palace was built in the early 17th century as the summer residence of the monarch but is now a museum. To the southeast, beyond the dock quarter of Christianshavn, is the largely residential suburb of Amager. The island of Amager, much of which is low-lying and marshy, is the site of Copenhagen's Kastrup airport, one of the largest in Europe.

Economy. Copenhagen is by far the largest manufac-

turing center in Denmark; its industries include metalworking, engineering, garment manufacturing, and food processing. Better known, although economically less important, are the city's breweries and china factories. There is also a large publishing industry. Historically, the city profited from the fact that Øresund offered the best navigable route between the Baltic and the North Sea. Ships sailing the waterway passed by the city and until 1857 were required to stop and pay a toll at Helsingör (Elsinor) 40 km (25 mi) to the north.

History. Copenhagen began to develop in the 12th century as a fortified fishing village. From about 1428 it was the residence of the Danish monarchs. Nevertheless, it did not grow significantly until about 1600, when the kingdom of Denmark began to play a more important role in European affairs. Much of the city was built of wood, and Copenhagen was devastated by fire several times, the worst of them in 1728 and 1795. Repeated destruction allowed the city to be replanned and rebuilt at intervals; today it is noteworthy among European cities for its wide boulevards and public parks and gardens. Among these is the Tivoli, a highly sophisticated amusement park laid out in 1843.

Copenhagen's involvement in the Napoleonic Wars, through its control of Øresund, resulted in the bombardment of the city by the British fleet in 1801 (under Lord Nelson) and again in 1807. Increasing trade led to the establishment of a free port in 1894, and Copenhagen became an intermediary trade center for the Baltic region. Its university was founded in 1479 by King Christian I.

copepod [koh'-puh-pahd] Copepods are minute CRUSTACEANS, subclass Copepoda, found in both salt and fresh water. Certain species of copepod provide an intermediate step in the oceanic food chain between phytoplankton and marine animals such as fish or whales. A free-living copepod, unlike most crustaceans, lacks compound eyes and a carapace, or external cover. It has five pairs of legs attached to the thorax and a divided, taillike appendage. Most parasitic copepods lose crustacean features and resemble larvae after entering the host, which is usually a fish.

Copernicus, Nicolaus [kuh-pur'-ni-kuhs, nik'-oh-luhs] Nicolaus Copernicus, b. Thorn (Toruń), Poland, Feb. 19, 1473, d. May 24, 1543, was destined to become, through the publication of his heliocentric theory 70 years later, one of the seminal figures in the history of scientific thought. The son of a prosperous merchant, after his father's death he was raised by a maternal uncle, who enabled him to enter the University of Kraków, then famous for its mathematics, philosophy, and astronomy curriculum. This experience stimulated the young Copernicus to study further liberal arts at Bologna (1496–1501), medicine at Padua, and law at the University of Ferrara, from which he emerged in 1503 with the doctorate in canon law. Shortly afterward he returned to Poland and eventually settled at the cathedral in Frauenberg, less than 160 km (100 mi) from his birthplace. Elected a canon of the church, Copernicus not only faithfully per-

The Polish astronomer Nicolaus Copernicus revolutionized science and the conception of the universe with his heliocentric theory of planetary movement, published as De revolutionibus orbium coelestium (1543).

formed his ecclesiastical duties, but also practiced medicine, wrote a treatise on monetary reform, and turned his attention to a subject in which he had long been interested—astronomy.

By May 1514, Copernicus had written and discreetly circulated in manuscript his *Commentariolus*, the first outline of those arguments eventually substantiated in *De revolutionibus orbium coelestium* (On the Revolutions of the Heavenly Spheres, 1543). This classic work challenged the geocentric cosmology that had been accepted dogmatically since the time of Aristotle. In direct opposition to Aristotle and to the 2d-century astronomer Ptolemy, Copernicus proposed that a rotating Earth revolving with the other planets about a stationary central Sun could account in a simpler way for the same observed phenomena of the daily rotation of the heavens, the annual movement of the Sun through the ecliptic, and the periodic retrograde motion of the planets.

In the midst of his radical reordering of the structure of the universe, Copernicus still adhered to the ancient Aristotelian doctrines of solid celestial spheres and perfect circular motion of heavenly bodies, and he held essentially intact the entire Aristotelian physics of motion. Moreover, with significant innovations, he clung to the Ptolemaic representation of planetary motion by means of complicated combinations of circles called epicycles. These aspects of the Copernican treatise do not mitigate the novelty or the impact of the final theory or the author's firm conviction that his system was an accurate representation of physical reality.

The enunciation of the heliocentric theory by Copernicus marked the beginning of the scientific revolution, and of a new view of a greatly enlarged universe. It was a shift away from the anthropocentrism of the ancient and medieval world. A scientific theory that reflected so profoundly on humanity was not welcomed by the church, and it was only after the publication (1540) of *Narratio prima* (A First Account), by an enthusiastic supporter named Rheticus, that the aged Copernicus agreed to commit to print the theory already outlined in 1514. An undocumented, but often repeated, story holds that Copernicus received a printed copy of his treatise on his deathbed.

Copland, Aaron [kohp'-land] Aaron Copland, b. Brooklyn, N.Y., Nov. 14, 1900, d. Dec. 2, 1990, was a leading American composer of the 20th century. He was the first of many American musicians to study with Nadia Boulanger in Paris (1921–24). On his return to the United States, he became identified with brash modernism. Copland later developed a folksy American style that won him a wide audience. He also taught and lectured extensively, wrote several books, and appeared frequently as a conductor of his own and other composers' music.

Copland is perhaps most famous for his superb ballet scores, such as *Billy the Kid* (1938), *Rodeo* (1942), and *Appalachian Spring* (1944), which are all based on American folklore. He also composed two operas, *The Second Hurricane* (1937) and *The Tender Land* (1954), as well as choral works and songs. His music for films includes that for *Of Mice and Men* (1939), *Our Town* (1940), *The Red Pony* (1948), and *The Heiress* (1949). Copland's *Piano Variations* (1930) is the most influential of his many solo and chamber works. Outstanding among his orchestral scores are the jazzy *Piano Concerto* (1927) and *Music for the Theatre* (1925), the *Clarinet Concerto* (1948) written for Benny Goodman, *El Salón México* (1936), the *Symphony No. 3* (1946) incorporating the famous "Fanfare for the Common Man," and *A Lincoln Portrait* (1942).

Aaron Copland, one of America's most versatile composers, has written such diverse works as the ballet Appalachian Spring *(1944) and the* film score for Steinbeck's Of Mice and Men *(1939). Incorporating jazz and folk elements, Copland has tried to make contemporary music acceptable to a large public by writing in a specifically American musical idiom.*

Copley, John Singleton [kohp'-lee] John Singleton Copley, b. Boston, July 3, 1738, d. Sept. 9, 1815,

The American artist John Singleton Copley created a style that established his place as one of the masters of the colonial period. Watson and the Shark *(1778) is representative of his work in historical genre painting. (Museum of Fine Arts, Boston.)*

was North America's first great portrait painter. Portraiture was in great demand in the colonies, and Copley excelled at this as had few other 18th-century American artists. His colonial portraits are remarkable for their verisimilitude. Among his best known are those of the Boston silversmiths *Nathaniel Hurd* (1766; Cleveland Museum of Art) and *Paul Revere* (c.1768; Museum of Fine Arts, Boston). Perhaps his most often reproduced portrait is that of his half-brother, Henry Pelham, *The Boy with the Squirrel* (c.1765; Worcester Art Museum, Mass.).

In 1774 and 1775, Copley made the painter's obligatory grand tour of Italy, and then he settled in London. Thereafter, even his portraits, such as *The Izard Family* (1775; Museum of Fine Arts, Boston), included such classical props as Greek vases, columns, and ruins in the background, a marked contrast to the elegant simplicity of such colonial portraits as *Mr. and Mrs. Thomas Mifflin* (1773; Historical Society of Pennsylvania, Philadelphia).

Copley remained in London, was elected an Associate Member of the Royal Academy in 1776, and, on receiving full membership in 1779, exhibited his famous *Watson and the Shark* (1778; Museum of Fine Arts, Boston), a dramatic depiction of a real event in Havana harbor and an early landmark of romanticized contemporary history painting. Equally popular during the same period was *The Death of the Earl of Chatham* (1780; Tate Gallery, London), showing a Romanized Pitt the Elder expiring amid robed peers. Although two portrait groups of 1785—one portraying Copley's own family and another, *The Three Daughters of George the III* (collection of H.M. Queen Elizabeth II)—are charming, the artist's fame as a portraitist rests on the more realistic and more spontaneous works he produced earlier in Boston.

copolymer   see PLASTICS

copper The chemical element copper is a reddish, ductile metal. Its symbol is Cu, its atomic number is 29, and its atomic weight is 63.546. Copper is a TRANSITION ELEMENT at the head of Group IB in the periodic table.

Copper was the first metal used by humans and is second only to iron in its utility through the ages. The name is derived from the Latin *cuprum*, "copper," from the earlier Latin *Cyprium*, "Cyprian metal." The discovery of the metal dates from prehistoric times, and it is estimated that copper was first used about 5000 BC or even earlier.

Natural Occurrence and Extraction. More than 160 minerals containing copper are known. Copper constitutes 70 parts per million of the Earth's crust and is present to the extent of 0.020–0.001 parts per million in seawater.

Copper in its native state—such as that found in the Lake Superior region of North America—is often so pure that it requires only melting with a flux to produce "lake copper," which for many years was the world standard for pure copper. About 80% of all copper mined today, however, is derived from low-grade ores containing 2% or less of the element.

Half of the world's copper deposits are in the form of CHALCOPYRITE ($CuFeS_2$) ore. All important copper-bearing ores fall into two main classes: oxidized ores and sulfide ores. Sulfide ores are more important commercially. Ores are removed either by open-pit or by underground mining. Ores containing as little as 0.4% copper can be mined profitably in open-pit mining, but underground mining is profitable only if an ore contains 0.7–6% copper.

The oxidized ores, such as CUPRITE (Cu_2O), can be reduced directly to metallic copper by heating with carbon in a furnace, but the sulfide ores, such as chalcopyrite, require a more complex treatment in which low-grade ores have to be enriched before smelting begins. This involves the ore-flotation process, in which the ore is crushed and powdered before it is agitated with water containing a foaming agent and an agent to make the copper-bearing particles water repellent. These particles accumulate in the froth on the surface of the flotation tank, and this froth is skimmed off and heated to about 800° C to remove some of the water as well as antimony, arsenic, and sulfur, which are also present. The residue is then mixed with silica and melted in a furnace at 1,400°–1,500° C. This produces two liquid layers: a lower layer of copper matte (cuprous sulfide mixed with iron sulfide and oxides), and an upper layer of silicate slag, which is drawn off. Silica or siliceous copper ore is added to the liquid matte in a converter, and air under pressure is blown through the liquid. This causes exothermic reactions to occur, with a consequent rise in temperature to between 1,220° and 1,350° C and production of slag-containing iron oxide and iron silicate.

Upon removal of the iron slag, the copper(I) sulfide that remains is reduced to copper by heating in a controlled amount of air:

$$Cu_2S + O_2 \rightarrow 2Cu + SO_2$$

The remaining molten copper, which is 98–99% pure, is either cast into blocks of blister copper or into anodes.

The final stage of purification is mainly by electrolytic refining, which yields copper of 99.95–99.97% purity. The impure copper is made the anode of an electrolytic cell that contains pure strips of copper as the cathode and an electrolyte of aqueous copper(II) sulfate. During electrolysis, copper is transferred from the anode to the cathode. An anode sludge containing silver and gold is produced during this process, and this increases its economic feasibility.

Physical and Chemical Properties. Copper melts at 1,083.4° ± 0.2° C (in a vacuum), boils at 2,567° C, and has a density of 8.96 at 20° C. The element has a hardness of 3, takes on a bright metallic luster, has a cubic crystal structure, and is malleable, ductile, and a good conductor of heat and electricity, second only to silver in electrical conductivity.

Copper exhibits oxidation states of +2 (the most common) and +1 (stable in aqueous solution only if part of a stable complex ion).

The outstanding feature of copper and the other metals of Group IB (gold and silver) is their resistance to chemical attack. Copper is slowly attacked by moist air, and its surface gradually becomes covered with the characteristic green patina that consists of the basic sulfate, $CuSo_4 \cdot Cu(OH)_2$. At about 300° C copper is attacked by air or oxygen, and a black coating of copper(II) oxide forms at the surface; at a temperature of 1,000° C copper(I) oxide is formed instead. Copper is not attacked by water, steam, or dilute nonoxidizing acids, such as dilute hydrochloric and dilute sulfuric acids. The metal is attacked by boiling concentrated hydrochloric acid with the evolution of hydrogen, by hot concentrated sulfuric acid, and by dilute or concentrated nitric acid.

Alloys of Copper. Copper mixes well with many elements, and more than 1,000 different alloys have been formed, several of which are technologically significant. The presence of the other element or elements can modify the hot or cold machining properties, tensile strength, corrosion fatigue, and wear resistance of the copper; it is also possible to create alloys of pleasing colors.

The best-known copper alloy is BRASS—that is, copper containing between 5% and 40% zinc. It possesses a high tensile strength, hardness, and wear resistance. The addition of 0.5–3% lead to a brass alloy (leaded brass) improves the machinability of brass, and brass containing 30–40% zinc and 1% tin (tin brass) has a high corrosion resistance.

Another useful alloy of copper is nickel silver, which consists of copper (55–65%), nickel (10–18%), and zinc (17–27%). It is used as a base for silver-plating items such as costume jewelry and tableware.

Phosphor bronze is formed by the addition of up to 0.35% of phosphorus to copper-tin alloys containing up to 10% tin. This alloy has great resiliency, fatigue endurance, hardness, and corrosion resistance; these properties make it suitable for use in springs and diaphragms.

Silicon bronze, consisting of 1–3% silicon, 95–96% copper, and small amounts of other metals—for example lead, tin, zinc, manganese, iron, or nickel—is as strong as mild steel and has a high resistance to corrosion. It is

Copper ores taken from open pits are usually mixtures of iron and copper sulfides. The process of copper refining consists of crushing the ore (1), then pulverizing it and mixing it with water (2). Frothing agents and air are added (3), and a froth of sulfides is removed from the surface of the mixture. A thickening tank (4) and a rotary suction filter (5) extract the water. The solids are heated (6), then mixed with fluxing agents and smelted (7). Iron oxide slag is removed (8). Air blown into a converter furnace (9) removes sulfur dioxide, and residual iron oxides are poured off (10). The copper melt is refined in a reverbatory furnace (11), and cast in slabs (12), which are used as anode plates in an electrolytic unit (13). The almost pure copper that is deposited on the cathodes is periodically removed and cast in bars (14).

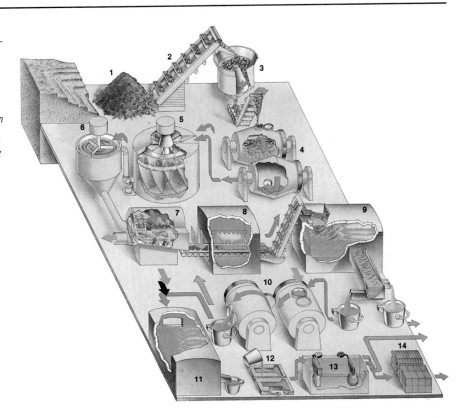

used in the production of equipment for chemical plants in which corrosive liquids are handled.

Relationship to Life Sciences. Copper is a trace element essential to the healthy life of many plants and animals, in which it usually occurs as part of the oxidizing enzymes, where the copper undergoes cyclic changes between Cu(I) and Cu(II) oxidation states.

The normal diet of humans includes between 2 mg and 5 mg of copper per day, exceeding the body maintenance requirements of about 2 mg per day. The hereditary deficiency of the protein ceruloplasmin, known as Wilson's disease, is associated with a pathological increase in the copper content of almost all tissues, particularly the brain and liver. Albino mammals lack the normal form of the copper-containing enzyme tyrosinase, which participates in the synthesis of the pigment melanin. Copper can be toxic in large quantities, especially to lower organisms such as bacilli, fungi, and algae.

Compounds of Copper. The most important simple salts of copper are copper(II) oxide, CuO, and copper(II) sulfate, $CuSO_4 \cdot 5H_2O$, also known as blue vitriol. On an industrial scale, copper(II) sulfate is obtained by forcing air through a hot mixture of copper and sulfuric acid. Copper, like other transition metals, forms a large number of organometallic compounds or COORDINATION COMPOUNDS.

Applications of Copper and Its Compounds. The electrical industry is a major consumer of copper. The metal is used for the windings of generators and for conveying electrical power. Its resistance to chemical attack and its high thermal conductivity make copper a useful metal for condensers in chemical plants and for car radiators. Copper tubing is widely employed in plumbing, and finely divided copper is used as an industrial catalyst in the oxidation of methanol to formaldehyde. Copper compounds, such as Fehling solution, are used in analytical tests for sugars.

Copper(II) sulfate has many industrial applications, including the preparation of Bordeaux mixture (a fungicide) and the manufacture of other copper compounds. It is also used in electroplating solutions, in textile dyeing, and as a timber preservative. Probably the earliest use of copper as a fungicide was in the form of copper sulfate solution employed as a seed dressing to destroy cereal disease, such as bunt.

The Copper Industry Today. The world's largest producer of copper currently is Chile. The United States, Canada, and the USSR are other major producers, followed by Zaire, Zambia, and Peru. Annual world mine production in the late 1980s totaled about 8 million metric tons.

Consumption of copper declined sharply in the early 1980s. In the United States alone, total consumption fell from a 1973 high of 2.2 million metric tons to 1.6 million in 1982; of this total, almost half was in the form of copper recovered from scrap. The worldwide recession of the early 1980s—when such heavy copper consumers as the housing and automobile industries experienced sharply lower sales—was partly responsible for the decline in copper use. In addition, new materials are increasingly replacing copper: plastic for pipe and tubing, lightweight aluminum for automobile parts.

As a result of the sharp decline in copper demand, many U.S. and Canadian producers either closed their facilities or curtailed production. The state of Arizona, the leading producer, was particularly hard hit; by 1986 employment in the copper industry there had dropped to less than 7,000 from a postwar high of 25,000. The closures, cutbacks, and wage reductions occasioned bitter, sometimes violent labor disputes.

The recession of the early 1980s was followed by an upswing in world economies, beginning in 1984. By 1988 copper consumption in the United States had soared to its highest point in a decade. U.S. mines reopened and miners were reemployed.

Copper wire for electric and electronic uses was the most important area of refined copper sales. Brass products, industrial machinery, automobiles and other forms of transport, and consumer products were all large copper consumers. In the fields where copper traditionally has been strong, only housing failed to revive.

Solvent extraction, a new copper refining technique, is proving highly successful. In a process resembling that recently developed for treating gold ores, low-grade copper ores—once considered valueless—are treated with a weak acid solution, and after being combined with other chemicals, the leachate is subjected to electrolysis. Copper derived from leachates is called "electrowon," and costs for electrowon copper are far below those for copper derived from smelting.

copperhead The North American copperhead, or highland moccasin, *Agkistrodon contortrix*, is a venomous PIT VIPER, subfamily Crotalinae, family Viperidae. It often congregates in large numbers during the fall in dens, where it spends the winter. The copperhead has a reddish brown head and contrasting light and dark brown or copper-colored bands. It bears from two to eight living young during the fall. Juveniles possess a bright yellow tail thought to function as a lure for frogs and lizards; adults consume primarily rodents. Copperheads are found

The copperhead is inoffensive unless disturbed, and its bite is not often fatal to humans. It prefers rocky regions.

from Massachusetts to Illinois, and south through the southern states (exclusive of peninsular Florida) to west Texas. Adults are generally less than 1 m (3 ft) in length. In Southeast Asia *copperhead* applies to a harmless rat snake, *Elaphe radiata*, and in Australia to the venomous *Denisonia superba*, a relative of the cobra.

copperheads *Copperhead* was a derogatory term used during the U.S. CIVIL WAR to refer to Northerners sympathetic to the Confederacy. The copperheads were strongest in the Midwest, where there were many people of Southern background and where a pro-Southern secret organization, the Knights of the Golden Circle, had flourished in the 1850s. During the war, this group was supposedly active on behalf of the Confederacy. The best known copperhead was Clement L. VALLANDIGHAM of Ohio.

Most copperheads were anti–African American, conservative "peace Democrats," who believed that President Abraham Lincoln's policies were destroying constitutional government and who opposed a stronger central government. They sensed that the war was inexorably changing the supposedly egalitarian, rural America of their youth. Although they won some local elections and influenced the Democratic party, the copperheads did not exert a major influence. For years after the war, however, the Democrats were tainted with charges of "copperheadism."

Coppola, Francis Ford [koh'-puh-luh] Francis Ford Coppola, b. Detroit, Apr. 7, 1939, made his name by directing the film *The Godfather* (1972). Among his previous work, *The Rain People* (1969), a sensitive study of a runaway wife, is thought by many to be his best film. Coppola departed from the florid style of *The Godfather* for the spareness of *The Conversation* (1974), then enlarged on his first success with *The Godfather, Part II* (1974), for which he won an Academy Award, and *Part III* (1990). *Apocalypse Now* (1979), a controversial film about the Vietnam War, takes its narrative structure from Conrad's novel *Heart of Darkness*. Other Coppola films include *Rumble Fish* (1983; adapted from a story by S. E. Hinton); *Gardens of Stone* (1987); *Peggy Sue Got Married* (1987), about a woman who returns to her adolescence; and *Tucker: The Man and His Dream* (1988), a portrait of the automobile designer.

copra SEE COCONUT

coprolite [kahp'-roh-lyt] Coprolites, fossilized animal dung, most often occur as rounded, tubular, or pelletlike masses of calcium phosphate in sedimentary rocks and are often found with fossilized fish, reptiles, and mammals. Since they may contain remnants of partly digested food, coprolites yield information about the anatomy and eating habits of the animal that left them.

See also: FOSSIL RECORD.

Coptic art and architecture [kahp'-tik] Coptic art was developed by the Christian community of Egypt, starting in the 3d century but especially between the 5th and 12th centuries; the term *Copt*, an Arabic word with Greek roots, identifies a native Christian of Egypt, as opposed to its Muslim or Greek Orthodox inhabitants. Derived from the indigenous folk art of Egypt, Coptic art was also related in its development to EARLY CHRISTIAN ART and BYZANTINE ART, and was influenced by ISLAMIC ART following the Arab conquest of Egypt (641). As a style, Coptic art tends toward abstract, schematic, two-dimensional forms, with a vigorous naïveté in the representation of figures.

Textiles form the richest heritage of Coptic art, although their portability raises problems of dating and place of manufacture. The majority are linen or wool tapestries, usually with a pattern of dark colors against a light background; flowers, fish, birds, animals, and *putti* ("cherubs") are often depicted. The *Birth of Aphrodite* tapestry (6th century; Louvre, Paris) combines a classical subject, traditional Nilotic imagery, and the folk style of Coptic art into a colorful design.

Works such as the stone relief *Christ Mounted between Two Angels* (9th century; Staatliche Museum, Berlin) exhibit the preference in Coptic sculpture for flat, linear forms with intricate surface patterns.

Coptic architecture is best preserved in the monastic complexes of Upper and Middle Egypt. The church of the White Monastery (Deir-el-Abiad) near Sohag, founded in 440 and still standing, is a typical example. A BASILICA with a longitudinal nave and flanking side aisles, it has an elaborate triconch apse on a trefoil, or clover-shaped plan, while its massive outer wall imitates the exterior of ancient Egyptian temples. Church interiors were often richly decorated with colored wall paintings, elaborate altarpieces, and friezes carved with exuberant floral motifs of Hellenistic origin.

This 6th-century ivory carving portraying Apollo's pursuit of Daphne reveals Hellenistic influences. Scenes from classical mythology, as well as from Christian tradition, were frequent subjects. Coptic art reached maturity during the 5th and 6th centuries. (Museo Nationale, Ravenna, Italy.)

Coptic church The Coptic church is the major Christian community in Egypt. The name *Coptic* is derived from the Greek word for Egyptian and reflects the national character of this ancient church, which goes back to the origins of Christianity. When the Christian church was torn apart by the 5th-century controversies on the identity of Christ, most Egyptian Christians sided with the Monophysite party, which held that Christ has one nature, a doctrine condemned at the Council of Chalcedon (451). MONOPHYSITISM is still formally affirmed by the Coptic church. *Coptic* is sometimes used improperly to refer to the Ethiopian church, which declared itself independent of the Coptic patriarch in 1959.

Coptic language   see AFROASIATIC LANGUAGES

copying machine   see ELECTROSTATIC PRINTING; MIMEOGRAPH

copyright A copyright is the exclusive right to publish and sell the expression embodied in a literary, musical, or artistic work, and of other works that involve original creative effort. In recent years copyright protection has been extended to computer programs and data bases, and copyrightlike protection to semiconductor chips. Copyright provides creators ("authors") and other rightsholders with broad rights to control the various modes of reproduction, public distribution, performance, display, and adaptation of their works ("authored works") or, at least, the right to exact payment for their use under the involuntary licenses imposed by the copyright statute. In limited cases, generally dealing with educational or charitable purposes, use of copyrighted material is permitted without permission of the copyright owner. Authors often grant rights to publishers and other producers. In the case of works created within the scope of an author's employment, the copyright belongs to the employer as a "work made for hire," as it may also by agreement in the case of some commissioned works.

History. The modern concept of copyright had its statutory beginnings in the British copyright law of 1710, known as the Statute of Anne, which for the first time both recognized the author's right to protection and statutorily established a limited term of protection, after which the work entered the public domain. In the United States the first federal copyright act, which followed British law and covered books, maps, and charts, was passed in 1790.

Throughout the 19th century U.S. copyright law was expanded to protect, successively, prints, music, photographs, paintings, drawings, and statuary, and expanded further in the 20th century to motion pictures, sound recordings, and computer programs. Over time, U.S. copyright law also expanded the scope of rights, including protection for public performances and displays of certain types of works.

Present-day U.S. copyright law is the result of two comprehensive recodifications of the federal statute in

1909 and 1976, and a third, less-sweeping revision in 1988. A principal purpose of the 1909 and 1976 revisions was to accommodate copyright to new technologies for creating and exploiting authored works, and the major purpose of the 1988 revision was to move toward meeting the requirements of the Berne Convention, an international treaty for the protection of copyright.

Because the copyright laws of countries differ, basic uniform copyright protection on a worldwide basis has become increasingly necessary and desirable. Established in 1886 and subsequently revised several times, the Berne Convention provides for certain minimum standards for copyright in those countries adhering to it. In addition, the Convention employs the principle of national treatment—that is, that a signatory country provide for eligible works from other countries protection at least as favorable as for those of the country itself. Although the United States did not adhere to Berne until 1989, it participated in the formulation of the Universal Copyright Convention (UCC), adopted at Geneva in 1952, and adhered to it. The UCC also embodies fundamental concepts of U.S. and European copyright law but provides for less rigorous minimum standards than Berne.

The U.S. Copyright Statute of 1976. The 1976 act, most of whose provisions remain in force today, covers "original works of authorship" that are "fixed in tangible form," whether published or unpublished—as for example, a manuscript, a dance notation, or a computer program on tape or disc. It thus extended federal copyright protection to works from the moment of their creation; under previous law such protection attached only at publication or, in the case of some unpublished works, at registration. Ideas, systems, methods, processes, and principles cannot be copyrighted, but their "literary expression" can be.

The owner of copyright has the exclusive rights: (1) to reproduce the copyrighted work in copies or phonorecords; (2) to prepare derivative works based on the copyrighted work; (3) to distribute copies of phonorecords of the copyrighted work to the public by sale or other transfer of ownership, or by rental, lease, or lending; (4) in the case of literary, musical, dramatic, and choreographic works, pantomimes, and motion pictures and other audiovisual works, to perform the copyrighted work publicly; and (5) in the case of literary, musical, dramatic, and choreographic works, pantomimes, and pictorial, graphic, or sculptural works, including the individual images of a motion picture or other audiovisual work, to display the copyrighted work publicly.

For works created on or after Jan. 1, 1978, the 1976 act measures the term of copyright (with some exceptions) by the life of the author(s) plus 50 years—instead of the previous term of 28 years (renewable for another 28)—measured usually from the date of first publication.

The U.S. Copyright Statute of 1988. This revision completed the endeavor, begun with the 1976 act, to bring U.S. law into condition to permit adherence to the Berne Convention. The 1988 statute distinguishes between works of U.S. origin and foreign works qualifying for protection in the United States under the national-treatment provisions of the Berne Convention ("Berne works"). The salient provisions of the 1988 revision eliminate for all works the previous requirement of copyright notice (usually the symbol © with the year of publication and the name of the copyright owner) and for Berne works only, the requirement of registration as a prerequisite for bringing suit.

▬

coquina [koh-kee'-nuh] Coquina is a form of LIMESTONE composed of broken fragments of fossil debris. Most fragments are about the size of gravel particles (greater than 2 mm/0.08 in) and are usually shell material—*coquina* is derived from the Spanish word meaning "cockle" or "shellfish"—that has been abraded during transport by marine currents and waves. Soft and highly porous, coquina fragments are easily broken. Deposits found in Florida have been used as roadbed material and as a masonry stone for homes.

▬

cor pulmonale [kohr' pul-muhn-al'-ee] Cor pulmonale is a chronic or acute disease of the heart, resulting from certain lung diseases, including emphysema, fungal and parasitic diseases, chronic bronchitis, tuberculosis, and diseases caused by prolonged inhalation of certain kinds of dust—such as silicosis, a disease that afflicts hardrock miners and stonecutters. Pathological changes in these lung diseases increase the resistance to blood flow in the lungs, leading to pulmonary hypertension. As a result, the right ventricle of the heart, which pumps blood to the lungs through the pulmonary arteries, must work harder. To compensate for the inefficient circulation the right heart enlarges, but eventually compensation reaches its limit and heart failure results.

▬

coral Corals comprise several species in the invertebrate phylum Coelenterata (or Cnidaria). Like all COELENTERATES, they are radially symmetrical and have an internal space for digestion, called a gastrovascular cavity, whose only opening is surrounded by tentacles to aid in food capture.

Corals are most often recognized by their stony skeletons, a calcium carbonate crystalline framework secreted by the epidermis of individual coral organisms. The skeleton provides a substratum to support the living organism, or polyp, and serves as a protective enclosure into which a polyp might retreat when threatened. Most corals are colonial, although a few are solitary. Individual polyps, usually under 3 mm (0.12 in) in diameter, can live together in enormous structures known as CORAL REEFS.

Reproduction. Coral colonies vary greatly in shape and form, depending on both the growth pattern and the arrangement of polyps within the colony. Colonies enlarge by asexual reproduction (budding off new polyps) or by sexual reproduction. A larval polyp, called a planula, settles and begins to secrete its calcium carbonate skeleton. All individual polyps become connected by a sheet of body wall, which includes an extension of the gastrovascular cavity and layers of the gastrodermis and epidermis.

Stony, or true, coral builds the reefs that so spectacularly enhance warm seas of the world. The staghorn coral is composed of hundreds of tiny polyps (A), which secrete outer skeletal limestone cups that surround their soft bodies. In a cross-section of an individual polyp (B), tentacles, which capture prey, surround a mouth that leads to the gullet. The polyp embeds itself in a limestone cup it built, and connecting tissue extends between polyps of a colony. New polyps arise either from the mouth (C) or the base (D) of an old polyp.

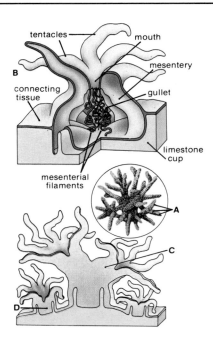

Stony Corals. Stony corals, or the true or hard corals, remove calcium from seawater and deposit it beneath the living tissue as a white, external skeleton of calcium carbonate (limestone). Many kinds of organisms bore into coral skeletons, leading to the coral's eventual death. Best known are the reef-forming corals that contain zooxanthellae, which aid in very rapid skeletal growth, as compared to non–reef-forming species, which exhibit slower growth.

Fire Corals. The fire, or stinging, corals belong to the class Hydrozoa, whereas all other corals belong to the class Anthozoa. Fire corals produce hard, smooth skeletons containing many tiny polyps. The skeleton is light brown because of zooxanthellae. The common name is derived from nematocysts that can inject poison through the skin. Fire corals bud off tiny, sexually reproducing jellyfish, and the fertilized egg becomes a planula larva that develops into a new colony.

coral reef   A coral reef is a wave-resistant underwater ridge or mound built of fragments of coral, coral sands, and solid limestone at or slightly below sea level. Coral may constitute less than half of the material in the reef, with other organisms such as coralline algae binding the various components together. Other organisms that live in the reef environment and add small amounts of material to the framework are *Halimeda* (a green alga), mollusks (snails or clams), bryozoans, foraminifera, echinoderms, brachiopods, and sponges.

Coral reefs have three forms: fringing reefs, barrier reefs, and atolls. Fringing reefs are located close to shore, separated from land by only shallow water. Barrier reefs lie farther offshore, separated from land by lagoons more than 10 m (about 30 ft) deep. Atolls, on the other hand, are found far offshore and comprise a ring-shaped reef enclosing a circular lagoon.

How Reefs Form

Corals are the critical organisms in reef formation, because their skeletons are the framework of reefs. Four environmental factors affect their growth: temperature, water depth, salinity, and wave action. Ideal temperature for optimum coral growth is about 23° to 27° C (73° to 80° F). Although some species will survive lower temperatures, corals normally do not grow where water temperature is below 18° C (65° F). The highest temperature that most coral will endure is 30° C (86° F). Western sides of ocean basins tend to be warmer and thus more favorable for coral growth. Most reef corals require shallow water to allow penetration of sunlight necessary for algal photosynthesis, which supplies the coral with necessary nutrients and oxygen. At greater depths (30 to 40 m/100 to 130 ft), coral growth is reduced and tends to become horizontal, hence more susceptible to erosion.

Corals normally grow in water whose salinity lies between 30 and 40 parts per thousand. High rates of rainfall and runoff from the mainland can kill coral reefs by reducing salinity and increasing the influx of sediment. Corals thrive in areas where strong wave action aerates

The resulting colony comprises many interconnected polyps that reproduce asexually as growth continues. Individual colonies derived from a single planula may comprise thousands of polyps.

Nutrition. Corals extend from protective skeletons, usually at night, to feed on plankton and other microorganisms. They capture food with nematocysts, which are specialized poison cells released from cells on their tentacles. Cilia around the mouth aid in catching suspended food as well. Many reef-building corals are found in association with small, round algal cells called zooxanthellae. Many tropical corals obtain energy from algae that live within their tissue and give the endodermal cells a brown or yellow color. These algae photosynthesize and transfer energy-containing compounds to their coral host and also remove excretory waste.

Gorgonian Coral. Among the more familiar corals are the gorgonian, or horny, corals of the order Gorgonacea. This group includes corals commonly known as sea feathers, sea fans, and the red coral. Members of the gorgonian coral group are often present in reefs. The body consists of an erect central rod of organic material called gorgonin, surrounded by a cylinder of calcareous spicules and by the polyp organisms, in branching, plantlike forms. The spicules contain a pigment that gives the gorgonian an orange or purple color. Yellow or brown colors may be caused by zooxanthellae. In *Corallium*, the red jewelry coral, the central rod of gordonin is replaced by a solid rod of fused red calcareous spicules.

Soft Corals. Soft corals differ from gorgonian corals in that they lack an axial skeleton. They derive their support from a gelatinous, spicule-filled mesoglea. Soft corals form rubbery, irregularly shaped colonies.

the water, thereby increasing the supply of food and oxygen. Waves also prevent silt from accumulating and suffocating the coral.

The calcium carbonate of which coral reefs are made is deposited in two ways: as reef framework and as unconsolidated sediment. The framework is provided by coral and some minor organisms and cemented by coralline algae. The unconsolidated sediment comprises eroded reef rock, sand, and gravel, and a small amount of silt and clay. The process by which reef rock is eroded, filled, and cemented is important in understanding reef accretion and sedimentation in both modern and ancient reefs.

Importance

Coral-reef environments are the subject of active research by geologists and biologists. Some of the world's largest oil and gas fields are in ancient fossilized coral reefs (for example, Zelten, located in Libya). By studying modern coral reefs, researchers hope to understand the mechanism of formation, migration, and entrapment of PETROLEUM in ancient reefs.

Atolls located in the South Pacific (Enewetak and Bikini) were sites for the testing of atomic and nuclear weapons during the late 1940s and early 1950s. Scientists have studied these atolls to determine the effects of the explosions on rocks and organisms. Geologists are particularly interested in how reef rock responded to the intense shock waves, whereas biologists are concerned with the effect radioactive fallout had on rich biologic communities.

Finally, coral reefs are an important research and teaching tool because they constitute a natural laboratory in which students can study interrelationships between organisms and their environment.

Coral-Reef Life

Coral reefs are most abundant in certain shallow, warm, tropical waters along the eastern coasts of continents (western sides of oceans) and around oceanic islands. Two distinctive coral-reef regions exist: the Caribbean and the Indo-Pacific. The latter covers a vast region, from the Red Sea through the Indian and Pacific oceans to the western coast of Panama.

Coral reefs are formed by colonial corals; not all corals contribute to the construction of reefs. Some are small and solitary. Corals that build reefs are called hermatypic. Coral reefs constitute a varied, complex structure that serves as a habitat for many other marine animals, including echinoderms, mollusks, crustaceans, and especially fish.

At first glance, coral reefs seem to be almost entirely lacking in plant life. The reef-building colonial corals, however, supply much of the photosynthetic basis for this rich community. The cells of hermatypic corals are packed with microscopic single-celled algae known as zooxanthellae. The association between coral and zooxanthellae is mutualistic—both partners benefit. The coral supplies the algae with shelter, and metabolic by-products of the algae are a major source of nutrients for the coral. As an additional source of food, corals capture plankton.

The coral-algal association accounts for the strange, plantlike structure of many reef-building corals. Corals spread out and compete for light just as terrestrial plants do. Overtopping by rapidly growing corals shades and kills slower-growing colonies. Some corals are able to damage and kill their neighbors by a digestive process should they come in contact. The plantlike nature of reef-building

Atolls, the most prominent product of coral growth, are ring-shaped chains of low-lying islands enclosing a lagoon. Found only in tropical seas, atolls are believed to have started with the development of a fringing reef (1) around the shallow shores of a volcanic island (A). At some point the volcano began subsiding (B), and corals grew upward and outward, creating a barrier reef (2). Eventually, the island summit sank below sea level (C), and only barrier reef islands (3) circling a lagoon (4) remained.

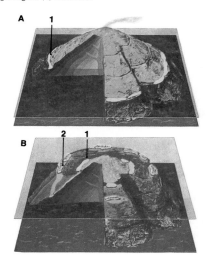

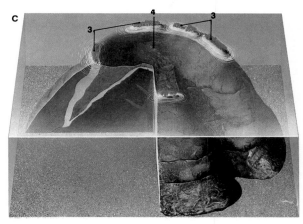

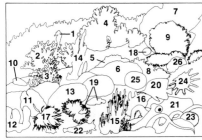

A coral reef supports a wide variety of life. A seahorse (1) *wraps its tail around a stag's horn coral* (2). *Other coral include: red coral* (3); *fire coral* (4); *organ-pipe coral* (5); *brain coral* (6); *and sea fans* (7). *Two forms of plant in a coral reef are seaweed* (8) *and reef alga* (9). *The cone shell* (10) *is a mollusk. The giant clam* (11) *grows to lengths of 150 cm (5 ft). Among the sponges are the* Callyspongia vaginalis (12); Cliona viridis (13), Axinella cannabina (14), Axinella (15), *and* Oscarella lobularis (16). *A burrowing sea anemone* (17) *attaches itself to the reef; another,* Actina equina (18), *is shown in a defense posture. The clown fish* (19) *lives among the tentacles of a sea anemone. A golden long-nosed butterfly fish* (20) *probes the coral for food. Other animals are the Atlantic octopus* (21); *the marine blenny* (22); *the crimson sea urchin* (23); *the crown-of-thorns starfish* (24); *the cake sea urchin* (25); *and a tropical sea slug* (26).

corals is the reason that reefs are found only in shallow waters. A few corals, lacking algae, form small colonies in deep water.

In response to environmental stress, some reef corals suffer from a condition known as "bleaching," in which they expel the algae, become weak, and sometimes die. Particularly widespread in the Caribbean region, this condition has damaged reef corals in all parts of the world.

Among the organisms occupying coral reefs, ECHINODERMS play an important role. The crown-of-thorns starfish is a major coral predator in the Indo-Pacific area, able to devastate large areas of living coral. Starfish population explosions, however, occur sporadically and are short-lived, which suggests that the crown-of-thorns is a natural part of the fluctuating buildup and breakdown of portions of coral reefs. This is not the case in other oceans, however. One objection to proposals for a sea-level canal through Central America is that it might unleash this voracious predator on Caribbean corals, which have never evolved any defenses.

Another important echinoderm is the spiny sea urchin, *Diadema*. This grazing urchin feeds both on algae growing on dead portions of the reef and on the sea grass that often surrounds shallow reefs.

The giant clam, *Tridacna*, is the most spectacular mollusk associated with coral reefs (in the Indo-Pacific area only). Like many corals, its tissues also contain zooxanthellae. Many other species of small bivalves, as well as many snails, are found among coral reefs. One snail, *Charonia*, is a major predator of the crown-of-thorns starfish.

Many Crustacea roam the surface of coral reefs. Large, brightly colored painted shrimp live in pairs and feed on the crown-of-thorns starfish. Another unusual crustacean is the gall crab. The female crab settles in a notch of a branching coral, and the coral grows around and permanently encases her. The vividly colored mantis shrimp occupies cavities in dead coral.

Among the most spectacular and visible life on the reefs are the numerous and beautiful fish. Some, such as the large PARROT FISH, feed on the living coral. DAMSELFISH, although small, defend territories from larger fish as well as from invertebrates and one another; otherwise, sea urchins and other herbivorous fish would soon eliminate their algal food supply.

Among other interesting fish species living on the reef are the poisonous stonefish and lionfish; moray eels, which dart out from crevices in the reef to attack their prey; and cleaner fish, which remove external parasites from the skin, gills, and mouth of most other reef fishes.

See also: BEACH AND COAST.

Coral Sea The Coral Sea is an arm of the Pacific Ocean, east of Australia and west of Vanuatu. In its waters near the Louisiade Archipelago, the United States won (May 7, 1942) the important naval Battle of the Coral Sea against Japan, halting its further expansion southward.

coral snake Three genera of venomous cobra-related New World snakes, *Micrurus, Micruroides*, and *Leptomicrurus* (family Elapidae), are commonly called coral snakes because of the bright rings of red, yellow, and black that most species possess. The approximately 40 species are mostly tropical, but two species occur in the

The eastern coral snake has wide bands of red and black that are separated by narrow yellow bands in a pattern unlike other red-black-and-yellow snakes. It is feared in the southern United States as a highly venomous reptile.

United States. The eastern coral snake, *Micrurus fulvius*, occurs from North Carolina south to Florida and west across the Gulf states to Texas and northern Mexico. It usually reaches an adult length of 50–75 cm (20–30 in). The small Arizona coral snake, *Micruroides euryxanthus*, is usually less than 50 cm (20 in). This species is found in southern Arizona and northern Mexico. All coral snakes lay eggs and prey mostly on reptiles, especially other snakes. They may be active day or night. Their venom is highly toxic, but the snakes are not aggressive and have very short fangs.

coral tree Coral trees, genus *Erythrina*, are about 100 species of deciduous, thorny trees and shrubs native to the tropics and subtropics. They have clusters of large, brilliantly hued flowers, usually red or orange; large seedpods; and simple, bright green leaves. They belong to the pea family, Leguminosae. A coral tree of Peru, *E. poeppigiana*, is often planted to shade coffee and cacao plants. The flowers of the Indian coral tree, *E. indica*, are used by Hawaiians to fashion leis.

Corbett, James J. James John Corbett, b. San Francisco, Sept. 1, 1866, d. Feb. 18, 1933, an American boxer, was the first recognized heavyweight champion under the Marquess of Queensberry rules, when in 1892 he knocked out John L. SULLIVAN in the 21st round of a bout in New Orleans. He fought rarely after winning the championship; tried acting, becoming known as Gentleman Jim; and in 1897 lost his title to Bob Fitzsimmons. Despite his fame, Corbett won only 20 fights, lost 5, drew 6, and had 2 no-decisions. He is credited with inventing the left hook. His autobiography, *The Roar of the Crowd*, was published in 1925.

Corbusier, Le see LE CORBUSIER

Corday, Charlotte Charlotte Corday, b. July 27, 1768, d. July 17, 1793, a poor but well-born Frenchwoman, assassinated the French revolutionary Jean Paul MARAT on July 13, 1793. A believer in reform, she lived in Caen, Normandy, where, after the expulsion of the GIRONDISTS from the National Convention (May–June 1793), she was induced by Girondist refugees from Paris to assist their cause. She went to Paris, gained access to Marat on the pretext of supplying information about Girondist dissidents, and stabbed him while he was bathing. She was guillotined.

Cordero, Angel [kohr-der'-oh] Angel Tomás Cordero, Jr., b. Santurce, Puerto Rico, May 8, 1942, is one of the most successful jockeys in the history of Thoroughbred racing, in terms of winners ridden and purses won. In 1968 he rode more winners (435) than any other U.S. jockey. A rough rider who has incurred frequent suspensions, Cordero is nevertheless respected in the racing world. He has won 6 Triple Crown races: the Kentucky Derby in 1974, 1976, and 1985 (aboard Cannonade, Bold Forbes, and Spend a Buck); the Preakness in 1980 and 1984 (on Codex and Gate Dancer); and the Belmont Stakes in 1976 (also on Bold Forbes).

cordierite [kohr'-dee-uh-ryt] Cordierite, or iolite, is a magnesium and iron aluminosilicate mineral, $(Mg,Fe)_2Al_4Si_5O_{18}$ (see SILICATE MINERALS). It forms short, blue glassy crystals with a hardness of 7 and a specific gravity of 2.5–2.8. Although found in some IGNEOUS ROCKS, cordierite is more common in GNEISS and SCHIST. The gemstone variety, dichroite, is colorless when viewed from one direction and violet when viewed from the other.

Córdoba (Argentina) [kohr'-doh-bah] Córdoba, a city in Argentina, is located in the central part of the country about 600 km (375 mi) northwest of Buenos Aires, on the Río Primero. Its population is 990,007 (1980). Córdoba is a major transportation hub and the commercial center for the surrounding agricultural region. Industries in Córdoba manufacture automobiles, food products, glass, leather, and textiles. The National University of Córdoba was established in 1613.

Córdoba was settled by the Spanish in 1573; it subsequently became a regional center for Jesuit missionaries and then a provincial capital. Colonial structures include the cathedral (completed 1758) and the convent of Santa Teresa.

Córdoba (Spain) Córdoba (English: Cordova), a city in Andalusia, southern Spain, lies at the foot of the Sierra Morena on the Guadalquivir River. It has a population of 298,372 (1987 est.). Industries include tourism, brewing, distilling, textile manufacture, and metal processing. It also markets the grain, cotton, and olives grown nearby. Settled by Iberians, it was part of a prosperous Roman colony in the 2d century BC. Conquered by Visigoths (572) and Moors (711), it became the capital of a Muslim caliphate in 756. Under the rule of the UMAYYADS the city was one of the largest and wealthiest in Europe, noted for its intellectual life, its architectural wonders and its splendid leather, silk, and gold craftsmanship. Ferdinand III of Castile captured the city in 1236 and imposed Christian culture on it without destroying its Moorish landmarks. Notable is the Great Mosque, called the Mezquita. Córdoba has an archaeological museum, a fine arts museum, and a university.

Cordobés, El see EL CORDOBÉS

cordon bleu [kohr-dohn' blu] The Cordon Bleu is a famous school of cooking in Paris, founded in 1895 by Marthe Distell to teach the principles of French cuisine to the daughters of upper-class families. Today it attracts amateur and professional cooks from throughout the world. The term *cordon bleu* is probably derived from the blue ribbons worn by knights of the Order of the Holy Ghost, a chivalric order renowned for the excellence of its table. The ribbon was bestowed by King Louis XV on Mme du Barry's chef, a woman, and for many years the decoration was given only to top-ranked female cooks.

Cordova see CÓRDOBA

corduroy Corduroy, an important apparel and upholstery fabric, may be identified by the cut-pile rib, or wale, that runs lengthwise down the fabric. Extra filling yarns float over a number of warp yarns to form either a plain or twill-weave ground. After weaving, the floating yarns are cut, and the pile is brushed and singed to produce a cord effect that may vary from a wide wale to a narrow pinwale. Corduroy can be given special crease-resistant, water-repellent, and spot-resistant finishes.

Corea, Chick Composer and pianist Armando Anthony "Chick" Corea, b. Chelsea, Mass., June 12, 1941, is among the most versatile and eclectic of contemporary jazz-rock musicians. He began his career by playing piano with local Latin bands, whose influence has remained strong in his work. After playing (1968–72) with Miles Davis's electronic jazz-rock group, he formed his own group, Return to Forever, and collaborated with numerous jazz and classical musicians. He formed a trio, Elektric Band, in 1985.

Corelli, Arcangelo [koh-rel'-lee, ahrk-ahn'jay-loh] Arcangelo Corelli, b. Feb. 17, 1653, d. Jan. 8, 1713, was a celebrated violinist and composer. He lived and worked in Rome from the early 1670s. From 1690 until his death he held the position of violin virtuoso and director of music for Rome's most active music patron, Cardinal Pietro Ottoboni. In 1700, Corelli became the leader of the instrumental section of the famous Roman musical society, the Academy of Santa Cecilia.

Corelli was the most celebrated composer of his time in the genres of trio sonata and concerto grosso. He is best known for his 48 trio sonatas for two violins and basso continuo (1681–94), his 12 solo violin sonatas (1700), and his 12 concerti grossi (composed before 1700 but published in 1714).

Corelli, Franco Equipped with a powerful tenor voice of great brilliance in the high range, the Italian Franco Corelli, b. Apr. 8, 1923, has excelled in such dramatic roles as Calaf in Giacomo Puccini's *Turandot* and Manrico in Giuseppe Verdi's *Il Trovatore*. Corelli learned to sing by listening to recordings. He made his debut as Don José in Georges Bizet's *Carmen* at Spoleto, Italy, in 1952, and appeared with Maria Callas in Spontini's *La Vestale* at La Scala the next year. He made his Metropolitan Opera debut in 1961.

Corfu [kohr-foo'] Corfu (modern Greek: Kerkyra) is a Greek island of 593 km² (229 mi²) and a population of 99,477 (1981) that lies in the Ionian Sea, just off of the coast of Epirus. Its name comes from the Greek word *coryphai*, meaning "crests." The island has mountain ranges in its northern and central regions and is flat in the south. Its capital city is the east-coast port of Corfu. Fertile land supports the cultivation of olives, figs, citrus fruit, grapes, and corn, and much of the land is worked by tenant farmers. Soap and textiles are manufactured.

In ancient legends, Corfu was known as Scheria. It was settled by Eretrians and later by Corinthians in 734 BC, before becoming an independent trading center. Because of its strategic location, it changed hands many times during the succeeding centuries. Part of the Napoleonic empire, it came under British protection in 1815, and in 1864 it became part of Greece. During World War II Corfu was occupied (1941–44) by Italians and then by Germans. In 1944, Corfu was returned to Greece.

coriander [kohr-ee-an'-dur] Coriander, *Coriandrum sativum* of the Umbelliferae, or carrot, family, is an annual herb native to southern Europe and widely cultivated for its small, fragrant fruits (coriander seeds) and its parsley-shaped leaves. Coriander seeds are a principal ingredient of CURRY and are used to flavor a wide range of foods. The plant's essential oil is used in beverages, candies, tobacco, and perfumes. The pungent leaves, known as cilantro or Chinese parsley, are a basic flavoring ingredient in Latin American and Oriental cooking.

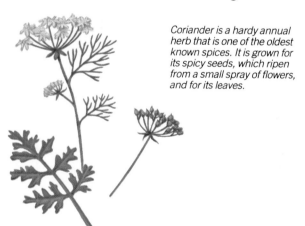

Coriander is a hardy annual herb that is one of the oldest known spices. It is grown for its spicy seeds, which ripen from a small spray of flowers, and for its leaves.

Corinth [kohr'-inth] Corinth, a city in the Peloponnesus, Greece, is a small seaport on the Isthmus of Corinth. Capital of the *nomos* (department) of Corinth, it has a population of 22,658 (1981). Because of the Corinth Canal, the city is a trade and transportation center, exporting locally grown fruits, raisins, and tobacco. It lies about 6 km (4 mi) east of the site of old Corinth, one of the great cities of the ancient world.

Old Corinth was founded by Dorian invaders in the 8th century BC. Its port flourished, and it became a thriving commercial center. One of its facilities was the Diolkos, a paved causeway used to draw ships across the isthmus on rollers. Corinth founded many colonies, including Syracuse in Sicily. It was allied with Sparta in the Peloponnesian War (431–404 BC) and with Athens in the Corinthian War (395–386 BC).

Destroyed by Romans in 146 BC, Corinth was rebuilt (44 BC) as a Roman colony and again prospered. During the Roman period Saint Paul established the Christian community there. Corinth was later held by Byzantines, Crusaders, Venetians, and Ottoman Turks. Old Corinth was destroyed by an earthquake in 1858, and the new city was then founded. The new city was also destroyed by an earthquake in 1928 and has since been entirely rebuilt.

Corinth, Isthmus of The Isthmus of Corinth is a narrow strip of land connecting central Greece to the Peloponnesus. Only 6.4 to 13 km (4 to 8 mi) wide, it has tempted canal builders since the Roman emperor Nero first tried to construct a canal in AD 67. The ancient Greeks dragged boats across it. The modern Corinth Canal, completed in 1893, shortens the journey from the Adriatic Sea to Piraeus by more than 320 km (202 mi).

Corinthians, Epistles to the [kohr-in'thee-uhnz] The two Epistles to the Corinthians in the New Testament were written by Saint PAUL from Ephesus, probably in AD 57, to the church he founded at Corinth, a cosmopolitan commercial city in central Greece. They were part of a lively exchange (there are references to other correspondence in 1 Cor. 5:9; 7:1; 2 Cor. 2:4) in which Paul clarified his teachings, rebuked the Corinthians for erroneous practices, and instructed them in Christian living.

The text of 2 Corinthians shows that relations between Paul and the Corinthians had deteriorated into open conflict. Most of chapters 1–7 reflect past conflict over the Corinthians' behavior, the rejection of Paul's apostolic authority by some, and subsequent reconciliation. Chapters 10–13 are an even more emotional defense of Paul's life and ministry against adversaries claiming to have authority above Paul's. Many scholars think that these chapters are another epistle, because they are so different from the preceding chapters.

Coriolanus, Gnaeus Marcius [kohr-ee-oh-lay' nuhs,gnay'-uhs mar'-shuhs] Gnaeus Marcius Coriolanus was a 5th-century BC Roman patrician who, according to legend, captured the Volscian town Corioli, from which he took his name. He left Rome when accused of misconduct for seeking to abolish the starving plebeians' tribunate in return for giving them grain, and led the Volscians against Rome until his mother and wife entreated him to stop. The Volscians then killed him. Shakespeare's play *Coriolanus* is based on Plutarch's version of his life.

Coriolis effect [kohr-ee-oh'-lis] The Coriolis effect, named for French physicist Gaspard Coriolis (1792–1843), is an imaginary force that appears to be exerted on an object moving within a rotating system. The apparent force is simply the ACCELERATION of the object caused by the rotation. For example, if a line were being drawn toward the center of a stationary wheel that then began to rotate, an observer in some way unaware of the rotation would note its effect as an apparent force being exerted at an angle to the progress of the line. This effect is seen on a large scale in the movement of winds and ocean currents on the rotating Earth. It dominates weather patterns, producing the counterclockwise flow observed around low-pressure zones in the Northern Hemisphere and the clockwise flow around such zones in the Southern Hemisphere.

In physics, the Coriolis effect is an example of the conservation of ANGULAR MOMENTUM. An object moving without any external force on it must move in such a way that its angular momentum remains constant. If a spinning object moves closer to its axis of rotation, its angular velocity must increase, as when a spinning skater's arms are pulled closer to the body, increasing the rate of spin. Similarly, the motion of a wind blowing northward along the surface of the Earth in the Northern Hemisphere reduces the distance of the air mass from the Earth's axis. Its angular velocity increases, forcing it to move eastward.

Cork (city) Cork, with a population of 173,694 (1986), is the second largest city in Ireland and seat of County Cork in southwestern Ireland. Located at the mouth of the Lee River at the head of Cork Harbor, the city is in a marshy valley area where the Lee splits to form an island that is the heart of the city. Heavy industries include car assembly and tire plants; there are also several breweries.

Tradition holds that the city was founded in the late 6th or early 7th century by St. Finbarr, who went there to kill the last dragon in Ireland and who built a monastery on the current south side of the city. Cork was taken by Henry II in 1172 and by Oliver Cromwell in 1649. The city is often called "Rebel Cork" because it was a center of the 19th-century Fenian movement and played an active part in the Irish struggle for independence. A famous landmark is the Shandon Steeple of St. Anne's Church, which contains the Bells of Shandon. Cork is the seat of University College (founded 1845; since 1908 part of the National University of Ireland). The Cork Film Festival is held each summer. The famous Blarney Castle is 8 km (5 mi) north of the city (see BLARNEY STONE).

Cork (county) Cork (Irish: *Corcaigh*) is a county in Münster province in southwestern Ireland, on the Atlantic coast. It is Ireland's largest county, covering 7,459 km² (2,880 mi²). Its population is 412,735 (1986). The city of Cork is the county seat. Inland hills slope from a maximum height of 682 m (2,237 ft) to a heavily indented coastline with numerous harbors. Livestock raising, farming (grains and sugar beets), tourism, and fishing are im-

portant. Most industries are concentrated around the city of Cork, and a large oil refinery is at Whitegate.

Cork was the center of the kingdom of Desmond until the 12th century, when it was invaded by Anglo-Normans.

cork Cork is the bark tissue of the cork oak, *Quercus suber*, an evergreen tree native to the Mediterranean area and cultivated in Spain and Portugal as well as in India and the western United States. When the tree is about 20 years old, it is stripped of its rough outer layer of bark. In another 8 to 11 years, the tree regenerates a layer of cork sheathing 25 to 50 mm (1 to 2 in) thick, which is also harvested. Regenerated cork from subsequent strippings improves in quality and quantity.

The cork oak tree has wide-spreading branches and acorns (right) similar to those of other oak species. Its bark (bottom) is used to make bottle stoppers and many other products.

The physical qualities of cork make it useful in a variety of products. Because it is resilient, cork is suitable for the cores of baseballs and for shoe soles. It makes waterproof bottle stoppers. Its hollow-celled structure makes it a buoyant material for use in floats and life preservers, and an excellent insulator and floor covering, since it is a poor conductor of heat and sound.

cork tree The cork tree, genus *Phellodendron*, is in the rue family, Rutaceae. Cork trees are native to eastern Asia and are grown as ornamentals because of their attractive, aromatic foliage. They produce black fruit, which remains attached to the tree long after the leaves have fallen. *P. amurense*, native to China and Japan, is used primarily as a shade tree, growing up to 15 m (50 ft) high. It grows into a broad, rounded shape with huge branches. The sexes are separate. The fruits of *P. chinense*, native to central China, are small drupes produced in grapelike clusters.

The common cormorant, a water bird, has the greatest range (almost worldwide) and is the largest of all cormorants. It is 100 cm (40 in) long and has a 1.5-m (60-in) wingspan.

cormorant The cormorant, a large aquatic bird of the order Pelecaniformes, family Phalacrocoracidae, is found throughout the world. It has webbed feet; short legs; a dark, elongated body; a long neck; and brightly colored, bare patches on its face. It is most common at the seashore but may also be found inland on large lakes and rivers. It feeds underwater on fish, crustaceans, and other aquatic life, often diving to great depths. It is sometimes used by humans in the Orient to catch fish. One species, the endangered *Nannopterum harrisi* of the Galápagos Islands, is flightless. The most common U.S. species is the double-crested cormorant, *Phalacrocorax auritus*; the adult is black, with an orange throat patch.

corn Corn, or maize, *Zea mays*, is an annual plant of the grass family, Gramineae. The largest of the cereals, it can reach heights of 4.5 m (15 ft). The stem, or cornstalk, is hard and jointed, resembling bamboo. The plant possesses both male and female flowers; the male flowers are borne in the tassel at the top of the stalk, and the female is a cluster, called a cob, at a joint of the stalk. The corn silks hanging from the husk of each cob are the pollen receptors; each thread of silk must receive a grain of pollen for its fruit, or kernel, to develop. A fertilized cob, or ear, contains eight or more rows of kernels. One to three or more cobs grow on each stalk.

Among the world's four most important crops (the others are wheat, rice, and potatoes), corn is one of the few economic plants native to America.

Origin of Corn

A type of primitive corn was used as a food in Mexico at least 7,000 years ago. No wild forms of corn have been found, and the origin of domesticated corn is a speculative and controversial issue.

In its present form, the corn plant is highly specialized and is unsuited for efficient, natural reproduction. Although the ear is specially constructed for producing high seed yields, the plant has no mechanism for broadcasting its seeds without human intervention. The processes of mutation, natural selection, and mass selection by the American Indians gradually transformed certain varieties of wild corn into the cultivated plant called maize.

Corn was unknown outside the New World before 1492, but the plant was extensively cultivated, in all its present forms, by the Indians of North and South America. Seed grains of Indian maize, brought to Europe and Africa by 16th-century explorers, were planted and eventually thrived throughout most of the world. Since the 1930s, the development of hybrid varieties of corn has resulted in greatly increased yields and improved quality. Today corn is considerably larger in cob size and in the number and weight of the kernels than the corn grown by the Indians.

Cultivation

Corn grows best in well-aerated, deep, warm loams containing an abundance of organic matter, nitrogen, phosphorus, and potassium. The crop thrives in areas with moderately high summer temperatures, warm nights, and adequate but not excessive rainfall that is well distributed during the growing season. Length of the growing season and length of day also influence production. The Corn Belt of the midwestern United States is ideally suited to these conditions.

In areas of intensive corn cultivation—especially in the Corn Belt where farms are large and the topography is relatively flat—mechanization has resulted in higher corn yields and greater crop-labor productivity. Many specialized machines are used throughout the Corn Belt. Among the most important are wheel-track planters, which dig the furrows, plant the seed, and cover it in one operation; mechanical corn pickers, which harvest only the ears (some machines shell the ears as well); and field choppers, which cut and chop the stalks into silage.

Pest control is accomplished through the use of pest-resistant hybrid varieties, proper cultivation, and the judicious use of HERBICIDES and pesticides (see PESTICIDES AND PEST CONTROL). Viral and other diseases have caused heavy crop losses during the past two decades, and plant geneticists are doing research on types of corn that are resistant to specific diseases and insects.

Types and Characteristics

Corn may be divided into several groups, each characterized by a difference in the character of the seeds.

Dent Corn. By far the most widely grown type, dent corn (so named because the seed has a depression, or dent, in the crown) furnishes millions of tons of grain for

Corn is one of the world's most important human and stock food crops. The four major color types of sweet corn are yellow, the most common; white; yellow and white, or bicolored; and black, which is the least popular.

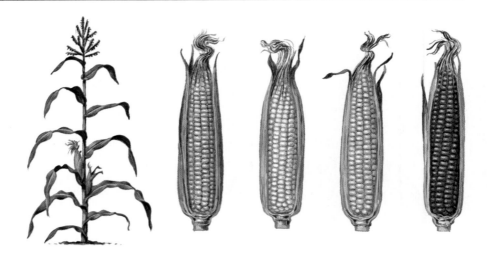

human and industrial use and for livestock feed. The soft starch extends to the summit of the seed, and the sides have a corneous starch. The characteristic denting is caused by rapid drying and shrinkage of the soft starch.

Flint Corn. The kernels of flint corn are hard and smooth and contain little soft starch. Flint corn is more widely grown in Europe, Asia, Central America, and South America than in the United States. In temperate zones, flint corn often matures earlier, germinates better, and has earlier plant vigor than do dent strains.

Popcorn. Popcorn, an extreme form of flint, contains only a small proportion of soft starch. A minor crop, it is grown primarily for human consumption as freshly popped corn and popcorn confections. The ability to pop seems to be conditioned by the quality of the horny endosperm, a tough, elastic material that resists the steam pressure generated within the heated kernel until it reaches explosive force.

Flour Corn. The kernels of flour corn are composed largely of soft starch and have little or no dent. Although it is now of little importance, flour corn has been widely grown in the drier sections of the United States and in the Andean region of South America. An old type of corn, it is frequently found in ancient Aztec and Incan graves. Because of the softness of the kernels, Indians were able to grind them for flour.

Sweet Corn. The kernels of sweet corn have a translucent, horny appearance when immature and are wrinkled when dry. The ears are eaten fresh or are canned. Sweet corn differs from dent corn by only one recessive gene, which prevents some sugar from being converted into starch. A considerable quantity is grown as a winter crop in the southern part of the United States.

Waxy Corn. The kernels of this corn are waxy in appearance. Its starch differs chemically from common corn starch. Corn having the recessive waxy gene was devel-

Corn is classified according to the character of its seed. (Left to right) Dent corn is fed to livestock and is processed into food and industrial products. Flint corn kernels are hard and resistant to disease and spoilage. Tough-skinned popcorn puffs when heated. Flour corn has a soft, chalky texture, even when dried. Sweet corn, with its soft yellow or white kernels, can be eaten directly from the ear.

 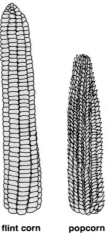   

dent corn　　**flint corn**　　**popcorn**　　**flour corn**　　**sweet corn**　　**pod corn**

oped in China. Waxy mutations have since occurred in American dent strains. Waxy hybrids are grown on a small scale to produce a starch similar to tapioca starch.

Pod Corn. Although not grown commercially, pod corn is of interest in studying the origin of corn, since it is thought to resemble varieties of primitive corn. Each kernel is enclosed in a pod or husk and the entire ear is also enclosed in a husk (as are the ears of other types of corn).

Development of Hybrids

Corn is well suited for genetic research, since it is easily grown and is adaptable to a wide range of environmental conditions. It has a large number of distinct hereditary variations. Inbreeding, or crossing, is simple and rapid, and hundreds of kernels may be obtained on one ear from a single pollination. Rates of mutation for specific genes can be measured, and the comparatively small number of relatively large chromosomes within the germ cell facilitates cytological studies.

Beginning in the 1920s, a method for breeding hybrid corn was developed, using crossbreeding between inbred lines. Normally, corn is cross-pollinated: pollen is carried from one plant to another by wind or by insects. Inbred corn is self-fertilized; that is, pollen from the tassel is used to fertilize the plant's silks, which are protected from chance pollination by other plants. Inbreeding is often continued through several generations, using only those progeny that show desirable characteristics. Producing cross-strains, or hybrids, by crossbreeding different varieties of inbred corn involves complex techniques. Since the 1930s, the results from breeding and cultivating hybrid corn have been spectacular.

Corn and such other monocot grains as rice and wheat proved less amenable to the standard GENETIC ENGINEERING techniques than did such broad-leaved dicots as tobacco and tomatoes. Scientists successfully introduced a foreign gene into corn for the first time in 1988, and researchers believe that this genetic manipulation will lead to the development of improved varieties of corn and other cereals.

A perennial variety of *teosinte*, a wild grass closely related to corn, has been discovered in the mountains of the state of Jalisco in Mexico. The variety, *Zea diploperennis*, carries only 20 chromosomes, as does corn; it is hoped that when the plants are crossbred, the new hybrid corn will grow perennially and also have the ability to tolerate moist and even wet soils.

Commercial Uses

Increased yields from the use of hybrids, as well as modern production practices, have made vast quantities of corn available for feeding livestock and for human consumption, as well as furnishing the raw materials for hundreds of industrial products. Because corn is deficient in protein, both in quantity and in quality, nutritional problems often arise when it makes up a large proportion of the diet. The development of high-oil, waxy, and modified protein corns is expected to improve the nutritional qualities of corn in the future. Major industrial users of corn are feed manufacturers, millers, and the distilling and fermentation industries. Corn oil is obtained from the germ of the kernel; corn sugars and syrups, from the starch contained in the endosperm.

See also: PLANT BREEDING.

corn dance   The term *corn dance* is applied to certain rituals of many Indian tribes of North America. Corn, traditionally a sacred plant to many Indians, needs plentiful rain to grow, and the dances are intended to induce rain, to promote fertility, or to thank the gods for the harvest. Corn dance rituals are associated especially with tribes of the arid Southwest, where Indians such as the HOPI and ZUÑI originally farmed without irrigation and thus were entirely dependent upon rain for the germination and growth of their crops. Among tribes of the southeastern United States, such as the CHICKASAW and the CREEK, the green corn dance, in celebration of the early harvest, was the most important ritual.

Corn Laws   In British history, the Corn Laws were regulations restricting the import and export of grain, especially wheat. The general purpose of such laws, which dated from the 12th century, was to ensure a stable supply of domestic grain and, later, to protect the British producers who, as large landowners, dominated Parliament. In 1815 a law was passed that allowed the import of foreign grain only after domestic wheat had reached the price of 80 shillings a quarter (about 3 hectoliters). This resulted in high bread prices at a time of considerable economic and social disruption following the Napoleonic Wars. It was not, however, until the formation (1839) of the Anti–Corn Law League by John BRIGHT and Richard COBDEN that effective opposition was mounted. In 1846 the Corn Laws were repealed by the government of Sir Robert PEEL.

See also: FREE TRADE.

Corneille, Pierre [kohr-nay']   Pierre Corneille, b. June 6, 1606, d. Oct. 1, 1684, along with his contemporary and rival, Jean Racine, ranks as France's greatest

Pierre Corneille, a 17th-century French dramatist, ushered in the neoclassical period in French drama with his major work, Le Cid *(1637).*

classical tragic dramatist. Born in Rouen, he was educated by Jesuits, studied law, entered the Rouen parlement in 1629 (the year his first play was written), and was a member of that judicial body for 21 years.

Although Corneille is regarded as the founder of French tragedy, six of his first eight plays, beginning with *Mélite* (c.1629), were comedies. In *La Place Royale* (1633–34) his comedy does not exclude seriousness. The hero abandons his proposed wife because he feels that love is only a phase in life and does not justify sacrificing duty and freedom. But the best examination of heroic motives occurs in *Le Cid* (1637), Corneille's masterpiece, which was influenced by Spanish tales of the famous 11th-century warrior known as EL CID. The problem of choice in *Le Cid* focuses on honor; in *Horace* (1640), on patriotism; in *Cinna* (1640–41), politics; and in *Polyeucte* (1642–43), religion. These four plays are considered Corneille's greatest achievements as a writer and thinker.

Opinion varies about the 21 plays that followed *Polyeucte*. At one time such plays as *Rodogune* (1644–45) were regarded as much less impressive masterpieces, and *Théodore* (1646) was his first failure. More recently, Corneille's admirers have claimed that his works, from the first comedy to the last tragedy, form a whole. In all of them Corneille combined support for absolute monarchy with a horror of tyranny. In his four best-known plays, the ruler is the arbiter who restores order or creates new order. In the later plays, the ruler becomes a rival of the hero and degenerates into a bloodthirsty tyrant who destroys the hero.

Nicomède (1651), described as tragedy, is actually a brilliantly ironic masterpiece in a new genre—the heroic comedy. *Pulchérie* (1672) and *Suréna*, Corneille's last play, produced in 1674, ten years before his death, are considered neglected masterpieces, as is *Théodore*.

Cornelius, Peter   Peter Cornelius, b. Dec. 24, 1824, d. Oct. 26, 1874, was an eminent German composer and writer. An advocate of Richard Wagner's music and an adherent of the Liszt-Wagner movement, Cornelius was befriended by Liszt, who conducted his masterpiece, the opera *The Barber of Baghdad*, in 1858 at Weimar. The failure of the opera led to Liszt's resignation as music director there. Cornelius joined Wagner in Munich in 1865, became a teacher at the Royal Music School in Munich, and enjoyed the patronage of Ludwig (or Louis) II, who was also Wagner's benefactor. He wrote the opera *Der Cid* in 1865, as well as many choral works and songs; he also wrote music criticism and poetry.

Cornell, Ezra   Ezra Cornell, b. Westchester Landing, N.Y., Jan. 11, 1807, d. Dec. 9, 1874, was an American businessman and the founder of the university named for him. He was associated with Samuel F. B. MORSE in constructing (1844) the first telegraph line, which ran from Washington, D.C., to Baltimore, Md. Over the next several years he built other telegraph lines and in 1855 was in-

strumental in unifying the lines and creating the Western Union Telegraph Company. He became interested in agriculture, and the Morrill Land Grant Act of 1862 enabled him to found (1865) Cornell University at Ithaca, N.Y. Cornell served in the New York state legislature from 1861 to 1867.

Cornell, Joseph   Joseph Cornell, b. Nyack, N.Y., Dec. 24, 1903, d. Dec. 29, 1972, was the first contemporary American artist to arrange "found objects" in glass-fronted wood boxes, thereby producing three-dimensional COLLAGES—or, as they became known, assemblages. In 1932, Cornell began juxtaposing memorabilia to form evocative, poetic metaphors. He used objects found in antique shops and secondhand bookstores, on beaches, and in backyards, to create miniature worlds that are both formally precise and filled with associational content. Cornell's use of repetition of a single image along a grid, as in *Flemish Child* (1942; ACA Gallery, New York City), and of photo-collages known as montages, along with his variations on a theme in a series of boxes, anticipated many artistic developments of the 1950s and 1960s. He was also a pioneer in the use of mirrors and of sound and movement (hand-manipulated) in the art of assemblage. Among Cornell's most famous works are those which refer to earlier works of art, such as *Medici Slot Machine* (1942; Mr. and Mrs. Bernard J. Reis Collection, New York City).

Joseph Cornell's Pipe and Glass Box (Eclipse Series) *demonstrates the surrealist method of creating artworks by rearranging everyday objects in unexpected conjunction. (Collection of the artist.)*

Cornell, Katharine   Katharine Cornell, b. Berlin, Germany, Feb. 16, 1893, d. June 9, 1974, is regarded as one of the finest American actresses of her time. Usually in association with her husband, producer-director Guthrie McClintic, she brought a rare artistic sense to the U.S. theater. Her most memorable role was as Elizabeth Barrett Browning in *The Barretts of Wimpole Street*

(1931). She published two autobiographies, *I Wanted to Be an Actress* (1939) and *Curtain Going Up* (1943).

Cornell University Established in 1865 by Ezra Cornell, Cornell University, located in Ithaca, N.Y., is the only private land-grant college and is a member of the IVY LEAGUE. The colleges of agriculture and life sciences, human ecology, and veterinary medicine and the school of industrial and labor relations are divisions of the State University of New York. The rest of Cornell, including a school of hotel administration, is privately controlled.

Corner Brook Corner Brook (1986 pop., 22,719) is the second largest city of Newfoundland province, Canada. It is located on the west coast of Newfoundland island, at the mouth of the Humber River. Settlement began there with the opening of a sawmill in 1864. The city's economy depends on paper and pulp mills, cement and gypsum plants, and salmon fishing.

cornet [kohr-net'] The cornet is a brass wind instrument resembling a TRUMPET but squatter in appearance and easier to play. Originating in the 1820s as a valved, circular posthorn, it soon emerged in its familiar, stubby trumpet form, although its bore was now wider and its mouthpiece deeper and more cupped than the trumpet's. The cornet's high, melodic tone and versatility make it particularly suitable for military bands. Although it is sometimes found in orchestras, especially French ones, the cornet is most often used for band and solo performances. The modern cornet has a range of about 2½ octaves.

The cornet, a three-valve brass wind instrument, was derived from the posthorn used on carriages.

cornett [kohr-net'] The cornett, or cornetto (not to be confused with the cornet), is a straight or slightly curved wooden wind instrument with fingerholes and a cup-shaped mouthpiece. In use from the 13th to the 19th century, it was popular in both church and ensemble music. Although the cornett is extremely difficult to play in tune, its sound—particularly that of the treble cornett—is mellow, yet with something of the trumpet's brightness.

Corning, Erastus Erastus Corning, b. Norwich, Conn., Dec. 14, 1794, d. Apr. 9, 1872, was the first president of the New York Central Railroad. During his professional life Corning was a merchant, iron manufacturer, railroad contractor, banker, land speculator, and political leader of considerable influence. He helped organize the Utica and Schenectady Railroad Company in 1833 and was active in promoting the formation of the New York Central Railroad Company in 1853. He was mayor of Albany, N.Y., a state senator, and a member of the U.S. House of Representatives for two terms. The town of Corning, N.Y., is named for him.

Cornish language see CELTIC LANGUAGES

Cornplanter Cornplanter, b. 1732 or 1740, d. 1836, was a famous SENECA Indian chief and statesman who, during the American Revolution, led his warriors against the colonists in several important campaigns. Of mixed Seneca and European blood, he was a half-brother of the Seneca prophet HANDSOME LAKE. Cornplanter eventually accepted the outcome of the Revolutionary War and became a staunch supporter of the United States.

corns see FOOT DISORDERS

Cornstalk Cornstalk, 1720?–1777, was a SHAWNEE war chief who fought English settlers in country west of the Appalachian Mountains during the colonial period. Sporadic fighting between Indians and frontiersmen who moved into territory west of the Kanawha River culminated (1774) in Lord Dunmore's War, named for the British governor of Virginia. On Oct. 10, 1774, Cornstalk led his warriors in a battle against the Virginians at Point Pleasant, in present-day West Virginia. The day-long fighting ended in defeat for the Indians, who were forced to cede contested land in Kentucky. In November 1777, Cornstalk was taken hostage and murdered by white settlers.

cornucopia [kohr-noo-koh'-pee-uh] The cornucopia, or horn of plenty, is a symbol of abundance. In Greek mythology, the infant Zeus was entrusted to the care of the daughters of King Melisseus and the goat-nymph Amalthea. In gratitude, Zeus broke off one of the goat's horns and gave it to Melisseus's daughters with the promise that it would be everlastingly full of food and drink.

Cornwall Cornwall is a county in the southwestern extremity of England. It is a peninsula bounded by the English Channel on the south and the Atlantic Ocean on the north and west, terminating at LAND'S END. Cornwall's population is 460,600 (1988 est.), and it covers 3,564 km^2 (1,376 mi^2). Although Bodmin is the county seat, Truro is the administrative center.

Most of Cornwall consists of rugged moorland that gradually declines in elevation to the heavily indented coastline. The SCILLY ISLANDS, located just offshore, are part of Cornwall. Dairy cattle are raised and fruits and vegetables grown. Tourism and tin and clay mining are also important. Falmouth, Fowey, and Penzance are industrial centers. Much of the scenic coast is protected from commercial development.

Cornwall was occupied by Romans, Saxons, and Celts before the Norman Conquest in 1066, after which it became an earldom. Since 1337 the heir to the British crown has held the title of duke of Cornwall.

Cornwallis, Charles Cornwallis, 1st Marquess

British general and colonial governor Charles Cornwallis, b. Dec. 31, 1738, d. Oct. 5, 1805, was the eldest son of the 1st Earl Cornwallis. He served in the Seven Years' War and became active politically with the Whigs in the House of Lords.

During the AMERICAN REVOLUTION Cornwallis served with distinction. In 1776 he subdued New Jersey and then triumphed at Brandywine and captured Philadelphia in 1777. As second in command to Sir Henry CLINTON, he advocated aggressive action in the South but was unable to realize his plans until 1780, when he captured Charleston and marched north. Cut off at Yorktown when Washington was reinforced by French troops, he capitulated on Oct. 19, 1781, thus effectively ending the war (see YORKTOWN CAMPAIGN).

Cornwallis was sent to India in 1786 as governor-general and commander in chief. He checked TIPPU SULTAN in Mysore and laid the administrative foundations of British rule in India. He also reformed the land and revenue systems and introduced a new criminal code (more humane than that of Britain), as well as a new court system.

Created marquess in 1792, Cornwallis returned to England the next year and joined the cabinet as master-general of ordnance in 1795. On the outbreak of rebellion in Ireland in 1798, he was sent there as viceroy and commander in chief. After pacifying the country, he aided Lord CASTLEREAGH in getting the Act of Union (unifying the Irish and British parliaments) through the Irish parliament. On the refusal of George III to permit CATHOLIC

The British military and political leader Charles Cornwallis initiated reforms both in the colonial administration of India, where he served (1786–93; 1805) as governor-general, and in Ireland, where he was viceroy from 1798 to 1801.

EMANCIPATION, however, he resigned (1801) as viceroy and from the cabinet.

corona   see SUN

Coronado, Francisco Vázquez de

[kohr-oh-nah'-doh]   Francisco Vázquez de Coronado, b. *c.*1510, d. Sept. 22, 1554, was a Spanish explorer of the American southwest. He sailed to Mexico with Viceroy Antonio de MENDOZA in 1535 and in 1538 was appointed governor of New Galicia. In February 1540, Coronado set out to explore the area north of the Rio Grande. He pushed forward to the pueblos of the ZUÑI tribes in a search for the fabled Seven Golden Cities of CÍBOLA and the riches of Gran Quivira. At the same time, a naval detachment led by Hernando de Alarcón sailed up the Gulf of California and into the COLORADO RIVER, and another party led by García López de Cárdenas discovered the GRAND CANYON on the river. When Coronado finally reached Quivira, in present-day Kansas, he found little wealth. He returned (1542) to Mexico, where his expedition was regarded as a failure. It is now recognized, however, as one of the greatest explorations.

coronary artery   see HEART

coronary artery disease   see ARTERIOSCLEROSIS

coronary disease   see HEART DISEASES

coronation

A coronation is a ceremony at which kings or queens are crowned on their accession to the throne. The practice of acknowledging new rulers by presenting them with the insignia of royal authority has existed since ancient times. In pre-Christian Europe, new chiefs were presented with a spear and a diadem, which symbolized their new power. With the spread of Christianity in Europe, new rites were added to the existing customs. A religious service of benediction was introduced into the ceremony in the early Middle Ages, and the anointing of the sovereign with oil or a mixture of oil and balsam became the main element in the ritual, a practice probably derived from the biblical accounts of the anointing of kings.

In England, where sovereigns have been crowned in Westminster Abbey since 1066, coronations still resemble medieval pageants. A major change, however, did take place in 1603, when at the coronation of James I the service was for the first time performed in the English language.

Coronation ceremonies in other countries followed traditions similar to, if not identical with, those in England. The medieval German kings customarily received the imperial crown from the pope in Rome. In continental Europe, only Norway and the Netherlands have kept the tradition of coronations. Coronation ceremonies were traditionally held to mark the election of a new pope as head of the Roman Catholic church. In 1978, Pope John Paul I replaced the papal coronation with a simple inaugural ceremony.

coroner A coroner is a public official whose principal function is to inquire into the causes and circumstances of any unnatural or otherwise suspicious death occurring within the coroner's jurisdiction. The coroner once had the power to investigate these deaths with the help of a jury and to issue warrants for the arrest of persons suspected of having caused a death by criminal means. Today the coroner is usually limited to ascertaining the cause of death. Most U.S. states have replaced the coroner's office with that of the medical examiner.

Corot, Jean Baptiste Camille [koh-roh'] Jean Baptiste Camille Corot, b. July 16, 1796, d. Feb. 22, 1875, was one of the greatest 19th-century French landscape painters. Although NEOCLASSICISM is evident in the subject matter, drawing technique, and palette of his early works, such as *Entrance to the Park at Saint-Cloud* (1823–24; private collection, Paris) and *Bridge at Narni* (1827; Louvre, Paris), Corot's spontaneity, as well as his intimate and romantic attitude toward nature, was already apparent. In sketching the Italian countryside during a visit from 1825 to 1828, he rejected neoclassical techniques in favor of heavy brushstrokes and dense impasto that conveyed his immediate impressions. Corot attained tonal harmony by mixing white lead paint with other hues,

Chartres Cathedral (1830), by the French painter Camille Corot, illustrates his masterly handling of composition. (Louvre, Paris.)

producing an extraordinary luminosity that lent substance to atmosphere and weight to volumes.

Corot frequently painted the region around his family's house at Ville d'Avray and at Fontainebleau. Paintings such as *Morning: Dance of the Nymphs* (1850–51; Louvre, Paris), executed in muted tones of pale green and silvery gray, exhibit overtones of melancholy and sadness; such personal moods distinguish Corot's art from the more objectified landscapes of the BARBIZON SCHOOL. During the summer he sketched *en plein air*, jotting down copious notes to be used during the winter, when he painted in the studio. Corot did not receive wide acceptance until the Exposition Universelle of 1855, when he won a first-class medal and Napoleon III purchased *Le Chariot: Recollections of Marcoussis* (1855; Louvre, Paris). This success provided him with numerous commissions over the next 20 years.

Corot's figure paintings, such as *Woman with a Pearl* (1868–70; Louvre, Paris), received little attention during his lifetime, despite his exceptional powers of modeling with broad passages of light and dark that gave his subjects a monumental fullness. It was his landscapes that were considered seminal to later 19th-century painting.

corporation A corporation is a business in which large numbers of people are organized so that their labor and capital are combined in a single venture. They may enter or withdraw from the venture at any time, leaving it to others to carry on. In law, a corporation is a single entity, a "person" that may sue or be sued without its members being held liable. Modern corporations include not only profit-making firms but also educational, scientific, recreational, charitable, and even religious organizations. Cities and towns incorporate themselves. Some activities of the federal government are carried on in corporate form, for example, the FEDERAL DEPOSIT INSURANCE CORPORATION and the TENNESSEE VALLEY AUTHORITY.

Development of the Corporation

The corporation is a result of two related yet distinct traditions. The first is the age-old penchant of people to join together in associations and engage in mutually beneficial activities. The second tradition began when the chartered company was established by sovereign states in western Europe in the late Middle Ages. Notable forerunners of the modern corporation were the great English trading companies of the 16th and 17th centuries, chartered by the crown or by act of Parliament. These JOINT-STOCK COMPANIES had a legal existence separate and distinct from that of their individual members. They also had the right to engage in commercial activities, including the exploration and colonization of new lands. By the end of the 17th century English lawyers had devised a new form of corporate organization that did not need an act of Parliament or the permission of the monarch. Combining contract and trust law, they established unchartered joint-stock companies that had all the attributes of the modern corporate form.

In the United States, after it gained independence

from Britain, corporations were chartered on an individual basis by state legislatures. Public dissatisfaction with this system grew. It placed a staggering burden on state legislatures; competing firms were jealous of the special privileges granted to some corporations; and the granting of special privileges was a concept alien to a democratic society.

The result was a shift toward a general enabling statute under which any group of persons could achieve corporate status simply by satisfying certain legal requirements. New York passed the first general corporation statute in 1811, and other states followed.

The Corporate Form of Enterprise

The corporation is distinguishable from other common forms of business enterprise, notably the proprietorship and the partnership. The sole proprietorship is a business that is owned by one person, whereas the partnership is an association of two or more persons. Although the corporation is more difficult and costly to organize than the proprietorship or the partnership, it has several advantages.

Limited Liability. Stockholders in a corporation are not legally responsible for the debts of the enterprise. Although they can lose their personal investment, they cannot be sued by the corporation's creditors. Individual proprietors and partners, however, are personally liable for their companies' debts and may be forced to sell other property to satisfy debts.

Legal Personality. The law treats a corporation as a person entitled to enter into contracts, to sue, and to be sued. The employees of the corporation are not held personally responsible for the acts of the corporation as a legal entity, although, under the law, they may be held responsible for acts committed as individuals.

Transferability of Ownership Interest. Ownership of a corporation is vested in its stockholders, who may sell their shares on the market whenever they wish. Thus, except when STOCK is held by a few individuals who choose not to sell it, the ownership of a corporation is constantly changing.

Continuity of Existence. Proprietorships and partnerships exist only as long as their owners are alive and as long as they continue the proprietorships or partnerships. In contrast, a corporation exists independently of its individual stockholders. Although corporations do not last forever, they can continue indefinitely at the will of their stockholders and creditors.

Concentration and Specialization of Management. Large corporations can employ professional managers with training and skills, a capability proprietors or partners may not have. Many large corporations are, in fact, run entirely by their hired managers.

Large Corporations

The size and economic power of some industrial agglomerations has long been a subject of controversy. Many of today's corporations have thousands of employees and control billions of dollars in assets. The 1988 combined annual revenues of the top five corporations was $402 billion, which is greater than the gross national product of all but a handful of countries in the world.

Mergers. Corporations began to grow large late in the 19th century. Between 1897 and 1902 a wave of mergers occurred, producing hundreds of large companies. These corporations subsequently grew larger, both by expansion and acquisition. A second wave of mergers occurred during the 1920s, reaching a peak of 1,250 in 1929. During the 1960s a third wave occurred; in 1969 about 2,500 mergers took place. Yet another wave that started in 1983 continued strongly through the 1980s; in 1985 alone a total of 3,165 mergers took place.

Mergers among corporations take several forms. In the horizontal merger, a company seeks to extend its share of the market by acquiring another firm in the same industry. In the vertical merger, a company moves forward or backward in the productive process, acquiring others engaged in producing raw materials or in selling to the final consumer—as, for example, when a steel company acquires coal mines and oil fields (a backward merger) or buys a bridge-building firm (a forward merger). In the 1960s mergers began to take place among companies in substantially different industries. These are called CONGLOMERATE mergers.

Merger Language. The growth of corporate mergers and takeovers has brought an associated set of buzz concepts and strategies—and new terms. "Junk bonds" are corporate bonds lacking an A rating from Moody's and Standard and Poor's investors' services. They are rated lower because the companies are deemed too highly leveraged in debt or their earnings are too low. "Leveraged buyout" is the purchase of assets or stock of a privately owned company, a public company, or a subsidiary or division of a private or publicly held company in which the purchaser uses a significant amount of debt and very little or no capital. A "poison pill" is an action by the management of a company threatened by takeover that makes acquiring the firm so expensive that the predator goes off to seek other game. "Shark repellants" are other measures used to fight off a pursuing firm, including changing the bylaws to make it more difficult to acquire the company. Thus the corporate charter and bylaws might be amended to require the controlling shareholder to obtain 80 to 95 percent approval for a takeover (a "super majority").

"Corporate raiders" are individuals who attempt to make a hostile takeover of or bids for a company at exorbitant prices. "Arbitragers" are securities specialists who buy stock of a target company on the hunch that a takeover effort will be successful or will elicit bids from the target or from another suitor. "Green mail" is the premium paid by a company above the market prices to buy back stock from a corporate raider. "White Knights" are corporations with which a target company might negotiate a friendly merger in order to forestall a hostile takeover.

Growth and Regulation. As corporations grew, many Americans became concerned that they were becoming too powerful. In 1890, Congress passed the SHERMAN ANTI-TRUST ACT, which made illegal any combination of or conspiracy among companies in restraint of trade. The meaning of "restraint of trade" was not clear. The Supreme Court adopted what it called the "rule of reason," holding that bigness alone was not in restraint of trade but only combinations that were intended to coerce or attack competitors. The Court did not condemn growth that was achieved by superior efficiency in management and production. Applying the rule of reason in 1911, the Court ordered the American Tobacco Company and Standard Oil to be broken up into separate companies; it left Eastman Kodak and International Harvester intact, however. Through other laws, Congress has sought to prevent large companies from using their power unfairly against competitors or consumers.

Defenders of the corporation point to its efficiency as a form of economic organization, arguing that the size of a corporation is no indication of its power, since every company faces competition within its particular industry. The three giants of the automobile industry—General Motors (GM), Ford, and Chrysler—compete vigorously for their share of the market, as well as facing strong competition from foreign manufacturers. The same is true of other industries in which a few large companies control 60% or more of the market; on the average, the share of the large companies in the total sales of their industries has not changed much over a period of time; in some cases it has decreased as other companies participated.

Ownership and Control

In addition to size, a striking characteristic of the modern corporation is that those who own it have little say in how it is run. Legally, stockholders have the power to determine the main policies of a company, since it is they who elect the board of directors. Ostensibly, the board of directors oversees the actions of the managers, whose job it is to carry out the board's decisions. In reality, the average person with a few shares of stock in GM or Exxon has no effective control over the company's policies. In many large corporations effective control is in the hands of management, which may select or change the board of directors as it sees fit.

Management excercises control by use of the proxy mechanism—a provision that allows stockholders who cannot attend the annual meeting to authorize management to cast their votes for them. Most stockholder meetings are so sparsely attended that a serious challenge to company policy can come only from holders of large blocks of stock or, as often happens, from banks to which the company owes money. Some corporations are controlled by family groups that own a sizable share—10% or more—of a corporation's common stock.

In recent years a new kind of stockholder has emerged: the large financial institution that holds stock for its clients. Included in these institutional investors are insurance companies, mutual funds, savings banks, employee pension funds, and the trust departments of commercial banks. In the late 1980s the institutional investor had about $2 trillion in assets in U.S. publicly owned corporations, primarily in the form of the pension fund. Pension funds own one-third of the equity of all publicly traded U.S. companies and 50% or more of the equity of the large ones. U.S. stock ownership has become more concentrated than ever before.

Multinational Corporations

The corporation has come full circle since it began. Just as the English trading companies of the 17th century set out to seize the commercial opportunities of overseas trade, the large industrial corporations of today look beyond the borders of their home countries for commercial opportunities. During the 20th century the multinational corporation, one that owns plants or business enterprises in more than one country, emerged—and flourished in the last decades of the century. These corporations began in the oil industry and in the mining of copper and nickel. In the years following World War I, U.S. automobile manufacturers began to acquire subsidiaries overseas, producing cars aimed at local markets. The multinational movement grew rapidly after World War II. Direct foreign investment, as the U.S. Department of Commerce calls investment by U.S. companies in other countries, grew from $11.8 billion in 1950 to $309 billion in 1987. Investment in Canada, in European countries, in Japan, and in other developed countries accounted for about three-quarters of the total; the flow was not one way. Foreign corporations also acquired subsidiaries in the United States.

Corporations form foreign subsidiaries for a number of reasons. Perhaps the major reason is to overcome barriers to foreign trade, such as tariffs and import quotas. The formation of the Common Market (see EUROPEAN COMMUNITY) was a great incentive to investment by U.S. companies in Europe, because it created an international market about the size of the U.S. market. Another motive in forming multinational corporations is the adaptation of products for local markets.

The growth of the multinationals has been viewed with alarm by some and hailed by others as a step forward. The French publisher Jean-Jacques Servan-Schreiber wrote in *The American Challenge* (1967; Eng. trans., 1968) that U.S. business interests in Europe had acquired the dimensions of a superpower, penetrating deeply into certain critical high-technology industries, such as computers and integrated circuits. Multinationals have also been criticized for pursuing their own interests while disregarding those of the countries in which they operate, as well as the interests of their home countries.

On the positive side, the multinationals are viewed as a unifying force in the world economy, enabling entrepreneurs of all nations to compete wherever economic conditions exist that are favorable to business. Thus, a watch company based in Hong Kong may combine Swiss technology and an Asian work force with a sales organization in the United States.

The world of the 1980s and '90s is different from the one described by the critics of the multinationals in the 1960s and '70s. Instead of dominating the world, the U.S. multinationals are struggling to hold their own—not only in foreign markets but also in their home markets. Multinational corporations have emerged from such Asian countries as Japan, South Korea, Taiwan, Hong Kong, and even India and the Philippines. Moreover, new global forces have appeared in the form of international agencies and internationally linked religious and other public interest groups that monitor the performance of multinational corporations to ensure that their activities benefit all concerned parties.

See also: BUSINESS ADMINISTRATION; CARTEL; GOVERNMENT REGULATION; MONOPOLY AND COMPETITION; PUBLIC UTILITY.

Corpus Christi [kohr'-puhs kris'-tee]   Corpus Christi is a port of entry on Corpus Christi Bay near the mouth of the Nueces River in southern Texas. The seat of Nueces County, Corpus Christi has a population of 257,453 (1990); the metropolitan-area population is 349,894. The city's fine landlocked harbor on the Gulf Intracoastal Waterway is connected to the Gulf of Mexico by a deepwater channel. It is also an oil and natural-gas center. Corpus Christi serves as the processing and commercial center for a fishing, cattle-ranching, and wheat-growing region. It has a university and a college and is the site of a naval-air training station. Much of the population is of Mexican descent. The city's warm climate and nearby beaches attract many tourists. The year-round resort islands of Padre and Mustang shelter the harbor.

The city was named for the bay that was sighted by Alonso de Pineda in 1519 on the feast of Corpus Christi. The bay area was settled by Spaniards about 1765, and a U.S. trading post was established there in 1838. The discovery of natural gas in 1913 and the development of the harbor in 1926 spurred the growth of the modern city.

Correggio [kohr-red'-joh]   Antonio Allegri, b. August 1489, d. Mar. 15, 1534, known as Correggio for his hometown, rapidly developed a personal style of painting that was even more sensuous and emotive than the art of Michelangelo. Correggio's earliest documented work, the *Madonna of St. Francis* (Gemäldegalerie, Dresden) dates from 1514. About 1519 he frescoed the ceiling of the Camera di San Paolo in Parma with an abstruse mythological allegory set into a trellislike framework reminiscent of Andrea Mantegna's experiments in perspective.

Between 1520 and 1524, Correggio frescoed the apse and dome of the church of San Giovanni Evangelista in Parma. The dome seems open to the sky as Christ, ringed by his apostles, ascends into the heavens. Correggio's work in Parma established his reputation, and thereafter orders for his paintings increased. In them, the dramatic and emotional content is intensified by fluttering clothing, diagonal compositions, and extravagant poses. His saints and angels are always charming, sometimes alluring. Two of his most famous religious paintings, *Madonna and Child with Saints Jerome and Mary Magdalen* (c.1529; Galleria Nazionale, Parma) and the *Adoration of the Shepherds* (1530; Gemäldegalerie, Dresden) are commonly known as *Il Giorno* ("day") and *La Notte* ("night"). In *La Notte* the infant Jesus is the source of intense light that illumines the entire painting and controls forms and colors.

Between 1526 and 1530, Correggio executed his most important church decoration, the *Assumption of the*

The Italian artist Correggio painted this ceiling fresco of the cupola of San Giovanni Evangelista in Parma in 1520–24.

Virgin, in the dome of the Cathedral of Parma. The apostles, whose foreshortening adds to the illusion of movement in space, stand around the drum of the dome and watch a ring of angels, swimming through clouds, carry the Virgin into the heavens. Correggio occupied his remaining days by illustrating the erotic series the *Loves of Jupiter* (c.1534; Kunsthistorisches Museum, Vienna).

Correggio deeply influenced Lanfranco and the Carracci brothers in the 17th century, and thus the formation of the baroque style (see BAROQUE ART AND ARCHITECTURE).

Corregidor [kuh-reg'-i-dor]   Corregidor is an island at the entrance to Manila Bay about 5 km (3 mi) off BATAAN Peninsula and is part of Cavite province of the Philippines. Its area is 5 km² (2 mi²). Of strategic importance, it was once called the Gibraltar of the East. The island served as a fortress and penal colony under the Spanish. After the Spanish-American War in 1898, the United States extended the fortifications, establishing Fort Mills and Kindley Field. During World War II, American and

Filipino forces on Corregidor made a last effort to resist the Japanese invasion of the Philippines. After the fall of Bataan on Apr. 9, 1942, U.S. forces on Corregidor had no way to receive supplies, and on May 6, Lt. Gen. Jonathan M. WAINWRIGHT surrendered with more than 10,000 troops, medical personnel, and civilians. Retaken in February 1945, the island became an official part of the Philippine Republic in 1947 and is now a national shrine.

correspondence principle In physics, the correspondence principle requires that a new theory explain all phenomena explained by the theory that it supersedes. Formulated in 1923 by physicist Niels BOHR, the correspondence principle reflects the relationship between 20th-century quantum theory and 19th-century classical theory and can be applied almost universally. As an example, classical mechanics, which can explain only large-scale physical systems, is seen to be merely a special case of quantum mechanics, which can explain large- and small-scale systems.

correspondence school Correspondence schools are a system of education in which instruction takes place through the mail. Although the original goal was to reach otherwise inaccessible pupils, the system also has the advantages of self-paced instruction, of not disrupting home or employment schedules, and of low cost. A higher ratio of students to teachers can be maintained than in ordinary schools, and less space is required. Correspondence programs are used extensively in Australia, Latin America, and Africa and are growing in Western Europe. Such programs often offer continuing education for adults.

Correspondence programs exist for all levels, from primary to technical and university education. Schools may be operated by government ministries, universities, or private companies. Many teachers work part-time, and programs vary widely in quality. The accrediting agency in the United States is the National Home Study Council, established in 1926. It had about 90 members in the late 1980s.

corrosion Corrosion is the natural deterioration or destruction of a material as a result of its interaction with its environment. The term is applied mostly to metals and particularly to their reaction with oxygen, or rusting; all materials, however, are subject to surface deterioration. Generally the processes are chemical or electrochemical, although physical and mechanical factors contribute to the corrosion.

Corrosion of metals is generally confined to the surface. In some cases, such as that of aluminum, a layer of oxide is formed that serves as a barrier to prevent further contact with oxygen, thus suppressing corrosion. The very thin oxide layer on iron protects the iron in dry air. In the presence of moisture, however, hydrates of iron oxide form, the iron becomes porous to oxygen, and corrosion proceeds.

Although some trace impurities in metal can acceler-ate corrosion, others inhibit it. Aluminum is added to brass to make it more corrosion-resistant. The most common means of thwarting corrosion is to apply a resistant surface coating.

Corsair The Vought F4U Corsair is a single-seated aircraft considered by many the finest naval fighter plane of World War II. It was in production for 11 years, and about 12,500 were built. Designed by a team directed by Rex B. Beisel, the Corsair had distinctive inverted-gull wings, which were necessary for adequate ground clearance of the large-diameter propeller. The propeller had to be large to utilize efficiently the high power of the Pratt and Whitney radial piston engine. The Corsair was modified to serve as a night-fighter, a fighter-bomber, and a reconnaissance aircraft.

The Chance-Vought F4U-1D Corsair, one of World War II's most effective dive-bomber planes, had a distinctive bent-wing configuration. The whistling sound generated by its wing air-intakes earned it the nickname "Whistling Death."

Corsica Corsica (French: Corse) is the fourth largest island (8,680 km²/3,352 mi²) in the Mediterranean Sea. It is situated 170 km (105 mi) southeast of France, 97 km (60 mi) west of the Italian mainland, and is separated from Sardinia by the Strait of Bonifacio. A region of France with its own elected assembly, Corsica is divided into the departments of Haute-Corse and Corse-du-Sud. An independence movement is active.

Most of the island is a crystalline massif carved by the major rivers (Golo, Gravone, Tavignano), with frequent gorges in the mountains. Maquis, a dense, nearly impenetrable scrub brush, is the most common vegetative cover at low and medium altitudes. Forests of pine, beech, birch, and chestnut are found at higher altitudes. Sheep are raised on the rugged Niolo plateau in the north, and cheese from their milk is an important Corsican export. The economy is based on agriculture (citrus fruit, tobacco, grapes), although tourism is becoming important. A third of the population of 247,300 (1988 est.) live in the two largest towns, AJACCIO, the capital, and Bastia, both of which are on the coast. Most inhabitants speak both French (the official language) and Corsican, which is an Italian dialect.

The Romans conquered Corsica in the 3d century BC and established agricultural colonies along the coasts.

Calvi, a small fishing village founded during the 13th century, is located on the Ligurian Sea in the Balagne region of northwestern Corsica.

These were destroyed during the Vandal, Lombard, and Saracen invasions between about AD 450 and 1050. Pisa and Genoa (until 1284) and Genoa and Aragon (until 1434) battled for control of the island. Genoa remained dominant from the 15th to the 18th century, when the Corsicans rebelled (1729) and established (1755) their own government under Pasquale PAOLI. The French conquered Corsica in 1769. During the French Revolution, Paoli returned to power and allied himself with the British, who occupied the island in 1794. Napoléon Bonaparte (a native Corsican) restored French rule in 1796.

Corso, Gregory   Gregory Corso, b. New York City, Mar. 26, 1930, a BEAT GENERATION poet, is known as the renegade of American poetry, especially for the angry surrealism of his second book, *Gasoline* (1958). Corso spent his youth as a delinquent and a vagabond. After serving a prison term for theft, he worked as a manual laborer and a merchant seaman. He arranged for his first volume of poems, *The Vestal Lady on Brattle* (1955), to be published through the subscriptions of friends. Other works include the verse volumes *Long Live Man* (1962), *Elegiac Feelings American* (1970), and *Herald of the Autochthonic Spirit* (1981) and the novel *American Express* (1961).

Cortázar, Julio [kohr-tah'-zar, hool'-ee-oh]   The Argentinian writer Julio Cortázar, b. Aug. 26, 1914, d. Feb. 12, 1984, was a leading figure in Latin American letters. *Rayuela* (1963; *Hopscotch*, 1966) has been described as one of the most important novels of this century. Cortázar often used fantasy and surrealism to depict the realities buried under the habits of daily life. His collections of short fiction include *Bestiario* (1951), *End of the Game* (1956; Eng. trans., 1967), *We Love Glenda So Much* (1981; Eng. trans., 1983), and *All Fires the Fire* (1966; Eng. trans. 1988). Among his novels are *The Winners* (1960; Eng. trans., 1965), *62: A Model Kit* (1968; Eng. trans., 1972), and *A Certain Lucas* (1979; Eng. trans., 1984).

Cortés, Hernán [kohr-tez', air-nahn']   Hernán Cortés, b. Medellín, Spain, 1485, d. Dec. 2, 1547, was the Spanish conqueror of Mexico. The child of low Spanish nobility, he was sent at age 14 to the University of Salamanca. Two years later he abandoned his education and in 1504 sailed to Santo Domingo to seek his fortune in the New World. He participated in the conquest of Cuba by Diego de VELÁZQUEZ DE CUÉLLAR and in 1519 led an expedition that, after renouncing Velázquez, set out to conquer Mexico.

Cortés explored the coast of Mexico, finally stopping near modern Veracruz, where he founded a city in order to legitimize his expedition. After gaining valuable information regarding the political situation in the highlands, Cortés marched inland, made an alliance with the Indians of Tlaxcala (the traditional enemies of the AZTECS), and began to pose as QUETZALCÓATL. The Indians believed that this legendary ruler and deity would eventually return to Mexico from the east. Consequently, MONTEZUMA II, the Aztec king, was too mystified to organize resistance, and the Spaniards entered TENOCHTITLÁN, the Aztec capital, unopposed in November 1519.

After several months Cortés went to the coast to defeat a rival Spanish force under Pánfilo de NARVÁEZ. When he

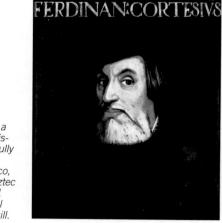

Hernán Cortés, a Spanish conquistador, successfully invaded and colonized Mexico, defeating the Aztec Empire by 1521 through political and strategic skill.

returned, he found the Aztecs, who had been brutalized by his lieutenant Pedro de ALVARADO, in revolt. Forced to withdraw, the Spanish suffered heavy losses on the so-called *noche triste* ("sad night") of June 30, 1520. Cortés, however, returned in 1521 to besiege Tenochtitlán. It fell, after 3 months, on Aug. 13, 1521—only because an epidemic killed many defenders.

The conquest thus completed, Cortés distributed the spoils, giving himself huge landholdings in various parts of Mexico. He returned several times to Spain, where he was entitled the marqués del Valle de Oaxaca. His other exploits included expeditions to Honduras (1524) and Baja California (1536) and participation in the unsuccessful Spanish attack on Algiers in 1541.

corticoid   see HORMONE, ANIMAL

corticosterone   see HORMONE, ANIMAL

cortisol   see HORMONE, ANIMAL

cortisone   see HORMONE, ANIMAL

Cortona, Pietro da [kohr-toh'-nah]   The architect and painter Pietro Berrettini, b. Nov. 1, 1596, d. May 16, 1669, known as Pietro da Cortona (after his birthplace), was a major figure in Italian baroque architecture. In Rome, Pietro painted (1633–39) the huge illusionistic ceiling frescoes of the great *salone* of the Barberini Palace. For Marcello Sacchetti, he built the Villa del Pigneto near Rome (1626–36).

From 1634 to 1638, Pietro was director of the Academia di San Luca, the artists' society in Rome. In 1634 he was given permission to build his tomb in the academy's church, San Martina e Luca. During the excavations, the body of St. Martina was discovered, and in 1635, Cardinal Barberini commissioned a new church for the site. This church, designed by Pietro, is a Greek-cross plan with apsidal endings.

One of Pietro's most ingenious Roman works was the new facade (1656–57) for the church of Santa Maria della Pace. The single-story church portico curves out into the piazza, and the body of the facade rises above and behind. A pair of concave wings encircles the facade. A similar plan was used by Giovanni BERNINI for the facade of Sant' Andrea al Quirinale, Rome. Pietro's other major work (1658–62) is the church of Santa Maria in Via Lata, Rome.

corundum [kuh-ruhn'-duhm]   Corundum is a widespread and common aluminum OXIDE MINERAL, Al_2O_3, varieties of which include the gemstones RUBY and SAPPHIRE and the abrasive material EMERY. Common corundum forms dull, opaque, hexagonal crystals with a hardness of 9 and a specific gravity of 4.0–4.1. It occurs in FELDSPATHOID-bearing igneous rocks, in recrystallized limestone, in PLACER DEPOSITS, and in certain metamorphic rocks.

Corythosaurus [kuh-rith-uh-sohr'-uhs]   *Corythosaurus* (Greek: *koryth-*, the stem of *korys*, "helmet"; *sauros*, "lizard"), a late Cretaceous duckbill (hadrosaurian) DINOSAUR of North America, reached a length of 950 cm (31 ft) and weighed up to 3.8 metric tons (more than 8,000 lb). The genus is characterized by a helmetlike crest con-

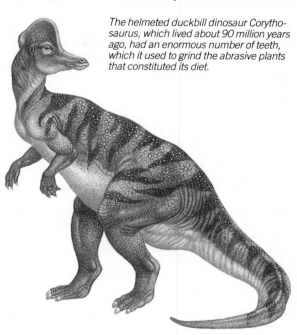

The helmeted duckbill dinosaur Corythosaurus, which lived about 90 million years ago, had an enormous number of teeth, which it used to grind the abrasive plants that constituted its diet.

taining convoluted loops of the nasal passage, a structure that some paleontologists believe was involved with vocalization. Like other hadrosaurs, *Corythosaurus* was a herbivore, equipped for its vegetarian diet with a flattened ducklike bill behind which batteries of several hundred

Common corundum includes all the opaque forms of dull, usually dark-colored, aluminum oxide minerals. Harder than any mineral except diamond, it is usually found as large six-sided crystals.

teeth were arranged in superimposed rows that functioned as a shearing device. A long, transversely flattened tail and evidence of webbed feet suggest that the animal lived mainly in water but could also walk on land. Specimens are most common in Alberta, western Canada, where occasional impressions of the skin on rock surrounding the skeletons reveal small, elevated scales arranged in geometric patterns.

Cosa, Juan de la   Juan de la Cosa, *c.*1460–1510, a Spanish navigator and geographer, drew the earliest surviving map showing the discoveries in the New World. Having sailed with Christopher COLUMBUS on his second voyage (1493) and with Alonso de Ojeda to the northeastern coast of South America (1499–1500), Cosa produced a world map, dated 1500, that included the Caribbean Sea and recorded John CABOT's voyage to Canada and Vasco da GAMA's route to India. Cosa was killed by Indians near Cartagena, Columbia, in 1510. Another Juan de la Cosa was the owner and master of the *Santa María* on Columbus's first voyage in 1492.

Cosby, Bill   William Henry Cosby, Jr., b. Philadelphia, July 12, 1937, is a television and film comedian. Cosby's interest in the education of children has led him to take a doctorate and to teach, as well as influencing his comedy material (the character Fat Albert, a Cosby invention, has been used in educational TV programs). It has also apparently influenced the many TV commercials Cosby has made. As the co-star of "I Spy" (1965–68) Cosby became the first black actor in a weekly TV dramatic series. He won three successive Emmys for the part, and several Grammys for recordings of his comedy routines. "The Cosby Show" (1984–   ), a family sitcom, became television's highest rated program.

cosecant   SEE TRIGONOMETRY

Cosell, Howard   Howard Cosell, b. Howard William Cohen in Winston-Salem, N.C., Mar. 25, 1920, is a sports announcer whose instructive but abrasive style made him a renowned sports-television personality. Cosell graduated from New York University Law School but stopped practicing law in 1956. He supported Muhammad Ali when the boxer was stripped of his title in 1967, and spoke out against racism in sports at the 1968 Olympics. Cosell was an announcer on ABC's Monday-night football during the 1970s. In the 1980s he severed his ties with boxing and stopped appearing regularly on television.

Cosgrave (family)   The Cosgraves are a family prominent in Irish politics. **William T. Cosgrave**, b. June 6, 1880, d. Nov. 16, 1965, was prime minister of the Irish Free State from 1922 to 1932. A member of Sinn Fein, he fought in the Easter Rising of 1916. He was elected to the British Parliament in 1918 and helped to establish the revolutionary parliament, Dáil Éirann. In 1919, Cosgrave became a minister in the revolutionary cabinet. He supported the 1921 treaty setting up the Irish Free State and in August 1922 succeeded Arthur GRIFFITH as prime minister. In 1932 his Cuman na nGeadheal party was defeated by Eamon DE VALERA's Fianna Fáil. Cosgrave remained leader of Cuman na nGeadheal (later Fine Gael) until 1945.

His son, **Liam Cosgrave**, b. April 30, 1920, was elected to the Dáil for Fine Gael in 1943. He served (1954–57) as minister of external affairs, and was leader of Fine Gael from 1965 to 1977. From 1973 to 1977 he was prime minister as head of a Fine Gael–Labour coalition government.

cosine   SEE TRIGONOMETRY

Cosmas and Damian, Saints   Cosmas and Damian are the patron saints of physicians. According to legend, they were twin brothers who were martyred (*c.*303) in Syria under the emperor Diocletian; nothing, however, is actually known of their lives. According to one story, they practiced medicine without accepting payment and hence were known as the "silverless ones." They were venerated in the East as early as the 5th century. Feast days: July 1 and Nov. 1 in the East; Sept. 26 (formerly Sept. 27) in the West.

cosmetics   Cosmetics are preparations used to change the appearance or enhance the beauty of the face, skin, and hair. Like perfumes, cosmetics were probably originally used as an adjunct to religious ritual.

History

Archaeological evidence suggests that prehistoric peoples knew how to find and prepare pigments and blend them with greasy substances that could be used to paint cave walls and to decorate the body. Body painting was a form of both adornment and magical protection.

Analysis of prehistoric pigments has revealed the use of as many as 17 colors. White was made from white lead, chalk, or gypsum.

Cosmetics in the Ancient World. Records left by the ancient civilizations of the Middle East show a consistent use of cosmetics. The Sumerians, Babylonians, Hebrews, and Egyptians employed similar preparations for similar purposes—ceremonial, medicinal, and ornamental. Face and body paints, as well as skin oils and unguents, have been found in pots, jars, sticks, and pencils, some from the 4th millennium BC. The ancient Middle Eastern civilizations lavished attention on the eyes, in part because the cosmetics used served as protection from flies and the Sun's glare. Lashes, lids, and eyebrows were painted black with kohl, a paste made from soot, antimony, or galena, a form of lead ore.

Henna was used as a hair dye and to dye the fingernails, the palms of the hands, and the soles of the feet. Scents and unguents, restricted at first to use in the ritu-

This painted lime-stone bust (c.365 BC) of Queen Nefertiti illustrates the use by ancient Egyptians of elegant, ornamental cosmetics. Both men and women of the upper classes used cosmetics to outline their eyebrows and eyelids. Cheek and lip colorings, as well as unguents and perfumes, were also widely used. (Staatliche Museum, Berlin.)

Women of the Roman Empire used cosmetics from Egypt and other parts of the Middle East to adorn the body and to signify social status. Hair dyes from France and Germany were often used to lighten the hair. This Pompeian fresco shows a servant attending to a young woman's coiffure.

als of mummification, became an important product in the Egyptian export trade. Raw essences were compounded and sold as perfumes, creams, and lotions.

India. Used to pay homage to the body, cosmetics and perfumes were also essential to the Indian woman, whose duty it was to appear alluring to her lover. In the famous Indian treatise on love, the KAMASUTRA (compiled between AD 100 and 600), women are advised to learn the arts of tattooing and of "coloring the teeth, garments, hair, nails, and bodies."

Greece and Rome. In contrast to the civilizations of northern Africa and Anatolia, the classical Greeks permitted few cosmetics, although Greek courtesans used imported perfumes, depilatories, rouges, and eye paint made of kohl. The early Romans scorned cosmetics as effete. By the time of the empire, however, the luxuries of the conquered eastern peoples had become not only desirable but symbols of status and wealth.

Medieval Europe. When the Roman influence in Europe finally vanished, Roman notions of personal cleanliness and adornment disappeared as well. It was only with the return of Crusaders and pilgrims from the east, and the beginnings of the Renaissance, that the ancient cosmetic arts were relearned and revived in Europe, first in the royal courts and much later among the common people. In spite of the church's disapproval, face paint again became fashionable among the nobility; for a time its use was restricted to the males of certain courts and to highborn ladies and courtesans.

The Beginnings of the Modern Era. France became a leader in developing the art of makeup (*maquillage*), and both men and women of rank used face powder, hair powder, and skin lotions. Although France continued to be considered the fount of artifice in cosmetics use, by the 16th century, the Italians, and particularly the Venetians, had become the major producers and purveyors of cosmetic preparations. As the desire for new and more

effective cosmetics grew, the number of dangerous or lethal preparations in common use increased; for example, fucus red, used for lip color, was actually red mercuric sulfide.

The peak of cosmetic use was reached in 18th-century Europe, especially in England and France, where both sexes attempted to reach an almost totally artificial appearance. Whitened faces were etched with blue to bring out the vein lines. The black velvet or silk beauty patch, invented to cover the blemishes left by smallpox, was increasingly used.

A gentlewoman of Elizabethan England used cosmetic lotions and facial masks, many of them containing low-grade poisons, to achieve the flawless alabaster complexion considered ideal.

Cloth beauty patches, designed to hide smallpox scars, became the vogue for men and women in 18th-century England and France.

The flamboyant use of cosmetics dimmed considerably after the French Revolution and the opening of the Victorian age. Men abandoned makeup almost entirely, and respectable women confined themselves to a touch of eau de cologne or a dab of white rice powder. By the 1880s, however, advances in technology—especially in printing—and the advent of advertising opened a new era in cosmetic history: the age of the testimonial. For example, the American cosmetic manufacturer Harriet Hubbard Ayer spent $50,000 to advertise her face cream and her claim that it was invented by the famous French beauty Madame Récamier. Encouraged by such advertising, women once again began to use cosmetics. Modern methods of mass production and packaging made them relatively inexpensive, and there is now a flourishing U.S. industry that produces cosmetics and toiletries for use by men as well as women.

Modern Cosmetics

Divided according to the method of their manufacture, most modern cosmetics fall into one of the following categories:

Powders. A face powder usually contains talc, chalk, kaolin, and mixtures of zinc oxide, titanium oxide, and various powdered pigments. Properly compounded, this mixture spreads easily, adheres to the skin, and absorbs some moisture. Cake makeup consists of face powder mixed with a dry gum, which is then moistened, compressed, and dried. Rouge in cake form is a compressed, pigmented powder.

Emulsions. Most skin preparations in cream or lotion form are emulsions, usually fine particles of oil dispersed in water. Vanishing cream is an oil-in-water emulsion made of a fatty acid such as stearic acid, with glycerin or propylene glycol. Vanishing creams penetrate the skin but leave no oily sheen. With added pigments, they are used as cosmetic foundation creams.

Cold creams are emulsions of mineral oil and water and are used to remove makeup or as a substitute for soap. Thinner emulsions, which contain more water relative to the oil content, are used as cleansing lotions and hand creams.

Lipsticks. Oils, such as castor oil, and waxes are melted together, mixed with pigments or dyes, melted again, and hardened in molds. Since the materials used in manufacturing lipsticks (and lip salves, which contain essentially the same ingredients without the coloring) are ultimately taken into the body, the choice of ingredients is limited to those which are known or assumed to be nontoxic.

Eye Makeup. Eyebrow pencils, eye shadow, and mascara are, like lipstick, compounds of oil, wax, and pigments. They, too, must be made of noninjurious materials.

Special Preparations. Cosmetic products may also include the following: deodorant and depilatory preparations; suntan lotions and creams that either protect the skin by screening it with a light-absorbing chemical, or that, because of their oily base, make possible a tan; shampoos, usually based on highly soluble detergents with additional perfumes and sometimes special ingredients to compensate for dry hair or dandruff; hair sprays, usually made from a resin (for example, shellac in a volatile solvent such as alcohol); nail preparations, including nail lacquers—a solution of nitrocellulose and colorants with resins and plasticizers to promote gloss and adhesion; and polish remover, a nitrocellulose solvent, usually acetone or ethyl acetate.

Cosmetics Safety. The production and sale of cosmetics in the United States was virtually unregulated until the passage of the Food, Drug and Cosmetics Act of 1938, which for the first time imposed penalties for products that were "adulterated" (that is, contained some dangerous or impure substance) or carried a deceptive label. Clear and accurate labeling of all ingredients—with the exception of flavorings, fragrances, and colors—was now required. By 1960 food and drug—but not cosmetics—manufacturers were expected to test new chemical substances before marketing products containing them. The Delaney Clause, added to the act in 1958, forbade the use of any substance found to produce cancer in laboratory animals.

The food and drug laws are administered by the Food and Drug Administration (FDA), sometimes in conjunction with the Department of Agriculture. With regard to cosmetics, the laws hold manufacturers responsible for selling products that are in compliance with the regulations.

The FDA may investigate a product but bears the responsibility for proving that a substance used in that product is harmful. The industry, however, has been largely self-policing in recent years.

cosmic rays   Cosmic rays are high-speed subatomic particles that pervade space. They are studied by scientists in a wide variety of disciplines. Galactic cosmic rays enter the solar system in equal numbers from all directions. Solar cosmic rays are emitted by the Sun, more or less continuously (low energy) or as discrete, explosive bursts (high energy).

After 1900 many attempts were made to explain the puzzling behavior of instruments used for studying X RAYS and radioactivity; these attempts culminated in the discovery of cosmic rays. In 1912 the Austrian physicist Victor Franz Hess, using ionization chambers in an open gondola, concluded that a mysterious ultrapenetrating radiation was probably coming from an extraterrestrial source. Hess received (1936) the Nobel Prize for physics for his discovery.

Originally thought to consist of exceedingly energetic electromagnetic radiation, cosmic rays were found to be particles, after experiments pioneered by the Dutch physicist Jacob Clay revealed that the amount of incoming radiation decreased as the detector approached the equator. This result proved that incoming cosmic rays are electrically charged particles, since electromagnetic waves would be unaffected by the action of the Earth's magnetic field.

Composition. The incident primary galactic cosmic rays (original particles) are chiefly positively charged nuclei of hydrogen atoms—that is, protons. Heavier nuclei, mainly those of helium (alpha particles), and smaller amounts of various other elements—some even from the heavy end of the chemical periodic table—are also present. The composition roughly reflects the relative abundance of the elements in the universe, but some exceptions exist, which are of great astrophysical interest. Electrons are also a primary component. The composition of solar cosmic rays differs significantly, in accord with the relative abundance of elements in the Sun. When primary cosmic rays collide with atmospheric particles, they create many types of secondary particles, including positrons, mesons, and hyperons. These particles form what are called cosmic-ray showers or cascade showers.

Detection. Various instruments are used to study the low-energy particle population of galactic, solar, and even planetary origin (that is, particles emanating from planetary magnetospheres). Equipment aboard spacecraft ranges from Geiger counters to elaborate combinations of solid-state and other highly sophisticated detectors that can determine charge, mass, and energy with remarkable precision. For example, the resolution of these detectors is sufficient for separating neighboring isotopes such as helium-3 and helium-4.

Ground-based equipment is used for long-term observations of the intensity of primary cosmic rays with energies above 10^9 electron-volts (eV). Three secondary components (nucleonic, hard, and soft) represent different primary energy regimes. Neutron monitors respond to the nucleonic component, produced by the primaries through a cascade process in the atmosphere; nucleons represent the lower end of the energy spectrum of relativistic pri-

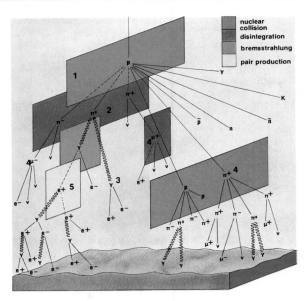

Cosmic rays are high-energy particles that enter the atmosphere from all directions in space. When these so-called primary cosmic rays, mainly high-speed protons, collide with air molecules, a shower of smaller subatomic particles (1) is produced. Among these secondary particles are neutrons (n), protons (p), neutral π mesons (π°), positively and negatively charged mesons (π⁺, π⁻), antiportons (p̄), heavy mesons (K), and hyperons (Y). A neutral π° meson is highly unstable and rapidly decays (2) into electromagnetic gamma rays (γ). Gamma rays that approach atomic nuclei may form positive and negative electrons (3). Charged mesons may strike other atmospheric nuclei (4) or decay into mu mesons (μ⁺, μ⁻) and neutrinos (ν). Electrons passing through strong electric fields of nuclei emit radiation (called bremsstrahlung) such as gamma rays (5); few of these secondary cosmic rays actually reach the Earth's surface.

mary particles (velocities near the speed of light). The hard component, consisting of muons, is associated with a somewhat higher mean energy that is raised by placing the detectors (called meson telescopes) underground. Finally, by a succession of interactions, the electromagnetic, or soft, component evolves into many associated particles. These are detected by extensive air shower (EAS) arrays.

Origin. Because most cosmic rays are charged, they are deflected by the magnetic field of our galaxy and approach the Earth from every direction. For this reason astronomers have not been able to locate cosmic-ray sources with accuracy, especially as the mechanisms of cosmic-ray production are not yet established. One likely speculation is that cosmic rays in the most common energy range—10^9 to 10^{13} eV—are the production of collisions between interstellar matter and the expanding remnants of SUPERNOVA explosions in our galaxy. More energetic cosmic rays may derive from other galactic objects such as Cygnus X-3, a known producer of X rays and radio waves. Cygnus X-3 is a double-star system in which one of the stars is thought to be a NEUTRON STAR that is producing high-energy protons as it absorbs material from its companion. Still more energetic cosmic rays, with energies of 10^{19} eV or higher, may derive from extragalactic sources such as the active galaxy M87, whose nucleus has been speculated to be a massive BLACK HOLE.

cosmology (astronomy) [kahz-mahl'-uh-jee]   Cosmology is the study of the origin, constitution, structure, and evolution of the universe. It makes use especially of the theories of GRAVITATION and RELATIVITY, Riemannian geometry, and the observation of EXTRAGALACTIC SYSTEMS. Interpreting the observational data requires an understanding of the evolutionary processes of individual galaxies; hence it involves the study of STELLAR EVOLUTION and INTERSTELLAR MATTER. The density and temperature of the universe in earlier stages are understood in terms of the interaction of matter, radiation, and other forms of energy, as explained by atomic, nuclear, and particle physics. Finally, because the SOLAR SYSTEM is a product of the star-formation process and is directly accessible, its study—by such disciplines as geophysics, geochemistry, and the physics of the solar system—yields a large amount of information useful in the study of the rest of the universe.

The term *cosmogony* is still sometimes used to distinguish the study of the origin of discrete celestial objects, particularly those of the solar system, from the study of the origin of the universe as a whole. Cosmogony may be considered a branch of cosmology.

History of Cosmology

Despite numerous historical creation accounts concerning the origin and nature of the universe, and despite important advances such as the development of the heliocentric world system in the 16th and 17th centuries and sidereal astronomy in the 18th and 19th centuries, the first decisive steps toward modern cosmology were not taken until the 20th century. As the century began the GALAXY was commonly believed to be an isolated system in which the stars of the Milky Way were arranged in the shape of a disk, with the Sun at its apparent center. Harlow Shapley discovered (1918) that the Sun is actually toward the edge of the system, and shortly afterward H. D. Curtis and others came to the conclusion that the Andromeda Nebula must be a separate star system similar to the Milky Way but at an unexpectedly great distance. By the 1920s it was recognized that many galaxies, or island universes, exist within the universe.

A 17th-century model of an Earth-centered universe reveals that astronomers had not yet accepted the Copernican Sun-centered system published in the previous century. The polar and equatorial circles represent the eight spheres in which the Moon, Mercury, Venus, Sun, Mars, Jupiter, Saturn, and the zodiacal constellations were conceived to be circling the Earth.

An old woodcut depicts a man who has journeyed to the end of a flat Earth to poke his head through the starry vault of the sky and view the machinery that moves the stars. During the Middle Ages the stars were thought to be fixed on a moving sphere that drove a series of smaller Earth-centered spheres to which the Sun, Moon, and planets were attached.

Meanwhile, in 1915, Albert EINSTEIN had published the famous general theory of relativity, which had many implications for cosmology. Soon afterward Einstein proposed a static model of the universe. Willem de Sitter proposed a cosmological model based on Einstein's theory, which allowed for either an expanding or contracting universe. In 1922, Aleksandr Friedmann derived a set of general cosmological models from Einstein's theory; it included Einstein's static model and de Sitter's dynamic model as particular cases. According to these mathematical solutions, the universe originated in and expanded from a single body of infinite density. Georges LEMAÎTRE (1927) and Arthur EDDINGTON (1930) put this concept forward as a physical theory, later known as the BIG BANG THEORY.

Based on RED-SHIFT data of galaxies, Edwin P. HUBBLE and Milton Humason discovered (1929) a linear relationship between the recession velocity v and the distance r of observed galaxies expressed in the equation $v = H_0 r$, where the constant of proportionality H_0 is now known as Hubble's constant. By 1936 this relationship had been extended to distances as large as several hundred million light-years, and the expansion of the universe and the general correctness of Einstein's theory of general relativity had been established.

George GAMOW and R. A. Alpher incorporated (1949) nuclear physics into the big bang model. They theorized that during the initial high-density state, radiation had dominated the universe, and from this they predicted that microwave background radiation would be found to exist. They also attempted to account for the origin of the elements by nuclear processes in the big bang. In 1965, R. W. Wilson and A. A. Penzias measured this background radiation, a feat for which they later received the Nobel Prize.

In 1963, Maarten Schmidt discovered the first two QUASARS, extremely distant objects whose rate of energy emission is many times that of an ordinary galaxy. Because of their distances, quasars are important objects for observational cosmology.

Constitution of the Universe

The visible structure of the universe consists of galaxies—our own galaxy and the extragalactic systems all composed of STARS and interstellar matter. The mean density of matter contributed by the known galaxies lies between 10^{-31} and 10^{-30} g/cm^3 (equivalent to one hydrogen atom in 17 and 1.7 cubic meters, respectively). Based on observations of stars in our galaxy, the chemical composition of this matter is found to be 75% hydrogen, 24% helium, and 1% other elements. Since the minimum density needed for a closed universe is about 10^{-29} g/cm^3, there is great interest in searching for matter in intergalactic space. This is the so-called missing-mass problem in cosmology. There are indications that intergalactic matter must exist within clusters of galaxies.

Age of the Universe

The age of the universe must be determined from the correct cosmological model, using Hubble's constant and the so-called deceleration parameter obtained from observations. The deceleration parameter cannot yet be measured reliably, but there are a number of ways by which the upper and lower limits to the age of the universe may be estimated.

In a thorough analysis of available red-shift data of galaxies, the American astronomer Alan Sandage derived a value for the Hubble constant of (55 ± 7) Km/(sec-megaparsec), giving the age of the universe as about 10 billion years.

The probable error of the Hubble constant in this estimate is about 10%. However, it must be realized that the Hubble constant is obtained from a chain of analyses, and many theoretical arguments are used. The estimated value of the Hubble constant may change significantly in the future, just as it did in the past, when it was believed to be much larger.

The age of the solar system may be determined by radiometric age-dating of meteorites, because fresh meteorites are good samples of the primordial matter of our solar system. When the ratios of lead isotopes in these samples are measured, an age of 4.6 billion years is obtained.

Using theories of element synthesis, and observing the ratios of ^{235}U to ^{238}U, and ^{232}Th to ^{238}U, William A. Fowler concluded that our galaxy must be at least 11.7 billion years old.

The age of star clusters can be estimated from the observed properties of their brightest main-sequence stars by using theories of stellar evolution. Using accurate stellar models computed by a number of other scientists, Sandage has determined the age of three old star clusters, M3, M15, and M92, giving their ages as 11.5 billion, 9.4 billion, and 9.7 billion years, respectively.

The age of the universe as determined from cosmological models is consistent with limits determined from isotope ratios and stellar evolution. The age of the universe may be placed in the range of 10 to 20 billion years.

Structure of the Universe

The most important feature of Einstein's theory of relativity is that it identifies gravitational fields with the geometrical structure of space and time. In contrast to Newton, Einstein proposed that the universe was a space-time continuum in which a type of NON-EUCLIDEAN GEOMETRY known as Riemannian geometry applies. To relate the source of gravitational fields—matter, energy, and pressure—to the geometrical structure of space and time, Einstein introduced ten equations. Friedmann found a complete set of solutions to these equations: the space-time structure (three-dimensional space plus one time dimension) may be described by a three-dimensional space whose curvature depends on time. If the curvature is positive, then the three-dimensional space has a finite (closed) volume and properties analogous to those of a

sphere. If the curvature is negative, then the three-dimensional space has an infinite (open) volume and properties analogous to those of a hyperboloid (saddle surface). An important feature of Friedmann's models is that there are no static solutions: the universe, as described by a three-dimensional space of positive, negative, or zero curvature, is expanding.

Origin of the Universe

All Friedmann-model universes begin from a singularity having infinite density, the starting point for the big bang theory. At a density of 10^{96} g/cm^3, the size of the universe would have been the size of a proton, with a radius of about 10^{-13} cm. Without resolving the infinite-density problem, it is possible to proceed with the assumption that the universe was created at a rather high density state, say at a density considerably below 10^{96} g/cm^3 but substantially greater than the density of a proton (approximately 10^{14} g/cm^3). In 1946, Gamow pointed out that

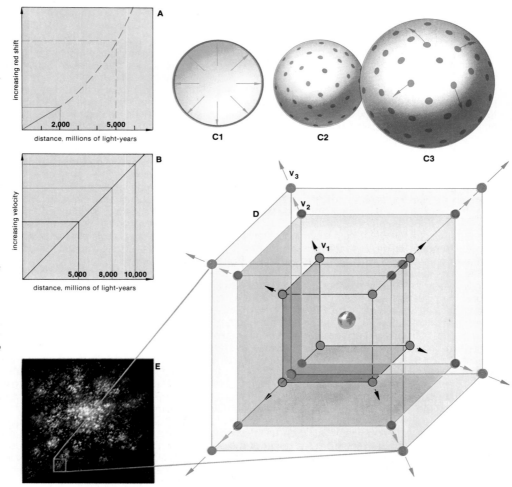

Astronomers have found that the spectral lines of all distant galaxies are shifted to the longer wavelengths, or the red end, of the spectrum. These red shifts increase as the distance of a galaxy from Earth increases (A). Assuming that the shifts are caused by the Doppler effect, the data indicate that all galaxies are moving away from Earth at a speed that increases in direct proportion to their distance (B). Actually, all galaxies are moving away from each other, and not from Earth as a center. If the universe is imagined as the surface of an expanding balloon (C1), and if galaxies are represented by spots (C2), then as the balloon expands, an observer on any one galaxy (red spot) would see all the other galaxies (blue spots) moving away in all directions (C3). An expanding universe in which galaxies appear to recede from Earth (D) may simply be part of a larger universe (E), the galaxies of which cannot be seen because they are so far that they are receding at the speed of light.

It is possible that the universe can occupy a finite volume yet have no boundaries. A two-dimensional analogy of such a closed universe would be the surface of a sphere; the sum of the angles of a large triangle on its surface is greater than 180°. In addition, a spacecraft traveling in a straight line would fly completely around this universe and return to its original launch point. Analogously, a triangle of astronomical dimensions in the universe, with angles totaling more than 180° (A), would reveal a closed universe. Similarly, an Earth spacecraft traveling along a straight-line course (B) would, after a finite time, return to its launch point from the opposite direction.

some time matter dominated radiation energy in density.

There are two strong indications that the early universe was in fact dominated by radiation. First, the residual microwave background radiation has been detected. Second, the abundance of helium in the universe is about 24% by mass. If all helium was created in stars, then at most 1% of matter would be in the form of helium. On the other hand, about 20–30% helium may have been produced at early epochs when the temperature was between 10^8 and 10^{10} K.

Galaxies and probably star clusters form only after matter-energy becomes dominant. This occurs about 100 million years after creation.

There is another cosmological theory known as the STEADY-STATE THEORY, conceived by Thomas Gold, Hermann Bondi, and Fred HOYLE. They modified the first cosmological principle by including time and stated the "perfect cosmological principle": the universe is homogeneous in space and time. According to their theory, the density of galaxies in space has always been constant. In order to account for the expansion of the universe, spontaneous creation of matter is assumed. The strongest evidence against the steady-state theory is its inability to account for the observed microwave background radiation. Although this theory is no longer accepted by most cosmologists as a valid model of the universe, it contributed much to the development of cosmological thinking.

Future of the Universe

If the universe is closed, the expansion will eventually stop, and red shifts will become blue shifts (contracting phase). After a certain time the universe will return to the state of being a singularity of infinite density and vanish

the early stages of the universe must have been dominated by radiation. As the universe expanded, the matter density decreased more slowly than the radiation-energy density decreased. Thus, after the universe had expanded for

Major theories of the origin and evolution of the universe include the big bang theory, a variant of this theory called the oscillating theory, and the steady-state theory. (A) The big bang theory states that 14 to 20 billion years ago, all matter in the universe was concentrated in a superdense, superhot core (1), which exploded. As the matter expanded and cooled (2), portions condensed into galaxies, which continue to move away from each other (3). (B) The oscillating theory adds that sufficient matter exists in the universe to halt the expansion and reverse it, so that all matter will return to the superdense state. Illustrations 4–7 are stages in one cycle. The steady-state theory says that the universe has no beginning and no end and assumes that matter is continuously created. The big bang theory predominates today, but a more inclusive one called the inflationary theory is now drawing much attention.

in a second big bang. Will the universe be re-created from this singularity again (oscillatory universe)? According to Einstein's theory, the answer is no. However, Einstein's theory is not likely to be valid when the density is too high. There is therefore no answer to this question as yet.

If the universe is open, the expansion will go on forever. Eventually all the energy of the stars will be used up, and the universe will expand forever in total darkness.

As already seen, there are great discrepancies in the determination of the curvature of the universe. Until these discrepancies are resolved, it will not be possible to predict the properties of the universe in the distant future.

Alternative Theories in Cosmology

A number of major developments took place in cosmology theory in the late 1970s and early 1980s based on the assumption that the evolution of the universe can be predicted from particle physics. Using the basic concepts of the big bang theory, these developments were largely devoted to understanding the processes at work in the first few moments of creation, when densities and temperatures were so great that conventional theories of matter are no longer applicable. As part of this effort, the British physicist Stephen HAWKING showed that matter could be spontaneously created at the so-called event horizon of a BLACK HOLE—that is, the point of proximity to a black hole at which the red shift is supposedly so great that light signals emitted there cannot reach an observer. Following Hawking's work, it was then shown that quantum fluctuations in an empty de Sitter space could create a virtual universe with negative gravitational energy. This virtual universe could exist for only a very few seconds, but by means of the so-called quantum TUNNEL EFFECT it could emerge as a real universe and expand to form the universe as it exists today.

This theory, then, provides an account of the creation of the universe within the framework of the big bang concept. According to this theory, the total energy of the universe is not necessarily zero. It may be positive (leading to an open universe) or negative (leading to a closed universe). The theory also requires a multidimensional space in which many four-dimensional subspaces are embedded. A separate universe could be created in each subspace by means of the quantum fluctuation processes, leading to the concept of a possible infinity of other universes. If our own universe were confined to one such subspace, however, there would be no way to find out if other universes actually exist.

The INFLATIONARY THEORY developed in the early 1980s by the American physicist Alan Guth is a further attempt to account for the first moments of creation in terms of quantum fluctuation processes. Such work aims to align cosmology with the so-called GRAND UNIFICATION THEORIES that seek to unite the FUNDAMENTAL INTERACTIONS of matter in a single formulation. One product of these attempts is the concept of cosmic "strings," defects in the fabric of space-time that linger from the first moments of the big bang. The strings would either extend infinitely or form closed loops. Essentially one-dimensional and under enormous tension, they would become increasingly massive the farther they stretched and could serve as sites for galaxy formation. Other theorists object to the concept of a singularity at the onset of creation, however, and are exploring exotic theories such as "negative pressure," a fifth fundamental interaction that might also account for the massive creation of matter in the early universe.

Many other possible models of the universe are also being explored by theorists. Some of them involve complex variations on the numbers of dimensions required to account for a universe that will satisfy both relativity and quantum mechanics within the confines of the big bang concept. Others, such as the "plasma cosmology" first advanced by Swedish astrophysicist Hannes ALFVÉN, move beyond the bounds of big bang theory and in the direction of the largely discarded steady-state theory. Plasma, called the fourth state of matter, is matter in the form of electrically charged particles (see PLASMA PHYSICS). Although observed only in isolated circumstances on Earth, it is the state in which most of the universe actually exists. According to plasma cosmologists, the magnetic and electrical properties of plasmas are sufficient to account for the large-scale structures of a universe without beginning or end. Supporters of this theory are mainly plasma physicists, although astronomers are taking notice of this concept.

Although such work is being done in the theoretical field, it remains necessary to resolve certain basic observational problems of cosmology. Among them are the discrepancy between the observed density of matter in the universe and the value of the deceleration parameter; the role of quasars in cosmological evolution, including their nature and energy source; the drastic differences between the magnitude–red shift relationships of quasars and galaxies; the paradoxical quasar-galaxy pairs (apparently adjacent objects with very different red shifts); and according to some studies, the grouping of galaxies on the surfaces of giant, bubblelike voids throughout the universe. Apparent discoveries of newly forming galaxies also call into question some basic assumptions of the big bang theory. These questions, difficult as they appear, are relatively no harder than the problems that confronted cosmologists at the beginning of the 20th century.

cosmology   (philosophy) see METAPHYSICS

cosmonaut   see ASTRONAUT

Cosmos   The name *Cosmos* is applied to a number of Soviet artificial satellite programs, most of them related to military functions. About 100 satellites named Cosmos are orbited each year. The Intercosmos program is a cooperative scientific effort involving East European experiments launched on Soviet spacecraft. The USSR has also launched satellites for various other nations. Other scientific satellites are flown under the Electron, Proton, and Prognoz series.

See also: SATELLITE, ARTIFICIAL; SPACE PROGRAMS, NATIONAL.

cosmos *Cosmos*, of the composite family, Compositae, is a genus of annual or perennial herbs native to Central America, Mexico, and the southwestern United States. The plants produce white, rose, or purple flowers similar to the DAISY. The plants have tall (1–3 m/3–10 ft), erect stems and feathery foliage.

The common cosmos is a popular, fast-growing annual, 1–2 m (3–6 ft) tall. It flowers in late summer and early autumn.

Cossacks [kahs'-aks]   The Cossacks (from a Turkic word meaning "adventurer" or "vagabond") constituted a paramilitary society that was employed by the Russians in the expansion of their empire. Between the 14th and 17th centuries, the Cossacks were freebooting runaway serfs and adventurers who worked as mercenaries. In exchange, they received land grants, tax exemptions, and other special dispensations. During the 18th, 19th, and 20th centuries, they evolved into 13 elite cavalry units that served on the Russian frontiers. By 1916, Cossacks numbered 4.4 million, 285,000 of whom were in the Russian army. Today, the name may be applied to as many as 3 million people living near the coasts of the Black and Azov seas. Émigré Cossacks reside in Europe and North America.

From the outset, Cossacks were of mixed origins and cultures that included Russian, Polish, Tatar, and other ethnic elements. Gradually they supplemented their military function with sedentary agriculture and stock raising. Before 1930, Cossack farms were among the biggest in the USSR. Even today, former Cossack villages (*stanitsy*) are large, some being composed of up to 20,000 persons.

Originally a semidemocratic, almost anarchistic social group, Cossack organization became military-hierarchical, with the officers (*hetmen*) attaining quasi-nobility status. Kinship was patrilineal and family management was patriarchal. By 1900, Cossack men wore distinctive military uniforms, with long coats, bullet pouches, and tall Caucasian hats. Invariably, they fought on horseback.

The alliance between the tsar and the Cossacks suffered from three major Cossack revolts (1670, 1707, and 1773). Strongly independent, the Cossacks, especially the largest contingent along the Don River (see DON COS-

SACKS), bitterly opposed Bolshevism and collectivization. The opposition was eventually crushed by the Stalinists, and thousands of Cossacks fled or were deported from the USSR before 1940. During World War II, remnant Cossack cavalry units fought well against the Germans.

cost accounting   see ACCOUNTING

cost-benefit analysis   Cost-benefit analysis is a method of estimating the rates of returns on public investment projects. Just as a private business firm tries to estimate the yield on an investment, so a community may wish to know what advantages it will receive from its expenditure on a park or a pollution control system.

Complex cost-benefit analysis has been used, for example, by the U.S. Army Corps of Engineers and the Bureau of Reclamation for estimating the total benefits to be expected from multipurpose river-development projects that combine electric power, flood prevention, irrigation, and improved navigation. This process involves estimating the commercial value of the power output, the property damage from past floods that will not occur again, the value of crops that will be produced on the irrigated land, and the probable increase in freight tonnage that will be carried by vessels on the river.

cost of living   see CONSUMER PRICE INDEX

Costa, Lúcio [kohs'-tah]   The Brazilian architect Lúcio Costa, b. Toulon, France, Feb. 27, 1902, is considered the father of modern Brazilian architecture and urban design. As the new director (1930) of the National School of Fine Arts in Rio de Janeiro, Costa played a major role in creating the national architecture of Brazil; he endeavored to make modern architecture regionalistic in intent and to adapt it to tropical environments. With Oscar NIEMEYER and others, he constructed the famous Ministry of Education building in Rio de Janeiro (1937–43), based on a plan of LE CORBUSIER. In 1957 he won the competition for the master plan for Brazil's new modern capital, BRASÍLIA. Among his other works are the Brazilian Pavilion at the New York World's Fair (1939), also designed with Niemeyer, and the block of apartments in Rio de Janeiro's Eduardo Guinle Park (1947–54).

Costa-Gavras, Henri [kaws'-tah-gahv'-rahs]   Henri Constantin Costa-Gavras, b. 1933 of Russo-Greek parents, is a French filmmaker noted for his political thrillers, many of them based on actual events. His films include *Z* (1969), about the 1963 assassination of a Greek liberal politician; *The Confession* (1970), concerning Stalinist repression in Czechoslovakia; and *State of Siege* (1973), about CIA involvement in police torture in Uruguay. *Missing* (1982) deals with the disappearance of an American during the 1973 coup in Chile. *Betrayed* (1988) is the director's fictional examination of a conspiratorial white-supremacist group in the Midwest. *Mu-*

REPUBLIC OF COSTA RICA

Land: Area: 50,700 km^2 (19,575 mi^2). Capital and largest city: San José (1989 est. pop., 284,550).

People: Population (1990 est.): 3,032,795. Density: 60 persons per km^2 (155 per mi^2). Distribution (1989): 45% urban, 55% rural. Official language: Spanish. Major religion: Roman Catholicism.

Government: Type: republic. Legislature: Legislative Assembly. Political subdivisions: 7 provinces.

Economy: GNP (1988): $4.7 billion; $1,630 per capita. Labor distribution (1987): agriculture—28%; public administration and services—23%; trade—16%; mining and manufacturing—17%; construction, transportation, and public utilities—7%. Foreign trade (1988): imports—$1.4 billion; exports—$1.3 billion. Currency: 1 colón = 100 centimos.

Education and Health: Literacy (1989): 93% of adult population. Universities (1990): 4. Hospital beds (1986): 7,382. Physicians (1984): 2,539. Life expectancy (1989): women—78; men—74. Infant mortality (1990): 16 per 1,000 live births.

sic Box (1989) addresses anti-Semitism and the fact that a loving father may also be a brutal war criminal.

Costa Rica [kohs'-tah ree'-kah]   Costa Rica is a Central American republic located north of Panama and possessing two seacoasts—on the Pacific Ocean in the west and on the Caribbean Sea in the east. The capital and largest city, SAN JOSÉ, is located in the central mountain valley. Costa Rica is notable among Latin American countries for its long-standing democratic form of government.

Land and People

Costa Rica is a mountainous country with broad coastal plains in the east and west. The Cordillera Central, which runs the length of the country from the northwest to the southeast, has several peaks more than 3,000 m (10,000 ft), including the Chirripó Grande (3,819 m/12,529 ft), the highest point in the country. The central plateau, or Meseta Central, reaches an altitude of 900 to 1,200 m (3,000 to 4,000 ft) and is the heartland of the country. The Caribbean coastal plain receives heavy rainfall (3,048 mm/120 in) during most of the year. Less rain falls on the Pacific plain, which annually averages 1,905 mm (75 in). Temperatures average 15° C (59° F) in the highlands to about 27° C (80° F) in the plains. About 25% of the land, mostly tropical dry forests, is under government protection.

The population is of predominantly European descent, particularly Spanish. The original Indian population was absorbed or otherwise disappeared during colonial times. A small number of people of African descent migrated to the Caribbean coast from Panama, where they had been laborers on the Panama Canal. Predominantly Roman Catholic, the country, until recently, had one of the highest rates of population growth in the world. The literacy rate is among the highest in Latin America. The country, which has no army, sustains extensive systems of education and health services. The University of Costa Rica was founded in 1843.

Economic Activity

Costa Rica is predominantly an agricultural country. Coffee, the nation's principal export, is produced on the small farms and plantations of the central plateau; bananas and other tropical fruits are grown on the larger coastal plantations of both shores. Food crops include maize (corn), rice, potatoes, and beans. The government has encouraged foreign investment in manufacturing and tourism to diversify the economy. Manufacturing now provides over 20% of national income.

The PAN AMERICAN HIGHWAY, which runs north-south through the middle of the country, has greatly facilitated the transport of goods to market. A railroad links San José to the ports of Limón on the Caribbean and Puntarenas on the Pacific. Food supplies must be supplemented by imports from neighboring countries and the United States. Fluctuating prices for agricultural exports and a large foreign debt led to periodic economic difficulties in the 1980s and early 1990s.

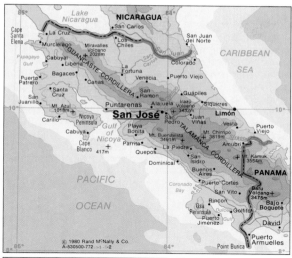

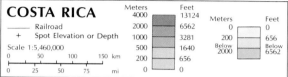

COSTA RICA

— Railroad
+ Spot Elevation or Depth

Scale 1:5,460,000

Meters	Feet
4000	13124
2000	6562
1000	3281
500	1640
200	656
0	0

Meters	Feet
200	656
Below 2000	Below 6562

This coffee finca (plantation) lies in the Meseta Central of Costa Rica, which is favored with extremely fertile volcanic soil. The region is best known for its high-grade coffee, the country's most valuable export crop.

Government and History

Costa Rica has a democratic form of government, electing a president and unicameral legislature once every four years. Voting is compulsory, and election day is a national holiday.

The area had only a small Indian population when Christopher Columbus sighted it in 1502. For 300 years it was a Spanish colony, governed as part of the viceroyalty of Mexico. When the colonies revolted in 1821, Costa Rica was included in the independent CENTRAL AMERICAN FEDERATION. This lasted until 1838, when each state decided to become independent. The first free elections were held in 1889, and the country has since, except for

brief interruptions in 1917 and 1948, remained a democratic republic. Two minor invasions by Nicaraguan rebels took place in 1948 and 1955; both provoked intervention by the Organization of American States.

Costa Rica has traditionally been hospitable to refugees from other Central American countries, and President Oscar ARIAS SÁNCHEZ (elected 1986) won the 1987 Nobel Peace Prize for his plan to end regional strife and civil war. Legally unable to seek a second term, he was succeeded in 1990 by Rafael Calderón, a critic of the peace plan.

Costain, Thomas B. [kahs'-tayn]   Thomas Bertram Costain, b. Brantford, Ontario, May 8, 1885, d. Oct. 8, 1965, was a Canadian novelist and journalist who edited

San José, a national and provincial capital, is the largest city in the Republic of Costa Rica. Founded by Spanish settlers in 1736, San José became the capital in 1823, when administrative offices were transferred from Cartago.

(1920–34) the *Saturday Evening Post*. His most widely read novels are *For My Great Folly* (1942), *The Black Rose* (1945; film, 1950), *High Towers* (1949), and *The Silver Chalice* (1952; film, 1954).

Costello, Lou   see ABBOTT AND COSTELLO

---

costume   Fashion and costume, collectively, constitute a minor art that can tell much about a people or culture and the times in which they lived. Although some now remote ages have left little or nothing in the way of written records, their pictorial arts nevertheless reveal what the clothing of these civilizations, or at least of their aristocratic classes, was like.

Ancient Times

Egypt. Because of the warm temperatures, Egyptian costumes were minimal. The usual fabric was linen, left in its natural off-white color, some of which was so finely woven that it was transparent. Men of the Old Kingdom (*c.*2686–2181 BC) wore belted loincloths wrapped around the waist; the loincloth was sometimes supplemented by a linen cape or an animal hide draped over the shoulders. By the time of the Middle Kingdom (*c.*2040–1786 BC), the loincloth had been lengthened into an intricately pleated skirt. Egyptian women wore linen tunics or skirts that extended from above or below the breast down to the ankle.

Wide collars and other adornments were of gold and

(Above) *The linen clothing worn in ancient Egypt was based on elongate lines. Women wore a long sheath, or* kalasiris; *men wore kilts or loincloths. The double kilt, which appeared during the 18th dynasty, featured a longer, transparent top kilt. Both men and women wore wigs, jewelry, and eye makeup.*

(Below) *The Minoan costume was one of the most unusual in the Mediterranean area. The women's bell-shaped skirts, comprised of horizontal flounced layers, were topped by small aprons that resembled men's loincloths. The short-sleeved, narrow-waisted bodice exposed the breasts.*

(Above) *The graceful dress of classical Greece was derived from a basic tunic. These tunics were oblong bolts of fabric pinned by brooches, or* fibulae. *On the left is a* chiton, *which was worn with a cloak, or* himation. *The woman's* peplos *was double-folded from neck to waist.*

(Below) *Roman men and women wore a* tunica *or a* stola, *long tunics based on the Greek* chiton. *The Greek* himation *appeared in Roman costume as the woman's* palla *and the man's* pallium. *The toga, adopted from the Etruscans, denoted Roman citizenship. Roman dress indicated social status.*

(Above) *Etruscan clothing resembled Greek dress and, in turn, had a stylistic influence on Roman fashion. Both sexes wore a tunic and a loose cloak, or* tebenna, *bordered by one band. The tebenna later evolved into the Roman toga, and the band, or* clavus, *became a mark of rank.*

(Above) *Byzantine garments were distinguished by luxurious materials and rich colors, a result of increased contact with the Orient. Both sexes wore tunics, but men also wore leggings or trousers (not shown). An embroidered square decorated the front edge of men's mantles.*

semiprecious stone, or of glass. Headdresses were decorated with elaborate depictions of birds or serpents in gold and with colorful stones signifying rank. Black wigs and cosmetics invariably completed the costume. Kohl, a dark pigment, was used by both men and women to outline the eyes and for protection against the sun. Sandals were worn by all ancient peoples, from the Egyptians to the Romans; the Greeks and Romans also wore leather boots.

Mesopotamia. The earliest documented people of the region, the Sumerians, are depicted in art as barefoot and wearing skirts of leather or goatskin; their heads are shaved. Others are shown wearing woolen robes and hats or turbans of curly lambswool. The Babylonians, who succeeded the Sumerians as masters of the region after

2300 BC, wore a type of tunic that later became the basic garment of the Romans. The Assyrians, who flourished from 1200 to 612 BC, adopted a similar but more elaborate attire that included tasseled robes embroidered with small, repeated patterns or rosettes. Men's hair was shoulder length and curled, as were their beards; they also wore hats resembling fezzes, that were decorated to indicate rank. Women's attire was similar, being differentiated by headbands made of wool or of stonework and gold.

Crete. The colorful and lively fashions of the Minoans seem closer in spirit to modern Western dress than any other examples known from ancient times. Women wore bell-shaped skirts with tiers and flounces and brief jackets that showed their breasts. Their hair was long and flowing. Young men went bare-chested, their only cloth-

(Above) *Richer fabric and ornamentation appeared during the Middle Ages, reflecting the new trade with the East. Women wore a shorter, wider-sleeved kirtle over a slim chemise; a mantle covered the head and shoulders. Men's cloaks were worn over medium-length tunics and trousers.*

(Below) *During the 12th century, women's tunics, now called* bliauts, *featured a full, draped skirt and belled sleeves. Men's* bliauts *were girdled once at the waist. Hose, or* chausses, *replaced men's leggings, and the toes of shoes became pointed. Women's veils were secured by a circlet.*

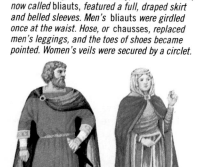

(Above) *By the 13th century, the sleeve had become part of the tunic, rising from the waist and falling gracefully to the wrist. Men's tunics were for ease of movement, and women's trained tunics billowed over the stomach. A woman's hair was bound in a wire net and topped by a linen cap.*

(Above) *The surcoat, a sleeveless over-tunic, became popular during the 14th century. It was lined with fur in winter. Under the surcoat could be seen the women's kirtles, more tailored to the body. Shoes with pointed toes, called* crackows *or* poulains, *appeared even in suits of armor.*

(Below) *The* houppelande *became fashionable during the 15th century. It was worn by men as an overcoat and by women as a gown. Unusual headdresses, elaborate turbans and* henins, *were adopted by both men and women. Headdress height was achieved by using wires and padded horns.*

(Above) *By the late 15th century, the Italian influence was evident. Exaggerated headgear proliferated for both sexes. Men's* houppelandes *were considerably shorter; full sleeves hung from padded shoulders and were slashed at the elbow. Women's* houppelandes *became more like gowns.*

ing a brief loincloth. Their hair, too, was worn long and was adorned with a small feathered hat.

Greece. Greek dress styles fall into two periods, the archaic and the classic. Archaic dress for women resembled clothing from the Near East, its point of origin. The *peplos*, the basic garment, consisted of two rectangles of wool held together at the shoulders by large pins. The material then fell straight or in folds to the ankles and was belted above the waist. After the Persians were driven from Greece in 479 BC, a reaction against Oriental fashion found expression in the wearing of the *chiton* of linen or wool. When the chiton was stitched together down the sides, it could be made to form short sleeves. For men, the chiton could be knee length. Both men and women draped a large rectangular robe, called a *himation*, over the chiton. Active young men wore a *chlamys*, a short robe held together at the right shoulder, leaving the right arm free.

Rome. The basic garment for Roman men was the toga. The size and shape of the toga, as well as the color of the border, indicated social position. Originally of white wool and undecorated, the toga became more elaborate during the late Empire, when gold-embroidered designs were added.

Women wore a simpler version of the toga called a *palla* and beneath that, a *tunica*. Costly silk, imported from China, was woven into women's costumes and was eventually used by men as well. Women's hairstyles were varied and elaborate: wigs and falls supplemented the

natural hair; and dyeing the hair blond became a fad during imperial times.

Byzantine Empire: Before 1204 AD. Byzantine costume was an elaboration of imperial Roman dress, with changes introduced as a result of Greek contacts with Persian and other Oriental peoples. At court, robes, now heavy with embroidery, were no longer soft-flowing. In some cases, gems were worked into the mantles and cloaks. Women wore softer robes of silk, with collars and crown-like headdresses encrusted with pearls and precious stones. Barbarian invaders from colder climates wore snugly fitted clothes, including trousers and hose, and these were adopted for wear under Byzantine tunics and robes.

The Middle Ages

Romanesque and Early Gothic: 1000–1350. Changes in fashion escalated in response to the novelties brought home from the East by the Crusaders. Rich fabrics such as satin, velvet, and brocade became available in Europe. The wood-block printing of fabrics was adopted, and by the 11th century buttons had also arrived from the East.

A fitted tunic remained the basic item of apparel for both men and women. An over-tunic, or *bliaut*, covered the under-tunic, and by 1200 tight lacing drew the woman's bliaut into a form-fitting shape which, girdled at the hips, created a long-waisted appearance. A mantle, hung from the back of the shoulders and descending to the ground, was worn outdoors.

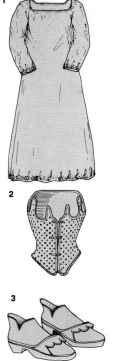
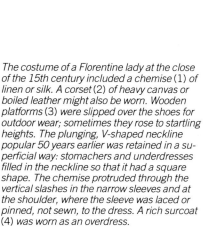

The costume of a Florentine lady at the close of the 15th century included a chemise (1) of linen or silk. A corset (2) of heavy canvas or boiled leather might also be worn. Wooden platforms (3) were slipped over the shoes for outdoor wear; sometimes they rose to startling heights. The plunging, V-shaped neckline popular 50 years earlier was retained in a superficial way: stomachers and underdresses filled in the neckline so that it had a square shape. The chemise protruded through the vertical slashes in the narrow sleeves and at the shoulder, where the sleeve was laced or pinned, not sewn, to the dress. A rich surcoat (4) was worn as an overdress.

The doublet, worn by men from the early 14th to the 17th century, was tight-fitting, sleeved, and belted; it replaced the bliaut over-tunic, which continued to be worn by the lower classes. A similar item was the *cotehardie*, which could be parti-colored or fur-lined, with the sleeves dagged, or scalloped, and often hanging to the ground. Heraldic devices provided additional color to the breast of the cotehardie.

Headdress for men included hoods or close-fitting caps tied under the chin. A tall cap with a pointed brim appeared after 1300. Through the 11th century, women's hair was worn free-flowing or braided, although it was veiled for church attendance. By 1200, married women covered their hair with veils and wore wimples under the throat. A *barbette*, or crownlike headband, secured the veil.

Late Gothic: 1350–1500. Led by the elegant courts of Burgundy, Paris, and Flanders, the fashion-conscious of the Continent lent themselves to frequent changes in style. By 1400 the *houppelande* had appeared; it was worn by both men and women as an outer garment (over a man's doublet and over a woman's tunic, or kirtle). Men's hose, fully exposed under the houppelande, ended in leather shoes that were extremely pointed at the toes.

Wooden pattens, or clogs, were donned for outdoor wear. Around 1400 tiny bells were added to belts and hoods. Men wore hoods with long trailing ends, called *liripipes*. These hoods could be drawn up and padded to create a turbanlike headgear, with the scalloped edges forming a cockscomb. By 1450 tall felt hats were adopted.

Around 1350, women wore their hair coiled on either side of the face and fitted into metal baskets. By the end of the century the fashion was to draw the coiled hair up with rolled pads, to create a *bicorne* that supported a veil. About 1420 a steeple hat, or *henin*, was worn, with the veil wound around it and left trailing. Women's hair was hidden under these elaborate dressings. Women completed their toilette by plucking their eyebrows and painting their cheeks with rouge.

The Renaissance and Baroque Eras

The Italian Renaissance: 1420–1520. In the mid-15th century, dress assumed a more natural appearance. The robe appeared, which was actually a dress with attached bodice and skirt. Men's doublets grew shorter and hose received greater emphasis. Hair reappeared, now elaborately trimmed with thin veils, ribbons, and jewels. The

Men's fashion in mid-15th-century Italy tended to be brief. The well-dressed man began his ensemble with an elegant silk or linen undershirt, worn under a pourpoint (1). The hose, often parti-colored, were laced to the pourpoint at the hem. The doublet (2), which had evolved into a mutton-sleeved garment of rich fabric, featured a skirt whose length varied from the thigh to the hip. The chaperon (3), a hat devised to look like a turban, still carried a liripipe, or long scarf. Shoes (4) were not as pointed as they were either before or after mid-century. Over all was worn a tabard, or jerkin (5), usually trimmed in fur and belted at the waist.

use of lace and perfume also became more common during the Renaissance.

The Later Renaissance. By 1490, Gothic dress in northern Europe had given way to the simpler styles of Renaissance Italy. The slashing of clothes began as a reaction to SUMPTUARY LAWS that decreed that commoners should wear clothing of only one color. To circumvent the law, men (and soon women as well) cut open the outer surfaces of their garments—doublets, sleeves, and hose—in this way exposing a contrasting color beneath. This lining could then be pulled through the slashing and puffed out to further emphasize the contrast.

Women's Gothic headdress was replaced before 1500 by a simple hood. This hood then became peaked, not unlike a playing card queen. Men's hats were broad, and some were trimmed with gems. Women's robes were expanding below the waistline; by 1550 hoops made of wire or wicker, held together with ribbons and tapes, were used for support. This was the beginning of a recurring fashion phenomenon. The hoopskirt, or farthingale, reached its maximum width around 1600, when it assumed a cartwheel or drum-shaped appearance. With puffed-out trunk hose, balloon sleeves, padded doublets, and the same large ruff collars, men achieved a similar appearance.

Baroque Fashions. Except in Spain, the farthingale was gone by 1620, although skirts remained bell-shaped. The millstone ruff also vanished, to be replaced among both men and women by a wide lace collar that sloped over the shoulders. The Cavalier look resulted from the ENGLISH CIVIL WAR and, on the Continent, the THIRTY YEARS' WAR. With its broad-topped boots, slashed doublets, and wide-brimmed hats, it dominated men's attire until 1660.

A new elegance followed that reflected the magnificence of Louis XIV's court at Versailles and, in England, the restoration of the monarchy. Men's jackets became longer and were trimmed with lace at the sleeves. High-heeled shoes replaced boots, and men took to wearing cascading shoulder-length wigs.

Both men and women wore the high-crowned Puritan hat until 1660, when women's bonnets appeared. Women wore their hair naturally, no longer than to the shoulder, and covered it with a kerchief. Waists were narrow

Italian styles dominated European fashion at the beginning of the 16th century. Men's hose, divided into upper and lower hose, were laced to the doublet. Women's fashions changed little in the early 1500s; full, high-waisted gowns with stomachers continued to be worn.

Spain's political ascendancy brought the rigid, somber styles of Spain to the fore. Under Spanish influence, raised and ruffled collars became fashionable, and the farthingale, or hoopskirt, came into wide use. Waistlines on both men's and women's clothing dropped to a low "V." Men's padded, bombasted breeches contributed to the overall rigidity of the style. Headdress, lavish ornamentation, and slashing continued as the height of fashion.

and skirts bell-shaped. Sleeves, although wide, tended to be three-quarter length. The outer gown was pulled back from the skirt front and, by 1680, formed a bustle, another fashion phenomenon that would emerge again toward the end of the next two centuries.

By 1680 women's height was accentuated by the *fontage*, a headdress of ribbon and lace that mounted to a height of a foot or more. Lace and ribbons were freely used and, except among the Puritans, colors were bright for both men and women.

The Eighteenth Century

Both dress and manners became comparatively relaxed in Europe during the 18th century. The stiff, almost architectural style of Louis XIV gave way to a rococo lightness. Although the hoopskirt reappeared, the period as a whole was conservative, classic in proportion and taste, as befitted an age of reason and enlightenment. The immense wigs worn by men in the years immediately preceding 1720 gave way to natural-sized powdered wigs. Typical attire for men included knee breeches, jackets with embroidered vests, and shirts decorated with a throat cloth, or cravat, the ancestor of the modern necktie. The hat for men throughout the century was the tricorn, a low-crowned hat with the brim turned up on three sides. By 1790 two other hats were common: a bicorn and a top hat similar to the 17th-century Puritan hat.

About 1730 hoops, known as panniers (or baskets), began to expand women's skirts laterally. By the 1750s this side expansion had reached its extreme width, only to subside a few years later. Except for formal dress, skirts were not always floor length. Silk stockings and shoes with medium-high heels adorned the legs and feet.

Extreme artificiality reappeared in the 1770s in the shape of women's powdered pompadour hairdos, which, rising to heights of more than a foot, were festooned with ribbons and flowers and sometimes even trimmed with miniature ships in full sail. In the next decade, a fuller, rounded hairdo was topped by an enormous hat or a lace cap. A pouter pigeon silhouette was created by a bustle pad in back of the skirt, and by a kerchief worn over the bodice in front.

A variety of stiff garments made up the fashion of mid-16th-century Spain. The high, frilled neck of the shirt (1) heralded the appearance of the ruff. Stuffed and slashed "pumpkin breeches" (2) were hooked to the doublet. A short jacket (3), with contrasting sleeves, was worn under the doublet (4), whose long waistline was comparable with women's elongate bodices. A short, full cape (5), fur-lined and brocaded, toques (6), leather gloves (7), and pointed shoes (8) completed the look. The Spanish woman's costume resembled two triangles. The basis of all dress was a chemise (9). Chopines (10), high-soled shoes, protected the hem from dirt. Drawers (11) were sometimes worn as well as chemises. Farthingales (12) spread throughout Europe and provided a conical form. Women's jackets (13) resembled those worn by men. An iron or bone structure known as a vasquine (14) was a frame to lengthen and stiffen the bodice. Slashed oversleeves appeared on the overdress (15).

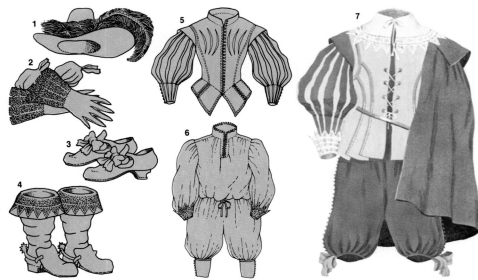

Burghers of early-17th-century Holland displayed their prosperity with this modish attire. (Right) The French cavalier fashion is reflected in the wide-brimmed felt hat (1) festooned with ostrich feathers. Lace was used to trim the cuffs of gauntlets (2), and red-soled shoes (3) were decorated with rosettes and ribbons. Wide-topped boots (4) were de rigueur, as were spurs. The doublet (5) was short, with longer skirts and four to six vertical slashes on the breast. The sleeves were slashed to reveal the undershirt (6), whose lacy cuffs and "falling band" collar were turned over the doublet. A buff leather jerkin and long, full cape covered the complete outfit (7).

(Below) Women's costumes were cut on horizontal lines. Lace, ribbons, and rosettes adorned gloves (8), drawers (9), and heeled shoes (10). A stomacher (11), pointed and richly decorated, filled the low-necked bodice (12). An overdress (13) featured half-sleeves split on the inner seam and tied on the outer seam with ribbons. Later in the century, women's sleeves rose to the elbow, and overskirts were raised to reveal the underskirts. Men's breeches widened into "petticoat breeches."

The Nineteenth Century

The French Revolution (1789–94) brought profound changes in fashion that lasted well into the 19th century. Because traditional aristocratic attire was suspect, the French upper classes turned in self-protection to the wearing of peasant costume or English country dress. In women's clothes, a neoclassic look based on a high-waisted "Grecian" dress that flowed simply from the bustline remained in fashion through the Napoleonic era until 1820. The simplicity and scantiness of this garb would not be seen again until the 1920s.

The baggy trousers worn by the radical republican *sans-culottes* early in the revolution proved only a prelude to the substitution of straight-hanging trousers for knee breeches among gentlemen by the turn of the century. This was an irreversible stylistic revolution, the only exceptions thereafter being jodhpurs for riding and the knickerbockers worn by men on the golf range and by American schoolboys.

Court dress gave way to less formal attire. Country dress, consisting of riding hat, jacket, and boots, became urbanized by 1800. Overcoats were also introduced. The top hat, once worn for protection by horseback riders, had become regulation street wear by 1820; by 1900, it constituted formal attire. The formal tailcoat of 1900 was also derived from what was street wear in 1820 and sportswear in 1780.

By 1860 men were wearing suits not unlike those worn by businessmen today. These replaced the frock coat and cutaway, which then became daytime formal attire. Cravats became smaller, developing into ascots, bow ties, and four-in-hand ties by 1900. Collars, which in 1800 rose to the chin, were gradually lowered and reduced in size.

Romantic influences, often inspired by a cult of the medieval, began to appear in the details of women's clothing after 1820. The waistline also reemerged in its anatomically appropriate place, the Grecian gown giving way to a bell-shaped skirt, which became progressively more voluminous with each decade until, by the 1850s, hoops or crinolines were once again in use to support its girth. By 1870 the crinoline had been replaced by a bustle, a stylistic flourish that pervaded women's fashions until 1890. Women's hats during the same period evolved from the large bonnet popular during the 1820s to the feather- and ribbon-trimmed hats of the 1870s and later. The silhouette presented by the 1890s woman would have shown a bell-shaped skirt, tight-corseted waist, and balloon sleeves.

(Above) *This couple (c.1630) display the conservative English version of French cavalier dress. Both wear the wide-brimmed plumed hat and the generous lace and linen trim. The sleeves and upper half of the man's doublet are slashed, and his knee-length breeches button on the side. The tabs on the woman's bodice mirror the skirt of the doublet. Elbow-length sleeves for women were just coming into vogue in England. (Below) The extravagant court of Louis XIV, the French Sun King, was reflected in the costume of the day. A full shirt (1) had tiers of puffs on the beribboned sleeves. Bloomerlike underbreeches (2) were worn under huge, flowing rhingraves, or petticoat breeches, which resembled skirts. Cannons (3) were lacy flounces worn just below the knees. A lace collar, or rabat (4), was worn over the doublet (5), which had shrunk to bolero size. The rhingraves (6) were decorated with generous loops of ribbon at the waist and on the sides. The full, layered outfit (7) was completed by a cape whose hem was tiered with lace. Hats (8) were carried so as not to disturb the elaborate wigs (9). Ribboned, tasseled canes and slender gloves (10) were fashionable, and boots were replaced by square-toed shoes (11) with flat, stiff bows.*

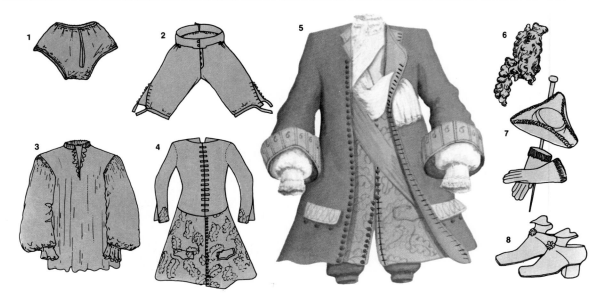

French fashion became more moderate toward the end of Louis XIV's reign. (Above) Flannel or linen drawers (1) with a front opening were worn under trim, knee-length breeches (2). Only the ruffled neck and belled lower sleeves of the shirt (3) were exposed. A long, patterned vest (4) was worn under the waistcoat, or justaucorps (5), which featured wide cuffs, flared skirts, and flapped pockets. A cravat and crossbelt were essential, as were the still-popular wig (6), cane, gloves, tricorn hat (7), and tongued shoes (8). By the mid-1700s, rococo fashion prevailed and fabrics were lighter and were designed in floral patterns. (Below) For women, the fan (9) was as important an accessory as were men's swords and walking sticks. The frilled "mob cap" (10) and heeled, pointed shoes (11) were also worn. A chemise (12) was worn beneath the underpetticoat with its elliptical hoop, or pannier (13), which was hinged at the side to enable the wearer to fit through doorways. The underpetticoat was calf-length and contained the pockets, which were reached through "placket holes" in the petticoat. The cane or whalebone corset (14) had hip pads that provided a perch for the hoops. The petticoat (15) was elaborately quilted and of a contrasting color to the gown. It and the stomacher (16) were revealed by the open front gown or sacque (17).

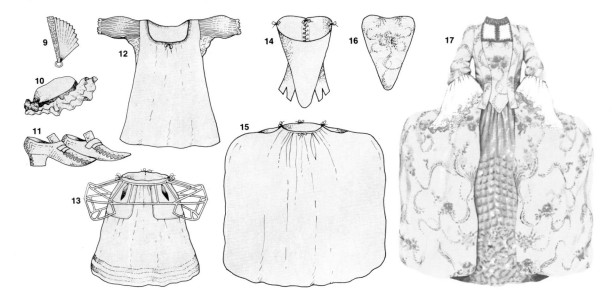

The Twentieth Century

Hobbled skirts and small turbans were introduced in 1910 by French couturier Paul Poiret. It was in this con- fining costume that the suffragists of England and Ameri- ca staged their first mass demonstrations for women's rights. The postwar period brought the long-waisted, bare-

(Above) The Marquise de Pompadour greatly influenced French fashion in the middle of the 18th century. The overdress-and-petticoat ensemble was continued and refined. A shorter vest, slimmer waist, and smaller wig delineated the new, more tailored cut of men's clothing.

(Below) English styles came into favor late in the 18th century. Hoops were replaced by bustles, and the bust was accentuated by the insertion of a neckcloth or a fichu. A modest cuff figured on men's sleeves. Hats were elaborate for both sexes.

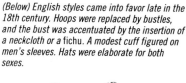

(Above) Fashion in postrevolutionary France favored the neoclassical look. Dresses, derived from English chemises, were high-waisted, columnar gowns with drawstring neck closures. Men's breeches extended to the ankle, in contrast to earlier knee breeches, and were tucked into boots.

(Above) British garments became more conservative as the 19th century came to an end. Cutaway coats remained popular. High collars, narrow sleeves, and tight breeches mirrored the French fashion. The spencer, a short, tailless jacket, was worn by both men and women. The general silhouette was full.

(Below) During the first quarter of the 19th century, the high-waisted, puffed-sleeve dress, shortened to the ankle, continued to be fashionable. Men's trousers underwent a change, however, hanging straight from the waist like women's dresses. Hemlines for both sexes ended at the ankle.

(Above) By 1850 the silhouette for both men and women had returned to that of an hourglass. Skirts were full, requiring numerous petticoats to maintain their voluminous shape. In men's wear the quality of the cut and the cloth were emphasized rather than innovation in style.

kneed look of the flappers. The short tubular dresses of 1925 and the simplicity of Coco CHANEL's fashions ended the excessive corseting that had characterized past fashions and the prohibition against revealing legs. The economics of the fashion industry might thereafter decree change for the sake of change, but women, except for their high-heeled shoes, never again submitted to the physical limitations imposed by entirely artificial shapes.

Skirts in the 20th century seemed to rise and fall according to the rhythm of the stock market. When Wall Street boomed, as it did in the 1920s, skirt lengths rose above the knee; with the crash of 1929, skirts plummeted, only to rise again during America's World War II prosperity. Christian DIOR's "New Look" of 1947 took the wartime padding out of shoulders and once again lowered the hemline; nevertheless, skirts crept steadily upward during the next 20 years, culminating in the daring miniskirt of the mid-1960s. Trouser-clad women seemed a permanent legacy of the cultural upheavals of that era.

Men's fashions during the 20th century reflected a steady trend toward the more casual and comfortable. The stiff collars in favor from 1880 to 1920, for instance, became steadily softer and more natural. The hat, once an essential of every well-groomed wardrobe, had virtually disappeared in the United States by 1960. Ties and trouser legs might widen or narrow, cuffs might come and go, but essentially men's clothing remained loose. The hippie, sexual, and political revolutions of the late 1960s

(Below) The slim silhouette of the 1870s gave way to a bustle in the early 1880s. Horizontal and diagonal lines characterized women's clothing. Men's clothes served mainly as foils for women's dresses. The derby, a single-breasted matched suit, and the standing collar continued to be worn.

(Above) Skirts reached surprising diameters during the 1860s. Ribbons, lace, and flowers adorned richly colored evening gowns, eclipsing the plain, wasp-waisted male dress. The extreme décolletage was permitted by the enormous skirts that prevented a suitor from drawing too near.

(Above) About 1900, women's figures were forced into an "S" shape by a new corset style. A gored skirt flared out from the waist and ended in a slight train. Full hairstyles and elaborate hats appeared. Men resumed wearing the frock coat, top hat, and wide trousers for formal occasions.

Conservative English fashions dominated men's styles by the latter half of the 19th century. Suits of matched material, originally called "ditto suits," appeared during the 1850s. Undershirts (1) and drawers (2) were usually woolen. The shirt (3) featured a standing collar. Suspenders (4) came into use. The vest (5) often matched the high-buttoned jacket (6). The cravat shrank to a narrow bow tie. A boxy, double-breasted overcoat (7) had a detachable hood or cape. Derby hats (8) appeared during the 1860s, as did high-buttoned shoes (9). Gloves (10) were still the mark of a well-dressed man.

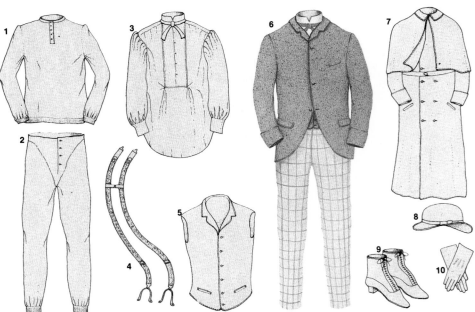

heralded a turn toward more androgynous, or unisex, clothing, and a return to the long hair, beards, and moustaches in favor throughout much of the 19th century.

cotangent   see TRIGONOMETRY

Côte d'Azur [koht dah-zuer']   The Côte d'Azur (English: Azure Coast) is the narrow coastal part of the department of Alpes-Maritimes in Provence, southeastern France. Strictly defined, it stretches from CANNES to Menton at the Italian border, but the term is often used synonymously with the RIVIERA (or French Riviera). The Côte d'Azur, where the white cliffs and headlands of the rugged, indented coast contrast with the often clear, blue sky and sea amid the lush subtropical vegetation, has become an almost continuous string of resorts. The most important are Monte Carlo in Monaco, Cannes, Antibes, and Menton. Fishing is important, and olives, grapes, citrus fruits, and flowers (for making perfumes) are grown. The eastern part of the Côte d'Azur, the county of Nice, was ceded to France by Italy in 1860.

Cotman, John Sell   The British artist John Sell Cotman, b. May 16, 1782, d. July 24, 1842, was the cofounder, with John CROME, of the Norwich School of landscape painting. Although he also worked in oils, he is best known today for his watercolors of pastoral scenes. Through a strong massing of lights and darks he often achieved strikingly fresh designs, paving the way for the freer and more realistic style of English landscape painting in the 19th century. His etchings of the architectural antiquities of England and Normandy, done between 1811 and 1822, are justly celebrated. Cotman's works are in the British Museum, which owns the well-known *Greta Bridge* (1805), and in the Victoria and Albert Museum in London.

Cotonou   [koh-toh-noo']   Cotonou, the largest city (1982 est. pop., 487,000) and port in the West African nation of Benin, is situated on the Gulf of Guinea. Its artificial deepwater port facilities (completed in the late 1960s), airport, and rail lines make it the major financial, communications, and distribution center of Benin. Manufactures include milled lumber, bicycles, processed food, textiles, and building materials. Offshore oil rigs operate nearby. Originally a small autonomous state, Cotonou was made part of the kingdom of Dahomey in the early 18th century. In 1851 the French established a trading post there, a base from which they expanded outward and eventually conquered the country.

Cotopaxi   [koh-toh-pah'-hee]   Cotopaxi is an active volcano in the Cordillera Central of the Andes in north central Ecuador. At 5,897 m (19,347 ft) it is considered the highest active volcano in the world. It is cone shaped and remains snow covered above 5,000 m (16,400 ft). The volcano continuously emits clouds of steam from its lava-filled crater.

The first recorded eruption was in 1532, but the most violent series occurred during the 18th century. Cotopaxi's slopes are covered with ash and rocks from its frequent eruptions. The volcano's most recent eruption was in 1928.

Cotte, Robert de   Robert de Cotte, b. 1656, d. July 15, 1735, is considered one of the originators of the French ROCOCO STYLE in architecture; he helped to popularize it in northern Europe as an influential consultant to German and Austrian architects. De Cotte began his career as assistant to Jules HARDOUIN-MANSART and in 1708 succeeded him as *premier architecte* of the Palace of VERSAILLES. In Paris, de Cotte participated in all of Hardouin-Mansart's major projects, such as the Church of the Invalides and the Place Vendôme, and designed many private residences. The finest of his commissions outside Paris was the Palais de Rohan (begun 1731; now the Municipal Museum) in Strasbourg.

cotton   Cotton is the most important vegetable fiber used for producing textiles. Its history as a cultivated plant began in the ancient civilizations of Egypt, India, and China. In the New World, cotton was known in Mexico as early as 5000 BC and in Peru by about 2500 BC. Today it is grown in more than 70 countries throughout the world.

The Cotton Plant

The cotton plant, genus *Gossypium*, belongs to the mallow family, some of whose other members are hibiscus, hollyhock, and okra. Although more than 30 species of cotton are in this genus, only three have commercial significance: *G. barbadense*, *G. herbaceum*, and *G. hirsutum*. The last of these is the most prominent and is known as upland cotton. About 99% of all U.S. cotton and 88% of all varieties grown worldwide are of this species. Its staple length (the average length of fiber) is between that of the other two species. *G. barbadense* includes all long staple cottons such as Sea Island, Egyptian, Peruvian, and the pimas. Their long, fine fibers can be woven into sheer, strong, lighter-weight fabrics. *G. herbaceum* has the shortest staple length and is a rather coarse fiber.

In its wild state cotton is a perennial, but in cultivation it must be planted annually. The cotton plant grows upright to a height of 1 to 2 m (3 to 6 ft). Because the flowers have both pollen-bearing stamens and an ovary with several ovules, the probability for self-pollination is high. Immediately after fertilization the boll, which contains seeds and fibers, begins to form. Individual fibers grow from cells on the surface of the seed. About three weeks after fertilization, fibers reach their full length, and they become thin-walled hollow tubes filled with plant juices. Then the plant begins to deposit layers of CELLULOSE (a complex carbohydrate constituting 95% of the weight of

Cotton, one of the world's most important crops, produces white fibrous bolls (lower right) *that are manufactured into a highly versatile textile. The plant has white flowers, which turn purple about two days after blooming.*

the mature fiber), at the rate of a layer a day for three more weeks, until maturity. When the boll finally bursts open, it contains up to 50 seeds with the fibers, called lint, attached. Short fuzz fibers, linters, are also attached to the seed. Linters have thicker walls and a larger diameter. If a lint fiber is of average length, 25.4 mm (1 in), the linters will be 2.5 to 5 mm (0.1 to 0.2 in) long.

Cotton Cultivation in the United States

Cotton grows in a temperate to hot climate and is therefore confined to the region from 47° north latitude to 30° south latitude. In the United States the area is a line from central California to southern South Carolina and south to the southern tip of Texas. It is believed that colonists planted cotton in Florida in 1556 and in Virginia in the early 1600s. Before the COTTON GIN was invented (1793) by Eli Whitney, seed was picked by hand and cotton processed primarily in the home.

Cotton Planting. Cotton requires fertile, well-drained soil, sufficient moisture, and warm to hot temperature (17°–27° C/62°–80° F) during the growing season. Today cotton is mechanically planted in rows, with seeds set at regular intervals or in small groups called hills. Seedlings must be thinned to leave only two or three plants in a hill, with hills about 30 cm (1 ft) apart. Cotton is thinned, or chopped, with hoes or with mechanical choppers. Weeds are removed at the same time, usually with herbicides. When the stem of the cotton plant is somewhat hardened, the rows can be flamed—fired by quick jets of flame that kill weeds without hurting the cotton. Fertilizers are vital for cotton growth and can be injected into the soil when the seed is planted.

Crop Protection. Disease-resistant strains of cotton and good cultivation practices can help control the many pests and diseases to which cotton is subject. The pests most difficult to eradicate are the boll WEEVIL and the pink bollworm; both cause huge crop losses when they are not controlled. Many insecticides have been used against the weevil, but because of unwanted side effects, or because the weevil develops resistance, new insecticides must constantly be found. The pink bollworm is present in huge numbers because the heavy pesticide campaigns against weevils also killed the insects that were the bollworm's natural enemies. It has proven even more difficult to control than the weevil.

Harvesting. About 16 to 25 weeks after planting, depending on variety and growing conditions, the bolls mature and burst open, and the fluffed-out cotton fibers dry and are ready for harvest. Today, 99% of U.S. cotton is mechanically harvested. Before the harvest, chemical defoliants strip the leaves, leaving the ripe cotton bolls accessible to the machine.

Ginning. In a modern installation, cotton is sucked into a drier, where excess moisture is removed, and then into a cleaner that separates the lint from debris picked up in the harvesting process. Finally it goes to the gin stand, where revolving teeth pull the lint through narrow steel gratings, leaving the seeds behind. The deseeded fiber is cleaned again and then fed to a gin press, where the cotton is pressed into bales. Baled cotton is either exported

Of all the insects that attack cotton, the boll weevil is the most destructive. With its long, curved snout, it bores into the cotton boll. The female lays eggs in this hole; as the larvae grow, they consume the boll's contents.

or sent to a SPINNING plant for processing into yarn.

Cottonseed. Cottonseed removed during ginning is shipped to an oil mill. There the linters are removed in a process similar to the original ginning operation. The principal uses of linters are in padding for upholstery, mattresses, photographic film, paper products, and surgical supplies.

Cottonseed accounts for two-thirds of the weight of usable material in the cotton boll. Major products from the seed are meal; hulls; and oil, which is used as a salad oil, in the preparation of shortening and margarine, and in the manufacture of cosmetics, soaps, detergents, and paints. Chemical treatment converts cottonseed oil into specialized fats and food coatings. Cottonseed meal, the residue from oil extraction, is a premier animal feed and,

The picking of cotton, once done by hand, is today almost completely mechanized. The cotton stripper shown here harvests the entire boll, then removes and discards the leaves and twigs, leaving the cotton fibers and seeds ready for ginning.

Early in the century cotton gins were located on plantations, but cotton is now shipped to nearby installations. Modern gins based on Eli Whitney's model provide a quick and efficient means of cleaning and deseeding large quantities of cotton.

to some extent, an organic fertilizer. Hulls are also used, primarily in animal feeds.

The Cotton Market

Since 1933 the U.S. government has acted to stabilize production and assure the farmer a fair profit on crops. Farmers have been paid for land diversion and conservation programs on diverted land; they have been subsidized for cotton grown for export, and they have received price supports.

Within the past quarter century, the increased use of SYNTHETIC FIBERS has greatly reduced the demand for cotton fabrics. Cotton offers unique qualities of comfort and wear, however, and consumer demand for all-cotton fabrics, or blends of cotton and synthetics, is on the rise once again.

Cotton, John   John Cotton, b. Dec. 4, 1584, d. Dec. 23, 1652, was a leading spokesman for early New England PURITANISM. Ordained a priest in the Church of England, he was for 20 years rector of a church in Boston, Lincolnshire. His rigorous Calvinism eventually brought him into conflict with church authorities, and in 1633 he emigrated to Massachusetts Bay Colony, where he became minister of the only church in Boston.

In subsequent years Cotton defended the doctrinal foundations of CONGREGATIONALISM against all opponents. Those who saw bishops as essential to church life found him arguing that true churches needed no such supervisors, only liberty for each congregation to control its own affairs. On the other hand, those championing complete freedom of conscience found that Cotton insisted on a Puritan monopoly.

cotton gin   The cotton gin is a device for removing the seeds from COTTON fiber. In ancient India a machine called a charka was developed to separate the seeds from the lint when the fiber was pulled through a set of rollers. The charka worked well on long-staple cotton, but variations of this machine used in colonial America could not be adapted for short-staple cotton. For the latter, cottonseed had to be removed by hand, work that was usually performed by slaves.

A machine for cleaning short-staple cotton was invented by Eli WHITNEY in 1793. His cotton engine consisted of spiked teeth mounted on a boxed revolving cylinder that, when turned by a crank, pulled the cotton fiber through small slotted openings so as to separate the seeds from the lint. Simultaneously a rotating brush, operated via a belt and pulleys, removed the fibrous lint from the projecting spikes. Although patented, the design was so widely imitated that Whitney gained only a modest financial reward from his invention.

The gin, with subsequent innovations, made the raising of short-staple cotton highly profitable and thereby revived the institution of slavery. Through the use of horse-drawn and water-powered gins, the ginning process was speeded up enormously. This permitted increased cotton production and lowered costs. As a result, cotton became the cheapest and most widely used textile fabric in the world.

With the advent of mechanical cotton pickers in the 20th century, it became necessary to refine the gin further. Among many modern improvements are devices for removing trash, drying, moisturizing, sorting, cleaning, and baling.

cottonmouth   SEE WATER MOCCASIN

cottonwood   The cottonwoods are deciduous hardwood trees that belong to the genus *Populus*, which also includes the aspens and poplars, in the WILLOW family, Salicaceace. Cottonwoods grow very rapidly and are distributed throughout the Northern Hemisphere, with approximately 10 species native to North America. In the semiarid western United States they are typically found on stream banks. Such exotic *Populus* species as the Lombardy poplar and the Simon poplar are used as street and shade trees in American cities. (See art on page 298.)

cotyledon   [kaht-uh-lee'-duhn]   The cotyledon is the SEED leaf—or one of the pair of leaves—of the embryo plant. The flowering plants, division Angiospermae, or Magnoliophyta, are divided into two classes—Monocotyledonae (or monocots) and Dicotyledonae (or dicots)—on the basis of the number of seed leaves, or cotyledons: the seed of the monocot has one cotyledon; the seed of the dicot, two. The name *cotyledon* is derived from the Greek *kotylēdōn*, meaning "cup-shaped hollow." The name may refer to the cuplike shape taken by the two cotyledons within the surrounding seed coat of a dicot seed; but the

The Eastern cottonwood, found mainly in the central United States, is the most characteristic representative of the genus. Shown are the leaf, about 13 cm (5 in) long; female catkin (bottom right) with fruit, flowers, and cotton-tufted seed; and male catkin (center). In summer a cottonwood releases huge clouds of wind-blown seed.

name is not so apt for the monocot seed, which has only one cotyledon. In dicots, such as the bean plant, the plump cotyledons serve as a source of food for the growing plant and, for a short time, as an organ for PHOTOSYNTHESIS. These cotyledons fall off soon after the food reserve is depleted and the young plant is ready to produce its own food. In monocots, such as the corn plant, the endosperm (the major portion of the monocot seed) is the basic food reserve. The cotyledon of the monocot absorbs food from the endosperm and makes it available to the growing parts of the plant.

See also: CLASSIFICATION, BIOLOGICAL; FLOWER; PLANT; POLLINATION.

coudé telescope [koo-day']   The coudé (French for "elbowed") astronomical TELESCOPE, which is usually a

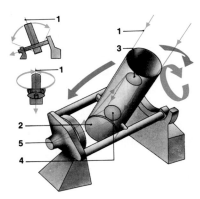

Using a telescope with a coudé system, the observer need not move as the telescope rotates. Incoming light rays (1) are reflected by the primary mirror (2) to a convex secondary mirror (3) below the prime focus. The secondary mirror reflects the light beam to a movable, flat mirror (4) which diverts the light to a stationary focus position (5) in a separate room.

reflector, is a special telescope system. It uses a series of mirrors to bring incoming light to a focus at an observing station that remains fixed regardless of the direction in which the telescope points. Large instruments, such as spectrographs and spectrum scanners, may be installed at the focus. Because the focal length is great (ratio typically f/30), the image scale is large and the illumination of extended objects low. An image rotator sometimes compensates the rotation of the image field as the telescope drives.

cougar   see PUMA

Coughlin, Charles E. [kawf'-lin]   A Roman Catholic priest, Charles Edward Coughlin, b. Hamilton, Ontario, Oct. 25, 1891, d. Oct. 27, 1979, broadcast a weekly radio program that drew millions of listeners across the United States during the 1930s. Coughlin was ordained in 1916 and served as pastor of the Shrine of the Little Flower in Royal Oak, Mich., from 1926 to 1966. Beginning his broadcasts in 1926, Coughlin became increasingly political. He was a vehement critic of the New Deal, advocating monetary inflation, calling for the nationalization of banks, and denouncing President Franklin D. Roosevelt's policies. His isolationism and anti-Semitism, which led him to blame Jewish financiers for engineering U.S. entry into World War II, persuaded the Catholic hierarchy to order him to cease all nonreligious activities in 1942.

coulomb [koo-lohm']   Named for Charles Coulomb, the coulomb is the unit of electric charge in the mks (meter-kilogram second) system of units. It is defined as the amount of charge transported by an electric current of one AMPERE flowing for one second and is approximately equal to the charge of 6.24×10^{18} electrons. The cgs (centimeter-gram-second) system uses two units of charge; one coulomb is equal to 3×10^9 statcoulomb and to 10^{-1} abcoulomb.

See also: ELECTROMAGNETIC UNITS; UNITS, PHYSICAL.

Coulomb, Charles Augustin de [koo-lohm']   The French physicist Charles Augustin de Coulomb, b. June 14, 1736, d. Aug. 23, 1806, discovered the law of force between two charged bodies. After 1781, Coulomb turned his attention to physics and published (1785–91) seven memoirs on electricity and magnetism. He adapted a torsion balance to measure electrical forces and demonstrated (1785) the inverse-square law of forces for the case of two bodies of opposite electrical charge. In 1787 he further proved the inverse-square law for attractive and repulsive forces in both electricity and magnetism, and he later showed that the force is also proportional to the product of the charges—a relationship now called COULOMB'S LAW. Coulomb may be considered to have extended Newtonian mechanics to a new realm of physics. The unit of electrical charge is named for him.

Charles Coulomb formulated Coulomb's law, a mathematical description of the electrostatic force between two charged particles.

Coulomb's law

Coulomb's law governs the forces of attraction or repulsion between electrical charges. Unlike charges attract and like charges repel. Coulomb demonstrated that the Coulomb force, F, of attraction or repulsion between two charges, q_1 and q_2, is proportional to the inverse square of the distance, r, separating the two charges, that is, F is proportional to $1/r^2$. In SI (Système International) units, Coulomb's law can be written $F = q_1 q_2 / 4\pi E r^2$, where the charges are in coulombs, the distances are in meters, and ε is the dielectric constant of the medium between the two charges. For free space, $E = E_0 = 8.85419 \times 10^{-12}$ farad/meter.

council, ecumenical

An ecumenical council gathers bishops and other representatives of the Christian church from all over the world to formulate positions intended to bind or influence the members everywhere. After the Protestant REFORMATION of the 16th century, it became impossible for Western Christians to convoke fully ecumenical councils, since those that have been held under papal auspices, the Council of TRENT (1545–63) and the First and Second VATICAN COUNCILS (1869–70, 1962–65), have excluded Protestants and Eastern Orthodox Christians.

History. According to the ACTS OF THE APOSTLES, the disciples of Jesus Christ called a council at Jerusalem to discuss stresses between two parties. One party stressed continuity between ancient Judaism and its law and the community that had gathered around Christ. The other stressed the mission of Christians to the whole inhabited world, with its preponderance of Gentiles (or non-Jews).

In Roman Catholic belief the bishop of Rome (pope) must always convoke a council, and after the bishops have voted, he must officially spread the decrees they pass.

It is not plausible to call any gathering since the Second Council of NICAEA (787) truly representative. Since that date, Eastern and Western churches, and since the 16th century Protestant and Catholic churches, have not

met together. Throughout the Middle Ages, even Western or Roman Catholics themselves debated the convoking and authority of councils. Although all the bishops and theologians agreed that the pope should have special prerogatives, for several centuries reformers claimed that when protesters had grievances, they could appeal from the pope to a council. Out of these reformist parties came a theory of CONCILIARISM, the idea that a council is ultimately above the pope. The Great Schism in 1378 brought this debate to a head, since there were then two and later three popes. The Council of Constance (1414–18) settled the division, but conciliar power was again limited when the pope declared the Council of BASEL (1431–37) heretical.

Three councils have been held since the Reformation. The first, at Trent, met over a period of 18 years to deal with the Protestant revolt; it was decisively anti-Protestant in its decrees. The First Vatican Council, convened at Rome in 1869–70, not only continued the attempts to define Roman Catholicism against the rest of ecumenical Christendom, but decreed that, in matters of faith and morals when he speaks officially and with clear intention to do so, the pope is infallible. The Second Vatican Council (1962–63), which also met in Rome, showed a different outlook. First, it invited observers from Orthodox and Protestant churches; second, the bishops did vote for a principle of collegiality, which gave higher status to their participation. Collegiality, however, did not effectively limit the supremacy of the pope.

Significance. The earlier councils have tremendous moral authority even if they are not seen as binding, and most Christians regard the CREEDS and statements they produced as authoritative or highly influential for subsequent statements of faith.

The Council of Trent, which met between 1545 and 1563, reformed doctrines and practices of the Roman Catholic church.

The councils that raise the greatest problems for modern ecumenical Christianity are those which were exclusively Roman Catholic: the Council of Trent and the First Vatican Council. Trent, which was a part of the Counter-Reformation, expressly countered Protestant teaching by asserting that the authority of the church was based on tradition as well as Scripture and rejecting the idea that humans are justified (saved) only by grace through faith. Unacceptable to all non–Roman Catholics was the definition of papal infallibility by the First Vatican Council.

Non–Roman Catholics in the modern world, through the World Council of Churches at its plenary conventions, have on occasion felt something of the ecumenical character of conciliar thought again. However, these assemblies lack authoritative power and gain credibility only through their power to persuade assent.

Council Bluffs

Council Bluffs (1990 pop., 54,315) is a suburban city in southwestern Iowa, on the Missouri River, across from Omaha, Nebr. It is the seat of Pottawattamie County and a trade and railroad center for a large agricultural region. The city's industries manufacture farm equipment. Settled by Mormons in 1846, the town was called Kanesville from 1848 to 1852. It was renamed in 1852 to commemorate Meriwether Lewis and William Clark's council with local Indians in 1804.

Council of Economic Advisers

The Council of Economic Advisers is part of the executive office of the president of the United States. It consists of three economists appointed by the president, who designates one of them as the chair. The council advises the president on economic policies and prepares the president's annual economic report to Congress.

The council was established under the Employment Act of 1946, which directed the president to follow economic policies that would "promote maximum employment, production, and purchasing power." In its early years the council had little influence. In the 1960s, however, under Walter Heller, it was instrumental in persuading Presidents Kennedy and Johnson to follow a policy of deficit spending in order to stimulate the national economy. In the 1970s the council took a more conservative stance in an effort to fight inflation. President Ronald Reagan considered abolishing the council but confirmed its retention early in 1985.

Council of Europe

The Council of Europe, headquartered in Strasbourg, France, is an organization founded in 1949 to achieve greater European unity. Its original membership of 10 (Belgium, Denmark, France, Ireland, Italy, Luxembourg, the Netherlands, Norway, Sweden, and the United Kingdom) has grown to 23.

The council consists of two main bodies: the Consultative (or Parliamentary) Assembly, composed of 170 representatives chosen by the national parliaments; and the Committee of Ministers, consisting of the foreign ministers of the member nations and their deputies. Among the most important of the council's other organs are the European Commission and European Court of Human Rights, which investigate and rule on, respectively, alleged violations of the European Convention on Human Rights, signed in 1950.

Council for Mutual Economic Assistance

The Council for Mutual Economic Assistance, or Comecon, is an organization established in January 1949 to coordinate the economies of the Soviet-bloc countries. Charter members were the USSR, Bulgaria, Czechoslovakia, Hungary, Poland, and Romania. Albania joined a month later but ceased to take part after 1961. East Germany joined in 1950 and Mongolia in 1962. In 1964, Yugoslavia agreed to participate as an associate member. Cuba became a full member in 1972 and Vietnam in 1978. Several other nations that had close economic ties to the Soviet bloc were given observer status.

In its early years Comecon sought to integrate the members' economies through supranational planning and a degree of specialization among the countries. By the 1980s, calls for greater integration were resisted by Hungary, with its liberalized economy, and by East Germany, with its trade links to the West. In 1990, following the breakup of the Soviet satellite system, Comecon underwent a fundamental change, voting to adopt a free-market trade policy.

Count of Monte Cristo, The

The Count of Monte Cristo (1844–45; several film versions), by Alexandre DUMAS *père*, master of the French historical novel, first appeared in serial form. Set in early 19th-century France, it is a swashbuckling, romantic tale of a young man's revenge on the people who had him unjustly condemned to prison for Bonapartist sympathies. The hero, Edmond Dantès, escapes from prison through courage, cunning, and a series of improbable events. On the island of Monte Cristo he discovers a fortune that enables him to plot revenge.

Counter-Reformation

The Counter-Reformation was the movement within the Roman Catholic church in the 16th and 17th centuries that tried to eliminate abuses within that church and to respond to the Protestant REFORMATION. Until recently historians tended to stress the negative elements in this movement, such as the INQUISITION and the INDEX of Forbidden Books, and to concentrate their attention on its political and military aspects. They now show greater appreciation for the high level of spirituality that animated many of its leaders.

The century before the outbreak of the Reformation was marked by increasing and widespread dismay with the venality of the bishops and their involvement in politics, with the ignorance and superstition of the lower clergy, with the laxity of religious orders, and with the sterility of academic theology. Movements for a return to the

In 1540, Ignatius of Loyola and his six followers received the approval of Pope Paul III for their new religious order, the Society of Jesus. The missionary and educational activities of the Jesuits consolidated the Roman Catholic efforts of the Counter-Reformation.

original observances within religious orders and the activity of outspoken critics of the papacy like Girolamo SAVONAROLA were symptomatic of the impulses for reform that characterized sectors of the Catholic church during these years.

Not until PAUL III became pope in 1534 did the Roman Catholic church receive the leadership it needed to coordinate these impulses and meet the challenge of the Protestants. This pope approved new religious orders like the JESUITS, and he convoked the Council of TRENT (1545–63) to deal with the doctrinal and disciplinary questions raised by the Protestant reformers.

The Counter-Reformation was activist, marked by enthusiasm for the evangelization of newly discovered territories, especially in North and South America; for the establishment of religious schools, where the Jesuits took the lead; and for the organization of works of charity and catechesis under the leadership of reformers like Saint Charles BORROMEO. The era also produced two of the greatest representatives of MYSTICISM—TERESA OF AVILA and JOHN OF THE CROSS.

counterculture   The counterculture, which arose in the United States during the 1960s and persisted into the 1970s, was a social revolt among middle-class youth. Opposition to the Vietnam War was at its core. It had both political and cultural aspects: participants in the cultural revolt were called hippies; the political movement was known as the New Left. Both groups believed that American business, government, and social institutions were corrupt.

The hippies, focusing on individual freedom, rejected the traditional family in favor of other arrangements

based on love; were often attracted to mystical, Oriental philosophies; and participated heavily in the use of such drugs as MARIJUANA and LSD. ROCK MUSIC helped popularize their alternative life-styles.

The New Left was spearheaded by Students for a Democratic Society (SDS), which pursued the ideal of participatory democracy and forged alliances with radical minority groups such as the BLACK PANTHER PARTY. Its principal focus was protest demonstrations in support of the civil rights movement and against the Vietnam War. Infiltration of radical groups by the FBI, terrorist actions by the Weathermen faction, and, above all, the end of the war led to the decline of the movement.

counterfeiting   Counterfeiting, in criminal law, is the act of copying or imitating a genuine object with the intent of unlawfully distributing the copy. The most commonly counterfeited object is money, but documents, works of art, and many other objects are also subject to counterfeiting, or forgery.

In the United States, counterfeiting money is a federal crime, for which punishment can be as much as 15 years in prison and a $5,000 fine. Counterfeit U.S. money is probably only a tiny fraction of the money in circulation. It is difficult to make real-looking bills and even more difficult to produce genuine-looking coins. The Secret Service, a division of the U.S. Treasury Department, is responsible for uncovering counterfeiters. Moreover, the present-day public has become more aware of how to detect counterfeits. To determine if a bill is counterfeit, place it next to a genuine bill and compare them. A real bill has red and blue fibers throughout the paper. The portrait on the front looks clear and distinct on a genuine bill, while a counterfeit portrait appears flat and dull, and background lines are usually broken or irregular. On a real bill, the serial numbers are evenly spaced and properly aligned.

counterpoint   In MUSIC, counterpoint is the art of combining two or more melodies in a way that makes musical sense; one melody is then spoken of as written "in counterpoint" to another. The adjective *contrapuntal* is used to describe this style of music. Counterpoint originated during the Middle Ages when musical notes were referred to as "points." The earliest form of counterpoint allowed hardly any melodic independence among the individual parts. By the end of the 13th century a fully developed contrapuntal style existed.

Counterpoint is a technique of organizing musical material that may become the basis of a complete piece; or counterpoint may be used intermittently, as the composer desires. Some musical forms, such as the canon and the FUGUE, are by their nature essentially contrapuntal.

See also: POLYPHONY.

countertenor   The male alto voice, neither CASTRATO nor FALSETTO, is the countertenor. Prized during earlier centuries, especially in England, where countertenors often sang the alto part in church music, the countertenor fell victim to the increasing number of women in choral societies after about 1800. In the 20th century, however, countertenors such as Alfred DELLER and Russell Oberlin revived the art.

country and western music   Country and western music is an American popular-music style that was once confined to the rural South and Southwest but is now commercially successful throughout the United States. In its present form, it blends two musical traditions: the styles of the southeastern states, with their strong heritage from the British Isles; and the music of the Southwest, especially Texas. Both styles were influenced by the BLUES and by black rural dance music.

In the late 1920s, the Carter family of Virginia, who sang traditional Appalachian material to a rolling guitar and autoharp accompaniment, achieved wide popularity. The Mississippi railroad man Jimmy C. Rodgers, whose style reflected more widespread influences, including the blues, became famous for his yodeling chorus ends.

The style called western swing—a blend of west Texas fiddle music with jazz and pop music—began to be heard nationally in the early 1930s. Bob Wills, a mandolin and fiddle player, formed the Texas Playboys in 1933, sometimes using horns and saxophones—rare instruments in rural music. Radio shows, records, and movies reached large, nonrural audiences throughout the country and made musicians such as Gene Autry, the "Singing Cowboy," and Roy Rogers into nationally famous names.

By the 1950s the GRAND OLE OPRY, a radio program originating in Nashville, Tenn., had become a national institution. The singer-songwriter Hank WILLIAMS wrote four million-seller songs in 1950, seven in 1951, and four

The original Grand Ole Opry House (Ryman Auditorium) in Nashville, Tenn., has been the unofficial capital of country music since 1925, when station WSM carried the first broadcast of the "Grand Ole Opry" radio show.

more in 1953. The mass popularity of country music led to a dilution of the style, but later the growing interest in bluegrass music restored some concern for authenticity.

During the 1960s and '70s country music continued to infiltrate other popular forms. The growth in importance of a country music center in Austin, Tex.—in competition with the increasingly conservative Nashville—was spurred by such singers as Willie Nelson. He combined country music with elements of the prevailing youth culture, a combination that resulted eventually in the formation of a style known as country rock, whose popular practitioners include Emmylou Harris, joined in recent years by such groups as Alabama. The 1960s also began the meteoric rise into national celebrity of three talented women singer-songwriters. Dolly Parton, Loretta Lynn, and Tammy Wynette have continued to sing country and western for well over two decades. Others who have maintained their popularity over many years include Merle Haggard and George Jones, both of whom sing in traditional country-western style.

In the mid-1980s, two competing country music styles came into prominence. Singers such as Kenny Rogers produced slick, bland, pop-country music. Also popular, however, were traditionalists such as Ricky Skaggs, John Anderson, and George Strait. A new, more eclectic generation of country singer-composers emerged in the late 1980s.

Johnny Cash, the deep-voiced country and western singer known to his fans as "the man in black," rose to national prominence during the late 1960s.

county A county is a territorial division and unit of local government in the United States, some Canadian provinces, the United Kingdom, and other parts of the English-speaking world. The county originated in England, where it evolved from the Anglo-Saxon shire. The medieval English county was presided over by a crown-appointed SHERIFF, assisted from the 14th century by appointed JUSTICES OF THE PEACE. From the 13th century to 1832 each county sent two representatives to Parliament. The Local Government Act of 1888 transferred local administrative responsibility to elected county councils. The Local Government Act of 1972 reorganized the counties of England and Wales outside London into 47 nonmetropolitan counties and 6 metropolitan counties; within the counties there are 369 districts. The London metropolitan area was divided into 32 BOROUGHS. Scotland is administered under a different system of regions.

In 1987 the United States had 3,042 counties; Texas had the most (254) and Delaware the fewest (3). The most populous county, with almost 8.9 million inhabitants (1990), is Los Angeles, Calif. Although most states are divided into counties (except Louisiana, which has 64 parishes, and Alaska, which has 23 boroughs), the county has been most important in the South and Midwest. In New England the TOWNSHIP remains the basic governmental unit.

Couperin (family) [koo-pur-an'] The Couperins, a distinguished family of French musicians, were active from the mid-17th century until the mid-19th century. Two of them are well remembered today as composers.

Louis Couperin, b. *c.*1626, d. Aug. 29, 1661, came to Paris about 1650 and, in 1655, became organist at Saint-Gervais. Although Louis wrote excellent chamber music, he is best known for his harpsichord pieces, to which he was among the first to apply the style and ornamentation of lute music. In his nearly 100 compositions for the organ, he helped shape the French classical organ style. At Louis's death, his brother Charles succeeded him at Saint-Gervais.

François Couperin le Grand, b. Nov. 10, 1668, d. Sept. 12, 1733, the son of Charles Couperin, was organist at Saint-Gervais from 1685 until his death. In 1693, Louis XIV appointed him organist at the Royal Chapel. Although he composed much church, chamber, and organ music of the highest quality, François is best known for his four books of harpsichord pieces (1713–30) which are the perfect expression of the French rococo style. Couperin wrote a revealing and influential book of instruction, *The Art of Playing the Harpsichord* (1716). The three intensely passionate *Leçons des Ténèbres* (*c.*1714–15) constitute the peak of Couperin's church music.

Courbet, Gustave [koor-bay'] Gustave Courbet, b. June 10, 1819, d. Dec. 31, 1877, was the foremost realist painter (see REALISM, art) of mid-19th-century France. During the 1840s, Courbet produced many canvases in a typically romantic style, including some com-

In reaction to the romantic art of his contemporaries, the French painter Gustave Courbet founded the school of realism in the mid-1800s. Bonjour, Monsieur Courbet!, *or* The Meeting *(1854), exemplifies his scenes of daily life. (Musée Fabre, Montpellier.)*

placent self-portraits such as *Self-Portrait with a Black Dog* (1842; Museum of the Petit Palais, Paris). His maturing as an artist coincided with the Revolution of 1848; in *After Dinner in Ornans* (1848–49; Palace of Fine Arts, Lille), exhibited at the Salon of 1849, Courbet painted an intimate genre scene (see GENRE PAINTING) on the monumental scale formerly reserved for paintings of historical and mythological subjects. This painting was followed rapidly by other major works, such as *The Burial at Ornans* (1849–50; Louvre, Paris) and *The Stone Breakers* (1850; destroyed), notable for their large scale and volumetric solidity.

During the 1850s and '60s, Courbet was the archetypical bohemian artist of radical political beliefs. Dissatisfied with his treatment by art juries, he took the revolutionary step of constructing pavilions to show his work at his own expense during the world's fairs of 1855 and 1867. Although his massive *The Artist's Studio* (1855; Louvre, Paris) was not well received, the popularity of his smaller landscapes, hunting scenes, still lifes, and nudes made him financially secure in the 1860s. Courbet's republican sympathies led to his involvement in the Paris Commune of 1871 and to his imprisonment following the collapse of the revolutionary government. He fled to Switzerland in 1873.

Courbet was perhaps the first painter of genre subjects to become the acknowledged leader of a major school. His example had a great influence on the impressionists (see IMPRESSIONISM) and, through them, on 20th-century art.

court A court is an agency of government that provides authoritative decisions in legal disputes brought to it for resolution. Courts are required not merely to decide disputes but to decide them fairly, in accordance with the law. Courts fulfill three important functions: (1) they resolve disputes that, while often routine, are crucial to those involved; (2) they provide protection from illegal actions by government and individuals; and (3) they occasionally resolve disputes of great political and social significance.

Work of the Courts

A dispute before a court is called a case, suit, or action. Civil cases are basically disputes over whether private legal rights have been violated, as, for example, whether a person has failed to keep promises made by signing a contract with another person. In a civil case, the plaintiff brings suit against the defendant, whereas a criminal case involves alleged violations of the public order. Although the victim of a crime is the one most directly affected, crimes are seen as a threat to the fabric of the whole society; therefore the government, acting for the people, prosecutes the defendant in a criminal case.

To resolve a dispute, a court must do two things. It must "find the facts" of the dispute (in other words, determine what actually happened), and it must apply the appropriate legal principles to the facts. For example, in a dispute over who should pay medical bills for injuries suffered in an automobile accident, a court will seek to determine whether the defendant's carelessness caused the plaintiff's injury. If so, the court, applying the law, will direct the defendant to compensate the plaintiff for the damages suffered.

One way of resolving a court case is by a trial, a public hearing in which lawyers for the parties present evidence and legal arguments. It should be emphasized that relatively few cases go to trial; the great majority of legal disputes are settled without resort to courts. Of the remainder, 90 percent are resolved before they reach trial. One reason is that the parties in a civil suit may agree to settle it by compromise, because each side fears that it may lose, or that what it may win at trial will not justify the expense of carrying the case that far. Similarly, a prosecutor may offer a criminal defendant the chance to avoid trial by admitting guilt to a lesser charge, thus escaping the more severe sentence that might be imposed were he found guilty after being tried on the original charge. Although this process of PLEA BARGAINING saves the court and the prosecutor valuable time, it may place unfair pressure on the defendant.

Participants in a Court. The most important court official is the judge; it is he or she who is ultimately responsible for the court's decisions. In a jury trial the judge interprets the law, and the JURY decides the facts of the case. Juries range in size from 6 to 12 citizens of the area in which the court is located. Jurors typically serve for periods up to a month.

Courts must usually rely on others to carry out their decisions. The executive branch of the government is responsible for maintaining prisons and other correctional institutions to which courts may sentence those found guilty of crimes. Convicted defendants who are not incarcerated, however, may be supervised by court-employed probation officers. In civil cases, the parties may carry out a court's decision by themselves; if not, the court may provide for taking a defendant's property, selling it, and turning the money over to the plaintiff. In complex cases such as those involving school desegregation, one of the court's difficult tasks is to ensure enforcement of its orders by the many parties involved. The executive branch may have to use its police resources to be certain that court orders are obeyed.

Jurisdiction. A court may act only in disputes within its jurisdiction. For example, a court in Texas cannot, as a rule, assert jurisdiction over a defendant who resides in Louisiana. Jurisdiction also involves the kinds of disputes that courts may hear; for example, not every court may grant a divorce.

More importantly, a court cannot reach out for a dispute to resolve merely because the judge thinks an injustice has been done. The dispute must be brought to the court in the form of a case. Furthermore, the parties must actually be in conflict. A person seeking advice on the legality of an act under consideration is expected to get the opinion of a lawyer rather than the decision of a court.

A party who is dissatisfied with the way a trial court has applied the law to the facts may appeal to a higher court to review the lower court's decision. The role of the appellate court is limited to determining whether the trial court has properly applied the law or whether it has erred in some way.

Common-Law Courts

The court systems of the United States and England share historical roots. During the 11th and 12th centuries the English king resolved disputes with the aid of his "court," as his advisors were called. Formal courts of law gradually developed to apply the king's law for him. During the 16th and 17th centuries the concept developed that the king himself should be subject to the law and the courts independent of the king.

As the English courts evolved, they began to study their earlier decisions for guidance. The law contained in these decisions came to be known as the COMMON LAW, and its traditions were inherited by other English-speaking countries.

Courts in the United States. The United States has 51 separate court systems. They include the federal court system, established and maintained by the national government, and the courts of the 50 states. Because of the separate state and federal systems, the United States is said to have a dual court system.

The federal court system is more limited in size and purpose than are the state courts. Federal courts have jurisdiction over five basic kinds of cases. They hear: (1) cases in which the United States is a party; and (2) cases involving foreign officials. In civil matters, if more than $10,000 is involved, they may also hear (3) cases with parties from different states, and (4) cases involving the CONSTITUTION OF THE UNITED STATES and federal laws. Federal courts also hear (5) "federal specialties," cases involving patents, copyrights, or bankruptcies.

State courts share jurisdiction with federal courts in

Jacques Yves Cousteau revolutionized oceanographic research in 1943, when he developed the aqualung, the first practical, self-contained, underwater breathing apparatus (SCUBA). Cousteau has become an international celebrity through his books and films about underwater life.

French navy as a midshipman. In 1936 Cousteau began studies of the ocean environment. He founded the undersea research group of the French navy in 1945. His technological innovations include underwater breathing equipment, or the aqualung, which he developed with Émil Gagnon, and the use of underwater photography. Cousteau has a strong commitment to the marine environment and has used television to promote a better understanding of the ocean and its life forms. Since 1957 Cousteau has been director of the Oceanographic Museum and Institute in Monaco. He is also secretary-general of the International Commission for the Scientific Exploration of the Mediterranean. Cousteau has published many books, among them *The Silent World* (1953; with Frédéric Dumas), *Cousteau's Amazon Journey* (1984; with Mose Richards), *Jacques Cousteau: The Ocean World* (1985), and *The Living Sea* (1988; with James Dugan).

Cousy, Bob [koo'-zee]   Robert Joseph Cousy, b. New York City, Aug. 9, 1928, is a basketball Hall-of-Famer best known for his leadership and playmaking on the great Boston Celtics teams, which won six National Basketball Association (NBA) championships in the 1950s and 1960s while he was with them. Cousy was a superb passer; he held the NBA record for assists when he retired. Cousy earned All-America honors at Holy Cross College in 1950, and then played professionally with the Celtics. With Boston he was named to the All-Pro team in 10 of his 13 seasons. In 1957 he was named the Most Valuable Player in basketball. In addition to passing, he was a fine scorer, averaging 18.4 points a game throughout his professional career.

Couture, Thomas [koo-tuer']   Thomas Couture, b. Dec. 21, 1815, d. Mar. 3, 1879, was an exceptionally gifted French painter who, in espousing an eclectic approach, produced a style between romanticism and neo-

classicism and between romanticism and realism. His early work, exploring moralizing themes and using innovative techniques, incarnated the *juste milieu* or "happy medium" outlook of the July Monarchy (1830–48) of Louis Philippe. Couture was an outstanding teacher and attracted an international student body to Paris. His most famous works were *Romans of the Decadence* (1847; Musée d'Orsay, Paris), which won wide acclaim at that year's Paris Salon, and *Enrollment of the Volunteers* (1848; Musée de l'Oise, Beauvais). Couture had a far-reaching impact as both artist and teacher on impressionism, postimpressionism (Georges Seurat and Paul Cézanne admired his work), symbolism, and the American Ashcan school.

couvade [koo-vahd']   The couvade is the custom whereby the father retires to his bed upon the birth of his offspring and imitates the actions of labor and childbirth. The term is derived from the French *couver* ("to hatch"). The couvade is found primarily in nonliterate societies, but it was also found in Europe. The purpose of the custom commonly is to protect the child from supernatural or ritual danger, but it also enables the father to show his empathy for the mother's childbirth role and to express general identification with the female role and with the newborn.

covalent bond   SEE CHEMICAL BOND

Covarrubias, Miguel   [koh-vahr-roo'-bee-ahs]
Miguel Covarrubias, b. Mexico City, 1904, d. Feb. 4, 1957, was a painter, caricaturist, and illustrator. In 1923 he went to New York City, where he became a noted stage designer and contributor of caricatures to such magazines as the *New Yorker* and *Vanity Fair*. His mural paintings include two large works in Mexico City's Hotel del Prado (1947). An ethnologist as well as an artist, Covarrubias wrote and illustrated *Island of Bali* (1937), based on his travels there. He also produced illustrated works on pre-Hispanic Mexican culture, including *Mexico South* (1946), *The Eagle, the Jaguar and the Serpent* (1954), and *Indian Art of Mexico and Central America* (1957).

covenant (law)   A covenant, in contract law, is a legally enforceable agreement between two or more persons to perform or to refrain from performing a certain act, or specifying that a given state of facts does or does not exist.

Covenants are most commonly found in deeds, used to guarantee title to property or to place restrictions on its use. Covenants are classified as dependent, concurrent, or independent. They are dependent when performance by one party is conditioned on and subject to performance by the other. Concurrent covenants must be performed at the same time by both parties. Independent covenants are such that a party need not perform his or her own covenant in order to recover damages for the other party's failure to perform his or her covenant.

covenant (religion)   Covenant is a legal concept often used in the Bible as a metaphor to describe the relationship between God and humankind. One type of ancient covenant that serves as a model for certain biblical passages is the royal grant. It is typical of such covenants that only the superior party binds himself; conditions are not imposed on the inferior party. The covenants God made with Noah (Genesis 9:8–17), Abraham (Genesis 15:18), and David (2 Samuel 7; 23:5) fit this pattern.

The Mosaic covenant (Exodus 19–24; Deuteronomy; Joshua 24) seems to have been modeled on another type of ancient covenant, the political treaty between a powerful king and his weaker vassal. Following the standard form of such treaties, God, the suzerain, reminds Israel, the vassal, how God has saved it, and Israel in response accepts the covenant stipulations. Israel is promised a blessing for obedience and a curse for breaking the covenant.

These two different conceptions of covenant, one stressing promise, the other obligation, eventually modified one another. Jesus Christ added a third model, that of a last will and testament. At the LAST SUPPER, he interpreted his own life and death as the perfect covenant (Matthew 26:28; Mark 14:24; Luke 22:20).

The idea of a covenant between God and humankind lies at the heart of the Bible. This idea explains the selection by Christians of the word testament, a synonym for covenant, in naming the two parts of their Bible.

Covenanters   The Covenanters were Scottish Presbyterians of the 17th century who subscribed to covenants (or bonds), the most famous being the National Covenant of 1638 and the Solemn League and Covenant of 1643. The National Covenant opposed the new liturgy introduced (1637) by King CHARLES I. This led to the abolition of episcopacy in Scotland and the BISHOPS' WARS (1639–41), in which the Scots successfully defended their religious freedom against Charles.

In the Solemn League and Covenant, the Scots pledged their support to the English parliamentarians in the ENGLISH CIVIL WAR with the hope that PRESBYTERIANISM would become the established church in England. This hope was not fulfilled. In fact, after the Restoration (1660), King CHARLES II restored the episcopacy and denounced the covenants as unlawful. Three revolts of the Covenanters (1666, 1679, 1685) were harshly repressed. After the Glorious Revolution of 1688, WILLIAM III reestablished the Presbyterian church in Scotland but did not renew the covenants.

Covent Garden   Covent Garden, a theater in London known primarily for its opera performances, opened on Dec. 7, 1732, on a site that was formerly a convent garden. George Frideric Handel introduced his oratorio *Messiah* to London at Covent Garden in 1743. The theater was twice destroyed by fire and rebuilt, once in 1808 and again in 1856. In 1892 it was renamed the Royal Opera House, Covent Garden, and since 1945 it has had its own resident opera and ballet companies, named "Royal Opera" since 1968 and "Royal Ballet" since 1956.

Coventry   Coventry (1988 est. pop., 306,200) is an industrial city in Warwickshire, central England, noted for its automobile and motorcycle manufacturing industries. The city grew around an abbey founded c.1043 by Lady GODIVA and her husband Leofric. Lady Godiva's legendary ride was made through the streets of the town. A cloth-weaving industry began there in the 13th century, and the city was the scene of the famous Coventry mystery plays in the 15th and 16th centuries. In modern times it became an industrial center. An air raid on Nov. 14, 1940, destroyed Coventry's center and gutted its cathedral (1373–1433). In a remarkable reconstruction, the ruined shell of the old cathedral is preserved as a shrine. It serves as the atrium for a new cathedral (constructed 1954–62) designed by Sir Basil Spence in the contemporary style. At the entrance is Sir Jacob EPSTEIN's bronze *Saint Michael*; tall stained-glass windows illuminate an enormous tapestry, *Christ in Glory* (1952–62), by Graham SUTHERLAND.

Coverdale, Miles   Miles Coverdale, b. 1488, d. Jan. 20, 1569, was an English Augustinian friar who is best remembered as a translator of the Bible. After embracing Lutheran teachings, he abandoned (1528) the order and preached against church practices such as confession. Forced to leave England, he went to the Continent, where he produced (1535) the first complete English Bible. With Richard Grafton he issued the "Great Bible" in 1539 under the patronage of Thomas CROMWELL. In 1551 he became bishop of Exeter, but he was exiled again after the succession (1553) of the Roman Catholic Queen Mary. He returned in 1559, continuing as a leader of the Puritan party.

covered wagon   see CONESTOGA

cow   see CATTLE AND CATTLE RAISING; DAIRYING

Coward, Sir Noel   Noel Pierce Coward, b. Dec. 16, 1899, d. Mar. 26, 1973, was an English playwright, actor, and master technician of the theater. Many of his nearly 60 plays, especially his sentimental and patriotic pieces and his witty drawing-room comedies, were filmed and are often revived. His works are distinguished for their craftsmanship and versatility.

His major comedies are *Hay Fever* (1925), portraying a family modeled on that of actress Laurette Taylor; *Private Lives* (1930; film, 1931), featuring quarrelsome Bohemian lovers who desert their new spouses to run off together; *Design for Living* (1933; film, 1933), depicting the ménage à trois of three artists; *Tonight at 8:30* (1935; film, 1953), ten one-acters, the most popular of which is *Still Life*, filmed as *Brief Encounter* (1946); and

Sir Noel Coward, an English actor, lyricist, and playwright, is best known for writing such sophisticated comedies as Blithe Spirit *(1941), which reflects his witty dialogue and deft sense of theatrical timing. Coward was knighted in 1970 by Queen Elizabeth.*

Blithe Spirit (1941; film, 1945), a witty comedy about a man haunted by his dead wives.

His other works include a twice-filmed (1933; 1940) romantic operetta, *Bitter Sweet* (1929); *Cavalcade* (1931; film, 1933), a nationalistic extravaganza; *In Which We Serve* (1942), a patriotic wartime film for which Coward received a special Academy Award (1942); and revues such as *Sigh No More* (1945). His last important play was *Nude with Violin* (1956), dramatizing a recently deceased artist's frauds.

cowbird   The cowbird is a New World BLACKBIRD of the family Icteridae and the genus *Molothrus*. Cowbirds often associate with livestock, feeding on insects they stir up. Most species lay their eggs in the nests of other, usually smaller, birds. If the host birds do not dispose of the im-

The brown-headed cowbird (female at top) *lays its eggs in nests of other birds. The young from these eggs grow rapidly and dominate the nestlings of their hosts. Few host nestlings survive if more than one cowbird are with them in the nest.*

posed egg or rebuild the nest to cover it, the hatchling cowbird will dispossess the hosts' young or starve them. The brown-headed cowbird, *M. ater*, usually 17 cm (7 in) long, is a migrant found in most of North America. The male is black with a brown head, and the female is dark gray.

cowboy   The cowboy of the American West, a dashing figure in popular novels and films, was in reality a poorly paid laborer engaged in difficult and usually monotonous work. During the years after the Civil War the range cattle industry developed first in Texas and, beginning in the 1870s, in the Southwest and on the northern Great Plains. Probably the majority of the ranch hands came from the South, and many had fought in the Civil War. Not all cowboys were whites; about a third were African Americans or Mexican Americans. For their techniques and equipment, cowboys drew on both the Spanish traditions of northern Mexico and southern Texas and those of the Gulf coastal states.

The work year centered on two events, the roundup and the long drive. Roundups were held in the spring and often also in the fall. After cowboys had herded cattle to a central location, they branded newborn calves, castrated and dehorned older animals, and, in the spring, chose the cattle to be taken to market. From 1865 to 1880 at least 3.5 million cattle were driven in herds of between 1,500 and 3,000 from southern Texas to cattle towns on rail lines in Kansas, Nebraska, and Wyoming. The route most frequently used was the CHISHOLM TRAIL, which went to Abilene, Kans. Working up to 20 hours a day, cowboys drove the animals from one watering place to the next,

This engraving (c.1885) by Charles M. Russell shows some of the distinctive clothing worn by American cowboys. The flat-brimmed hat afforded protection against the elements, and the neck kerchief could be pulled over the face during dust storms. Heavy gloves protected the hands from rein or rope burns, and because much of the cowboy's work was done in areas of heavy cactus growth, leather boots and leg chaps were often worn.

guarding against predators, straying cattle, and stampedes at night. For his hard and dirty work the typical cowboy earned between $25 and $40 a month.

By about 1890 the era of the old-fashioned cowboy came to an end. At this point, however, dime novels and works such as Owen WISTER's *The Virginian* (1902) began presenting to a nostalgic public the stalwart, romantic cowboy hero who continues to dominate popular accounts of the West.

Cowell, Henry

Henry Dixon Cowell, b. Menlo Park, Calif., Mar. 11, 1897, d. Dec. 10, 1965, was one of the most prolific and influential American composers of his generation. His musical innovations often shocked listeners. In his piano music, for example, he introduced the *tone-cluster*, in which the fist, palm, or forearm is used to strike a group of keys simultaneously. In the 1930s he was one of the earliest composers of ALEATORY, or chance, music, in which the performers are given a major creative role. Cowell composed 20 symphonies, works for many different combinations of chamber ensemble, choral music, band music, and songs.

Cowley, Abraham

Abraham Cowley, b. 1618, d. July 28, 1667, was an English metaphysical poet and essayist whose colorful life included careers as a Royalist spy and as a botanist. He wrote his first volume of poems, *Poetical Blossoms* (1633), at the age of 15. The love poems in his most important volume, *The Mistress* (1647), resemble the more complex verse of John Donne. *Miscellanies* (1657) contains odes modeled on those of Pindar; his essays, including "Of Myself," imitate those of Montaigne.

Cowley, Malcolm

Malcolm Cowley, b. Belasno, Pa., Aug. 24, 1898, d. Mar. 27, 1989, was a Harvard-educated literary critic and editor, best known for his memoirs of literary life in Paris and New York in the 1920s and 1930s. *Exile's Return* (1934; rev. ed. 1951) and its sequels, *A Second Flowering* (1973) and *And I Worked at the Writer's Trade* (1978), concern the LOST GENERATION of American writers. For many years the literary editor for Viking Press and the *New Republic*, Cowley discovered novelist John Cheever and was instrumental in reviving William Faulkner's declining reputation during the 1940s.

cowpea

The cowpea, or black-eyed pea, *Vigna unguiculata*, is a member of the legume family, Leguminosae. Native to Asia and Africa, it is grown for human food, for animal forage, and as a soil-improving crop. The plant is a trailing, or semitrailing, annual. It bears pendant pods 20 to 30 cm (8 to 12 in) in length on long, stout petioles. The seeds often have a dark spot, or eye. The cowpea thrives in hot climates and has drought tolerance, but it is quite susceptible to frost.

The cowpea, or black-eyed pea, grows up to 3.7 m (12 ft) long, taking about 70 days to mature. The pods are about 20–30 cm (8–12 in) long and contain about 9–12 peas each.

Cowpens, Battle of

[kow'-penz] The Battle of Cowpens was an American victory during the American Revolution. On Jan. 17, 1781, Brig. Gen. Daniel MORGAN, with about 1,000 men, met a British force of 1,100 under Col. Banastre Tarleton at the Cow Pens, north of present Spartanburg, S.C. By a combination of skillful tactics and the deadly fire of his riflemen, Morgan defeated Tarleton, inflicting over 200 casualties and capturing most of the rest of the British forces. He lost only about 70 of his own men.

Cowper, William

[koo'-pur] William Cowper, b. Nov. 26, 1731, d. Apr. 25, 1800, an English poet of the age of sensibility, is noted especially for his long poem *The Task* (1785), which conveys a sense of God's presence in the world. Always sickly, he suffered the first of many fits

William Cowper, an 18th-century English poet, is best remembered for poems praising the simplicity of rural living and for works describing the English countryside.

of insanity when threatened with an examination for a government post. He entered an asylum, where he found comfort in Calvinist evangelicalism. Later he joined the pious family of a clergyman, Morley Unwin, whose wife, Mary, became the object of devotion in many of his poems. Cowper moved to Olney in 1767 to be closer to John Newton, a noted evangelical preacher. The two men collaborated on the *Olney Hymns* (1779), a projected series of 348 hymns, including "God Moves in a Mysterious Way," but the project was interrupted when Cowper suffered another attack of insanity, convincing him he was damned beyond redemption. When Cowper recovered, he turned more to poetry to ward off melancholia, and in 1782 he published his *Poems*, which included satiric and didactic verse as well as his popular comic ballad, "The Diverting History of John Gilpin." Shortly before his death he wrote his most powerful and painful poem, "The Cast-away," asserting his own damned state.

cowpox Cowpox, a contagious disease that affects cows, is caused by the VACCINIA virus. It causes pus-filled lesions to occur on the skin, especially on the teats and udder. Cowpox can be acquired in a mild form by humans. The English physician Edward JENNER discovered that dairy workers who had had cowpox were immune to SMALLPOX, a serious disease. He therefore advocated and first experimented in 1796 with the deliberate infection, or vaccination, of people with cowpox as protection against smallpox. The technique is still in use.

cowrie see MOLLUSK

cowslip The European cowslip, *Primula veris*, is a wildflower of the primrose genus. Native to alpine regions of Europe, it has leaves that grow close to the ground and bright yellow flowers borne on a long stem. The American cowslip, or shooting star, genus *Dodecathon*, resembles the European cowslip except that the petals of its flowers turn backward. Other American wildflowers sometimes called cowslips include the marsh marigold, *Caltha palustris*, which has clusters of yellow flowers; and the Virginia bluebell, *Mertensia virginica*, which has blue flowers borne in hanging clusters.

Cox, Archibald Archibald Cox, b. Plainfield, N.J., May 17, 1912, a professor of law at Harvard University, was appointed (May 1973) special prosecutor to investigate the WATERGATE scandal. When he pressed President Richard NIXON to release tape recordings of conversations held in the president's office, Nixon ordered U.S. Attorney General Elliot Richardson to fire Cox. Richardson and his deputy, William D. Ruckelshaus, both refused and then resigned, leaving the task to Solicitor General Robert M. Bork. This sequence of events became known as the "Saturday Night massacre." In 1980, Cox was elected chairman of the citizens' lobby COMMON CAUSE.

Cox, James M. James Middleton Cox, b. Butler County, Ohio, Mar. 31, 1870, d. July 15, 1957, was a U.S. political leader who was the Democratic candidate for president in 1920. An Ohio newspaper publisher, Cox served (1909–13) in the U.S. House of Representatives and was twice governor of Ohio (1913–15, 1917–21). He was a strong supporter of President Woodrow Wilson and of U.S. membership in the League of Nations. Cox was nominated to run for the presidency in 1920; his running mate was Franklin D. Roosevelt. Cox was soundly defeated by the Republican candidate, Warren G. Harding.

Coxe, Tench Tench Coxe, b. May 22, 1755, d. July 16, 1824, was influential in the early development of U.S. economic policies. The son of a Philadelphia merchant, he entered his father's business and, upon U.S. independence, turned to politics. He was made assistant secretary of the treasury (1789), commissioner of revenue (1792–97), and purveyor of public supplies (1803–12). Coxe was one of the economic nationalists around Alexander HAMILTON who believed in the need for a strong central government and the development of manufacturing.

Coxey's Army Coxey's Army was a contingent of unemployed workers who marched on Washington, D.C., in 1894. The group was organized by the reformer Jacob S. Coxey (1854–1951), hence its nickname; its official name was the Commonweal of Christ. Its purpose was to protest the unemployment that followed the Panic of 1893 and to lobby for laws creating legal currency to be spent on road building and other public improvements. The army, about 100 strong, left Massilon, Ohio, on Easter Sunday 1894. When it arrived in Washington on May 1, it had grown to only 500 and was immediately broken up by the police.

coyote [ky-yoht'-ee] The coyote, *Canis latrans*, is a carnivorous mammal belonging to the dog family, Canidae, order Carnivora. Coyotes are smaller than gray wolves

The coyote is an intelligent, adaptable animal capable of running at speeds up to 64 km/h (40 mph). North American Indian lore includes folktales about Coyote, the cunning trickster.

but overlap in size with red wolves and domestic dogs. The nose pad is narrower and the ears are longer than those of the wolf. Adult males weigh from 8 to 20 kg (18 to 44 lb); females are slightly smaller. Color varies, but coyotes are usually gray. Coyotes communicate by howling. Their sense of smell is well developed.

Originally, coyotes inhabited open country and grasslands in the southwestern United States and Mexico. Their range has expanded in recent history, and they now are found in a variety of habitats from Central America to northern Alaska and throughout the United States and most of Canada. Their diet is extremely diverse, and they take advantage of .whatever is available, including rodents, rabbits, birds, insects, and fruit. They sometimes eat domestic animals. Much of their winter diet is carrion. Females breed between January and March and produce an average of six pups per litter.

Coysevox, Antoine [kwahz-voh']

Antoine Coysevox, b. Sept. 29, 1640, d. Oct. 10, 1720, was the most highly esteemed and prolific sculptor at the court of Louis XIV of France. By 1666 he had been appointed *sculpteur du roi*. He became a professor at the Royal Academy of Painting and Sculpture in 1678 and its director in 1702.

Coysevox's mature style, notable in the *Tomb of Cardinal Mazarin* (1689–93; Louvre, Paris), displays a reconciliation of baroque exuberance with classical restraint. He is best known, however, for his portraits, which retain their individual character despite an official, grand manner, as can be seen in the *Grand Dauphin* (c.1680; Versailles). The informality and playfulness of such late works as the garden statues at Marly (1701–07) influenced the development of rococo style in the 18th century.

Cozens (family) [kuhz'-uhnz]

Alexander Cozens and his son and pupil, John Robert Cozens, were English landscape artists whose surviving works consist almost entirely of watercolors and drawings. Both father and son exerted considerable influence on other English artists, largely through their unorthodox approaches to and techniques of landscape painting.

Alexander Cozens, b. 1717, d. Apr. 23, 1786, often used abstraction as a starting point for his compositions. His technique was to cover the paper with what he called "blots," arbitrarily placed landscape elements, and to develop an imaginary landscape from them, usually in monochrome. Cozen's unique methods may be what make his work so powerful, if somewhat coarse. He published numerous treatises on drawing techniques.

John Robert Cozens, b. 1752, d. December 1797, continued his father's work in imaginative landscape compositions; his most important contribution was to demonstrate that watercolor landscapes can convey far more than mere topography. His brooding, almost menacing drawings of mountains, clouds, and atmospheric effects foreshadow the work of J. M. W. Turner, John Constable, and Thomas Girtin. Although his father may

be said to have invented "elegiac" English landscape painting, the younger Cozens brought to it an air of sublimity and an emotional content that, through its influence on other artists, made it a major development in English painting, leading to romanticism.

Cozzens, James Gould [kuhz'-uhnz]

James Gould Cozzens, b. Chicago, Aug. 19, 1903, d. Aug. 9, 1978, was an American novelist whose carefully crafted works usually study upper-middle-class professional men facing crisis and compromise. His books include *The Last Adam* (1933), *Men and Brethren* (1936), *The Just and the Unjust* (1942), the 1949 Pulitzer Prize–winning *Guard of Honor* (1948), and the popular *By Love Possessed* (1957).

crab

Crabs comprise about 4,500 species of ARTHROPODS in the order Decapoda, class Crustacea. They are characterized by a flattened, broad body covered by a shell, or carapace. The shell is actually an outgrowth of one segment of the head region. Crabs are found throughout the world, chiefly in marine waters, but they also inhabit fresh water and land. Crabs have as many as 19 pairs of appendages, five pairs of which are developed into walking legs. The first pair of walking legs, the chelipeds, is generally modified into claws by the extension of part of the next-to-last joint up along the last joint to form a pincer. The true crabs, Brachyura, differ from the hermit crabs, Anomura, in having a small, flaplike tail carried flexed beneath the body.

Crabs range in size from the pea crab, family Pinnotheridae, which inhabits living oyster shells and may be less than 1.5 mm (0.06 in) from leg tip to leg tip, to the Japanese spider crab, *Macrocheira kaempferi*, which may be 3.5 m (12 ft) from leg tip to leg tip.

Life Cycle. The crab's reproductive organs open to the

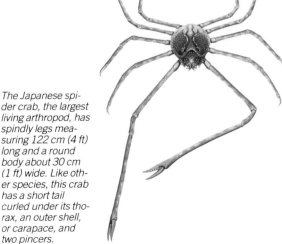

The Japanese spider crab, the largest living arthropod, has spindly legs measuring 122 cm (4 ft) long and a round body about 30 cm (1 ft) wide. Like other species, this crab has a short tail curled under its thorax, an outer shell, or carapace, and two pincers.

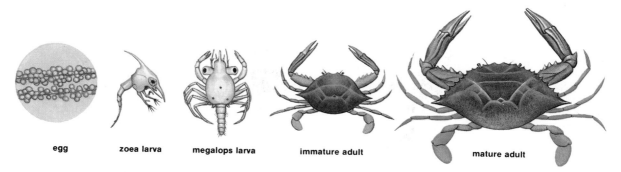

egg   zoea larva   megalops larva   immature adult   mature adult

The life cycle of the blue crab is typical of most true crabs and involves several stages of development before the crab matures into an adult. An egg hatches as a free-swimming zoea larva. The zoea larva molts several times, developing into a megalops larva, which has a prominent, tail-like abdomen. The megalops larva molts once, assuming an adultlike form that slowly grows to full maturity.

outside at the base of the last pair of walking legs in the male and at the base of the middle pair of walking legs in the female. In most species, the female carries the eggs cemented to her underside and protected by the flexed tail.

The developing crabs pass through four stages, two of which occur while still in the egg. Most crabs hatch at the third stage and then change into the fourth stage before assuming adult form. In some crabs, such as the freshwater *Potamon*, the young hatch as miniatures of the adult. Crabs grow by shedding, or molting, their hard shells. The blue crab, *Callinectes sapidus*, is believed to live about 3 years. The English crab *Cancer* has reached at least 12 years of age.

Behavior. Most crabs feed on small fish or worms or else scavenge along the shore or sea bottom. The tree-climbing robber crab, *Birgus*, however, feeds on coconut meat, which it obtains by drilling through the "eye" of the coconut with its powerful claws; the tree crab, *Aratus pisonii*, feeds to some extent on mangrove leaves.

Many crabs dig or inhabit burrows, but *Hypoconcha* carries half of a clamshell over its body. *Dromia* cuts out and attaches a roof of living sponge to its back. Crabs communicate with one another by several means, including claw waving and drumming. Stone crabs, *Menippe*, and others stridulate much like crickets by bending and rubbing the first walking leg against itself or against ridges on the body.

Several crabs are prized as food, including the Alaska king crab, *Paralithodes camtschatica*; the blue crab; and the Dungeness crab, *Cancer magister*. Soft-shelled crabs are newly molted crabs whose new shells have not yet hardened.

The internal structure (left) of a mitten crab is representative of true crabs and includes gills for breathing and a simple heart. The external skeleton (right) consists, in part, of a hard shell, or carapace, which extends from the mouth to the abdomen. The first pair of legs is modified into claws, and the paddlelike 5th pair of legs is used mainly for swimming.

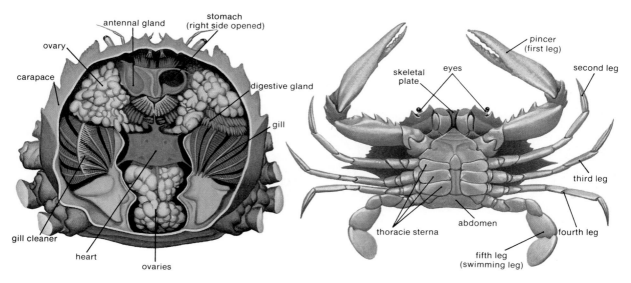

crab apple   The crab apple tree is grown primarily as an ornamental tree. The fruit tends to be acid and bitter, although it may be used in making jellies and preserves, and in Europe is often made into cider. Although the fruit of native American species remains green even when ripe, some hybrids and Oriental crab apples produce fruit that turns red, yellow, or purple in the fall. Crab apples and APPLES constitute the commercial fruit-bearing branch of the genus *Malus*, family Rosaceae.

Crab nebula   The Crab nebula is a peculiar gaseous nebula in the constellation Taurus. It is the remnant of a SUPERNOVA in 1054, which was so bright that it was visible even in the daytime. The name of the nebula comes from its supposed resemblance to a crab.

One of the brightest radio sources in the sky, the Crab nebula consists of two interpenetrating systems, a system of narrow filaments immersed in an amorphous region. The system of filaments is expanding with a velocity of about 1,200 km/sec. This expansion rate has helped to determine its distance as about 5,000 light-years.

In 1968 a PULSAR was identified near the center of the Crab nebula. It emits pulses of radio waves, optical waves, gamma rays, and X rays. The period is about 33 milliseconds, so short and so regular that it must be due to the rotation of a very dense NEUTRON STAR.

The Crab nebula is a luminous, expanding mass of gas and particles ejected by a supernova explosion in AD 1054. The star that exploded lies within the nebula and has evolved into a pulsar.

Crabbe, George   George Crabbe, b. Dec. 24, 1754, d. Feb. 3, 1832, was an English poet who left his medical practice to pursue a writer's career. With the help of Edmund BURKE he published his didactic poem *The Library* (1781). Working as a village cleric, Crabbe wrote his best-known works—the harsh, realistic poetic narratives *The Village* (1783), *The Borough* (1810), *Tales in Verse* (1812), and *Tales of the Hall* (1819). The poems dissect the grim life of what he called the "middling classes," and he was widely respected by the English romantic writers.

crack   see COCAINE

Cracow   see KRAKÓW

craft   Crafts are handmade objects created for utility, for decoration, or as a vehicle for the maker's imagination. At their best, crafts can link skill and substance—the product of the craftsperson's training and mastery of tools and techniques coupled with an understanding of natural and synthetic materials.

The crafts are categorized within the visual arts, which include sculpture and painting and other GRAPHIC ARTS. The term DECORATIVE ARTS is used interchangeably with that of crafts. The maker of crafts may be titled craftsperson, artisan, designer-craftsperson, artist-craftsperson, or various terms depending on the specialization. FOLK ART, while handmade, is distinguished from crafts by its naïveté and the fact that its makers are usually untutored in their art.

The range of crafts is broad—from the clay vessels of ancient Greece to contemporary containers that deal more with the "idea" of vessel than with function. Although many contemporary craft objects are not functional, they generally have their roots in function. Crafts mirror the age in which they are produced, embodying the knowledge, styles, and customs that exist in a given place at a given time.

History

The earliest handmade objects were chipped flint and bone cutting tools and weapons used by prehistoric peoples. These and successive objects—baskets, leather garments, pottery, woven materials, wooden objects, jewelry, and metalwork—mark human development and reflect ways of life and beliefs. In the Islamic world and in China, India, and Japan, craftspeople excelled in many crafts.

Fine craftsmanship flourished in Europe with the rise of monastic workshops in the Middle Ages. By the 13th century, GUILDS for specialized crafts were well established. During the Renaissance a distinction grew between painters and sculptors—considered intellectual and inspired—and craftspeople, who were judged as being bound by traditional manual skills. This view has lingered without basis into the 20th century and underlies the terms *fine art* and *minor art*.

Until the Industrial Revolution in the 18th century,

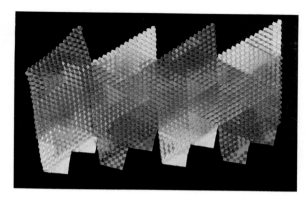

Crafts in America have experienced a revival in recent years. The many gifted artisans of today work in a variety of materials. Some find expression through age-old techniques; others utilize modern scientific advances. (Left) Triple Image *(1981),* contemporary wall hanging by Sherri Smith, is made of hand-plaited and dyed cotton webbing.

(Above) *Harvey Littleton's* Red Interrupted Descending Form *(1983),* of barium-potash glass with multiple cased color overlays, emphasizes the play of light and color on a simple shape. Littleton, who taught at the University of Wisconsin from 1951 to 1977, is considered a founder of the American studio glass movement.

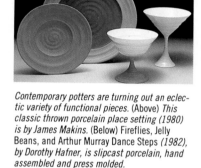

Contemporary potters are turning out an eclectic variety of functional pieces. (Above) *This classic thrown porcelain place setting (1980) is by James Makins.* (Below) Fireflies, Jelly Beans, and Arthur Murray Dance Steps *(1982),* by Dorothy Hafner, is slipcast porcelain, hand assembled and press molded.

(Above) *Douglass Howell made this flax sketchbook in 1966. Some of Howell's textured papers look like paintings made of fiber, and his artists' papers have been used by Jackson Pollock and Joan Miró.*

(Above) Plant Stand *(1981)* exemplifies Albert Paley's sculptural approach to metalwork; his pieces are noted for their fluid lines and integrated forms. Paley's jewelry and larger pieces are designed to relate to avant-garde fashion and high-tech architecture.

(Below) Group of 3 Manzanitas *(1982)* is by Del Stubbs. The vessels of green manzanita wood were turned on a lathe.

(Left) Cone Series: Bracelet No. 2 *(1983),* by Rachelle Thiewes, combines silver and 14k and 18k gold. The designer used form, line, and the play of light on metal to create dramatic impact.

most objects were handmade. The machine age led to a rapid decline of handwork, which came to be produced mostly at a luxury level and in the home. By the mid-19th century the array of machine-made products lacking standards of design stimulated the emergence of the English ARTS AND CRAFTS MOVEMENT, which is considered the precursor of modern crafts.

Contemporary Crafts

At a point in history when the machine can supply all of people's physical needs, handcrafts might seem an anachronism, except when thought of as a means of sustaining traditions, countering the uniformity of mass production, and providing an outlet for artistic self-expression. All of these roles define the place of crafts in the 20th century.

In Japan, the heritage of craft is preserved by an attitude of respect and government support. In the Third World, traditional crafts are being eroded by industrialization and the pressures of the tourist market.

In the West, the crafts have been closely tied to universities and art schools, where contemporary craftspeople receive their training and where many teach in addition to creating their own work or designing for industry. The independent, self-supporting studio craftsperson is much in evidence.

The crafts revival in the United States that began in the late 19th century took its design cue from the Arts and Crafts Movement and from successive styles such as ART NOUVEAU and ART DECO. The German Bauhaus school, Scandinavian design, Japanese folk art, pre-Columbian art, and American Indian craft art have been important influences on American craftspeople, as have ABSTRACT EXPRESSIONISM and POP ART. Whether producing a "line" of products or one-of-a-kind objects, the professional craftsperson today is able to work imaginatively with materials in many processes to create art.

See also: BASKETRY; FURNITURE; GLASSWARE, DECORATIVE; GOLD AND SILVER WORK; IRONWORK, ORNAMENTAL; JEWELRY; NEEDLEWORK; POTTERY AND PORCELAIN; TAPESTRY; WOOD CARVING; and other articles on individual crafts and regional art and architecture.

craft union   see LABOR UNION

▬

Craig, Gordon   Edward Gordon Craig, b. Jan. 16, 1872, d. July 29, 1966, an English scene designer, producer, actor, and writer about the theater, exerted a pervasive influence on modern theater with his stagecraft and his theories on theater.

Son of the famous actress Dame Ellen Alice Terry, Craig made (1889) his stage debut under the aegis of the actor and manager Sir Henry Irving. His imaginative staging of Purcell's opera *Dido and Aeneas* (1900) was followed by Handel's *Acis and Galatea* (1902) and Ibsen's *The Vikings in Helgeland* (1903). Craig attracted international attention with innovative productions—stage designs that emphasized portable structural elements and

the use of light to create atmosphere. In his best-known book, *The Art of the Theatre* (1905), he first set forth his developing theories on the theater of the future. In Italy he founded and edited (1908–29) his theatrical journal, *The Mask*, and established (1913) his School for the Arts of the Theatre. World War I forced him to close the school. Craig later published *The Theatre Advancing* (1919), *Scene* (1923), and theatrical biographies, and he designed stage sets for theaters on both sides of the Atlantic.

See also: THEATER ARCHITECTURE AND STAGING.

▬

Craig, Sir James   James Henry Craig, b. 1748, d. Jan. 12, 1812, was a British soldier and governor-general (1807–11) of Canada. He took part in the battles of Bunker Hill and Saratoga in the American Revolution and the capture (1795) of the Cape of Good Hope from the Dutch. As governor of Canada, Craig was in continuous conflict with the Quebec Assembly.

▬

Cram, Ralph Adams   Ralph Adams Cram, b. Hampton Falls, N.H., Dec. 16, 1863, d. Sept. 22, 1942, was an architect best known for ecclesiastical architecture in the late Gothic Revival style. His greatest achievement is the Cathedral of Saint John the Divine in New York City (begun 1911; incomplete). Between 1892 and 1913, Cram was associated with the firm of Cram, Goodhue and Ferguson, which won the competition to rebuild the U.S. Military Academy at West Point. In 1913, Bertram Goodhue formed his own firm, while Cram and Ferguson continued to build churches and college buildings primarily in the Gothic style.

▬

Cranach, Lucas, the Elder   [krah'-nahk]   Lucas Cranach the Elder, b. 1472, d. Oct. 16, 1553, was the distinctive German painter and engraver who may have initiated the DANUBE SCHOOL of romantic landscapes. *Rest on the Flight into Egypt* (1504; Staatliche Museen, Berlin) exemplifies the fairy-talelike moods and intensely warm colors characteristic of these landscapes. From 1500 to 1504, in Vienna, he painted portraits for academic patrons, including the diptych of *Dr. Johannes Cuspinian and Anna Cuspinian* (1502–03; Oskar Reinhart collection, Winterthur, Switzerland). These are the first German portraits containing a landscape background contributing to the mood of each subject.

Because Cranach's paintings frequently echoed motifs of Albrecht DÜRER, Michael PACHER, and others, many paintings were mistakenly attributed to other artists until the late 19th and early 20th centuries. An early masterpiece, the *Crucifixion* (1503; Alte Pinakothek, Munich) was thought until 1895 to have been executed by Matthias GRÜNEWALD.

In 1504, Frederick III, elector of Saxony, invited Cranach to become court painter at his residence in Wittenberg, the small town in northern Germany that soon became renowned as the birthplace of the Reformation.

The nude figures in Lucas Cranach the Elder's painting Caritas *(1537) glow against the dark leafy background. Cranach's nudes made up a significant portion of his work, both in his mythological and imaginative paintings and, often, in his portraits of biblical figures. (Koninklijk Museum, Antwerp.)*

September harvest in this Massachusetts cranberry bog begins with flooding the bog, which releases the ripe berries, causing them to float on the surface. The fruit is then pushed onto a mechanical conveyor (foreground) *and loaded on trucks.*

There Cranach became a close friend of Martin Luther and other Protestant reformers, and he often depicted them in paintings, engravings, and woodcuts. As Wittenberg court painter, Cranach received commissions for religious altarpieces; erotic, sensuous nudes; engravings; still lifes; and portraits of the court. Because he increasingly relied on his large workshop, these court paintings became more stereotypical and facile. Before 1520 such paintings as the *Torgau Altarpiece* (1509; Staedel Institute, Frankfurt) and *Reclining Nymph* (1518; Museum der bildenden Künste, Leipzig) display influences of Quentin MASSYS and Jan GOSSAERT, as well as of Flemish and Italian Renaissance artists. After 1520, however, Cranach frequently used a delicate, curvilinear style, derived from late Gothic MANNERISM as evident in his mythological nudes *Apollo and Diana* (1530; Staatliche Museen, Berlin) and *Venus* (1532; Staedel Institute, Frankfurt). Upon his death in 1553, Cranach's son Lucas the Younger, b. Oct. 4, 1515, d. Jan. 27, 1586, formerly an assistant in Cranach's studio, succeeded him as court painter.

cranberry The commercial cranberry, *Vaccinium macrocarpon,* is a creeping evergreen plant of the heath family, whose red, acidic fruit is used in sauces and jellies and in a variety of fruit juice beverages. Native to the bogs and marshes of the northern United States, the cranberry was first cultivated in Massachusetts and is now an important fruit crop in Wisconsin, New Jersey, Washington, and Oregon as well. Cultivation involves planting cuttings in 7.5 to 10 cm (3 to 4 in) of sand laid over moist, acid soil. The planting area is flooded for a day or two to set the cuttings securely. Each winter the bog is reflooded to protect the plants from frost injury. Plants mature in four to five years, and the crop is harvested in September. The newest harvesting technique is to flood the bog and churn the water to shake loose the fruit, which is scooped up as it floats to the surface.

crane (bird)   Cranes are any of several wading birds comprising the 15 species of the family Gruidae, order

Cranes are long-legged, bulky, omnivorous wading birds. The sandhill crane (foreground) *is fairly common in North America, but the whooping crane* (rear) *is considered an endangered species.*

The crowned crane, with its gold feather crown and contrasting white and black face and body, is a distinctively colored species found in central and southern Africa. Unlike other cranes, the crowned crane sometimes nests in low trees.

Gruiformes. They are found in North America and throughout much of the Old World. The plumage is usually brown, gray, or white. Such species as the crowned crane, *Balearica pavonina*, of Africa are particularly striking in appearance, and many species have unfeathered areas, sometimes brightly colored, around the head. Cranes often have loud, resonant cries. The trachea, or windpipe, in some species is convoluted into the keel of the sternum, a condition that facilitates the production of sound. Most cranes are terrestrial, preferring marshy conditions. They feed on plant materials and a wide variety of small animals. Their nests, usually containing two eggs, are on the ground in marshy areas. The crowned crane, however, may nest in low trees.

At least five crane species are in danger of extinction; these include the WHOOPING CRANE, *Grus americana*, the tallest bird found in the United States and Canada.

crane (machine) see DERRICK AND CRANE

Crane, Hart   The American poet Harold Hart Crane, b. Garrottsville, Ohio, July 21, 1899, d. Apr. 27, 1932, became known for complex and carefully crafted verse. The first of the two volumes of poetry published in his lifetime, *White Buildings* (1926), attracted some critical attention. Although Crane wrote some effective short lyrics, he is best known for *The Bridge* (1930), an ambitious epic poem in which he hoped to encompass the totality of American visions and myths. It won the annual *Poetry* award in 1930. In *The Bridge* Crane moves spatially and temporally back and forth through the American experience. With the unifying flux of the water beneath and a metropolis around it, the Brooklyn Bridge serves as the poem's central symbol. While on a Guggenheim Fellowship in Mexico, Crane jumped overboard from a steamer taking him back to New York and drowned.

Crane, Stephen   Stephen Crane, b. Newark, N.J., Nov. 1, 1871, d. June 5, 1900, was an American fiction writer, poet, and journalist. An avant-garde experimenter, he is generally considered the herald of 20th-century naturalism.

Crane was the youngest child of a Methodist minister, who died when the boy was eight years of age. In his teens, Crane acquired some newspaper experience working for an older brother who had a reporting agency in Asbury Park, N.J.; for the rest of his life, journalism was Crane's profession.

Eking out a hand-to-mouth existence while living in the Bowery, Crane rewrote a novel he had drafted in college. When no publisher would print it, he borrowed money from his brother to pay for a private printing, which appeared in 1893 as *Maggie: A Girl of the Streets* under the pseudonym Johnston Smith. The book was a total break with tradition in subject matter and style, and it did not sell, although it was favorably noticed by some literary figures. With their aid, Crane's Civil War novel, THE RED BADGE OF COURAGE, was commercially published in 1895. A masterpiece of realistic imagination—the author had never seen combat—it was an immediate success. Crane followed with the *Black Riders and Other Lines* (1895), a volume of poetry.

As a successful novelist, Crane was relieved of his professional worries and given better newspaper assignments. In 1896 he published *The Little Regiment, and Other Episodes of the American Civil War*, as well as *George's Mother*, another New York novel with a Bowery background. In January 1897, on a gun-running expedition to Cuba, Crane was shipwrecked and spent two days in an open dinghy with three other men. The resulting title story of *The Open Boat, and Other Tales of Adventure* (1898) conveys his basic view of the status of humans: pitiful little beings in the midst of hostile or indifferent nature, victims of capricious fate. This view is also apparent in the sardonic pictures of human society drawn in "The Monster" (1899), "The Blue Hotel" (1899), and "The Bride Comes to Yellow Sky" (1898).

Crane covered the Greco-Turkish War of 1897 and the

Stephen Crane, a novelist, poet, and writer of short stories, influenced American literature with his realistic fiction. The Red Badge of Courage (1895), about a young soldier's struggle to overcome his fears in a Civil War battle, earned Crane an international following.

Spanish-American War of 1898 as a war correspondent; he recorded his experiences in *Active Service* (1899) and *Wounds in the Rain: War Stories* (1900). In 1898, already tubercular, he moved with his mistress, the former proprietor of a brothel, to England. He died at a German spa while seeking a cure for his tuberculosis.

Crane, Walter   Walter Crane, b. Aug. 15, 1845, d. Mar. 14, 1915, was a prominent English painter, designer, and illustrator of children's books. He was apprenticed to a London wood engraver in his youth. Like many late-19th-century artists, he was strongly influenced by Japanese prints, and he used his own interpretations of their techniques to illustrate a number of books from 1868 to 1911. Crane's Japanese style, much imitated by other illustrators, became very fashionable in England.

Crane's work, especially his wallpaper and textile designs, reflects his connections with the ARTS AND CRAFTS MOVEMENT. He was the first president of the Art Workers' Guild and founder of the influential Arts and Crafts Exhibition Society, as well as principal of the Royal College of Art. His most important series of book illustrations were for *The Frog Prince* (1874) and for Edmund Spenser's *The Faerie Queene* (1894–96). Crane's work also shows the influence of the Pre-Raphaelites and of his adherence to the teaching of John Ruskin.

crane fly   Crane flies are members of the insect family Tipulidae, of the order Diptera (true flies). Adult crane flies resemble large mosquitoes and may reach 2 to 3 cm (about 1 in) in length. Their mouthparts are often formed into snouts and can neither chew nor pierce. Larval forms are aquatic and feed on decaying matter; adults may feed on flower nectar. Other families of Diptera often called crane flies are the Trichoceridae, Tanyderidae, and Ptychopteridae.

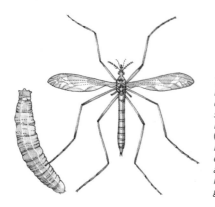

The giant crane fly resembles a mosquito by having a slender body and long legs. Its larva (left), *known as a leather jacket, damages lawns and crops by feeding on the roots of grass and grains.*

Cranmer, Thomas   Thomas Cranmer, b. July 2, 1489, d. March 21, 1556, was one of the principal fig-

Thomas Cranmer, English ecclesiastic and the first Anglican archbishop of Canterbury, contributed greatly to the development of the Church of England during the 16th century by promoting doctrinal and structural reformation and by composing (1549) much of the first Book of Common Prayer.

ures in the English REFORMATION. After studying at Cambridge, he taught theology and was ordained (1523) a priest. When King HENRY VIII sought the annulment of his marriage to CATHERINE OF ARAGON, Cranmer suggested (1529) that he obtain the opinion of the universities of Europe to strengthen his position. Henry commissioned Cranmer to carry out this plan and subsequently (1531) sent him to Germany to win the support of the Protestant princes.

In 1533, Cranmer was named archbishop of Canterbury and immediately pronounced Henry's marriage to Catherine annulled and his marriage to Anne Boleyn legal. He later invalidated the marriage to Anne (1536) and that to Anne of Cleves (1540) and played a leading role in the proceedings against Catherine Howard in 1542.

Cranmer promoted the Reformation theologically, supporting the English Bible translation of 1537–40 and opposing Henry VIII's *Six Articles* in 1539, in which the king reasserted such Catholic doctrines as transubstantiation in the Eucharist and the enforced celibacy of the clergy. Under King EDWARD VI, he promoted the first BOOK OF COMMON PRAYER (1549) and its 1552 revision, contributing substantially to both. He also produced the confession of 1553 called the Forty-two Articles (the basis of the THIRTY-NINE ARTICLES).

When Edward died in 1553, Cranmer supported the succession of the Protestant Lady Jane GREY. However, the throne passed to the Catholic MARY I, who sent Cranmer to the Tower of London, where he was burned at the stake for treason and heresy.

crannog   see LAKE DWELLING

Cranston   The city of Cranston (1990 pop., 76,060) is located on the Pawtuxet River in Rhode Island. Providence adjoins it to the north. Its manufactures include machinery, textiles, chemicals, and beverages. Cranston was settled about 1636.

The black crappie, also called the calico, or strawberry, bass, is an important clear-water game fish.

crappie The crappie, a fish native to the eastern United States, is related to the sunfish and bass (family Centrarchidae). There are two species: the white crappie, *Pomoxis annularis*, and the black crappie, *P. nigromaculatus*. They usually do not exceed 30 cm (12 in) in length but may reach 53 cm (21 in). Crappies inhabit streams but are most important as a sport fish. Their growth will be stunted if the fish are overcrowded or underfed. Thus, they must be managed in artificial reservoirs in order to provide enough large crappies for sport fishing.

Crashaw, Richard The English poet Richard Crashaw, b. *c.*1613, d. Aug. 21, 1649, was the chief proponent of the baroque style in English poetry. Crashaw was a fellow of Peterhouse College in Cambridge and was curate of Little St. Mary's church in the same city. Self-exiled to France in 1644 because of his High Church leanings, he became a Roman Catholic. He died in Italy.

His principal volumes of poetry, *Steps to the Temple* and *Delights of the Muses*, were published together in 1646. These secular and religious poems are characterized by sensuous, often violent imagery, using exaggeration and paradox to describe experiences of mysticism and religious passion.

Crassus, Marcus Licinius [kras'-uhs] Marcus Licinius Crassus, b. 115 or 114 BC, was known as the richest man in ancient Rome, although Pompey and Caesar amassed greater fortunes. Crassus's chief concern was the restoration of his family's prestige after the deaths of his father and a brother at the hands of Gaius MARIUS.

After exile (85–83) in Spain, Crassus joined Lucius Cornelius SULLA in the civil war. Later, however, he lost favor with Sulla and Sulla's successors and built his own personal following. In 72 BC, Crassus was chosen to put down the slave revolt of SPARTACUS. Although it was his generalship that defeated Spartacus, his rival POMPEY THE GREAT claimed credit for the victory. Crassus nonetheless joined Pompey in a successful campaign for the consulship of 70.

From 69 to 60 BC, Crassus tried to outbid all rivals for prestige. As censor, he proposed (65) citizenship for the Transpadane Gauls and annexation of Egypt but was blocked by CICERO and others. In 61 BC, Crassus probably helped bribe jurors in the trial of Publius CLODIUS, and he cooperated with Pompey's enemies in the Senate. Julius CAESAR, however, persuaded him to join Pompey in establishing the First Triumvirate (late 60/early 59). Later slighted by his partners, Crassus forced a renegotiation of the coalition at Luca (April 56). As co-consul with Pompey in 55, Crassus set out to make war on PARTHIA. Trapped by the Parthians near Carrhae, he perished in 53 BC.

crater see METEORITE CRATERS; VOLCANO

Crater Lake Crater Lake is in southern Oregon, on the crest of the southern Cascade Range at an altitude of 1,879 m (6,164 ft). It lies in a crater caused by the explosion of an ancient volcano that geologists call Mount Mazama. The lake is 10 km (6 mi) in diameter and 42 km (26 mi) in circumference. Its greatest depth is 589 m (1,932 ft).

The lake was originally called Deep Blue Lake because of its sapphire blue color in sunlight. There is no inlet or outlet. The lake was created and is maintained by precipitation. Lava walls 152 to 610 m (500 to 2,000 ft) high surround it. Near the west shore is Wizard Island, a small and newer cratered cone 237 m (776 ft) high. Prospectors discovered the lake in 1853. In 1902 the lake and a surrounding area of 64,895 ha (160,290 acres) were designated as Crater Lake National Park.

Craters of the Moon National Monument see NATIONAL PARKS

Crawford, Isabella Valancy Isabella Valancy Crawford, b. Ireland, Dec. 25, 1850, d. Feb. 12, 1887, was Canada's first distinguished woman poet. Her love for the pioneer life of her youth is evident from her earliest poems. *Old Spookses' Pass, Malcolm's Katie and Other Poems* was published in 1884. Crawford's last years were spent in poverty, and her collected poems were published only in 1905, establishing her reputation posthumously.

Crawford, Joan Joan Crawford, b. Lucille Le Sueur in San Antonio, Tex., Mar. 23, 1908, d. May 10, 1977, was a film star especially noted for her portrayals of strong-willed women. Crawford became the personification of Hollywood's most glamorous era and starred in more than 80 films. Among the best known are *The Women* (1939); *Mildred Pierce* (1945), for which she won an Academy Award; and *The Best of Everything* (1959).

Crawford, William H. William Harris Crawford, b. Feb. 24, 1772, d. Sept. 15, 1834, was a U.S. senator, secretary of the treasury, and presidential candidate. He entered the Georgia legislature in 1803 and in 1807 was elected to the Senate, where he became a popular and influential leader. He was minister to France (1813–15), secretary of war (1815–16), and then secretary of the treasury until 1825. The bitter rivalry between Crawford, Henry CLAY, and Andrew JACKSON for the presidency in 1824 was largely instrumental in the destruction of the old Democratic-Republican party. With support only in the South, he ran third in the field of four, and the presidency went to John Quincy ADAMS.

Craxi, Bettino [krak'-see]   Bettino Craxi, b. Feb. 24, 1934, Italy's first Socialist prime minister (1983–87), gave his country four years of unprecedented political stability, remaining in office longer than any other Italian premier of the post–World War II era. Under Craxi's leadership the economy improved dramatically. Relying on an alliance of middle-of-the-road "laic" parties, he also loosened ties between church and state by means of a new concordat (1984) with the Vatican.

crayfish   Crayfish, also known as crawfish, order Decapoda, are freshwater CRUSTACEAN arthropods that look like small lobsters. They comprise the families Astacidae, Parastacidae, and Austroastracidae. Crayfish range in length from 2 to 40 cm (0.8 to 16 in). Their thin, hard exoskeleton is usually brownish green, but may also be white, pink, or blue. They live in streams and ponds throughout the world, hiding under stones during the day and feeding at night. They eat decaying plant and animal matter and small fish, snails, insect larvae, and worms.

In many parts of the world crayfish are eaten as food and used as live fish-bait. In the United States their use as food is limited chiefly to areas around the Mississippi River basin.

Crazy Horse   The Indian chief Crazy Horse, d. Sept. 5, 1877, is revered by the Oglala SIOUX (Teton Lakota) Indians as one of their greatest warriors. He led the resistance to the U.S. government's forced settlement of the Sioux on the Pine Ridge reservation. Together with SITTING BULL, Crazy Horse and others lived off the reservation, hunting freely and harassing traditional enemies (the Crow and Blackfoot) and the white invaders swarming into the Black Hills, the sacred land of the Sioux, where gold was discovered in 1874.

When all the Sioux were ordered back to the reservation in December 1875, Crazy Horse engaged General George CROOK in battle. A series of confrontations ensued, including the famous Battle of the LITTLE BIGHORN (June 25, 1876), in which George Armstrong CUSTER and his 7th Cavalry were overwhelmed. After a winter of extreme hardship, Crazy Horse was finally persuaded to surrender by his uncle SPOTTED TAIL. He and his band of warriors, numbering about 1,000, entered Fort Robinson in May 1877. Crazy Horse was imprisoned, and while struggling to escape, he was stabbed in the back and killed.

Creasey, John [kree'-zee]   An English detective-mystery writer, John Creasey, b. Sept. 17, 1908, d. June 10, 1973, wrote nearly 600 novels under 28 pseudonyms. Among the most popular of his series' heroes were George Gideon (by J. J. Marric), the Baron (by Anthony Morton), Patrick Dawlish (by Gordon Ashe), and Roger West and the Toff (under his own name). Creasey was a skilled technician who could write various styles of books, from the potboiler to the serious police procedural. One of the latter, *Gideon's Fire* (1961), won the 1962 Edgar Allan Poe Award.

creation accounts   Creation refers to the act or acts by which the world came into existence. Since earliest times almost all societies have conceived one or more accounts of creation; these narratives, either oral or written, constitute a major theme in MYTHOLOGY. For an outline of scientific ideas concerning the origin of the cosmos, see COSMOLOGY.

Myths of Creation

Creation myths, also sometimes called cosmogonic myths, have been classified geographically (for example, creation myths of Australia, Africa, or South America) or in terms of their cultural-historical context; by this method, myths of hunter-gatherer societies, of simple and advanced agriculturists, or of cultures with urban traditions would be classified together. Creation myths have also been classified on the basis of a common linguistic and ideological orientation, as in the pioneering work by the French philologist Georges Dumézil. In recent studies, creation myths are often classified on the basis of a dominant motif or underlying structure.

Creator Deity. Virtually all creation myths emphasize the power of a creator deity. It is the power that is able to bring forth new beings, and thus creator deities are sources of fertility and fecundity. The creation myths of hunter-gatherer peoples are filled with symbols of the sky, landscape, and animals. In one example creation is attributed to the activities of the sun and moon, which, because they are too close together, divide the heavens between them and thus create day and night. Such symbolism of "up thereness" reflects a mode of transcendent religious orientation basic to many of these nomadic societies.

Among the Mbuti Pygmies of the Ituri forest in Zaire, there is a creator god (the Father or Grandfather) who is superior to the deities of the hunt or other deities manifested in sky symbolism. In one of their myths it is stated that after the Father created the world and human beings, he lived among the humans on earth. During this period there was no trouble or strife in the world, animals were friendly, and human existence was paradisiacal. After an act of disobedience by the humans, the world turned against them, animals and plants became enemies, and the deity Father departed from them back into the sky. Humans then began to search for the deity who had departed. They thought that they had rediscovered the deity in the moon but found the moon to be only a mask of their god. The Pygmies identify the forest in which they now live as an archetype of their former paradise.

In the creation myth of the San (Bushmen) of the Kalahari Desert, another hunter-gatherer culture, the supreme being, called Cagn, is symbolized by an insect (the mantis), who created all the animals and assigned colors and names to them. Cagn is said to dwell wherever antelope herds are grazing, and the eland is said to be Cagn's first-born. Because of this close relationship, Cagn is also a lord and protector of animals.

Emergence from the Earth. In many creation myths the manifestation of the power to create is expressed in the form of the earth mother. The earth is seen as a source of latent powers that bring forth new creation. In a creation myth of the Navajo Indians of North America, embryonic beings within the earth undergo a gradual metamorphosis as they pass upward through stages—each is identified with a direction and a color—until they finally emerge as humans on the face of the earth.

The Australian Aborigines refer to a creative period before the actual creation of the world as the *Alcheringa*, the time of the Dreaming. Among the aboriginal Aranda people, the earth was believed to be desolate during the period of the Dreaming, while, beneath the earth, the moon and the sun and a multitude of uncreated supernatural beings slumbered.

At a certain moment marking the beginning of creation, these supernatural beings awoke from their sleep and broke through the surface of the earth. The sun also came forth from underneath the earth giving light and warmth to these new emergents. Some of these beings rose up in animal forms, others as men and women, and others as plants.

World Parents. In other creation myths, the primary forms are symbolized by world parents who form a primordial unity. In some cases offspring initially have no separate identity, as in the Babylonian creation epic, ENUMA ELISH, or in the Polynesian myth of Rangi and Papa. At some moment in the narrative, tensions or even open warfare break out between the offspring and the parents. In the Enuma Elish, the parents are defeated in the war between the generations, and the earth forms from the mutilated body of the primeval mother.

The Cosmic Egg. The cosmic egg is another widespread primordial symbol of creation. In almost every form of the egg symbol, two elements are involved: the egg as a symbol of fertility, and the egg as a symbol of perfection. In the myths of the Near East and China, the cosmic egg is brought forth not by an egg-laying life-giver in animal shape but by the spontaneous action of the creator or primordial being. This implies that the egg symbolism is not simply a projection of natural forms on the cosmos, but is in fact a kind of philosophical reflection.

Other round or ovoid shapes related to the egg, such as coconuts and calabashes, often serve the same function as eggs in cosmological accounts. A story in Plato's *Symposium* relates that the first beings were round entities. Their perfection and strength caused the gods to fear their power. Thus, Zeus cut the creatures in half; each half then sought its other half in order to restore the lost unity. A similar theme appears in the myth of creation from a cosmic egg narrated by the West African Dogon people. The cosmic egg originally contained twins who were to become perfect androgynous beings. Because one of the twins broke out of the egg prematurely and this plan was thwarted, humans were forced to live with the imperfection of two sexes; males and females come together in sexual union in imitation of the archetype of perfection of the original creation.

Creatio ex Nihilo. The notion that creation came from nothing (*creatio ex nihilo*) appears in several accounts of creation. The biblical story of creation contained in the Book of GENESIS begins with a formless, watery chaos that God shapes into the ordered world. The hymn of creation from India's epic Rig Veda (see VEDAS) describes the primordial situation as one of neither existence nor nonexistence and further states that no one, not even the gods, knows who produced the universe. In marked contrast is an Egyptian myth attributing creation to the deity Khepri. In this myth Khepri states that when he came into being, being itself came into being; all other beings were then produced from his actions and his body; but before him there was only nonbeing.

Among the Polynesians, creation myths emphasize the dimensions of void space and the qualities of darkness as the primordial structures of creation. In these myths, the initial state of darkness and void in which the deity dwells is later transformed and the forms of the universe then emerge. Creation is thus predicated on a void or a nothingness—a reality totally different from any form or substance of the created order. In addition, the deities who create from nothing or emerge from this void are given a new and special kind of power; for although creators of the world, they remain distinct from it in their originative form.

The Earth-Diver. In a number of creation myths, an earth-diver—usually an animal, crab, fish, or tortoise—dives into the depths of water, bringing up a small amount of earth, out of which the entire universe is made. In these myths, water appears as the primordial matter of creation, although beneath the waters there is earth. Water is the symbol of the uncreated universe, a kind of pregnant chaos.

In creation myths of this kind, which are prominent in North American Indian mythology, especially among the Huron, a marked dualism is notable in the inertia of water expressing a passive resistance to the establishment of solidity. This dualism is often further expressed within the myth by the antagonism between an older and younger brother, or a greater and lesser spirit. The creation is usually accomplished by the younger brother or the lesser spirit with the cooperation of the earth-diver.

creationism   Creationism is the name popularly given to the view of fundamentalist Christians that the biblical account of the origin of life is literally true and that the theory of evolution, first elaborated by Charles DARWIN and basic to modern biology, must therefore be false. In the 1920s, U.S. fundamentalists pressed for state laws banning the teaching of evolution in public schools, but the ridicule that attended the famous SCOPES TRIAL (1925) in Tennessee effectively crippled this effort. FUNDAMENTALISM experienced renewed activism in the late 1960s, and creationists began to demand that the biblical creation account be taught in the schools as a theory of equal validity to evolution; the teaching of evolution alone, they claimed, violated religious freedom by promoting a "rival religion"—secular humanism. In some states creationist policies and legislation went into effect but in the 1970s were overturned by the courts; the movement nevertheless influenced curriculum planning and textbook content. Equal-treatment laws passed subsequently have been found both by federal courts and by the U.S. Supreme Court to be unconstitutional.

Creationists have also sought to advance their views on scientific grounds through such organizations as the Creation Research Society, founded in 1963, which supports publication of "creation science" papers; these have been rejected by established scientific journals for lack of scientific coherency and documentation. A few members of the scientific community have also developed counterevolutionary arguments, such as modern forms of the Panspermia Theory, but are not necessarily in accord with fundamentalist aims.

Crébillon

Crébillon [kray-bee-ohn'] Prosper de Crébillon, b. Jan. 13, 1674, d. June 17, 1762, was a highly esteemed French dramatist of the 18th century, credited with introducing melodramatic elements into traditional French tragedy. His *Rhadamiste et Zénobie* (1711) and other tragedies make use of violence, frenzied action, and complicated situations. Crébillon could also be tender and lyrical, as in his *Électre* (1708).

credit see BANKING SYSTEM

credit, letter of see LETTER OF CREDIT

credit agency

credit agency Credit agencies are companies that provide information about the credit worthiness of prospective borrowers. There are two types of credit agencies: those which provide credit information on individual buyers and those which give data on business firms. Dun & Bradstreet is the best-known U.S. company giving credit ratings on businesses. Credit information on individuals is supplied by TRW Inc., the International Credit Association, the Associated Credit Bureaus, and others.

A credit agency collects information on the character, income level, outstanding debts, and capital of credit applicants. Recent federal and state laws have strictly regulated the methods by which this information is collected. The decision on allowing credit is made by the agency's client. Some credit agencies provide collection services on past-due accounts.

credit card

credit card A credit card allows its holder to buy on credit from stores, restaurants, and other providers of goods and services. The credit-card holder pays the company issuing the card for those purchases, and the company reimburses the providers. With a "charge card," a customer may purchase items from a particular store, or gasoline of a particular brand. Both types of card offer the customer the option of paying the full amount of the monthly debt balance, or of paying only a portion per month, repaying the remainder at an annual interest rate as high as 18–21%.

Many credit-card companies impose an annual fee on credit-card holders. All charge retailers a fee—typically, about 3 percent of the purchase price—for each credit-card purchase. The cost to retailers—totaling several billion dollars—is "folded into" the retail price of all goods and services sold by the firms that accept credit cards from their customers.

Crédit Mobilier of America

Crédit Mobilier of America [kre'-dit moh-bil-ee-ay'] The Crédit Mobilier was a construction company founded in 1864 to build the Union Pacific Railroad (see TRANSCONTINENTAL RAILROAD). The ownership of the Crédit Mobilier was identical with that of the railroad, but railroad officials let contracts to the construction company at inflated prices, paid for from congressional subsidies to the Union Pacific. The promoters, including Congressman Oakes Ames of Massachusetts, were later charged with making enormous profits. Ames sold his fellow members of Congress shares of stock in Crédit Mobilier at less than par value, from which they received huge dividends. In 1872 these transactions, involving among others Vice-President Schuyler COLFAX and Congressman James A. GARFIELD of Ohio, became public knowledge. The House of Representatives condemned Ames, considered the impeachment of Colfax, and published the names of lawmakers with whom Ames had dealt. The Crédit Mobilier episode came to symbolize the lax ethical standards of the post–Civil War era.

credit union

credit union A credit union is a cooperative financial institution funded by the pooled savings of its members, to whom it makes low-interest personal loans. Credit societies for the owners of small businesses and others who could not obtain loans through the banks of the time were established in the 19th century in Germany and Italy. The first U.S. credit union was founded in New Hampshire in 1909. By 1990 approximately 15,000 credit unions, most of them small institutions with assets under $5 million, had been formed by groups of people who share a common bond: they are employees of a particular organization or members of a labor union, a church, or an occupational group. Owned entirely by its members, a credit union elects its officials, who often serve without pay. Savings accounts pay interest at rates set by the members. Low-interest, short-term loans to members are made principally for automobile purchases, home improvements, and personal needs. Credit unions also provide financial services equivalent to those offered by commercial institutions, such as interest-bearing checking accounts and savings certificates. All U.S. credit unions operate under federal or state charters.

Cree The Cree are North American Indians who spoke an Algonquian language and formerly inhabited the boreal forests south and west of the Hudson Bay and Lake Nipigon regions of Canada. As hunters and prime suppliers of pelts, they were early drawn into the fur trade with the French and English. By the mid-17th century a series of western and northern migrations were underway that eventually saw Cree bands scattered from near Lake Mistissani in northern Quebec to the foothills of the Canadian Rockies.

Their extensive migrations and fur-trapping activities brought them into frequent conflict with their tribal neighbors. Allied with the ASSINIBOIN in Manitoba, they drove the Skisika and their allies from the Saskatchewan River valley. Three distinctive groups evolved, the Woodland Cree, Swampy Cree, and the Plains Cree, the latter subsisting as mounted buffalo-hunters on the northern plains. Many of the Plains Cree intermarried with the French, creating the distinctive métis subculture of the Red River valley. In 1986 the Cree population was estimated to number about 122,000.

creed A creed is a brief, authorized summary of the Christian doctrine sometimes recited in church services as an affirmation of faith. Formulations of the Christian faith, presumably taken as the basis of teaching and evangelization, are found in the New Testament, although in a rudimentary form.

Of the two classical creeds, the Apostles' Creed belongs in its essential content to the apostolic age, although it is not the work of the Apostles. It had its origin in the form of a confession of faith used in the instruction of catechumens and in the liturgy of BAPTISM. The creed may have been learned by heart and at first transmitted orally (to protect it from profanation). It is based on a formula current at Rome c.200, although its present form did not appear before the 6th century. It is used by Roman Catholics and many Protestant churches but has never been accepted by the Eastern Orthodox churches.

The other classical creed, the Nicene, was an expression of the faith of the church as defined at the Councils of Nicaea (325) and Constantinople (381). Based probably on the baptismal creed of Jerusalem, the Niceno-Constantinopolitan Creed contained a fuller statement concerning Christ and the Holy Spirit than the earlier formula. Its use in eucharistic worship is not much earlier than the 5th century. The so-called *Filioque* ("and the Son") clause, expressing the double procession of the Spirit, was added at the Third Council of Toledo (589). The Nicene Creed is used by Roman Catholics, many Protestants, and the Eastern Orthodox; the last, however, reject the *Filioque* clause.

The Athanasian Creed (sometimes known as the *Quicumque*, from the opening Latin word) was first clearly referred to in the 6th century, and the attribution to ATHANASIUS is untenable. It is Latin in origin, and in the Middle Ages it was regularly used in church services, although it is now infrequently recited.

See also: CHALCEDON, COUNCIL OF; CONSTANTINOPLE, COUNCILS OF; EPHESUS, COUNCIL OF; NICAEA, COUNCILS OF.

Creek The Creek are a North American Indian people who formerly occupied land along the waterways of present-day Georgia and Alabama. A settled, agricultural people, in 1750 they numbered about 20,000 and lived in 50 towns, loosely organized as the Creek Confederacy, composed predominantly of Muskhogean-speaking tribes.

Each Creek town had a public square, where the annual CORN DANCE ceremony was performed and around which rectangular frame buildings were erected. Nearby was the *chunkey* yard, where the ritual ball games were played in summer. Townspeople's homes were built in the surrounding forest. In nearby fields the women raised crops, principally maize, squash, and beans. The men were hunters and fishers.

By 1750, European trade goods had been introduced by the French and by the British, with whom the Creek were allied in the 18th century. During the so-called Creek War of 1813–14, Andrew JACKSON annihilated the Creek forces at Horseshoe Bend, Ala., on Mar. 27, 1814, whereby the Indians were forced to cede their choicest land to the United States. In 1832 they ceded their remaining land east of the Mississippi River. From 1836 to 1840 the Creek were removed to INDIAN TERRITORY in present-day Oklahoma, where they formed one of the FIVE CIVILIZED TRIBES. The Creek Nation was formed in 1839, but it was dissolved (1907) when Oklahoma entered the Union. In 1987 more than 54,600 Creek resided on or near the Oklahoma reservation.

Creeley, Robert Robert White Creeley, b. Arlington, Mass., May 21, 1926, is linked with the BLACK MOUNTAIN SCHOOL OF POETRY; his poems deal with states of mind and feelings as they shape fundamental senses of self-definition. Working from a set of artistic principles called Projectivism (first enunciated by Charles OLSON), Creeley often defies the ordinary expectations associated with lyric poetry. His volumes include *For Love* (1962), *Words* (1965), *Pieces* (1968), *A Day Book* (1972), *Later* (1979), *Memory Gardens* (1986), and *The Collected Poems of Robert Creeley* (1982). He has also published short and long fiction, a journal of a trip to the Far East, and *The Collected Prose of Robert Creeley* (1984).

creeper Creeper is a common name for the birds of the family Certhiidae, but it is also applied to some unrelated species that also creep about on trees, rocks, or walls. The true creepers, however, are mostly small (12–18 cm/4.75–7 in), with long toes and long, sharp, curved claws. The brown creeper, *Certhia familiaris*, ranges over

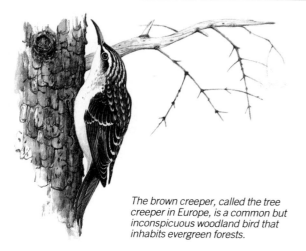

The brown creeper, called the tree creeper in Europe, is a common but inconspicuous woodland bird that inhabits evergreen forests.

most of the temperate Northern Hemisphere. It is small (13 cm/5 in) and is streaked with brown above and white below. It has a long, thin, decurved bill and a stiff tail, which it uses as a prop as it spirals up tree trunks.

cremation Cremation, the disposal of a corpse by fire or intense heat, is an ancient practice that originated during the Stone Age. As a mode of final disposition, it is widely practiced in many parts of the world. In the FUNERAL CUSTOMS of the Hindus of India, cremation is used almost exclusively. In the Western world it is generally accepted. Its practice in the United States, however, remains statistically low. Cremation is forbidden in Orthodox Judaism and only recently has been approved by the Roman Catholic church.

An early method of cremation involved placing the corpse on a wood pyre. In modern crematories the process is accomplished by the direct application to the body of intense heat in a large ovenlike structure called a retort. The bone fragments, which usually are reduced to 0.9 to 1.8 kg (2 to 4 lb) in weight, are then pulverized and placed in a cremation urn.

See also: SUTTEE.

Crémazie, Octave [kray-mah-zee', awk-tahv'] Octave Crémazie, b. Quebec, Apr. 16, 1827, d. Jan. 16, 1879, is considered French Canada's first national poet. Influenced by French romanticism, he worked to preserve early French-Canadian literature and encouraged some of its best writers. Because of business reverses, he left Canada in 1862 for Paris where, under the pseudonym Jules Fontaine, he wrote *Siège de Paris* (1870). His *Oeuvres complètes* was published in 1892.

Cremona [kray-moh'-nah] Cremona (1981 pop., 80,758) is the capital city of Cremona province in the Lombardy region of northern Italy. Situated on the Po RIVER southeast of Milan, it is an agricultural market and manufacturing center for textiles, pianos, and farming machinery. Founded by Rome in the 3d century BC, it was a free commune during the Middle Ages and was later held by Milan, Spain, and Austria before being incorporated into an independent Italy. Violins and violas made here between the 16th and 18th centuries by the AMATI and GUARNERI families and Antonio STRADIVARI are world famous.

creole [kree'-ohl] Creole languages are fully formed languages that develop from a PIDGIN and gradually become the primary language of a linguistic community. As the domains of the pidgin expand, often with the development of a LINGUA FRANCA used between different groups, it becomes more complex. When the pidgin replaces the community's original language, it is called a creole.

Widely distributed throughout the world, creolized languages are native to between 10 and 15 million people. Different creoles share many common features, such as an outward simplicity and regularity that is believed to reflect universal linguistic processes.

Most creole languages have vocabularies derived from major European languages. When a creole coexists with the language on which it is lexically based, it blends with the base language to form a decreolization continuum. Except for the English-based Tok Pisin that has semiofficial status in Papua New Guinea, and the French-based Creole endowed with a semicodified orthography in Haiti, creoles still bear the stigma of their pidgin origin and association with slavery and social inferiority.

Creoles [kree'-ohlz] Creoles are the native-born descendants of early French, Spanish, and Portuguese settlers in Latin America, the West Indies, and the southern United States. Derived from the Portuguese *crioulo* ("raised at the home of the master, domestic"), the term came into use in the 16th century to distinguish persons born in the New World colonies of European parents from New World residents of European birth. Later, the term designated persons of European descent, whether white or of mixed blood, as distinguished from those of African or aboriginal American descent.

The meaning of the term *Creole* varies considerably in different regions. In some Latin American countries, notably Mexico, it denotes local-born persons of pure Spanish extraction. In the West Indies, the term is applied to descendants of any European settlers, and in the Guianas, it refers to descendants of African slaves. In Louisiana, the term refers to French-speaking white descendants of early French or Spanish settlers; less commonly, it is applied to mulattoes speaking a creolized version of French and Spanish.

The Creoles in the Old South of the United States lived between Baton Rouge, La., and the Gulf Coast, and in small communities in eastern Missouri and southern

Alabama. As landowners and slaveholders during the antebellum period, they were perceived as aristocrats who took pride in gracious living and courtly manners. Although largely absorbed into the mainstream American culture, Creole traditions survive in Louisiana's Civil Code and its Spanish colonial architecture; in gumbo, pralines, and other cuisine specialties; and in the New Orleans Mardi Gras festivities.

creosote [kree'-uh-soht]   Creosote is the name for two different oily liquids, products of the distillation of either COAL TAR or the tar of hardwoods such as beechwood. Coal-tar creosote is a poisonous organic compound used primarily as a wood preservative. Wood-tar creosote, which consists largely of phenolic compounds, is used for pharmaceutical purposes, as an antiseptic, and as a flavor additive. Creosote can build up in improperly installed stoves and flues and create a fire hazard.

creosote bush   Creosote bush is the common name of *Larrea tridentata*, a strongly scented evergreen in the caltrop family, Zygophyllaceae. It is native to the hot, dry areas of Mexico and the southwestern United States, where it grows to heights of 3 m (10 ft). Its compound leaves, divided into two small leaflets, contain a resin with an odor resembling creosote. An individual bush can live for up to 100 years, but its manner of propagation makes the plant a candidate for the world's oldest living organism. As a bush grows, its main stem forms rooted lobes that develop their own branches. This process is repeated, forming a spreading ring around the original plants as they die. Because all of the plants in a ring are genetically identical clones, they may be considered a single organism. One such ring, in the Mojave Desert, has been radiocarbon-dated as about 11,700 years old, far older than the most ancient BRISTLECONE PINE. Other plants that propagate by cloning, however, may prove older still.

Crerar, Henry   Henry Duncan Graham Crerar, b. Hamilton, Ontario, Apr. 28, 1888, d. Apr. 1, 1965, was a Canadian general during World War II. After serving as an artillery officer in World War I, Crerar was appointed chief of the Canadian general staff in 1940. He served (1943–44) in Italy and commanded the First Canadian Army in the Normandy landings and during its advance (1944–45) across the Low Countries into Germany.

Crerar, Thomas Alexander   Thomas Alexander Crerar, b. Molesworth, Ontario, June 17, 1876, d. Apr. 11, 1975, was a Canadian political leader. Elected (1917) to Parliament as a Liberal, he served (1917–19) as minister of agriculture in Sir Robert Borden's Union government. Shifting leftward, he founded (1920) the Progressive party, an amalgamation of farm parties, which, after the election of December 1921, formed the second largest group in the House of Commons. In No-

vember 1922, Crerar retired to private life. He was later minister of mines and resources (1936–45) in the government of William Lyon Mackenzie KING and served (1945–66) in the Senate.

cress   Cress is the common name of various annual and perennial herbs of the mustard family, Cruciferae. They are used in salads and garnishes for the stimulating flavor of their leaves. One of the best-known cresses is watercress, *Nasturtium officinale*. The scientific name should not be confused with the common name "nasturtium," applied to garden flowers of the genus *Tropaeolum*. Watercress is native to Europe but has become naturalized in springs and wet ground in temperate climates. It is an aquatic plant with floating or creeping stems that root easily at the nodes. Young leaves are usually roundish or oval, with unbroken margins. Mature leaves are compound, consisting of 3 to 11 rounded or oval leaflets, each resembling a single young leaf. Watercress can be grown easily from seed or propagated from bits of stem.

Garden cress, or peppergrass, *Lepidium sativum*, is an Asiatic annual cress that grows to heights of 60 cm (2 ft). It is popular in Europe and is becoming so in the United States. This plant grows rapidly from seed and makes an attractive and tasty salad or garnish. Its seeds are sown thickly in narrow rows 25 to 30 cm (10 to 12 in) apart in early spring. Winter cress or upland cress, *Barbarea verna praecox*, is a biennial that grows to heights of 60 cm; native to Europe but naturalized throughout the United States, it is sometimes cultivated for its leaves. Bitter cress, *Cardamine pratensis*, a widely distributed perennial, grows to heights of 50 cm (20 in).

Cretaceous Period   see EARTH, GEOLOGICAL HISTORY OF; GEOLOGIC TIME

Crete   Crete (Greek: Kríti), a constituent part of Greece, is an island lying between southern Greece and Turkey, separating the Aegean Sea from the Mediterranean. The largest of the Greek islands, it has an area of 8,260 km^2 (3,189 mi^2) and a population of 502,166 (1981). The island is about 245 km (152 mi) from west to east but does not exceed 56 km (35 mi) from north to south. Very mountainous, it rises at Mount Ida to 2,456 m (8,058 ft).

Crete has hot, dry, summers, and mild, rainy winters. Although less than one-third of the island is cultivated, agriculture is the primary occupation. Olives, grapes, and cereals predominate; grazing is important in the mountains. Most peasants own their land. Industrial development has lagged because of the absence of railroads. Almost one-third of the population is urban, but towns are small; IRÁKLION is the largest. A substantial migration of young people to the mainland has occurred in recent years.

Crete was the center of an important Bronze Age culture called Minoan (after the legendary King MINOS) that existed c.2500–c.1100 BC. Elaborate settlements and

The ancient palace complex at Knossos, near the northern coast of Crete, was excavated and partially reconstructed by the British archaeologist Sir Arthur Evans.

palaces were built, notably at KNOSSOS, during this period. Crete played an important role in the transmission of ancient Near Eastern civilization to Europe, but lay only on the fringe of classical Greek culture. Later a part of the Roman and Byzantine empires, the island subsequently was occupied by Venetians and, in 1669, by Ottoman Turks, against whom the Cretans successfully revolted in 1898. Crete was joined to Greece in 1913. The island was occupied by German troops during World War II.

See also: AEGEAN CIVILIZATION.

cretinism see ENDOCRINE SYSTEM, DISEASES OF THE

Crèvecoeur, Michel Guillaume Jean de [krev-kur'] Using the pen name J. Hector St. Jean de Crèvecoeur, Michel Guillaume Jean de Crèvecoeur, b. Jan. 31, 1735, d. Nov. 12, 1813, was a French author whose *Letters from an American Farmer* (1782) popularized the idea that America was a "melting pot" and that Americans constituted a new race. After his enthusiasm and personal life had been shattered by the American Revolution, he became the kind of displaced person about whom he wrote so movingly in *Sketches of Eighteenth-Century America* (published 1925).

---

crib death Crib death, or Sudden Infant Death Syndrome (SIDS), is the sudden unexpected death of an infant between 2 weeks and 1 year old, due to unknown causes. About 95% of all cases occur between 2 and 4 months of age. The incidence of SIDS worldwide averages about 1.5 per 1,000 live births, and the syndrome is responsible for at least 7,000 infant deaths annually in the United States. Most such deaths occur in apparently healthy infants. The risk of SIDS is higher for male in-

fants than for females; higher in low-birthweight infants, particularly premature babies; higher in infants born to mothers who had used narcotic drugs during pregnancy; and higher in babies with recent respiratory infections, which may be related to the more frequent occurrence of SIDS that has been observed during the cold winter months.

Various neurophysiologic, metabolic, cardiorespiratory, endocrine, and immunologic disturbances have been suggested to explain SIDS. Recent research has shown pathologic changes consistent with chronically reduced oxygen levels in the blood, possibly related to failure—observed in some babies—of a fetal form of hemoglobin to switch over to normal hemoglobin A. In a small percentage of cases, an enzyme defect that prevents the infant body from metabolizing fat for the energy needed by the brain may be at fault. About 60% of SIDS victims die in respiratory failure, and 30% or more succumb to circulatory failure, so no single explanation applies to all cases.

---

cribbage Cribbage, a 17th-century card game, is scored on a board with 4 rows of 30 holes each, plus 2 or 4 holes (the game holes) at one end. Once around the board completes a 61-point game; twice around completes a 121-point game. To begin, 6 cards are dealt, alternately and face down, to the players, and the remaining cards are set aside until the hand is finished. Each player must decide which 4 cards to keep and which 2 to put aside, face down. The 4 discards become a third hand—the crib—which is added to the dealer's score when the hand ends.

The nondealer cuts the cards, then turns over the top card of the lower deck—the starter—and places it on top of the deck. The nondealer next places a card face up on the table and announces its value. The dealer then shows a card and announces the total count of the two cards. The nondealer plays the second card and announces the total of the three cards played so far. Play alternates in this manner until a card is played, bringing the total to 31, which entitles that player to peg 2 points. If a player cannot play a card without exceeding 31, this player says "go" and the opponent continues to play until 31 is reached or until play cannot proceed without exceeding 31. After a 31, or "go," is reached, the players complete the hand by playing their remaining cards, again alternately and with 31 as their aim.

Crick, Francis Francis Harry Compton Crick, b. June 8, 1916, English physicist and biochemist, collaborated with James D. WATSON and Maurice Wilkins to determine the molecular structure of DNA, or deoxyribonucleic acid, for which they shared the 1962 Nobel Prize for physiology or medicine.

After studying the early X-ray diffraction studies of Wilkins on biological macromolecules, Watson and Crick were convinced that nucleic acids were constructed as a helix (shaped like a spiral staircase). Working with the knowledge that chromosomes form replicas during cell division and that a chromosome was believed to be a string of DNA molecules, they concluded that the DNA molecule must form a replica of itself. By 1953, Watson and Crick had determined the structure of DNA—a complementary double helix—and published their work. They showed that each single helix of DNA served as a model for its complementary helix, and that the two resultant strains unwound from the double helix during replication of the cell. These extremely important findings opened the way to many advances in GENETICS.

Crick then studied how nucleotide sequences in DNA translate into amino acid sequences of a particular protein, working with other famous geneticists to try to break this GENETIC CODE. He also studied virus structure and bacterial viruses and later turned to brain research. Among his sometimes controversial writings are *Of Molecules and Men* (1966), *Life Itself* (1982), and *What Mad Pursuit* (1988).

Cricket equipment has been standardized in size, shape, and composition for almost 200 years. The bat's striking surface is almost flat; the other surface is a triangular wedge.

cricket (game)

cricket (game)   Cricket is a bat-and-ball, team game played during the summer in the British Isles and in several countries influenced by the British, such as Australia, New Zealand, India, Pakistan, Sri Lanka, South Africa, and West Indian nations.

Cricket is played between two teams of 11 players on a grassy field 122 to 152 m (400 to 500 ft) long and at least 68 m (225 ft) wide. In the center of the field, 20 m (66 ft) apart, are two wickets (see diagram above), each consisting of three stumps (wooden poles). Wooden bails lie in grooves on top of them. (The pitch area—see diagram below—is also sometimes referred to as the wicket.) The object of the defending team is for one player, the bowler, to throw the ball without bending the elbow and strike the wicket to dislodge the bails. The other team's batsman protects the wicket with a paddlelike bat and also tries to score runs.

One complete run through both teams' batting orders is an inning, and games, or matches, comprise one or two innings, determined beforehand. A single match may last several hours to several days.

The game starts with the defending team surrounding the wickets, some players close to the wickets, others in the outer portion of the field. One member of the other team stands at each wicket; the two players comprise a batting team. The bowler bowls from behind the bowling crease. If the batsman hits the ball, he or she can elect to run to the other wicket. In that case, both batsmen must run and reach the opposite wickets without being put out. If they are successful, one run is scored. They can continue to run between the wickets, scoring further runs, as long as they judge it to be safe. A great batsman may score more than 100 runs.

The two diagrams below illustrate a cricket pitch (left) and the positions taken by the fielders of the defending team on a cricket field (right). The fielding positions are chosen according to whether batsman and bowler are left-handed or right-handed. The area of the pitch is determined by the positioning of the two wickets and is marked at each end by whitewashed lines, or creases.

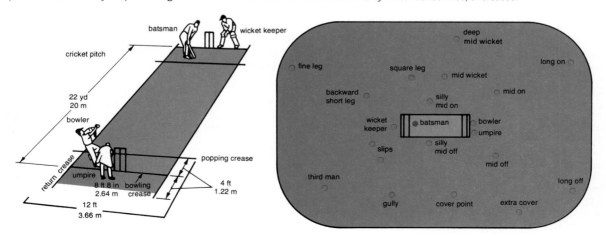

A batsman is put out if the bowled ball hits the wicket, if the hit ball is caught on the fly, if the fielder hits the wicket with the ball while the batsman is between wickets, or if a batsman's body obstructs the ball (a situation called "lbw," leg before wicket). The batter may hit the ball in any direction. If it is not intercepted and crosses the boundary of the field, the batter automatically scores 4 runs for a ball on the ground or 6 runs for a ball in the air. The bowling of 6 balls constitutes an over, at the end of which the fielding positions are reversed and the bowling resumes from the other end of the pitch—to the other batsman, unless a single run has just caused the batters to exchange wickets.

The rules of cricket, a complicated game, have evolved over several centuries. The game's exact origins are unknown, but in England it dates back to at least c.1300. International matches lasting 5 days are called "test matches," and the test between England and Australia, dating from 1882, is known as "the Ashes." In 1975 a World Cup series of 1-day matches, played every 4 years, was introduced.

An adult female house cricket is shown carrying a female nymph on its back. Peoples in various parts of the world believe that finding a cricket in the house is a sign of good luck.

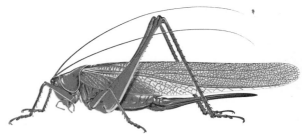

A great green cricket blends into surrounding foliage because of its green skin color and leaflike wings. It creates its familiar chirp by scraping a vein on its right forewing against its left forewing. This cricket lives in coastal areas of Europe.

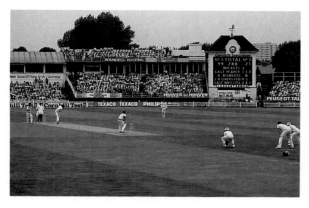

In this test match between England and the West Indies, the bowler has just released the ball toward the batsman in hopes of hitting his wicket. The batsman's job is twofold: to protect the wicket and to hit the ball in such a way that he and his batting partner can score runs.

Most crickets have a single annual generation. Eggs are laid in the autumn, usually overwinter in soil, then hatch out tiny nymphs that look like miniature adults. The nymphs eat leaves or roots and go through a series of molts until they reach the adult stage.

Crickets vary considerably. The best-known kinds are the dark, cylindrical field crickets often seen outdoors under boards and other debris. The house cricket enters houses in Europe and parts of the United States. Tree crickets are pale green and lay eggs in holes cut into twigs, thereby damaging trees. Mole crickets burrow with enlarged forelegs and are pests of vegetables in sandy soils.

cricket (insect)   The cricket is a slender, chirping, jumping insect closely related to grasshoppers and cockroaches. True crickets belong to the arthropod phylum, order Orthoptera, and are usually green or brown, with long antennae.

Most crickets have wings, and the males (and some females) "chirp" or "sing" by rapidly drawing a filelike structure on one forewing over a thickened vein on the opposing wing. Usually these sounds are made at night, although some crickets sing by day from dense vegetation. The sounds attract mates, and chirping males also defend territory, sometimes by physical combat. (Cricket fighting is a popular sport in the Orient.) Both sexes have auditory organs on their forelegs.

crime   In the broadest legal sense, a crime in most countries is an act committed in violation of a law forbidding it and for which a court may impose a variety of punishments including imprisonment, death, fine, or removal from office.

A fundamental categorization divides criminal acts into two classes, *mala in se* and *mala prohibita*. Some offenses, such as HOMICIDE, are considered to be "wrong in themselves" (*mala in se*) and inherently evil. On the other hand, *mala prohibita* offenses, such as drug abuse or gambling, are considered criminal because society seeks to regulate these particular types of behavior. Such offenses often drift in and out of the legal codes, their status determined by current public opinion.

Ideally, the punishment for crimes should be scaled according to the severity of the offenses. Murder, for example, is widely considered an offense meriting the death penalty—in which case it is called a capital offense—or life imprisonment. Some harmful offenses, however, do not bring so serious a punishment as others. White-collar offenses, despite the fact that they often involve large sums of money and affect great numbers of people, commonly bring shorter terms of imprisonment than do armed robbery or burglary. The reason for this disparity is often the social status of the offender: a bank president who has embezzled bank funds is not usually viewed as a common criminal.

The French sociologist Émile DURKHEIM considered crime to be a "normal" social phenomenon in the sense that it has existed in all societies throughout history. Durkheim felt that *mala prohibita* crimes function in society as a means of defining the limits of acceptable behavior, serving as a vehicle for social change by extending and testing those boundaries. Western society's present liberal attitudes toward sexual behavior, for example, have emerged out of an era when certain sexual acts were classified as criminal. Abortion provides another example of a shift in public perception of what constitutes a crime. In 1973 the U.S. Supreme Court (in ROE V. WADE) decriminalized abortion, declaring it instead to be a right guaranteed women under the Constitution. That decision would have been impossible 20 years earlier.

Criminal Intent

Once it has been established that a person has committed a criminal act, the law then questions the intent (MENS REA) of the actor, in effect inquiring whether the offender intended to cause harm by committing the act. The answer to this question helps to determine not only the question of guilt or innocence but also the severity of the punishment, if any.

Mens rea has played a major role in the development of the insanity defense (see INSANITY, LEGAL), which is derived from an 1843 English case in which a man named M'Naghten shot and killed a member of Parliament. M'Naghten was tried and acquitted because the jury found him not guilty by reason of insanity (NGRI). After a public protest, the judges of the Queen's Bench (an appeals court) formulated a standard to determine mental responsibility that became known as the M'Naghten Rule. It states that, in order to acquit, "It must be clearly proved that, at the time of committing the act, the party accused was laboring under such a defect of reason, from disease of the mind, as not to know the nature and quality of the act he was doing or, if he did know it, that he did not know it was wrong." The "right and wrong" test has become the basis for most legal statutes dealing with intent.

The insanity defense, however, has been controversial because it seems to offer a legal loophole that permits the obviously guilty to escape just punishment. Commitment to a mental institution is the most common result of the NGRI verdict, and—despite the fact that competency hearings that could result in release are required by law—persons so committed often serve longer sentences than their counterparts in penal institutions.

Certain states, such as Michigan, have abolished the insanity defense in favor of a plea of "guilty but insane," by which the court recognizes the mental deficiencies of the accused, and the accused accepts his or her legal responsibility for the act. Persons found to be "guilty but insane" receive sentences that include treatment in a mental hospital. If they are released as cured, the time during which they have received treatment is counted as part of their total sentence, which they must complete in prison.

Classification of Crime

The basic legal distinction between crimes is that separating felonies from misdemeanors. In general, a FELONY is a serious offense punishable by death or imprisonment in a state or federal facility. A MISDEMEANOR is a less serious act that is punishable by a fine or imprisonment for less than one year.

Another basic categorization of crime is based on criminological theory and is commonly used to detect patterns in the crime rate. This classification divides crime broadly into two categories: crimes against the person and crimes against property. Crimes against the person are predatory in nature: the offender intends, threatens, or commits physical harm against the victim. Such crimes include homicide, RAPE, and armed robbery. Crimes against property involve no physical threat, and include ARSON, BURGLARY, LARCENY, and auto theft.

These classifications do not, of course, cover all types of crime. Recently, criminologists have focused on crimes committed by the government in violation of the rights of citizens: wiretapping, police brutality, bribery, and conspiracies such as the Watergate crimes of the Nixon administration.

A related category of crime is the type that the U.S. criminologist Edwin H. Sutherland (1885–1950) termed "WHITE-COLLAR CRIME." Sutherland defined white-collar crimes as violations of the criminal law committed during the course of their occupational activities by persons of upper socioeconomic status. Such acts as EMBEZZLEMENT, price-fixing, industrial pollution, and computer fraud fall within this class. Sutherland held that these acts must be considered criminal—regardless of the status of the offender—because they are recognized by the law as harmful, often affect large numbers of victims, and are usually the result of willful and intentional behavior. Studies have estimated that white-collar crimes have a far greater financial impact on society than does any other type of crime.

A final category of crime is the victimless crime, which includes drunkenness, drug addiction, prostitution, and gambling. The use of the term *victimless* is an extremely qualified one. It refers to acts committed by consenting adults in private; the acts involve only the participants and are not harmful to others. If harm occurs, it is inflicted only upon the willing participants. Victimless crimes are often characterized by the exchange of sought-after goods and services, and they generate huge amounts of illegal income. It has been argued, however, that no crime is victimless. The drug addict suffers physical and emotional harm and often commits property crimes to obtain money for buying drugs. Prostitution and pornography damage property values, and their existence often breeds lawlessness and leads to other, more serious types of crime. Finally, the revenue gained by these acts is often funneled to ORGANIZED CRIME.

The term *organized crime* refers to a system of crime in which a group of individuals create and maintain a corporatelike organization, its members each having recognized responsibilities and obligations. Such criminal operations attempt to gain monopolistic control of certain types of criminal enterprises—the marketing of illegal drugs, for example—which are capable of generating large profits. These organizations often use the funds gained by criminal activities to take over legitimate businesses, and they routinely employ force and violence to maintain internal and external control. Although the mobs' enormous wealth has tended to protect their members from the law, convictions were obtained in three out of four major organized-crime trials held in New York in 1986–87. (See also MAFIA.)

Measuring the Extent of Crime

The development of accurate measures of crime has been the most difficult task faced by criminologists and those engaged in law enforcement. The oldest U.S. statistical analysis of certain types of crime is the Uniform Crime Report (UCR), which has been issued annually since 1930 by the Federal Bureau of Investigation. Individual law-enforcement agencies are responsible for the collection of the crime data assembled by the FBI. The statistics measure only "crimes known to the police." In order for a crime to be included in the UCR, it must have been reported to the police by the victim or a witness, or directly observed by the police themselves.

The best-known portion of the UCR is the Crime Index, in which eight major crime categories are listed: murder, rape, robbery, aggravated assault, burglary, larceny, motor vehicle theft, and arson. Data are also included on the age, sex, and race of persons arrested; the percentages of crimes that are "cleared by arrest"; and the rate of crime per 100,000 U.S. inhabitants.

Much criticism has been directed at the UCR statistics. The data, it is charged, are open to manipulation by law enforcement agencies that have a vested interest in demonstrating reduced crime rates or in obtaining more funds should crime rates be shown to have risen. Some doubt exists as to whether all the reporting agencies count the same offense in the same manner. Perhaps the most common complaint is that the figures change along with changing police practices. If a police agency were to concentrate on apprehending the sellers of stolen goods (or if citizens began to report all robbery or theft incidents), the number of Index crimes in those categories would rise sharply.

To counteract this problem, the U.S. Bureau of Justice Statistics issues the National Crime Survey (NCS), an an-nual report on household crime victimization based on census surveys rather than on individual complaints. It is believed that these interview/surveys give a more accurate picture of the amount of crime that occurs by uncovering unreported crimes.

Compared with other countries that keep crime statistics, the United States has the highest rate per 100,000 population for reported murders, rapes, and robberies. It is important to remember, however, that the incidence of crime is influenced by such factors as industrialization, urbanization, drug and alcohol abuse, unemployment, and the availability of firearms. The U.S. population possesses more firearms than any other population group and has an extremely high rate of alcohol and drug abuse. The effect of periods of high unemployment and the influence of television and movie representations of violence are issues that have not yet been definitively studied.

Criminology and the Causes of Crime

Criminology is the scientific study of crime and criminal behavior. Although there are several contemporary schools of criminological theory, they all share a common goal: the search for the causes of criminal behavior in the hope that this information can lead to policies that will be effective in handling or even eliminating crime.

The earliest criminologists were late-18th-century thinkers concerned with humanizing the highly arbitrary and harsh systems of criminal punishment of the time. The Italian economist Cesare Bonesana BECCARIA and the English philosopher Jeremy BENTHAM both emphasized the deterrent effect of punishment on potential criminals. The theory evolved by the classical school posits the existence of a rational humanity possessing free will whose primary motivation is to maximize pleasure and minimize pain. Classical theorists reasoned that if a rational person knows that a particular, painful punishment will almost certainly follow the commission of a particular crime, he or she will not commit the crime. This line of thought led to the attempt to establish elaborate categorical systems in which each crime had its punishment equivalent and which prefigured the fixed-term sentences that are increasingly imposed today. The belief that everyone has the capacity to make rational choices still influences the field of criminology.

A later influential body of criminological thought was the positivist school, founded in the late 19th century by the Italian psychiatrist and anthropologist Cesare Lombroso. Responding to the new evolutionary theories of Charles Darwin, Lombroso embarked on a detailed physiological study of convicts to determine if criminal behavior was biologically determined. Lombroso found that his convicts possessed certain physical characteristics to a greater degree than did the general population. Although his findings were later refuted, his use of the scientific method and his emphasis on the multiple environmental causes of crime had a great impact on criminology and the development of the ideal of rehabilitation. The biological approach pioneered by Lombroso is used today in such studies as the link between learning disabilities and crime, and the relationship between diet and assaultive behavior.

Twentieth-century criminologists have been profoundly influenced by the work of such sociologists as Durkheim; by the psychological theories of Sigmund Freud and his followers; and by the case-study approach inspired by Freud and first used by criminologists in the 1920s in work on juvenile delinquency, where possible environmental and genetic causes of criminal behavior were examined.

In the 1930s, Edwin H. Sutherland propounded his theory of differential association, which attributed the genesis of criminality to the social environment of the offender. Sutherland believed that criminal behavior is learned and that persons who live in a milieu that contains more criminals than law-abiding citizens are likely to become criminals themselves. This line of thought led Sutherland and his followers to believe that some transformation of the social structure is necessary in order to eliminate the root causes of crime.

Theorists of the radical, or Marxist, school of criminology believe that the ruling classes designate certain types of behavior as criminal in an attempt to secure the capitalist system. Thus, the criminal justice system is in their eyes largely a means to maintain the status quo by suppressing the proletariat. This school also calls for change in the social structure in order to eliminate crime.

Another social structural theory, labeling theory, relates to the manner in which criminal law is enforced and is primarily concerned with the explanation of JUVENILE DELINQUENCY and the commission of status offenses—that is, acts that are considered to be criminal if they are committed by a juvenile but are not considered criminal if committed by an adult. Running away, for example, is a status offense. Enforcement of the punishment for a status offense, it was found, could lead to a juvenile's committing further and more serious offenses. In effect, enforcement of the law created rather than prevented crime. This theory has influenced the decriminalization of most status offenses, although decriminalization has produced its own problems.

Control of Crime

Strategies for crime control and crime prevention have shifted over the years. Since the mid-19th century a major goal of U.S. CRIMINAL JUSTICE practices has been the rehabilitation of the prisoner. To this end, at the discretion of the trial judge, a convicted criminal has often received an indeterminate sentence under the terms of which he or she might be given an early release from prison, perhaps under the supervision of a PAROLE officer; or might, instead, be sentenced to PROBATION rather than imprisonment. In addition, the use of CAPITAL PUNISHMENT steadily declined in the United States; in a 1972 decision the Supreme Court banned its use under the then-existing state statutes, requiring instead (in 1976) laws that carefully defined what crimes merited capital punishment along with standardized judicial proceedings for imposing it. In more recent years, however, public attitudes toward crime and criminals have hardened, and in

1984, Congress ordered the drawing up of sentencing guidelines for judges in federal courts. Capital punishment is once again increasing.

The theoretical justifications for these changes emphasize the principles of retribution and deterrence in the punishments meted out to criminals. Retributionists assert that punishment functions as an expression of the desire of citizens to maintain social order and as a demonstration of social disapproval of criminal acts. They believe that swift and certain punishment prevents criminal behavior by warning potential offenders of the likely consequences of crime and by persuading the punished criminal not to repeat the crime.

A related theory, the doctrine of incapacitation, holds that it is not possible to rehabilitate criminals and therefore offenders should be incarcerated as long as possible. Further, if the greatest amount of serious crime is committed by repeat offenders (recidivists), then such a step should also reduce the crime rate. The theory implicitly assumes that there is a fixed supply of criminals.

Incapacitation and deterrence theories support the adoption of habitual offender laws, whereby persons who are convicted of a serious offense for a second or third time receive a harsher penalty than first offenders. Deterrence is the basis for laws such as California's "use a gun, go to prison" legislation, under which offenders convicted of a felony while using a firearm automatically draw a prison term.

There are no easy solutions to the problem of crime. Hard-line policies, such as determinate sentencing, are not cheap. They have aggravated overcrowded conditions in prisons and increased the already heavy costs of incarceration.

▬

Crime and Punishment   *Crime and Punishment* (1866), a psychological masterpiece by the Russian novelist Fyodor DOSTOYEVSKY, mixes such contemporary 19th-century themes as the anonymous, alienating power of society with the universal problems of crime, guilt, and redemption. Raskolnikov, an impoverished student in Saint Petersburg, kills and robs a grasping old woman pawnbroker, but his ostensible motives serve merely to introduce the author's exploration of the nature of justice and truth. Raskolnikov ultimately decides to accept punishment through his love for the young prostitute Sonya, whose life is one of suffering and remorse.

▬

Crimea   [kry-mee'-uh]   The Crimea is a peninsula on the north coast of the Black Sea, forming an oblast within Ukraine. Crimea covers an area of 27,000 km² (10,400 mi²) and has a population of 2,277,000 (1983 est.). The capital of the oblast is Simferopol, with a population of 333,000 (1986 est.). The peninsula is a flat plain that is bounded along the southeast coast by the Crimean Mountains, which rise to 1,545 m (5,068 ft).

Although the Crimea is administratively part of Ukraine, Russians are in the majority. Because of the pleasant climate, the population has been growing rapid-

(Left) The map indicates the location of the Crimea, a peninsula on the northern shore of the Black Sea in the Ukrainian Republic of the USSR. Its relatively warm climate, beaches, and pleasant scenery have made the Crimea a popular resort area.

CRIMEAN WAR

ly through inmigration. The principal cities, besides the capital city of Simferopol, are the naval base of SEVASTOPOL, the industrial city of Kerch, and the beach resorts of Yevpatoriya and Yalta. The Crimea has iron mines near Kerch and a chemical industry in the north. Fishing is an important industry. The principal crops are wheat in the northern steppe and grapes (for wine), fruits, and essential oils along the southeast coast.

Because of its exposed, strategic position, the Crimea has had a turbulent history. The south coast was colonized by the ancient Greeks, and the Hellenistic kingdom of the Cimmerian Bosporus existed from the 5th to the 2d century BC. The Turks seized the peninsula in 1475. Under Russian rule after 1783, it was the scene of the CRIMEAN WAR (1853–56). During the Soviet period, a Crimean autonomous republic was established, but during World War II the Crimean TATAR minority was accused of collaborating with the Germans, was exiled to Central Asia, and had its republic abolished. The Crimea was made an oblast in 1945.

Crimean War   The Crimean War of 1853–56 was one of a series of RUSSO-TURKISH WARS, but it differed from the others as a result of British and French involvement. Diplomatic concerns associated with the long-standing EASTERN QUESTION lay behind the conflict. Tsarist Russia continued to seek expansion of influence in the Balkans at the expense of the OTTOMAN EMPIRE. Britain, in turn, deemed the preservation of the Ottoman Empire vital for British imperial interests in the eastern Mediterranean and Asia. The worst prospect for British strategic and economic interests was Russian control of Constantinople and the Straits. France, under NAPOLEON III, supported Roman Catholic interests in the Holy Places of Turkish-controlled Palestine. Tsarist Russia, the patron of the Eastern Orthodox population in the Ottoman Empire, viewed French demands in Constantinople for greater concessions—specifically access to certain Christian shrines—as losses for the Orthodox.

Tensions increased during 1853 as Russia sought reassertion of its protectorship over the 12 million Orthodox subjects of the Ottoman Empire. Long negotiations failed to resolve the problems, and in early July, Russia occu-

pied the Danubian principalities of Moldavia and Walachia, then under Turkish jurisdiction. Turkey protested, and Britain and France ordered their fleets to the entrance of the Dardanelles. On November 3, the Russians destroyed the Turkish fleet at Sinope, and Britain and France declared war on Russia on Mar. 28, 1854. To divert the war from its borders, Austria ordered Russian evacuation of the principalities, to which Russia agreed, not wishing to face still another enemy. A joint Anglo-French-Turkish expedition was sent against the Russian fortress at SEVASTOPOL, on the tip of the Crimean peninsula.

Neither side distinguished itself during the war. Far more men died of disease than of battlefield wounds. The conflict introduced women in the important role of army nurses under the effective direction of Florence NIGHTINGALE. Alfred, Lord Tennyson's poem The CHARGE OF THE LIGHT BRIGADE recorded the blunders of the Battle of BALAKLAVA (Oct. 25, 1854) for future generations. The Battle of Inkerman (Nov. 5, 1854) was another costly victory for the allies.

At Balaklava a British light cavalry brigade made a heroic but senseless charge against Russian field artillery and lost over a third of its men. Despite the heavy losses, the Allies blocked the Russian attempt to break the siege of Sevastopol.

(Left) *Last-minute farewells are exchanged between British soldiers bound for the Crimean front and their wives in Henry Nelson O'Neill's* Eastward Ho *(1857). Popular support for the war waned as British casualties, resulting more from disease than from combat, increased.* (Right) *This Russian redoubt was overrun when the Allied forces captured Sevastopol in September 1855.*

The fall of Sevastopol in September 1855 and an Austrian threat to intervene forced Russia to yield to stiff peace demands incorporated in the Treaty of Paris (Mar. 30, 1856). Russia had to accept the demilitarization and neutralization of the Black Sea, thereby ensuring the continuation of British maritime dominance in the eastern Mediterranean. The Russians abandoned their claims to the exclusive protectorship over Balkan Christians; similarly, Russia's protectorate over the Danubian principalities and Serbia was replaced by a collective guarantee of the great powers. Finally, southern Bessarabia was returned to Moldavia, thus cutting off Russia's access to the important Danube River.

criminal justice   Criminal justice comprises all the means used to enforce those standards of conduct which are deemed necessary to protect individuals and to maintain general community well-being. In broad terms, a system of criminal justice creates the laws governing social behavior, attempts to prevent violations of the laws, and apprehends, judges, and punishes those who do violate them. Thus, criminal-justice systems typically have four components: the legislative arm to create laws, the POLICE to enforce the laws, the COURTS to determine if any laws have truly been broken and to prescribe penalties for illegal behavior, and the corrections system to administer penalties (see PRISON). In the United States these components do not form a "system" in any functionally organized sense. Rather they are embodied in a huge network of agencies scattered throughout various federal, state, county, and municipal governmental units. These agen-cies exercise broad discretionary powers in a decentralized, uncoordinated fashion, often competing with each other for scarce resources. By contrast, England and Wales have a centrally organized national police force, a single judicial hierarchy, and a national correctional system.

Criminal Laws and Courts. Criminal laws or codes define what types of conduct are criminal and establish penalties for such behavior. In the United States each state and territory is empowered to legislate its own criminal statutes, within the restrictions laid down by the U.S. Constitution, and to set the penalties for breaking them. There are approximately 17,000 state and local courts and 90 federal courts. About 90 percent of all criminal cases are under the jurisdiction of the minor, or lower, trial courts, which are generally empowered to hear MIS-DEMEANOR cases—crimes punishable by a maximum sentence of a fine or one year in jail. Major trial courts hear FELONY cases—more serious crimes punishable by a sentence of at least one year in a prison. (See CRIME for an analysis of the categories into which criminal acts fall.) Federal courts hear cases that involve constitutional issues, such as CIVIL RIGHTS, or offenses against federal laws, such as the banking laws.

Arrest and Bail Proceedings. When police officers have probable cause to believe that a certain individual has violated a law, they are legally empowered to make an arrest. (In some jurisdictions a GRAND JURY may be convened to determine whether there is probable cause and if an arrest should be made.) Arrested persons are generally taken into police custody until arraignment.

At the arraignment the charges are formally filed with the court and read to the defendant. The latter is informed of his or her rights (see MIRANDA V. ARIZONA) and furnished counsel if he or she does not already have it (see GIDEON V. WAINWRIGHT; LEGAL AID), and his or her plea is entered. With a plea of guilty, the defendant automatically waives the right to a trial and may be sentenced by a judge there and then. If the accused pleads not guilty, a trial date is set. The defendant may then be released on recognizance (that is, he or she signs an undertaking to appear at all court hearings), returned to custody to await trial, or released on the payment of a money or property bond called a BAIL bond. Bail is forfeited if the defendant does not appear at all appointed court hearings. Defendants may post the full amount of the bond themselves, obtain aid from family and friends, or purchase the services of a bail-bond agent. Bail-bond agents post the full amount of the bond in exchange for a nonrefundable fee, usually 10 percent of the bond.

The bail privilege may be withheld from persons accused of murder or treason. Reformers suggest that it also be withheld from those judged to be violent or habitual criminals and those who would be likely to commit new crimes if released. Frequently, a judge will set bail at a very high figure, effectively denying the bail privilege.

Plea Bargaining. More than 90 percent of all criminal cases never reach the formal trial stage. They are adjudicated by way of guilty pleas in a process known as PLEA BARGAINING, which involves negotiations among the prosecutor, the defendant, and the defendant's counsel that lead to the defendant's entering a guilty plea in exchange for a reduction in charges or the prosecutor's promise to recommend a more lenient sentence. The process may take place at the arraignment, at the preliminary hearing—if there is one—or during the TRIAL itself. A defendant who plea-bargains and pleads guilty may not receive the trial to which he has a constitutional right. Guilty pleas, however, do relieve the courts, which could not possibly handle the trials of all accused persons. Prosecutors are often willing to accept plea bargaining, particularly when the case against a defendant rests on weak evidence or less than credible witnesses, and a trial may therefore result in an acquittal.

If the defendant is charged with a felony, a preliminary hearing, a formal examination of the evidence by the court, may be held as part of the trial process. If the judge determines that there is probable cause to believe that a criminal act was committed, the case is bound over for trial. If probable cause is found to be lacking, the defendant may be released, although he or she is not protected against further prosecution for alleged criminal activity arising from the incident for which the arrest was made.

Trial and Appeal. The Constitution provides the right to a trial by JURY in all cases punishable by more than six months of imprisonment. The defendant, however, may request a trial by a judge.

A verdict of guilty does not end a defendant's legal recourse, for a new trial may be requested from the original trial court, or the case may be appealed to a higher court. In most jurisdictions a defendant has the right to at least one APPEAL, the result of which may be either the sustaining of the original trial ruling or a reversal of the decision and the ordering of a new trial. If a constitutional violation of personal rights is claimed, the case may enter the federal-court system, but only after all state-court appellate opportunities have been exhausted.

Sentencing. With the indeterminate sentence, which has been the predominant sentencing form in the United States for more than a century, minimum and maximum penalties for every criminal category have been established by each state, and judges are given the power to select sentences within those extremes as specific case circumstances require. Some states permit sentences to exceed or fall short of the mandated limits if there are unique circumstances surrounding a particular case. Concern with documented cases of abuse of this discretionary power has led many states to tighten control over the sentencing process through the adoption of various forms of determinate sentencing, whereby sentences are definitively fixed by state statute for each type of criminal offense.

The decision to grant PROBATION is made by the judge and is usually based on the report of an investigating official, which includes information on the defendant's previous criminal record and other factors indicating the probability of his or her rehabilitation.

Criminal Justice in Other Western Countries. U.S. and English law are derived from the same body of COMMON LAW, and thus many similarities exist between the two systems of criminal justice. Both systems grant the rights to counsel and to a public trial by jury. The English system, however, more severely limits rights to appeal conviction and more often practices preventive detention by refusing bail. Newspapers and other media are severely restricted in the information they may publish about ongoing trials, in order to assure defendants' privacy until a verdict is obtained and to protect juries from possible prejudicing.

In the countries of continental Europe, whose legal systems are based on CIVIL LAW, the most striking difference in criminal justice practices lies in the investigation process. Responsibility for case investigations usually rests with the judge, who—with the assistance and cooperation of the suspect—clarifies disputed facts and plays a key role in determining whether a case should be prosecuted. Trials are held before a judicial tribunal from which rights to appeal are limited. Trial by jury is no longer practiced in Germany, France, and the Netherlands. Other civil-law countries use juries only for cases of major crimes or for political crimes against the state.

Trial by jury—except for occasional petty criminal cases—does not exist in Communist countries. In the USSR, cases are usually tried before a bench composed of one professional and two lay judges, and decisions are reached by majority vote. Most criminal cases are tried in people's courts, which are the lowest regularly sitting city or county tribunals.

criminology   see CRIME

crinoid [kry'-noyd]   Crinoids, a form of ECHINODERM, are invertebrate marine animals having a cuplike enclosing sac, or theca, at the end of a narrow stem. Branching arms growing from the theca gather food from the surrounding water and expose soft tissue for respiration. The stem, rooted to the seafloor, is about 0.6 m (2 ft) long in some modern animals. Modern crinoids also include floating animals without stems. The FOSSIL RECORD of these creatures extends back to the Cambrian Period, but stemmed crinoids nearly became extinct by the end of the Paleozoic Era (see GEOLOGIC TIME; EXTINCTION). Modern forms include feather stars and sea lilies; in the mid-1980s a stemmed crinoid (subclass Inadunata) thought to have been long extinct was found in the Indian Ocean.

Cripps, Sir Stafford   Richard Stafford Cripps, b. Apr. 24, 1889, d. Apr. 21, 1952, a British political leader, was responsible for the economic reconstruction of Britain immediately after World War II. Although a radical socialist in the 1930s, Cripps was appointed ambassador to the USSR (1940–42) and lord privy seal and minister of aircraft production (1942–45) in the war cabinet. As president of the Board of Trade (1945–47) and then minister of economic affairs and chancellor of the exchequer (1947–50) in the postwar Labour government, he instituted a program of tight economic controls that earned him the nickname "Austerity Cripps."

Remembered chiefly for his economic austerity program while chancellor of the exchequer (1947–50) in Britain's postwar Labour government, Sir Stafford Cripps was earlier known as a Labour rebel. He served (1929–31) as solicitor general but was expelled (1939) from the party for his radicalism.

Crispi, Francesco   Francesco Crispi, b. Oct. 4, 1819, d. Aug. 12, 1901, was a Sicilian politician and premier of Italy. During the RISORGIMENTO he first supported the republican movement for Italian unification led by Giuseppe Mazzini. He organized an abortive uprising in Sicily in 1848, and in 1860 he helped Giuseppe Garibaldi overthrow the Bourbon monarchy of the Two Sicilies. Later, he gave up republicanism and accepted national unification under the house of Savoy.

A leader of the parliamentary left, Crispi was twice premier (1887–91 and 1893–96). He became increasingly repressive and embarked on a policy of imperialism in Africa. His government fell after a humiliating Italian defeat by Ethiopian forces at Adowa on Mar. 1, 1896.

cristobalite [kris-toh'-buh-lyt]   Cristobalite, a form of QUARTZ stable only at high temperatures, has the crystal structure of most other SILICA MINERALS. Cross-linkage of SiO_4 units yields isometric (high temperature) or tetragonal (lower temperature) crystals. The crystals, which are colorless or white, form from alteration of volcanic glass, such as OBSIDIAN, and are also found in meteorites and lunar rocks.

critical constants   The critical constants of a substance are its critical temperature, T_c; critical pressure, P_c; and critical volume, V_c. All describe the substance at its critical point—the temperature above which the substance, in its gaseous phase, cannot be liquefied no matter how much pressure is applied. This temperature is the critical temperature; the pressure required to liquefy the gas at this temperature is the critical pressure; and the volume that one mole of gas would occupy at critical temperature and critical pressure is the critical volume.
See also: PHASE EQUILIBRIUM.

critical mass   see CHAIN REACTION; FISSION, NUCLEAR

criticism, literary   The term *literary criticism,* broadly used today to encompass any discourse on literature, includes three distinguishable but overlapping fields of inquiry—literary history, literary theory, and evaluative criticism. In literary history, literature is viewed as part of a historical process. In literary theory, or poetics, an attempt is made to describe the principles of literature, its GENRES, and its techniques and functions. Literary criticism in the narrow sense of evaluative criticism concerns the study and analysis of specific works and their authors. This judgmental role is often singled out as the particular task of literary criticism and is a view sanctioned by the etymology of the term, which is derived from the Greek *krinein,* "to judge." The term *kritikos* as "a judge of literature" originated as early as the end of the 4th century BC.
  History of Criticism. Although literary questions are formally discussed in many of the dialogues of PLATO, the *Poetics* of ARISTOTLE is the fundamental text of literary criticism. In the *Poetics,* Aristotle defined the aim of literature as imitation (*mimesis*). He describes the form and plot of certain Greek tragedies and alludes to the effect of tragedy as "purgation." He pays no attention to the author. LONGINUS's treatise *On the Sublime* speaks, rather, of the soul, the greatness of the author, as the standard of literature. These two treatises, and the rather casual verse epistle of HORACE, the *Art of Poetry,* are the source of the dictum that literature should both please and instruct. Although the tradition of Roman rhetoric and the craft of making verses was alive during the Middle Ages, the an-

cient authors were not rediscovered until the Renaissance, when the doctrine known as NEOCLASSICISM took form.

Several stages occurred in the development of this doctrine: an early reliance on the authority of the ancients, a plea for identifying the principles of the ancients with the voices of reason, and an increasing reliance on taste, conceived to be that of an educated elite. Broadly speaking, however, no great change took place; neoclassicism, the critical doctrine that culminates in the works of Samuel JOHNSON during the late 18th century, is derived from Renaissance theory.

The classical system was dissolved during the second half of the 18th century by a new historical sense. Particularly in Germany, as demonstrated in the works of Johann Gottfried von HERDER and the two SCHLEGEL brothers, the classical tradition was rejected in favor of a view of each work as a product of its time and place. In this view, criticism can be used to understand a work and surrender to its particular beauty; it cannot be used to judge literature by an eternal standard. Immanuel KANT formulated a compromise: taste, he grants in the *Critique of Judgment* (1790), is individual, but it claims universality and appeals to common sense.

In the 19th century the historical view triumphed despite many attempts to anchor judgment in new principles. Samuel Taylor COLERIDGE tried to distinguish critically between fancy and imagination. Others, such as William HAZLITT, relied on their personal reactions and developed procedures that have been called impressionistic. Walter PATER advanced an aesthetic movement advocating art for its own sake. Most theorists, however, tried to give a causal explanation of the course of literature. The approach of Hippolyte Adolphe TAINE, for example, which looked for a milieu, a moment, and a race (or nation), was most influential. MARXISM, proponents of which look for economic and social causes, is in the same tradition.

The 20th century has been an era of enormous expansion and diversity in literary criticism. Italy, the USSR, and the United States have played increasingly significant roles. Totally new methods have been developed from related disciplines. Marxist criticism, which prevailed in Eastern Europe, found many adherents in the West. Freudian psychoanalysis was applied to literature. Carl JUNG's speculations on archetypes in the collective unconscious inspired a search for myths in all literature. A new and rigorous stylistic criticism has developed under the influence of modern linguistics. A psychological and anthropological approach has been taken by Northrop FRYE, who attempts to trace similarities in the literary patterns of different cultures. In Russia and later in Czechoslovakia a new, formal study of literature called STRUCTURALISM has flourished and has had an impact in both France and the United States. A form of philosophical criticism that draws its inspiration from EXISTENTIALISM has had a great impact. Spokesmen of MODERNISM such as T. S. ELIOT in England and Paul VALÉRY in France have profoundly altered taste.

Methods of Criticism. The methods of criticism vary with its functions. Literary works may be described mere-

ly to communicate some idea of their content or effect, but critics also interpret a work and develop the tools to do so. They analyze sound patterns and meters; styles; devices such as metaphors, character, and plot; and the ideas that emerge from the work. They analyze tone and any particular individuality that can be evoked or defined. Interpretation leads finally to a decision about artistic merit and often to judgments about the moral, political, religious, or philosophical implications of a work.

True to the traditional pattern, most modern critics do not see a work in complete isolation; they study it in relation to its presumed causes or at least its antecedents. Since the author is the most obvious cause, the author's life, personality, psychology, and experiences are the concern of biographical criticism. Critics who engage in historical criticism look for the antecedents of writings in the history of literature. They study a work in the tradition of a specific genre or form even if it revolts against its predecessors. Finally, critics may study the social setting of an author's works. They trace the author's roots and contacts in a specific society, time, or locale. They relate the works to trends in the other arts, to philosophy, theology, politics, economics, and other human activities. In *Essays in the History of Ideas* (1948), for example, Arthur O. Lovejoy (1873–1962) integrates philosophy and literature in a study of intellectual history.

Study has increasingly been devoted to the effect of literature on society. The almost endless questions bring out clashes of views that have been debated throughout history. Some of these debates are still unsettled. For instance, the question about the nature of literature has been answered either by considering literature as an art that induces aesthetic enjoyment and contemplation or by considering literature as communication, in no way different from the ordinary functions of language. The New Critics (see NEW CRITICISM), including Cleanth BROOKS and Robert Penn WARREN, say that literary works should be examined autonomously by close textual reading. Another question in any theory of criticism is that of subjectivity versus objectivity. The subjective view is that all criticism is just airing of personal opinions. The objective view is that absolute standards, or at least determinants in the text, exist to which the critic must adhere.

The variety of voices today is so great that the situation has been compared with the Tower of Babel, with its mutually incompatible languages. Never before has there been such a ferment in criticism, and critics have never before attracted so much attention and fervent loyalty. (See DECONSTRUCTION for an example of a recent school of criticism that has received notice well beyond academia.) Indeed, some scholars argue that this is the age of criticism, since literary critics now often function not only as specialists in literature but also as general critics of society and civilization.

See also: AESTHETICISM; AESTHETICS; CLASSICISM; DECADENCE.

Critique of Pure Reason   The *Critique of Pure Reason* (1781), a philosophical treatise by the German philosopher Immanuel KANT (1724–1804), is perhaps the single most influential work of modern philosophy. In it, Kant attempted to reconcile the opposing views of RATIONALISM and EMPIRICISM. Like the empiricists, Kant argued that knowledge is limited to that which can be experienced (the world of phenomena); but he also maintained, along with the rationalists, that pure reason is necessary to make order out of knowledge. Thus, whatever order the individual finds in the universe is really only that which is imposed on it by the human reasoning capacity itself. NOUMENA (things-in-themselves), however, remain forever unknowable.

Crittenden Compromise [krit'-uhn-duhn]

On Dec. 18, 1860, two days before South Carolina became the first state to secede from the Union, Sen. John J. Crittenden (1787–1863) of Kentucky offered several constitutional amendments in an unsuccessful last-ditch effort to stave off the split between slave and free states. Crittenden proposed amendments permanently to permit and protect slavery south of the MISSOURI COMPROMISE line of 36°30' and permanently to bar slavery north of that line. He also proposed enforcement of the FUGITIVE SLAVE LAW and federal compensation to slave owners losing slaves because of the actions of Northerners.

Crittenden's proposals had the backing of some moderates, especially those in border states who were aware that war would ravage their region. However, the compromise failed to win strong support from either North or South. President-elect Abraham LINCOLN refused to consider any arrangement that would open new territory to slavery. The measure quickly failed, and secession and Civil War soon followed.

Cro-Magnon man [kroh'-mag'-nuhn]

Cro-Magnon man is the name given a well-known population of prehistoric humans who lived in late Pleistocene times. Skeletal remains of this type were first discovered in 1868 when some road builders, working in Dordogne department, southern France, accidentally opened a prehistoric rock shelter. Stone tools and ancient hearths were found beside human bones at the site.

Since the discovery at Cro-Magnon, additional human skeletons have been found at a number of European sites. The human remains do not differ significantly from those discovered at Cro-Magnon, so this name is now generally employed in referring to all such anatomically modern humans found in Europe and the Middle East, from their rather sudden appearance about 40,000–30,000 years ago to the end of the Pleistocene Epoch, some 10,000 years ago.

In contrast to the earlier NEANDERTHALERS, the Cro-Magnons, who are classified as *Homo sapiens sapiens*, possessed such modern human features as higher, more vertical foreheads, indicating a modern configuration of the frontal lobes of the brain, reduced brow ridges, small-

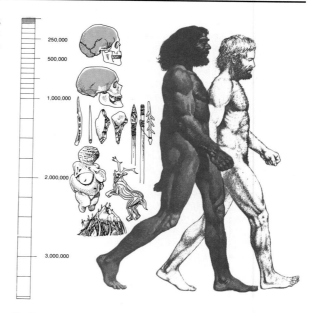

The first representatives of modern Homo sapiens are known as Cro-Magnon man, named for the cave in France where their fossil remains were discovered in 1868. Various Cro-Magnon populations of seminomadic tool-making hunters inhabited parts of Europe, Asia, and North Africa from about 50,000 to 10,000 BC. The comparative illustration—based on reconstructed skulls and skeletal remains—suggests that the Cro-Magnons closely resembled modern humans; Cro-Magnon man was slightly taller and had broader facial features.

er faces and teeth, and a chin. The anatomy of these early modern humans was not identical, however, to that of present Europeans in all respects. Their skeletons show greater muscularity, suggesting they were employed in much more strenuous activities than those of most modern peoples, and among the skeletal finds skull features vary considerably.

Far more is known about the culture of the early Cro-Magnons than about any other prehistoric humans. Beautifully made stone tools as well as artifacts of bone and wood belonging to the Upper Paleolithic AURIGNACIAN, PERIGORDIAN, and Magdalenian traditions have been identified from numerous sites in Europe.

The efficiency of Cro-Magnon hunting methods is reflected in the vast numbers of animal bones piled up at some of the sites. At Solutré in France, for example, the remains of more than 10,000 horses have been found, and at Dolní Věstonice in Czechoslovakia, a large number of bones from extinct mammoths litter the site.

The numerous Cro-Magnon burial sites that have been found reveal that these groups, like the preceding Neanderthalers, engaged in various ritual activities. Objects of ivory and shell sometimes adorned the ochre-stained bodies of the deceased, who were often buried in mass graves. Moreover, with the advent of the Cro-Magnon people, the first examples of PREHISTORIC ART—cave paintings and engravings—appeared in the Old World.

The Venus of Laussel (c.21,000 BC), a relief carving of a faceless female figure, was discovered in a Cro-Magnon rock shelter in southern France. Its exaggerated sexuality led anthropologists to suggest that the figure may represent a fertility goddess.

Croatia [kroh-ay'-shuh]   Croatia, the traditional homeland of the Slavic people called Croats, is one of the six constituent republics of Yugoslavia and has a population of 4,679,000 (1988 est.). Occupying the western part of the country, Croatia covers 56,537 km² (21,829 mi²), and also includes the historic regions of DALMATIA, most of ISTRIA, and Slavonia. Much of northern Croatia is a flat plain, drained by the SAVA and Drava rivers, tributaries of the Danube. In the south, the DINARIC ALPS, reaching about 1,500 m (4,900 ft), border the Adriatic Sea coast. ZAGREB is Croatia's capital and largest city.

An important industrial republic, Croatia has textile, chemical, food-processing, and petroleum-refining industries, located primarily in the cities of DUBROVNIK, RIJEKA, SPLIT, and ZADAR, as well as Zagreb. Tourism is important to the economy, especially along the coast. Croatia is Yugoslavia's leading producer of coal. The most fertile agricultural land is located in the northeast, on the Pannonian plain.

The Croats are mostly Roman Catholic, unlike their

This illustration of life in a Cro-Magnon camp is based on evidence unearthed at Ostrava-Petřkovice in Moravia. The camp existed during the Paleolithic Period (Old Stone Age) more than 25,000 years ago. The Cro-Magnon hunters who inhabited the site were tool-making nomads whose existence depended on their prowess in stalking native reindeer and mammoths. The tribesman (foreground) *carving a talisman is especially significant; the earliest examples of prehistoric art are of Cro-Magnon origin. Cave paintings and sculptures from other Cro-Magnon sites suggest that sewn animal skins were worn. Shelters at Ostrava-Petřkovice consisted of conical tents that could be dismantled and transported as the hunters moved on. These tents were probably fashioned from animal hides and were buttressed against the elements with bones and tusks.*

Croatia, located in northwest Yugoslavia, is the second largest of Yugoslavia's six constituent republics and the country's most industrialized republic.

closely related neighbors, the Serbs, who are Eastern Orthodox. The Croats speak Serbo-Croatian, writing it with Roman characters, rather than Cyrillic characters as the Serbs do.

The Croats settled the region during the 7th century and established an independent kingdom during the 10th century. They were, however, conquered in turn by the Hungarians (1091), Turks (1526), and Austrians (1849). Before the creation of Yugoslavia following World War I, the Croats were the most prosperous of the South Slavs. Subsequently overshadowed by the Serbs, some Croats have launched a vigorous nationalist movement, demanding independence from Yugoslavia.

See also: BALKANS.

Croce, Arlene [kroh'-chay]   Arlene Croce, b. Providence, R.I., May 5, 1934, the dance critic for the *New Yorker*, is perhaps the most rigorous and widely respected dance critic in the United States. After writing film criticism for various specialty journals in the United States

and abroad, she founded *Ballet Review* in 1965, serving as its editor until 1978. She had written extensively for this journal and for the English *Dancing Times* (1969–71) before joining the *New Yorker* in 1973.

Croce, Benedetto   Benedetto Croce, b. Feb. 22, 1866, d. Nov. 20, 1952, was an Italian philosopher, critic, and historian. Independently wealthy, he lived and studied privately in Naples. An interest in Karl MARX led to a long collaboration with the idealist Giovanni GENTILE. Croce was minister of education (1920–21), but the advent of Fascism, which he attacked, brought his retirement from public life and ended his association with Gentile.

Croce's masterwork, translated into English as *Philosophy of Spirit*, consists of four volumes: *Aesthetics* (1902), *Logic* (1905), *Philosophy of the Practical* (1909), and *History: Its Theory and Practice* (1917). He held that there is a universal human spirit, which is fourfold: intuitive, conceptual, vital, and moral. Intuition appears in artistic activity, and conceptual thought probes history. Vitality displays itself in legal, economic, and scientific systems, and morality allows humans to realize themselves as free moral individuals. According to Croce, history displays the realizations of humans' theoretical grasp (art and history) in practical activities (law, economics, science, and ethics).

crochet [kroh-shay']   Crochet (from the French *crocheter*, "to hook") is a needlecraft that probably originated in 18th-century France from a type of chain-stitch embroidery called tambour work. Once used only for

All stitches of crochet needlework are based on the simple chain stitch shown here. The yarn is knotted and the crochet hook is inserted through the knot (far left). The yarn is held with one hand while the other works the hook to catch the loose yarn and draw it back through the original knot (left), to form two loops (right). This step continues until a chain of the desired length is formed (far right). To form the single crochet stitch, the hook is inserted in the second loop from the end of the chain (far left). The loose yarn is hooked and drawn through each individual loop of the previously formed chain (left). This is repeated (right) until the end of the chain is reached. To form the second row, it is necessary to chain one stitch (far right) before continuing to interlock the yarn as before.

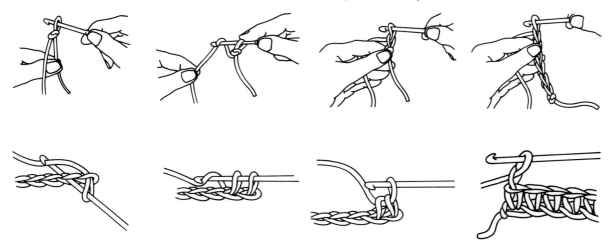

making decorative edgings and lace imitations, the technique is now also used to make complete garments. In crocheting, a hook is used to draw individual loops through previously made loops, and each new loop locks the preceding one in place. Crochet stitches range from simple loops to complex and ornate configurations and are worked in back-and-forth rows or in rounds to create a fabric.

American politician and adventurer Davy Crockett served (1827–31; 1833–35) in the U.S. Congress, but his place in American history is as a folk hero rather than as a political figure. His legendary status was assured as much by his own tales of backwoods adventure as by his heroic death (1836) at the Alamo.

Crockett, Davy   Davy Crockett, b. Limestone, Tenn., Aug. 17, 1786, d. Mar. 6, 1836, was one of America's most colorful frontiersmen and folk heros. Coming from a poor pioneer family, he received no real education as a child but picked up the skills of a hunter, scout, and woodsman. He served (1813–14) under Andrew Jackson in the wars against the Creek Indians. After returning to Tennessee to farm, he was appointed (1817) a local magistrate, an office that required him to learn to read and write more proficiently. Elected a "colonel" in the militia, he also served two terms (1821–25) in the Tennessee legislature and defended the squatter rights of his west Tennessee constituents.

As a U.S. congressman (1827–31, 1833–35), Crockett won a reputation as an amusing, shrewd, and outspoken backwoodsman, and it was in Washington that the legend of the man as a coonskin-hatted bear hunter, Indian fighter, and tall-tale teller was promoted by his Whig allies to compete with President Jackson's image as a democrat. Crockett's opposition to Jackson's Indian-removal policies estranged him from the Democratic party, and this disagreement cost him his fourth bid for election in 1834. His bitterness over the defeat inspired him to leave (1836) Tennessee for Texas, where he died defending the ALAMO during the TEXAS REVOLUTION.

crocodile   Crocodiles are large amphibious reptiles related to ALLIGATORS, CAIMANS, and GAVIALS. They are dis-tinguished by a notch at the side of the snout that exposes the elongate fourth tooth of the lower jaw, thus giving a crocodile's face its typical expression. Crocodiles are found in tropical Africa, Australia, and Asia; in the islands of the western Pacific Ocean; and in the tropical parts of North and South America. The range of the American crocodile extends from the southern tip of Florida to tropical South America.

The smallest species is the broad-fronted, or dwarf, crocodile, *Osteolaemus tetraspis*, of West Africa, which seldom exceeds lengths of 1.5 m (5 ft); the largest is probably the saltwater crocodile, *Crocodylus porosus*, of southeastern Asia, with a length of up to 6 m (20 ft), although some reports give up to 9 m (30 ft). Several species, including the American and the Nile crocodiles, are known to have also reached lengths of up to 6 m (20 ft) and to weigh a ton or more.

Crocodiles swim or float on the surface of the water, exposing only their eyes, nostrils, flat tail, and webbed toes. A fleshy valve in the throat allows them to open their mouths in the water without choking. The nostrils and ears can also be closed to keep out water. Besides the normal upper and lower eyelids, crocodiles have a transparent third eyelid, the nictitating membrane, which allows them to see underwater. Crocodiles swim by moving their tails.

Most crocodiles hunt at night and bask during the day; hungry crocodiles hunt during the day as well. Generally, they feed on other vertebrate animals. Crocodiles vary among species in the prey they prefer. Some broad-fronted crocodiles typically feed on frogs, birds, and small

The crocodile family includes crocodiles (top), alligators, caimans, and gavials, all of which are aquatic and carnivorous. The American alligator (A) differs from the African crocodile (B), by having a wider snout. A gavial (C), a small member of the crocodile family, which is found in India, has an extremely long, narrow snout. Caimans (not shown) are small South American reptiles that resemble most closely the alligators.

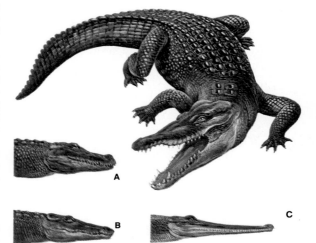

mammals, whereas specialized narrow-snouted crocodiles feed primarily on fish. Such large species as the saltwater crocodile and the Nile crocodile often catch large animals—for example, antelopes, deer, and hogs—and are known to attack humans.

The female crocodile lays her eggs in nests made of vegetation or in sand banks and remains with them until the heat of the Sun causes them to hatch about three months later. It is believed that she digs up the young when they begin to call and either carries them in her mouth or leads them to the water.

Crocodiles originated during the late Triassic Period, 200 million years ago. During the Cretaceous Period, about 120 million years ago, crocodiles existed that were so large—12 m (40 ft) or more—that they may have preyed on dinosaurs.

Crocodiles belong to the family Crocodylidae, order Crocodylia. The 11 species that exist today belong to three genera: *Tomistoma*, the false gavial of the Malaya Peninsula, Sumatra, and western Borneo; *Osteolaemus*, the broad-fronted crocodile of West Africa; and *Crocodylus* (nine species), the true crocodile. Several species of crocodile, including the American crocodile, *C. acutus*, are in danger of extinction, their existence threatened by habitat loss and hide hunters.

crocus   *Crocus* is the generic name of hardy, corm-forming herbs belonging to the iris family, Iridaceae. The genus comprises about 80 species native to the Mediterranean region and to Southwest Asia. They are grown primarily as ornamentals for their brightly colored, usually single flowers, ranging from yellow through lavender and blue to white. (The species *Crocus sativus* is also cultivated because its stigmas yield SAFFRON, an important food dye and flavoring.) Crocuses may be divided into two main groups, spring-flowering and fall-flowering, of which the former are the more popular because they appear early in spring, before most other flowers.

Crocus neapolitanus, a variant of the Dutch crocus, is a popular perennial herb that is a traditional harbinger of spring. It is frequently planted in a naturalistic setting.

Croesus, King of Lydia [kree'-suhs]   Croesus, d. 546 BC, was the last king of LYDIA. He succeeded his father, Alyattes, about 560. Famous for his great wealth gained by trade, he instituted the first official government coinage. After capturing Ephesus and other Ionian cities, Croesus tried to limit the growing strength of Persia but was attacked and eventually captured by CYRUS THE GREAT. According to legend, Croesus either was thrown or threw himself on a burning pyre but was saved by Apollo. He apparently survived to become an official at the Persian court.

Crohn's disease   Crohn's disease, or regional ENTERITIS, is one form of the severe and potentially fatal chronic disorder called inflammatory bowel disease (see COLITIS). Crohn's disease mainly affects the wall of the small intestine but can occur anywhere along the digestive tract. The inflammation causes episodes of pain, diarrhea, constipation, and appetite loss and may lead to problems such as mouth sores, arthritis, and liver, skin, or eye damage. Internal bleeding and other results may require surgical intervention. The cause of the disorder remains unknown. Because the symptoms resemble those of other conditions, Crohn's disease is sometimes hard to diagnose. Drug treatments include steroids and sulfasalazine. Both can have serious side effects.

Crome, John   John Crome, b. Norwich, England, Dec. 22, 1768, d. Apr. 22, 1821, was a founder of the Norwich school of watercolorists. He was often called "Old Crome" to distinguish him from his son, John Berney Crome. He became a drawing teacher in the Norwich schools and soon was surrounded with numerous disciples.

In addition to WATERCOLORS, Crome painted in oils and etched. His watercolors usually consist of drawings in pencil or chalk with color added in simple, muted washes, although some of his later work is stronger. He considered his pleasing etchings to be mere studies. His oil landscapes are now considered to be among the more powerful and original works of the period, and are admired for their effective color and economy of composition.

Cromer, Evelyn Baring, 1st Earl of   Evelyn Baring, 1st earl of Cromer, b. Feb. 26, 1841, d. Jan. 29, 1917, was a British administrator in Egypt. He first served (1877–80) in Egypt as a commissioner of the public debt and then as controller general. When he returned as British consul general in 1883, the presence of a British occupation force made him de facto ruler of Egypt. Cromer instituted substantial administrative reforms, fostered economic development, and inaugurated joint Anglo-Egyptian rule of the Sudan after British reconquest of that area (1898). Retiring (1907) to England, he wrote *Modern Egypt* (1908) and other works.

cromlech   see MEGALITH

Oliver Cromwell, who ruled England, Scotland, and Ireland under the Republican Commonwealth and Protectorate (1649–58), rose to prominence as a parliamentarian general during the English Civil War. He was among the first European leaders to proclaim religious toleration, although his regime was marked by considerable repression.

Cromwell, Oliver   Oliver Cromwell, b. Huntingdon, Apr. 25, 1599, d. Sept. 3, 1658, was one of the most important figures in British history, a great general, and lord protector of the Commonwealth, or republic, of England, Scotland, and Ireland for five years. Elected to Parliament in 1628, Cromwell made his mark by attacking the bishops of the Church of England, and in 1640 he was chosen to represent Cambridge in the Long Parliament. Once again he attacked the bishops, urging their total abolition and advocating purification of the church by abandoning the Book of Common Prayer and instituting more sermons.

As war between King Charles I and Parliament approached, Cromwell raised a cavalry regiment (called the Ironsides) at Huntingdon. In the English Civil War, after winning most of East Anglia for Parliament, Cromwell was appointed lieutenant general and helped defeat the royalists in the Battle of Marston Moor (1644). In 1645 he took part in the decisive victory at Naseby and, as second in command to Sir Thomas Fairfax, took Oxford in 1646, thus ending the first civil war. When the largely Presbyterian Parliament quarreled with its army, Cromwell, himself an Independent (congregationalist), sided with the sectarian soldiers. After defeating the Scots, who had allied with the king, at Preston in 1648, he decided that Charles was responsible for renewing the civil war and pressed for his trial and execution.

During 1649–51, Cromwell fought successfully in Ireland and Scotland, replacing Fairfax as commander in chief in 1650. When he perceived that the Rump Parliament (the remnant of the Long Parliament) was not pressing on with the reform of the church and state and was antagonistic to the army, he forcibly dissolved it (1653). Subsequently, a written constitution, the Instrument of Government, was drawn up by a group of army officers. It made Cromwell lord protector to govern the country with the aid of a council of state and a single-chamber Parliament.

Before the first protectoral Parliament met, Cromwell and his council carried out many valuable reforms, particularly of the law. His second Parliament offered to make him king in 1657, an offer that he refused.

Fashioning a first-class army and a large navy, Cromwell caused the Commonwealth to be recognized as a great power in Europe. England was victorious in the First Anglo-Dutch War (1652–54) and acquired Jamaica and Dunkerque. At home Cromwell succeeded in establishing a broad church with complete freedom for all Christian sects. His building up of the national prestige and his tolerance in religious matters—which was extended to the Jews, who were allowed to settle in England for the first time since 1290—were his outstanding achievements. He grew more tolerant in his last years and, although an avowed Puritan, did not ban music, wine, or dancing at his court. He was buried with pomp in Westminster Abbey, but his corpse was disinterred, hanged, and beheaded by order of King Charles II in 1661.

Cromwell, Thomas, 1st Earl of Essex   Thomas Cromwell, b. c.1485, d. July 28, 1540, was the principal minister in the English government under Henry VIII from about 1531 until 1540. He was the son of a clothworker and tavern keeper. In his youth he traveled on the Continent, working as a mercenary soldier and in trade. After his return to England he entered the service of Thomas, Cardinal Wolsey, the most important figure in the state as well as in the English church from 1513 to 1529. As an administrator for Wolsey, Cromwell was largely responsible for the establishment of Cardinal's College, Oxford, now known as Christ Church.

In 1529, Wolsey fell from power because of his inability to secure Henry VIII's divorce from Catherine of Aragon. Cromwell then attached himself directly to the royal court. He was chiefly responsible for drafting the legislation that severed England from the Roman Catholic church and made it possible for the archbishop of Canterbury, as primate of the Church of England, to annul

Thomas Cromwell began his political career as a protégé of Cardinal Wolsey and rose to become chief minister of King Henry VIII about 1531. Cromwell designed the legislation that created the national Church of England, carried out the dissolution of the monasteries, and reorganized the administration of England.

Henry's marriage. From 1536 on he supervised the suppression of the monasteries and the confiscation of their wealth. Cromwell was also active in government finance, an area in which he instituted important reforms, and in developing progressive economic and social policies. In April 1540 he was created earl of Essex.

Cromwell negotiated Henry VIII's marriage to ANNE OF CLEVES, which took place in January 1540. However, Henry was dissatisfied with Anne's appearance and insisted on a divorce almost immediately. Cromwell's enemies, especially Thomas Howard, duke of Norfolk, took advantage of this situation to procure Cromwell's downfall. He was arrested, charged with treason and heresy, and beheaded in London.

Cronkite, Walter   Walter Leland Cronkite, Jr., b. St. Joseph, Mo., Nov. 4, 1916, often called the most trusted journalist in the United States, was the anchorman of "The CBS Evening News" from 1962 to 1981. After attending the University of Texas and working as a reporter for the *Houston Post*, he joined the United Press (UP) in 1939 and was a war correspondent during World War II. He spent two years after the war as UP's Moscow bureau chief and joined the Columbia Broadcasting System in 1950. Aside from newscasting, Cronkite was host of the Emmy Award–winning television series "The 20th Century" (1957–66) and "The 21st Century" (1967–69).

Cronus [kroh'-nuhs]   In Greek mythology, Cronus was the youngest of the TITANS, the 12 children of URANUS (Heaven) and Earth. Cronus became supreme ruler by killing his father. He then married his sister Rhea.

As soon as Rhea bore children, Cronus swallowed them, lest they usurp his power. In this way he temporarily disposed of HESTIA, DEMETER, HERA, HADES, and POSEIDON. When the sixth child, ZEUS, was born, Rhea hid him and gave Cronus a stone wrapped in swaddling clothes to swallow. After Zeus grew to manhood, he returned to his father and gave him an emetic, causing Cronus to regurgitate all the children he had swallowed. A 10-year struggle followed between the children of Cronus, led by Zeus, and the Titans, led by Cronus. Eventually the Titans were defeated, and Cronus was exiled. The poet Hesiod tells the story of Cronus in the *Theogony* and the *Works and Days*. Later, the old Roman agrarian god SATURN became identified with Cronus.

Cronyn, Hume [kroh'-nin]   Hume Cronyn, b. London, Ont., July 18, 1911, a versatile Canadian stage and screen actor, won the 1964 Tony Award for his performance as Polonius in *Hamlet* and a 1973 Obie award for the title role in *Krapp's Last Tape*. Together with his wife, Jessica Tandy, he starred in the 1977 Pulitzer Prize–winning play *The Gin Game* and in *The Fourposter* (1951). He has also appeared in Shakespeare's *Richard III* (1965), in plays by Chekhov and Molière, and in many films.

Crook, George   George Crook, b. near Dayton, Ohio, Sept. 23, 1829, d. Mar. 21, 1890, was a U.S. general in the American Indian campaigns; he was known for his skillful and respectful dealings with the Indians. After quelling Indian uprisings in Idaho and Arizona, he played an important role in the Sioux War of 1876. He returned (1882) to Arizona to subdue the Chiricahua Apaches under GERONIMO, pursuing them into Mexico and returning most of them to their reservation in 1883. Geronimo later escaped with a band of followers, and Crook's Indian policies were severely criticized. For the last two years of his life, Crook commanded the Division of the Missouri.

Crookes, Sir William   The English experimentalist William Crookes, b. June 17, 1832, d. Apr. 4, 1919, contributed to many of the new fields of physics and chemistry that emerged in the late 19th century. His investigations of the photographic process in the 1850s motivated his work in the new science of spectroscopy. Using its techniques, Crookes discovered (1861) the element thallium.

Crookes invented the radiometer in 1875 and, beginning in 1878, investigated electrical discharges through highly evacuated "Crookes tubes." At the age of 68, Crookes invented a device that detected alpha particles emitted from radioactive material.

Cropsey, Jaspar   Jaspar Francis Cropsey, b. Rossville, N.Y., Feb. 18, 1823, d. June 22, 1900, was a prominent member of the HUDSON RIVER SCHOOL of American landscape painters. He formed his style under the influence of the romantic landscapes of Thomas COLE, founder of the school. During a 7-year stay in England (1856–63) Cropsey, considerably influenced by the works of the Pre-Raphaelites, turned toward a stronger realism of detail. He was perhaps the greatest colorist of the Hudson River school; his depictions of the glories of the American autumn were especially popular in both the United States and England. One of the finest of these is *Catskill Mountain House* (1855; Minneapolis Institute of Arts, Minneapolis, Minn.).

croquet [kroh-kay']   Croquet is a game for individuals or for 2 teams of 2 players each, in which mallets are used to drive balls through wickets (also called hoops) in a prescribed sequence. The playing surface is a level lawn. The equipment comprises 1 peg, 6 wire wickets, 4 colored wooden balls, and wooden mallets.

The object of the game is to drive the ball with the face of the mallet through the 6 wickets (each in two directions) and hit the center peg. The side that hits the peg first wins, and the number of strokes taken to do this is immaterial. A player continues to strike until he or she fails to pass through a wicket, or to hit an opponent's ball. Hitting an opponent's ball (called a "roquet") entitles the player to two more strokes; passing through a wicket enti-

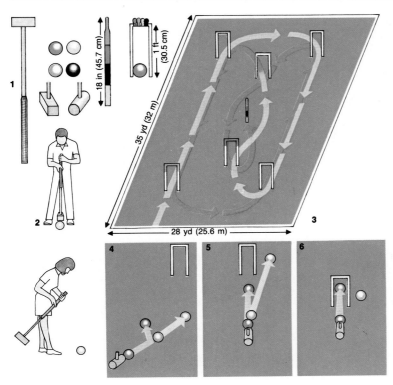

Several versions of the game known as croquet exist in the United States, but standard English croquet, described and illustrated in this article, is more strictly regulated than its popular counterparts in the United States. Standard equipment (1) for the game, all of a specified size and color, includes wooden mallets, the 4 balls always used in both double and single play, a single peg, and 6 narrow hoops, or wickets. These are topped by color clips to designate the position of each ball. Two standard strokes (2), the center and side styles, are commonly used. The course (3), of specified dimensions, is run twice, following the circuit indicated in pink for the first run and in red for the second. The outcome of the game depends largely on skilled use of the roquet (4), a legal strike with one's ball of any of the other balls on the court. This results in 2 extra shots: the croquet stroke (5), in which the ball is placed in contact with the "roqueted" ball and struck so that both move; and the continuation stroke (6), an ordinary free shot. Whenever a hoop is run, as shown, the player receives an extra shot in which he or she may again roquet the other balls. In English croquet, it is possible for an expert player to complete a round before an opponent scores.

tles the player to one more stroke, with which another roquet can be made, and so on. A first-class player may complete the course before the opposing team has played a stroke.

Croquet is popularly supposed to have developed from the game of *paille-maille*, played in France during the 17th century. The modern form of the game was devised in England in 1857. Two popular variants of croquet, roque and lawn croquet, are played in the United States.

Crosby, Bing Harry Lillis "Bing" Crosby, b. Tacoma, Wash., May 2, 1904, d. Oct. 14, 1977, was the most popular singer in the United States from the 1930s to the 1950s. The star of 58 films and a radio show, he made more than 1,000 recordings, including the world's bestseller, "White Christmas" (1942).

Crosby joined Paul Whiteman's band in 1927 as one of The Rhythm Boys, a vocal trio. His unique "crooning" style brought him fame as a soloist in the early 1930s. In films his easygoing personality made him a perennial box-office star and an Academy Award winner for *Going My Way* (1944). He remained a popular singer and actor until his death.

cross The cross is among the oldest and most universal symbols. In preliterate societies it often represented a conjunction of dualities. The horizontal arm was associated with the terrestrial, worldly, feminine, temporal, destructive, negative, passive, and death, while the vertical arm connoted the celestial, spiritual, masculine, eternal, creative, positive, active, and life. Often symbolic of the four astrological elements of earth, water, fire, and air, a cross was also perceived as the cosmic axis from which radiated the spatial dimensions of height, length, width, and breadth, as well as the directions of north, east, south, and west.

The *ankh* (*crux ansata*) was an ancient Egyptian T-shaped cross surmounted with a loop. It symbolized the creative energies of the male and female and the essence of life. The simple T-shaped cross (*crux commissa*) is named for the Greek letter tau. It is often referred to as the Old Testament cross because Moses supposedly placed a brazen serpent on a T cross (Num. 21:6–9), and the Israelites on Passover eve marked their doors with blood-drawn tau crosses to identify themselves as Yahweh's followers.

In ancient Asian, European, and pre-Columbian American civilizations the left-directed swastika (*crux gammata*) appears to have been symbolic of solar power and movement. Hindus see it as a sign of the resigned spirit, whereas Buddhists deem it an emblem of the Buddha's mind. The German Nazis adopted a right-directed swastika for their party logo, believing it to be an ancient Nordic symbol.

Tau Cross

Crux Ansata

Greek Cross

Swastika

Chi-Rho

Latin Cross

St. Andrew's Cross

Celtic Cross

Cross Paty

Maltese Cross

Papal Cross

Cross of Lorraine

The image of the cross has a long multicultural history. It is most prominent in religious iconography and is the primary symbol of Christianity. The cross also served as a heraldic symbol of power and protection.

The erect pole and crossbar used to crucify Jesus Christ became the principal symbol of Christianity. A cross stood for both the actual Crucifixion and the concept of the Christian church. More than 50 variants were to develop, but the most important are the Greek cross, with its equilateral arms, and the Latin cross, with a vertical arm traversed near the top by a shorter horizontal arm.

Two graduated crossbars indicate the Lorraine cross associated with archbishops and patriarchs, whereas the Papal cross has three graduated crossbars. A commonly used Eastern Orthodox variant of the cross of Lorraine has an additional crossbar diagonally placed near the base.

The cross was not widely depicted before the 4th century AD, when Christianity became the official religion of the Roman Empire. Earlier, when Christians were often persecuted, the cross was frequently disguised as an anchor, or some other mundane object. Second-century Christians, however, had already begun to make the sign of the cross as a gesture of identification, blessing, and warding off of evil. In the Roman church the sign of the cross was made from left to right and in Eastern Orthodox churches from right to left.

A crucifix is a cross bearing a painted or sculpted image of Christ. Crucifixes first appeared in the 5th century, and from the 9th century on medieval artists aimed at a realistic portrayal of Christ's suffering. The Renaissance created a fashion for a more ideally conceived imagery that dramatically returned to pathos under the emotional taste of the baroque period. During the Reformation, Protestants generally repudiated the use of representational religious imagery; the crucifix became associated with Roman Catholicism.

When the art of HERALDRY developed in medieval Europe, various types of Christian crosses were employed as symbols, or charges, in the designing of coats-of-arms. A cross with equal arms and a diagonal cross, or saltire, were the most traditional heraldic forms. Many of the insignias for medieval and Renaissance chivalric orders were crosses: the Maltese cross, for example, was the heraldic symbol of the Knights of Malta (the Hospitalers). The flags of Switzerland, Greece, and the Scandinavian countries display various crosses. The British Union Jack was designed to unify the diagonal crosses of Saint Patrick (Ireland) and Saint Andrew (Scotland) with the rectilinear cross of Saint George (England). A Saint Andrew's cross dominated the American Confederate flag, and it was subsequently incorporated into the state flags of some former Confederacy members.

During the 19th and 20th centuries many decorations awarded for military distinction were crosses. The German Iron Cross, the French Croix de Guerre (War Cross), the English Victoria Cross, and the American Distinguished Service Crosses of the army, navy, and air force are among the most significant medals that have been awarded for battle bravery.

cross-country   SEE TRACK AND FIELD

cross-eye   SEE STRABISMUS

cross-section   In nuclear physics, a cross-section is the probability of occurrence of a particular nuclear process—such as a nuclear reaction, scattering, or fission—when a nuclear particle or radiation passes through matter. It can be visualized in terms of a cross-sectional, or target, area presented by each nucleus within the matter. If the nucleus is considered a sphere of radius R, and the incident particle as a point projectile, then the target area presented is a circular disk of area πR^2. If the particle passes anywhere within this area, the reaction will occur. The radius R of a nucleus is of the order of 10^{-12} cm; hence the target area is 10^{-24} cm^2, defined as one barn.

The symbol σ (sigma) is used to denote the cross-section. It depends on the type of target nucleus, the type and energy of the incident particle, and the number of atoms for each unit area. Typical cross-sections for nuclear processes range from millibarns to several thousand barns.

crossbill   Crossbills are any of three species of small (15-cm/6-in) birds of the finch family, Fringillidae, genus *Loxia*. They have twisted bills that cross at the tips. The adult male red crossbill, *L. curvirostra*, is brick red with black wings and tail. The white-winged crossbill, *L. leucoptera*, is paler red with white bars on its wings. Females of both species are drab olive and yellow with dark back

The red crossbill (male in front) *uses uniquely adapted and characteristic crossed bills to feed on its only food: seeds that the bird extracts from cones.*

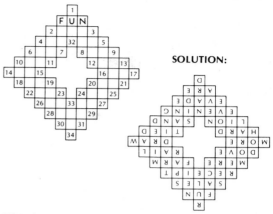

SOLUTION:

Fill in the squares of the puzzle so that the words spelled by the letters agree with these definitions:

2-3.	What bargain hunters enjoy.	6-22.	What we all should be.
4-5.	A written acknowledgement.		
6-7.	Such and nothing more.	4-26.	A daydream.
10-11.	A bird.	2-11.	A talon.
14-15.	Opposed to less.	19-28.	A pigeon.
18-19.	What this puzzle is.	F-7.	Part of your head.
22-23.	An animal of prey.	23-30.	A river in Russia.
26-27.	The close of a day.	1-32.	To govern.
28-29.	Elude.	33-34.	An aromatic plant.
30-31.	The plural of is.	N-8.	A fist.
8-9.	To cultivate.	24-31.	To agree with.
12-13.	A bar of wood or iron.	3-12.	Part of a ship.
16-17.	What artists learn to do.	20-29.	One.
20-21.	Fastened.	5-27.	Exchanging.
24-25.	Found on the seashore.	9-25.	To sink in mud.
10-18.	The fiber of the gomuti palm.	13-21.	A boy.

markings. Both nest in coniferous forests of much of the Northern Hemisphere. The parrot crossbill, *L. pytyopsittacus*, is a European species.

crossbow   see BOW AND ARROW

crossword puzzle   The first crossword puzzle was created by Arthur Wynne, a newspaper editor, who was searching for something new to include in the Sunday magazine section of his paper, the *New York World*. Using a basic word square and dictionary, he created a diamond-shaped trifle of words and clues, which appeared in the *World* on Dec. 21, 1913.

Eventually the standard rectangular format was established; largely because of the demands of the *World's* readers, a list of formal rules was developed. In 1920, Margaret Petherbridge was hired as secretary to the editor of the magazine section. One of her duties was to see that the puzzles appeared without typographical errors. She became so adept at her job that in 1924 she collaborated in compiling the *Crossword Puzzle Book.* In 1926, she married John Farrar, the publisher. As Margaret Farrar she became, in 1942, the first crossword puzzle editor of the *New York Times* and remained in that position until her retirement in 1969.

Geographically, crosswords differ in both style and content. According to Margaret Farrar, the British style accepts many unkeyed words with no cross clues, eliminates most short words, and favors difficult or punning definitions. In the United States, however, more conservative rules apply. The puzzles must be what is called an overall interlock, allowing no unkeyed letters at all. Black squares must be kept down to about one-sixth of the total number of squares, two-letter words are not allowed, and a low word count is attempted, since the longer the

words, the harder the puzzle. The real quality of a crossword puzzle is based on the cleverness of its word combinations and its creator's ability to compose challenging and diverse clues.

crotalaria [kroht-uh-lair'-ee-uh]   *Crotalaria* is a genus of shrubs and herbs of the pea family, Leguminosae. More than 500 species inhabit the warm regions of the world. Some species are cultivated as ornamentals; others are grown for forage or as ground cover. *C. juncea* produces sunn hemp, which is an important fiber of Asia. *C. spectabilis*, from Southeast Asia, is grown as an ornamental; it produces large, showy clusters of purplish-streaked yellow flowers.

croton [kroh'-tuhn]   Croton is the common name for plants of genera *Codiaeum* and *Croton* in the spurge family, Euphorbiaceae. Members of the *Codiaeum* genus are tropical shrubs. Combinations of yellow, green, red, pink, and purple are found in their leaves. Most of the

The garden croton, originally of the Malayan archipelago and Pacific islands, is a widely cultivated evergreen shrub known for its attractive foliage. It grows to 2–3 m (6–10 ft) in the tropics but is usually cut to less than 0.5 m (1.5ft) when potted.

many garden and houseplant varieties were originally selections from *C. variegatum*, variety *pictum*. All members of the tropical and subtropical genus *Croton* are trees. Croton oil, a purgative, is extracted from *C. tiglium*, and *C. eluteria* yields cascarilla bark, also of medicinal value.

croup [kroop] Croup is an acute inflammation of the air passages, especially the larynx, in young children. The disorder is caused by various viruses, particularly the parainfluenza virus, or by bacteria. The primary symptoms are coughing, hoarseness, and noisy, difficult breathing, which can sometimes be alleviated with steam inhalations. If the infection is bacterial, antibiotics are given. Insertion of a tube into the windpipe is sometimes necessary.

Crouse, Russel see LINDSAY, HOWARD, AND CROUSE, RUSSEL

Crow The Crow, a North American Indian tribe, call themselves the Absoraka, which in their Siouan language means "bird people." In the 18th century they separated from the HIDATSA, who were agriculturists living in sedentary villages along the Missouri River. They ranged westward to the Rocky Mountains, becoming famous as hunters and warriors and later as scouts for the U.S. Army.

Like other Plains peoples, the Crow depended on the buffalo for food and skins and on the horse for mobility. They lived in portable TEPEES, used parfleche, or rawhide, for containers, moccasins, shields, and other objects, and practiced the SUN DANCE ritual.

The Crow grew only one crop, tobacco. Many traditional ceremonies, including those of the tobacco society, are still performed by the Crow Indians, who today live on the Crow Indian reservation in Montana and number 5,900 (1987 est.).

crow The crow is a large, mostly black bird of the family Corvidae and the genus *Corvus*, which also includes

the common RAVEN, *C. corax*. It is found throughout much of the Northern Hemisphere and is the largest (66 cm/26 in) of the perching, or song, birds. The common crow, *C. brachyrhynchos*, of North America is about 50 cm (20 in) long, all black and stout-bodied, and has a heavy bill. It is abundant from coast to coast (except in the Great Basin area) and from Canada to Mexico; it retreats to southern ranges in winter.

Among the most intelligent and wary of birds, crows may become a nuisance when they gather in huge communal roosts, sometimes numbering hundreds of thousands. Omnivorous and aggressive, they may prey on other birds and their eggs, and they are often destructive to crops. They are beneficial, however, in helping to control insects and small rodents.

The common crow is adaptive and intelligent. It can be tamed and can mimic human speech; research indicates that it is able to solve uncomplicated puzzles.

Crowfoot Crowfoot, b. 1830, d. Apr. 25, 1890, a chief of the Canadian BLACKFOOT Indians, is remembered as a peacemaker and advocate of conciliation with the Canadian government. He was born into the Blood tribe but grew up among the Blackfoot. His Indian name was Isapo-muxika, meaning "Crow Indian's Big Foot," shortened by interpreters to "Crowfoot." As a Blackfoot leader he was a skillful orator and diplomat, acting as envoy to eastern Canada and negotiator between warring Plains tribes and métis (persons of mixed Indian and European ancestry). His adopted son was the notable Cree Indian chief POUNDMAKER.

crucifix see CROSS

crucifixion Crucifixion was a method of execution used by the Romans to punish slaves and foreigners. Hung from a crossbar astride an upright peg, the naked victim was allowed to hang as a public spectacle until dead. No vital organs were damaged, and death was slow agony. Prior to crucifixion, the victim was scourged and made to carry the crossbar to the execution site. The crucifixion of JESUS CHRIST followed this order of events (Mark 15:15; John 19:17).

Though closely associated with Rome, crucifixion originated with the Phoenicians and Persians. It was practiced from the 6th century BC until the 4th century AD. The Roman emperor Constantine I banned crucifixion in 337.

Because Jesus was crucified, the CROSS has assumed theological significance for Christians. It symbolizes reconciliation with God through faith in Christ.

crucifixion thorn　The crucifixion thorn, or Christ thorn, is one of several shrubs or small trees in the BUCKHORN family, Rhamnaceae. (The name also refers to three families of shrubs or small trees in southwestern North America.) The prickly branches of the crucifixion thorn may have been used to make Christ's crown of thorns, thus its name. The name is usually applied to the Jerusalem thorn, *Paliurus spina-christi*, a Eurasian tree that reaches a height of 6.3 m (20 ft) and bears clusters of small greenish yellow flowers. Each flower ripens into a dry, woody fruit that somewhat resembles a tiny human head wearing a wide-brimmed hat. The range of the crucifixion thorn is southern Europe to northern China.

Also commonly called crucifixion thorn is a kind of jujube—*Ziziphus spina-christi*. This small tree grows from northern Africa to western Asia and bears small yellow flowers and small fleshy round or oval fruit.

crude oil　see PETROLEUM

Cruikshank, George [krook'-shank]　George Cruikshank, b. Sept. 27, 1792, d. Feb. 1, 1878, was the most famous member of an English family of artists and caricaturists. His early cartoons, in the style of James GILLRAY, were mostly directed against Napoleon I, but they also mercilessly lampooned King George IV. Before long he developed his own highly characteristic style.

Cruikshank's works are legion, varying from watercolors to etchings that illustrate the evils of drink. His masterly book illustrations include those for Charles Dickens's *Oliver Twist* and for the novels of W. Harrison Ainsworth. His watercolors, which are often delightfully fantastic, include superb preliminary drawings for his illustrations.

Cruikshank was fortunate to work at a time when book, newspaper, and magazine illustrations were coming into great demand, for the first time in the history of print. He was among the most brilliant of an era of great illustrators.

cruise missile　The cruise missile is a small pilotless aircraft armed, usually, with a nuclear warhead. Powered by a turbofan jet engine and equipped with both an inertial guidance system and a computer and radar for maintaining its course, the missile has a range of up to 3,200 km (2,000 mi) and a speed of approximately 800 km/h (500 mph); it flies at altitudes of between 15 and 100 m (50 and 330 ft).

Cruise missiles have been developed by a number of nations. The most advanced are those produced by the United States: the Air-Launched Cruise Missile (ALCM), which is carried and launched from a bomber; and the Tomahawk, which may be launched from a ship or submarine, or from the ground (GLCM). Over water, the missile follows a preprogrammed flight path under the control of its inertial guidance system. A Terrain Contour Matching system (TERCOM) controls the missile over

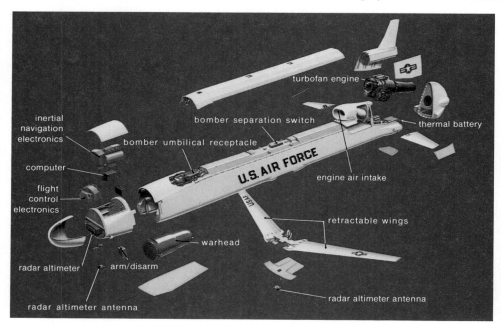

An exploded view of a U.S. ALCM reveals major components and their locations. The missile is designed to be launched from an airborne bomber and to cruise under control of an on-board computer after launching. The missile has a length of 4.27 m (14 ft) and a wing span of 2.90 m (9.5 ft).

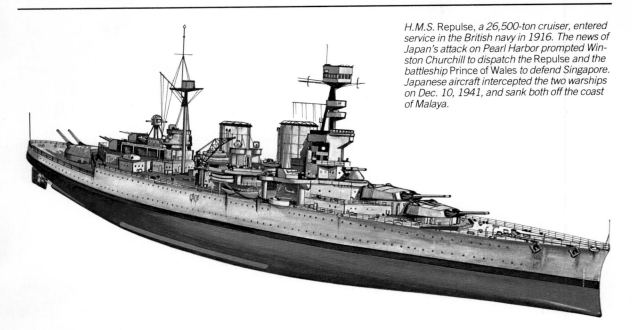

H.M.S. Repulse, *a 26,500-ton cruiser, entered service in the British navy in 1916. The news of Japan's attack on Pearl Harbor prompted Winston Churchill to dispatch the* Repulse *and the battleship* Prince of Wales *to defend Singapore. Japanese aircraft intercepted the two warships on Dec. 10, 1941, and sank both off the coast of Malaya.*

land. In conjunction with a radar altimeter, TERCOM matches the terrain below the missile with a digital map of the area and corrects the missile's flight path. The digital map is derived from existing intelligence reconnaissance sources and stored, together with target data and routes, on magnetic tapes that are read into the missile before launch.

The successful operational capabilities of cruise missiles were proven in the GULF WAR, when they were launched from U.S. ships in the region and struck targets in Iraq with great accuracy.

Completed Air-Launched Cruise Missiles (ALCMs) are given a final inspection before shipment.

cruiser   Originally a descriptive term for the swift-sailing warships that scouted for the main battle fleet, the cruiser, by the late 1800s, had come to signify a specific type of ship intermediate in size between the BATTLESHIP and the DESTROYER.

Since the 1950s, guided missiles have replaced guns as the main battery of the cruiser. Partly as a result of this, and partly because missiles can penetrate armor of great thickness, armored cruisers are no longer built. In addition, antisubmarine cruisers have assumed the traditional role of the destroyer, particularly in the Soviet navy. The U.S. Navy, which is the main proponent of the cruiser, aside from the USSR, has commissioned several nuclear-powered, guided-missile cruisers, beginning in 1961 with the U.S.S. *Long Beach*, the first nuclear-powered surface warship.

Crumb, George   The composer George Henry Crumb, b. Charleston, W.Va., Oct. 24, 1929, won the Pulitzer Prize for music in 1968 for his orchestral work *Echoes of Time and the River*. To create a magical atmosphere in his music, Crumb uses unusual instruments, such as the musical saw, the African thumb piano, tuned water glasses, and Jew's harps. His best-known works include *Ancient Voices of Children* (1970), one of his many works that set to music the poetry of Federico García Lorca, and *Star Child* (1977), for children's chorus.

Crusades   The Crusades were Christian military expeditions undertaken between the 11th and the 14th century to recapture the Holy Land from the Muslims. The

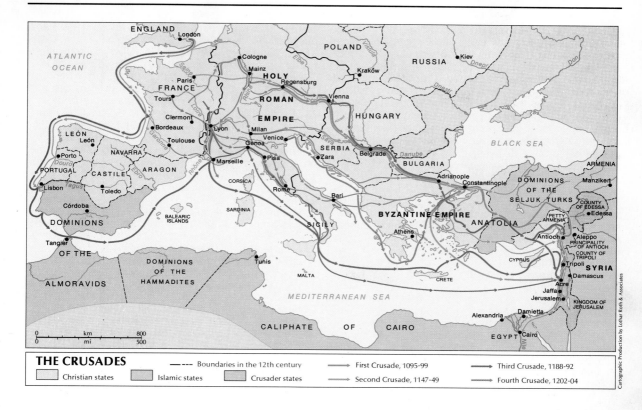

THE CRUSADES

- Boundaries in the 12th century
- Christian states
- Islamic states
- Crusader states
- First Crusade, 1095-99
- Second Crusade, 1147-49
- Third Crusade, 1188-92
- Fourth Crusade, 1202-04

Cartographic Production by Lothar Roth & Associates

word *crusade*, which is derived from the Latin *crux* ("cross"), is a reference to the biblical injunction that Christians carry their cross (Matt. 10:38). Crusaders wore a red cloth cross sewn on their tunics to indicate that they had assumed the cross and were soldiers of Christ.

Causes

The causes of the Crusades were many and complex, but prevailing religious beliefs were clearly of major importance. The Crusaders continued an older tradition of the PILGRIMAGE to the Holy Land, which was often imposed as a penance; now, however, they assumed a dual role as pilgrims and warriors. Such an armed pilgrimage was regarded as a justifiable war, because it was fought to recapture the places sacred to Christians.

Jerusalem had been under Muslim rule since the 7th century, but pilgrimages were not cut off until the 11th century, when the SELJUK Turks began to interfere with Christian pilgrims. For Christians, the very name of Jerusalem evoked visions of the end of time and of the heavenly city. Papal encouragement, the hope of eternal merit, and the offer of INDULGENCES motivated thousands to enroll in the cause.

The Crusades also were a response to appeals for help from the BYZANTINE EMPIRE, threatened by the advance of the Seljuk Turks. The year 1071 had seen both the capture of Jerusalem and the decisive defeat of the Byzantine army. In addition, the hopes of the PAPACY for the reunifi-

cation of East and West, the nobility's hunger for land at a time of crop failures, population pressure in the West, and an alternative to warfare at home were major impulses.

The Crusades were equally a result of economic circumstances. Many participants were lured by the fabulous riches of the East; a campaign abroad appealed as a means of escaping from the pressures of feudal society, in which the younger sons in a family often lacked economic opportunities. The Crusades also were seen as a means of establishing and extending trade routes.

The Campaigns

First Crusade (1096–99). The First Crusade was launched by Pope URBAN II. Urban spoke of the need to help the Christian East and to stop the desecration of the holy places, and stressed the moral duty of keeping the "Peace of God" at home. He appealed for volunteers to set out for Jerusalem and promised remission of ecclesiastical penances as an incentive. Bands of poorly armed pilgrims, most of them inexperienced and poor, set out for Constantinople under PETER THE HERMIT and Walter the Penniless even before the army gathered. Some began by massacring Jews in the Rhine valley. Many perished on their way east, and the rest were destroyed by the Muslims when they crossed into Anatolia.

The main army, mostly French and Norman knights under baronial leadership—GODFREY OF BOUILLON, Baldwin of Flanders, Raymond of Toulouse, Robert of Normandy, Bohemond of Taranto, and others—assembled at Constantinople and proceeded on a long, arduous march through Anatolia. They captured Antioch (June 3, 1098) and finally Jerusalem (July 15, 1099) in savage battles. By the end of the campaign, four Crusader states had been formed along the Syrian and Palestinian coast: the County of Edessa, the Principality of Antioch, the County of Tripoli, and the Kingdom of Jerusalem, where Baldwin was crowned king. Continuing rivalry among the leaders and the other nobles, however, undermined any chance of consolidating these acquisitions almost from the beginning. (See JERUSALEM, LATIN KINGDOM OF.)

The Second Crusade (1147–49). The next Crusade had its immediate cause in the loss (1144) of Edessa to the Muslims of Mosul and Aleppo. Challenged by Saint BERNARD OF CLAIRVAUX, King LOUIS VII of France and the German King CONRAD III tried to lead separate armies through Anatolia. The only success of this Crusade was the capture (1147) of Lisbon, Portugal, by English and Frisian Crusaders on their way to the East by ship.

The Third Crusade (1188–92). The Third Crusade was a response to the conquest (1187) of almost all of Palestine, including Jerusalem, by Sultan SALADIN, who had consolidated Muslim power in Mesopotamia, Syria, and Egypt. The Crusade's illustrious leadership included King PHILIP II of France, Holy Roman Emperor FREDERICK I, and King RICHARD I of England. Frederick, however, drowned en route in Cilicia, and the Crusading effort disintegrated through attrition and lack of cooperation.

The Fourth Crusade (1202–04). Pope INNOCENT III attempted to reorganize the Crusading efforts under papal auspices. But lack of funds to pay for the passage of the 10,000 Crusaders in Venice forced a diversion of the mostly French army. (See CONSTANTINOPLE, LATIN EMPIRE OF.)

Other Crusades. During the 13th century several attempts were made to revive the declining enthusiasm for Crusades. The Muslims, however, were in firm control of Syria and Palestine, and their devotion to *jihad* ("holy war") against the Europeans strengthened their resolve. The Fourth Crusade was followed by the tragic episode of the CHILDREN'S CRUSADE (1212), in which thousands of children perished from hunger and disease or were sold into slavery on their way to the Mediterranean. During a peaceful expedition to the Holy Land (the Sixth Crusade, 1228–29), Holy Roman Emperor FREDERICK II negotiated the return of important pilgrimage sites (among them Jerusalem, Bethlehem, Lydda, and perhaps Nazareth) without bloodshed. Frederick crowned himself king of Jerusalem, but the city was retaken by the Muslims in 1244.

King LOUIS IX of France led two Crusades. The first, with 15,000 or 25,000 troops, was directed against Egypt (the Seventh Crusade, 1248–54). While he was in the East, Louis tried to form an alliance with the MONGOLS against the Muslims. A second campaign against the sultan of Tunis in North Africa (the Eighth Crusade, 1270) was equally unsuccessful. In the meantime, Jaffa and Antioch were lost to the MAMELUKE Sultan Baybars (1268). The last Christian bastion on the Syrian coast, Acre, was stormed by the sultan in 1291.

During the 13th century, Crusades were increasingly

The siege of Jerusalem, the culmination of the First Crusade, was preceded by more than a month of preparations by forces outside the city walls. Captured in July 1099, the city remained in Crusader hands until its reconquest by the Sultan Saladin in 1187.

The conquest of Jerusalem in AD 1099, portrayed in this English miniature of the late Middle Ages, was the culmination of the First Crusade. (British Museum, London.)

ple, in the use of indulgences). On the other hand, the Crusades did stimulate religious enthusiasm on a broad scale. They inspired a great literature in Latin and in the vernacular, especially the Romance languages. Contacts with the Muslim world started to replace ignorance about other cultures and religions with a certain respect for them. The idea of religious conversion by force gave way to a new emphasis on apologetics and mission. Peter the Venerable, an abbot of Cluny, had the Koran translated into Latin (1143), and Saint FRANCIS OF ASSISI tried in person to convert the sultan of Damietta during the Fifth Crusade. Later FRANCISCANS continued the concern for mission to the Muslims.

Politically, the Crusades did not effect much change. The Crusader states and the Latin Empire of Constantinople were short-lived. Only the military orders founded in the East (the HOSPITALERS, TEMPLARS, and TEUTONIC KNIGHTS) had an appreciable influence on later European politics. Today only the ruins of Crusader castles remain as evidence of the knights' presence in the East. More than 100 castles and fortresses were built, the majority during the defensive phase after the Second Crusade (KRAK DES CHEVALIERS, Chastel Blanc, Château Pèlerin, Margat, Monfort).

Economically, the Crusades imposed huge burdens on the clergy and the laity. The growing economy of western Europe was drained of funds in support of the expeditions. At times the papacy was unable to support any other causes effectively. Still, the Crusades furthered the rapid growth of a money economy, of banking, and of new methods of taxation. The widening of the geographical horizon prepared Europe for the discoveries of the modern age. Trade, architecture, and the growing urban culture, particularly in France and Italy, were stimulated through the Crusades, and Islamic science, philosophy, and medicine deeply influenced intellectual life in the West. Much of this influence, however, came through contacts with the Muslims in Spain and Sicily; the Crusaders in the East generally remained isolated from the surrounding culture.

Fortresses such as this one near Aleppo, Syria, were built by the Crusading orders of the Knights Hospitaler and the Knights Templar during the 12th century in order to secure territories wrested from the Muslims during the First, and most successful, Crusade.

used by the papacy against foes in the West. A precedent had been set by the Crusade against the Slavic pagan Wends in Germany (1147) and the granting of Crusaders' indulgences for the fight against Muslims in Spain. These Crusades were followed by Crusades against the ALBIGENSES (heretics in southern France; 1209–29) and the Baltic Prussians and Lithuanians. The French ANGEVINS took Sicily from the German HOHENSTAUFEN dynasty as Crusaders with papal consent. This use of Crusades as mere tools of power politics continued into the 14th and 15th centuries.

Results

The results of the Crusades are difficult to assess. In religious terms, they hardened Muslim attitudes toward Christians. At the same time, doubts were raised among Christians about God's will, the church's authority, and the role of the papacy. Religious fervor yielded to disinterest, skepticism, and a growing legalism (as, for exam-

The anatomy of a male crayfish is typical of most shrimplike crustaceans. The head has two pairs of sensory antennae and a pair of eyes on movable stalks. The appendages, or pereiopods, of the thorax include four pairs of walking legs and one pair of clawbearing chelipeds. In the open circulatory system blood flows from the heart through the arteries and returns into open sinuses. The digestive system has a stomach for grinding food and a gland for chemical processing. The antennal gland is the main excretory organ.

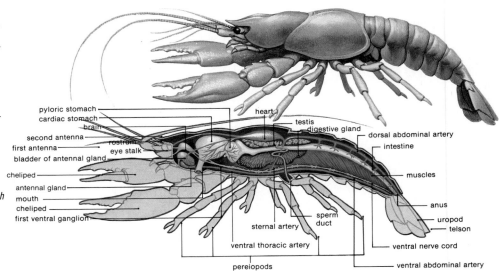

pyloric stomach
cardiac stomach
brain
second antenna
first antenna
rostrum
bladder of antennal gland
eye stalk
cheliped
antennal gland
mouth
cheliped
first ventral ganglion
heart
testis
digestive gland
dorsal abdominal artery
intestine
muscles
anus
uropod
telson
ventral nerve cord
sperm duct
sternal artery
ventral thoracic artery
pereiopods
ventral abdominal artery

crustacean Crustaceans are largely aquatic invertebrate animals in the phylum Arthropoda, class Crustacea, and include BARNACLES, CRABS, CRAYFISH, LOBSTERS, SHRIMPS, and terrestrial wood lice. Members of the class Crustacea, consisting of about 30,000 species, have evolved a variety of body forms and behaviors to cope with both aquatic and terrestrial environments.

Crustaceans are characterized by a shell, or integument, formed by calcified cuticle, which includes glands and pigment granules called chromatophores. The head contains five pairs of appendages, including two pairs of sensory antennae (a distinguishing feature for the class), a pair of mandibles, and first and second maxillae used as mouthparts. The trunk consists of a thorax—often covered by a dorsal carapace, a cuticular extension of the head overhanging the body sides—and a variable number of appendages modified in different species for swimming, crawling, grasping, egg-brooding, and food manipulation. An abdomen follows, often with appendages and terminal fanlike segments, or uropods.

Feeding habits of crustaceans range from filter feeding to scavenging and from herbivorous to carnivorous, especially in larger species. A few species of crustaceans are internal or external parasites.

The generalized crustacean digestive system varies from a simple tube in primitive forms to a highly specialized system of chambers and diverticula, each with a specialized function in digestion. The circulatory system usually consists of a dorsal thoracic heart, tubular or spherical, from which blood is pumped to a system of arteries and open sinuses. In some groups the heart or arteries, or both, are absent. The nervous system shows a central, ladderlike arrangement of ganglia, with a concentration of ganglia in the head region, and a variety of peripheral sensory structures. Crustaceans usually mate through copulation, the male clasping the female with a specialized appendage.

Crux Crux, the Southern Cross, is a small CONSTELLATION in the shape of a cross in the Southern Hemisphere. Like the BIG DIPPER in the Northern Hemisphere, Crux is used as a rough navigational aid, because the long arm of the cross points directly to the south celestial pole. Located in a brilliant region of the Milky Way, it contains an enormous dust cloud, known as the Coalsack, which obscures part of the Galaxy.

Cry, the Beloved Country In *Cry, the Beloved Country* (1948), South African novelist Alan PATON laments social conditions in his homeland. The novel depicts the dual tragedy of oppressed blacks and of whites who become tyrannical out of fear and greed. It tells the story of a simple black parson, Stephen Kumalo, whose search for his son Absalom takes him through the black slums of Johannesburg, where he encounters the soul-destroying conditions under which his people are forced to live. Eventually Kumalo finds his son in prison, where he is awaiting trial for the murder of a white man who, ironically, was one of the few Europeans to oppose South African racism.

cryobiology [kry'-oh-by-ah'-luh-jee] Cryobiology is the scientific study of the effects of extreme cold on living tissue. Practical applications include storage of frozen, viable tissues and organs for later transplantation, destruction of diseased tissue by extremely cold probes (cryosurgery), and the development of crop plants that are more resistant to the effects of cold.

cryogenics [kry-oh-jen'-iks]   Cryogenics is the study of the properties of matter at low temperatures. The term *cryogenics* is derived from the Greek *kryos*, meaning "icy cold," but it applies to temperatures far below that of common ice. The highest temperature dealt with by cryogenics is about -100° C (-148° F). The lowest is the unattainable ABSOLUTE ZERO temperature of -273.15° C (-459.67° F). It is standard practice in cryogenic studies to express temperatures in this range by using the Kelvin temperature scale; absolute zero is 0 K, and water freezes at 273.15 K. Thus the cryogenic range extends from about 173 K to a fraction of a Kelvin above absolute zero.

The study of cryogenics began about 1877, when the Swiss physicist Rasul Pictet and the French engineer Louis P. Cailletet simultaneously liquefied oxygen for the first time at a temperature of 90 K.

In 1898, a major advance in cryogenics was achieved by a British professor, James DEWAR, who succeeded in liquefying hydrogen gas and devised a double-walled vacuum storage vessel, known as the Dewar flask. Although special methods have produced temperatures down to about 40 millionths of a degree Kelvin above absolute zero, using sodium gas, it is a fundamental theorem of THERMODYNAMICS that absolute zero can be approached but can never actually be reached.

Superconductivity and Superfluidity. It had been known for many years that the electrical resistivity of metals decreases with falling temperatures. Nevertheless, many were surprised when Kamerlingh Onnes discovered in 1911 that the resistance of pure mercury undergoes a sharp drop just below liquid helium temperatures and then vanishes. The same phenomenon of SUPERCONDUCTIVITY was subsequently observed in other metals. The enormous potential value of electricity flow when resistive losses are zero is demonstrated by the superconducting electromagnets used in particle ACCELERATOR and FUSION ENERGY research as well as in NUCLEAR MAGNETIC RESONANCE IMAGING devices in hospitals. Other fields of application include electronics, where high-speed cryogenic computer memories and communication devices are in various stages of research and development.

Closely related to superconductivity is the phenomenon of SUPERFLUIDITY, a strange behavior of liquid helium. Liquid helium cooled below 2.2 K becomes an elusive superfluid that runs uphill, escapes many solid containers, and generally defies the ordinary principles of fluid mechanics. Such spectacular effects occur because the superfluid displays essentially none of the viscous tendencies that are characteristic of all common fluids. The explanation of these effects depends on quantum rather than classical physics and is still under intensive investigation.

Cryobiology. Another application of modern cryogenics is the study and use of low-temperature biological materials. Developments in this field, known as CRYOBIOLOGY, have led to modern methods of preserving blood, semen, and other biological materials at and below temperatures obtained by the use of liquid nitrogen. In surgery, a cryogenic scalpel can deaden or destroy tissues with a high degree of accuracy.

Cryopumping. The availability of cryogenic materials has made it possible to attain an extremely high vacuum by using a process known as cryopumping. In this process, the residual gases left in a vacuum vessel by conventional pumping methods are literally frozen out on low-temperature coils. Cryopumping is important in high-vacuum research and is particularly useful in devices used to simulate the vacuum environment of outer space.

Other Applications. Large-scale cryogenic operations are currently being used to transport energy in the form of liquefied natural gas. The processing, handling, and preservation of food by cryogenic means is a major industry, providing both frozen and freeze-dried foodstuffs. Other applications of modern cryogenics are in chemical synthesis and catalysis, gas separation, metals fabrication, and miscellaneous uses ranging from fire fighting to the drilling of oil wells.

Liquid hydrogen plays a role in high-energy physics studies and, along with liquid oxygen, powers rocket engines for space research. Present laboratory studies are directed toward characterizing material properties at cryogenic temperatures. Related research in solid-state physics has shown a superconductivity effect in organometallic compounds. Other research examines the phenomena of cryogenic heat transfer and boiling, and explores low-temperature MAGNETOHYDRODYNAMICS (MHD).

See also: HEAT AND HEAT TRANSFER.

cryolite [kry'-oh-lyt]   Cryolite is a sodium aluminum fluoride (Na_3AlF_6) mineral that is colorless to white and has a waxy luster, a specific gravity of 2.95, and a hardness of 2.5. The only known major deposit is in southwestern Greenland. Cryolite was the chief ore of ALUMINUM until about 1900, when it was replaced by BAUXITE. It is used now as a solvent or flux in the electrolytic production of aluminum.

crypt   A crypt (from the Greek word for hidden or secret place) is a vaulted subterranean area beneath a church that is used for purposes other than storage. The crypt may be a chapel or a complete lower church, or it may contain only altars for worship. Tombs, especially those of martyrs connected with the church, are often found in the crypt. In classical church architecture, the crypt was located under the eastern end of the building. In Greek temples, the equivalent of the crypt is the naos.

cryptology   Cryptology, the branch of knowledge that concerns secret writing or communications in code or cipher, originated in human desire to communicate secretly and is as old as writing itself. The word derives from the Greek *kryptos* ("hidden") and *logos* ("word").

Early History of Secret Writing

Methods of secret communication were developed in ancient Egypt, Mesopotamia, India, and China. About 400 BC the Spartans used the scytale, a cylindrical rod around which the sender wrapped a length of parchment or papyrus in a spiral. Words were then written lengthwise along the rod, one letter on each revolution of the strip. Once unrolled, the strip showed nothing but a succession of meaningless letters; to be read, the strip had to be wrapped around a rod of exactly the same diameter as the first. Julius Caesar is said to have used a simple letter-substitution method in his correspondence, consisting of writing the ordinary alphabet from left to right, and beneath, another normal alphabet shifting three letters.

In 1470, Leon Battista Alberti published *Trattati in cifra,* in which he described a cipher disk capable of enciphering a small code. Most authorities, however, consider Johannes Trithemius, abbot of Spanheim in Germany, to be the father of modern cryptography. In 1510, Trithemius wrote *Polygraphia,* the first printed work on cryptology. He introduced for the first time the concept of a square table, or tableau, in which the normal alphabet was successively shifted. For example, the first letter might be enciphered with the first shifted alphabet, the second letter with the second, and so on.

Technical Aspects of Cryptology

Cryptology is divided into two general fields, cryptography and cryptanalysis. Cryptography concerns the methods of converting plaintext (also known as cleartext) into ciphertext. Ciphertext messages are called cryptograms. Cryptanalysis concerns the methods of solving or reading cryptograms without their keys.

Today cryptologists agree that a number of cryptographic systems are analytically unsolvable. Cryptographic systems in which a key is used only once, known as holocryptic systems, can be mathematically proven to be unsolvable. Other systems, especially those using electrical devices, can often be completely secure from a practical viewpoint. Even so-called paper-and-pencil systems can be constructed for which analytic solutions are virtually impossible. Nonetheless, the most theoretically secure cryptographic system can be vulnerable to solution if the system is incorrectly used or if there is a physical compromise of the system.

Codes. When cryptographic treatment is applied to plaintext elements of irregular length, the cryptographic system is called a code. The letters or digits that replace the irregular length plaintext elements are termed code groups. The plaintext elements with their accompanying code groups are found in a code book. If both the plaintext elements and the code groups run simultaneously in alphabetic or numerical order in the code book, the code is said to be one-part. If, however, the plaintext elements are in alphabetic order, and the code groups are not in order, or vice versa, the code is said to be two-part. In a one-part code the same book is used for both encoding and decoding. In a two-part code, one section is required for encoding and one for decoding.

Ciphers. When cryptographic treatment is applied to plaintext elements of regular length, usually single letters or pairs of letters (digraphs), the cryptographic system is called a cipher. In a transposition cipher the plaintext letters are transposed following a prearranged plan; for example, odd letters written on one line and even letters on another. To facilitate transmission, the ciphertext is usually written in five-letter groups. This kind of a transposition is a railfence cipher.

The Zimmermann telegram is an example of a numerical code-group system. The telegram was sent in January 1917 by the German foreign minister Arthur Zimmermann to the German ambassador in Mexico. Its interception and decipherment by the British revealed German designs for cooperation with Mexico against the United States and was partly responsible for America's entry into World War I.

This Renaissance cipher disk was designed by the Italian cryptologist Giovanni Porta. The inner disk rotates against the stationary outer disk, enabling the symbols to encipher the original letters and numbers.

Transposition ciphers may use geometrical figures. Thus, for instance, writing the plaintext normally into a rectangle, then reading the ciphertext down the columns from left to right produces a simple transposition cipher. In a substitution cipher the plaintext letters are replaced by other, usually different, letters. If the symmetry is broken and plaintext letters are replaced by mixed letters, security increases. Such a system is called a monoalphabetic substitution cipher or simple substitution cipher. But a message may be enciphered with more than one ciphertext alphabet, using perhaps a cipher square or tableau, such as the square table of Trithemius. Such a system is called a polyalphabetic substitution cipher.

Cryptanalysis. Cryptanalysis is the analytic solution of cryptographic systems without knowledge of the key. Most governments attempt to read the secret messages of their enemies or potential enemies because of the wealth of intelligence information they provide. Cryptanalytic successes are rarely revealed, though, because to do so would cause the enemies to change their cryptographic systems.

Enigma, the cryptographic machine used by the Germans during World War II, was broken by means of cryptanalysis. The code word "Ultra" was used by the Allies to designate information derived from German secret messages. In addition, U.S. success in reading Japanese codes during World War II helped shorten the war and save American lives.

Cryptanalysis is successful principally because plaintext is not random. Not only do individual letters and words occur with definite frequencies, but certain letters and words appear together with predictable frequencies. As cryptographic systems become more complicated, however, sophisticated cryptanalytic techniques are required. Today the computer's ability to store millions of pieces of information is both an invaluable aid in cryptanalysis and itself an incentive to the development of highly complex cryptographic systems, because of the wide range of sensitive information in computer databanks. Such data are stored in ciphers so complex that only other computers can decipher them. Governments, banks, and manufacturers primarily make use of encryption systems that are based on the difficulty involved in factoring large numbers, as compared with the difficulty in finding out whether those numbers are primes (see PRIME NUMBER). Primes are used in coding systems by computer networks, which encrypt their data so that only those authorized users who have the proper "key," or number, can decode the transmitted information.

The DES (data encryption standard) system developed by IBM and approved in 1976 by the U.S. National Bureau of Standards for governmental use employs a variable 56-bit "key." In DES, which has been widely adopted commercially, plaintext is converted into ciphertext by the encrypting operations of substitution and transposition, repeating the operations several times by means of special techniques that make the codes particularly hard to break. DES, however, shares with earlier systems the vulnerability inherent in a key exchange between a sender and a receiver. Other new systems, such as the so-called public-key systems, bypass the problem by making use of both a public encryption key and a secret decryption key that can be generated locally by the authorized receiver of the data.

In 1988 a group of U.S. researchers using hundreds of computers was able to factor a 100-digit number in just 26 days, a feat thought to be impossible a decade earlier. The ever-increasing power of computers and the development of more sophisticated factoring methods are forcing cryptographers to choose even larger and more cumbersome numbers on which to base code keys.

---

crystal A crystal is solid MINERAL matter bounded by plane surfaces that intersect each other at particular angles. Matter in which the internal arrangement of atoms or molecules is regularly repeated is said to be crystalline. Crystallography, the study of the crystalline state, contributes to fields as diverse as biochemistry, materials engineering, ceramics, and synthetic gem production. The work of René-Just HAÜY in the late 18th and early 19th centuries elevated crystallography to a science. "Haüy's Law" or the "law of rational indices" states that when a crystal is considered to have a framework of three intersecting axes, all faces of the crystal can be described by numerical indices related to the intercepts of the faces on these axes. Haüy's work led to the concept of the unit cell, a basic tenet and integral part of modern crystallography.

The Unit Cell

The search for the shape of the unit cell was vigorously pursued by 19th-century crystallographers, who believed that a single shape would explain all forms of all types of crystals. Haüy, correctly recognizing that this was impossible, held that there were three "integrant molecules": the tetrahedron, the triangular prism, and the parallelepi-

Calcite, or calcium carbonate, has been observed in more than 300 crystalline forms, a few of which are displayed in this agglomerate. No matter what the shape of the original crystal may be, it always breaks into fragments with the same rhombohedral symmetry.

pedon. Precise measurement of interfacial angles, however, showed that the concept of three "integrant molecules" was untenable.

Haüy's work had formed a basis from which later scientists were able to begin constructing a geometrically exact discipline. Christian Weiss (1780–1856) set about classifying crystals on the basis of the axes of reference that he defined, as well as on symmetry elements inferred from them. Dividing crystals into systems on the basis of their axes and symmetry elements, Weiss was able to distinguish the hexagonal, orthorhombic, tetragonal, and ISOMETRIC SYSTEMS (without naming them as such).

The Crystal Systems

Investigations of the geometrical theory of crystals continued throughout the latter half of the 19th century. Eventually, all 7 crystal systems were recognized and classified on the basis of the three axes first delineated by Haüy and on the apparent symmetry of the forms derived therefrom. A complete delineation of the 32 crystal classes, or "point groups," was published (1848) by Auguste Bravais (1811–63). Bravais investigated the types of geometric figures formed by points distributed regularly in space, demonstrating that points with varying symmetry and geometry could be grouped in only 14 ways and yet allow continuous repetition in space. These 14 "lattices" could be grouped by symmetry so that 7 different lattice symmetries corresponding to the 7 crystal systems could be recognized. By combining the 14 lattices with symmetry operations, exactly 32 symmetry groupings resulted.

Leonard Sohncke (1842–97) recognized two additional symmetry elements, and in the late 1880s Russia's

Geometrical and X-ray diffraction studies of crystals have shown them to comprise a number of regularly repeating stacks of submicroscopic building blocks, or unit cells. Each unit cell is composed of atoms, ions, or molecules arranged in one of seven different systems. In the case of quartz, or silicon dioxide, crystals (A), hexagonal groups of atoms in the same plane (1) are stacked above each other to form a hexagonal unit cell (2). Ions (3) in halite, or sodium chloride, crystals (B) are fixed at the corners of a cubic unit cell (4).

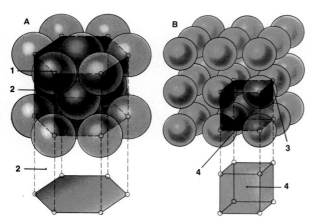

Crystals belonging to the isometric, or cubic, system have three axes of equal length at right angles to each other. This system (1) is characterized by nine planes of symmetry—three rectangular and six diagonal—each dividing the body into two mirror-image parts. Garnets (2) are cubic forms. An isometric crystal also has a number of axes of symmetry (3), or lines about which a crystal may be rotated so that a given appearance (line, angle, or face) is seen two (2-fold) or more times: three 4-fold axes (A), four 3-fold axes (B), and six 2-fold axes (C).

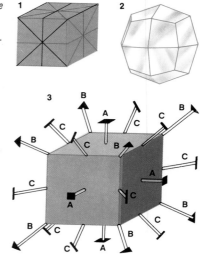

Evgraf Stepanovich Federov (1853–1919) outlined the 230 space groups that were thought to represent all possible combinations of lattice-type and symmetry operations. This classification scheme held until 1982, when a new type of fivefold symmetry was discovered in an aluminum-manganese alloy. It contained 20-sided, or icosahedral, structures that showed long-range positional order but repeated in an apparently random, or "quasiperiodic," manner that did not allow for rotational symmetry. Several such solids, now called quasicrystals, have since been found, and the fact that they exhibit fivefold symmetry has been verified. The manner in which they form remains a subject of debate, however, since they require at least two different types of unit cell to achieve long-range order.

X-Ray Diffraction

Max Theodor von Laue (1879–1960), a German physicist, was the first to think of bombarding a crystal with X rays in order to reveal the arrangement of atoms within. He reasoned that crystals should diffract X rays in much the same way that a closely ruled grating diffracts light. This prediction was borne out when two graduate students in physics at the University of Munich, experimenting on a copper sulfate crystal, produced (1912) the first tangible evidence of the internal order of crystalline matter. Thereafter, X-ray diffraction methods developed rapidly, and their use on powdered materials is now a standard identification technique in every materials laboratory. X-ray diffraction of single crystals has led to the determination of such complex structures as hemoglobin and DNA, thereby revolutionizing the fields of biochemistry and medicine.

Modern Crystallography

Crystallographers can now use transmission electron microscopy (see ELECTRON MICROSCOPE) and field ion emis-

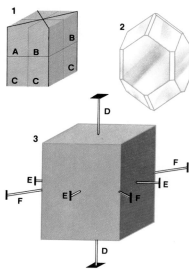

(Left) *The tetragonal system includes all crystals with three axes at right angles to each other, two of which are of equal length. It has five planes of symmetry (1): a horizontal plane cutting the crystal in half (A), two vertical planes bisecting opposite vertical faces (B), and two vertical planes passing through opposite vertical edges (C). An example (2) is N (CH$_3$)$_4$ I. Axes of symmetry (3) includes a 4-fold vertical axes (D), two 2-fold horizontal face axes (E), and two 2-fold horizontal edge axes (F).*

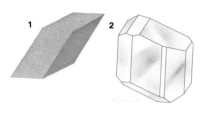

(Left) *The triclinic system includes all crystals with three unequal axes intersecting each other at oblique angles (1). Hydrated iron sulfate (2) is an example of a mineral crystallizing in the triclinic system. Minerals belonging to this system are relatively simple to identify, because they have only a center of symmetry and neither planes nor axes of symmetry (3).*

(Right) *The hexagonal system includes crystals with a vertical axis of variable length and three equal horizontal axes intersecting at 120° angles. The seven planes of symmetry (1) consist of a bisecting horizontal plane (A), three vertical planes bisecting opposite vertical faces (B), and three vertical planes passing through opposite vertical edges (C). Beryl (2) is a hexagonal crystal. Symmetry axes (3) include a 6-fold vertical axis (D) and three 2-fold central horizontal face axes (E) and edge axes (F).*

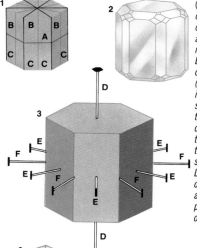

(Right) *The orthorhombic, or rhombic, system includes crystals with three axes of unequal length at right angles to each other. Because any axis can be chosen as the vertical (principal) axis, confusion in classification often results. Orthorhombic crystals have three axial planes of symmetry (1): a horizontal bisecting plane (A) and two vertical planes (B) bisecting opposite faces. Lead sulfate crystals are orthorhombic (2). Three axes of 2-fold symmetry (C) pass through the middle of opposite faces (3).*

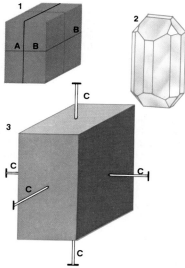

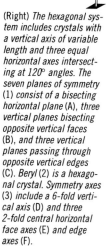

(Left) *The monoclinic system includes all crystals with three axes of unequal length; two intersect at an oblique angle, whereas the third axis is perpendicular to them. In addition to a center of symmetry, the monoclinic system (1) possesses a single axial plane of symmetry (A), which passes through the two axes intersecting at an angle, and/or a single twofold axis of symmetry (B) through the center of the parallelogram faces (3). Sodium bicarbonate (2) crystallizes in the monoclinic system.*

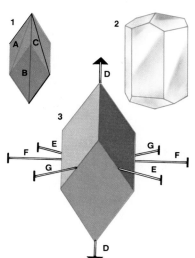

(Left) *The trigonal, or rhombohedral, system includes all crystals with three axes of equal length and equal angles other than 90°. The unit cell is similar to that obtained by stretching or compressing a cube along a diagonal (1). Trigonal crystals have three vertical planes of symmetry (A, B, C). Calcite (2) is representative of this system. Axes of symmetry (3) consist of the principal axis (D), which has 3-fold symmetry, and three lateral 2-fold axes (E, F, G) that join the centers of opposite edges.*

sion imaging and diffraction to study crystals. Today, features as small as 1.4 ANGSTROMS can be imaged and photographed, and pictures of actual atomic crystal arrangement appear routinely in the crystallographic literature. The knowledge obtained has applications in almost every field of science and technology. The production of pure or specifically designed crystals, for example, is essential for SEMICONDUCTOR technology, INTEGRATED CIRCUITS, and systems employing PIEZOELECTRICITY. Methods for producing such crystals now include advanced techniques such as molecular-beam EPITAXY and, potentially, the use of the gravity-free environment of outer space.

Crystal Palace   Built to house the Great Exhibition of 1851 in London, the Crystal Palace was probably the most prophetic building of the 19th century. An immense enclosure of glass and iron, it measured 124 by 563 m (408 by 1,848 ft) overall in ground plan, embraced 91,960 m^2 (989,884 ft^2) of floor area, and contained 83,610 m^2 (900,000 ft^2) of glass.

Sir Joseph PAXTON conceived the Crystal Palace and worked out its general form, but the preparation of working drawings and the construction were carried out by William Barlow, William Cubitt, Sir Charles Fox, C. H. Wild, and others.

The entire structure, a masterpiece of CAST-IRON ARCHITECTURE, was designed on the basis of a 7.3-m (24-ft) module and erected in Hyde Park, London, of prefabricated elements with bolted connections. The building was dismantled and reerected (1852–54) at Sydenham, South London, after the exhibition. In 1936 the building was destroyed by fire.

The Crystal Palace was the first work of distinctly modern architecture, the first great iron-framed, glass-walled building, and an early work of prefabrication built on a scale appropriate to the modern city. It foreshadowed the curtain-walled buildings of the mid-20th century.

The Crystal Palace anticipated modern European and American architecture. It was the first building to use a cast-iron framework and to be made of prefabricated parts.

Ctenophora   see COMB JELLY; INVERTEBRATE

Ctesibius   [ti-sib'-ee-uhs]   Ctesibius (fl. 2d century BC), a Greek Alexandrian, was described as a mechanical genius whose inventiveness was limited only by the restrictions of the world he lived in. Using the power of water and air, he devised a water organ, whose airpipes were operated by the weight of falling water; an air-powered catapult; and a force pump.

Ctesibius is perhaps best remembered for the CLEPSYDRA, or water clock. Although he did not actually invent it, he greatly improved it. While none of his writings survives, later inventors, including HERO OF ALEXANDRIA and the Roman engineer VITRUVIUS, mention him in their works.

Ctesiphon   [tes'-i-fahn]   The ancient Parthian and Sassanian city of Ctesiphon, now bisected by the Tigris, lies about 32 km (20 mi) southeast of Baghdad, Iraq. The site became important during the 1st century BC as the winter residence of the Parthian ARSACID dynasty. It was sacked (AD 165) by the Romans but survived to become the great winter capital of the SASSANIANS.

The most important surviving monument is the Taq-Kisra, the great hall of the Sassanian palace, probably built by KHOSRU I (r. 531–79). Its huge single-span vault of unreinforced brickwork, known as the Arch of Ctesiphon, is among the finest architectural achievements of the Sassanians.

Cuauhtémoc   [koo-ow-tay'-mawk]   Cuauhtémoc, c.1495–1525, became ruler of the AZTECS in 1521, during the siege of TENOCHTITLÁN, and led the final desperate resistance of that city against the Spanish conquistadors. After weeks of street fighting, he surrendered to Hernán CORTES. This act marked the end of the Aztec empire and the beginning of Spanish dominion in Mexico.

Cuauhtémoc was first treated kindly by the Spanish, then imprisoned and tortured, and finally hanged during Cortes's march to Honduras, on a charge of plotting treachery.

Cuba   Cuba, the largest island in the Antilles archipelago in the Caribbean Sea, is located 145 km (90 mi) south of the United States across the Florida Straits. Positioned between the Gulf of Mexico and the Atlantic Ocean, Cuba was discovered by Christopher Columbus on Oct. 27, 1492, during his first trip to the New World, and it remained a Spanish colony until 1898. Cuban governments were mostly authoritarian, with brief periods of democratic rule in the 1940s and early 1950s. The triumph of Fidel CASTRO's guerrilla movement in 1959 ushered in the Cuban revolution and the creation of the only Communist state in the Americas. Resisting the worldwide disintegration of Communist regimes, Cuba in the early 1990s was one of the last few orthodox Marxist countries.

AT A GLANCE

REPUBLIC OF CUBA

Land: Area: 114,524 km^2 (44,218 mi^2). Capital and largest city: Havana (1988 est. pop., 2,059,223).

People: Population (1989 est.): 10,500,000. Density: 92 persons per km^2 (237 per mi^2). Distribution (1989): 72% urban, 28% rural. Official language: Spanish. Major religion: Roman Catholicism.

Government: Communist one-party state. Legislature: National Assembly of People's Power. Political subdivisions: 14 provinces, 1 special municipality.

Economy: GNP (1989): $20.9 billion; $2,000 per capita. Labor distribution (1988): services—30%; manufacturing, mining, and utilities—22%; agriculture—20%; trade—11%. Foreign trade (1988): imports—$7.6 billion; exports—$5.5 billion; Currency 1 Cuban peso = 100 centavos.

Education and Health: Literacy (1988): 96% of adult population. Universities (1984): 4. Hospital beds (1986): 54,028. Physicians (1986) 25,567. Life expectancy (1990): women—78; men—73. Infant mortality (1990): 12 per 1,000 live births.

Land and Resources

Cuba is about 1,200 km (750 mi) long, with a median width of 97 km (60 mi) and a maximum width of 200 km (125 mi). The republic includes the Isle of Youth (formerly, Isle of Pines) to the south and numerous keys and islets.

Topography. The island's topography is varied. Sixty percent of the total surface is plain, with the rest in hillsides and mountain ranges. Pico Turquino, in the Sierra Maestra range in the southeast, reaches to 1,994 m (6,542 ft) and is the highest peak. Other important ranges are the Escambray in central Cuba and the Sierra de los Órganos in the island's western part. The longest river is the Cauto, running for 257 km (160 mi) in a westerly direction across Santiago de Cuba and Granma provinces. Beaches on Cuba's northern coast, such as Varadero, are known for their pure white sand and clear blue green waters. Several deep-water ports, such as HAVANA, SANTIAGO DE CUBA, and CIENFUEGOS handle the nation's foreign commerce.

Climate. A moderate and balmy climate prevails. Seasonal median temperatures range from 18° C (66° F) to 30° C (86° F), but humidity is often high. The rainy season runs from May to October, and dry weather prevails between December and April.

Resources. Cuba has extensive nickel reserves. Cobalt, iron, manganese, and copper are also found. There is little oil, but domestic production totals between 3% and 4% of consumption requirements. The government is carrying out a nuclear-power program, and hydroelectric energy is generated.

People

Cuba's principal racial groups are mulattoes (mixed black and white), whites, and blacks. Ethnic or racial conflict is quite rare. Spanish is the national language, and Roman Catholicism the nominal religion, but Marxist-Leninist ideology dominates secular life.

Demography. The capital, Havana, is the largest city, accounting for nearly 20% of Cuba's total population. Santiago de Cuba is the second largest city, followed by CAMAGUEY. The population is mostly young, and the country does not have a high rate of population growth.

Education and Health. The government is in charge of all educational institutions; private and religious education has been abolished. School attendance is mandatory, and Cuba has one of the highest literacy rates in Latin America. Political criteria affect admission to the universities, but education is free for all citizens. Technical and scientific subjects are emphasized over more traditional studies. The University of Havana is the leading institution of higher learning, but Cuba has 40 institutions of advanced training.

The government-run health system is recognized as one of the best in the Third World, with most services provided free. (Almost 25% of the government's budget goes for education and public health.) The provision of health care is highly decentralized: residents have access to services in neighborhoods, schools, and the workplace, as well as in clinics and hospitals. Hundreds of Cuban doctors, nurses, and specialists serve in several Third World countries.

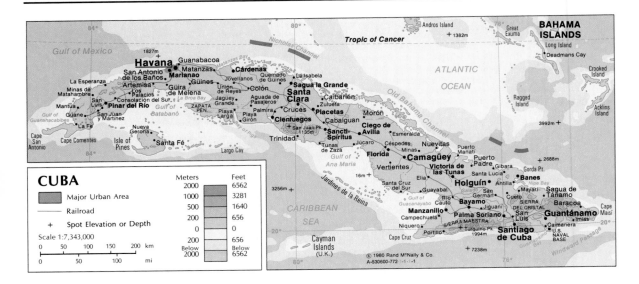

CUBA

		Meters	Feet
	Major Urban Area	2000	6562
		1000	3281
	Railroad	500	1640
+	Spot Elevation or Depth	200	656
		0	0

Scale 1:7,343,000

0   50   100   150   200 km

0   50   100   mi

200 / Below 2000 — 656 / Below 6562

© 1980 Rand McNally & Co.
A-530600-772 -1- -1- -1

The Arts. Artistic expression is conditioned by political criteria, and the culture is affected by Marxist ideology as well as by traditional Spanish and African influences. Expression is watched by the state, dissent is proscribed, and nonconformity is frowned on. Ideological pressures and subtle forms of censorship affect the content of literature, cinema, and theater. Many writers and artists have left Cuba; an exception was the novelist Alejo Carpentier. Another of Cuba's leading cultural figures is the prima ballerina Alicia ALONSO, who founded the Ballet de Cuba.

Economic Activity

Sugar is the principal cash crop, and sugar exports bring in 85–90% of total foreign exchange earnings. The industry employs nearly 500,000 workers. In the late 19th and early 20th centuries, U.S. ownership of sugar mills and lands was common, but domestic capital also participated in production. Since 1959 the industry has been nationalized and, to some extent, modernized. Factories, utilities, large farms, and most other units of production were also nationalized in the 1960s. Government planners determine what is to be produced by industry and agriculture; prices are regulated, and quotas established for farms, factories, sugar mills, and so on. The government emphasizes the production of collective goods over consumer items. Scarcity prevails, but basic needs are met. Despite modest rates of economic growth in the 1980s, Cuba has fallen short of production goals in sugar, citrus fruits, tobacco, and other commodities.

Manufacturing and Mining. Nickel is the principal mineral, accounting for two-thirds of all mineral output. Cuba is one of the world's largest exporters of nickel, and it has the fourth largest reserves. Oil, copper, chrome, and salt are mined in small quantities. Steel is also manufactured, but imports are necessary. Other manufactures include foodstuffs, canned fruits and vegetables, and canned fish. Cement is produced, as are textiles and light equipment.

Agriculture and Fishing. Potatoes, rice, sweet potatoes,

Havana, situated in northwestern Cuba on the Gulf of Mexico, is the nation's capital and leading seaport. The city was founded by Spanish conquistadors during the 16th century.

Cuban citizens parade through the streets of Havana on May Day, an important holiday honoring workers observed in many Socialist and Communist nations. In 1961, Cuba's socialist leader, Fidel Castro, announced his conversion to communism and his intention to pattern Cuba's government and economy after the Soviet model.

and eggs make up the bulk of nonsugar agriculture. Tobacco and citrus are produced and exported; tobacco is grown mostly on small, private farms. State farms and collective farms organize rural producers. Cattle raising has not been successful, and meat and milk are rationed. Fish production has risen.

Foreign Trade. Until the late 1980s, 85% of Cuba's trade was with the Communist bloc, but the upheaval in the Soviet Union and Eastern Europe has disrupted this pattern. Cuba must import foodstuffs, machinery, and transportation equipment, as well as most of its oil, pharmaceuticals, chemicals, tires, steel, and spare parts. Japan, Canada, and Spain are Cuba's main noncommunist trading partners. Cuba consistently runs a deficit in its foreign trade, which adversely affects its credit standing and financial health.

Government

Cuba is a one-party state, with the Cuban Communist party (PCC) as the only legally recognized party. The party's position is dominant; it oversees all aspects of government and national life. Total party membership is about 485,000.

Cuba's socialist constitution came into effect in 1976. The Organs of People's Power (OPP) function as local governments in each of 169 municipalities. OPP delegates elect deputies to provincial assemblies and to the 500-member National Assembly. The latter is not independent; rather, it ratifies the policies of the leadership. Cuban president Fidel Castro is head of both state and government; he is also first secretary of the PCC and commander in chief of the armed forces.

History

Indian tribes, who lived by subsistence agriculture and fishing, inhabited Cuba at the time of its discovery

(1492) by Columbus. The Spaniards quickly conquered the Indians. Cruel treatment and disease destroyed many Indians, who supplied the labor for Cuba's early development. Gradually, the cultivation and processing of sugar came to dominate the economy, linking Cuba to world markets. Hundreds of thousands of black slaves were imported over two centuries, and slave labor contributed to the expansion of the sugar industry.

Minor rebellions and conspiracies were common in the 19th century, but Cuban efforts to wrench free from Spain did not succeed until 1898. The TEN YEARS' WAR (1868–78) proved a bloody and costly affair, as did the War of Independence (1895–98), in which the United States finally intervened (see SPANISH-AMERICAN WAR). The leaders of the independence movement were Jose MARTÍ,

Tobacco, Cuba's second most valuable export crop, is dried in the sun before being removed to a shed (upper right) for curing. Cuba is famous for its hand-rolled cigars (habanos) made from high-grade tobacco grown in Pinar del Río.

Soviet-built machinery has been important in Cuba's efforts to increase its harvest of sugarcane. This crop, the country's leading agricultural product, accounts for more than four-fifths of Cuba's revenue from exports.

Máximo Gómez, and Antonio Maceo. The United States occupied Cuba from 1898 to 1902 and then turned Cuba into a protectorate after independence. U.S. capital flowed into Cuba, and the United States exercised substantial political influence.

In 1906, 1912, and 1917, U.S. military contingents returned to Cuba to restore stability and protect private interests. A progressive constitution went into effect in 1940, ushering in a period of democracy. The democratic interlude under presidents Fulgencio BATISTA, Ramón GRAU SAN MARTÍN, and Carlos Prío Socarrás lasted until 1952, when a coup by Batista restored authoritarian rule. Insurrectional movements emerged in the 1950s, and Batista was overthrown by Fidel Castro's guerrillas in 1959.

A nationalist and popular revolution moved forward, substantially supported by the middle class. The revolutionary regime enacted reform laws and proceeded to change the character of society. It soon became evident that a radical socialist revolution was underway. The regime successfully challenged U.S. economic and political interests, and it obtained economic and military assistance from the Soviet Union. The regime's power is unchallenged, but not all of its policies are well received. One million Cubans have left since 1959.

Washington and Havana are suspicious of each other. Relations were broken in 1961, and the situation was more strained after the BAY OF PIGS INVASION and the CUBAN MISSILE CRISIS. In 1962, Cuba was suspended from the Organization of American States (it has since reestablished relations with several Latin American countries). The U.S. embargo imposed on Cuba in 1962 is in effect, but its utility is marginal. The massive exodus of 125,000 Cubans from the port of Mariel in 1980 and the U.S. invasion of Grenada in 1983 have frozen relations.

Furthermore, in the rapidly changing international situation in the early 1990s, Cuba has been losing many of its friends. The unraveling of communism in the Soviet Union, the collapse of Eastern European Communist regimes, and the electoral defeat of Sandinistas in Nicaragua have left Cuba rather isolated. Fidel Castro, however, persists in maintaining that the country needs neither GLASNOST nor PERESTROIKA.

Cuban Missile Crisis   The Cuban Missile Crisis occurred in October 1962, after U.S. intelligence reconnaissance flights verified reports that the USSR was constructing launching sites for medium-range and intermediate-range nuclear missiles on the island of Cuba. The USSR apparently hoped to achieve a more favorable balance of power, to protect the Cuban Communist government of Fidel Castro (which the United States had attempted to overthrow in the abortive Bay of Pigs invasion of 1961), to gain greater diplomatic leverage vis-à-vis the United States, to damage U.S. credibility, and to achieve greater influence in Latin America.

President John F. KENNEDY rejected military advice for a full-scale surprise attack on Cuba and instead delivered a public ultimatum to the USSR on October 22. He declared a "quarantine," or naval blockade, of Cuba and demanded withdrawal of all offensive missiles. After nearly two weeks of unprecedented tension, the Soviet government of Nikita Khrushchev yielded. Kennedy, in return, agreed to refrain from attempting an overthrow of Castro's government. Despite this concession, all sides regarded the outcome as a substantial victory for the United States, and Kennedy won a reputation as a formidable international statesman. The USSR began a long-term effort to strengthen its military capability, but in the immediate future both nations sought to relax hostilities.

In the late 1980s several unique conferences of U.S., Soviet, and Cuban officials and scholars contributed new revelations and perspective to the historical record of the crisis.

This aerial photograph, taken by a U-2 reconnaissance plane, was presented by the U.S. government in 1962 as evidence that the Soviet Union had installed intermediate-range ballistic missiles in Cuba.

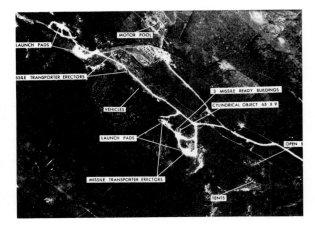

Cuban tree frog   The Cuban tree frog, *Osteopilus septentrionalis,* family Hylidae, is the largest tree frog in the United States. Females, which are larger than males, attain 5–13 cm (2–5 in) in length. The species is native to Cuba, the Isle of Pines, and the Bahama and Cayman islands, but it has been introduced, possibly as a stowaway in produce, into Puerto Rico, south Florida, and the Florida Keys. It has a rough, warty skin and large toe disks. The males have loud, raucous voices.

cube   In geometry, a cube is a solid bounded by six plane faces (a hexahedron) that are all congruent squares. It may also be defined as a regular POLYHEDRON having six faces. A cube has 8 vertices and 12 edges. For a cube having edges of length *a*, the volume is $V = a^3$. In algebra, the cube of a quantity is its third power, as $4 \times 4 \times 4 = 4^3 = 64$.

cubism   Cubism was a completely new, nonimitative style of painting and sculpture that was cofounded by Pablo PICASSO and Georges BRAQUE in 1908 and survived in its purest form until the mid-1920s. Cubism had an impact on art in general that extended far beyond the existence of the painting style itself; it paved the way for other art revolutions, such as DADA and SURREALISM, and was seminal to much of ABSTRACT ART. It also fostered newer modes of art, such as FUTURISM and Orphism, and even affected the formal structure of styles whose origins had predated cubism, such as expressionism.

Picasso and Braque found the precedents and initial concepts for cubism in two art sources. One was primitive art—African tribal masks, Iberian sculpture, and Egyptian bas-reliefs. The other influence was the work of Paul CÉZANNE, especially his late still lifes and landscapes. Cézanne had introduced a new geometrization of forms as well as new spatial relationships that finally broke with the Renaissance traditions of perspective. In 1907, Picasso synthesized these two sources in his seminal painting *Les Demoiselles d'Avignon* (1906–07; Museum of Modern Art, New York City). Braque, one of the few artists to see and understand Picasso's painting at the time, im-

mediately transformed his style from a Fauvist (see FAUVISM) to an early cubist idiom. In March 1909 the French critic Louis Vauxcelles, reviewing the Salon des Indépendants, referred disparagingly to Braque's style as one that "reduces everything to little cubes"; hence, cubism.

Cubism developed from the early phase of 1908–09 to the more complex and systematic style of 1910–12, known as analytic cubism, implying intense analysis of all elements in a painting. It consisted of facets, or cubes, arranged in superimposed, transparent planes with clearly defined edges that established mass, space, and the implication of movement. During this period, Picasso and Braque employed a palette of muted greens, grays, browns, and ochers. Despite this radical method of painting, the subject matter consisted of traditional landscapes, portraits, and still lifes. Fragments of the faces, guitars, or wine glasses that were the subject of these works can be detected through the shifting facets or contours.

The dissolving, overlapping shapes of these paintings have suggested to some scholars that the objects were

(Above) *Picasso's* Les Demoiselles d'Avignon *(1906–07) introduced the movement that became known as cubism. In this painting Picasso abandoned conventional perspective by fragmenting the subjects into distorted planes and forms. (Museum of Modern Art, New York.)*

(Left) *The French avant-garde painter Georges Braque's fragmentation of natural elements in* Still Life with Erik Satie Score *(c.1920) is typical of cubist painting. Braque's inclusion of literal materials in his work mirrors the techniques of collage and papier collé. (Musée d'Art Moderne, Paris.)*

seen from multiple viewpoints at the same time. Picasso and Braque, however, frequently denied the notion of multiple viewpoints; they explained that the cubist structure was developed as a means of providing all the essential information regarding a three-dimensional object within a two-dimensional canvas.

When Picasso and Braque invented COLLAGES and *papiers collés* in 1912, they initiated the study of color and light within a cubist oil painting, a stage known as synthetic cubism (1912–14). The introduction of bright color resulted in the further flattening of space and the elaboration of the picture surface with such decorative devices as the stippling technique derived from pointillism.

By 1910 other painters had joined the cubist movement, including Juan GRIS, Fernand LÉGER, Albert GLEIZES, and Jean Metzinger. Others, such as Robert DELAUNAY, Marcel DUCHAMP, and Joan MIRÓ moved through cubism into exceptionally personal styles. Cubism was introduced to the United States with the ARMORY SHOW of 1913. Notable American cubists included Max WEBER and Stuart DAVIS. In 1909, Picasso began to create a cubist sculpture. Other sculptors who followed in the cubist idiom were Aleksandr ARCHIPENKO, Henri LAURENS, and Jacques LIPCHITZ.

Cuchulain [koo-hoo'-lin]   Cuchulain was the mythical hero of the Old Irish Gaelic epic *Táin Bó Cúalnge* (The Cattle Raid of Cooley) from the cycle of tales centering on the kingdom of Ulster. Though not a god, Cuchulain was capable of superhuman feats. He was killed by three druids at the command of Medb, queen of Connacht, after his enemies offered him a meal of dog's flesh, forcing him to violate one of two resolutions: never to refuse a meal and never to eat dog's flesh.

cuckoo   The name *cuckoo* is used for some of the 127 species of birds of the cuckoo family, Cuculidae, order

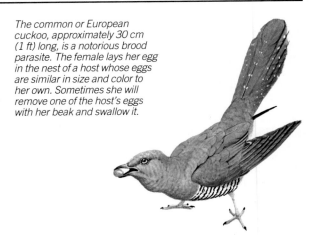

The common or European cuckoo, approximately 30 cm (1 ft) long, is a notorious brood parasite. The female lays her egg in the nest of a host whose eggs are similar in size and color to her own. Sometimes she will remove one of the host's eggs with her beak and swallow it.

Cuculiformes. Some cuckoos are known to be brood parasites—birds that build no nest of their own but leave their eggs in the nest of other birds, which then rear the young. Nest parasitism is characteristic of less than half of all cuckoo species. Some cuckoos are arboreal, but others, such as the ROADRUNNER of the southwestern United States, are poor fliers. The arboreal types are insectivorous; the larger, ground types feed on snakes, lizards, small rodents, and other birds.

Most cuckoos are drab gray or brown and have long tails and down-curved bills. The glossy cuckoos, however, are a striking emerald green.

cucumber   The cucumber, *Cucumis sativus*, is a vine fruit that can be eaten fresh or pickled. A member of the Cucurbitaceae family and related to melons and squash-

The cucumber is a popular warm-weather plant. The slicing cucumber (bottom) is longer and darker than the pickling variety (middle). The vine (top) generally grows to about 2.4 m (8 ft) long, although newer bush varieties require less space.

The two cuckoos common to North America are about 30 cm (1 ft) long. They are the eastern black-billed cuckoo (left) and the western yellow-billed cuckoo, also called the "rain crow" because its repeated call purportedly signals a storm.

es, it is native to northwestern India.

The plant is a frost-tender annual that thrives in temperatures of 20° to 30° C (69° to 86° F). It has large, triangular leaves borne on branched, trailing stems; its separate staminate and pistillate flowers are pollinated by bees. The fruit is harvested in the immature stage, 50 to 70 days after planting.

Long and dark-green slicing types such as Marketmore are grown for marketing. Light-green and shorter types such as SMR 58 are grown for pickling. A new type bearing only pistillate flowers produces high, early yields. Specialized cultivars that produce seedless fruit are used for greenhouse culture.

cucumber tree   see MAGNOLIA

Cuenca [kweng'-kah]   Cuenca is the capital of Azuay province in south central Ecuador. It lies on the PAN AMERICAN HIGHWAY about 109 km (68 mi) southeast of Guayaquil, at an altitude of 2,596 m (8,517 ft). The population is 218,490 (1989 est.). The city is a center of a farming and cattle-raising area. Panama hats and leather are manufactured there. Cuenca was established by Spaniards in 1557 on the site of an Indian village.

Cuernavaca [kwair-nah-vah'-kah]   Cuernavaca is the capital of Morelos state in south central Mexico and is an agricultural and manufacturing center. It is located at an altitude of about 1,500 m (5,000 ft), giving it a mild climate that makes it a popular resort area. The population is 232,355 (1983 est.) and includes many foreign retirees. A favorite vacation spot even for Aztec nobles, the city was captured by the Spanish under Hernán CORTÉS before 1521. The center of the town has a small square and the large Jardin de los Heros plaza, the 18th-century Borda gardens, and one of the oldest cathedrals in Mexico, commissioned by Cortés in 1529. The Cortés Palace (1531) contains murals by Diego RIVERA. Murals by David Alfaro SIQUEIROS are in the Casino de la Selva hotel. Near the railroad station is the Teopanzolco Pyramid, believed to be built by Tlahuican Indians and uncovered in 1910. Institutes of learning include the University of Morelos (1953), the regional Fine Arts Institute, and the Institute for Mexican Studies.

Cueva, Juan de la [kway'-vah]   Juan de la Cueva, 1550?–1610, was a major figure in the creation of Spanish national drama. His 14 surviving tragedies and comedies, of which the best known is *El infamador* (The False Accuser), were first performed on the Sevillian stage from 1579 to 1581. He also wrote an important verse treatise on literary and dramatic theory, the *Ejemplar poético* (Poetic Guidebook, 1606).

Cuevas, José Luis [kway'-vahs]   José Luis Cuevas, b. Feb. 26, 1934, is a leading Mexican expressionist painter. Using the stark tonal contrasts of line drawing and the improvisatory energy of ink washes, Cuevas presents writhing, distorted figures in depressed and terrifying settings. His art is a violent protest against the inhumane underside of ordinary society.

Cukor, George [koo'-kohr]   George Cukor, b. New York City, July 7, 1899, d. Jan. 24, 1983, was a film director esteemed for the taste and literacy of his work. He had extensive stage experience before going to Hollywood in 1929, where he directed *Dinner at Eight* (1933), *Little Women* (1933), and *Camille* (1936). Cukor showed his versatility in such films as the urbane comedy *The Philadelphia Story* (1940) and in such thrillers as *Gaslight* (1944) and *A Double Life* (1947). His later films include the comedies *Adam's Rib* (1949) and *Pat and Mike* (1952) and the innovative *A Star Is Born* (1954). Katharine Hepburn, a Cukor discovery, shared a long career with the director, from her first Hollywood film, *A Bill of Divorcement* (1932), through the 1979 television remake of *The Corn Is Green*. Cukor won an Academy Award for *My Fair Lady* (1964). His last film was the comedy *Rich and Famous* (1981).

The Philadelphia Story *(1940), starring* (left to right) *James Stewart, Ruth Hussey, John Howard, Katharine Hepburn, and Cary Grant, established George Cukor as a master of sophisticated comedy.*

Culbertson, Ely   Ely Culbertson, b. Romania, July 22, 1891, d. Dec. 27, 1955, was one of America's finest contract bridge players. An unknown club player in 1930, he challenged a pair of British experts to play against him and his wife, Josephine. To finance the trip to England, he wrote his *Blue Book,* detailing the bidding system they used. The couple won, and soon their system became popular. Culbertson enhanced his reputation by winning a challenge match in 1931, playing with his wife against expert Sydney Lenz and several different partners.

Culiacán [koo-lee-ah-kahn'] Culiacán (1983 est. pop., 560,011) is the capital of Sinaloa state in western Mexico, situated at the base of the Sierra Madre Occidental. Surrounded by irrigated agricultural land and linked to the Pacific port of Altata 65 km (40 mi) away, Culiacán is a commercial and transportation center. The University of Sinaloa (1873) is there. Culiacán was founded in 1531 by the Spanish.

Cullen, Countee   Countee Cullen, b. New York, May 30, 1903, d. Jan. 9, 1946, was a black American poet whose sensuous lyric verse was a major contribution to the 1920s literary movement known as the HARLEM RENAISSANCE. Although influenced stylistically by Keats, Cullen found his themes in the life of his race. *Color* (1925), *Copper Sun* (1927), *The Ballad of the Brown Girl* (1927), and *The Black Christ* (1929) are among his verse collections. His novel, *One Way to Heaven*, appeared in 1932.

cults   see RELIGIOUS CULTS

Cultural Revolution   The Great Socialist Cultural Revolution was begun in 1966 by MAO ZEDONG (Mao Tse-tung) as a means of revitalizing China's revolutionary zeal. Radical students, organized and trained as Red Guards, staged demonstrations and led often-violent attacks on the four "olds": old ideas, old culture, old customs, and old habits. During the mass campaign against intellectuals and things foreign, those accused of being "bad elements" or "revisionists" were forced to perform manual labor and publicly humiliated in "struggle meetings." By 1968, with China on the verge of civil war as radical factions fought one another, the Red Guards were disbanded, and the army was brought in to restore order while continuing the revolution. The Cultural Revolution damaged the credibility and morale of the Communist party. It officially ended in 1969, but many of its excesses continued until Mao's death, in 1976. JIANG QING (Chiang Ch'ing), Mao's wife, was a leader of the Cultural Revolution. Those purged during this period included LIU SHAOQI (Liu Shao-ch'i) and DENG XIAOPING (Teng Hsiao-p'ing). Many thousands died.

culture   Anthropologists and other social scientists define human culture as learned behavior acquired by individuals as members of a social group. The concept of culture was first explicitly defined in 1871 by the British anthropologist Edward B. TYLOR. He used the term to refer to "that complex whole which includes knowledge, belief, art, morals, law, custom and any other capabilities and habits acquired by man as a member of society." Since then, anthropologists have offered numerous refinements and variations on this definition, but all have agreed that culture is learned behavior in contrast to genetically endowed behavior.

Each human society has a body of norms governing behavior and other knowledge to which an individual is socialized, or enculturated, beginning at birth. Just as the culture of specific societies around the world can be discussed, culture can also be considered as the sum total of human knowledge and acquired behavior of humankind. In this sense, there is a body of knowledge that is not shared by all human societies at any time nor by all individuals of any society. Agriculture is an important aspect of human culture that many hunter-gatherer and pastoral societies do not traditionally share.

Transmission of Culture. Human societies consist of organized groups of individuals, usually of both sexes and all ages, which have a set of behavioral rules that are transmitted from one generation to another. All human behavior is either entirely learned or drastically modified by social learning. Even such strong biological drives or instincts as sex and hunger are modified by culture. Sexual behavior is channeled by TABOOS in virtually all human societies, and even hungry people may refuse food that violates their religious taboos and DIETARY LAWS or is considered repugnant in their culture. Humankind's overwhelming dependence on learned behavior is made possible by certain unique biological features, particularly the relatively long life cycle and the extended period of CHILD DEVELOPMENT during which the child is dependent on and educated by parents and other adults.

The emergence of language was the giant step that made possible the remarkable complexity of human culture. All human cultures are based on language, and all human languages, even those of nonliterate peoples, are sufficiently complex to transmit the full totality of a human culture. Likewise, any language is flexible enough to expand in vocabulary and structure as the culture of society becomes more complex. Children acquire the culture of their society mainly through language. A child of any race or biological type can learn any human language and, through that language, acquire any human culture.

Cultural Diversity. In spite of the great diversity of human cultures around the world, in all societies certain universals of culture reflect basic responses to the needs of human beings as social animals. These universals include a primary means of subsistence—for example, hunting and gathering, agriculture, industrialized labor; some form of the primary FAMILY; a system of KINSHIP; a set of rules of social conduct; religion; material culture (tools, weapons, clothing); forms of art; and many other institutions that indicate the common adaptations of all human societies to varied natural environments.

A culture pattern generally refers to a set of cultural traits or elements that form an interrelated system. The plow is an element of a culture pattern that originally consisted of the plow itself, the domestic animals used to draw the plow, the Old World cereal crops such as wheat or barley, the cultivation of fields larger than gardens, and the use of fertilizers from the dung of domestic animals. As a culture pattern, plow agriculture and its associated elements diffused from the Middle East about 5000 BC. Such culture patterns persist over time; yet as they are spread from one culture to another, new elements are frequently added. Today, plow agriculture as a culture pattern has incorporated new crops such as peanuts, soybeans, and other vegetables and new forms of synthetic fertilizers.

The term *culture pattern* is also sometimes used to mean the coherent configuration of behavior, customs, institutions, and values that characterize culture or civilization.

Customs and behavior that are considered sinful in one culture may be totally acceptable, even praised, in another. Most anthropologists view human cultures in terms of cultural relativism, the concept that all cultures are orderly systems within which customs and institutions are rational in their own terms. Thus the Hindu belief that prohibits the consumption of beef and guarantees special treatment of cows can be seen as functional and rational, not only within the religious tradition of the sacred cow, but also in terms of the usefulness of the cow as a traction animal and as a source of dung for fertilizer and fuel. Most anthropologists would also admit that human cultures sometimes contain customs and values counter to human welfare; some examples are slavery, head-hunting, and cannibalism.

Cultural Evolution. The evolution of human culture is closely linked to the development of technology, through which humankind has exploited the environment in increasingly complex ways (see TECHNOLOGY, HISTORY OF). In the 19th century many pioneering anthropologists and sociologists theorized that each human culture passed through specific stages of evolution. The American anthropologist Lewis Henry MORGAN postulated a three-part development consisting of an initial stage that he called savagery, when humankind collected seeds and nuts; followed by barbarism, when humankind cultivated grains, used some metal tools, and lived in permanent dwellings; and finally, by civilization, initiated by the invention of the phonetic alphabet and writing. Anthropologists, archaeologists, and historians no longer believe that every culture necessarily progresses through every stage. Obviously a simple society composed of a few hundred individuals in the Amazon rain forest could not independently develop a complex system of irrigation-based agriculture or be able to manufacture automobiles. However, through culture contact or acculturation, so-called Stone Age peoples can learn to drive and maintain automobiles and tractors soon after such mechanized devices are introduced into their cultures. Human culture can thus be said to be accretive, that is, it can spread from one society to another according to a society's ability to absorb new ideas, institutions, and technologies.

Cultural Diffusion. Elements of culture are spread from society to society through direct or indirect contact among groups, a process known as DIFFUSION. With the continuing improvement of communications and modes of travel, the interchange of culture elements has increased drastically. Great cultural differences still exist, however, not only among nations but within the boundaries of nations from one ethnic group to another (see CULTURE AREA). Moreover, not all aspects of a culture diffuse with the same rapidity and ease. A steel axe is more

efficient than a stone axe and, when available, will be borrowed at once by the culture into which it is introduced. A political system, a religion, or an ideal of what is beautiful, however, is more resistant to diffusion than are material aspects.

See also: ANTHROPOLOGY; ARCHAEOLOGY; CIVILIZATION; PREHISTORIC HUMANS.

—

Culture and Anarchy In his essay *Culture and Anarchy* (1869), the English poet and critic Matthew ARNOLD addressed himself to the problems arising from the extension of voting rights to the working class. Using irony as a tool, he characterized British society as consisting of Barbarians (upper class), Philistines (middle class), and Populace (working class). Hope for a righteous society, he held, resided in the influence of people of culture, defenders of beauty and truth whom he called "the true apostles of equality."

—

culture area A culture area is a geographic region within which the human population shares similar culture traits, patterns of cultural ecology, and a similar way of life. Culture traits include anything that has material form, a recognized function, or an acknowledged value to the culturally related group. Patterns of cultural ecology may be seen in patterns of land division and use, settlement, transportation, resource utilization, architecture, and plant and animal husbandry. Culture hearths are well-defined culture core areas where a cluster of traits is most fully developed.

The culture area concept is used by anthropologists, geographers, and other social scientists as a means of identifying, classifying, and better understanding human culture within a specific spatial dimension. Although attempts have been made to identify culture areas on a global scale, most scholars tend to define culture areas within continental, or even smaller, geographic regions.

Scholars frequently disagree on the number and the precise spatial distribution of culture areas. Within most primary, or first-order, culture areas, second- and often third-order culture realms may also be identified. The European culture area, for example, can easily be subdivided into at least three distinct subcultural units: the Mediterranean, Northwestern, and Eastern realms, each of which has peripheral transitional belts. Further cultural distinctions can be made on the basis of ethnic (national) and linguistic blocs existing within each realm.

—

culture lag A culture lag is an aspect of a culture preserved from the past that is out of keeping with a contemporary way of life. In the process of culture change, certain elements that change more slowly than others tend to persist in a society even after more efficient or rational elements have been developed to replace them. The term *culture lag* was first used by the sociologist William F. Ogburn in 1922.

culture shock   Social scientists use the term *culture shock* to denote the feeling of depression, often expressed as homesickness, caused by living in a foreign environment. Faced with an unknown or poorly understood foreign language and confused by different codes of conduct, unfamiliar foods, and even unfamiliar physical surroundings, the traveler or new resident may look upon the people and the unaccustomed behavior with distaste, and sometimes with fear. Culture shock, when recognized as such, passes.

Cumae   [kue'-mee]   Cumae, an ancient city near Naples, was perhaps the earliest Greek colony in Italy. It was probably founded *c.*750 BC by Chalcis. Cumae prospered, founding and dominating a number of other Greek colonies. Its hero, and later tyrant, Aristodemus, held off Etruscan invaders in the 6th century BC, and Cumae kept its supremacy until 421 BC when it was taken by the Sabelli. Cumae subsequently came under Roman control, and its inhabitants eventually became full citizens of Rome in the 2d century BC. Although gradually eclipsed by other cities, it survived until the 13th century AD. Cumae's extensive archaeological remains include the cave where the Cumaean Sybil of Apollo probably delivered her prophesies.

Cumans   The Cumans (or Kumans) were a nomadic people of Turkish origin, who from the 11th to the 13th century established a powerful empire in southern Russia (where they were called Polovtsi). The period of Cuman conquest began *c.*1030, and within a century the Cumans ruled from the Volga to the Danube River. During the 12th century, based in Kiev, they were a continual threat to Hungary and the Byzantine Empire. In the 13th century, however, they faced an increasingly powerful Hungarian kingdom, and their rule was broken by attacks from the east by Mongols. The tribes were dispersed, some joining the Khanate of the GOLDEN HORDE.

Cumberland   see CUMBRIA

Cumberland, Richard   Richard Cumberland, b. Cambridge, England, Feb. 19, 1732, d. May 7, 1811, was a popular 18th-century playwright. Although he aspired to write tragedy, only two efforts in this vein, *The Jew* (1794) and *The Wheel of Fortune* (1795), were well received. He enjoyed greater success with sentimental comedies such as *The Brothers* (1769), *The West Indian* (1771), and *The Fashionable Lover* (1772). His *Memoirs* (1806–07) contains interesting material on his association with the actor, manager, and playwright David Garrick and on his life as a government official and diplomat.

Cumberland Gap   At an altitude of 500 m (1,640 ft), the Cumberland Gap is a natural pass in the Cumberland Plateau of the Allegheny ridge. Named for the duke of Cumberland, son of George II, it is located between Middlesboro, Ky., and the town of Cumberland Gap, Tenn., near the point where Kentucky, Tennessee, and Virginia meet. The Wilderness Road blazed by Daniel BOONE, which became a main route for westward migration, runs through the gap. Since 1955 this road has been part of the Cumberland Gap National Historical Park.

Cumberland Plateau   The Cumberland Plateau is the western portion of the Appalachian mountain system, a southern extension of the Allegheny Plateau. It stretches about 725 km (450 mi) from southern West Virginia into Alabama. Its average elevation is about 450 to 600 m (1,500 to 2,000 ft). The Cumberland Mountains rise on its southeastern border. Big Black Mountain in Kentucky is the highest peak (1,263 m/4,145 ft).

Cumberland River   The Cumberland River, a major source of hydroelectric power, is formed in southeastern Kentucky by the confluence of the Poor and Clover forks and flows southwest into Tennessee. At Nashville it turns northwest and reenters Kentucky to join the Ohio River at Smithland. The Cumberland is 1,106 km (687 mi) long. Near its mouth a canal 2.5 km (1.5 mi) long links it to the Tennessee River. Dams of the TENNESSEE VALLEY AUTHORITY have created many reservoirs, including Lake Cumberland in Kentucky, which is 160 km (100 mi) long, and Lake Barkley in Kentucky and Tennessee.

During the Civil War the Cumberland was strategically valuable to both sides. The Union capture of Fort Donelson, Tenn., in February 1862 was an important victory, giving Union forces a waterway deep into the South.

Cumbria   [kuhm'-bree-uh]   Cumbria is a county in northwestern England, bounded by Scotland to the north and the Irish Sea to the west. It covers 6,807 km^2 (2,628 m^2), and the population is 489,200 (1988 est.). CARLISLE is the administrative center. Encompassing the LAKE DISTRICT, the area is crossed by the Cumbrian Mountains, which reach 978 m (3,208 ft) at Scafell Pike, the highest point in England. Farming takes place in the valleys of the rivers Derwent, Esk, and Kent. Coal, gypsum, iron, lead, and silver are mined. Industries include shipbuilding, fishing, and the production of nuclear power. Cumbria was created in 1974 from parts of the former counties of LANCASHIRE and YORKSHIRE and all of Cumberland and Westmorland.

cumin   [kuhm'-in]   Cumin is an annual herb, *Cuminum cyminum*, in the family Umbelliferae, cultivated for its small fragrant seeds. Ground cumin is added to curries, chili powders, and chutneys and is used to flavor meats, pickles, cheese, and sausages. Its essential oil is used in seasonings, pickles, and meat sauces; as an aromatic in perfumes; and as a flavoring in liqueurs. Native to the

Mediterranean region, cumin is cultivated in Morocco, Turkey, Spain, the USSR, Iran, and India. Black cumin, *Nigella sativa*, is used in curries and cheeses.

Cummings, E. E. Edward Estlin Cummings, b. Cambridge, Mass., Oct. 14, 1894, d. Sept. 3, 1962, was a poet, playwright, prose writer, and painter whose vital transcendental vision found embodiment in a startling array of innovative artistic devices, where typography, punctuation, grammar, syntax, diction, imagery, and rhythm were often pushed to their limits.

After completing his B.A. and M.A. in English and classics at Harvard University by 1916, Cummings volunteered for the Norton-Harjes Ambulance Corps in France during World War I. He wrote letters back home criticizing the conduct of the war, and the nervous French censors had him arrested and sent (1917) to a detention center, where he remained for three months before being released. This harrowing prison-camp experience became the basis of his first published book, *The Enormous Room* (1922), one of the best American works to come out of that war. Written as a journal of his prison stay, it is heightened by an already experimental prose style and a hatred of the bureaucracy that could treat helpless and innocent civilians so cruelly. On his return from France to the United States, refusing his family's wish that he seek a commission, Cummings was drafted into the army until shortly after the 1918 Armistice. He depicts military life satirically in such poems as "i sing of Olaf glad and big" (1931).

After the war, Cummings devoted himself entirely to his writing and painting, publishing 11 books of poems—with a posthumous volume appearing the year after his death. All are collected in *Complete Poems 1913–1962* (1972).

The American poet E. E. Cummings, though most widely known as an innovative experimentalist with verse forms and language, was also an accomplished painter, as evidenced by this self-portrait. Although Cummings was famous for, among other things, his typographically striking poetry, it should also be noted that he made extensive use of traditional, metered and rhymed forms, especially the sonnet.

He also published a second antibureaucracy journal, this time of his journey to the Soviet Union, entitled *EIMI* (Greek for "I Am"), in 1933, as well as several plays—*HIM* (1927), *Anthropos: The Future of Art* (1930; 1945), and *Santa Claus: A Morality* (1946)—and a scenario for a ballet called *Tom* (1935), based on *Uncle Tom's Cabin*. His lectures and essays are to be found in *i: SIX NONLECTURES* (1953) and *E. E. Cummings: A Miscellany* (1958; rev. ed. 1965); a group of stories for children entitled *Fairy Tales* appeared in 1965; and some correspondence was published in *Selected Letters* (1969).

---

cumulonimbus clouds see THUNDERSTORM

Cumulus clouds can form when warm, moist air rising from the sun-heated ground encounters the cooler temperatures of higher elevations. These low-lying, domelike clouds take their name from the Latin word meaning "heap."

---

cumulus clouds [kue'-mue-luhs] Cumulus CLOUDS, composed of water droplets, and often ice crystals in their upper levels, are puffy on top of a uniformly flat base. They appear brilliantly white in direct sunlight but dark gray in shadow. Over land these clouds form most frequently during the day when the ground is heated strongly by the sun, whereas over the oceans the diurnal variations are much less marked, with a slightly greater frequency of formation after midnight. Several categories of cumulus may be described. Cumulus humilis clouds, composed of small water droplets, have little vertical development and can be seen on bright, sunny days. Cumulus congestus clouds, which develop from cumulus humilis, have considerable vertical development, often reaching 6 km (3.7 mi) or higher. Ice often forms in their upper levels. Continued development results in cumulonimbus clouds.

Cuna [koo'-nuh] Cuna, a Chibchan-speaking Indian people who number about 20,000, inhabit the San Blas

Islands off the eastern coast of Panama. They moved there in the mid-19th century, possibly because of the encroachment of the Chocó and Catío, but small Cuna groups still live on the mainland. Until the 1960s, Cuna prohibited strangers from staying overnight on their islands. There is a high incidence of albinism, about 0.7 percent, among the Cuna.

Cuna live in small villages. Men hunt and fish, but agriculture—maize, beans, squash, rice, and citrus fruits—is the mainstay. In Cuna society descent, inheritance, and succession to status are reckoned through the maternal line. Men wield authority, especially in the public sphere, but only by virtue of their status in a matrilineal descent group. Cuna have an anthropomorphic concept of divinity and believe that shamans guide their souls through eight layers of an underworld and eight layers of heaven.

Cunard, Sir Samuel [kue-nard']

Samuel Cunard, b. Halifax, Nova Scotia, Nov. 21, 1787, d. Apr. 28, 1865, was the founder of the Cunard Line. He owned whalers that went from Nova Scotia to the Pacific. In 1839, with the aid of British associates, he established the British and North American Royal Mail Steam Packet Company, which contracted with the British government to carry mail to and from Liverpool, Halifax, Boston, and Quebec in steamboats. The first vessel, the *Britannia*, crossed from Liverpool to Halifax in July 1840, taking 13 days. By 1847 ten ships were making the run. Cunard was created a baronet in 1859.

cuneiform [kue-nee'-i-form]

Cuneiform (from the Latin *cuneus*, "wedge," and *forma*, "shape") is a system of WRITING used for a number of ancient Near Eastern languages from c.3000 BC until the 1st century AD. Primarily a Mesopotamian system, cuneiform was inscribed on clay, stone, metal, and other hard materials.

Cuneiform script originated in SUMER (south Mesopot-

Cuneiform was commonly impressed into tablets of wet clay with a sharp reed stylus, forming the angular symbols that replaced earlier pictographic inscriptions. The tablets, sun-dried or baked in kilns, are important records of ancient Near East cultures.

original pictograph	later pictograph	early Babylonian	Assyrian	Original or derived meaning
				bird
				fish
				ox
				grain
				to stand to go

Ancient New Eastern script evolved from the Sumerian pictographic writing of about 3500 BC to the cuneiform used by the Babylonians and Assyrians of the 2d and 1st millennia BC. As it evolved, cuneiform symbols were rotated from vertical to horizontal.

amia) c.3000 BC, where it had developed from the earliest known form of writing, called pictographic writing, found on clay tablets at the ancient city of URUK. The earliest Sumerian pictographic writing, which seems to have been used for administrative purposes in compiling lists of objects, dates from the mid-4th millennium BC. Gradual simplification and standardization of the pictures led to a linear style better suited to inscribing on clay. During the 3d millennium BC, the increased use of a writing stylus made of reed, wood, or bone with a narrow, rectangular head gave the symbols a more regular and wedge-shaped appearance. At about the same time, it was found that writing could be done far more efficiently by changing the earlier system of working from right to left in columns to working from left to right in lines and by moving the angle of the signs 90 degrees, so that the sign pictures then appeared horizontally instead of vertically.

In the mid-3d millennium BC, sometime after their arrival in Mesopotamia, the Semitic Akkadians adopted the Sumerian cuneiform script, as did the neighboring Canaanites and Elamites of roughly the same period. Cuneiform continued to be used, for their own dialects, by the later Babylonians and Assyrians. Under HAMMURABI of Babylon, in the 18th century BC, most of the extant records of Sumerian and Babylonian literature and scientific knowledge were written in cuneiform. Some of the finest cuneiform writing is found in the 9th- to 7th-century BC Neo-Assyrian libraries, such as that of Ashurbanipal (668–626 BC) at NINEVEH.

During the 2d millennium BC, Akkadian, written in cuneiform, became the lingua franca of the Ancient Near East, and it was from this time onward that cuneiform script was adopted by the Kassites, Hittites, Hurrians, Mitanni, Urartians, and Persians to write their own languages. The decipherment of cuneiform, largely owing to the work of Sir Henry Creswicke Rawlinson in the 19th century, was one of the major advances in Near Eastern archaeology.

Cunningham, Glenn Glenn Cunningham, b. Elkhart, Kans., Aug. 4, 1909, d. Mar. 10, 1988, was a U.S. distance runner who became the most famous miler of the 1930s. After overcoming severe leg burns suffered in a schoolhouse fire, Cunningham established national high school, collegiate, national, and world (1934) records for the mile. His best time was 4:04.4, for an indoor mile in 1938. At a time when 4:10 in the mile had been bettered on only 31 occasions, Cunningham held 12 of those clockings. In the 1932 and 1936 Olympics he ran the 1,500-meters race, placing fourth and second, respectively.

Cunningham, Imogen Imogen Cunningham, b. Portland, Oreg., Apr. 12, 1883, d. June 24, 1976, was a noted member of Group f/64, an association of West Coast photographers that favored sharply focused prints. She did not, however, limit her work to a single method. Cunningham also printed multiple and negative images and made prints in the softly focused romantic style. She is noted for her portrait work and her evocative photographs of flowers.

Cunningham, Merce Considered a revolutionary in the history of MODERN DANCE, Mercier "Merce" Cunningham, b. Centralia, Wash., Apr. 16, 1919, whose works have often been the subject of controversy, has been an innovative force in the dance world. As a soloist with Martha Graham's company (1939–45), he created roles in such works as *Appalachian Spring*. In 1942, Cunningham began to give independent solo concerts, working with John CAGE, his musical collaborator throughout his career. He formed his own company in 1953. Cunningham has choreographed dozens of works for his company, including *Minutiae* (1954), *Winterbranch* (1964), *Walkaround Time* (1968), *Rebus* (1975), *Inlets* (1977), and *Five Stone Wind* (1988) for the stage, and such works as *Fielding the Sixes* (1980) and *Coast Zone* (1983), designed specifically for film or videotape.

From the beginning of his career, Cunningham affirmed the right of dance to be its own subject matter, and asserted its independence from musical accompaniment. His later work focused on pure movement and chance process; it is often performed without decor. In 1985 the MacArthur Foundation awarded Cunningham a "genius" grant.

Cuomo, Mario [kwoh-moh] Mario Matthew Cuomo, b. Queens, N.Y., June 15, 1932, was elected Democratic governor of New York in 1982. Cuomo served as secretary of state (1975–79) and lieutenant governor (1979–83)

under Gov. Hugh Carey. In 1982 he won an upset victory over New York City mayor Edward Koch in the party's gubernatorial primary and went on to win the election; he was reelected in 1986 and 1990.

Cupid see EROS (mythology)

cupola see DOME

cuprite [koop'-ryt] Cuprite, copper oxide, Cu_2O, is a common ore mineral formed by oxidation of SULFIDE MINERALS in the upper zones of copper veins. It forms soft, octahedral crystals and granular masses that are various shades of red; parallel, elongated ruby-red needles are called chalcotrichite, and brick-red earthy masses are called tile ore.

Curaçao [koo-rah-sah'-oh] Located in the south Caribbean Sea, 97 km (60 mi) north of the Venezuelan coast and about 1,125 km (700 mi) southeast of Cuba, Curaçao is the largest island of the Netherlands Antilles, which is an autonomous part of the Netherlands. The population is 152,240 (1988). The total area is 444 km^2 (171 mi^2), and the highest point (372 m/1,220 ft) is located on the northern part of the island. The population is mainly West Indian, with a large component of Dutch. The capital is WILLEMSTAD, where the best natural harbor lies. Curaçao's economy was based on oil refining until the worldwide oil glut of the mid-1980s. Tourism is important, and phosphates are mined. Curaçao was discovered in 1499 by Spanish explorers and was settled first by the Spanish, then by the Dutch, from 1634.

curare [kue-rah'-ree] Curare is an ALKALOID derived from a number of South American plants, such as *Strychos toxifera* and species of *Chondrodendron*. One of its constituents has important medical uses as a relaxant, helpful in surgical anesthesia and in facilitating such diagnostic procedures as laryngoscopy and endoscopy. It is also used to relieve spastic paralysis and to treat some mental disorders.

Curare was first known in the form of various arrow poisons used by the Indians of the Amazon and Orinoco river basins to paralyze and kill wild animals. (The word *curare* is derived from the Indian *woorari*, meaning "poison.") The essential structure of tubocurarine, the constituent of these poisons that produces the physiological activity associated with curare, was established in 1935. A more powerful semisynthetic dimethyl derivative of tubocurarine is now used medicinally. Given intravenously, it relaxes muscles by blocking impulses between nerve and muscle, apparently by preventing the acceptance of acetylcholine by muscle fiber.

curassow [kur'-uh-soh] Curassows, family Cracidae, order Galliformes, are large, turkeylike birds that inhabit

The great curassow, 95 cm (38 in) tall, is found in the forests of America from southern Mexico to Ecuador.

the lower levels of dense tropical and subtropical forests from Mexico to Argentina. Most curassows have bushy crests, and the males of most of the 13 species are adorned with knobs or wattles of blue, yellow, or red at the base of the bill. The males are black with white bellies, and their song resembles a hoot. The females are either similar in color or a combination of brown, black, and white. They lay two eggs in nests that are built low in the undergrowth. Curassows' large size makes them favorite targets of hunters, and some species are now rare.

Curia, Roman   The Roman Curia is the name given to the central administrative organs of the ROMAN CATHOLIC CHURCH, headquartered in VATICAN CITY. Although its origins go back to the Middle Ages, the curia was first organized by Pope Sixtus V (1588) and was reorganized by Pius X (1908) and Paul VI (1967). It consists of the Secretariat of State, the Sacred Council of the Public Affairs of the Church, ten congregations (Doctrine of the Faith, Oriental Churches, Bishops, Discipline of the Sacraments, Divine Worship, Causes of Saints, Clergy, Religious and Secular Institutes, Catholic Education, and Evangelization of Peoples), three judicial bodies (the Sacred Apostolic Penitentiary, the Apostolic Signatura, and the Sacred Roman Rota), three secretariats governing relations with non-Catholics, and a number of other lesser offices.

Curie, Marie and Pierre [kue-ree']   Pierre and Marie Curie are best known for their pioneering work in the study of RADIOACTIVITY, which led to their discovery in 1898 of the elements RADIUM and POLONIUM. Marie Curie, b. Maria Skłodowska in Warsaw, Poland, Nov. 7, 1867, d. July 4, 1934, studied mathematics and physics at the Sorbonne in Paris, earning degrees in both subjects in 1893 and 1894. In the spring of 1894 she met the physicist Pierre Curie. They married a year later, and

Marie subsequently gave birth to two daughters, Irène (1897) and Ève (1904).

Pierre Curie, b. Paris, May 15, 1859, d. Apr. 19, 1906, obtained his doctorate the year he was married, but he had already distinguished himself (along with his brother Jacques) in the study of the properties of crystals. He discovered the phenomenon of PIEZOELECTRICITY, studied the magnetic properties of materials, and discovered that there exists a critical temperature above which the magnetic properties disappear, now known as the Curie temperature.

Since 1882, Pierre had headed the laboratory at the École de Physique et de Chimie Industrielle in Paris, and it was there that both Marie and Pierre continued to work after their marriage. For her doctoral thesis, Madame Curie decided to study the mysterious radiation that had been discovered in 1896 by Henri Becquerel. With the aid of an electrometer built by Pierre and Jacques, Marie measured the strength of the radiation emitted from uranium compounds and found it proportional to the uranium content, constant over a long period of time and uninfluenced by external conditions. She detected a similar immutable radiation in the compounds of thorium. While checking these results, she made the unexpected discovery that uranium pitchblende and the mineral chalcolite emitted about four times as much radiation as could be expected from their uranium content. In 1898 she therefore drew the revolutionary conclusion that pitchblende contains a small amount of an unknown radiating element.

Pierre Curie immediately understood the importance of this supposition and joined his wife's work. In the course of their research over the next year, they discovered two new spontaneously radiating elements, which they named polonium (after Marie's native country) and radium.

In 1903, Marie Curie obtained her doctorate for a thesis on radioactive substances, and with her husband and Henri Becquerel she won the Nobel Prize for physics for the joint discovery of radioactivity. The following year

The discoveries of Marie and Pierre Curie, shown here in their laboratory, marked the beginning of modern studies in radioactivity. The Curies shared the 1903 Nobel Prize for physics, and Marie Curie received (1911) the prize for chemistry, for the isolation of radium.

Pierre was appointed professor at the Sorbonne, and Marie became his assistant. Two years later he was killed, run down by a wagon in a Paris street. Grief-stricken, Marie put all her energy into continuing the work she and Pierre had begun together, becoming head of his laboratory at the Sorbonne and the first woman lecturer at the university. In 1908 she was appointed professor. For the isolation of pure radium, Marie Curie received a second Nobel Prize in 1911, this time for chemistry.

During World War I, Madame Curie dedicated herself entirely to the development of the use of X rays in medicine. In 1918 she took upon herself the direction of the scientific department of the Radium Institute, which she had planned with her husband, and where her daughter Irène Joliot-Curie (see JOLIOT-CURIE, FRÉDÉRIC AND IRÈNE) worked with her husband. Marie's research for the rest of her life was dedicated to the chemistry of radioactive materials and their medical applications.

The work of Marie and Pierre Curie, which by its nature dealt with changes in the atomic nucleus, led the way toward the modern understanding of the atom as an entity that can be split to release enormous energy.

Curie temperature   see MAGNETISM

Curitiba [koo-ree-tee'-bah]   The capital and largest city (1985 pop., 1,279,205) of the southeastern Brazilian state of Paraná, Curitiba is located at an elevation of 914 m (3,000 ft) in the Serra do Mar. The city has grown rapidly since 1900 because of the influx of German, Italian, Polish, Slav, Syrian, and Japanese immigrants. Manufactured products include paper, furniture, textiles, and cement. Curitiba is also a processing center for maté, lumber, and cattle. Founded in 1654 as a gold-mining camp, the city became the state capital in 1854.

---

curium [kuer'-ee-uhm]   Curium is a chemical element, a radioactive metal of the ACTINIDE SERIES in Group IIIB of the periodic table. Its symbol is Cm, its atomic number is 96, and its atomic weight is 247 (stablest isotope). Curium does not occur naturally. It was first produced in 1944, when Glenn T. SEABORG, A. Ghiorso, R. A. James, and L. O. Morgan bombarded plutonium-239 with helium ions and formed the mass-242 isotope of element 96. It was named for the French scientists Marie and Pierre CURIE. Curium is a silvery, hard, brittle metal. Curium-244, with a half-life of about 18 years, can be used as a heat source for compact thermoelectric power generation.

---

curlew [kurl'-yoo]   The curlew, genus *Numenius,* is a shorebird of the sandpiper family, Scolopacida. It has a long, downcurved bill and is usually mottled, with brown, gray, or buff stripes. The curlew inhabits marshes, beaches, mudflats, and prairies.

The whimbrel, *N. phaeopus,* formerly called the Hudsonian curlew, is a migrant of almost worldwide distribu-

The long-billed curlew, also called sicklebill, is the largest North American shorebird. The female lays 3 to 4 eggs at a time, and the young are tended by both parents.

tion. About 43 cm (17 in) long, it is distinguished by its bold head striping. The larger (61-cm/24-in), buff-colored, long-billed curlew, *N. americanus,* inhabits western North and Central America; its bill length varies but may exceed one-third of the bird's total length. Curlews feed on small aquatic life on the beaches and on insects and seeds in the grasslands. The Eskimo curlew of the west coast of the Americas may recently have become extinct.

Curley, James M.   James Michael Curley, b. Boston, Nov. 20, 1874, d. Nov. 12, 1958, was the longtime Democratic boss of Boston. Noted for his colorful personality and political shrewdness, he served as mayor of Boston (1914–18, 1922–26, 1930–34, 1947–50), governor of Massachusetts (1935–37), and a congressman (1911–14, 1943–47). In 1947, Curley was sent to prison for mail fraud. He continued as mayor, and President Harry S. Truman commuted his sentence after five months, issuing a full pardon in 1950. Curley's 1949 campaign for mayor, which ended in his defeat, is the subject of Edwin O'Connor's novel *The Last Hurrah* (1956).

---

curling   The sport of curling—bowling a stone with a handle toward a target laid out on ice—resembles shuffleboard in its general pattern of play. The sport probably originated in Scotland, where a curling stone dated 1551 was found in Dunblane. Brought to North America in the early 19th century, the game was standardized in 1838. Canada—where curling's popularity is greatest—the United States, and several European nations regularly participate in international competition, and curling was a demonstration sport at the 1988 Winter Olympics.

Teams of four compete in bonspiels (competitions) on a rink with two houses of four concentric circles, the centers of which are called tees or buttons. Each player curls two stones per end (round), with the players alternating by team. A game usually lasts 10 ends, played in alternating directions.

The skip (captain), who curls last, calls for the weight (amount of force) and type of curl he or she thinks necessary. He or she also carries a broom, used to point out and sweep clean the stone's path. The team with the stone closest to the tee scores 1 point for each of its stones inside the house and closer to the tee than any opponent's stone.

curly-coated retriever   The curly-coated retriever is a breed of dog believed to be the result of crossing the Irish water spaniel with the retrieving setter in the mid-19th century. Its exact origin, however, is unknown. Strong and intelligent, the curly-coated retriever stands about 58 cm (23 in) at the shoulder and weighs about 31.8 kg (70 lb). The coat, which is almost waterproof, is a thick mass of tight, crisp curls. It is either black or liver. A Curly-Coated Retriever Club was founded in 1896 in England, and the first pair was exported to the United States in 1907.

The curly-coated retriever is a large sporting dog bred from the Irish water spaniel and a retrieving setter. The retriever is a popular breed in New Zealand, where it is used to retrieve waterfowl.

currant   The currant is a hardy shrub in the genus *Ribes*, of the family Saxifraga. The genus includes about 150 species, of which the European black currant and the red currant are most important in cultivation. The European black currant is an alternate host for white pine blister rust, and planting is prohibited in many states to protect white pine forests. Consequently, currants are little cultivated in North America. Most of the world production is in Europe. Most of the production is processed into juice, which is popular for its flavor and high vitamin content.

currency   see MONEY

current, electric   see CIRCUIT, ELECTRIC; ELECTRICITY

curriculum   A curriculum is a plan for what is to be taught in schools. Curriculum studies is a field of inquiry into how school programs are developed, implemented, and evaluated. Using methods from diverse fields, curriculum scholars investigate such questions as what should be studied in schools, what is likely to be learned as the result of the activities provided by a particular school, how to develop a practical curriculum, and what forces affect what is taught in school.

Some educators are oriented toward outcome, viewing curriculum as a structured series of learning goals. This achievement-oriented approach is evident in national educational planning. For example, the USSR's advancement in science and technology in the late 1950s prompted the adoption of more school courses in those fields in the United States. Other educators include in a curriculum all the opportunities for learning. This approach addresses both intended and unintended outcomes but pays greater attention to the activities of schooling than to particular achievements. Curricula in more liberal schools can include courses such as film studies that are generally considered extracurricular in more conservative institutions.

Ever since schools were established, curricula have been discussed, debated, and changed. The curriculum of PLATO's Academy in ancient Greece revolved around gymnastics, literature, music, mathematics, and, eventually, philosophy. Ancient Roman EDUCATION took on aspects of Greek education and eventually came to be the basis of European education in the Middle Ages. Liberal arts curricula in medieval universities consisted of the *trivium* (grammar, logic, and rhetoric) and the *quadrivium* (arithmetic, astronomy, geometry, and music). Today a liberal arts curriculum encompassing the humanities, social sciences, physical and biological sciences, and mathematics forms the basis of a general education.

The swamp currant, a shrub native to the northern United States, produces tart berries. American Indians used dried currants to make pemmican, a paste of dried meat, berries, and melted fat.

Some educators have argued for curriculum goals related to subject matter, some for goals related to society, and still others for goals related to the student. Examples of U.S. colleges with divergent approaches to learning include the California Institute of Technology, whose curriculum is devoted almost exclusively to science and technology; and St. John's College in Annapolis, Md., whose curriculum has as its core the GREAT BOOKS PROGRAM. PROGESSIVE EDUCATION emphasizes a student's interests, experiences, and abilities and deemphasizes any binding, predefined curriculum.

Controversies about curriculum often arise from different conceptions of what schools are supposed to do. When the curriculum stresses academic disciplines, critics frequently complain that it neglects personal growth or fails to prepare youths for jobs; others have criticized cultural bias—"Eurocentrism"—in elementary and high schools.

In many countries the central government controls or oversees the curriculum. This is true in the USSR, although each republic is responsible for its schools' curricula. In Britain, before 1988, local education authorities could make extensive choices about the curriculum; the Education Reform Act of that year established a core national curriculum. As a result of a rigid and often archaic education system and curriculum, French state universities were reformed and refounded in 1970 and given academic autonomy and independence under the ministry of education. In the United States, many subjects in public schools on all levels are mandated by local and state governments. The federal government plays a role in curriculum change and emphasis at all education levels by enabling federal agencies such as the NATIONAL SCIENCE FOUNDATION to provide funds for curriculum development and change.

Currier and Ives   Currier and Ives is the name of a famous American printmaking partnership of the 19th century. The partners were **Nathaniel Currier**, b. Roxbury,

The Currier & Ives lithograph Rocky Mountains, *depicting a westward-bound wagon train, is among the thousands of illustrations published by the New York City firm between 1857 and 1907. (Museum of the City of New York.)*

Mass., Mar. 17, 1813, d. Nov. 20, 1888, and **James Merritt Ives**, b. New York City, Mar. 5, 1824, d. Jan. 3, 1895. The firm of Currier and Ives, created in 1857, was known for its evocative color lithographs of 19th-century American subjects. The prints, which were hand colored, featured themes of popular interest such as sporting events, frontier life, and political occasions. More than 7,000 were published from 1840 to 1890. The firm ceased to exist in 1907.

curry   A blend of several spices, curry serves as a basic condiment of India. Most curries have coriander as a base, with the addition of other spices such as turmeric, fenugreek, cumin, red and black pepper, ginger, and cloves. The spices are ground, blended, and cooked in clarified butter (ghee) or oil. Prepared curry powder is a concession to European tastes and to the Western desire for convenience. Cooking in Indonesia and in some parts of southern China is also dependent on curry as a flavoring.

Curry, John Steuart   John Steuart Curry, b. Dunavant, Kans., Nov. 14, 1897, d. Aug. 19, 1946, was a leading painter in the American regionalist movement in the first half of the 20th century. Curry and his fellow midwestern painters Thomas Hart BENTON and Grant

The Flying Codonas, by the prominent American regionalist artist John Steuart Curry, was one of a series that the artist painted while traveling with a circus during 1932. (Whitney Museum, New York City.)

WOOD battled successfully for critical acceptance of American subject matter in serious art. More than most regionalists, Curry saw rural life in highly dramatic terms and portrayed religious events, floods, tornadoes, circuses, and fights to the death between animals with uncompromising realism. He achieved his first success with *Baptism in Kansas* (1928; Whitney Museum, New York City). Curry worked on Works Progress Administration projects in the 1930s, executing murals for the Department of Justice in Washington, D.C., the Kansas State Capitol in Topeka, and the University of Wisconsin in Madison, where he was artist-in-residence for the last decade of his life.

Curtin, John   John Joseph Curtin, b. Jan. 8, 1885, d. July 5, 1945, was prime minister of Australia during most of World War II. A trade unionist, he edited the *Westralian Worker* from 1917 until he entered the federal parliament in 1928. Becoming leader of the disarrayed Labor party in 1935, he restored party unity and in October 1941 became prime minister. With the threat of Japanese invasion in 1942, Curtin recalled Australian troops from the Middle East and imposed tight economic and labor controls to maximize the nation's war effort. At the same time he established close ties with the U.S. government, and Australia became the base of the Allied operations to drive back the Japanese. Curtin's government also initiated farsighted welfare and economic policies for postwar reconstruction.

Curtis, Benjamin Robbins   Benjamin Robbins Curtis, b. Watertown, Mass., Nov. 4, 1809, d. Sept. 15, 1874, was an associate justice of the Supreme Court of the United States from 1851 to 1857. He dissented in DRED SCOTT V. SANDFORD, declaring Scott to be a free man, and resigned soon thereafter. In 1868 he led the defense in the impeachment trial of President Andrew JOHNSON.

Curtis, Charles   Charles Curtis, b. North Topeka, Kans., Jan. 25, 1860, d. Feb. 8, 1936, was the 31st vice-president of the United States (1929–33). A conservative Republican lawyer from Kansas, Curtis sat (1893–1907) in the U.S. House of Representatives. He then entered the Senate, where he served from 1907 to 1913 and again from 1915 to 1929. In 1928, Herbert Hoover, the Republican presidential candidate, chose Curtis as his running mate. They won overwhelmingly, but four years later the same team was badly defeated by the Democratic candidates, Franklin D. Roosevelt and John Nance Garner.

Curtis, Cyrus H. K.   Cyrus Hermann Kotzschmar Curtis, b. Portland, Maine, June 18, 1850, d. June 7, 1933, founded the Curtis Publishing Company, which in his lifetime became one of the largest magazine groups in the world.

After his family home was lost in the Portland fire of 1866, Curtis moved to Boston, where he worked in a dry-goods store and sold advertising space for newspapers. In 1872 he started the weekly *People's Ledger*, and in 1879 the Philadelphia *Tribune and Farmer*, featuring a woman's supplement edited by his wife. Noting the supplement's popularity, he sold his interest in the paper and in 1883 founded the *Ladies Home Journal*.

By advertising judiciously and by offering unprecedented fees for articles, Curtis secured notable contributors and a wide readership for the *Journal*. In 1893 circulation passed 1 million; four years later Curtis acquired the failing *Saturday Evening Post*, and in 1911 the *Country Gentlemen*. The popularity of his magazines owed much to his choice of editors: Edward William BOK for the *Journal* and George Lorimer for the *Post*.

Curtiss, Glenn Hammond   An American pioneer in aviation, Glenn Curtiss, b. Hammondsport, N.Y., May 21, 1878, d. July 23, 1930, began as a bicycle mechanic and motorcycle racer. In 1904 he built a motor for the *California Arrow*, a dirigible. This led him to study and experiment with heavier-than-air craft, and in 1908 he won the *Scientific American* trophy for a 1-km (0.6-mi) flight in his airplane *June Bug*. In 1911 he flew the first successful seaplane, and in 1912 he built the first flying boat. During World War I his factories turned out thousands of military seaplanes. His NC-4 flying boat, developed for the navy, made the first transatlantic flight in 1919. Curtiss is also credited with inventing the aileron, the flap on the trailing edge of a plane's wing that is used for rolling or banking on turns.

Curtiss Jenny   The Curtiss JN series of single-engine biplane trainers, nicknamed the "Jenny," became the United States's most well-known World War I two-seat trainer. It combined the best structural features of the Model J and the Model N. In 1916 mass production of the JN-4 began. The JN-4D version that followed had a wingspan of 13.4 m (44 ft) and was powered by a 90-

The Curtiss JN-4 biplane, known as "Jenny," was a slow, stable, two-seater airplane first produced in the United States in 1916 to train prospective pilots for European duty during World War I.

horsepower Curtiss OX-5 engine. Several variants of the JN-4D were produced. After the war, Jennys were shifted to civilian aviation and were used in BARNSTORMING, in air shows, and for private transportation.

curvature   The curvature of a CURVE, at a given point on that curve, is the rate at which the direction of the curve is changing with respect to the arc length at that point. Curvature may be thought of as a measure of how rapidly a curve deviates from its TANGENT line. A straight line has a constant direction; thus its curvature is zero at every point on it. The curvature of a circle is constant and is equal to the reciprocal of its radius—the larger the radius, the smaller the curvature.

curve   A curve is the path, or locus, of a point moving in space. Intuitively, a plane curve is a figure that can be traced without lifting a pencil from the paper. It is a subset of a plane; that is, all the points of the curve lie in a plane. A curve that does not lie in a plane is called a skew curve, a twisted curve, or a space curve.

If the curve can be traced so that no point is traced more than once, except possibly the starting or ending point, it is a simple curve. If it can be traced, starting and ending at the same point without retracing more than isolated points, it is a closed curve.

Curzon, George Nathaniel Curzon, 1st Marquess [kur'-zuhn]   George Nathaniel Curzon, 1st Marquess Curzon of Kedleston, b. Jan. 11, 1859, d. Mar. 20, 1925, was the British viceroy of India from 1899 to 1905 and British foreign secretary from 1919 to 1924. A Conservative member of Parliament from 1886 to 1898, Curzon had traveled widely in Asia before being sent to India as viceroy at the age of 39. He undertook important administrative reforms, but his partition of Bengal in 1905 provoked Hindu agitation. Embroiled in a dispute with Herbert KITCHENER over control of the Indian army,

The British statesman Lord Curzon served as viceroy of India (1899–1905) and foreign secretary (1919–24). In both positions he proved to be an adept executive, initiating administrative and educational reforms in India and realizing the Treaty of Lausanne in the Middle East.

he resigned (1905) after the London government sided with Kitchener.

After 10 years in political exile, Curzon became (1916) a leading figure in the coalition war cabinet and displayed high executive capacity. As foreign secretary from 1919, he had bitter disagreements with David LLOYD GEORGE, the prime minister. Continuing in office after the Conservatives came to power in 1922, Curzon skillfully handled a threatening crisis in the Middle East (see LAUSANNE, TREATY OF). He was greatly disappointed, however, not to be appointed prime minister when Andrew Bonar LAW resigned in May 1923.

cuscus [kuhs'-kuhs]   A cuscus is a marsupial of the genus *Phalanger*, family Phalangeridae, and is similar to the monkey. Seven species of these nocturnal, slow-moving tree-dwellers are found in Australia, New Guinea, and the nearby islands. In some species, the sexes are differentiated by color. Cuscus vary in length from 33 to 64 cm (13 to 25 in), have a prehensile tail 23 to 61 cm (9 to 24 in) long, and weigh 7 to 16 kg (15 to 35 lb). They feed mainly on fruits and leaves.

The spotted cuscus is a slow-moving marsupial that superficially resembles a monkey. Its tail, part of which is bare, is used to grasp branches and other objects.

Cush   Cush, or Kush, was the ancient kingdom of NUBIA in North Africa in what is now the Sudan. Its rulers conquered Upper Egypt during the 8th century BC and established a capital at Napata. King Piankhi (r. *c.*751–716 BC) also won Lower Egypt, but his son Taharka (d. 663 BC) was expelled from the north by the Assyrians. In the 6th century BC the Cushite capital was transferred to MEROË. The state flourished there until AD *c.*350, when it was overrun by the Ethiopians.

Cushing, Caleb   Caleb Cushing, b. Salisbury, Mass., Jan. 17, 1800, d. Jan. 2, 1879, was the first U.S. commissioner to China, where in 1844 he negotiated a treaty opening Chinese ports to American trade. He also served in Congress (1835–43), as attorney general (1853–57), as U.S. counsel in the arbitration of the Alabama Claims (1871–72; see ALABAMA, ship) and as minister to Spain (1874–77). Cushing was pro-South on the slavery issue but opposed secession and became an unofficial advisor to Abraham Lincoln during the Civil War.

Cushing, Harvey W.

Harvey Williams Cushing, b. New Haven, Conn., Apr. 8, 1869, d. Oct. 7, 1939, a pioneer in neurosurgery, developed many techniques for brain and spinal cord surgery. Studying the pituitary gland, Cushing described a condition now known as Cushing's syndrome in which symptoms such as fatty deposits in the face, neck, and abdomen, muscular weakness, and masculinization in women are caused by an overactivity in part of the anterior pituitary gland (hyperadrenalism). Cushing won the Pulitzer Prize in 1925 for his biography of the British clinician Sir William OSLER.

Cushing, Richard James

Richard James Cushing, b. Boston, Aug. 24, 1895, d. Nov. 2, 1970, was a Roman Catholic bishop and cardinal. Named archbishop of Boston in 1944, he was elevated to the cardinalate in 1958. Cushing did not tolerate dissent within his archdiocese; he excommunicated a Jesuit priest and his followers over the correct interpretation of the precept that there is no salvation outside the church. At the same time he endeared himself to many through his dedication to the poor.

Cushitic languages   see AFROASIATIC LANGUAGES

custard apple

The custard apple is one of two species, or a hybrid, of fruits in the *Annona* genus of trees

The custard apple tree is native to tropical America and thrives in warm-climate gardens. It bears lotuslike flowers and warty green fruit that turns brown.

and shrubs, family Annonaceae. In southern Florida, the term is applied to the pond apple, *A. glabra*, and the bullock's-heart, *A. reticulata*; in Australia, it is applied to the atemoya, a cultivated hybrid of the cherimoya, *A. cherimola*, and the sugar apple, or sweetsop, *A. squamosa*. The soursop, or guanabana, *A. muricata*, of South America, and the North American PAPAW, *Asimina triloba*, are related species. Cherimoyas grow at moderate altitudes in Andean South America and have been introduced into Spain and California. The sugar apple grows near sea level in tropical America and has been introduced into Florida and tropical Asia.

General George Custer, whose 1876 defeat by the Sioux at the Little Bighorn River cost the lives of more than 250 soldiers, was acclaimed for his Civil War exploits. Courageous but imprudent, Custer was once court-martialed; he later led a gold-seeking expedition into sacred Indian territory.

Custer, George Armstrong

Gen. George Armstrong Custer, b. New Rumley, Ohio, Dec. 5, 1839, d. June 25, 1876, was an American cavalry officer, most famous for his "last stand" in the Battle of the LITTLE BIGHORN. Custer attended West Point, from which he graduated last in the class of 1861. During the Civil War he proved himself a daring and brilliant cavalry officer in the Union Army and rose to the rank of major general.

After the war, Custer was sent to the Indian frontier. In 1867 he was court-martialed for disobeying orders and suspended. Reinstated the following year, he was given command of the Seventh Cavalry and sent against the Southern Cheyenne. On Nov. 27, 1868, his force surprised the peaceful encampment of BLACK KETTLE on the Washita River in the western Indian territory. Most of the Indians, including Black Kettle, were killed, and their village was burned.

In 1869, Custer was transferred to the SIOUX country and assigned to the protection of survey crews working on the Northern Pacific Railroad. In 1874 he was placed in command of an expedition to the Black Hills, a sacred portion of the Sioux reservation, where gold was rumored to exist. When the rumors were confirmed, miners inundated the area. Refusing to sell or lease the hills, the

Sioux were ordered to abandon the area. Again they refused, and troops were sent to force their retreat. One of these contingents, led by Custer, rode into an ambush on the Little Bighorn River on June 25, 1876. None of Custer's force survived; more than 250 men were killed in this last major Indian victory in North America.

■
customs union   A customs union is an agreement between separate countries to remove tariffs on imports from each other and to impose common tariffs on imports from the rest of the world. The best-known customs union was the ZOLLVEREIN, formed (1834–71) by independent German states. A present-day organization that began as a customs union is the European Common Market (see EUROPEAN COMMUNITY [EC]), established in 1958. The members started by removing tariffs on trade with each other and establishing a common tariff wall on trade with other countries. This was accomplished by 1968, and the EC entered a second stage of developing an economic union in which labor and capital, as well as goods, could move freely from one country to another and their economic policies would be coordinated. Another customs union was the Benelux Union of Belgium, the Netherlands, and Luxembourg, formed in 1948 and subsequently absorbed in the EC.

A more common type of trade arrangement is the free trade zone, in which the object is only to abolish tariffs among the members; examples are the EUROPEAN FREE TRADE ASSOCIATION and the Latin American Integration Association.

■
Cuthbert, Saint   Cuthbert, c.635–687, was a Celtic monk and missionary bishop. After becoming bishop of Lindisfarne (685), he spent the next two years in extensive missionary work, performing so many healing miracles that he became known as the "wonderworker of Britain." Feast day: March 20.

■
Cutler, Manasseh   Manasseh Cutler, b. Killingly, Conn., May 13, 1742, d. July 28, 1823, was an American Congregationalist clergyman, scientist, and colonizer of Ohio. Ordained in 1771, he began a long ministry at Ipswich, Mass. Extraordinarily versatile, he also took up medicine, astronomy, and botany; among his scientific endeavors was the first systematic account of New England flora. In 1786, Cutler helped found the OHIO COMPANY OF ASSOCIATES. He negotiated the purchase from Congress of territory along the Ohio River and pressed for passage of the Ordinance of 1787, which set up a territorial government for the whole NORTHWEST TERRITORY. Cutler served in Congress from 1801 to 1805.

cutlery   see SWORD AND KNIFE

cutter   see SHIP; SHIPBUILDING

cuttlefish   see MOLLUSK

■
Cuvier, Georges, Baron [kue-vee-ay']   Georges, Baron Cuvier, b. Aug. 23, 1769, d. May 13, 1832, was a French naturalist and anatomist who made important contributions to comparative ANATOMY and vertebrate paleontology. Impressed with what he perceived as the orderliness of nature, Cuvier studied the anatomy of various animals and concluded that a "correlation of parts" in organisms separated them from other organisms and species, thus enabling them to function in an integrated and harmonious way. Cuvier studied fossils and was the first to classify them. He also reconstructed skeletons of extinct animals.

Cuvier was an antievolutionist. He believed that all species had been created, and that some became extinct as the result of catastrophes, such as great floods, on the surface of the Earth. Paradoxically, his findings in anatomy and paleontology were later used to support the theory of EVOLUTION. Cuvier expressed his beliefs in such works as *Leçons d'anatomie comparée* (1800–05), in which, with the help of other naturalists, he presented all that was then known about comparative anatomy; and *Recherches sur les ossements fossiles* (1812), the earliest systematic account of paleontology.

■
Cuvilliés, François [kue-vee-es']   François Cuvilliés, 1695–1768, was a Walloon architect-designer whose work exemplifies the south German ROCOCO STYLE at its best. A dwarf who had joined the household of Max Emmanuel, elector of Bavaria, as playmate of the elector's children, Cuvilliés was recognized for his talents and given the opportunity to train in architecture. He became architect to the Bavarian court in 1725.

The most imaginative designer of his day, Cuvilliés is best known for the state apartments (*Reiche Zimmer*) he created (1730–37) at Munich's Residenz palace; for the charming Amalienburg Pavilion (1734–39) on the grounds of the Nymphenburg Palace; for the Residenztheater (1751–53); and for the facade of Munich's Theatinerkirche (1765–68). The use of white grounds and gold decorative motifs to create dramatic contrasts, less subtle than the work in French rooms of the period, gave his work the extra element of flamboyance familiar in the Rhineland and Bavaria.

■
Cuyp, Aelbert [koyp, al'-bairt]   A major Dutch landscape painter, Aelbert Cuyp, b. October 1620, d. July 31, 1691, is best known for his river views of the Maas at Dordrecht, and paintings of animals, particularly cattle, at the river's edge. His early landscapes reflect the influence of Jan van GOYEN and Salomon van Ruisdael, who introduced tonality to Dutch landscape in the 1620s.

Cuyp's work is suffused with a distinctive yellow coloration that becomes an atmospheric, golden sunlight in the mature paintings. The Italianate richness of this later work brought Cuyp international recognition, although he never traveled outside Holland. With Jacob van RUISDAEL and Meindert HOBBEMA, Aelbert Cuyp represents the best

River Landscape *(c.1650) is one of many pastoral scenes painted by Dutch artist Aelbert Cuyp. A 17th-century painter of the baroque period, he depicted the Dutch countryside with a poetic use of light and atmosphere.*

of the classical phase of 17th-century Dutch landscape painting. He was a prolific painter, although in his late years he produced few works. Among his masterpieces is *View of Dordrecht* (National Gallery, London).

Cuza, Alexandru Ion [koo'-zah, ahl-ek-sahn'droo yawn] Alexandru Ion Cuza, b. Mar. 20, 1820, d. May 15, 1873, was the first prince of Romania. A member of an old Moldavian family, he took part in the 1848 patriotic movement in MOLDAVIA (then tributary to Turkey but under Russian protection). On Jan. 17, 1859, he was elected prince (hospodar) of Moldavia, and on February 5 he became prince of WALACHIA. This double election brought about the unification of the two Romanian principalities. Cuza emancipated (1864) the serfs, promulgated legal codes, and founded the universities of Bucha-rest and Iaşi. Nonetheless, a conspiracy, organized mainly by the BRĂTIANU family, forced him to abdicate on Feb. 23, 1866.

Cuzco [koo'-skoh] Cuzco, the capital of Cuzco province in southern Peru, was the capital of the INCA empire from its beginnings in the 14th century until the Spanish conquest in 1533. The city is known for its Inca ruins and Spanish colonial architecture. Situated at an altitude of 3,416 m (11,207 ft) in a broad valley of the Andes, it is the busy hub of a thickly populated agricultural region where sheep are raised and cereals and tobacco are grown. The population of 255,683 (1985 est.) is predominantly Indian, and the city, with its open markets, adobe houses, and narrow, winding cobblestone streets, is Indian in character. Quechua, the Inca language, is still widely spoken.

Inca tribes are believed to have come to Cuzco from the Lake Titicaca region in about the 11th century. The legendary founder of the city was MANCO CAPAC, first of the Inca rulers. The name *Cuzco* is Quechua for "navel," and the city was the hub from which the famous Inca road network radiated. Designed in the form of a puma, with the 15th-century fortress of SACSAHUAMAN as the head, the Inca capital is especially known for its architecture of enormous cut-stone blocks fitted so perfectly that no mortar was needed. Coricancha, the temple of the Sun, and the fortress of Sacsahuaman are the most outstanding examples of this type of construction.

Cuzco was plundered by Francisco PIZARRO in 1533. The Spaniards built a new city on the ruins of the old, adorning the magnificent edifices with the looted wealth. Under Spanish rule Cuzco flourished as an art center, home of the renowned Cuzqueño school of painting.

cyanide [sy'-uh-nyd] A cyanide is any chemical compound containing the C≡N group, such as sodium cya-

Sacsahuaman, an Inca fortress located on a steep hill to the west of Cuzco, is thought to have doubled as a storage facility in time of peace and a safe haven during war. Construction, which began after 1438, was nearly completed at the time of Spanish conquest. No mortar was used in the walls of close-fitting stones, which now stand 16 m (52 ft) high and were once higher. The retaining walls shown here run in a zigzag pattern for about 550 m (1,805 ft).

nide, NaCN, and hydrogen cyanide, HCN. The simple ionic cyanides have chemical properties similar to those of chlorides, typically forming soluble salts. When dissociation of these molecules occurs, the cyanide ion CN⁻ is released. An organic compound may also contain the CN group, in which case it is joined to a carbon atom by a covalent bond. Such compounds are generally called NITRILES, for example, ACRYLONITRILE, CH_2=CHCN.

The simple cyanides are extremely toxic. Hydrogen cyanide, also known as hydrocyanic acid and prussic acid, is a fast-acting poison that can be ingested, inhaled, or absorbed through the skin. Its effect is to inhibit the enzymes that reduce oxidized CYTOCHROME, preventing cells from using oxygen.

Symptoms of acute cyanide poisoning include dizziness, nausea, and loss of consciousness. Fatalities can be prevented by treatment with antidotes—inhalation of amyl nitrite followed by injections of sodium nitrite and sodium thiosulphate solution—but the poison kills so quickly that the treatment must begin within minutes after exposure.

The cyanide ion tends to form complexes with transition metal ions, such as gold, silver, iron, nickel, and cadmium. This property makes cyanides very useful for the economic extraction of gold and silver from low-grade ores.

cyanobacteria SEE BLUE-GREEN ALGAE

cyanogen [sy-an'-oh-jen] Cyanogen, C_2N_2, a colorless, highly toxic gas with a pungent odor, is used in the synthesis of some fumigants and insecticides. It can be prepared by heating mercuric cyanide, by a reaction between sodium cyanide and copper sulfate, or by dehydrating ammonium oxalate with phosphorus pentoxide. Cyanogen bromide, BrCN, and cyanogen chloride, ClCN, were used as poison gases during World War I.

cyanosis [sy-uh-noh'-sis] Cyanosis is a condition caused by an insufficient amount of oxygen in the arterial blood. A bluish color in the skin and mucous membranes is characteristic. Cyanosis may occur when the air passages to the lung are obstructed, when hemoglobin in red blood cells loses its ability to bind or hold oxygen because of exposure to carbon monoxide, or when an individual has congenitally abnormal hemoglobin with a decreased ability to bind oxygen. Another cause is a congenital condition, such as a hole in the wall between the right and left ventricles of the heart, that prevents the heart from delivering enough blood to the lungs for the exchange of gas. An infant born with such a condition is called a blue baby. Surgical correction of this defect is necessary and is highly successful.

Cybele [sib'-uh-lee] Cybele was the great mother goddess of ancient Anatolia worshiped for her control over fertility, untamed nature, and the welfare of her subjects. Like her Semitic counterpart Ishtar, she was associated in myth and rite with a young consort, Attis (Tammuz in Babylonia), who before his death castrated himself out of

This Roman altar (AD 295) shows Cybele in a chariot pulled by two lions, which symbolize the bestial nature of her cult. Her whip, an emblem of power, was used by her priests for self-flagellation. The worship of Cybele was one of Rome's official state cults.

devotion to her. Attis died beneath a pine tree, violets springing from his blood drops. The spring festival honoring her commemorated Attis's death and culminated in a joyful celebration of resurrection. In art, Cybele is typically portrayed as crowned, enthroned, and attended by lions.

cybernetics [sy-bur-net'-iks] Cybernetics is a term formerly used to describe an interdisciplinary approach to the study of control and communication in animals, humans, machines, and organizations. The word *cybernetics* was coined by U.S. mathematician Norbert WIENER in 1946. The original concept grew out of Wiener's and his colleague Julian Bigelow's work on antiaircraft guns during World War II, which utilized FEEDBACK.

Feedback is utilized in devices that rely on information from the surrounding environment to fulfill their functions. Much of the early work in cybernetics focused on the use of feedback and other forms of communication by SERVOMECHANISMS, COMPUTERS, and all kinds of AUTOMATION.

Collaborating with physiologist Arturo Rosenblueth, Wiener demonstrated that cybernetics could be useful in an analysis of the human nervous system. Because of this psychological application of the theory, cybernetics attracted the interest of psychologists and psychiatrists, who saw some forms of mental illness as being analogous to a machine that performs poorly due to faulty feedback.

A major impetus to the development of cybernetics in the late 1940s and early 1950s came from the burgeoning science of computers. Not only did the computer suggest itself as a model of the nervous system, but it was also seen as a tool for developing and studying models of other complex systems. This area of study eventually became more widely known as ARTIFICIAL INTELLIGENCE.

Cybernetics was also influenced by (and influenced in return) INFORMATION THEORY, which is concerned with the measurement of the flow of information from an information source to a destination and with controlling error in transmission.

In the first few decades after Wiener conceived of it, cybernetics was influential to a wide variety of disciplines, among them the study of historical systems, cognitive science, linguistics, and automata theory (see AU-

TOMATA, THEORY OF). Cybernetics as a separate discipline gradually declined as the insights it offered were absorbed naturally into the framework of other fields.

The cycad (also called sago palm, although not a true palm) is a slow-growing evergreen. The leaves are commonly used in floral arrangements. The trunk is about 3 m (10 ft) high.

cycad [sy'-kad] Cycads are a group of GYMNOSPERMS (nonflowering seed plants) recognized primarily by the male and female cones that appear on separate trees and by their feathery evergreen leaves. The leaves usually occur as a crown at the top of the trunk and give the plants a palmlike appearance. Along with the ginkgos, cycads are considered primitive gymnosperms because motile sperm are involved in fertilization. In contrast, conifers and gnetums are more advanced gymnosperms, with nonmotile sperm. Cycads are small trees, averaging 2.5 to 3.5 m (8 to 12 ft) in height. The tallest cycad (*Macrozamia hopei*) on record, however, was about 18 m (60 ft).

The more than 70 living species of cycads are generally classified into nine genera and a single family, Cycadaceae. Two genera, *Dioon* and *Ceratozamia*, are found in Mexico; *Microcycas* (one species) is found only in western Cuba, and it is in danger of becoming extinct. The largest genus (about 28 species), and one of the most widely distributed, is *Zamia*. It ranges from Florida and the West Indies through Central America and the Andes into Chile. *Macrozamia* and *Bowenia* are found only in Australia. *Encephalartos* (about 14 species) and *Stangeria* (one species) occur only in southern Africa. *Cycas* (about 15 species) is widely distributed, ranging from Australia to the Pacific islands in the north and to India, China, Japan, and Madagascar.

Several genera are popular ornamentals, especially *Zamia*, *Cycas*, and *Encephalartos*. The underground stem of *Zamia* is a source of flour for the Seminole Indians of Florida.

Cycads apparently evolved from the Cycadofilicales ("seed ferns") late in the Pennsylvanian Period, about 300 million years ago. During the Mesozoic, some 65 to 225 million years ago, cycads reached their greatest development, becoming abundant and widely distributed.

After that, and until the present, they gradually declined in number. Today cycads are confined to tropical and subtropical regions.

Cyclades [sy'-kluh-deez] The Cyclades comprise more than 200 rocky volcanic Greek islands in the Aegean Sea. The area is 2,590 km^2 (1,000 mi^2), of which Náxos, the largest island, constitutes about one-sixth. Other major members of the group are Ándros, Tínos, Syros (Síros), Melos, (Mílos), Páros, and THERA (Thíra), often popularly associated with the lost city of Atlantis. The population is 88,458 (1981), and the islands are administered from Hermoupolis, on Syros. The name comes from the Greek for "encircling," because the ancients thought of the islands as surrounding sacred DELOS.

The Cyclades are a resort area; grapes, olives, wheat, fruits, and tobacco are raised by irrigation. Exports include marble, manganese, iron ore, hides, wines, and tobacco.

The Cyclades were the site of an Early Bronze Age civilization known for its art, particularly white marble statuettes distinguished by their stylized character and taut, elegant lines. These Cycladic figures were normally quite small, but some of them approached life-size. Details were often added to them in red and blue paint. The Cyclades were conquered by the Ottoman Turks in 1566 and became part of independent Greece in 1829.

cyclamates   SEE SWEETENER, ARTIFICIAL

cyclamen [sy'-kluh-muhn] Cyclamen, genus *Cyclamen*, is both the common and the scientific name of about 15 species of European and Middle Eastern plants in the primrose family, Primulaceae. The species *C. persicum*, or florist's cyclamen, is grown extensively as a greenhouse plant. The flower petals of cyclamens turn sharply backward, and the heart-shaped leaves are mottled with white along the veins.

Florist's cyclamen is a houseplant that blooms from mid-autumn to mid-spring. Some varieties can flower year round. It bears large, sweet-smelling flowers, each on a separate stalk. Colors of the flowers are usually pink, red violet, or white. The leaves are broad and deep green with white markings.

cyclic AMP   Cyclic AMP (3',5'-adenosine monophosphate) is a nucleotide, present in most living cells, that has a crucial role in regulating a great variety of processes. In bacteria it stimulates the synthesis of enzymes necessary for reproduction. In amoebas and slime molds it directs individual cells to aggregate and form a single colony. In higher animals and humans it receives the regulatory messages in HORMONES and conveys them to the mechanisms that control cell METABOLISM. Hormones, or "first messengers," travel from their cells of origin to the cells of their target organs, where they then act to alter the concentration of cyclic AMP. Cyclic AMP then does the work of the hormone inside the cell, and for this reason it has come to be called the "second messenger."

Cyclic AMP is believed to stimulate the release of certain hormones—for example, adrenocorticotropic hormone, thyroid-stimulating hormone, and glucagon. It is also believed to regulate gene expression, gastric secretion, water reabsorption in the kidney, and the transmission of electrical impulses in nerve tissue and heart muscle.

The biological function of cyclic AMP was not discovered until the late 1950s, when Earl W. Sutherland and T. W. Rall established one of its roles. In 1971, Sutherland received a Nobel Prize for his part in this research.

cyclic compounds   In organic chemistry, cyclic compounds are those having a closed chain, or ring, of atoms. ALICYCLIC COMPOUNDS have only carbon atoms constituting the ring structure; cycloalkanes have single bonds linking the carbon atoms, cycloalkenes have one or more double bonds, and cycloalkynes have at least one triple bond. AROMATIC COMPOUNDS are those compounds whose carbon rings contain alternating double and single bonds; the basic aromatic compound is BENZENE. Molecules whose rings contain one or more elements other than carbon are known as HETEROCYCLIC COMPOUNDS.

The smallest possible cyclic compounds are those which consist of three-membered rings, such as cyclopropane and ethylene oxide. Any number of atoms can constitute the ring of a cyclic compound. Large rings are not easily synthesized from open-chain compounds, however, because of the low probability that reactive groups on the two fairly remote ends will come together. Six-membered ring compounds of all classes are the dominant species in nature.

Benzene (C_6H_6) and its homologous heterocycles, such as pyridine, C_5H_5N, are planar structures. These aromatic structures are highly stabilized by the phenomenon known as RESONANCE, which is important in determining molecular stability. Carbon rings can be fused together to form larger polycyclic structures. Aromatic examples of such molecules are anthracene and naphthalene.

cycling   Cycling is both a sport and a noncompetitive pastime. As a test of endurance and speed, sport cycling is practiced particularly in Europe. As a form of exercise and recreation, cycling is almost universal. A racing BICYCLE used in road competitions is made of lightweight alloys and weighs no more than 9.5 kg (21 lb). It is equipped with lightweight tubular tires, gears, and metal-treaded pedals to hold the racer's feet in place. A sprinting or track bicycle weighs 5–6.8 kg (11–15 lb) and is a fixed-gear (1-speed) brakeless model; it offers savings in wind resistance and 7.3–7.6 m (24–25 ft) per pedal turn.

The first bicycle race was held at the Parc de St. Cloud, France, in 1868. Recognized world championships were first held in 1893. As competition became

Cyclists are massed at the beginning of the Tour de France, one of the single most arduous of all competitive athletic events. In 1985 the Frenchman Bernard Hinault became only the third man in history to win his fifth Tour de France. Greg LeMond emerged in the mid-1980s as the best American racer ever and one of the best in the world.

more widespread, the Union Cycliste Internationale (UCI) was established in 1900 to govern all amateur and professional events. The United States, France, Italy, Belgium, and Switzerland were charter members of this group, which now represents over 110 nations. Winners are currently established in 14 categories. The Olympic Games has competitions in both road and track racing for a total of 8 events. The Tour de France is cycling's most famous international event. Started in 1903 by Henri Desgrange, the stage race covers a course that varies from about 4,000 km to 4,800 km (2,500 mi to 3,000 mi) over roads and mountain passes throughout France and portions of five neighboring countries. The 3-week event attracts the greatest cyclists; the winner is generally acknowledged as the world's best cyclist. Eddy MERCKX of Belgium and Jacques Anquetil and Bernard Hinault of France have each won the event five times. Other major international races include the Giro d'Italia, the Vuelta a Espagna, and the Milan–San Remo. Merckx holds the record for number of victories in these and other road races. Major road races in the Western Hemisphere include the Tour du St. Laurent, the Québec Montréal, and the Coors Classic. Track events, races held on a specially constructed symmetrical and oval surface with two straight sections, include both individual and tandem sprint races; motor-paced races (not as popular today), in which the cyclists race for distance or against time in the protective wake of a motorcycle; and time trials (1,000 m against the clock).

cyclohexane [sy-kloh-hek'-sayn]   Cyclohexane, C_6H_{12}, is a colorless, volatile, flammable, liquid organic compound used as a solvent for fats, oils, and resins. It is also an important raw material for the manufacture of adipic acid (a component of nylon 6,6) and caprolactam (the building block of nylon 6). Cyclohexane, a cyclic ALIPHATIC COMPOUND, is produced by the reaction of benzene with hydrogen or by the refining of petroleum.

cycloid   A cycloid is a type of plane curve; an everyday example is the curve described by a point on the rim of a rolling wheel. Mathematically, a cycloid is defined as the plane curve generated by a point P fixed on the circumference of a circle as the circle rolls without slipping along a straight line.

cyclone and anticyclone   Cyclones and anticyclones are circulation systems in the ATMOSPHERE that can be considered, alternatively, as either producing, or resulting from, the intermediate zones of high and low pressure between the equator and the poles. In cyclones, the central pressure is lower than that of the surrounding environment, and the flow of circulation is clockwise in the Southern Hemisphere and counterclockwise in the Northern Hemisphere. Cyclones are characterized by low-level convergence and ascending air within the system. An anticyclone system has the opposite characteristics— the central pressure is higher than that of its surroundings, the flow is counterclockwise in the Southern Hemisphere and clockwise in the Northern Hemisphere, and anticyclones are usually characterized by low-level divergence and subsiding air.

Semipermanent Systems. Semipermanent systems rarely vary during an entire season. Examples include the Bermuda High in the northern subtropical region, and the Siberian High and the Aleutian Low, which dominate the winter in the middle and high latitudes of Asia and North America.

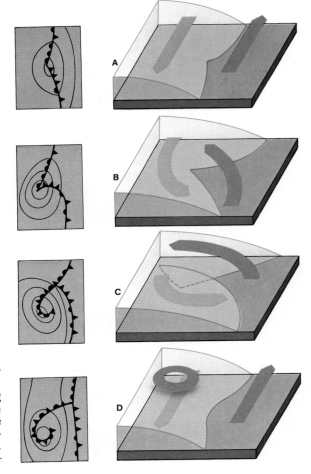

A cyclone begins to develop (A) when a mass of cold air (blue) slides past a mass of warm air (red) and the two begin to spiral around each other (B). The line along which the cold air encroaches on the warm, known as a cold front, is represented on weather maps (left column) by triangular teeth; the opposite—a warm front—is shown as solid semicircles. The cyclone moves around the low-pressure center that forms between the two air masses. As the fast-moving cold front overtakes the slower warm front, an occluded front (C), symbolized by alternating teeth and semicircles, forms, and the warm air mass is lifted off the ground, after which the cyclone usually dissipates (D).

The subtropical high-pressure belts coincide with the descending legs of the Hadley cells. They develop in direct response to surface heating anomalies, such as those produced by the differential heating of continents and oceans or by variations in the surface temperature of the sea. Because of the effect of the Hadley cell, the entire subtropics remain at a fairly high pressure throughout the year.

Surface-pressure anomalies develop at higher latitudes by similar processes. During summer the land areas are considerably warmer than the adjacent oceans, producing rising motion over the land and subsidence over the oceans. The resulting pressure gradient, produced by the temperature distribution, causes cool ocean air to flow toward the warm land surface. The CORIOLIS EFFECT deviates the flow, producing cyclonic flow over the land and anticyclonic flow over the sea. During winter the situation is reversed. The land cools quickly, having little stored heat. Consequently, high-pressure regions form over the land while low-pressure regions dominate the ocean. The clear atmosphere of the subsident region allows the land surface to continue cooling. The loss of heat is compensated for by an increase of energy that flows into the system as warm air from the oceanic low-pressure region. When the amount of energy radiated to space matches the inflow, an equilibrium is reached, but by that time deep high-pressure region has developed.

Transient Systems. The second group consists of transient cyclones and anticyclones associated with weather systems. Located in the equatorial and middle latitudes, they may grow, mature, and decay within a few days.

Depressions in middle latitudes are cyclonic systems that develop rapidly and move eastward against the basic westerly flow, over distances from 500 to 2,000 km (300 to 1,200 mi). Central pressures often fall below 990 millibars (mb). Inclement weather, strong winds (connected to the high-pressure gradient), and squalls are associated with such mid-latitude systems, which result from basic instabilities of a heated and rotating atmosphere. Because of the Coriolis effect, the upper tropospheric flow toward the pole in the Hadley cell is forced eastward, developing strong WESTERLIES. The air accelerates as it moves progressively poleward. As warm air moves poleward, cold air moves equatorward, producing adjacent pools of warm and cold air. Pressures from the resultant large east-west temperature gradient cause a cyclonic circulation around the low-pressure center and anticyclonic flow around the high.

In the tropics, cyclonic systems known as tropical depressions may develop with central pressures less than 2 mb lower than the environment. Associated with periods of intense rain, these systems usually move westward. Those which intensify significantly (pressures falling below 950 mb) are called tropical cyclones or hurricanes (see HURRICANE AND TYPHOON). Because of their relatively small horizontal scale, the pressure gradient is tighter and winds are more intense than in mid-latitude systems.

Cyclops [sy'-klahps]   In Greek mythology a Cyclops was a one-eyed giant. There are two traditions about the Cyclopes. According to Hesiod they were the three sons of Uranus and Gaea who fashioned thunderbolts for Zeus, the trident for Poseidon, and the cap of invisibility for Hades. According to Homer the Cyclopes were savage shepherds who inhabited caves and rocky caverns. Their leader, POLYPHEMUS, is said to have devoured several of Odysseus's crew before the survivors managed to blind the monster.

cyclosporine   Cyclosporines, a family of drugs used in medicine to aid TRANSPLANTATION operations, are derived from the Norwegian fungus *Tolypocladium inflatum.* The most common form is called cyclosporine A. In 1972 the Swiss biochemist Jean F. Borel discovered that cyclosporines selectively suppress certain components of the immune system. Most important, they block the activity of the lymphocytes called T-helper cells, which initiate the function of cytotoxic T cells. The latter, along with the BLOOD cells called monocytes or macrophages, are thought to be responsible for the rejection of grafted tissues. With cyclosporine, grafted organs are rejected less often than they had been with earlier antirejection drugs. Patients also suffer fewer of the infections that can cause illness and death after such operations. Cyclosporine can produce severe kidney damage, however, and must be used carefully. It was approved for clinical use in the United States in 1984. Various trials have since been conducted of other drugs in combination with cyclosporine to reduce its potential toxicity.

cyclostomi   see AGNATHA

cyclotron   see ACCELERATOR, PARTICLE

Cygnus [sig'-nuhs]   Cygnus the Swan is a constellation located in the Northern Hemisphere. It is also known as the Northern Cross because five of its brightest stars form a cross in the sky. At the foot of the cross is the bright double star Albireo, which can be resolved with a small telescope. The constellation also contains the North American Nebula and the Pelican Nebula, visible only with a large telescope.

cylinder   The term *cylinder* refers to both a cylindrical surface and the solid bounded by a cylindrical surface and two parallel planes, called the bases. To define a cylindrical surface, consider any simple, closed curve in a plane and a (straight) line L—called the generator, or generatrix—that intersects the curve. A cylindrical surface is the surface consisting of all lines parallel to line L that intersect the curve; the curve is called the directrix. The directrix need not be a circle. If it is, the cylinder is a circular cylinder. A right circular cylinder is the most common type; an example is a tin can. The volume of any cylinder is the product of the area of its base and its height, or altitude (the perpendicular distance between the parallel planes bounding the cylinder).

cymbals Cymbals are slightly concave thin metal plates of indefinite pitch. They are used in the percussion section of bands and orchestras, singly or in pairs, the player striking the two together or hitting one with a beater. Their modern orchestral use dates from the late 18th century. Orchestral cymbals are usually at least 36 cm (14 in) in diameter. Lightweight, thinner cymbals, suspended from a stand or attached to the trap-drum set, are used in jazz and rock bands.

Cymru see WALES

Cynewulf [kin'-uh-wulf] Cynewulf was an Anglo-Saxon poet who flourished in Northumbria or Mercia about the early 9th century. Several didactic works found in late 10th-century manuscripts have been attributed to him, including *Elene, Juliana*, and the cycle known as *Christ*, which treats the ascension, incarnation, and last judgment. He is one of the few Anglo-Saxon poets whose name is known, since he gave this away as a sort of acronym in his works.

Cynics [sin'-iks] The Cynics were adherents of a Greek philosophic school founded in the 4th century BC by Antisthenes; its best-known member was DIOGENES OF SINOPE. Antisthenes held that happiness is achieved by cultivating virtue for its own sake. This is attained by a life free of dependence on possessions and pleasures.

The Cynics admired SOCRATES for his self-sufficiency and his indifference to unnecessary luxury and possessions. A good life, they taught, involves a return to nature, giving up the decadence of civilized urban life and living simply and strenuously. The Cynics are important in the history of philosophy because of their influence, both in Greece and Rome, on STOICISM.

cypress Cypresses are coniferous evergreen trees belonging to approximately 20 species in the cypress family, Cupressaceae. They are found in the New World from Oregon to Mexico and Costa Rica, and in the Old World from the Mediterranean region to China and the Himalayas. Italian cypresses, *Cupressus sempervirens*, are tall, columnlike trees that are found throughout the forests of the Mediterranean. Formal in appearance, they are planted extensively in Mediterranean cities.

Cypress leaves are scalelike, forming four uniform rows, and are finely toothed on the margin. The fruit consists of globe-shaped woody or leathery cones that mature at the end of the second season. Monterey cypresses, *Cupressus macrocarpa*, are native only to a coastal strip below Monterey Bay in California. They have been planted throughout Europe, South America, Australia, and New Zealand. Having conical form when young, they develop into sturdy, low-spreading trees that withstand wind and salt injury. Arizona cypresses, *Cupressus arizonica*, are grown in the mountains of the southwestern United

The Italian cypress, native to southern Europe and western Asia, grows to a height of 24 m (80 ft). Its durable and long-lasting wood was used to construct the doors of Saint Peter's Basilica in Rome.

Also commonly called the Italian cypress, this columnar variant is actually a cultivar of the original species developed and propagated by the cultivation of specially selected seedlings. It grows to a height of 30 m (100 ft) and bears cones up to 4 cm (1.6 in) in diameter. This cypress is often used in formal gardens.

States and northern Mexico and are popularly used as Christmas trees throughout the southern United States.

Cyprian, Saint [sip'-ree-uhn] Cyprian, b. *c.*200, d. Sept. 14, 258, was bishop of Carthage and one of the major theologians of the early African church. Following his election (*c.*248) as bishop, Cyprian was forced to flee Carthage during the persecutions (249–51) of Emperor Decius. After his return Cyprian favored the readmission to the church of Christians who had failed to stand firm during the persecution. He opposed the schism of NOVATIAN, who believed that lapsed Christians should be permanently excluded. In the renewed persecution of Valerian's reign, Cyprian was beheaded near Carthage.

Cyprian's writing reflects the influence of TERTULLIAN, whom he held in high esteem. His best-known work is *De ecclesiae unitate* (On the Unity of the Church), in which he stressed the role of the bishop in deciding local church matters, although he gave the Roman church a position of preeminence. Feast day: Sept. 16 (Western); Aug. 31 (Eastern).

Cyprus [sy'-pruhs] Cyprus is an island state in the eastern Mediterranean Sea, 97 km (60 mi) west of the

AT A GLANCE

REPUBLIC OF CYPRUS

Land: Area: 9,251 km^2 (3,572 mi^2). Capital and largest city: Nicosia (1989 est. pop., 166,900).

People: Population (1990 est.): 700,000. Density: 75.7 persons per km^2 (196 per mi^2). Distribution (1990): 62% urban, 38% rural. Official languages: Greek, Turkish. Major religions: Greek Orthodoxy, Islam.

Government: Type: republic; northeast (Turkish Republic of Northern Cyprus) under de facto control of a Turkish Cypriot administration. Legislature: House of Representatives; Turkish Legislative Assembly. Political subdivisions: Republic of Cyprus— 5 districts; Turkish zone—3 districts.

Economy: GDP (1988): $4.2 billion; $6,100 per capita. Labor distribution, Republic of Cyprus (1988): agriculture—13.8%; manufacturing—17.8%; mining—0.3%; construction—8.6%; public utilities—0.5%; transport and communications—5.4%; trade—20.4%; finance—4.9%; public administration, defense, services—17.3%; other—10.8%; Turkish zone (1986): agriculture, forestry, and fishing—32%; industry—10%; construction—7%; trade and tourism—9%; transport and communications—7%; financial and personal services—11%; public services—24%. Foreign trade (1988): imports—$1.9 billion; exports—$709 million. Currency: 1 Cyprus pound = 100 cents; 1 Turkish lira = 100 kurus.

Education and Health: Literacy (1987): 99% of adult population. Universities (1990): 1. Hospital beds, Republic of Cyprus (1987): 4,256; Turkish zone, 761. Physicians, Republic of Cyprus (1987): 1,195; Turkish zone, 219. Life expectancy (1989): women—80; men—74. Infant mortality (1989): 8 per 1,000 live births.

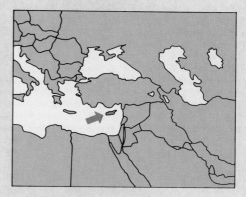

coast of Syria and 64 km (40 mi) south of Turkey. It has an area of 9,251 km^2 (3,572 mi^2). The island is 225 km (140 mi) from east to west and at most 97 km (60 mi) from north to south. It is compact in shape except for a long tapering peninsula to the northeast. Turkish-Greek animosities led to the establishment (1974–75) of an autonomous Turkish sector in the northern third of the island, which in 1983 proclaimed its independence.

Land

Topographically, Cyprus consists of two mountain masses (on the north and south) and a central lowland. The Kyrenia Range lies close to the north coast and consists mainly of limestone. To the south is the Mesaöria Plain, in which the densest population is found. The southern half of the island is occupied by the rugged Troödos Mountains, composed mainly of volcanic and igneous rocks and reaching a maximum elevation of 1,953 m (6,407 ft).

The climate is Mediterranean. Temperatures vary with elevation, but January averages are about 10° C (50° F)

and those of July about 27° C (80° F). Rainfall, which occurs mainly in winter, is rarely more than 380 mm (15 in) in the lowlands but is higher in the mountains. Surface drainage is by short, small streams that are usually dry in summer. The native vegetation consists mainly of drought-resistant scrub and conifers (including eucalyptus, pine, acacia, and cypress).

People and Economy

The population of the island is divided into Greek and Turkish communities. The Greeks make up about 77% of the total, and about 18% of the population are Turkish, who live mainly in the north of the island. Ethnic and linguistic differences are reinforced by religious differences: the Greeks are almost exclusively Orthodox Christians; the Turks, Muslims. There has always been hostility between the two communities, varying with the degree of support the Greeks have received from Greece and the Turks from Turkey. Much of the population is rural and agricultural. Apart from NICOSIA, the capital, and Limassol and Famagusta, the towns are very small.

The economy is basically agricultural, with fruits and vegetables the chief exports. Farming is highly mechanized, and irrigation is widely used. Although Cyprus has been known since prehistoric times for its minerals (the word *copper* is derived from the island's name)—copper, iron pyrites, chrome, and asbestos once made up more than a third of all exports—mining is no longer economically important.

The dislocations caused by the partition of 1975 stimulated the growth of the construction industry. Textile manufacturing and other light industries have expanded rapidly in recent times in the Greek sector, which has also become a banking, telecommunications, and trade center for international corporations dealing with the Middle East. The Turkish sector's recovery from partition has been hampered by a shortage of skilled labor and a lack of trade and diplomatic links to the outside world. Tourism, a major source of foreign exchange throughout the island, has returned to normal.

History and Government

Because of its key location in the eastern Mediterranean, Cyprus played an important role in the early history of civilization and was, during the 2d millennium BC, an important source of copper for Egypt and the Middle East. Cultural influences of Mycenaean Greece spread to

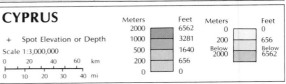

Kyrenia (Girne in Turkish), a resort city and the chief seaport of Turkish Cyprus, is located on the northern coast of Cyprus.

the island, but from about 800 BC Phoenician influence became more prominent. In 709 BC, Cyprus submitted to the Assyrian king SARGON II. The decline of Assyrian power was followed by a period of Persian domination, and it was not until ALEXANDER THE GREAT conquered the region in the 4th century BC that Cyprus was united politically with the rest of the Greek world. At this time Cyprus consisted mainly of city-states held together under the sovereignty of Alexander's successors. In 58 BC the island was annexed by the Roman Empire.

Cyprus was visited by Saint PAUL and was Christianized at an early date. Remains of a number of early basilican churches may still be seen. With the division of the Roman Empire, Cyprus came under the control of Byzantine emperors, who continued to rule it until it was occupied (1191) during the Third Crusade by RICHARD I of England. The island was given (1192) to Guy de Lusignan, who founded a French-speaking monarchy. From this time Italian merchants assumed an increasingly important role on the island, which eventually came under Venetian control in 1489. The ruined castles and Gothic churches of Cyprus date from this period.

Cyprus was, however, subjected to repeated attacks by the Turks, who in 1570–71 overran the island. It remained under Turkish rule until 1878, and during this period many Turks settled on the island. The British occupied Cyprus by agreement with the Turkish sultan in 1878 in order to support Turkey against Russia. In 1914 it was formally annexed by Great Britain. Soon afterward a movement developed among the Greek Cypriots for union (*enosis*) with Greece, a movement that became more powerful after World War II. At the same time Archbishop MAKARIOS III became the leader of the movement for an independent Cyprus.

In 1959, Cyprus gained independence after a period of guerrilla war, but Great Britain retained its military bases. Extremist elements still demanded union with Greece, while the Turks favored the division of the island along ethnic lines. Fear that the Greek government was preparing to annex Cyprus led to a Turkish invasion in 1974 and the forcible partition (1975) of the island. The Greek sector, known as the Republic of Cyprus, is led by President George Vassiliou, elected in 1988. The Turkish zone, under the leadership of Rauf Denktash, declared itself the Turkish Republic of Northern Cyprus in 1983 but is recognized only by Turkey. UN-sponsored talks on reunification between Vassiliou and Denktash began in August 1988.

■

Cyrano de Bergerac [sir'-uh-noh duh bur'-zhur-ak] A heroic comedy by Edmond ROSTAND, *Cyrano de Bergerac* (1897; Eng. trans., 1898; films, 1925 and 1950) is loosely based on the life of Savinien Cyrano de Bergerac. The play, written in both blank and unrhymed verse, idealistically portrays the charming, valiant, and witty Cyrano—master duelist, soldier, poet, and philosopher. Despite his many victories, Cyrano believes that his overly long nose will discourage love in Roxane, the woman he admires. Honor and friendship prevent him from declaring his passion. Only before dying does he avow his love. Despite its sentimentality, *Cyrano* is a lyrical study in praise of love, fidelity, honor, and heroism.

■

Cyrano de Bergerac, Savinien [see-rah-noh' duh bair-zhair-ahk, sah-veen-yan'] Savinien Cyrano de Bergerac, b. Mar. 6, 1619, d. July 28, 1655, was a 17th-century French novelist, satirist, and an audacious freethinker. Cyrano's masterworks are his two satirical novels, published in 1657 and 1662 and translated together as *Voyages to the Moon and the Sun* in 1687. Other works include an obscene comedy, *Le pédant joué* (The Pedant Imitated, 1645), and a classical tragedy, *La mort d'Agrippine* (The Death of Agrippina, 1654). Noted also for his dueling and his long nose, the real Cyrano was the inspiration for Edmond Rostand's play *Cyrano de Bergerac* (1897; Eng. trans., 1898).

Cyrenaica see CYRENE

■

Cyrenaics [sir-i-nay'-iks] The Cyrenaics were Greek philosophers who taught a form of HEDONISM in the late 4th and early 3d centuries BC. Cyrenaic thought was formulated by Aristippus, a pupil of SOCRATES, but the school flourished principally under his grandson, Aristippus the Younger. Stressing the Socratic virtue of self-mastery, Aristippus reached ethical conclusions different from those of Socrates and claimed that the only intrinsic good is pleasure—not just the absence of pain, but positively enjoyable sensation (see EPICUREANISM).

■

Cyrene [sy-ree'-nee] The city of Cyrene, named after a local spring nymph, dominated a huge area of North Africa from the 6th century BC to the 4th century AD. Located in modern Libya, the site covers a ridge 8 km (5 mi) from the sea and 176 km (110 mi) northeast of Benghazi.

Cyrene was settled in c.630 BC by Greek colonists from THERA. Ruled by kings (the Battiads) for 100 years, the city-state prospered from the production of wheat, oil, wool, and silphium (a medicinal plant). It was renowned for its schools of medicine and philosophy (see CYRENAICS).

After rule by the Persians (525–479), Alexander the Great (331–323), and the Ptolemaic kings of Egypt (323–96), Cyrene became part of the Roman province of CYRENAICA in 74 BC. With the exception of a devastating Jewish revolt in AD 115, the Roman city remained prosperous through the 4th century. Thereafter it succumbed to invasion by the nomadic tribes of the desert.

■

Cyril of Alexandria, Saint Cyril, b. c.375, d. June 27, 444, a theologian and patriarch of Alexandria from 412 to 444, is remembered for his vigorous opposition to NESTORIANISM. Nestorius, patriarch of Constantinople, taught that two persons dwelt in Jesus Christ, one human and one divine, and on this ground he denied that the Virgin Mary could be called *Theotokos*, or "God-bearer." Cyril defended the term *Theotokos* and thus brought into the open a long-standing rivalry between the Alexandrian church and that of Antioch, which supported Nestorius.

Because Cyril taught a union of natures in Christ, the proponents of MONOPHYSITISM claimed his authority for their doctrines. Nonetheless, his teachings are considered orthodox. He is one of the Doctors of the Church. Feast Day: June 9 (Eastern); June 27 (Western).

■

Cyril of Jerusalem, Saint Cyril, c.315–c.386, bishop of Jerusalem, was a leader of the early church in the struggle against ARIANISM. He was exiled (357) from his see by Acacius, the Arian bishop of Caesarea, but reinstated (359) by the Council of Seleucia. Subsequently, he was banished two more times. One of the Doctors of the Church, Cyril was the author of 24 *Catecheses*, theological treatises important to the study of the development of Christian doctrine. Feast day: Mar. 18.

■

Cyril and Methodius, Saints Cyril, b. c.826, d. Feb. 14, 869, and Methodius, b. c.815, d. Apr. 6, 884, were Greek missionaries and linguists, known as the "Apostles to the Slavs." They were brothers and members of a noble family of Thessaloníki. In 862, Emperor Michael III sent them to Moravia, where they taught and celebrated the liturgy in the Slavonic vernacular, now known as Old Church Slavonic. To translate the Bible into this previously unwritten language, the brothers invented an alphabet based on Greek characters. The Cyrillic alphabet used in modern Slavic languages was attributed to St. Cyril, but it was probably the work of his followers.

Cyril died in Rome, where the brothers had gone to defend themselves against German bishops who wanted to enforce the use of the Latin liturgy among the Slavs. Methodius was consecrated an archbishop. Feast day: May 11 (Eastern); Feb. 14 (Western).

Cyrillic alphabet [sir-il′-ik] The Cyrillic alphabet is the system of characters used in the writing of some Slavic languages, such as Russian, Ukrainian, Byelorussian, Bulgarian, and Serbian. It has also been adopted as the written form of several minority tongues in the USSR: Azerbaijani, Kazakh, Kirgiz, and Uzbek, among others.

Cyrus the Great, King of Persia Cyrus, 599–530 BC, founded the ACHAEMENID Persian empire and ruled it from 549 to 530 BC. His father was Cambyses I, a prince in Persis (modern Fars province). His mother, according to Herodotus, was the daughter of Astyages, king of the Medes, who ruled the Persians. Cyrus revolted against his overlord and defeated him, after which the Achaemenid empire was founded. Cyrus first conquered the Iranians who opposed him and then marched against CROESUS, king of Lydia (in present-day Turkey). Cyrus defeated him and captured his capital, SARDIS. After consolidating his rule over the Ionian Greek cities on the coast of the Aegean Sea, he turned to BABYLONIA.

The conquest of the great and ancient city of BABYLON in 539 BC made Cyrus the ruler of a vast domain from the Mediterranean Sea to the borders of India. Cyrus is famous in the Old Testament for freeing the Jewish captives in Babylonia and sending them home. Cyrus then marched to central Asia, where he was killed in a battle with nomads. He was succeeded by his eldest son, Cambyses II.

The Greek author XENOPHON wrote a fanciful biography of Cyrus that depicted him as an ideal ruler. The subject of many legends, he came to be considered the father of the Iranian monarchy.

See also: PERSIA, ANCIENT.

Cyrus the Younger Cyrus, b. after 424 BC, the son of Darius II and younger brother of ARTAXERXES II, attempted to seize the Persian throne from his brother after Darius's death in 404 BC. The governor of several Anatolian provinces, Cyrus there hired Greek mercenaries and, with other troops, advanced to meet Artaxerxes. The decisive battle was fought at Cunaxa in Babylonia on Sept. 3, 401. At first, Cyrus's Greek mercenaries seemed to have won the battle, but Cyrus lost his life in trying personally to kill his brother. XENAPHON praised Cyrus in his account of the retreat of the 10,000 Greeks, the *Anabasis*.

cyst A cyst is an abnormal sac or cavity that contains a liquid or semisolid material and that is enclosed by a membrane. Cysts commonly occur in the sebaceous, or oil, glands of the skin, ovaries, sweat glands, esophagus, or breasts. Sebaceous cysts, also called whiteheads, occur when the oil glands are blocked and secretions from them cannot escape. When the ducts of sweat or mammary glands are blocked, retention cysts may develop. Most cysts are harmless and may be safely left alone. If, however, they become so large that they press against adjacent tissue, they may be removed surgically.

cystic fibrosis Cystic fibrosis is a GENETIC DISEASE of childhood that is characterized by respiratory and digestive problems and is usually fatal. The faulty gene involved must be inherited from both parents. The disease is the most common inherited disease among Caucasians; the average life span of its victims is only about 24 years. Cystic fibrosis apparently is caused by the inability of chloride ions to cross the specialized epithelial cells of salivary, mucus, and sweat glands, and the pancreas. Effects include heavy production of thick mucus in respiratory tracts, which increases susceptibility to respiratory infections; 90 percent of all patients die of chronic lung disease. Secretions that block pancreatic ducts cause important digestive enzymes to fail to reach the small intestine. Treatment is directed toward relief of symptoms, and no cure is yet known. The discovery in 1989 of the gene that causes cystic fibrosis offers hope for improved treatments and genetic screening, but finding a cure is complicated by the increasing number of gene mutations found to be capable of causing the disease.

cystinuria see KIDNEY DISEASE

cystitis [sis-ty′-tis] Cystitis is an inflammation of the wall and lining of the urinary bladder that may be due to bacterial infection or to mechanical abrasion from microcrystals of calcium phosphate in urine. Usually caused by bacterial infection, it is particularly prevalent in women during childbearing years, especially during pregnancy. In addition, certain drugs, such as methenamine mandelate, nitrofurantoin, and cyclophosphamide, may irritate the bladder; the inflammation subsides when these drugs are discontinued. Symptoms of cystitis include frequent and painful urination, cloudy or bloody urine, or both, and pain and tenderness over the bladder.

Occasionally, no specific cause can be found, and a thorough medical evaluation is necessary because of the rare possibility that cancer in the bladder wall is involved. In this case, the internal surface of the bladder is inspected by passing a narrow optical instrument called a cystoscope through the urethra into the bladder. A biopsy is done by removing a small piece of tissue for microscopic examination. Most cystitis cases respond to therapy. Usually, antibiotics are used.

cytochrome [sy′-tuh-krohm] Cytochromes are a group of proteins that contain heme, or iron, and that play a major role in cellular respiration, the process by which energy is transferred within cells. They serve as electron carriers in the electron-transport chain, a series of complex enzymes found in all cells of animals, plants, and eukaryotic microorganisms that have respiratory systems dependent on oxygen. In animal cells, cytochromes are located in the endoplasmic reticulum and in the inner membrane of MITOCHONDRIA, the so-called powerhouses of the animal cell. In plants, they occur chiefly in chloroplasts, structures essential to photosynthesis.

cytokinin   see HORMONE, PLANT

cytology [sy-tahl'-uh-jee]   Cytology is the science of the microscopic anatomy, physiology, and biochemistry of the CELL. According to the cell theory, all organisms are composed of cells and cell products. The theory was formulated (1838–39) by Jacob Mathias Schleiden and Theodor SCHWANN. In 1855, Rudolf Virchow recognized that cells arise only from preexisting cells.

Many important discoveries were made in cytology before 1900. The German embryologist Oscar Hertwig described (1876) the union of eggs and sperm in FERTILIZATION, and Polish botanist Eduard Strasburger described (1884) fertilization in flowering plants. French biologist Edouard-Gérard Balbiani described the giant chromosomes of the fruit fly in 1881, seven years before German anatomist Wilhelm von Waldeyer suggested the name *chromosomes* for threadlike bodies present in the cell nucleus. The process of cell division, visible with the light microscope, was also described before 1900.

By 1941, Belgian-American biochemist Albert Claude, using differential centrifugation, a technique introduced in 1934, was processing cells to isolate organelles, or membrane-enclosed structures, such as MITOCHONDRIA, to determine their function. Today particles smaller than 0.02 μm are isolated, using refined ultracentrifugation techniques.

A new era in cell research began when preparation techniques were devised to permit the study of cells by electron microscopy. In 1953, Romanian-American physiologist George Palade, who shared the 1974 Nobel Prize for physiology or medicine, published the first description of the ultrastructure of mitochondria. Thereafter many cell parts were revealed with remarkable clarity.

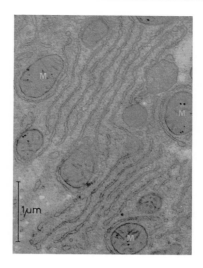

This electron microphotograph of a section of cytoplasm shows mitochondria (M), which supply energy to the cell. The endoplasmic reticulum appears as a network of membranes; the granules on its surface are ribosomes.

Radioactive isotopes have been used to tag chemical substances so that pathways of METABOLISM can be traced, and complex reactions in PHOTOSYNTHESIS and cellular respiration have become clearer as a result.

A laser beam focused on a minute cell part is used in microsurgery. Culture of plant and animal cells permits observation of these living, growing units outside the body.

cytoplasm [sy'-toh-plazm]   The cytoplasm of CELLS of EUKARYOTE organisms (protists and higher plants and animals) includes all the material bounded by the plasma membrane but outside the nucleus. It is packed with membrane-bound organelles, including mitochondria, chloroplasts (in green plants), the Golgi apparatus, lysosomes, endoplasmic reticulum, and ribosomes. The organelles contribute to cell maintenance by processing food and extracting chemical energy, transferring the energy to other cell parts, and producing compounds needed by the cell or to be sent to other cells. By contrast, cells of PROKARYOTE organisms (bacteria and blue-green algae) are divided into a nucleuslike body and the surrounding cytoplasm that is crowded with ribosomes but no membrane-bound organelles; this cytoplasmic matrix is called ground substance.

Czartoryski, Adam Jerzy [char-toh-ris'-kee]   A member of a distinguished Polish princely family, Adam Jerzy Czartoryski, b. Jan. 14, 1770, d. July 15, 1861, worked for the restoration of the Polish state after its third partition (1795) by Russia, Prussia, and Austria. He went to Russia where he served (1804–06) as foreign minister to Emperor ALEXANDER I. At the Congress of Vienna (1815), Czartoryski achieved the creation of the nucleic kingdom of Poland with Alexander as king. Disillusioned with the Russian policy in Poland, he joined the abortive insurrection of 1830–31. Later, in Paris, he continued diplomatic agitation for Poland's restitution.

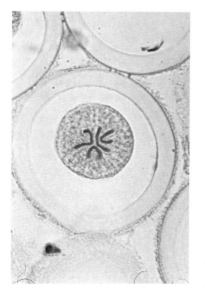

During mitosis (cell division), chromosomes become coiled and folded and are visible in the light microscope as distinct entities. In the stage known as metaphase, the chromosomes align in the center of the cell along structures called spindle fibers. Their study is facilitated by the use of the drug colchicine, which dissolves the spindle and interrupts the division process.

Czech language see SLAVIC LANGUAGES

■
Czech literature The first Czech writer of stature to use his native language rather than Latin or German was the religious reformer John Huss (Jan Hus). Humanistically oriented members of the Bohemian Brethren, the religious order that evolved out of Huss's teachings, refined the language even further. Their main achievement, the Kralice Bible (1588), occupies the position in Czech culture that the King James translation occupies in the English-speaking world. The Brethren's foremost thinker, the philosopher and reformer Jan Ámos Komenský (COMENIUS), also made an important contribution to Czech literature with his baroque allegory *The Labyrinth of the World and the Paradise of the Heart* (1631; Eng. trans., 1901).

With the Thirty Years' War (1618–48) and the Counter-Reformation, Czech as a literary language fell into disuse. Paradoxically, it was a Jesuit, Josef Dobrovský, who led the 19th-century renaissance, which included the translations and dictionaries of Josef Jungmann, the folk-poetry adaptations of F. L. Čelakovský and Karel Jaromír Erben, and the pan-Slavic sonnets of Jan Kollár. Original literary works also appeared: Karel Hynek Mácha's lyrical epic, *May* (1836), Božena Němcová's scenes from country life (typified by the novel *Babička*, 1855), Karel Havlíček Borovský's anti-Habsburg satirical verse, Jan Neruda's humorous sketches of Prague customs (1878), and Alois Jirásek's monumental historical novels.

By 1900 the influence of modernism was being felt. The prolific PARNASSIAN poet Jaroslav Vrchlický was followed by the decadent novelist Julius Zeyer and the symbolist poets Antonín Sova and Otokar Březina. Modernism survived World War I, veering to the left during the First Czechoslovak Republic (1918–38), when poetism (an original Czech movement combining features of futurism and Dada) and later surrealism came to the fore in the poetry and prose of such poets as Vítězslav Nezval and Karel Teige. The First Republic also saw the publication of the two works of Czech literature best known abroad: Karel ČAPEK's *R.U.R.* (1923), a play about the dangers of technology, and Jaroslav HAŠEK's *The Good Soldier Schweik* (1920–23), a satirical antiwar novel.

With the country under Soviet influence after World War II, the doctrine of SOCIALIST REALISM came into force, resulting in a spate of factory and farm novels. The strict censorship imposed by Czechoslovakia's Communist government drove many writers into exile, among them Milan KUNDERA, Jan Beneš, Pavel Kohout, and Josef Škvorecký. The poet Jaroslav Seifert (1901–86), however, winner of the Nobel Prize for literature in 1984, remained in his homeland and continued to publish there. Freedom of expression was restored with the end of Communist rule in 1989, and the playwright Václav HAVEL, jailed by the Communists for his dissenting views, was elected (1990) the country's president.

■
Czech music The Czechs, or Bohemians, the dominant ethnic group of Czechoslovakia, have one of the richest musical traditions of any of the Slavic peoples. Bohemia, an independent Czech state dating from the 9th century, began to fall under German influence in the later Middle Ages and was conquered by Habsburg Austria during the Thirty Years' War (1618–48). The HUSSITE movement of the 15th century temporarily reasserted the native tradition and generated a striking literature of hymns and devotional songs. In the 18th century Bohemia produced several generations of brilliant composers, but most of them made their reputations in foreign countries. Johan Stamitz (see STAMITZ family) and Franz Xaver Richter (1709–89) were leaders of the German Mannheim school, which influenced the transition from the baroque to the classical style of music. Jiří Antonín BENDA worked in Thuringia. Jan Ladislav Dussek (1760–1812) and Antonín Reicha (1770–1836) won success in Italy, England, France, and other parts of Europe. Prague, the Bohemian capital, was a major musical center in the 18th century, but its character was Austrian rather than Czech.

The central figure of the mid-19th-century national revival was Bedřich SMETANA, who, drawing on folk sources, almost single-handedly created a modern Czech musical style. In the next generation, Antonín DVOŘÁK, whose work combined cosmopolitanism with an unselfconscious nationalism, emerged as one of the most renowned composers of his day. Recognized and befriended by Dvořák, Leoš JANÁČEK, whose creative period came after 1900, had a unique style based on the speech patterns of his native district of Moravia.

The best-known Czech composer of the 1920s and 1930s was the French-influenced cosmopolitan Bohuslav MARTINŮ. After World War II and the advent of Communism in Czechoslovakia, some of the country's leading musical talents emigrated, including Karel Husa, who settled in the United States.

■
Czechoslovakia [chek-uhs-loh-vah'-kee-uh] Czechoslovakia is located at the heart of Europe. Bordered by Poland on the north, Germany on the north and west, the Soviet Union on the east, and Hungary and Austria on the south, it has long been at the crossroads of East and West. Established as an independent state in 1918, Czechoslovakia was dismembered by Germany prior to and during World War II and ruled from 1948 to 1989 by a Communist government. After the Communists were forced out (November 1989), free multiparty elections in June 1990 legitimated an interim government headed by Václav HAVEL, signaling Czechoslovakia's return to democracy.

Land and Resources

The Czech lands of BOHEMIA and MORAVIA, which constitute the western part of the country, are characterized by the Bohemian Highlands, which are bordered by the SUDETEN and the Ore mountains (Krušné hory) on the north and the Bohemian Forest (Český les) and Šumava Mountains on the west. East of Moravia is SLOVAKIA. Its landscape is dominated by the CARPATHIAN MOUNTAINS, which include Gerlach Peak (2,663 m/8,737 ft), the highest

AT A GLANCE

CZECH AND SLOVAK FEDERAL REPUBLIC

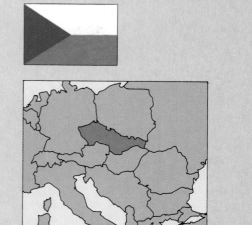

Land: Area: 127,869 km² (49,370 mi²). Capital and largest city: Prague (1989 est. pop., 1,211,207).

People: Population (1990 est.): 15,700,000. Density: 123.3 persons per km² (318 per mi²). Distribution (1990 est.): 75% urban, 25% rural. Official languages: Czech, Slovak. Major religions: Roman Catholicism, Protestantism.

Government: Type: republic. Legislature: Federal Assembly. Political subdivisions: 2 autonomous republics, 10 regions, 2 cities with regional status.

Economy: GNP (1988): $158.2 billion; $10,130 per capita. Labor distribution (1987): agriculture—12.3%; industry—36.9%; construction, communications, and other—50.8%. Foreign trade (1987): imports—$23.9 billion; exports—$23.5 billion; Currency 1 koruna = 100 haleru.

Education and Health: Literacy (1990): 100% of adult population. Universities (1990): 5. Hospital beds (1988): 155,082. Physicians (1988) 48,711. Life expectancy (1990): 71. Infant mortality (1989): 11.9 per 1,000 live births.

point in the country. Approximately 17% of Czechoslovakia has soils unsuitable for farming; only 8% of the soil is of the best quality for cultivation.

Drainage. Czechoslovakia's drainage is provided by the DANUBE, ELBE (Labe), and ODER (Odra) rivers. Tributaries of the Elbe include the Vltava (Moldau), the Berounka, the Ohře, and the Sázava; those of the Danube include the Morava, the Váh, the Hron, and the Ipel.

Climate. Czechoslovakia lies within a comparatively temperate zone marked by a transition from maritime to continental climate and by substantial variations of temperature and precipitation according to elevation. Winters are generally cold, with many days of subfreezing weather. Summers are moderately warm: temperatures seldom rise above 27° C (80° F). Annual precipitation ranges from 450 to 1,030 mm (18 to 41 in).

Vegetation and Animal Life. The prevalent feature of the flora is forests, which consist mostly of coniferous trees such as spruce and fir, mixed in lower-lying areas with deciduous trees such as oak, beech, birch, and linden.

The main quadrupeds are hares, roe deer, foxes, squirrels, weasels, and muskrat. Wild boars survive in some remote areas of Slovakia. Deer, bears, and lynx live mostly in reservations. Partridge, doves, pheasant, wild geese, blackbirds, swallows, and storks are abundant. The most common fish are carp, trout, pike, and perch.

One of the legacies of the Communist period has been tremendous ecological damage: most rivers are polluted, forests have been destroyed by acid rain, and air pollution

in northwest Bohemia has caused widespread health problems.

Resources. Czechoslovakia is relatively poor in natural resources. The primary domestic source of energy, soft coal, is expensive to mine and causes air pollution when burned as a fuel. Uranium, lead, copper, and iron ores are also found within the country. Most energy supplies and raw materials needed for manufacturing have been imported, in the past, primarily from the Soviet Union and other East European socialist countries.

People

Czechoslovakia has been a multiethnic state from its inception, but the redrawing of borders after World War II and the forced expulsion of the Sudeten Germans and many Hungarians simplified the country's ethnic composition. At present, the Czechs, who account for 64% of the population, and the Slovaks, who constitute 31%, are the two major ethnic groups. The remainder are Hungarians, Gypsies, Ukrainians, Poles, and Germans. The official languages of the state are Czech and Slovak. The principal cities include PRAGUE, the country's capital, BRATISLAVA, the capital of Slovakia, BRNO, OSTRAVA, KOŠICE, and PLZEŇ.

Tensions between Czechs and Slovaks, which were held in check by the Communist government, have come to the surface since the collapse of Communist rule. Other national groups have also begun to voice new demands in the changed political situation.

Prague, the capital and most populous city of Czechoslovakia, contains many architectural and historical landmarks. The Hradčany castle complex (right), begun as a fortress during the 9th century, contains St. Vitus's Cathedral. Today the castle is the residence of Czechoslovakia's president. The 17th- and 18th-century Church of St. Nicholas (left) is renowned for its baroque architecture.

Religion. Although religion was suppressed during the Communist period, many Czechs and Slovaks continued to identify themselves as believers. Roman Catholicism is the faith of the majority, but there is also an important Protestant tradition. The 19th-century Czech national movement was closely identified with this tradition, exemplified by the medieval Czech religious reformer John Huss. Protestant intellectuals also played an important role in Slovakia's national movement.

Education and Health Care. Prior to World War II, Czechoslovakia's literacy rates and educational levels approximated those in developed West European states. The subordination of education to political ends under Communist rule led to a decline in quality, and the new government is now reforming the school system.

Socialized since 1948, basic medical care has been widely available in Czechoslovakia, but lack of contact with Western medical circles for 40 years and the shortage of hard currency have caused medicine to lag behind in specialized areas. Although privatization in health care is envisioned, in the near future most medical care will still be provided by the state sector.

The Arts. Czechoslovakia traditionally has been a strong contributor to European culture. Prague has been a center of cultural life during various periods, and Czech and Slovak musicians, composers, architects, artists, and writers have made enduring contributions to their fields. Even during the Communist period, particularly the 1960s, artists, filmmakers, and writers took advantage of changing political conditions to try to expand the limits of permissible expression. The Czech New Wave in cinema is the best known of these efforts. (See also CZECH LITERATURE; CZECH MUSIC.)

Economy

Czechoslovakia's level of economic development is among the highest in central and eastern Europe, but the performance of the economy was hampered by the high degree of centralization and political interference in economic life that characterized the Communist period. Czech and Slovak Communist leaders copied Soviet economic practice and organization when they came to power in 1948. They completed the nationalization of economic assets begun in 1945, collectivized agriculture, and set up a central economic planning system. They also emulated Soviet emphasis on heavy industry, mining, and manufacturing, and neglected agriculture and light industry. Agriculture, although almost entirely collectivized, performed fairly well in the last years of Communist rule. Manufacturing and other branches of industry were handicapped by obsolete equipment, aging industrial plants, and shortages of raw materials, energy, and labor resources. The transportation network was expanded in the early days of Communist rule, but it proved inadequate to the demands placed upon it. The communication system, although relatively advanced for the region at the beginning of the Communist period, failed to keep pace with the country's development. These factors, as well as the impact of negative trends in the world economy in the 1970s, led to a decline in economic performance. Although Czechoslovakia did not experience the acute economic crises such as occurred in Poland, the standard of living stagnated during the late 1970s and 1980s. Political leaders acknowledged the need for economic reform, but little was actually accomplished before 1989.

Under the post-Communist government, measures have been enacted to privatize industry and agriculture and to facilitate foreign investment in the economy. Plans have been made to change the country's trading patterns, which until 1989 were very heavily oriented to the Soviet Union and other socialist countries, and to reintegrate Czechoslovakia into the world economy.

Government and Politics

The Czechoslovakian government in place between 1948 and November 1989 was modeled on Soviet political institutions and practices. Although several small political parties were allowed to exist, the only real political force was the Communist party. The legal system and judiciary were subordinated to political ends, and opposition to the system was prevented by the secret police. Unified mass organizations dominated by the party replaced the wealth of voluntary associations and interest groups that had existed previously. All areas of life, including education, culture, the arts, science, and leisure activities were politicized. In the late 1960s, intellectuals and party leaders, including Alexander DUBČEK, tried to reform this system in what came to be known as the "Prague spring," or "socialism with a human face." The USSR and its East European allies, however, fearing that the reform would spread to their countries, invaded Czechoslovakia with Warsaw Pact troops on Aug. 21, 1968, deposing Dubček and installing Gustáv HUSÁK in his place. Czechoslovakia then experienced nearly 20 years of political stagnation, broken only by the underground activities of the dissident group Charter 77.

This situation changed dramatically in 1989. Czechoslovakia was one of the last of the central European countries to take advantage of the new possibilities created by the liberal policies of Soviet president Mikhail GORBACHEV. Mass protests inspired by the examples of neighboring Poland and Hungary were begun by students on Nov. 17, 1989, and quickly spread to other sectors of the population. Dissident leaders, who, along with young people, had become active in openly challenging the regime during the previous two years, formed a new umbrella organization, the Civic Forum, and within 23 days the Communist leadership headed by Miloš Jakeš had resigned, the party had renounced its monopoly of power, and compulsory Marxist-Leninist education had been abolished at all levels. The choice of dissident playwright Václav Havel as president of the republic in late December capped the victory of democratic forces. In parliamentary elections held in June 1990, the Civic Forum and its Slovak counterpart, Public Against Violence, won control of the Federal Assembly.

History

Until the end of World War I the area that is now Czechoslovakia was part of the empire of AUSTRIA-HUNGARY. The

Farming settlements are found throughout this highland valley in the Low Tatras of eastern Czechoslovakia. In addition to rye, oats, and potatoes, a substantial amount of lumber and wood products are obtained from the region's forests.

previous history of the Czechs differed considerably from that of the Slovaks. Bohemia and Moravia, under Austrian rule, were major industrial centers, while Slovakia, which was part of Hungary, was an undeveloped agrarian region. Political conditions were also different in the two areas. The Czech and Slovak national movements reflected these contrasts. Conditions were much better for the development of a mass national movement in the Czech lands than in Slovakia. The roots of Czech nationalism go back to the 18th century, when philologists and educators, aided in part by German-speaking nobles, sought to propagate use of the Czech language and pride in the Czech nation. These efforts were followed by the development of a mass movement in the last half of the 19th century. Taking advantage of the opportunities for limited participation in political life available under Austrian rule, Czech leaders such as František PALACKÝ; founded numerous patriotic, self-help organizations that provided a chance for many of their compatriots to participate in communal life even prior to independence. In Slovakia, on the other hand, Hungarian rule was harsher, and an attempt was made to Magyarize the Slovaks. Slovak nationalism came to be a mass-based movement only after 1918.

The period between the two world wars saw the flowering of democracy in Czechoslovakia. Of all the new states established in central Europe after 1918, only Czechoslovakia had a democratic government. Despite regional disparities, its level of development was much higher than that of neighboring states. The population was by and large literate and contained fewer alienated groups. The impact of these conditions was augmented by the political values of Czechoslovakia's leaders. Under President Tomáš MASARYK, Czech and Slovak politicians promoted progressive social and economic conditions that served to diffuse discontent.

The weak spot of the interwar republic proved to be ethnic relations. The dissatisfaction of the large German minority, centered in the SUDETENLAND, became the pretext that led to the dissolution of the Czechoslovak state by Nazi Germany after the MUNICH CONFERENCE of 1938. Growing Slovak resentment over what was perceived to be domination by the more numerous Czech population eventually led to the establishment of a puppet Slovak state under Hitler's tutelage in 1939.

Following the defeat of Germany in 1945, Czechoslovakia was reestablished with its pre-1938 borders, except for RUTHENIA (Carpatho-Ukraine), which was ceded to the USSR. Eduard BENEŠ, the prewar president who had led the Czechoslovak liberation movement abroad, resumed his position as head of state. Soviet influence was predominant, however, enabling the Communists to seize control (February 1948) and convert the country into a satellite of the USSR.

The new regime, headed by Klement GOTTWALD, Antonín Zápotocký, and Rudolf Slánský, sovietized the economy and engaged in a struggle with the Catholic church that ended with the arrest and internment (1949) of Archbishop Josef Beran of Prague. In 1952 Gottwald engineered a purge in which Slánský and ten other party leaders were executed. From Zápotocký's death (1957) until the "Prague spring" of 1968 the government was controlled by Antonín Novotný.

Czerny, Carl [chair'-nee]   Carl Czerny, b. Feb. 20, 1791, d. July 15, 1857, was an Austrian pianist, teacher, and composer whose books of piano exercises have been used by generations of music students. After studies with Beethoven (1800–03), Czerny began a long career of teaching and giving occasional recitals. Among his pupils were Liszt, Kullak, and Leschetizky. Although Czerny's reputation today is based largely on his many piano studies, he composed in virtually all the forms of his time (his published works number almost 1,000) and wrote treatises on performance practice and music history.

Częstochowa [ches-tuh-koh'-vuh]   Częstochowa is an industrial city of Katowice province in south central Poland, about 200 km (125 mi) south of Warsaw. Its population is 252,900 (1988 est.). Iron and steel, textiles, chemicals, and paper are manufactured there. Częstochowa Technical University was founded in 1949. Pilgrims go to the city to visit the Jasna Góra monastery and its shrine of the Black Madonna, symbols of Poland's nationhood.

Dd

GERMAN-GOTHIC	RUSSIAN-CYRILLIC	CLASSICAL LATIN	EARLY LATIN	ETRUSCAN	CLASSICAL GREEK	EARLY GREEK	EARLY ARAMAIC	EARLY HEBREW	PHOENICIAN

D *D/d* is the fourth letter of the English alphabet and holds the same position in all modern alphabets derived from the Latin. The position and form of the letter in the Latin alphabet were in turn derived from the Greek by way of the Etruscan. The Greeks call the letter *delta*. The name, form, and position of the letter were taken by the Greeks, along with the rest of the alphabet, from a Semitic writing system—probably Phoenician but possibly Aramaic. The Semitic name of the sign is *daleth*.

The letter *D/d* represents a consonant sound produced in English speech by placing the tongue against the ridge behind the teeth. In English, the *-ed* of the past tense and past participle is often pronounced as *t* when it follows a voiceless consonant. Thus *stopped* is pronounced as if it were spelled *stopt*, and *passed* has the same pronunciation as *past*. Otherwise, final *d* and *t* are distinct, as in *send, sent* and *fad, fat*. The sound is often much reduced or completely silent when preceded by *n* or *l* and followed by most other consonants, as in *handsome*.

D Day see WORLD WAR II

da Gama, Vasco see GAMA, VASCO DA

Da Nang Da Nang (called by its French name, Tourane, before 1954) is a municipality in Quang Nam-Da Nang province in the densely settled central coastal lowlands of Vietnam. It has a population of 492,194. Located on the main railroad and highway of Vietnam, it is also a seaport with a fine harbor situated on the Bay of Da Nang, an arm of the South China Sea. It is about 80 km (50 mi) southeast of Hue. In 1787 the city was ceded to the French. During the Vietnam War, Da Nang was the site of a huge U.S. military base (built 1965), and it fell to North Vietnamese forces on Mar. 30, 1975. Da Nang has an important textile industry and it is also the site of the Cham Museum.

Da Ponte, Lorenzo [dah-pawn'-tay, lor-ent'-soh] Lorenzo Da Ponte, b. Emanuele Conegliano on Mar. 10, 1749, d. Aug. 17, 1838, was an Italian poet and librettist who collaborated with Mozart on three of the greatest operas of the 18th century: *The Marriage of Figaro* (1786), *DON GIOVANNI* (1787), and *Così fan tutte* (1790). Da Ponte, whose name was changed at baptism, studied for the priesthood, but after becoming involved in a scandal in Venice in 1779 he moved to Vienna, where he was appointed court poet to Emperor Joseph II. At the emperor's death in 1790, Da Ponte was forced to leave Vienna. He settled in London, but in 1805 he left England secretly and fled to the United States. From 1825 to 1837, Da Ponte was a professor of Italian literature at Columbia University. In 1825 he and Manuel García were among the first to present Italian opera in America.

da Vinci, Leonardo see LEONARDO DA VINCI

Dacca see DHAKA

dace [days] Dace is a common name for several species of minnow that inhabit clear, rapid streams throughout Europe and North America. These small, slender fish live in schools and feed on underwater plants, water insects, and small crustaceans. The common European dace, *Leuciscus leuciscus*, is a small-headed, silvery minnow that grows to 30 cm (12 in) long.

North American dace are smaller and consist of some species of *Phoxinus*, including the redbelly dace; redside and rosyside dace of the genus *Clinostomus*; and several species of *Rhinichthys*. Although the dace is not tasty, fishers consider angling for the European dace challenging.

The European dace inhabits lowland waters throughout northern Europe and into Siberia. The spawning period lasts from March to May, and the female lays her eggs on aquatic plants.

Dachau [dahk'-ow] Dachau (1986 est. pop., 32,682) is a town in Bavaria, southern Germany, that from 1933 to 1945 was the site of a Nazi concentration camp. On the Amper River about 18 km (11 mi) northwest of Munich, it has several industries, including machine shops, paper mills, printing shops, breweries, textile mills, and factories that produce ceramics and electrical equipment.

An old market town that dates back to about 800, Dachau was chartered in 1391. Notable landmarks include the 16th-century castle and a 17th-century town hall and church. The first Nazi concentration camp was established on the outskirts of the town in March 1933. From that time until the camp was liberated by U.S. troops on Apr. 29, 1945, more than 200,000 people from numerous countries were detained there, and perhaps 70,000 were killed or died of starvation or disease. Chapels and a museum commemorate the victims.

■

dachshund [dahks'-hund]   The dachshund is a long-bodied, short-legged dog with hanging ears, a slightly arched muzzle, and a tapering tail. The breed is recognized in two sizes: miniature, under 4.5 kg (10 lb), and standard, up to about 11 kg (25 lb). Heights range from 13 to 23 cm (5 to 9 in) at the shoulder. Three coat types exist: longhaired, shorthaired, and wirehaired. Coat colors and patterns vary from dark solids to light and dappled.

The dachshund was developed in Germany several hundred years ago to hunt badger and other animals that retreated into underground burrows; *dachshund* means "badger dog" in German. The breed's long, low-slung body enabled it to follow small game into a burrow and either keep it at bay or drive it out.

The dachshund (German for "badger dog") is a short-legged breed originally used to hunt badgers by following them into their burrows.

Dacron   see SYNTHETIC FIBERS

dactyl   see VERSIFICATION

■

Dada   Dada was an international, avant-garde art and literary movement that flourished between 1915 and 1922. The Dadaists' declared purpose was to protest the senseless violence of World War I, which they believed had made all established moral and aesthetic values meaningless. The term itself means "hobbyhorse" in French and was supposedly chosen at random from the dictionary. Dada promulgated antiart and nonsense, declaring that art did not depend in any way on established rules or on craftsmanship; the only law was that of chance, and the only reality that of the imagination. Dada

L.H.O.O.Q. (1919), Marcel Duchamp's desecration of Leonardo da Vinci's masterpiece, has become a symbol of Dada's rejection of the European artistic tradition. The work's seemingly enigmatic title, when pronounced in French, forms the sentence Elle a chaud au cul *("She has hot pants"). (Collection of Mrs. Mary Sisler, New York City.)*

appeared nearly simultaneously in Zurich, New York City, and Paris and soon took hold in Germany. It finally concentrated in Paris.

Dada Art.   In Zurich, where political exiles of all kinds took refuge during World War I, Dada was initiated by Hugo Ball, a German actor and playwright; Jean ARP, an Alsatian painter and poet; Richard Huelsenbeck, a German poet; Marcel Janco, a Romanian artist; and Tristan TZARA, a Romanian poet. Together they founded the Cabaret Voltaire—a theater, literary gathering place, and exhibition center. They offered scandalous and mysterious entertainments, lectured, and exhibited together a variety of such artists as Arp, Giorgio de CHIRICO, Max ERNST, Wassily KANDINSKY, Paul KLEE, and Pablo PICASSO. Arp illustrated the works of Huelsenbeck and Tzara and created a new type of COLLAGE by tearing pieces of colored paper and arranging them according to chance. In 1918, Tzara wrote the manifesto for the movement.

Marcel DUCHAMP, who in 1915 had moved to New York City and in the same year coined the term "ready-made," was the chief anticipator of Dada. For his ready-mades, Duchamp took such mundane objects as snow shovels, urinals, and bottle racks, gave them titles, and signed them, thus turning their context from utility to aesthetics. Francis PICABIA worked with Duchamp and with Man RAY in New York on the Dada review *291*; Picabia then founded the *391* review in Barcelona in 1917.

In 1919, Max Ernst launched Dadaism in Cologne with his friend Jean Arp. Ernst's type of collage technique was an important contribution to the Dada cause, as was the collage-painting of Kurt SCHWITTERS, the chief figure of Dada in Hanover, Germany, who called Dada *Merz*, "something cast-off, junk."

Dada emerged as a group activity in Paris when a Dada salon opened at the Montaigne Gallery in 1922. Dada has had a long and significant influence in art to the present.

Dada Literature. Dada found literary expression in France—principally in the form of nonsense poems and random combinations of words—with the writings of Louis ARAGON, André BRETON, and Paul ÉLUARD. They founded the revue *Littérature* in 1919; it was published until 1924. These writers soon abandoned the Dada movement, however, and turned to SURREALISM.

daddy longlegs

Daddy longlegs, or harvestman, is the common name for members of the arachnid order Phalangida (in some classifications, Opiliones). Daddy longlegs are related to spiders but have only two eyes, located toward the rear of the head (cephalothorax). The daddy longlegs has a segmented, oval body, up to 2 cm (0.8 in) long, that is supported on eight very slender legs, up to 16 cm (6.3 in) long. The second pair of legs carry sense organs and may be waved in the air to detect vibrations. Most daddy longlegs are omnivorous, feeding on plant juices and insects, and none spin webs. Adults live through the winter only in warmer climates.

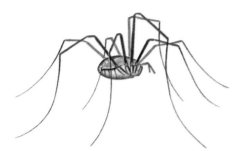

The daddy longlegs is one of several oval-bodied arachnids that have no constriction, or waist, between thorax and abdomen.

Daedalus (mythology)

In Greek mythology, Daedalus was a sculptor, architect, and inventor revered as the personification of arts and crafts. Credited with many inventions, Daedalus feared that his nephew Talus would surpass him in originality. He threw Talus from the Acropolis in Athens and then fled to Crete where he built a labyrinth to house the MINOTAUR for King MINOS. Later imprisoned by Minos, Daedalus escaped with his son, Icarus, on wings of waxed feathers. Icarus, however, flew too close to the Sun; his wings melted, and he fell into the sea. Daedalus settled alone in Sicily.

daffodil

Daffodil is the common name for any plant of the genus *Narcissus*, but correctly refers to larger, hardy, single-flowered, trumpet types of NARCISSUS, most of which are various shades of yellow. The JONQUIL, *N. jonquilla*, is similar to the daffodil and often mistaken for it. The Peruvian daffodil is a species of a bulbous spider-lily plant, *Hymenocallis narcissiflora*. It has white flowers with green stripes.

Dafydd ap Gwilym [dah'-vith ahp gwil'-im]

Dafydd ap Gwilym, *c.*1320–*c.*1380, generally regarded as the greatest of the 14th-century Welsh poets, was a master of technique and the first to exploit the *cywdd* form. This form consists of rhyming couplets with 7-syllable lines and an uneven stress pattern. Dafydd embellished most of his lines with the *cynghanedd*, a scheme of sound correspondences that involved alliteration, shifting accents, and internal rhyme. For future centuries his influence on Welsh poetry was so great that Gerard Manley Hopkins described the *cynghanedd* as having a major impact upon his own experiments.

Daghestan [dah-guh-stahn']

Daghestan (also Dagestan) is a region in eastern Caucasia, on the Caspian Sea, constituted politically as the Daghestan Autonomous Soviet Socialist Republic, one of the 16 autonomous republics in the Russian republic of the Soviet Union. Its area is 50,250 km^2 (19,400 mi^2), and its population is 1,729,000 (1989 est. pop., 315,000). The capital is Makhachkala (1989 est. pop., 315,000).

The name, which means "land of mountains" in Turkish, reflects the region's topography, in which isolated mountain valleys separated by outliers of the Caucasus Mountains shelter a wide variety of distinctive peoples. Daghestan is one of the least urbanized regions in the USSR. Vineyards and orchards are the basis for winemaking and fruit-canning industries. Some petroleum and natural gas is mined along the Caspian coast.

Dagon [day'-gahn]

Dagon, or Dagan, known in the Bible as the chief god of the Philistines, was worshipped in Mesopotamia in very early times, probably as a deity associated with good weather and agricultural fertility. His consort was called Shalash. Especially popular at Mari in the late 17th century BC, Dagan's cult passed from Mesopotamia to the Canaanites, and from them to the Philistines.

The daffodil N. pseudonarcissus, a springtime narcissus of temperate climates, produces long-bladed leaves and large, yellow flowers. It is closely related to the jonquil and to the tazetta narcissus.

Louis Daguerre helped develop modern photography when he perfected (1837) his daguerrotype, the first permanent photographic image. This process produced an original image on a silver-coated copper plate that was exposed to iodine vapor.

Daguerre, Louis J. M. [dah-gair']

Louis Jacques Mandé Daguerre, b. Cormeilles, France, Nov. 18, 1787, d. July 10, 1851, is the most famous of the several men who invented PHOTOGRAPHY in the 1830s. His process, the DAGUERREOTYPE, which produced a permanent image on silver-coated copper plate treated with iodine vapor, was bought by the French government and announced publicly on Aug. 19, 1839.

In 1824, Daguerre began attempts to fix chemically the image of the CAMERA OBSCURA, which was already widely used as an aid to sketching. He made only minor progress until, in 1826, he heard of similar research by Joseph Nicéphore NIÉPCE and, in 1829, joined him in a partnership. Niépce had achieved a crude photograph in 1822. Daguerre, however, did not succeed in perfecting a daguerreotype until 1837, four years after Niépce's death.

The invention was received with surprise and acclaim and was soon being used widely. Because Daguerre's process could not produce copies, it was soon replaced by William Henry Fox Talbot's calotype, which could produce many prints from a single negative.

daguerreotype [duh-gair'-oh-tipe]

The daguerreotype, invented in 1837 by the French artist Louis J. M. DAGUERRE, was the first practical form of reproduction in PHOTOGRAPHY. A daguerreotype was made on a silver-plated sheet of copper made light-sensitive by prior exposure to vapors that produced silver iodide. The plate was next exposed in a modified CAMERA OBSCURA, then treated with mercury vapors. Since the portions of the plate exposed to the light had changed back to silver, the mercury joined with the silver to form an amalgam, which was the image. The remaining silver iodide was removed by washing, originally with a salt solution but later with sodium hyposulfite. Costly and time-consuming, daguerreotypes were, nevertheless, superbly detailed. The process, although popular, was soon replaced.

Dahlberg, Edward

Edward Dahlberg, b. Boston, July 22, 1900, d. Feb. 27, 1977, was acclaimed as a pioneer of proletarian fiction following publication of his autobiographical novels *Bottom Dogs* (1929), *From Flushing to Calvary* (1932), and *Those Who Perish* (1934). Thirty years later he produced his finest work, *Because I Was Flesh* (1964), the story of his youthful tribulations, and became celebrated as "the curmudgeon of American letters" for his unremitting, quirkish attacks on the decline of Western literature and American culture. His *Confessions of Edward Dahlberg* appeared in 1971.

Dahlgren, John Adolphus Bernard

John A. Dahlgren, b. Philadelphia, Pa., Nov. 13, 1809, d. July 12, 1870, was a U.S. admiral who invented (1851) the Dahlgren gun, a type of ordnance used in the Union navy during the Civil War. Commandant of the Washington Navy Yard and chief of the Bureau of Ordnance, Dahlgren was appointed commander of the South Atlantic Blockading Squadron in 1863 and cooperated with Gen. William T. Sherman in the capture of Savannah in 1864. His son, Col. Ulric Dahlgren (1842–64) was killed in Dahlgren's Raid, an unsuccessful attempt to take Richmond in March 1864.

dahlia

Dahlias, genus *Dahlia*, are any of several perennial, tuberous, flowering plants that belong to the composite family, Compositae. The large flowers appear in most colors except blue. Dahlias were first discovered

Dahlia hybrids are widely different in appearance. Among several varieties are (A) formal decorative; (B) single petaled; (C) anemone petaled; (D) pompon miniature; and (E) cactus.

in the mountains of Mexico in the 16th century by a Spanish expedition and were later named in honor of Andreas Dahl, a Swedish botanist. In colder climates, the tubers are dug up and stored over the winter.

Dahomey   see BENIN

Daimler, Gottlieb [dime'-lur] Gottlieb Wilhelm Daimler, b. Mar. 17, 1834, d. Mar. 6, 1900, was a German inventor and engineer who in 1885 constructed and patented the first high-speed INTERNAL-COMBUSTION ENGINE. He also devised a CARBURETOR so that the engine could run on liquid gasoline instead of gas. He fitted his engine onto a bicycle (1885), making what was probably the first MOTORCYCLE; and powered a carriage with his engine (1886), creating one of the first AUTOMOBILES powered by an internal-combustion engine. (Karl BENZ is generally credited with being first the year before.) In 1890, Daimler founded the Daimler Motor Company, which later became Daimler-Benz and Company (1926).

Dairen   see DALIAN

dairying   Dairying is the branch of farming devoted to the production of MILK. Although many trades and industries are involved in the making of butter, cheese, yogurt, and the other by-products of milk, the term *dairying* refers explicitly to the type of farm where the main work is the care, feeding, and milking of cows that have been bred as milk rather than meat producers (see CATTLE AND CATTLE RAISING for a discussion of the types of cattle bred primarily for meat). Questions of optimum dairy-herd size and breed, of the best types of barn housing, of the most efficacious and economical feeds, of disease and stress prevention, and of government milk-price supports and subsidies are the issues that most occupy the dairy farmer, in both North America and Europe, the continents with the largest dairying industries. Although the cow is by far the most generous milk producer, BUFFALO, GOATS, and SHEEP also supply a small fraction of the world milk total.

Dairy Cow Breeds

In North America the major breeds of dairy cows are Holstein-Friesian, Jersey, Guernsey, Brown Swiss, and Ayrshire—all breeds that originated in Europe. The Milking Shorthorn, a variety of a type of beef cattle, is a dual-purpose breed, producing both meat and milk in quantity. Holsteins are also valued as meat producers; in fact, in western Europe they are used as a prime beef breed.

In the late 1980s, milk production per cow in the United States averaged over 6,350 kg (14,000 lb) annually. Holstein-Friesians (called Holsteins in the United States, Friesians in Europe) produce the greatest quantities of milk. Fat solids and nonfat milk solids are characteristically highest with Jerseys and lowest with Holsteins.

Dairying implements were used until the mid-19th century, when dairy products were first processed in commercial plants in the United States. Cream for butter making was skimmed from the milk with a perforated scoop (1) and agitated in hand-operated churns, such as the plunger (2), barrel (3), or box (4) churn. The butter was kneaded with butter workers (5), and decorative designs were imprinted with butter stamps (6). By 1850 the curd agitator (7) and cutter (8), which separated liquid whey from the solids used for cheese, had been replaced by a larger, more efficient apparatus (9). The cheese press (10) was used to remove excess moisture from the ripening cheese. The product was stored in small barrels (11).

The Dairying Process

Lactation, the production of milk, begins at freshening, when the cow bears a calf. The production period usually lasts 305 days. Milk production peaks about 2 months after freshening, then drops by about 5% per month. Some 60 to 90 days after freshening, the cow may be rebred. Cows have a gestation period of about 280 days.

Dairy cows are mature enough to bear calves at about 2 years of age. Thereafter, they are gradually culled, or removed from the herd, for insufficient production (33%), failure to breed (27%), or mastitis, an inflammation of the udder usually caused by bacterial infection.

The cow's ability to produce large quantities of milk is the product of millennia of selection and careful breeding. The cow's four large mammary glands contain alveoli, specialized cells that filter constituents of milk from the bloodstream as it passes through the udder (see also BREAST; MAMMAL).

Milking. Cows must be milked at regular intervals, usually twice a day. Milk is removed through the teats, elongated nipples at the end of each mammary gland. Nursing calves and milking machines remove milk by suction. (Hand milking removes the milk by squeezing the teat.) The flexible tubes of a milking machine are placed on the teats. A suction-creating vacuum is applied; the milk flows into volumetric (weigh) jars or through milk meters, which measure the quantity of milk produced, and then through pipes to a storage and cooling tank.

Breeding. The average milking life of a cow in a commercial herd is slightly more than three lactations (although some cows produce well for eight to ten lactations.) Thus, about one-fourth of the herd must be replaced each year.

Cows can conceive only during an estrous period that occurs about every 21 days. Since bulls are seldom kept with cows, dairy operators must detect the estrous period and either artificially inseminate or provide a bull for mating.

(Right) *In the milking parlor, each cow's output flows through a volumetric (weigh) jar, which measures quantity and allows daily production records to be maintained.* (Below) *At the processing plant, a technician checks the temperature of a giant vat of milk. At this stage, milk is usually skimmed of its cream, which is added back before the milk is pasteurized and homogenized.*

By means of ARTIFICIAL INSEMINATION a cow can be impregnated with the semen of a bull that is not kept at the same dairy. Semen can be frozen in liquid nitrogen, stored for long periods, and transported. Progeny testing helps to identify superior bulls as sires—that is, those bulls likely to transmit to their female offspring the desirable traits of high milk yield and high milk-fat content.

Although artificial insemination is the most common method of breeding dairy cattle, other more sophisticated methods have come into use in recent years. Prize cows may be hormonally induced to produce many eggs at a single ovulation, and these are fertilized through artificial insemination. The embryos are flushed out of the cow 6 to 8 days after insemination, and each viable embryo is transferred to a surrogate mother-cow, where it develops normally and is born 9 months after the embryo transfer. Eggs may also be fertilized in vitro, and embryos can now be kept frozen, like sperm, in liquid nitrogen until their transfer to surrogate dams. Finally, techniques for splitting, or cloning, embryos have been successful in producing multiple identical calves from a single embryo. (See also ANIMAL HUSBANDRY.)

Pasturage and Forage. Cows and goats, as well as

At this Wisconsin dairy farm, cows feed at a trough filled at regular intervals by an automatic mechanism that draws grain down from the silo in the background.

Half-gallon containers travel down the bottling line, to be filled and sealed in a totally automated operation.

sheep, deer, and camels, have four stomach cavities. The largest cavity, the rumen, contains billions of bacteria and protozoans, specially adapted to digest cellulose and to synthesize proteins from nonprotein nitrogen sources such as urea. Thus, they supply a means of digesting forages that are not digestible by humans and other animals with simple stomachs. These ruminants, therefore, provide a vital means of harvesting vast quantities of pasture from land that cannot be cultivated. Because pastures are seldom available year-round, and because land values are too high in some locations to allow for pastures, farmers also use HAY and silage as forages for cows. High-protein grain supplements fortified with soybean or cottonseed meal and added minerals are added to forages.

Impact of Biotechnology. The number of dairy cows in the United States dropped from 25 million in 1945 to 10 million in the late 1980s. Milk yield per cow soared, however, from an annual 2,080 kg (4,600 lb) in 1945 to today's average 6,350 kg (14,000 lb). Much of this advance is the result of the strides in biotechnology, which permit the kinds of sophisticated breeding techniques described above.

Other advances include genetic improvements in forages that will increase forage digestibility, and genetic manipulation that will alter the protein proportions in milk, making some supplies more appropriate for cheese production, for example, or more digestible for human infants.

The use of biotechnology is not problem-free, however. A case in point is the issue of bovine somatotropin (BST). BST is a lactation-increasing hormone produced naturally in cows. Artificial BST is made in large quantities by genetically altered bacteria; when given to cows it significantly improves their efficiency of using feed and their productivity. Its use has created controversy in the short time it has been commercially available. Questions con-

cerning its health effects on humans have been raised. Many farmers fear that the use of BST will overload an already oversupplied milk market, increase farm costs, and lower milk prices, driving smaller dairy farmers out of business. Finally, use of BST may keep U.S. dairy products out of the trans-European market created by the European Economic Community.

U.S. Milk Industry

Dairy owners may sell raw milk directly to private firms. More frequently, they either market milk through their own cooperative organizations, which sell it to private firms for processing, or manufacture the finished products themselves. Dairy cooperatives provide a strong voice for dairy owners through the National Milk Producers Federation, which represents milk producers and cooperatives in dealing with federal agencies on issues relating to the production, processing, importing, marketing, and pricing of milk.

U.S. farmers produce far more milk than the nation can consume. The federal government, through the Department of Agriculture (USDA), seeks to ensure a stable supply of milk and to maintain orderly marketing procedures. It buys milk—in the form of butter, cheese, and nonfat dried milk—that has not been sold commercially, in effect establishing minimum prices. Massive quantities of federally owned dairy products have been stored in government warehouses or given away in federal food programs. The USDA has tried many tactics in attempting to cut back the price-support program, which remains a sensitive political issue.

daisy   Daisy is the common name for many different members of the composite family, Compositae. The name originally referred to the English daisy, *Bellis perennis*, a

The name daisy *is derived from an English corruption of "day's eye." Illustrated are the Dahlberg daisy* (left) *and the true English daisy* (right).

Dakar, on the Cape Verde peninsula, is the westernmost city on the African mainland. The capital of French West Africa from 1902 to 1958, Dakar has been the capital of Senegal since 1960, when the country became independent.

Eurasian perennial seldom exceeding 15 cm (6 in) in height. Its flowers have yellow centers and white or rose outer petals. In the United States, daisy more often refers to *Chrysanthemum leucanthemum*, another Eurasian perennial that grows to 1 m (3 ft) high and bears flowers with yellow centers and white outer petals. Both species now grow wild in North America. Other daisies are the prairie daisy, *Aphanostephus skirrhobasis*; Shasta daisy, *C. superbum*; and Spanish daisy, *Bellis rotundifolia*.

Dakar [dah-kar'] Dakar (1985 est. pop. 1,382,000), the capital city of Senegal, is located on the southern tip of the Cape Verde Peninsula, near Africa's westernmost point. Dakar is a major African port where textiles, leather goods, flour, and peanut, fish, and petroleum products are manufactured. It is the site of several fine museums and of Cheikh Anta Diop University (1949; formerly the University of Dakar).

In 1677 the French occupied Gorée, an island near Dakar, but the mainland was not settled until the mid-19th century. In 1885 the first railroad in West Africa linked Dakar with the interior. Dakar became the capital of French West Africa in 1904, of the Mali Federation in 1959, and of independent Senegal in 1960. Growth has been rapid since World War II.

Dakota see SIOUX

Daladier, Édouard [dah-lahd-yay', ay-dwar'] As leader of the Radical party and premier three times during the 1930s, Édouard Daladier, b. June 18, 1884, d. Oct. 10, 1970, exercised a critical influence over prewar French politics. He entered parliament in 1919, served in French cabinets from 1924 on, and was premier from January to October 1933 and again in January 1934. In 1936 he helped bring the Radical party into a coalition with the Socialists and Communists, although he later turned against Léon BLUM's Popular Front policies.

As premier for the third time after April 1938, Daladier signed the Munich Pact on Sept. 30, 1938 (see MUNICH CONFERENCE), breaking France's commitment to support the territorial integrity of Czechoslovakia. In March 1940 he was replaced by his rival Paul Reynaud, and in September was arrested by the VICHY GOVERNMENT. When he returned from imprisonment (1943–45) in Germany, he again led his party and served as a deputy (1946–58).

Dalai Lama [dah'-ly lah'-muh] Dalai Lama is the title of the religious leader of TIBETAN BUDDHISM, who was also, until 1959, temporal ruler of TIBET. Each Dalai Lama is believed to be the reincarnation of his predecessor. When one dies, the new incarnation (identified partly by his ability to pick out possessions of the former Dalai Lama) is sought among newly born boys. The Dalai Lama is also regarded as an emanation of the BODHISATTVA Avalokitesvara.

The first Dalai Lama was Gan-den Trup-pa (1391-1474), head of the dominant Ge-luk-pa (Yellow Hat) monastic sect and founder of the Tashi Lhunpo monastery. He and his successor, however, did not actually bear the title *Dalai*, which was first bestowed on the third Dalai Lama (1543–88) by a Mongol prince in 1578 and applied retroactively.

The 14th Dalai Lama, b. Tenzin Gyatso, 1935, was installed in 1940. He remained in Tibet from the Chinese

The 14th Dalai Lama (1935–) established a government in exile in Dharmsala, India, in 1959 and has worked to preserve Tibetan culture. In 1989 he was awarded the Nobel Peace Prize.

takeover in 1950 until 1959, when he fled to India following an abortive Tibetan revolt against Chinese Communist rule. He established a Tibetan government-in-exile in Dharmsala, India, and has worked to preserve Tibetan arts, scriptures, and medicine. In 1989 he was awarded the Nobel Peace Prize for his nonviolent struggle to end Chinese domination of his homeland.

Tibet's secondary spiritual leader is the Panchen Lama. The 10th Panchen Lama (1939–89) served as nominal ruler of Tibet from 1959 until 1964. He was imprisoned during the CULTURAL REVOLUTION but later was returned to favor.

Dalcroze, Émile Jaques [dahl-krohz'] Émile Jaques Dalcroze (or Émile Jaques-Dalcroze), b. July 6, 1865, d. July 1, 1950, was a Swiss composer, music teacher, and originator of the system of rhythmic education known as EURHYTHMICS. He studied composition in Vienna and Paris before joining (1892) the faculty at the Conservatory of Music in Geneva, where he began his experiments based on the theory that the source of musical rhythm is in the body. In 1910, Dalcroze established his own school at Hellerau, Germany. From 1914 until his death, Dalcroze taught in Geneva. Although he was primarily a musician, his theories combining movement and dance greatly influenced theater, modern dance, ballet, and physical therapy.

Daley, Arthur Arthur John Daley, b. New York City, July 31, 1904, d. Jan 3, 1974, was, from 1942 until his death, author of the "Sports of the Times" column in the *New York Times*, for which he won a 1956 Pulitzer Prize. His other awards include the 1961 Grantland Rice Memorial Award for outstanding sportswriting. Daley joined the *Times* in 1926. His books include *Sports of the Times* (1959) and *Pro Football's Hall of Fame* (1963).

Daley, Richard J. The American politician Richard Joseph Daley, b. Chicago, May 15, 1902, d. Dec. 20, 1976, served as Democratic mayor of Chicago from 1955 to 1976. He was considered the last of the old-time big city political bosses. Daley was admitted to the bar in 1933 and rose through the ranks of the Cook County (Chicago) Democratic club, serving in the state legislature from 1936 to 1946. After being elected mayor, he quickly consolidated his power and ruled Illinois Democratic politics virtually single-handedly for the rest of his life. His support was avidly sought by Democrats aspiring to the presidential nomination and was crucial to several victorious nominees. Daley's son, Richard M. Daley, b. Chicago, Apr. 24, 1942, was elected mayor of Chicago in 1989.

Dalhousie, James Andrew Broun Ramsay, 1st Marquess of [dal-hoo'-zee] Lord Dalhousie, b. Apr. 22, 1812, d. Dec. 19, 1860, governor-general of India from 1847 to 1856, laid the foundations for direct

Richard Daley served continuously as mayor of Chicago from 1955 until his death in 1976. His machine-based administration was noted for its efficiency. Daley became the focus of national attention during the 1968 Democratic party convention, held in Chicago, when his city's police brutally put down anti–Vietnam War protesters.

British rule over the subcontinent. He annexed Punjab (1849) by force and lower Burma (1852) through aggressive diplomacy. He also annexed several states, including Satara (1848), Jaipur and Sambalpur (1849), and Nagpur (1854), whose rulers had died without heirs.

In 1856, Dalhousie took over Oudh on the ground that it had been misgoverned, thus helping to precipitate the INDIAN MUTINY of 1857. Dalhousie's changes, which in effect dismantled the system of government developed by the British East India Company, were preserved under the system of direct rule by the British crown instituted in 1858. Dalhousie was also responsible for social reforms and the construction of India's first railroad.

Dalí, Salvador [dah-lee'] The Spanish painter Salvador Dalí, b. May 11, 1904, d. Jan. 23, 1989, was a leader of SURREALISM. He studied (1921–26) at the San Fernando Academy of Fine Arts in Madrid and associated with such future Spanish modernists as Federico GARCÍA LORCA and Luis BUÑUEL. His early work was influenced by the Italian futurists and by the metaphysical paintings of Giorgio de CHIRICO. Dalí, however, pointed to his Catalan sense of fantasy and his megalomania as his true motivating forces.

Moving to Paris, he frequented the Café Cyrano, the headquarters of the Parisian surrealists, and in 1929 first exhibited his own surrealist paintings. He studied the writings of Sigmund Freud and subsequently declared an ambition to "systemize confusion." Such paintings as *Persistence of Memory*, popularly known as *Soft Watches* (1931; Museum of Modern Art, New York City), and *The Sacrament of the Last Supper* (1955; National Gallery, Washington, D.C.) have become widely known and part of the definitive record of 20th-century art. Displaying an early technical virtuosity, Dalí worked in several media,

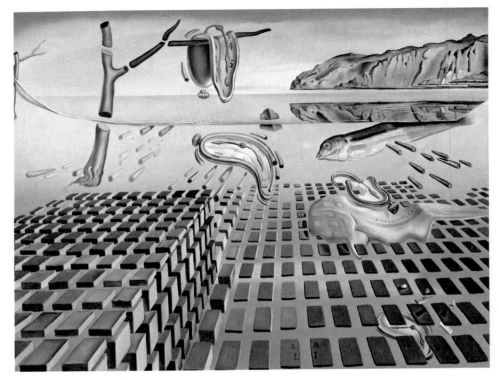

Salvador Dalí's surrealistic *Chromosome of a Highly Colored Fish's Eye Starting the Harmonious Disintegration of the Persistence of Memory (1952–54; private collection)* uses illusionistic techniques and takes ordinary objects out of their expected settings, distorting them and combining them in unusual juxtapositions.

including jewelry, advertisements, beer-bottle design, ballet sets and costumes, and, in collaboration with Buñuel, the famous surrealist films *Un Chien andalou* (An Andalusian Dog, 1928) and *L'Age d'or* (The Age of Gold, 1931). His personal eccentricities—flowing capes, handlebar mustache, and popping eyes—made him recognized around the world.

Dalian (Ta-lien) [tah-lee-ahn]   Dalian, formerly known as Dairen (1988 est. pop., 2,280,000), is a component of the Chinese municipality of LÜDA (Lü-ta), which encompasses Dalian and Lüshun. Dalian occupies the eastern portion of the Liaodong Peninsula's tip at the entrance to the Bo Hai (Gulf of Zhili). The city serves as an entry port for Manchuria and is connected to the interior by rail. Ships, cement, steel, transportation equipment, and cotton textiles are produced. Soybean processing and petroleum refining are also important.

The history of known settlement in Dalian dates from the 2nd-century BC occupation by the Han dynasty. Subsequently, the area was occupied by the Tang dynasty (7th century), the Ming dynasty (15th century), and the Manchu dynasty (1633-1911). Russia occupied the city in 1897, renaming it Dalny, but Japan was awarded the area after the Russian defeat in the Russo-Japanese War (1904-05). After World War II, Dalian was returned to China.

Dallapiccola, Luigi [dahl-lah-pik'-koh-lah]   Luigi Dallapiccola, b. Feb. 3, 1904, d. Feb. 19, 1975, was one of Italy's most significant avant-garde composers. During World War II he was persecuted by the Italian government because, although he was a devout Catholic, his wife was Jewish. This experience profoundly influenced his life and music. In 1939 he adopted the twelve-tone system of composing, using it, however, in his own way. His works include the choral pieces *Songs of Captivity* (1938–41) and *Songs of Liberation* (1955), the opera *The Prisoner* (1944–48), *Variations for Orchestra* (1954), *Christmas Cantata* (1957), the opera *Ulysses* (1969), and *Sicut umbra* for mezzo-soprano and 12 instruments (1970).

Dallas   Dallas is the seat of Dallas County and the second largest city in Texas. Located on the flat prairies in the northeastern part of the state, it sprawls on both sides of the Trinity River. Dallas, with an area exceeding 775 km^2 (300 mi^2), has a population of 1,006,877 (1990). Its rate of growth between 1980 and 1990 was 11.3%. The population of the combined metropolitan areas of Dallas and nearby FORT WORTH is 3,885,415. Nearly 30% of the population are black, and 12% are of Hispanic origin.

Dallas is a good example of a gateway city, serving as a hub through which goods, services, people, and, ultimately, ideas are channeled. Its gateway function is indi-

Dallas, located in northeastern Texas, is that state's second largest city and part of a large metropolitan complex that includes the city of Fort Worth. Dallas grew rapidly through the mid-1980s, benefiting from the population trend that brought large numbers of people to the "Sunbelt" region of the U.S. South and Southwest.

cated by the quantity of wholesale business, the concentration of insurance companies and financial institutions, the large number of national and regional corporate headquarters and state and U.S. government departmental offices, and the daily passenger flow through the Dallas–Fort Worth Regional Airport. Although commerce and finance dominate, manufacturing is also important, particularly in the aerospace, petroleum, electronics, food-processing, and apparel industries.

Dallas is also a center of the region's cultural and educational activities. Educational institutions include Southern Methodist University (1911), University of Dallas (1955), Bishop College (1881), Baylor University School of Dentistry (1905), and University of Texas Southwestern Medical Center at Dallas (1943). Prominent cultural institutions include the Museum of Fine Arts (1903); Dallas Theater center (1959); Dallas Symphony (1900), housed in the Morton H. Meyerson Symphony Center (1989); and Dallas Opera (1957). Other areas of interest include the downtown, the Arts district, and McKinney Strip—all served by the McKinney Trolley. The Texas State Fair is held in Dallas, and the city is the site of the Cotton Bowl stadium.

Dallas's first settler, John Neely Bryan, built a log cabin near the Trinity River in 1841. Five years later a village was laid out and a county organized; both were named for George Mifflin Dallas, then vice-president of the United States. The town was incorporated in 1856 and a city charter granted in 1871. Dallas was a supply center for Southern troops during the Civil War. Most of its pre–World War II development was a result of its position as a commercial center for a succession of businesses—railroads in the 1870s; cotton; oil after the east Texas oilfield was discovered in 1930; and insurance. President John F. Kennedy was assassinated in Dallas on Nov. 22, 1963. A permanent exhibit on the event, titled "The Sixth Floor," opened in Dallas in 1989.

Dallas, George Mifflin   George Mifflin Dallas, b. Philadelphia, July 10, 1792, d. Dec. 31, 1864, was U.S. vice-president (1845–49) under James K. POLK. He was the son of Alexander J. Dallas (1759–1817), who had been secretary of the treasury (1814–16). A Democrat, Dallas held various local offices in Pennsylvania before serving in the U.S. Senate (1831–33) and as minister to Russia (1837–39). As vice-president he presided over the Senate debates on the Mexican War and the Wilmot Proviso. Dallas was later minister to Great Britain (1856–61). He secured an agreement clarifying Britain's role in Central America and a disavowal of Britain's traditional claim to the right of searching at sea the ships of other nations.

Dalmatia [dal-may'-shuh]   Dalmatia, a coastal region along the Adriatic Sea, is a province of CROATIA, one of the constituent republics of Yugoslavia. It extends from the Albanian border on the south to ZADAR on the north and includes many offshore islands. Mountains rise abruptly from the sea, and the coast is dotted with inlets and bays. The Dinaric Alps separate Dalmatia from Bosnia and Hercegovina to the east.

Dalmatia has a population of 902,000 (1981 est.). DUBROVNIK, SPLIT, and Zadar are the principal cities. Tourism is now of prime economic importance. Wine is the major product, and some olives and vegetables are also grown. Much hydroelectric power is generated from the region's swift rivers.

dalmatian   The dalmatian is a shorthaired dog with distinctive black or deep brown (liver-colored) spots on a

The dalmatian, with its unique coloring, became fashionable in 19th-century England because its speed and stamina enabled it to accompany horse-drawn coaches.

white coat. It ranges in size from 48 to 58.5 cm (19 to 23 in) high at the shoulders and weighs about 25 kg (55 lb). The breed is believed to have originated in Dalmatia, now a part of Yugoslavia, where it was used as a general-purpose hunting dog. In the mid-1800s the breed was brought to England, where it became known as a carriage dog because it was trained to trot alongside a horse and carriage or sit beside the driver. This association led to its fame as a firehouse dog in the United States, where it accompanied the firemen and their horse-drawn fire engines.

Dalou, Aimé Jules [dah-loo'] Aimé Jules Dalou, b. Dec. 31, 1838, d. Apr. 15, 1902, was a French sculptor best known for his *Triumph of the Republic* in the Place de la Nation, Paris. Although he began exhibiting at the Salon in 1861, Dalou earned his living by creating ornamental sculpture for large private houses. He found an appreciative audience in London for his portraits and genre pieces. Dalou worked for 20 years on the *Triumph of the Republic*, unveiled in 1899.

Dalton, John The English teacher, chemist, and physicist John Dalton, b. Sept. 6, 1766, d. July 27, 1844, is best known for developing the ancient concept of ATOMS into a scientific theory that has become a foundation of modern chemistry.

Throughout his life Dalton was interested in the Earth's atmosphere, and he recorded more than 200,000 atmospheric observations in his notebooks. These observations led Dalton to study gases, and from the results of his experiments he was able to formulate his atomic theory. In a book on meteorology, he concluded that the aurora borealis is a magnetic phenomenon; he also explained the condensation of dew and gave a table of vapor pressures of water at various temperatures. His law of partial pressures was included in a paper (1803) on gas solubilities.

Dalton's atomic theory was expressed in public lectures in 1803 and later in his *New System of Chemical Philosophy* (1808). This theory incorporated some fea-

John Dalton, a British chemist and physicist, developed the atomic theory, which postulates that all elements are composed of particles, or atoms, identical in size and weight. Among Dalton's other achievements was the first description of color blindness, an optical condition he suffered from, which is sometimes called Daltonism.

tures that have since been discarded, but the realization that each atom has a characteristic mass and that atoms of elements are unchanged in chemical processes has served chemists to the present day.

See also: CHEMISTRY, HISTORY OF.

Dalton's law Dalton's law, named for the English chemist John DALTON (1766–1844), states that the pressure exerted by a gaseous mixture is equal to the sum of the partial pressures of its components. The partial pressure of a gas is the pressure it would exert if it alone occupied the entire volume of a mixture. Dalton's law applies only to ideal gases, but it holds closely enough for real gases. It is used in chemistry and thermodynamics to study the properties of gaseous mixtures.

See also: GAS LAWS.

Daly, Augustin John Augustin Daly, b. Plymouth, N.C., July 20, 1838, d. June 7, 1899, was an American playwright and theater manager who wrote and adapted about 90 plays. These include *Leah the Forsaken* (1862), about anti-Semitism; *Under the Gaslight* (1867), a melodrama; and *Horizon* (1871), a frontier drama. Many of the great stars of the age appeared in theaters that Daly managed after 1869 in New York and London. He disapproved, however, of the star system and emphasized ensemble performances and stage realism. Premieres of his productions were considered major social events.

Daly, Marcus Irish-born Marcus Daly, b. Dec. 5, 1841, d. Nov. 12, 1900, founded the Anaconda Copper Mining Company. While prospecting in the West he discovered (1876) what he believed to be a silver mine at Butte, Mont. He formed a company to work the mine, but the silver gave out. When the site proved to be rich in copper, he bought out neighboring silver mines, built a smelter, and soon became a multimillionaire. He founded the city of Anaconda, Mont., and acquired banks, power plants, irrigation systems, railroads, and timberlands. Powerful in the Democratic party, he supported William Jennings Bryan in the 1896 presidential election.

dam A dam is a barrier built across a water course to hold back or control the water flow. Dams may be classified according to the functions they serve, and in general terms, a dam is either a storage, diversion, or detention dam. Storage dams are constructed to impound water in periods of surplus supply for use in periods of deficient supply. For example, many small dams impound the spring runoff for later use in the summer dry season. In addition, storage dams may provide a WATER SUPPLY, or an improved habitat for fish and wildlife; they may store water for use in hydroelectric power generation, or for IRRIGATION; or they may be units in a flood control project (see FLOODS AND FLOOD CONTROL).

The specific purpose to be served by a storage dam

A laborer adds his clay-filled bag to complete (1987) a huge earth dam on the Feni River in Bangladesh. The final 1,300-m (0.8-mi) closure was finished during the 7 hours of a low tide.

tion developments and for diversion from a stream to a distant storage reservoir. Detention dams are constructed to minimize the effect of sudden floods and to trap sediment.

Overflow dams are designed to carry water discharge over their crests, and they must be made of materials that will not be eroded by such discharges. Nonoverflow dams are those designed not to be overtopped, and they may include earth and rock in their structure. Often the two types are combined to form a composite structure consisting of, for example, an overflow concrete gravity dam with dikes of earthfill construction.

To prevent a dam from being overtopped, spillway structures are designed to carry off excess water. In earthfill dams, with crests that cannot survive overtopping, spillways are essential and are usually built as separate structures—often a shaft or tunnel adjacent to the dam. With concrete gravity dams, the downstream side of the structure acts as the spillway.

will influence its design and determine the amount of reservoir storage needed. Where multiple purposes are involved—where, for instance, a dam stores water both for power and for irrigation—a reservoir allocation is usually made for each of the separate uses. The volume of storage, in turn, establishes the height and width of the dam.

Diversion dams are ordinarily constructed to provide sufficient water pressure for carrying water into ditches, canals, or other conveyance systems. Such dams, which are generally shorter than storage dams, are used for irriga-

Dam Design and Structure

The most common classification of dams is based on the materials used in their structure and on their basic design.

Earthfill and Rockfill Dams. The development of modern excavating, hauling, and compacting equipment for earth materials has made massive earthfill dams economical. The Rogun and Nurek dams in the USSR, the world's highest, are earthfill structures. Canada's Syncrude Tailings, which will be the world's most massive

(Below left) *An earthfill dam is begun by digging a trench (1) in a firm bedrock foundation and laying down an initial waterproof layer of compressed clay. Successive layers of compacted clay are laid until the trench is filled (2). A broad-based core (3) of compressed clay is built on this foundation to above high-water level and is supported on both sides with earth (4). The upstream slope (5) is covered with gravel (6) and surfaced with rock slabs (7). The downstream slope (8) is turfed (9), and a spillway (10) is added to handle overflow during a flood. (Below right) In building a rockfill or any other dam, a temporary, or coffer, dam is constructed (1), and the river is diverted around the dam site through tunnels (2) in the riverbank. The area behind the coffer dam is then filled with an inclined layer of thoroughly compacted rocks (3). The steep, concave upstream face (4) is covered with carefully graded crushed rock (5) and then with a layer of impervious material (6), which is grouted into the bedrock (7) to prevent seepage under the dam Finally, a spillway (8) is added to the downstream slope.*

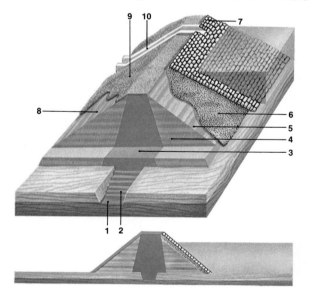

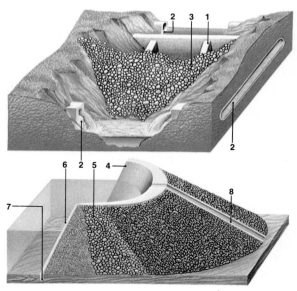

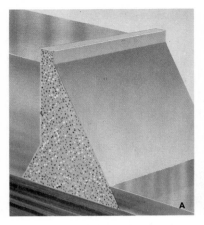 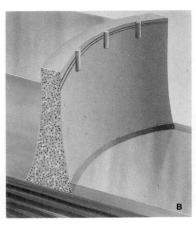 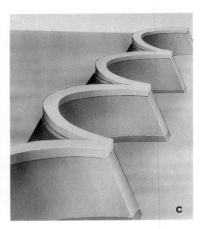

The three basic types of concrete dams are gravity, arch, and buttress dams. The gravity dam (A) is the most commonly built, and relies primarily on its great weight to withstand the tremendous pressure of the water that it holds back. The arch dam (B) is usually built in a narrow canyon and is curved into the flow of water, so that the water pressure is transferred to the canyon walls. The buttress dam (C) usually consists of a series of 45° sloping arches on the upstream side and supporting concrete buttresses on the downstream side. The slanting arches and buttresses transmit the water pressure to the foundations. Sometimes, flat concrete slabs are used instead of arches.

when completed, is also an earthfill structure.

Earthfill dams typically have a water-impermeable clay core, and a water cutoff wall from their base to bedrock to prevent underground seepage. During construction, the stream or river must be diverted either through the damsite by means of a conduit or around it by means of a tunnel.

Earthfill dams require supplementary structures to serve as spillways for discharging water from behind the dam. If sufficient spillway capacity is not provided, an earthfill dam may be damaged or even destroyed by the erosive action of water flowing over its crest. Unless special precautions are taken, such dams are also subject to serious damage or even failure, due to water seepage through or under the dam (see TETON DAM).

The rockfill dam, essentially an embankment like the earthfill dam, uses rock instead of earth to provide stability. It has an impervious, watertight membrane, usually an upstream facing of impervious soil, concrete paving, or steel plates; or it may have a thin interior core of impervious soil.

The rockfill dam must also be provided with a spillway of adequate capacity to prevent overtopping. Its foundation is usually rock or compact sand and gravel and is designed to prevent settlement that is great enough to rupture the watertight membrane.

Concrete Gravity Dams. The concrete gravity dam is designed to resist the pressure of reservoir water by sheer weight. Its shape differs from that of the earthfill or rockfill dam in that its inward, water-facing side is perpendicular to the water surface; in profile, the dam forms a right-angled triangle. (Earthfill and rockfill dams usually have long, gradual slopes on both sides.)

Gravity dams are used to hold back large volumes of water and are adapted to sites where there is a sound rock foundation. Until the early 1900s they were constructed of stone, but modern gravity dams are usually concrete.

Concrete Arch Dams. Concrete arch dams are built in narrow, steep-walled canyons, where the canyon walls can take up the thrust exerted by the arch and the pressure of the water. Such dams can be extraordinarily thin. VAIONT DAM is 265 m (828 ft) high, but only 22.7 m (75 ft) thick at its base. Concrete buttress dams are composed of multiple arches reinforced with buttresses. They are usually relatively low dams, built on solid rock beds across a wide river valley. Concrete is saved by using steel buttresses to support the series of smaller concrete arches.

Auxiliary Structures. In addition to the spillway, most dams incorporate several other structures designed to hold or release water. The reservoir, the water-holding area created by the dam, is regulated according to the dam's primary function. For irrigation purposes the reservoir may be filled during spring floods and the water held until the summer, when it is released to irrigate growing crops. The reservoir water level of a flood-control dam is kept low to conserve capacity for floodwaters. To generate hydroelectric power, reservoirs are kept as full as possible, and many power dams use an auxiliary reservoir downstream, from which water can be pumped back to the higher reservoir for additional water power.

Water is drawn out of the reservoir through gate openings in the dam face. The most usual gate form is one that can be raised vertically; more recent gate types use floating roller caissons that move up and down to control the water flow.

Since a dam effectively blocks the passage of fish, many dams construct stepped pools, which allow fish to bypass the dam. A series of fish locks, like the canal locks used for ship passage, may also be used to permit fish to pass both upstream and downstream.

History

Early agricultural civilizations based in river valleys built dams to control flooding and to provide water for irrigation.

The Greek historian Herodotus mentions a dam built across the Nile River about 2900 BC to protect the city of Memphis from inundation. A rockfill structure on the Orontes River in Syria, built about 1300 BC, still functions to irrigate fields near the city of Homs. Desert peoples often constructed dams across narrow, dry-stream channels, or *wadis*, to conserve the product of brief, intense rainstorms. The remains of many ancient dams are found throughout the Middle East, along with traces of such other water-retaining structures as tanks and stone cisterns. The Romans built dams throughout their empire.

Dam construction in Europe came to a halt after the end of the Roman Empire. It was reborn as a science in the 19th century. In particular, the mid-19th century studies of soil mechanics by Scottish engineer W. J. M. Rankine allowed the erection of dams whose height no longer needed to be matched by their bulk in order to withstand stress. The French Furens Dam (1861–66) is generally cited as the first dam built on the basis of modern engineering principles. It was a stone masonry structure, curved in cross section, standing 52 m (164 ft) high.

The Dam-Building Era

The first years of the 20th century saw many large dams built in both Europe and the United States. In the United States the Federal Reclamation Act of 1902 opened an unprecedented period of dam building. The act established the Reclamation Service (now the Bureau of Reclamation) and authorized the building of irrigation

Water cascades down La Grande 2 spillway at Quebec's monumental James Bay hydroelectric complex. Eight giant roller gates open to evacuate water from the reservoir behind the dam during flood periods.

When it reaches full capacity in the early 1990s, the hollow gravity Itaipu Dam on the upper Paranà River between Brazil and Paraguay will generate 12,600 MW, the world's largest output.

projects. The construction of dams to impound water for irrigation was followed, in the 1930s, by projects of much greater scope that were intended to affect whole river basins. The Boulder Canyon Project on the Colorado River, for example—with the HOOVER DAM as its major structure—was designed with multiple purposes: irrigation, power production, flood control, municipal water supply, and recreation are among the most important. The dams built under the TENNESSEE VALLEY AUTHORITY in the 1930s provide other notable examples of multiuse structures functioning to control river waters over a broad region.

There are about 50,000 dams presently operating in the United States. With the exception of two unfinished undertakings, however—the Central Arizona Project and the Central Utah Project—few large dams are planned for the future. (See HYDROELECTRIC POWER for a review of the environmental effects of large-dam construction.)

The ASWAN HIGH DAM in Egypt, completed in 1970, provides irrigation and power generation. The Itaipú Dam on the Paraná River between Paraguay and Brazil is the world's largest hydroelectric complex, with 18 giant turbines generating an ultimate capacity of 12,600 megawatts. Begun in 1975, it required about 30,000 workers and cost nearly $15 billion. Turkey's Ataturk Dam will be another of the world's largest when it is finished in the mid-1990s.

Dam, Carl Henrik   The Danish biochemist Carl Peter Henrik Dam, b. Feb. 21, 1895, d. June 17, 1976, discovered vitamin K. While studying cholesterol formation in chickens, Dam found (1934) that for proper blood clotting to take place, a certain substance, which he named vitamin K, is necessary in the diet. He then studied the medical uses of vitamin K preparations and found that these preparations could help prevent hemorrhage during some types of surgery and in newborns who initially lack the intestinal bacteria that synthesize vitamin K. Dam shared the 1943 Nobel Prize for physiology or medicine with Edward DOISY, who isolated and studied the chemical properties of vitamin K.

damages Damages are compensation recovered in the courts by someone who has suffered loss or injury to person, property, or other rights because of the unlawful act or negligence of another. Damages are either compensatory or punitive.

Compensatory damages make good or replace the loss suffered by the wronged party. They are subdivided into general and special damages. General damages are awarded for losses resulting from a wrong or injury without reference to the special circumstances of the plaintiff (the complaining party), such as physical pain or injury and mental anguish. Special damages are awarded to compensate for the natural but not necessary result of a wrong or injury, as when someone has incurred hospital expenses or loss of earnings.

Punitive or exemplary damages are damages on a higher scale, awarded to punish a wrongdoer for wanton or malicious acts. Some statutes, such as U.S. antitrust laws, specify triple damages as a way of punishing violators and encouraging private persons to bring suit against them.

Daman see GOA

Damascus [duh-mas'-kuhs] Damascus (Arabic: Dimashq), the capital and largest city of Syria, is situated on the Barada and Awaj rivers 85 km (53 mi) southeast of Beirut, Lebanon. The municipality population is 1,361,000 (1989 est.).

Contemporary City. The Barada River divides the city. South of the river lies the partially walled old city, containing the major mosques and markets and the Meidan, Christian, and Druze quarters. The new town lies north of the river and contains most government buildings, hospitals, hotels, and factories.

Traditional handicraft industries, including mother-of-pearl mosaics, silk brocades (from which the name *damask* is derived), copper goods, and blown glass, are still important. The city gave its name to a finely decorated steel that was formerly produced there. Newer industries include cement, food processing, furniture, glassworks, clothing, leather, and printing. Tourism is spurred by the presence of many historical and religious sites. Damascus is also the center of an important wholesale trade among the eastern Arab countries.

The city's educational institutions include the University of Damascus (1923) and the Arab Academy. Among the city's many mosques is the Umayyad (or Great) Mosque (AD 705), the fourth holiest in Islam. Other historical sites include a Roman citadel, the tomb of Saladin, and the monastery of Suleiman the Magnificent.

History. Damascus, which is often said to be the world's oldest continuously inhabited city, has obscure origins, but it is known to have been the capital of the ARAMAEAN kingdom until it fell to the Assyrians in 732 BC. In 333 BC the city came under the rule of ALEXANDER THE GREAT, who was succeeded by the SELEUCIDS. Hellenistic influence was overlaid with Roman culture after the Roman takeover in 64 BC. Damascus became a Christian

The Umayyad (or Great) Mosque of Damascus, one of the holiest of Islamic shrines, was built on the orders of Caliph al-Walid during the early 8th century.

city while it was still under Roman rule. The BYZANTINE EMPIRE took control in the 4th century. Damascus fell to the Arabs in 635 and was the capital of the CALIPHATE from 661 until 750. It was a center for SALADIN's opposition to the Crusaders in the 12th century.

Captured (1260) by the MONGOLS and sacked (c.1400) by TIMUR, Damascus became part of the OTTOMAN EMPIRE in 1516. In 1918 it was liberated from Turkish rule by the Arab Legion and the World War I Allied forces. After years of political tension under the French League of Nations' mandate (1920–41), Damascus became the capital of independent Syria during World War II.

damask [dam'-uhsk] Damask is a fabric with a flat, woven design that appears on both sides of the cloth. The technique of weaving it was first devised by the Chinese and was introduced into Europe from Damascus during the Middle Ages. Damask was originally made wholly of silk, but later linen damask became the specialty of such flax-growing countries as France and Belgium. Today the cloth is made from many different fibers.

Its flat design distinguishes damask from brocade, where the pattern is raised above the surface of the fabric. Double damask has more threads per inch than single damask. Most damasks are used for table linens or, in heavier weights, as upholstery and drapery fabrics.

d'Amboise, Jacques [dahm-bwahz'] Jacques d'Amboise, b. Dedham, Mass., July 28, 1934, was one of the first male dancers born and trained in the United States to capture the public's eye. He joined NEW YORK CITY BALLET in 1950, having trained in its School of American Ballet. By 1953 he was dancing principal roles in ballets ranging from *Stars and Stripes* to *Apollo*. He choreographed several works for the company and also appeared in movies. He founded the National Dance Institute in 1976.

Damien, Father [dahm-yan']   Father Damien was the religious name of Joseph de Veuster, b. Jan. 3, 1840, d. Apr. 15, 1889. He was a Belgian Roman Catholic missionary famous for his work among the lepers on the island of Molokai, Hawaii. He not only ministered to the spiritual needs of the lepers but also dressed their sores, provided shelter and food, and buried them. Even after he had contracted leprosy himself, Father Damien continued his work until he became too ill to do so. In 1965, Father Damien was nominated by the state of Hawaii for a place of honor in the Statuary Hall of the Capitol in Washington, D.C.

Damocles [dam'-uh-kleez]   In Greek legend, Damocles, a courtier of Dionysius the Elder, tyrant of Syracuse, repeatedly extolled the ruler's happy life. One day at a lavish banquet given by Dionysius, Damocles looked up to see a sword suspended by a single hair over his head. He then realized that power and wealth are perilous possessions. Any impending disaster is now referred to as the "sword of Damocles."

Damon and Pythias [day'-muhn, pith'-ee-uhs]   Damon and Pythias (or Phintias), citizens of Syracuse in the 4th century BC, were celebrated for their loyalty to each other. When Pythias was sentenced to death he received permission to set his affairs in order, on the condition that Damon take his place as a pledge against his return. This mutual display of trust and devotion inspired the emperor to pardon Pythias.

Dampier, William [dam'-pir]   William Dampier, b. c.1652, d. March 1715, was an English seafarer and buccaneer. Sent to sea as a young man, he later became a buccaneer, chiefly along the Pacific coast of South and Central America. Dampier acquired a knowledge of hydrography, pilotage, and winds, which he used to produce surveys, maps, and charts. Recognizing his skills as a navigator, the British Admiralty sent him on an expedition (1699–1701) during which he explored the coasts of Australia, New Britain, and New Guinea.

damping   see MOTION, HARMONIC

Damrosch, Walter [dam'-rahsh]   Walter Johannes Damrosch, b. Jan. 30, 1862, d. Dec. 22, 1950, was a German-American pianist, conductor, and composer who lived and worked in New York City. He took over direction of the Oratorio Society from his father, Leopold (1832–1885), who had founded it in 1874, and had his own opera company from 1894 to 1899. He was musical director and conductor (1903–27) of the New York Symphony Society, a precursor of the NEW YORK PHILHARMONIC. His brother, Frank (1859–1937), was a noted choral conductor and music administrator.

damselfish   Damselfish, or demoisellefish, are small, aggressive, territorial fish found chiefly in shallow tropical seas. The more than 200 species of damselfish constitute the family Pomacentridae. Hardy in captivity and often strikingly colored, they are popular aquarium animals.

The body of a damselfish is compressed, and the single dorsal fin is spined. Almost alone among fishes of the order Perciformes, nearly all species have a single nostril opening on each side. Damselfish feed on invertebrates and smaller fish, and they spawn several times a year. Members of the subfamily Amphiprioninae, called clown fish, live commensally with certain SEA ANEMONES, swimming safely among the stinging tentacles. Common names of other damselfish include the beaugregory, garibaldi, and sergeant major.

The bicolor damselfish (bottom) is strikingly colored. The genus Abudefduf, however, including the blue damselfish (center) is generally dull. Clownfish (top) live symbiotically with sea anemones.

damselfly   Damselflies are members of the suborder Zygoptera of the insect order Odonata (dragonflies and damselflies). They are slender, often brilliantly colored insects and are fluttery in flight. They rest with their four wings held together above the back. The thorax of adults is rectangular and tilted 70° to 80° out of the body line. Adults feed on insects captured in flight; the nymphs are aquatic and have three leaflike gills at the end of the abdomen.

ILLUSTRATION CREDITS

The following list credits or acknowledges, by page, the source of illustrations used in this volume. When two or more illustrations appear on one page, they are credited individually left to right, top to bottom; their credits are separated by semicolons. When both the photographer or artist and an agency or other source are given for an illustration, they are usually separated by a slash. Those illustrations not cited below are credited on the page on which they appear, either in the caption or alongside the illustration itself.